STUDIES IN MEDIEVAL
LEGAL THOUGHT

STUDIES IN MEDIEVAL LEGAL THOUGHT

Public Law and the State, 1100-1322

BY GAINES POST

PRINCETON, NEW JERSEY

PRINCETON UNIVERSITY PRESS

1964

To My Wife

ABBREVIATIONS USED IN FOOTNOTES

A.H.R.   *American Historical Review*

C.A.H.   *Cambridge Ancient History*

C.M.H.   *Cambridge Medieval History*

Chartularium   *Chartularium Universitatis Parisiensis*

E.H.R.   *English Historical Review*

H.L.R.   *Harvard Law Review*

L.Q.R.   *Law Quarterly Review*

M.G.H.   *Monumenta Germaniae Historica*

M.P.L.   Migne, *Patrologia Latina*

Jaffe-Loewenfeld (JL)   *Regesta pontificum romanorum* (see Bibl. B. iii)

Potthast   *Regesta pontificum romanorum* (see Bibl. B. iii)

S.C.   Stubbs, *Select Charters* (see Bibl. B. iii)

Abbreviations relating to Roman and Canon Law (see *Corpus Iuris Civilis, Corpus Juris Canonici,* and *Quinque Compilationes Antiquae,* in Bibl. A. i and ii, B. i and ii):

Auth.   *Authentica* (one of *Authenticae,* or *Novellae*)

C.   *Causa* (*Causae* in *Decretum Gratiani*)

C.   *Codex*

Comp. I, II, III, IV, V   *Compilatio I,* etc.

D.   *Digestum* (*Digest*)

Decr. Greg. IX   *Decretales Gregorii IX*

Decretum   *Decretum Gratiani*

Dist.   *Distinctio* (*Distinctiones* in the *Decretum*)

ff.   *Digestum* (medieval abbreviation derived from *D.*)

Glos. ord.   *Glossa ordinaria*

Inst.   *Institutiones*

l.   *lex, lege*

t.   *titulus, titulo*

PREFACE

"DER STAAT ALS KUNSTWERK"—"The State as a Work of Art"—such is the title of the first section of the famous classic by Jakob Burckhardt, *Die Kultur der Renaissance in Italien*. My studies, too, deal in large part with the use of legal and political reason and skill in the creation of the State; as early as the twelfth century John of Salisbury thought of the Republic as a work of art imitating nature; and in the twelfth and thirteenth centuries kings and jurists were anticipating the political science of the Italian Renaissance in their growing intellectual awareness of what they were doing in the realm of public law. To use the words of Burckhardt, however, seemed presumptuous. His book is a work of art in itself; mine is a prosaic collection of miscellaneous studies. Besides, the choice of such a title would have persuaded the reader that I intended deliberately to engage in a clever *tour de force* in order to deny that there was an Italian Renaissance. The title I have decided upon, therefore, *Studies in Medieval Legal Thought*, is the proper one.

It is proper in another sense. The emphasis is on the legal thought that resulted from the great revival of the Roman law at Bologna, and on its influence on medieval "constitutionalism." General political theory is neglected—partly because legal ideas were of greater practical influence than political theory in royal courts and councils, and partly because numerous histories of medieval political theories, but not of the concepts belonging directly to the realm of public law, are available. To be sure, Gierke, the Carlyles, McIlwain, d'Entrèves, Ullmann, and, above all, Ernst Kantorowicz, have paid some attention to the laws and the jurists. But I have concentrated on the legal at the expense of political thought, leaving it to scholars more learned than I to make the great synthesis. If political theory finds little place, political (and economic and social) history also is wanting. This is unfortunate, of course. But these are *Studies*, not a history of law and politics.

In a Preface the author should, I suppose, apologize for all the weaknesses of the book. But apologies, like lawsuits, should not be multiplied and become *immortales*; nor should they constitute a boastful *humilitas*. A few explanations, however, are necessary.

In the period under investigation, what we call "State" was called *Imperium, Regnum, Respublica,* and *Civitas.* But since a *Regnum,* for example, was often treated as an abstract entity or body, even a corporate body, that was superior to king or government and all the members, and was in many respects the supreme subject of public law, it is surely no distortion to use our own term, "State," instead of the medieval term. The word "State," therefore, is capitalized in order to distinguish it from "state" in such a context as "state of the Realm" or "state of the Republic." This is because the "state" is the *status,* or public welfare, or even government, of the *Regnum* as State. It should be understood that not only *status* but many other terms belonging to the public law of our period have special meanings in the realm of private law. For example, every man in the Middle Ages was given a *status* related to his position in society, and every man who held rights in property had a *status,* an estate. Men enjoyed, unless they lost it by sinful and criminal acts, a natural *dignitas.* In feudalism *honor* had its particular significance. But these and similar terms will be considered in this work only in the context of public law.

I must explain, moreover, why I have deliberately avoided consistency in the spelling of proper names. If there is any rule followed, it is that of custom insofar as I know what the customary methods are among scholars in Britain, Canada, and the United States. For example, with regard to the names of legists and canonists, I give them in the Latin spelling unless they are better known in the English or other vernacular versions: Irnerius and Accursius, not Irnerio and Accursio or Accorso; Vincentius Hispanus, not Vincent of Spain; Johannes Teutonicus, not John the German; but Odofredo, not Odofredus, and Jacques de Révigny, not Jacobus de Ravanis. As for the names of political writers, theologians, philosophers, and others, custom again prevails: John of Salisbury, not Johannes Saresberiensis; Thomas Aquinas, not Tommaso d'Aquino; Gérard d'Abbeville, not Gerald of Abbeville; and Marsiglio (not Marsilius) of Padua. Of course custom is not a guide in the case of names that are given in different ways by scholars in England and America—so Peter of Auvergne or Pierre d'Auvergne. In such cases I surrender to the French (or Italian or German) spelling. Naturally, just as in the case of place names, consistent inconsistency is difficult to maintain.

It has been impossible to check for accuracy most of the quotations from the manuscripts and from rare editions of the sixteenth century. For the most part I could not depend on microfilm, which is a poor means of reproducing large pages with the glosses copied or printed in small lettering and in the margins; besides, the glosses of interest are widely scattered throughout many folios, and it is difficult to turn the film to the right places. Even the best photostats often fail to give a clear enough reproduction of glosses copied in the margins that suffered from the binding of the manuscripts. And I could not return to European libraries in order to verify my transcriptions of the Latin texts. Thus, although I have always tried to copy accurately and recheck at the time of copying, no doubt there are too many textual errors. At any rate I am convinced that the errors are not serious enough to betray the original thought of the authors.

Where the subject matter is well known, I have not tried to refer at all points to such standard authorities on medieval political theories as the Carlyles, Gierke, McIlwain, and Ernst Kantorowicz. Nor have I tried completely to revise my older studies by taking into consideration all the excellent scholarship that has been devoted to the problems since I treated them. To all whom I have neglected I offer my sincere apologies. My excuse is, apart from the duties of teaching and engaging in the *vita activa* of a large university, that no one, unless he can make use of research assistants, can possibly keep up with all the scholarly publications of interest.

Finally, a few words about the repetitiousness involved in

stating and restating the principal theme of public law. Inevitably, when one publishes articles over a long period of time, one repeats earlier conclusions in order to give a setting to each of the new aspects of the subject. I have retained some of these repetitions, partly because I wish to make it clear that the influence of the Roman law on medieval institutions and on the development of public law and the State is not something to be dismissed as superficial; partly because *status* and *utilitas publica*, for example, have a bearing on nearly every topic presented; and partly because I have to some degree followed the method of medieval commentators on the two laws.

So much for explanations. Now I am happy to express my appreciation for all the help that has enabled me to write these *Studies*. Among the many who have offered critical advice and have given encouragement by their interest, may the following accept my gratitude: Charles H. McIlwain, Joseph R. Strayer, Ernst H. Kantorowicz,* Sir Maurice Powicke,* Stephan Kuttner (who has also given me references and sources that I had overlooked), Brian Tierney, and R. Stuart Hoyt. My thanks go also to those learned editors of periodicals in which most of the following studies originally appeared as articles. They have corrected many errors and have offered many useful suggestions: Charles R. D. Miller, editor of *Speculum*; Stephan Kuttner, editor of *Traditio*, of *The Jurist*, and of *Seminar*; and Fritz Ernst, editor of *Die Welt als Geschichte*. Moreover, they have generously permitted me to use the articles for this book—and I also thank Johannes Quasten, coeditor of *Traditio*, for adding his special permission. Of course the Mediaeval Academy of America, the Fordham University Press, and the editors of the periodicals mentioned reserve all rights of copyright to what appeared in the original articles.

The research and writing are my own, but I could never have found the time and money to carry on the work had it not been for generous grants from universities and foundations.

* It is sad now to record the death of Sir Maurice Powicke and Professor Ernst H. Kantorowicz. May these *Studies* in some small measure do honor to their memory.

GAINES POST

November 11, 1963

Therefore I wish to thank Harvard University for summer aid for research in Europe in 1932 and 1934; the Graduate School of the University of Wisconsin for leaves-of-absence and grants-in-aid; the John Simon Guggenheim Memorial Foundation and the Conference Board of Associated Research Councils (Fulbright Awards) for fellowships supplementing other awards and enabling me to do research in European libraries in 1951-1952 and 1955-1956; and the Institute for Advanced Study for a fellowship in 1959-1960.

Finally, to Miss Geraldine Hinkel, of the University of Wisconsin, goes my gratitude for typing much of the manuscript. Miss R. Miriam Brokaw and Mrs. William Hanle, of the Princeton University Press, by their constructive corrections, deserve my special thanks.

Boncompagno, a famous professor of the notarial art at Bologna in the early thirteenth century, boasted of creating a new science. I can make no such boast, for the science of medieval legal and constitutional history has long since been well established. But I hope that, by referring to a considerable body of the legal thought of the twelfth and thirteenth centuries, I have contributed interpretations that are interesting and constructive.

GAINES POST

Madison, Wis.,
February 10, 1963

CONTENTS

CONTENTS

INTRODUCTION

INTRODUCTION

ALMOST forty years ago Charles Homer Haskins applied the word renaissance to the twelfth century. Whether or not it was a renaissance, the twelfth century was in fact a period of great creative activity. The revival of political, economic, and social life, along with the appearance of new learning, new schools, and new literatures and styles of art and architecture, signified the beginnings, in the West, of modern European civilization. In the thirteenth century what had begun in the twelfth arrived at such maturity that it is safe to say that early modern Europe was coming into being.

Among the institutions and fields of knowledge created by medieval men, the university and the State and the legal science that aided in the creation of both were, as much as the rise of an active economy and the organization of towns, important manifestations of the new age. While accepting and respecting tradition and believing in the unchanging higher law of nature that came from God, kings, statesmen, and men of learning confidently applied reason and skill to the work of introducing order into society and societies, into feudal kingdoms, Italian communes, and lesser communities of the clergy and laity. Long before the recovery of Aristotle's *Politics*, the naturalness of living in politically and legally organized communities of corporate guilds, chapters, towns, and States was recognized both in practice and in legal thought. Nature itself sanctioned the use of human reason and art to create new laws for the social and political life on earth—provided always, of course, that the new did not violate the will of God.[1]

At the very time when merchants, artisans, townsmen, and schoolmen were forming their associations for mutual aid and protection, the study of the Roman and Canon law at Bologna introduced lawyers, jurists, and secular and ecclesiastical au-

---

[1] Treated in chs. X and XI.

thorities to the legal thought of Rome on corporations. When kings were trying to overcome the anarchy of feudalism, the new legal science furnished those principles of public law that helped them convert their realms into States. And when the problem of the relations between corporations and corporate communities on the one side and the authority of the heads of Church and State on the other needed to be solved, the Roman law offered much of the solution. It provided for the legal capacity of a corporation to act as a private person and to defend the rights of both the individual members and the corporate body as a whole. By means of the Roman law on agency these rights could be represented in secular and ecclesiastical courts. The Roman law, moreover, furnished a theory of consent according to which the representatives of corporate communities could appear in royal courts and councils and defend the rights of their constituents before consenting to the superior right of the prince, the supreme judge, to make the final decision.[2] As a result, the development of corporations and agency speeded the binding of communities to the central government at the same time it extended the king's authority more effectively into all parts of the realm. A further consequence of the process was, by the late

[2] A distinguished historian of English constitutional developments in our period, Professor R. Stuart Hoyt, is not sure that "romanesque terminology" was important in the rise of representation and of the royal authority (*Speculum*, XXIX, 370); and he doubts that such representatives as knights, burgesses, proctors, and other agents understood the Romano-canonical procedures. As for the question of what the representatives understood, no doubt most of them were ignorant of the meaning of the legal terms in their mandates, as they were of the problems of public law and the State. But what they understood is not so important as what members of the royal government understood. The fact is that it was the royal courts and councils which had to understand the law and interpret it and make the final decisions. But royal justices and counsellors had some knowledge, even in England, of principles of the Roman law, and they advised the king. Decisions were of course influenced by political and economic situations, but they were made by men who appreciated and knew legal procedures and the theories of public law. To use an analogy: if I go to court in a lawsuit it is presumed that I have no understanding of the law; I must submit to the law as interpreted by the court. It hardly matters that English knights or their representatives knew nothing about *plena potestas* and *quod omnes tangit* (yet they probably learned something about them in meetings of shire courts); what matters is that the royal government ordered them to bring full powers to consent to what would be done by the king in his court in his council in his Parliament. The king, by consulting his counsellors and judges who were expert in the law, knew the law; he had "omnia iura in scrinio pectoris sui." (Cf. below, ch. VII, nn. 64 and 71.)

thirteenth century, the early, in some respects premature, triumph of those Roman principles of public law and the State which prevented Roman corporatism from becoming a new kind of localism.

Part I of these Studies is devoted to the examination of the Roman and Canon law in order to show how legal ideas played an important role in the development of corporations and corporate agency; how the representation of towns and other communities, some of which were not true corporations but which acquired the right to elect agents to act in their name, began to reflect the Roman law on corporations and naturally appeared first in Italy rather than in Spain; and how representation by agents given "full powers of attorney" in Parliament, Cortes, and (a little later) Estates General, was not a democratic but a royal institution in which the judicial, administrative, and legislative prerogative of the king was superior to all the private rights represented and defended. In Chapter 1 the history of the legal recognition of a guild, the corporation of the University of Paris, illustrates not only the use of the two laws in favor of the members of a rising community of students and professors, but also the necessary dependence of the corporate body on the highest authority. His interest in the law of corporations and agency thus aroused, thereafter the author began to consider the problem of the rise of other corporate communities and when they were first represented, in the new Roman style, by specially chosen agents in the feudal assemblies summoned by kings and popes in Italy and Spain (Ch. II). But it was necessary also to study the legal nature of representation and of the powers of the representatives in relation to the public right of the prince to summon them and in relation to the law on the right of consent (Chs. III and IV). At once it became evident that the nature of consent in assemblies could be interpreted only in the context of the theory and practice of the royal authority.

In Part II, Chs. V-XI, therefore, we turn from communities and representation to the community of the realm and to the problems of public law and the State. For representative assemblies were summoned because, as the royal documents abundantly reveal, the monarch intended to deal with a weighty business (*ardua negotia*) that was common to the "state of the king" and the "state of the realm" and was vital to the public welfare and safety. But the concepts of the *status regis* and the *status regni*, it developed, belonged not to feudal law and custom but to the public law, and the public law was the law of the State. Magna Carta and feudal contract could not by themselves explain representation and consent in Parliament. The public interest which it was the king's duty and right to maintain subordinated private rights and consent to the "right of State." What was the public interest? What constituted the public authority? Did cases of public emergency or necessity enhance the powers that belonged to king and crown? And were these powers the "estate royal"? What was the *status* or "state" of the realm? Finally, what was the public law, and what was the nature of the State with which it was concerned? Again the author turned to the Roman law, as interpreted by the legists and canonists of the twelfth and thirteenth centuries, in order to find answers to such questions and in order to learn whether the public law of Rome affected England, the land of the common law, as well as monarchies on the Continent.

Inevitably, then, to understand medieval assemblies, to understand the nature of the consent of representatives, we always return to the problems of the public authority and public law, to the relation between individual rights and the "right of State," between communities and the community of the realm. But again, what is the public law, and what is the State? Perhaps a paper written fifteen years ago and now slightly revised will state the problems and the major premise of these *Studies*.[3]

[3] The substance of this part of the Introduction was read before the Riccobono Seminar in 1947, and published under the title, "The Theory of Public Law and the State," in *Seminar* (Annual Extraordinary Number of *The Jurist*), VI (1948), 42-59. I refer chiefly to the following: Otto Gierke, *Das deutsche Genossenschaftsrecht*, 4 vols.—vol. III bears on my subject; Gierke, *Political Theories of the Middle Age*, part of the above work, transl. by F. W. Maitland; Fritz Kern, *Kingship and Law in the Middle Ages*, transl. by S. B. Chrimes; Georges de Lagarde, "Individualisme et corporatisme au moyen âge," in *L'Organisation corporative du moyen âge*, Etudes . . . pour l'histoire des assemblées d'états, II; E. Lousse, *L'Etat corporatif au moyen âge*; C. H. McIlwain, *Constitutionalism Ancient and Modern*; F. Meinecke, *Die Idee der Staatsräson*; T. F. T. Plucknett, *Concise History of the Common Law*, 2nd ed.; F. Pollock and F. W. Maitland, *History of*

Walter Map, trying to explain the *curia regis* in the twelfth century, impatiently exclaimed: "God knows what it is!" It is equally hard to explain the nature of the public law and the State even in our time. The public law, of course, should have as its province what is public as opposed to what is private; but sometimes it is as difficult to distinguish between public and private as it is to separate clearly the realms of body and soul. And what is the State? Is it something real, yet abstract, existing apart from the government and the collectivity of all members of the community of the nation? Is it the nation itself? Or is it a merely fictitious person, a juridical convenience? What is "reason of State"? I do not know, and I shall therefore make no attempt to indulge in logical definitions or in profound philosophizing about public law and the State. To paraphrase Terence (*Phormio*, II, 4, 454: "Quot homines, tot sententiae"—a passage that I learned from medieval lawyers, who loved to quote it), so many philosophers of law and the State, so many definitions!

For the present purpose, it is sufficient to observe that Hans Kelsen, one of the greatest authorities on the modern State and the public law, defined the State as a juristic entity, a personification of the national legal order, a politically organized society, and a subject of rights and duties.[4] Its rights are largely public rights, asserted in terms of the public welfare and the common utility. And the public law, let me add, is not only the law that deals with the public authority and the public welfare; it is at

---

English Law, 2nd ed., 2 vols.; J. R. Strayer, "Laicization of French and English Society in the Thirteenth Century," *Speculum*, XV (1940), 76-86; Helene Wieruszowski, *Vom Imperium zum nationalen Königtum*, Beiheft 30, *Historische Zeitschrift*, 1933.

Important as the feudal background is, I have neglected it in these *Studies*. But for feudalism in the development of the State see above all H. Mitteis, *Lehnrecht und Staatsgewalt*; and *Der Staat des hohen Mittelalters*, 3rd ed. Mitteis does not emphasize the revival of the Roman public law—nor is the Roman law stressed sufficiently by other historians of feudal monarchies.

Now (in 1963) the references given in the studies published during the past fifteen years can be consulted below, to chs. V-XI, where it will be noted how Sir Maurice Powicke, Joseph R. Strayer, Ernst Kantorowicz, and others have increasingly recognized that the State and its public law were appearing in the twelfth and thirteenth centuries. See also the Bibliography for their studies.

[4] *General Theory of Law and State*, pp. 181-206; cf. McIver, *Modern State*, pp. 3-22.

times the government, the constitutional order, without which the State is nothing.[5] At any rate, we can understand that when the "public welfare clause" is invoked in connection with the building of highways or with necessary preparations for war, private rights inevitably must yield. The public interest, sometimes tyrannically, demands it. Evidently the "public welfare clause" is connected with the "right of State"; and the State, whatever it is, is thus superior to all individuals and individual rights. The State is above the law of the land which protects private rights. In times of grave crisis, of a national emergency, of necessity, it is certain that the government of the United States can do extraordinary things which normally the law of the land does not permit. And yet even then the public "right of State" must have some regard for the rights of private citizens.

In Germany and Italy we have seen the extreme logical application of the idea that the State is above the law—and normally rather than in emergencies. The State of Nazi Germany and Fascist Italy was the culmination of that amoral necessity or "reason of State" which, some historians claim, first appeared in the Italian Renaissance. In 1914 Bethmann-Hollweg asserted the principle in the words "Necessity knows no law" in order to justify the German violation of the neutrality of Belgium.

All of these expressions—"public" or "common utility" or "welfare," "emergency," "necessity," "necessity knows no law," and "reason of the *status* or public welfare"—are to be found in the twelfth and thirteenth centuries. The purpose of this study is to point to their origin in the Roman law,[6] to show how the

---

[5] See the excellent remarks by Professor Antonio Marongiu, *Storia del diritto pubblico. Principi e istituti di governo in Italia dalla metà del IX all metà del XIX secolo*, pp. 10-30. Note also Ernest Barker's definition of public law (in his trans. of Otto Gierke, *Natural Law*, p. 36): "Public law . . . is what we call Constitutional Law—the law concerned with the rights and duties of the State. It is contrasted with private law, which deals with the rights and duties of subjects *inter se*." This is but another way of putting Ulpian's famous definition, *D.* 1, 1, 1, 2, which will be quoted often enough in these *Studies*.

[6] Yet Professor Walter Ullmann, in his *Principles of Government and Politics in the Middle Ages*, p. 133, says that "this principle of *publica utilitas* was in the final analysis probably evolved from the (Germanic) *mundeburdium*, the supreme protection, inherent in the theocratic king." To be sure, the idea that the king should rule for the public and common welfare by protecting people and

legists and canonists used them to develop the early modern theory of public law and the State; and to observe how kings, emperors, and popes were employing the new terminology to justify their claim to an authority that represented the public and common welfare and the *status* (state) of Realm or Church and was therefore above human if not natural law.

The great Otto Gierke recognized that in the fourteenth century some of these terms and concepts were current among legists like Bartolus and Baldus, and among publicists like John of Paris, Marsiglio of Padua, and William of Ockham. And he admitted that in them the modern theory of the public law and the State found its beginning. Yet the public law was still confused with the private, for the corporate theory of Empire, Church, and kingdoms and lesser communities was a part of private law; and the heads of these corporate bodies ruled by private as much as by public law.[7] Even the right of expropriation of property for evident utility and necessity was not a fully public right (here Gierke follows Georg Meyer). Nor was taxation, since it grew out of the law on expropriation or confiscation, and was subordinate to the private law that protected private property.

As for the State, except possibly in the case of the Empire, there was no medieval concept of it until the time of Bartolus.

churches was well known in the barbarian kingdoms. But it was already ancient—indeed, it is an ageless ideal of every kind of government, whatever the practice; and theocracy has nothing to do with it except to indicate that the king may assert that his power comes from God and that he has the right, for the sake of the public welfare, to govern the clergy as well as the laity. But in the terms and concepts used in the barbarian kingdoms, *publica utilitas* and *status regni* were a survival of the tradition of the imperial authority in the Roman Empire. On the survival of some concept of public law Professor Floyd S. Lear has made fundamental studies, a few of which I refer to below, ch. IV, n. 66; see also Lear's "The Public Law of the Visigothic Code," *Speculum*, XXVI (1951), 1-23, "Treason and Related Offenses in the Anglo-Saxon Dooms," *Rice Institute Pamphlet*, XXXVII (1950), 1-20, and "The Literature on Public Law in Germanic Custom," *Rice Inst. Pamphlet*, XLII (1955), 90-110. In any case, the Roman law, not to mention Cicero, abundantly expressed the concept that the principal duty of the government was the achievement of the public utility of the State. Naturally the revival of the Latin classics and of the Roman law in the twelfth century resulted in a new emphasis on the *utilitas publica* or *status* of the Republic or *Regnum*.

[7] See the good criticism of Gierke by Mrs. Ewart Lewis, "Organic Tendencies in Medieval Political Thought," in *American Political Science Review*, XXXII (1938), 849-876.

This was true, first, because of the prevailing corporate theory. If the corporation of a kingdom was not a real, but merely a fictive, person, how could it be a State, existing apart from the members and acting as an entity outside and above the law? It was true, in the second place, because all corporate communities were a hierarchy from the smallest to the all-inclusive whole, the Empire and the Church; and in the third place because the corporate community was a subject of the law and was subordinate to moral principles. (In general, Lagarde and Lousse have recently stated a theory of medieval representation that rests on similar presuppositions.) Even when Bartolus in the fourteenth century declared that not only the Empire but kingdoms and Italian city-states were true republics and independent of the Empire, these communities were not true States, for they were still controlled by Christian moral principles.

Gierke, it seems to me, is so obsessed with the corporate theory and the desire to make the State a real person superior to moral values and the law, that he feels that otherwise no State exists either in theory or in reality. Indeed, I sometimes think that one of the principal errors of modern scholarship on medieval law and institutions has been that of interpreting in accordance with contemporary notions. I prefer rather to find out if there was a *medieval* conception of the State, just as I prefer to believe that there is a State of the United States even if it is not completely above and outside the citizens, the law, and some morality.

But Gierke at least admits, if hesitantly, that a theory of public law and the State began to appear in the later Middle Ages. Kern, however, a great authority on medieval kingship, refuses to recognize any kind of State or public law in the modern sense. The objective law, he says, was simply the sum of all the subjective rights of the people, and it was prior to and above the State. The State was "muzzled" by private rights; it could not adapt the law of the community and private rights to meet its necessities; it could not interfere with private rights for the benefit of the community as a whole. Private rights, especially property rights, were sacred, and the government could not set them aside by new law. Since taxation was sequestration of property, the State could not raise taxes without the free consent of all concerned. (He forgets that in the United States the State is assumed to exist and yet in theory it can tax only with the free consent of the people.) "The State itself had no rights *sui generis.*" There was, in short, no public law and no State.

Authorities on medieval England come to a like conclusion—Pollock and Maitland holding that public law was merged into private law, no line being drawn between the king's public and private capacities; Plucknett, that matters of public law (the prerogative of the Crown, the means of extraordinary taxation) were intimately connected with the land and were regarded from the point of view of private property law; McIlwain, that private rights and public law are so interwoven that the line is hard to draw between such *libertates praescriptae* as belong to the king alone as a part of the "government" over which he has *plenam potestatem et liberum regimen*—in the phrase of St. Louis—and, on the other hand, those prescriptive rights of tenants or subjects which are wholly outside and beyond the legitimate bounds of royal administration and fall properly under *jurisdictio*, not under *gubernaculum.*

Yet Pollock and Maitland admit, by implication, that if all law was private law, what was private could also be public. For we must not distinguish too sharply between the governmental powers of a sovereign State and the proprietary rights of a supreme landlord, between a tax and a rent. If all land was held of the king and rents were paid, it was owned as much as in the modern State in which heavy land-taxes diminish the taxpayers' ownership. Thus royal right over the land was similar to public right, "eminent domain," today. (And I would add the reflection that it is absurd to suppose that there is much more absolute private ownership of property in our own country today than in medieval feudalism; for the public utility farmers have to sell their land for the construction of a highway or an artificial lake, and, as we shall see, this theory, revived along with the Roman law, was being stated in the thirteenth century.) McIlwain, too, offers a compromise. Observing how in the Roman Empire public and private law had in theory the same ultimate source, the will of the people, he says that the public law, as stated in the *Institutes*, pertains to the State *(status rei Romanae)*, that is, to the people who are the State. Since the State is no abstraction apart from the people, the rights of State are the rights of the people collectively and individually. For public and private rights, therefore, the subject was the natural person. Roman constitutionalism consisted in the fact that the law, public and private, was binding on the government because, deriving from the people, it protected individual rights. If the public law was the law of the State, the State was not a separate entity superior to the individuals in it. This Roman constitutionalism, containing the idea of a State and a public law, reinforced medieval constitutionalism as a result of the legal renaissance of the twelfth century. Thus, in thirteenth-century England, although private and public rights and law were closely connected, the Roman influence may be seen in the emphasis by Bracton on the consent of the people to the law, and on the obligation of the king to rule according to the law; and in his theory of public and private law, and of the power of the prince. But McIlwain concludes that there is no State, that is, no community of the people as a whole which had a right in itself that was superior to private rights.

In short, the authorities referred to, from Gierke to McIlwain and Lagarde and Lousse, are too absorbed in the importance of private rights, and in the cellular, corporate nature of medieval society, to appreciate how not only Roman and Canon lawyers but kings and popes frequently appealed to the "public welfare clause," the "state of the realm" *(status regni)*, and the "state of the Church" *(status Ecclesiae)*, and thus demanded a sacrifice of private rights and of the law that protected them; how, indeed, they were, in an earlier period than generally supposed, developing the theory and practice of public law and the State.

The legists started building their theories, naturally, on the foundation of Roman law, although Aristotle was of some influence by the end of the thirteenth century. They started with Ulpian's famous statement *(D.* 1, 1, 1, 2; also *Inst.* 1, 1): "Public law pertains to the *status rei Romanae*; private, to the utility of individuals. Public law relates to religion, priests, and magistrates." On this, as early as 1228, a glossator even seemed to personify *status,* saying that public law exists "to preserve the state, lest it perish." But probably, like others, he meant the public welfare of the Empire. For Odofredo a little later asserted that the public law pertains chiefly to the *status* of the whole Empire, and the glossators in Accursius' *Glossa ordinaria* related *status* to the public utility. Like Azo, they held that if private law pertains primarily to the utility of individuals, it pertains secondarily to the public utility, since it interests the *Respublica* (the State) that no one should misuse his property. Contrariwise, what is primarily public, secondarily pertains to the utility of individuals. Accursius added that it is for the utility or welfare of individuals that the Republic be preserved unharmed— an approach to the frequently expressed idea that the common utility is essentially the safety of all collectively and individually. Odofredo said, in adding to the thought of the glossators, that one of the concerns of the Republic is that its subjects be rich, even though property belongs to private law.

The public law, then, dealt with the public or common utility and safety, with the *status* of the State. In the sense that the public utility was generally a higher good than private (this was also the opinion of the scholastic philosophers, particularly of St. Thomas Aquinas—the salvation of one's soul is the only private right that is superior to the public utility, except in the case of a bishop, who cannot, said Pope Innocent III, resign his office to save his own soul if he is needed to help others to salvation), in this sense the State, the true bearer of the public utility, was superior to its subjects considered individually and collectively.

It follows that public law must deal more specifically with the means of assuring the *status* of the *Respublica.* The concept of public law was attached to the public authority, the government, which existed to administer the State for the common utility, good, and safety of all, which interpreted the public law and the common welfare, and which therefore had a certain prerogative that made it superior, in an emergency or necessity, to the private law and private rights. Therefore, as Odofredo put it, summing up Azo and the glossators, it was of public interest to have *sacra*, churches and priests to save people from their sins, and to protect priests from injury; and to have magistrates, for laws would be of no value without men to administer justice. Public law, then, dealt with the Church and the clergy, and with the office of magistrates. The *Glossa ordinaria* added the *fiscus* and fiscal law to the realm of public law.

Since national representation arose particularly in connection with taxation, it is interesting that fiscal matters pertaining to the Empire and the emperor were treated as a part of public law. The glossators, to *C.* 10, 1, *De iure fisci*, observed how the public law dealt with the repression of crime and the preservation of the law of the Republic, and at the same time protected the rights of the prince, one of whose rights was that of the *fiscus*. The ruler's jurisdiction belonged to public law; but so did the *fiscus*, even though it was the emperor's right and was of less public concern than criminal jurisdiction. This was true in part because the *fiscus* was public as a result of being enriched by penalties imposed for crimes, and because jurisdiction belonged to the public authority. Yet the *fiscus* was also a private right of the emperor as a private person.

Accursius, however, clearly made the *fiscus* public; it was the treasury of the Empire, not the patrimony of the emperor; and while it kept the accounts of the emperor and empress, it succeeded to the old public treasury (*res Romana*) and thus belonged to public law. Criminal jurisdiction and the fines and confiscations of property imposed by the *fiscus* were therefore regulated by public law. For these aspects of government pertained to the public welfare, to the *status* of the Empire, the *Respublica*.

But if the *fiscus* was public, was taxation? Placentinus and other legists, commenting on *C.* 10 and *C.* 1, 2, asserted that when the prince went on a campaign, all, even the clergy and monks, should help him with their property; and (*C.* 1, 3) that when it was for the public utility, e.g., the transport of supplies by ship, the emperor might exact extraordinary services from churches with the consent of the prelates. Moreover (to *C.* 4, 62, 1) a provincial governor might raise new taxes if the consent of the emperor and the common utility and necessity or poverty of the province were concomitant. They all held that extraordinary taxation belonged to public law since it was for the common utility and necessity of defense.

Similarly the *Glossa ordinaria* reflected this relationship between the *fiscus*, new taxation, public law, and common utility and necessity. For example, to *C.* 10, 48, 1, in which the Emperors Honorius and Theodosius declared that all, rich and poor alike, with no exception by special privilege, must aid in the provision and transportation of supplies for the war in Illyricum (*ad necessitates Illyricanas*), a gloss stated that even the emperor and empress were not exempt from the burden. This anticipated Baldus, who in the fourteenth century, to *C.* 10, 25, 2, said that a tax imposed for the public utility, i.e., the necessity of defending a province, touched all equally, but in proportion to their wealth in immovables, livestock, or money.

Taxation in a case of necessity, for the defense of province or Empire, for the common safety of all and the protection of all property (as Baldus said in the comment just referred to), and thus for the common utility, clearly belonged to the realm of public law. So also did the *fiscus* as the public treasury which controlled taxation levied publicly for the common welfare. Such taxation for the defense of the whole community was levied likewise in order to preserve the *status* of the community, be it province or Empire—or kingdom, since in a kingdom, some lawyers of the thirteenth century held, the king had all the public authority that the emperor had in the Empire: "Rex est imperator in regno suo." The king thus had the right to demand extraordinary taxes for the defense of the land in a case of necessity and public utility, for the prince administered and judged, if according to the law, for the common good of all. But the consent of all was required because all were touched by the necessity of a general tax for the common safety. Hence, at this point *quod omnes tangit,* a famous Romano-canonical maxim, became a principle of public law while remaining at the same time one of private law. Thus, public law was recognized in the kingdom—and in the Church—as well as in the Empire.

In their treatment of public law, therefore, the legists included the right of the public authority to tax for the *status* or public utility of the community. This power of taxation was not an outgrowth of the right of expropriation by the public authority, because it was not confiscation, and the consent of those taxed was more clearly involved. If the power to tax came under the scope of public law, so the power to legislate. This is not the place to discuss the medieval theory of legislation as law-finding rather than law-making. But in the thirteenth century the legists certainly held that the right to make statutes, general laws for the common utility, belonged to the public authority by public law, even though the consent of prelates and nobles (or, in the Italian republic, the consent of the leading citizens) was necessary. The power to legislate belonged to the ruler as the public authority, and general laws were made for the *status* or public utility of empire, kingdom, or city state. Moreover, the power of jurisdiction, as we have seen, was a part of the public law on magistracy, and jurisdiction in the Middle Ages was not clearly distinguished from legislation as law-finding. But all the same, there was a theory of law-making in the antique-modern sense. This theory derived in part from passages in *Code* and *Digest* on legislation by the Roman emperor for emergencies not covered by the old body of law, and on the making of new laws for new matters not decided by the old law, if "evident utility" exists. The legists interpreted "evident utility" as the common utility of all subjects and as a case of necessity. By doing so they showed that the public authority existed to meet emergencies, new situations, in order to maintain the common welfare or *status,* in the field of legislation as in that of taxation. Indeed, at least one famous legist, Odofredo, made extraordinary taxation a part of legislation. Commenting on *D.* 1, 4, 2, he said that *constitutiones* have to be made for new cases (*de rebus novis*) not decided by the old law; but they should not be made for new cases decided by the old law if the result was a departure from what had long seemed equitable (*equum*), unless the evident utility of the people demanded them. Then he added, by way of example, that no one should impose new *vectigalia* on his subjects unless "evidens utilitas" was manifest; and he referred for additional authority to *C.*

4, 62, 1ff., in which laws new *vectigalia* were prohibited unless the emperor decided that they were necessary.

On the relation of public law to taxation and legislation for the *status* or public utility of all in the community and of the community as a whole I have referred, for the thirteenth century, only to Azo, the *Glossa Ordinaria,* and Odofredo; I have not consulted all their glosses on many passages in *Institutes, Digest,* and *Code* which they cite as cross references. But a sufficient number of opinions has been given to show that by 1265 they had a real concept of public law. They could understand that, as Ulpian said, public law is that branch of law which deals with the public welfare, *status,* of the Republic and with the public authority, while private law deals primarily with the interest of individuals. They could understand that since the *status* of the community can be preserved only if there is a government which has the power to administer, legislate, judge, and tax, therefore the public law is divided into constitutional, administrative, and criminal law. In the *Code* in particular they found much public law relating to matters ecclesiastical, constitutional, fiscal, military, criminal, and municipal. They had a sufficient grasp of Roman law to appreciate the distinction between public and private.

This is evident in still another fashion. We have noted how, in the legal and political theories of the thirteenth century, the Roman emphasis on common or public utility was repeated, how the public utility was always placed, except occasionally in purely spiritual affairs like personal salvation, above private interests. This public utility, when asserted of Empire, Church, or kingdom, was the *status* for which the public law existed. Therefore, just as the legists preferred the public utility to private, they asserted that the public law cannot be changed by private agreements. For Papinian had said, *D.* 2, 14, 38: "Public law cannot be changed by the contracts of private individuals"; and this was repeated as a *regula iuris, D.* 50, 17, 45, 1: "A private agreement does not repeal (*derogat*) public law." The *Glossa ordinaria* to Papinian's statement offers the explanation that a private agreement is invalid against that part of public law which pertains both to the public authority and to the public utility, as in the case of the *fiscus,* or which relates to the public utility and safety of all in common; but permissible if against that part of public law which relates to private interests but is public by authority—although some say that private agreements must not be made against the public law which issues from the public authority for private interests.

It follows in part from this that when for the public welfare, the defense of the realm, a king asked for an extraordinary tax to meet the necessity, special privileges, immunities, and liberties, such as exemptions even of churches from taxation, all of which amounted to private contracts between king and individuals and corporations, were not valid. They must yield to the superior right of the public welfare, of the *status regni.* And all exempt persons and churches, if the government could demonstrate the existence of real necessity, must contribute their share of the subsidy.

The canonists in this period, *ca.* 1150-1265, are important, too, for their theory of public law in Church and State. They naturally discussed the question of the lay taxation of the clergy in terms of public necessity and utility. For in 1179 and 1215 the Third and Fourth Lateran Councils decided that cities (Italian communes) could tax the clergy if the common utility and necessity were evident and if the pope (this in 1215) was first consulted and gave his consent. The canon lawyers and royal governments quickly interpreted this to mean that the same law applied to kingdoms. From the 1220's on, in fact, until the time of Boniface VIII, we find the kings of England and France repeatedly obtaining papal permission to tax their clergy for the common utility in the emergency or necessity of a just war of defense. Popes, too, appealed to the case of necessity, that is, the defense of Christendom by means of a just war or Crusade against the infidel, the heretic, or Frederick II and Manfred, in order to compel the clergy to consent to special subsidies. In the Canon law, then, one finds the admission that in times of emergency the community includes clergy and churches. As we have seen, this thought goes back to late Roman imperial legislation and was discussed by the legists. In fact, it is, along with the Roman theory that the public law em-

braces the supervision of churches and the clergy, the essential
basis of the increasingly frequent assertions from 1250 on, by
men like Pierre Dubois, Marsiglio of Padua, William of Ockham, and the legists of the fourteenth century, that the State
is all-embracing and is therefore in special cases above the
Church. Thus if the Canon law maintained that the Church,
with papal consent, contributed voluntarily to the necessities of
a kingdom and was in theory still independent of the royal authority, Boniface VIII discovered in 1295-1296 that he *had* to
consent to the extraordinary taxation of the English and French
clergy by Edward I and Philip IV. Ironically, each of these
monarchs claimed that his necessity was a just war of defense
against the other.

There was, then, a theory of public law in the twelfth and
thirteenth centuries. Cicero, Roman jurisconsults, St. Augustine, and St. Thomas Aquinas all agreed that the common good
or utility was superior to private rights and interests; that governments existed to maintain the public welfare or *status* of
the Republic. Emphasizing passages in the *Corpus Iuris Civilis*,
the legists and canonists concluded that the public law pertained
to the *status* or public and common welfare and to the government necessary to achieve and maintain it. In other words, the
raison d'être of a king or prince was the preservation of the
status, state, of the *Respublica* or kingdom. Indeed, by the *ius
publicum* it belonged to the prerogative of the prince, said a
canonist of the late twelfth century, to protect the Republic
and provide it with *sacra*, priests, and magistrates.[8] The prerogative, then, was the public authority of the ruler; it was, we shall
see, the public "estate royal," the *status regis*, which was essential to the preservation of the *status regni*.[9]

Although it was chiefly the subject of public law, the *status*
or public and common welfare of the State was normally coin-
cident with the private welfare of all the members of the State.

---

[8] In the *Summa* "Antiquitate et tempore" (see Kuttner, *Repertorium*, pp.
178f.), to *Decretum*, Dist. 1, c.11: the *ius publicum* which pertains to the *Respublica* "est quod est de prerogativa imperatoris et sacerdotum et aliorum, quorum
precipue est tueri enim rempublicam et ei providere in sacris . . . et sacerdotibus
. . . et magistratibus"; Vat., MS Pal. 678.

[9] See below, chs. v-vii.

For normally the ruler was preserving the common welfare of all—and the common welfare was essential to the public welfare of the realm as a whole—when he maintained law and justice and protected private rights in his courts.[10] Normally, indeed, the king and the prerogative were subordinate to the private law of the land, even though the private law, receiving its validity from the right of the king to enforce it, was public by authority. In emergencies, however, when the welfare and safety of realm and people were endangered, the public law was superior to private law. In times of dire emergency the public welfare of the community as a whole was a public right that was above all private rights, liberties, and privileges. As the *status* of the realm, it was all-embracing and superior to the *status* either of the ruler or of any of his subjects, individual or corporate. The *status Reipublicae (regni)*, therefore, belonged definitely to public law, as did the prerogative of the king, which was essentially the right and duty to administer, judge, and legislate for the common and public welfare.

If, then, there was a concept of public law, was it accompanied by a theory of the State? We cannot answer this question without asking another question: were the *status*, or public welfare, the public law, and the right of the government to assure the *status Reipublicae*, above that law which in medieval theory was presumed to be sovereign? For in the modern sense the State is sometimes above the law of the land, above private law; and a concept of the State could hardly exist in the Middle Ages if the law was absolutely sovereign.

The answer, again, is that in the emergency of a danger that threatened the safety of all, the ruler had a superior right to take such action as would ensure the public welfare or safety, that is, maintain the *status* or state of the realm. This emergency was a case of necessity—usually, as I have had occasion to say above, a just war of defense. Now the case of necessity, Meinecke

10 *Utilitas communis* and *utilitas publica* often meant the same thing. Here I make the distinction that was made by the legists when they sometimes held that *communis* refers to the welfare of the individual members, *publica* to the welfare of the corporate body of the State as a whole and considered apart from the individual members. But they were not consistent; see below, ch. VIII, n. 24, for a brief discussion of the problem.

has shown, was asserted by Machiavelli as a part of his theory of the State: the State is above all; and the prince, to assure the noble end of the State, has the right to use any means to meet the necessity and preserve the State. Necessity is Guicciardini's reason of State. But it had its medieval background—Meinecke finding the earliest statement in the maxim, "necessity knows no law," in the late fourteenth century—in Gerson; Helene Wieruszowski finding it stated, along with public utility, in the time of Frederick II.

Actually it goes back farther—if not to the Greeks, at any rate to Mark 2, 25-26; and above all to the *Corpus Iuris Canonici* and the *Corpus Iuris Civilis*. A pseudo-Isidorian canon in Gratian (*De cons.*, Dist. 1, c. 11) uses the very expression, "quoniam necessitas non habet legem"; decretists and decretalists from the late twelfth century on state the maxim and in their glosses explain its meaning in connection with the equitable interpretation of the law. For example, the necessity of hunger, says one, excuses theft; poverty, says another, knows no law; and the law ends, says a glossator, when necessity begins. Azo in his *Brocardica* discusses the rule and gives many citations *pro* and *con* to *Code* and *Digest*. To *D.* 9, 2, 4, where we find that it is lawful to kill a thief in the night (the correspondence to *Exod.* 22, 2-3, had been noted by St. Augustine and was discussed by the canonists) because "natural reason" permits one to defend oneself against danger, Accursius gives complete approval.

Here, "Necessity knows no law" was a principle of private law. But because of the theory of the just war, that is, the right of the kingdom to defend itself against the aggressor (St. Augustine stated it, as did the scholastic philosophers), the case of necessity became a principle of public law in the thirteenth century; the equivalent of "just cause," "evident utility," and the common welfare, it was perforce connected with the preservation of the *status regni*. From the twelfth century on, the kings of France and England appealed to necessity as the justification for demanding extraordinary taxes. As we have seen, the Church had already recognized the validity of necessity in the lay taxation of the clergy. No wonder, then, that in the late thirteenth century French lawyers, not only Beaumanoir and Pierre Dubois, but royal councillors like Pierre Flot and William of Nogaret, were asserting that in a case of necessity the defense of the kingdom and all its members was a superior right of the *status regni*; and that if "what touched all must be approved of all," the king had the right to compel all, even the clergy, to consent to measures taken to meet the danger.

At the same time, the situation of "international wars," necessity, public welfare, and the rise of powerful monarchies broke down the corporate hierarchy of communities within the Empire. Each great kingdom, like England or France, by the middle of the thirteenth century was independent of the Empire in theory and practice alike. And at the end of the century each was independent of the Church—and even above the Church, except in purely spiritual matters.[11]

When, therefore, a king stated that a great danger, emergency, or necessity had arisen that touched king and kingdom, the *status regis et regni*, and the common welfare and safety, he was reflecting the terminology and theory developed by the legists and canonists.

At this point we again perceive a conscious, intelligent theory of public law. The public law was that law which pertained to the public and common welfare of the kingdom; and when the common welfare or safety was threatened, the public law was above the private. In this sense necessity was a part of the public law, and thus "necessity knew no *private* law." In cases of necessity, to be sure, the public law was still closely related to private law, since all interested parties had the right to represent their rights before the government. Nonetheless, added to the traditional rights of the crown, the use of reason of State, the "reason of the public welfare" and the "reason of necessity" made the royal prerogative superior to the private right of consent.

Does all this imply a theory of the State? My conclusion is that it does. Although normally *status* meant the condition or standing of individuals, classes, or regions, in connection with the public law it meant the common welfare and public utility of the whole community of the kingdom. A tautology, indeed,

[11] See ch. x.

was involved in this meaning, for the *status* was the public welfare and the *Respublica* alike. It was what would be called, in seventeenth-century England, the commonweal, the Commonwealth, or the State of the Commonwealth. In French terms it was both the *commun profit* and the *chose publique*.

Not yet, in the thirteenth century, was the "state of the realm" completely personified as the highest juridical entity. But *Respublica, Regnum,* and *Civitas* had become public corporate bodies which by the fiction of law could act and could be defended. Naturally, no juristic person whether public or private can do or suffer anything. Kings and governments, however, already acted in the name of the Realm, the State as a whole; and the State had become something that was above and different from the individual collectivity of all the members, including the king as head. If the *status regni (lestat du roialme* in the Statute of York, 1322) still meant the public welfare of the Realm, the Realm was the State, the public welfare of which must be maintained. Since the public welfare was called *status,* and was inseparable from the public interest—the substance and end of the Realm itself—gradually *status* came to be the word used not only for the *utilitas publica* and the indispensable public authority of the royal government, but also for the abstract community of the Realm. *Regnum* became *Status,* the Realm the State. It is interesting that we still speak of the "state of the Republic," the "state of the nation," and of the State.

On the foundation of the two laws and of the rise of feudal monarchies, the theory, and some practice, of public law and the State thus arose in the twelfth and thirteenth centuries. Private rights and privileges remained powerful and enjoyed a recrudescence in localism and privileged orders in the fourteenth century and later. At times, in periods of war and civil dissension, they weakened the public authority of kings and threatened the very survival of the State.[12] But the ideas and

12 Naturally I cannot attempt to outline the history of the failures of the public order of the State and of the public authority of the king in the fourteenth and fifteenth centuries. At times, in France for example, king and realm meant little except in the continuity of the ideas and ideal of the public law symbolized by the crown. As late as the eighteenth century, local and individual privileges

ideal of the State and public order, of a public and constitutional law, were constantly at hand to remind statesmen of their right to reconstitute the State.

---

and local resistance to the commands of the central government made the State weak. On this see in general the excellent book by R. R. Palmer, *The Age of the Democratic Revolution*. To return to the fourteenth century, in France, after the time of Philip IV, particularly in the period of the disasters of the Hundred Years' War and the Black Death, there was far less of a State than in the thirteenth century. *Plena potestas, quod omnes tangit,* and *status regni* apparently no longer manifested the power as well as the theoretical right of the king to obtain more than haphazard and sporadic consent, chiefly in local assemblies, to extraordinary taxes. In England the situation was different, but even there the legal thought I have investigated needs study in relation to the political events. For the situation in France see, besides C. H. Taylor in Strayer and Taylor, *Studies*, Fredric Cheyette, "Procurations by Large-Scale Communities in Fourteenth-Century France," *Speculum*, xxxvii (1962), 18-31.

PART I
CORPORATE COMMUNITY, REPRESENTATION, AND CONSENT

CHAPTER I ✦ PARISIAN MASTERS AS

A CORPORATION, 1200-1246[1]

E BEGIN with the corporation in order to understand the early history of the medieval creation of the University and to show how in the early thirteenth century the corporate community and its representation by agents developed in response to the revival of the Roman and Canon law and to the political, social, economic, and cultural needs of men. But if we begin with the corporation, we do not end with the interpretation that the *esprit corporatif* was an obstacle to a higher ordering of society in Church and State. The rise of the University of Paris as a corporation was not a-chieved without the subordination of the corporate body and its members to the public law of the Church. Similarly, when in subsequent chapters we study the rise of the representation of towns and shires in royal courts and assemblies, we shall observe that community and corporate rights, and the individual rights of the members, submitted increasingly to the public welfare (*status*) of the State and to the public authority of the prince.

In the first half of the thirteenth century the masters in the schools at Paris won measurably in a struggle for corporate free-dom from the direct control of the cathedral chapter and the bishop. Whether they could form a corporation was a matter of doubt to canonists in the second decade of the century;[2] that they could do so was still a source of mild surprise a generation later.[3] When they received legal recognition as a corporation

[1] This study first appeared in *Speculum*, IX (1934), 421-445.

[2] Johannes Teutonicus, gloss ad v. *de iure communi* (*Compilatio IV*, 1, t. *De procuratoribus*, c.2; *Decr. Greg. IX* 1, 38, 7): "Dubitationis causa hec fuit [whether the *scolares* at Paris could elect procurators *ad litem*], quia scolares non videntur constituere universitatem, cum causam vel ius universitatis non sint a principe consecuti . . ." (Bamberg, MS Can. 23, fol. 12ᵛ). He concludes that they could; see below, n. 86.

[3] Henry of Susa (Hostiensis), *Summa*, 5, t. *De magistris*: "Porro si universitas

is even now a subject of controversy.[4] The problem of the rise of the corporation or *universitas* of masters at Paris therefore merits reconsideration. How and when the new corporation appeared and became legal can be understood only after a careful study of contemporary theories and definitions and of the extent to which the body of masters, in the terminology of the period, in their functions and organization, in their legal competency (through procuration) in the procedure of ecclesiastical courts,[5] and in the recognition of their collectivity by the papacy,

---

magistrorum et scolarium consideretur, certum est quod singularium scientiarum modi et studia sunt diversa, et tamen unum corpus faciunt, et insimul coherent, et insimul coniunguntur."

[4] H. Denifle held that the essential University of Paris, the society of masters, was flourishing by 1209 and that a corporation of students was legally recognized by 1215, *Universitäten*, pp. 63-131, 68f., 76-82, 86-88, 91, 129-131; cf. Denifle and E. Chatelain, *Chartularium Universitatis Parisiensis*, I, ixf. His conclusions were, on the whole, accepted by Rashdall, *Universities of Europe in the Middle Ages*, I, 288, 293-325. See now the new ed. of Rashdall by Powicke and Emden, I, 292-343. My references are mainly to the old ed.; I refer to the Powicke-Emden ed. only when it is necessary to indicate corrections of Rashdall's work.

Louis Halphen reconsidered the problem and concluded that the corporation was not fully and definitively recognized by the papacy until 1231-1246, "Les débuts de l'Université de Paris," *Studi Medievali, Nuova Serie*, II (1929), 134-139; "Les universités au XIIIe siècle," *Revue historique*, CLXVI (1931), 222; and *L'Essor de l'Europe (Peuples et Civilizations*, VI, Paris, 1932), 322. Here M. Halphen seems to recognize the University as existing before 1231, but only as an "association générale" and as a "collectivité," not as a fully legal corporation. This divergence in opinions is largely a result of different conceptions of a corporation in the first half of the thirteenth century. Denifle and Rashdall tend to accept as a legal corporation one which acts as such before it has obtained its complete organization and which is only tacitly recognized by superior authorities through privileges. M. Halphen would postpone legality until all the functions are exercised and all the privileges obtained which were deemed necessary in a later period of the development of corporation theory. Since he himself admits that the whole subject merits further study (*Studi Medievali*, II, 139), and has (along with Denifle and Rashdall) neglected the corporation as it acted in the courts and was treated in legal practice, I feel that further considerations, based on contemporary opinions and legal procedure, are needed.

[5] The masters and students and their corporation were subject to Canon law; Rashdall, *Universities*, I, 292f.; *Chartularium*, I, Introd., no. 15; *Decr. Greg. IX* 2, 2, 9—on which Bernard of Parma, *Casus*: "Nota, quod dicitur in ista decr. speciale est parisius in favorem universitatis," Paris, MS lat. 3965, fol. 50v; and a gloss: "scolares parisienses conquesti sunt quod quando conveniebantur vel conveniebant, non recipiebantur canones allegati, sed consuetudo terre, unde super hoc providetur"; in an *Apparatus* to *Decr. Greg. IX* (BN, MS lat. 3949), 2, 2, 9. Cf. *Chartularium*, I, Introd., no. 15, n. 2, "scolares." The statements above, while late, strengthen the evidence that Celestine III had in mind especially students at Paris; but see Denifle, *Univ.*, p. 680 n. 88. See the privilege of Philip Augustus, 1200, *Chartularium*, I, no. 1; and M. M. Davy, "La situation juridique des étu-

corresponded to a corporation in thirteenth-century thought and practice.

1. Theories and Definitions

In general, the conceptions of a corporation held by civil and canon lawyers of the thirteenth century were lacking in precision.[6] A corporation might be called a *corpus, universitas, communitas, collegium, societas,*[7] or even (by Pillius) a *consortium* or *schola,*[8] and it was vaguely defined as a *collectio personarum plurium,*[9] or "plurium corporum inter se distantium, uno nomine specialiter eis deputata."[10] Three persons or more in a profession[11] could form a *collegium*[12] for the purpose of securing justice for each member, but the *collegium* must be recognized either by common law[13] or by the "tacit or express approval" of a superior authority.[14] Such a corporation could elect its own officers and representatives,[15] could within certain

---

diants de l'Université de Paris au XIIIe siècle," *Revue d'Histoire de l'Eglise de France,* xvii (1931), 298f., 310f.

[6] Gierke, *Deutsche Genossenschaftsrecht,* iii, 192, 247f. Cited hereafter as Gierke, iii.

[7] *Ibid.,* 193, 248.   [8] *Ibid.,* 193.

[9] Pillius (*ca.* 1192), Gierke, iii, 193.

[10] Hugolinus, *ibid.,* 193; cf. gloss ad v. *unum corpus* (*Compilatio III,* 1, t. *De constitutionibus* c. 1; *Decr. Greg. IX,* 1, 2, 6: "Corporum tria genera distinguuntur in iure civili, unumquodque uno spiritu continetur, ut homo, lignum, lapis, et sumitur species large; aliud quod coherentibus partibus constat, ut domus, navis; tercium quod ex partibus distantibus constat, ut populus, collegium, grex . . ." (Paris, BN, MS lat. 15398, fol. 106[r]). Henry of Susa, *Summa,* 1, t. *De sindico*: *universitas,* "collectio plurium corporum racionabilium speciali nomine attributo"; *collegium,* "plurium personarum collectio simul inhabitantium speciali nomine attributo."

[11] Azo: "magistri ergo possunt eligere consules quia ipsi exercent professionem"; Accursius: "magistri ergo possunt eligere, quia ipsi exercent professionem, et sic fit Parisius"; Denifle, *Univ.,* p. 170, nn. 425-427.

[12] Gloss ad v. *in congregatione* (*Comp. I,* 1, t. *De electione,* c. 1; *Decr.,* 1, 6, 1): "Nota quod duo faciunt congregationem, ut hic, tres collegium, ff. de verbi significatione, Neratius [*D.* 50, 16, 85]"; Halle, Universitätsbibl., MS Ye 80; and Alanus, ad v. *donum ratum* (*Comp. I,* 1, t. *De consuetudine,* c.2; *Decr.,* 3, 24, 3): "Est contra ff. de verbi sign., Neratius, ubi dicitur quod non nisi tres faciunt collegium, quod verum est quoad contestationem ipsius; durare tamen potest in uno. Al."; Halle, MS Ye 52. For later opinions see Gierke, iii, 287 n. 125.

[13] Hugolinus and others, Gierke, iii, 207f.

[14] *Ibid.,* 208, and, for the statement of Innocent IV, p. 289. For an ecclesiastical corporation, the authority of the bishop was needed, but not for a corporation of masters or students; so also Henry of Susa, *Summa,* 1, t. *De sindico.*

[15] Gierke, iii, 208, 228, 304f.

limits make statutes,[16] could possess property,[17] and could, as a legal person,[18] sue and be sued through a *syndicus* or *procurator*.[19] In detail these conceptions varied from time to time, and developed in step with the evolution of corporations and legal procedure.

2. TERMINOLOGY

If the term *consortium* has small legal significance with Pillius, it is at least interesting that it is used in a corporate sense in papal letters to the masters at Paris in 1208-1209[20] and as late as 1253[21] and 1255.[22] We find *communitas scolarium* used in 1207,[23] and *communio magistrorum* and *societas magistrorum* in the next two years.[24] But the term *universitas*, in the strict

16 *Ibid.*, 215f., 307-328.

17 *Ibid.*, 209f., 291-301.

18 Roffredus of Beneventum held that a representative could not function in court for a *pars universitatis*, for the "universitas est quoddam individuum, unde partes non habet" (*ibid.*, 204). But the conception of the fictitious person is first fully expressed by Innocent IV (pp. 278-282).

19 *Ibid.*, 232, 309, 336f., 338, 340f. Henry of Susa emphasizes the rights of owning property (*res communes*), having a common chest or purse (*arca communis*), and of having a "sindicum vel actorem per quos agant atque respondeant," *Summa*, I, t. *De sindico*; cf. *D.* 3, 4, 1, 1, where the same rights are stressed.

20 *Chartularium*, I, 68. Rashdall, *Universities*, I, 293f. (292f.), and Denifle, *Chartularium*, I, ix, find an earlier use of *consortium* in 1170-1175 in the life of John, Abbot of St. Albans (1195-1214), by Thomas of Walsingham, *Gesta Abbatum Sancti Albani*, ed. H. T. Riley, I, 217, "in juventute . . . ad electorum consortium magistrorum meruit attingere." But these words belong to Matthew Paris, not, probably, to the original annals of the monastery (see Riley's introduction, pp. xf.), and should not be attached to the masters of 1170-1175.

21 *Chartularium*, I, nos. 222 and 224; on the restoration of the Friars regent in theology "ad statum pristinum et ad collegium magistrorum ac Universitatis consortium" (p. 247).

22 *Ibid.*, pp. 284, 285ff., 293, where Alexander IV uses the terms *collegium* and *consortium Universitatis*, and also *consortium magistrorum*, while the masters and students use *collegium Universitatis* and *consortium magistrorum*; cf. p. 243.

23 *Ibid.*, p. 65; statute of the bishop and cathedral chapter of Paris.

24 *Ibid.*, pp. 67f. Halphen, *Studi Medievali*, II, 135, objects to attaching any significance to the expression used by Innocent III, "ex tunc beneficio societatis eorum [magistrorum] in magistralibus privaretur," on the ground that Master G. was excluded not from a corporation but merely from association with other masters and from the enjoyment of the advantages of this association. Apparently M. Halphen does not reflect that the main purpose of a corporation was to secure for each member certain professional advantages, and that it must regulate membership; cf. *infra*, nn. 43-51. In 1253 the University expelled the two Dominican regents in theology (*Chartularium*, I, nos. 219, 222, 230, 247); Alexander IV describes the expulsion in the terms used almost fifty years earlier by Innocent III, "eos beneficio societatis in magistralibus," *ibid.*, p. 280. Deprivation

sense of corporation as opposed to any group of persons (as in *Noverit universitas vestra*), was that which was most often used to designate the whole body of masters and students—that is, the masters of the four Faculties[25]—acting as a legal person.[26] In the first original instrument drawn up in their name, 1221, the masters term themselves "nos universitas magistrorum et scolarium Parisiensium."[27] More important is the terminology in the text of papal letters and legatine ordinances relating to the masters and students: *universitas vestra* and *magistrorum,* 1208-1209;[28] *vestra universitas,* 1210-1213;[29] *universitas magis-*

---

of magisterial rights was serious; it was the loss of all rights in the corporation. Although until 1213 an expelled master could continue to teach in the diocese, since his license to teach was obtained from the chancellor, after 1213 the chancellor could not grant the license to a candidate not approved by the masters, *ibid.,* I, no. 16. These magisterial rights are listed by Henry of Susa (cited by Bernard of Parma, glosses on *Decretals of Gregory IX*), ad v. *in magistralibus* (*Decr.,* 1, 2, 11): "i.e., in consiliis, exequiis, conventibus, examinationibus, et licentiis dandis, et aliis tractatibus et libertatibus magistrorum. hos.," BN, MS lat. 3949, fol. 7ʳ.

25 Rashdall, *Universities,* I, 322 (321) ff. The masters in the Faculty of Arts were often at the same time students in the higher Faculties of Medicine, Canon Law, and Theology. That the masters constituted the University is shown by the fact that they appointed procurators and petitioned for a seal; see below, nn. 95-102 and part 5 of this study.

26 About 1214 Guillaume le Breton speaks of the *universitas scolarium* and its action against Amaury de Bène before 1204 or 1207; H. F. Delaborde, *Œuvres de Rigord et Guillaume le Breton,* (Paris, 1882), I, 231: Amaury "accessit ad summum pontificem, qui, audita ejus propositione et universitatis scolarium contradictione, sententiavit contra ipsum. Redit ergo Parisius, et compellitur ab Universitate confiteri ore quod in contrarium predicte opinioni sue sentiret." But the words *ab Universitate* cannot be proved to be by Guillaume le Breton; *ibid.,* II, iv-v, and xxxvii, on the date of the manuscripts; Rashdall, *Universities,* I, 300f. (299) n. 1. On the date of the *Gesta* of Guillaume, see A. Molinier, *Les Sources de l'Histoire de France,* I, iii, 4.

27 *Chartularium,* I, no. 42.

28 *Ibid.,* pp. 67f. Halphen, *Studi Medievali,* II, 135, thinks that the vaguer meaning is intended because the decretal is addressed "Universis doctoribus sacre pagine, decretorum et liberalium artium," failing to note that the *universitas magistrorum* is enforcing its statutes and expelling Master G. from the *consortium* and *societas* of the masters. His further objection, that the decretal is not dated, is without foundation, for it appears in the Register of Innocent III, *an.* 11, and in *Compilatio III,* 2, 15, 12 (*Decr. Greg. IX* 1, 2, 11); Schulte, *Quellen und Literatur,* I, 87; cf. *Chartularium,* I, 68, note; Kuttner, *Repertorium,* on *Comp. III.*

29 *Chartularium,* I, no. 24, "interdum vestra universitas ad agendum et respondendum commode interesse non potest"; decretal of Innocent III granting to the "scolaribus Parisiensibus" the right of electing a procurator for litigation. Contrary to Halphen, *Studi Medievali,* II, 135, who holds that the word *universi-*

trorum et scolarium, 1215,[30] 1221,[31] and 1222;[32] *doctorum et discipulorum Parisiensium universitas* and *universitas doctorum*, 1219;[33] *magistri et universitas scolarium*, 1228;[34] *universitas scolarium*, 1231;[35] and *universitas magistrorum vel scolarium*, 1231.[36] Not until 1245 does the address of an original papal bull directed to the masters and students contain the word *universitas*.[37] This late appearance, however, of the term *universitas* in the address cannot be taken as the first possible date of a legal corporation,[38] for the usual form of address, which was

tas here is used in a general sense, I think that a corporate sense is indicated by the fact that procuration was granted in response to a petition (on petitions, *infra*, nn. 91, 103-105), and that the *universitas* could have a procurator. The canonists refuse the right of procuration to an illegal corporation—Johannes Teutonicus and Innocent IV (*infra*, n. 86). Thus not *any* collectivity could have a procurator, and the moment Innocent III recognized that the masters at Paris could have one they constituted a corporation. A suit of the abbot against the men of Saint-Gilles in 1257 illustrates the connection of procuration with incorporation; E. Bligny-Bondurand, *Les Coutumes de Saint-Gilles*, Paris, 1915, p. 183. I owe this reference to Professor C. H. Taylor. In the French royal courts, however, as in the English, communities of all kinds could act as corporations and send representatives to courts and assemblies; see below, ch. III.

30 *Chartularium*, I, no. 20, p. 79, statutes of Cardinal Robert de Courçon, apostolic legate, for the University. Strangely, Halphen, *loc. cit.*, asserts that these statutes do not mention the University; yet it is decreed that transgressors should appear "coram universitatem magistrorum et scolarium, vel coram aliquibus ab Universitate constitutis."

31 *Ibid.*, no. 41; "sigillo nomine universitatis magistrorum et scolarium nuper facto."

32 *Ibid.*, no. 45; Honorius III prohibits sentences of excommunication "in universitatem magistrorum et scolarium."

33 *Ibid.*, no. 31; chiefly on procuration.

34 *Ibid.*, no. 58; confirmation of articles of the settlement of a struggle with the bishop and chancellor.

35 *Ibid.*, 137; statutes and privileges of Gregory IX; for the *universitas scolarium* two masters are to receive the chancellor's oath.

36 *Ibid.*, no. 95; prohibition of excommunication of this *universitas* or its officer; cf. no. 113.

37 *Ibid.*, no. 135, "dilectis filiis magistris et universitati scolarium Parisiensium." On the back of the document is the address, "Universitas parisiensis," probably written by a chancery official. From this time on, it is found in varying combinations: in the formula just given, or with "doctoribus" in place of "magistris," 1247, 1253, and 1254 (I, nos. 169, 222, 225, and 237); or "dil. fil. universitati magistrorum et scolarium" (1259, I, nos. 349 and 350); or "dil. fil. Universitati Parisiensi" (first in 1263, I, no. 382).

38 Halphen, *Studi Medievali*, II, 135, thinks that because the decretal of Innocent III, 1208-1209 (*Chartularium*, I, no. 8), was addressed "universis doctoribus," it related not to a university but merely to all the doctors. Yet, in the text the pope speaks of the *universitas, societas,* and *consortium magistrorum*, which has its statutes and expels members. It could be equally maintained 'hat

the earliest and continued to be used after the new formula appeared, was "universis magistris et scolaribus," 1215,[39] or "dilectis filiis magistris et scolaribus," 1217;[40] or, preferably, "dil. fil. universis magistris et scolaribus Parisiensibus (Parisius commorantibus)," 1220.[41] By 1215, then, nearly all the terms used by lawyers for corporations are found in the sources relating to the masters at Paris.[42] But a final conclusion cannot be drawn from terminology alone; more important than terminology, which is not fixed, is the question, when did the masters act as a legal corporation?

3. FUNCTIONS AND PRIVILEGES

A corporation of any importance could control its membership by establishing rules and regulations with which the apprentices or students must conform in order to be admitted into the guild. At Paris the chancellor of the cathedral chapter granted the license to teach, or the formal recognition of the

---

Alexander IV's *Quasi lignum vitae* in 1255 does not refer to a corporation—although the terms *universitas, consortium,* and *collegium* are evident in the text—because it is addressed "dil. fil. universis magistris et scolaribus Paris" (*ibid.*, I, no. 247). But Halphen concedes that the University of Paris was legally constituted in 1231, when Gregory IX addressed the *Parens scientiarum* "dil. fil. universis magistris scolaribus Paris" (*Chartularium,* I, 136).

[39] *Chartularium,* I, no. 20.

[40] *Ibid.,* no. 25; thereafter, 1246, 1252, 1259 (I, nos. 162, 215, 343).

[41] *Ibid.,* no. 36; for later examples, nos. 40, 79, 113, 143, 165, 207, 211, 247, 271, 383, 512. In papal bulls not preserved in the original we find "universis magistris et scolaribus Paris." as early as 1205 (I, no. 3), "universis doctoribus etc." in 1208-1209 (no. 8), and "scolaribus Parisiensibus" in 1210-1212 (no. 24).

Guido Faba in his *Summa Dictaminis* notes how papal privileges should be addressed to masters and students at Bologna: "exemplum: Gregorius, etc. . . . dilectis filiis doctoribus et magistris et universitati scolarium Bononie commorancium," Rockinger, *Briefsteller und Formelbücher,* 198, n. 2. But no bull of Gregory IX to the masters and students at Paris is addressed to a *universitas;* the first is from Innocent IV, 1245. The University of Bologna was nearer Rome, and most of the notaries and *scriptores* in the papal chancery were trained in Italy; hence, probably, since the students constituted the University of Bologna, such addresses as "dil. fil. magistris et universitati scolarium Paris.," 1245; the address given in *Compilatio IV* for the decretal *Quia in causis,* 1210-1212 (*Chartularium* I, no. 24), "Scolaribus Paris.," is perhaps owing to the misunderstanding of the compiler of this collection who was probably a canonist of Bologna (cf. Schulte, *Quellen,* I, 89). In their own documents the masters at Paris term themselves *universitas magistrorum et scolarium, Chartularium,* I, nos. 42, 62, 136, 219, 230, 355, 462, 477, 478.

[42] *Collegium* and *corpus* are the exceptions; they are not used, so far as I know, until 1253-1254; *Chartularium,* I, 247, 253, 284.

fitness of the apprentice student to enter the profession of teaching as a member of the society of masters. His control of the license, at first arbitrary, was limited by Alexander III[43] and reduced to a formality as a result of litigation in 1212-1213 between the masters and the chancellor before judges delegated by Innocent III.[44] Henceforth the chancellor must confer the *licentia docendi* on all candidates examined and recommended by the majority of the masters of the Faculties of Theology, Canon and Civil Law,[45] or Medicine, or by the majority of six masters chosen from the Faculty of Arts.[46] This arrangement was simplified but maintained in its essentials by Gregory IX.[47] Examined and approved by the masters of his Faculty, and licensed by the chancellor, the new member of the society of masters must observe the customs and obey the statutes of the guild. We learn from a decretal of Innocent III, *Ex litteris*, 1208-1209,[48] that the masters of theology, Canon law, and liberal arts had elected eight from their body to put into statutes their customs in the matters of costume, the order of lectures and disputations, and funerals,[49] and to submit them all to an oath of obedience. All but one, a Master G., took the oath; and the masters decreed the deprivation of the privileges of their society of any disobedient colleague who refused to appear within three days, after three summonses, before the *universitas magistrorum*. Master G. was expelled, but later decided to take the oath. Some of the masters, however, thought that he could

43 See my study, "Alexander III, the *Licentia Docendi*," *Haskins Anniversary Essays*, pp. 260-263, 268-275.

44 *Chartularium*, I, nos. 14, 16, 17, 18.

45 Only Canon law after 1219; *ibid.*, p. 92.

46 *Ibid.*, no. 16. The terms of this settlement were confirmed by the Cardinal-Legate Robert de Courçon in 1215; *ibid.*, no. 20.

47 *Ibid.*, no. 79, p. 137; *an.* 1231. Another arrangement was made in 1225-1226, but its terms are lost; *ibid.*, nos. 45, n. 3, and 58. In 1219-1222 the chancellor tried to refuse the license, and the students had recourse to the abbot of Sainte-Geneviève; this action, sanctioned by Honorius III, still further weakened the authority of the chancellor; *ibid.*, nos. 41, p. 99, and 45, p. 103.

48 *Ibid.*, no. 8, from *Compilatio III*, 2, t. 15, c. 12 (*Decr. Greg. IX* 1, 2, 11).

49 *Chartularium*, I, 67; some of the masters of arts had violated the customs of their elders, "habitu videlicet inhonesto, in lectionum et disputationum ordine non servato, et pio usu in celebrandis exequiis decedentium clericorum jam quasi penitus negligenter omisso." Tancred, the canonist, remarks, ad v. *inhonesto* (*Comp. III*, 2, 15, c. 12), "forte capas manicatas portando, cum doctores consueverint capas clausas deferre" (Leipzig, Universitätsbibl., MS 968, fol. 164).

not be readmitted to membership until he obtained a mandate from the pope ordering them to restore him to their body, since their decree and oath of expulsion permitted of no reconsideration. So Innocent III declared that the decree of deprivation was not intended *in perpetuum*,[50] and ordered the masters to readmit Master G. to their *consortium in magistralibus*.[51] It

---

[50] Cf. gloss ad v. *in perpetuum* (*Comp. III*, 2, e. t., c. Ex litteris): "sed quid si simpliciter dictum esset, presumeretur in perpetuum esse statutum, ut C. de penis, servus [*C*. 9, 47, 10]; unde si per imperitiam non statuissent tempus, videtur quod. x. annis deberet esse privatus, ff. e., sine prefinito tempore [*D*. 48, 19, 23]"; BN, MS lat. 15398, fol. 145ᵛ. This point is discussed more fully by Innocent IV, *Apparatus*, 1, t. *De constitutionibus*, c. Ex litteris: ". . . ubi propter contumaciam tantum amovetur que ut dicit hic penam perpetuam non meretur sed quousque peniteat vel satisfaciat tunc iuramentum et privatio eius temporale intelligitur, i.e., quousque satisfaciat quia iuramentum est secundum ius interpretandum."

[51] Vincentius Hispanus remarks, ad v. *admittatis*, c. Ex litteris: "Non obstante isto mandato, si quid medio tempore deliquisset, ipse possit repelli, supra, de ces. c. ult., ar. ff. de transac. cum aquiliana [*D*. 2, 15, 5]"; Chartres, MS lat. 384 (formerly 462), fol. 172ᵛ; MS Vat. lat. 1378, fol. 47ᵛ. Another gloss, by Vincentius, ad v. *in eodem statu*, seems to imply that Master G. was not deprived of his license to teach but only of association with the masters: "id est, docendi officio non renu[n]cians, si cum renunciaret ex inde non esset ei pena, non habere communionem magistrorum; vel in eo statu, id est, exclusus a communione, quasi diceret non se ingerens improbe simile xviij. d. si episcopus metropolitanus [*Decretum*, Dist. 18, c. 13]"; MS Vat. lat. 1378, fol. 47. Henry of Susa thus lists magisterial rights, gloss ad v. *in magistralibus*: "i.e., in consiliis, exequiis, conventibus, examinationibus, et licentiis dandis, et aliis tractatibus et libertatibus magistrorum hos.," BN, MS lat. 3949, fol. 7.
An interesting interpretation of this decretal is given in a *Casus Decretalium* of the middle of the century (probably by Bernardus Parmensis or Bernardus Compostellanus junior; cf. Schulte, *Quellen*, II, 114, 118), BN, MS lat. 16543, fol. 5ᵛ (to *Decr.* 1, 2, 11): "*Ex litteris*. Casus. Magistri liberalium artium parisius commorantes a consuetudine antiqua in quibusdam articulis deviaverant. Ipsi volentes consuetudinem pristinam reformare, iuramento interposito statuerunt (iuraverunt), quod si quis magistrorum ordinationi universitatis ipsorum duceret (induceret) resistendum tertio commonitus infra triduum universitate parere contempneret, ex tunc consorcio aliorum in magistralibus privaretur; propter quod magister G. communione ipsorum fuit privatus, tandem voluit redire et obedire universitati. Utrum deberet (debeat) recipi dubitabatur: quidam dicebant quod sic debebat (debet) remanere privatus; alii dicebant quod recipiendus erat, ex quo volebat satisfacere; alii dicebant quod no posset recipi propter iuramentum absque licentia domini pape. Unde papa consultus respondet, quia (quod) constitutum non fuit ut huius[modi] privatio imperpetuum duraret (perduraret), et tam de iure quam de consuetudine ecclesie existit ut, qui propter contumaciam aliorum communione privatur, cum satisfacere voluerit, restitui debeat. Mandat dominus papa quod dictum magistrum obedire volentem admittant in magistralibus ad consorcium universitatis.
"Nota, quod qui simpliciter a communione aliorum excluditur propter contumaciam, debet recipi cum satisfacere voluerit. Item, nota, quod iuramentum benigne interpretandum est." The variant readings are from MS lat. 16544, fol 3ᵛ.

can hardly be doubted that the pope herein tacitly recognized the right of the masters to have statutes and to enforce them. In commenting on this decretal, the canonists who glossed the *Compilatio III* raise no objection to their right to make statutes;[52] instead they admit that the masters had a corporate *voluntas* in imposing on all members of the corporation an oath of obedience to the statutes.[53] In causing statutes to be drawn up the masters acted as one body, for the validity of such statutes depended on the *consensus communis*.[54] But according to Honorius III, a cathedral chapter could not make new statutes without the consent of the bishop.[55] On a similar reservation the bishop and chancellor of Paris in 1219-1225 based their contestation of the right of the masters, without their consent, to make common cause through *constitutiones* and other obligations under oath,[56] in spite of the attitude of Innocent III and his legate, Robert de Courçon, who in 1215 provided that the masters could by *obligationes* and *constitutiones* made under

52 Johannes Galensis, Johannes Teutonicus, Silvester, Vincentius, Laurentius, and Tancred; Schulte, *Quellen*, I, 229; Fr. Gillman, *Archiv für katholisches Kirchentrecht*, CV (1925), 488-565; CVI (1926), 149-155; CIX (1929), 598-641; CX (1930), 157-186; CXII (1932), 99-110; CXIII (1933), 99, 480, n. 2; and Kuttner, *Repertorium*, pp. 355-368. When the *Ex litteris* was incorporated into the *Decretals of Gregory IX* in 1234, it was placed under a different *titulus, De constitutionibus*, instead of the old t. *De iureiurando* in *Comp. III*, for it was then recognized as being important in showing the right of corporations to make statutes, and Henry of Susa so discusses it, *Summa*, I, t. *De constitutionibus*: "Quis possit constitutionem facere? . . . Item universitas clericorum seu magistrorum. infra. e. ex litteris. Item civitas sive universitas instit. de iur. natu. . . . Idem credo de quolibet collegio approbato. infra. e. que in ecclesiarum. et c. ex litteris et de hoc nota infra de syndico." Likewise Abbas Antiquus (1260-1275; Schulte, *Quellen*, II, 130f.), on the *Ex litteris*: "Nota magistros facere universitatem"; Denifle, *Univ.*, I, 172 n. 434. Cf. Henry of Susa, *Commentaria*, I, t. 38, c. 7.

53 Gloss ad v. *iuramento interposito*, c. Ex litteris: "Notabis hic quod parere debetur universitate, qui de eius voluntate compromittit;" BN, MS lat. 15398, fol. 145ᵛ.

54 Gierke, III, 312f.; *consensus communis* was demanded by Laurentius as early as about 1210 (p. 313, n. 204; cf. p. 314 n. 207); Lanfrankus, in Gierke, but wrongly; see Kuttner, *Repertorium*, pp. 326 n. 1, 356 n. 5.

55 Honorius III, *Decr. Greg. IX* 1, 4, 9; also Innocent IV, Gierke, III, 307 n. 187. Cf. Damasus (1210-1215): "Et universitas videtur quod constituere possit . . . dummodo non sit const. talis, per quam inferatur onus aliis et ad constituentes non extendatur, tunc enim valeret. . . . Causa constituendi est, malitiae coercitio . . . et novae quaestionis iudicialis definitio"; *Summa*, ed. Schulte, "Literaturgeschichte der Compilationes Antiquae," *Sitzungsberichte d. Kais. Akademie der Wissenschaften zu Wien, Philos.-Hist. Cl.*, LXVI (1871), 145.

56 *Chartularium*, I, 87, 89, 98.

oath regulate costume, lectures and disputations, funerals, house-rents, and the method of obtaining justice for students.[57] The litigation was settled in 1225 or 1226,[58] and in 1231 Gregory IX granted to the masters the privilege of regulating the same matters and of punishing rebellious colleagues "per subtractionem societatis."[59] Here is final papal confirmation of the very matters which Innocent III and a papal legate had confirmed either tacitly or expressly twenty years earlier.[60] In 1215, at latest, therefore, the masters were recognized by the papacy as a *universitas magistrorum et scolarium* insofar as this *universitas* could enact statutes and enforce obedience to them.[61] To that extent their *universitas* was a *collegium licitum*.[62]

For the administration and enforcement of its rules a corporation could elect officers.[63] As early as 1208-1209 the masters at Paris had elected eight sworn men from their body to enforce their statutes.[64] In 1212-1213 they chose three masters to represent them, in arranging an agreement with three representatives chosen by the chancellor, before judges delegated by the pope.[65] In 1215 the Cardinal-Legate Robert de Courçon or-

---

[57] *Ibid.*, p. 79.

[58] *Ibid.*, nos. 45, n. 3, and 58; a compromise, the terms of which are lost.

[59] *Ibid.*, p. 137.

[60] That Gregory IX did not innovate seems to be certain from the fact that he based his statutes on earlier privileges; in 1230 he ordered the masters to send to Rome by their procurators authenticated copies of all privileges granted to them in the past by popes or kings (*ibid.*, no. 75); among these copies must have been the privilege of Philip Augustus of 1200, the compromise of 1213 (*ibid.*, no. 16), and the statutes of Robert de Courçon of 1215.

[61] "Omnes qui contumaciter contra hec statuta nostra venire presumpserint, nisi infra quindecim dies a die transgressionis coram universitate magistrorum et scolarium, vel coram aliquibus ab Universitate constitutis presumptionem suam curaverint emendare, legationis qua fungimur auctoritate vinculo excommunicationis innodavimus"; Statutes of Robert de Courçon, 1215, which he promulgated as a result of a special mandate from the pope; *Chartularium*, I, 78f.

[62] To *Decr. Greg. IX* 1, 2, 6: "nam quodlibet licitum collegium potest facere statutum de his quae ad se spectant"; Gierke, III, 307 n. 190.

[63] Gierke, III, 208, 304; cf. Denifle, *Univ.*, I, 170.

[64] *Chartularium*, I, no. 8. But Master G. submitted to four representatives, perhaps of the Nations; cf. Rashdall, I, 313 n. 2, who, Professor F. M. Powicke decides, is probably wrong in saying that here is possibly an early trace of the Nations and their four Proctors (Rashdall, ed. Powicke and Emden, I, 312 n. 1). I now agree with Powicke that the four may have been proctors as agents rather than heads of the Nations.

[65] *Ibid.*, no. 16; these were arbitrators, acting by the authority of the judges delegate, cf. *Decr. Greg. IX* 1, 43, 9.

dered that violators of the statutes should appear before the *universitas* of masters and students, or "coram aliquibus ab Universitate constitutis."[66] In 1229 the whole University elected twenty-one provisors who were to act "communi consensu et voluntate."[67] The opinion of Azo and Accursius, that the masters could elect officers, is therefore not surprising.[68] By the agreement of 1213 with the chancellor, the Faculty of Arts was to elect three masters each half-year for approving candidates for the license.[69] In 1219 the masters of arts, who later with their students constituted the Four Nations,[70] had their proctors;[71] and by 1249 there was a rector of the Nations,[72] who because of the greater number of the masters and students of arts and their initiative became the common head of the whole University.[73] Before 1219 the masters of the four Faculties acted as a body; thereafter the masters of arts often act for the other masters, and develop within the University a corporation of their own which succeeds in becoming the most important part of the University. Nevertheless all of the masters act as a corporate body in 1229, 1230-1231, 1237, and later.[74] Thus the development of the organization of the University was slow, starting with a general body which broke up into several bodies or corporations within a corporation. But the fact that there was no common head in the first two decades of the century should not be taken to mean that there was no legal corporation before 1220, for civil and Canon law recognized acephalous corporations.[75] What is important is that the masters did have officers by

[66] *Chartularium*, p. 79.

[67] *Ibid.*, no. 62.

[68] Above, nn. 11-15.

[69] *Chartularium*, p. 76. In 1218 three doctors of theology, to whom Honorius III addresses a bull, seem to be representing the Faculty of Theology; no. 27.

[70] Rashdall, *Universities*, I, 316, 319 n. 5; cf. G. C. Boyce, *The English-German Nation in the University of Paris*, pp. 26f.

[71] Rashdall, *Universities*, I, 313f.; *Chartularium*, p. 89. The election of these officers was suspended *lite pendente* by Honorius III in 1222, *ibid.*, p. 103; but it is doubtful that the masters obeyed. These *procuratores* are still possibly the legal representatives or agents, not the Proctors, of the Four Nations (see above, n. 64). Kibre, *Nations*, has not treated this problem.

[72] Rashdall, *Universities*, I, 316; cf. *Chartularium*, p. 215.

[73] *Ibid.*, p. 215; Rashdall, *Universities*, I, 322.

[74] *Chartularium*, I, nos. 62, 75, 79, 115, 117, 121, 132, 144, 219, 230, etc.

[75] Denifle, *Univ.*, I, 129 and 170, nn. 425-427; Gierke, III, 304f.; Rashdall, I, 294 n. 2.

1210 and 1213, officers recognized by the papacy and not suspended by Honorius III in 1222 *lite pendente.*[76]

Of the other rights pertaining to a corporation—property, immunity from excommunication, and legal competency—the first two may be treated briefly. In 1219 the masters possessed property, for they deeded a church and (in 1221) their rights in other property to the Dominicans.[77] But if a corporation could own property, it need not follow that the masters did not constitute a corporation before they had possessions in common.[78] Nor need it be concluded that they had no legal corporation before they procured special privileges of immunity from excommunication as a body in 1231,[79] 1237,[80] and 1246,[81] since in the earlier period the theory of the impossibility of excommunicating a corporation had not been stated.[82]

4. LEGAL COMPETENCY: PROCURATION

Of all the privileges enjoyed by a corporation perhaps the most important was that of acting in the courts as a juristic person. Obviously, when the masters were in conflict with the bishop and chancellor, they could not all carry petitions and appeals to the pope, or appear as plaintiffs or defendants in the courts of judges delegate. To petition, to sue or be sued, or to

[76] *Chartularium*, I, no. 45.

[77] *Ibid.*, nos. 34 and 42.

[78] I have been unable to determine how long before 1219 the masters had property.

[79] *Chartularium*, I, no. 95: Gregory IX, "indulgemus, ut nullus in universitatem magistrorum vel scolarium seu rectorum (*sic*) vel procuratorem eorum aut quemquam alium pro facto vel occasione Universitatis excommunicationis, suspensionis, vel interdicti sententias audeat promulgare absque sedis apostolice licentia speciali."

[80] *Ibid.*, no. 113.

[81] *Ibid.*, no. 162. It should be observed that already in 1219-1222 Honorius III had forbidden the excommunication of the University or its members; *ibid.*, nos. 31 and 45, pp. 90 and 103. Thus in spite of sentences of excommunication pronounced by the bishop and chancellor, the University could act in the courts at this time.

[82] Gregory IX approached the theory, *Decr.* 1, 38, 15; and Innocent IV so interpreted his decretal, "quia universitas, cujus nomine agitur, excommunicari non potest"; Gierke, III, 278. In the Council of Lyons, 1245, Innocent IV prohibited the excommunication of corporations, *Liber Sextus*, 5, 11, 5. Cf. Gierke, III, 280f., 348; and the *Consuetudines Curiae Romanae* (1245-1246): "et est ratio, quod non excommunicatur universitas, cum excommunicatio sit eternae mortis dampnatio et universitas non habeat animam, ideo excommunicari non potest"; ed. L. Wahrmund, *Archiv für katholisches Kirchenrecht*, LXXIX (1899), 11.

appeal *lite contestata*, they must do so with a common will and purpose through an elected representative. For such a body a procurator was indispensable.[83] Civil and Canon law recognized that an individual (*dominus*) could stand trial or cause to stand trial through his procurator,[84] and that a *universitas* or *collegium* could for the same purpose appoint a *syndicus* or *actor*.[85] This distinction between the *procurator* and the *syndicus* had no real importance in Canon law after about 1215,[86] and was not

[83] Cf. Gierke, III, 231f., 338 n. 291, Innocent IV.

[84] Bamberg *Ordo Iudiciarius* (1180-1185): "Procurator is est, qui aliena ministranda suscepit negotia mandato domini rei vel litis. . . . In civili causa omnis permittitur communi iure per procuratorem causam agere vel defendere. . . . Procuratorem constituunt homo liber, pater familias et hoc rationabiliter, mentis compos, dominus rei vel causae," ed. Schulte, Vienna *Sitzungsberichte, Philos.-Hist. Cl.*, LXX (1872), 298. Tancred, *Ordo Iudiciarius* (1214-1216), t. 6, *De procur.*: "Quia in omni iudicio tres personae ad minus sunt necessariae, scilicet iudex, actor et reus . . . , et interdum reus vel actor causae suae tractandae interesse non valet per se, sed per procuratorem, syndicum vel actorem interesse potest . . . §1. Procurator est, qui aliena negotia, unum vel plura, mandato sibi a domino facto gerenda gratuito suscipit"; ed. Bergmann, *Pillii, Tancredi, Gratiae Libri de Judiciorum Ordine*, p. 114.

[85] Bamberg *Ordo Iudiciarius, De procuratoribus*: "ubi vero collegium convenitur, vel experitur, unus vel duo de collegio ad agendum vel respondendum instituantur, ceteri de collegio ad testimonium admittuntur"; Schulte, *Sitzungsber.*, LXX, 298. Bernard of Pavia, *Summa Decretalium* (1191-1198), t. xxixa, §1: "Syndicus est actor universitatis, i.e., qui constitutus est ad agendas causas universitatis, sive in agendo sive in repondendo. . . . §4 . . . syndicus et ad unam causam et ad omnes constitui potest"; ed. Laspeyres, *Bernardi Papiensis Faventini Episcopi Summa Decretalium*; idem, "Potest autem fieri syndicus etiam qui non est de ipsa universitate"; Halle, Universitätsbibl., MS Ye 80, fol. 13ᵛ. Tancred, gloss ad c. 1, *Comp. I*, 1, 29 (*Decr. Greg. IX*, 1, 39, 1): "Sindicus est qui pro universitate agit, et iurabit de calumpnia, sicut tutor, cum uterque legitimam habeat administrationem . . . t."; Paris, BN, MS lat. 15399, fol. 12; *idem, Ordo*: "Syndicus est ille, qui constituitur ad agendum vel defendendum causas nomine universitatis; syndicus graece, latine defensor dicitur. . . . Actor similiter ad agendas vel defendendas causas universitatis constituitur," but the "actor tantum ad lites praesentes constituitur et cum decreto . . . ; syndicus vero . . . ad lites praesentes et futuras et sine decreto. . . . Sola universitas vel collegium constituere potest syndicum vel actorem, . . . vel is, cui universitas potestatem dederit eligendi"; Bergmann, *Pillii, Tancredi, etc.*, pp. 123f. Cf. Boncompagno, *Rhetorica Novissima*, ed. Gaudenzi, *Bibliotheca Iuridica Medii Aevi*, II, 259; William of Drogheda, *Summa Aurea*, ed. Wahrmund, *Quellen*, II, ii, 176f., says that the *syndicus* acts for individuals belonging to a *universitas*, while the *actor* "universitatis causam agit" (p. 178).

[86] About 1218 Johannes Teutonicus, referring to the decretal of Innocent III granting the *scolares* at Paris the right to elect proctors (*Chartularium*, I, no. 24), admitted that "secundum canones universitas constituit procuratorem et per ipsum iurat, ut supra, de iuram. calump., cum causam [*Comp. III*, 1, 26, 1; *Decr. Greg. IX* 2, 7, 6; the reference is to litigation between the archbishop of Ravenna and the commune of Faenza, both parties being represented by proctors]. Jo.";

made in the practice of the law in the Roman Court and in courts of judges delegate after about 1200.[87] We may therefore speak of the procurator of a *universitas*, whether he was called *nuntius*,[88] or "sindicus, sive yconomus, sive axinus, sive etiam

---

Bamberg, MS Can. 23, fol. 12ᵛ; MS Vat. lat. 1377, fol. 290ᵛ; Leipzig, Universitätsbibl., MS lat. 968; this gloss is ad v. *de iure communi, Comp. IV*, 1, t. *De procur.*, c. Quia in causis (*Decr. Greg. IX* 1, 38, 7). Saxon *Summa Prosarum Dictaminis* (1234-1241): "Item statuitur procurator universitatis vel collegii vel alicuius communis, qui in iure sindicus appellatur. . . . Procurator in solidum et in totum est is quem quis in una causa procuratorem constituit ad litigandum"; Rockinger, *Briefsteller*, pp. 205, 227. Anonymous addition (1224-1234; Schulte, *Quellen*, I, 204) in a *Libellus Ordinis Iudiciarii*, Paris, BN, MS lat. 18240 (wrongly attributed to Ricardus Anglicus; it is a reworking of Tancred's *Ordo*, for the *prooemium* literally follows that of Tancred, fol. 1ᵛ; cf. Bergmann, *op.cit.*, pp. v and note 15, and 89): "Nota quod licet universitas habet constituere syndicum vel actorem, tamen nichilominus quandoque constituit procuratorem, ut extra. de procurator. quia [*quod* in MS] in causis, ubi dicitur, quod universitas parisiensium peciit a domino papa ut sibi liceat in causis suis procuratorem constituere; et respondet papa, quod licet id de iure communi possint facere, ex quo postulabant sibi specialiter indulgeri, constituendi procuratorem liberam habeant facultatem . . ." (fol. 9ᵛ); also, "Ad hoc potest dici, quod in omnibus allegatis capitulis syndicus vel actor appellatur procurator, ut probatur x. 3. de probat. 2. 11. c. licet. 4 [*Decr. Greg. IX* 2, 19, 9]; x. 3. de praescript. 2. 17. c. 1 [*Decr.* 2, 26, 11, Innocent III], ubi iidem appellantur syndici et procuratores. . . . Vel dicas, quod in hoc attenditur loci consuetudo, utrum sc. constitui debeat syndicus vel actor, aut procurator"; Bergmann, *op.cit.*, pp. 123f. n. 6. Geoffrey of Trani, *Summa super Titulis Decretalium*: "Sindicus est procurator universitatis ad iudicia constitutus"; BN, MS lat. 18224, fol. 70ᵛ. Bernardus Parmensis: "Nota quod universitas potest constituere procuratorem, non obstante quod dicitur procurator est qui domini mandato negocia administrat. . . . Sed universitas loco domini habetur. . . . Secundum canones non est differentia in vocabulario, dummodo constet quod habeat potestatem agendi vel deffendendi"; BN, MS lat. 3949, fol. 60 (on the *Decretals of Gregory IX*, to 1, 38, 7); cf. the opinion of William of Drogheda, *Summa Aurea*: "Verumtamen actor ab universitate constitutus fungitur partibus procuratoris"; he then distinguishes between the *syndicus* and the *actor*, Wahrmund, *Quellen*, II, ii, 177, 178.

[87] *Decr. Greg. IX* 1, 41, 2; 2, 7, 6; 1, 38, 7. See also the preceding note. Cf. R. von Heckel, "Das Aufkommen der ständigen Prokuratoren an der Päpstlichen Kurie im 13 Jht.," *Miscellanea Francesco Ehrle*, II, 300. There is one example of a "procurator universitatis" as early as the time of Clement III, *Decr. Greg. IX* 2, 19, 5; and the Bamberg *Ordo* speaks of the *collegium* as having a *procurator*, Schulte, *Sitzungsber.*, LXX, 298.

[88] Honorius III in 1219 speaks of the *nuntius* sent by the masters at Paris to Rome "ad prosecutionem appellationis," *Chartularium*, I, 89; in 1259 there is a reference to the *nuntii et procuratores* of the masters in the time of Honorius III, *ibid.*, p. 379; cf. I, 354. The term *nuntius* used likewise in connection with appeals by Alexander III, *Decr. Greg. IX* 2, 28, 30; it appears in connection with petitions in the Chancery Ordinances of the time of Innocent III, *procurator* in those of the time of Gregory IX; Tangl, *Päpstlichen Kanzleiordnungen*, pp. 54f., Constitutio III, Art. 7 and 12; cf. von Heckel, *Miscel. Ehrle*, II, 300, 305-311, 313-315. For Innocent III's rules for *nuntii*, see also *Decr. Greg. IX* 5, 20, 4.

nullum nomen."[89] Whatever his title, this representative of a corporation was chosen by the whole *universitas* or by the *maior et sanior pars* of at least two-thirds of the members in assembly.[90] In the name of the corporation the procurator as plaintiff presented petitions or *libelli*[91] in initiating and prosecuting suits, and as defendant stood trial. He called witnesses, took the oath that the action was brought or the defense offered in good faith (*juramentum calumniae*), received the sentence of the court, and appealed to a higher court or judge.[92] He might be ap-

[89] Henry of Susa, *Summa*, 1, t. *De procur.*: "sive dicatur procurator, sive sindicus, . . . nullum nomen exprimatur, nichil obstat, dummodo de mente constituentis liqueat." Cf. Gierke, III, 341, n. 30.

[90] Tancred, *Ordo*, t. *De syndico et actore*: "Defensores constitui debent a tota universitate vel a maiori parte, ita tamen quod duae partes ad minus intersint in constituendo ipsum . . .; sed [non] est necesse, quod omnes, qui intersint, consentiant; sufficit enim, quod maior pars consentiat in eum," Bergmann, *op.cit.*, p. 125. Paris *Libellus Ordinis Iudiciarii*, t. *De sindico*: "Constitui debet sindicus et actor a tota universitate vel a maiori et saniori parte capituli, ita tamen quod due partes ad minus intersint in constituendo ipsum"; BN, MS lat. 18240, fol. 9ᵛ.

[91] The *libellus* was "quaedam carticella seu cedula, quae continet intentionem actoris vel accusatoris, et talis libellus dicitur alio loco libellus responsionis in causa civili." In some places, "puta Romae, dicitur petitio." Bernardus Dorna, *Summa Libellorum*, ed. Wahrmund, *Quellen*, I, i, 3; this *Summa* was written 1213-1217, or 1215 (p. xxi). Cf. *Decr. Greg. IX* 2, 3, 1; and Pillius, *Summa*, Bergmann, p. 4.

[92] Tancred, *Ordo*, t. *De syndico et actore*: "Officium syndici vel actoris est causas universitatis tractare ac defendere universitatem. . . . Item . . . iurant de calumnia. . . . Contestatur litem et interrogatur de facto, et omnia facit in causa, sicut legitimus dominus litis; et eius confessioni stabitur; et sententia in persona eius formatur"; t. *De iuramento calumniae*: "cum quis iurat, se bona fide et non calumniandi animo agere vel respondere. . . . Calumnia est falsa petitio vel iniusta repulsio scienter facta. . . . Procurator vero de calumnia no iurat. Decretalis tamen videtur contradicere X. 3. e. t. 1, 26, c. un. [*Decr. Greg. IX* 2, 7, 6]. Sed dico quod syndici appellantur ibi procuratores, quoniam universitas procuratorem non facit ad causam, sed syndicum vel actorem . . . ; et praeterea canon omnes tales personas procuratores appellat"; Bergmann, *Pillii, etc.*, pp. 125f., 201, 204. Johannes Teutonicus: "est hoc verum, quod secundum canones universitas constituit procuratorem et per ipsum iurat, ut supra, de iuram. calump. cum causam [*Decr. Greg. IX* 2, 7, 6]"; Bamberg, MS Can. 23, fol. 12ᵛ. The Saxon *Summa Prosarum Dictaminis*: "Procurator universitatis . . . qui universitatis negocia procuranda sumit in genere, et in ipsius nomine universitas condempnatur. . . . Statuitur etiam procurator ad impetrandum, ad contradicendum, ad appellandum, et ad iudices eligendos"; Rockinger, *Briefsteller*, pp. 226, 227; cf. William of Drogheda, *Summa Aurea*, ed. Wahrmund, *Quellen*, II, ii, 9f.

On the *juramentum calumniae* cf. O. Riedner's discussion of the authorship of the *Ordo "Invocato Christi Nomine"* (last quarter of twelfth century) in his review of Wahrmund, *Quellen*, v, in *Zeitschrift der Savigny-Stiftung für Rechtsgeschichte, Kan.-Abtlg.*, XXI (1932), 491: according to Pillius, the consul takes the oath for a *civitas*, but in the presence and with the consent of the *maior pars*

pointed for one case only, or for several.[93] But, to be accepted by the court as a *bona fide* representative, the procurator must present an authentic mandate from his *dominus* which showed that the *dominus* or corporation would ratify his actions and submit to the sentence of the court for or against him.[94]

When the masters at Paris first sent a procurator to the Roman Court cannot be stated with confidence, since their mandates for procuration and written petitions have not come down to us.[95] They may have elected procurators as early as 1192,[96]

---

universitatis, "ut sic ipsa quodammodo iurare videatur universitas"; but the *Ordo "Invocato Christi Nomine"* decides that the *universitas (civitas, municipium, ecclesia,* or any *collegium*) or *maior pars* need not take the oath, "quoniam satis videtur maior pars iurare, cum defensores aut consules vel actor seu syndicus universitatis aut syndicus electus a collegio vel prelati vel yconomi ecclesiarum et aliorum locorum religiosorum iurant." Cf. *Decr. Greg. IX* 2, 7, 4 and 6.

On appeals, Tancred, *Ordo*, t. 5, *De appellationibus*, says that anyone can appeal "cuius interest, vel cui mandatum est, vel qui negotium gerit alienum"; the procurator, who has a mandate and "negotium gerit alienum," can therefore appeal. Appeals can be made from judges ordinary or delegate, normally *gradatim* (from archdeacon to bishop, from bishop to archbishop, from archbishop to pope); but to the pope "potest ab audientia cuiuslibet iudicis appellari." Bergmann, *op.cit.*, pp. 291-293. Cf. Honorius III, *Decr. Greg. IX* 2, 28, 63; Gregory IX, *Decr.*, 2, 28, 70.

[93] Bernard of Pavia, *Summa*, ed. Laspeyres, p. 25, *syndicus;* Tancred, *Ordo*, t. 6, *procurator*, ed. Bergmann, p. 114; and p. 115, "constituitur procurator praesens et absens; in lite praesente, et futura; pure et in perpetuum in diem et ad diem, et sub conditione; per nuntium et per epistolam"; the *actor* "ad lites praesentes," the *syndicus* "ad lites praesentes et futuras" (p. 124); but a gloss ad c. un., t. *De sindico* makes this distinction, "procurator agit paucas, sed sindicus omnes," BN, MS lat. 15398, fol. 218ʳ.

But no permanent procurator for all suits of his *dominus* could reside at the Roman Court until toward the end of the reign of Gregory IX (von Heckel, *Miscel. Ehrle*, II, 315-320), and thus a magnate, a church, a chapter, or any *collegium* having lawsuits at Rome had to appoint a new procurator for each case in the time of Innocent III (Constitutio II, Art. 9, Tangl, *Kanzleiordnungen*, p. 54), for two years in the time of Gregory IX (Const. II, Art. 12, *ibid.*, p. 55); the two-year rule still exists in a *Consuetudines Curiae Romanae* of 1245-1246 (Wahrmund, *Archiv für katholisches Kirchenrecht*, LXXIX, 18), but is no longer enforced (von Heckel, *loc.cit.*).

[94] A discussion of the mandate and the means of authenticating it will be given below in connection with the question of the seal.

[95] One trace of a procuratorial mandate of 1233 remains from a Register of the seventeenth century, *Chartularium*, I, no. 100.

[96] Stephen of Tournai, in a letter to the Cardinal-Bishop of Ostia, Octavian: "Si quis adversus eum [the Abbot of St. Germain-des-Près] in curia domini pape moverit questionem, maxime super memoria rixe, que hoc anno inter homines Sancti Germani et scolares mota est, in qua et unus scolarium per insaniam rusticorum cecidit, excusabilem habete predictum virum . . . "; *Chartularium*, I, Introd., no. 47.

1200-1207,[97] and 1208.[98] In 1210-1213 the masters had serious need for a procurator in their litigation with the chancellor. Perhaps the chancellor attempted to prevent the masters from carrying their case to the Roman Court by contesting their right to elect a procurator *ad litem*.[99] Anyhow, in response to their petition, Innocent III granted their *universitas* the right to appoint a procurator "ad agendum et respondendum," although by common law or right they could already do so.[100] This indulgence,[101] although addressed to the *scolares*, was made to the masters, not to the students.[102]

[97] Guillaume le Breton: Amaury de Bène († 1204 or 1207) "accessit ad summum pontificem, qui, audita ejus propositione et universitatis scholarium contradictione, sententiavit contra ipsum"; Delaborde, *Œuvres de Rigord et Guillaume le Breton*, I, 231.

[98] The masters petitioned the pope for a decision on the case of Master G. (above, to nn. 49-51), *Chartularium*, I, 67: "Ex litteris vestre devotionis accepimus"; "Unde nobis humiliter supplicastis." Someone must have carried their petition to Rome.

[99] P. Viollet thinks that the "University" demanded procuration because it did not yet have a seal and was therefore not yet an "authentic person" and could not yet be represented by a procurator without a special privilege (see below, on the mandate and seal, §5), *Établissements de Saint Louis*, IV, 229, and II, 345.

[100] The decretal *Quia in causis* (*Comp. IV*, 1, 16, 2; *Decr. Greg. IX* 1, 38, 7); *Chartularium*, I, no. 24, where it is dated 1210-1216 or 1214-1216; but I think it may be more closely connected with the litigation of 1210-1213.

[101] About forty years later, Henry of Susa put this decretal in the class of privileges, *Summa*, 5, t. *De privilegiis*: the *privilegium* is a "privatum sive singulare ius uni vel pluribus specialiter indultum, nec enim est privilegium nisi aliquid indulgeat speciale. . . . Plerunque tamen id quod de iure communi competit indulgetur . . . supra, de procura., quia in causis, sed tunc exponi debet, indulgemus, id est, indultum esse ostendimus. Vel id operatur, quia magis consuevit timeri quod specialiter cavetur, quam quod generaliter indulgetur; nam per bullas magis terrentur homines [perhaps the chancellor of Paris also!] licet ius commune contineant, quam per iura. . . . Item quia plerique sciunt privilegia talia qui ignorant iura. Item quia iura male observentur, et ideo per privilegia innovantur." In 1210-1215 (Schulte, *Quellen*, I, 205) Tancred, gloss ad vv. *ut libere sibi liceat appellare* (*Comp. I*, 1, *De rescriptis*, c. 1; *Decr. Greg. IX* 1, 3, 1), says that "quod de iure communi competit, privilegio non debet impetrari," but in this case "ista indulgentia, ut aliquid valeat, ita intelligetur concessum, ut liceat ei appellare ubique ubi ius inhibet appellationem . . . T."; BN, MS lat. 15398, fol. 3. Hence, we may conjecture that the masters, because of the opposition of the chancellor, may have sought a privilege for what common law or right already permitted—"videtur tamen quod istam indulgentiam petere per privilegium superfluum sit"; gloss ad *Quia in causis*, Chartres, MS lat. 384 (formerly 462), fol. 254ᵛ—this gloss in a later hand than the other glosses in the MS. Kibre, *Scholarly Privileges*, does not treat this subject.

[102] Rashdall, *Universities*, I, 302, accepts this interpretation without explaining why. The decretal bears the address "Scolaribus Parisiensibus"; hence Denifle, *Universitäten*, I, 86-88, assumes that the students, not the masters, were granted the right to elect proctors, and concludes that the opinion of Johannes Teutoni-

Having secured the right to appoint a procurator, the masters
started a suit in 1210-1212 against the chancellor by sending
someone, *nuntius* or procurator, to Rome with their petition

---

cus (cited below, in this note) had no connection with the masters. But the
decretal was evidently intended for the masters. It is not preserved in the
original, and the address comes from *Compilatio IV*, compiled partly from the
papal Register, which was kept by chancery officials who often abbreviated
addresses, or who as Italians perhaps thought that the *universitas* at Paris consisted of students, as it did at Bologna. The two other papal letters before
1250 addressed "Scolaribus Paris." are not originals; of these two the first
(*Chartularium*, I, no. 29, *an.* 1219) clearly pertains to *scolares* as students
seeking the license to teach, but the second (I, no. 116, *an.* 1237) orders the
scolares to pay a debt contracted in 1222-1225 (*infra*, n. 124) for the expenses
of four procurators sent to the Roman Court. In this the masters are
intended, for it was the masters of arts and other faculties who were active in
collecting money and electing procurators (*Chartularium*, I, 89f., 103; cf. p. 379).
All other papal letters, whether originals or copies, are addressed to the masters
or masters and students (above, nn. 25-36); and, of these, several deal with procuration in a manner which permits no doubt that it was mainly the masters who
were concerned in appointing procurators (*ibid.*, nos. 31, 45, 75, 95, 113, 162, 330).
When the masters petitioned for a *sigillum ad causas* before 1246, it was the
"magistri iiijor facultatum" who did so (*ibid.*, no. 113, note, and no. 165).

Furthermore, Innocent III had studied at Paris (*ibid.*, no. 17, Introd., and
no. 14; Rigord, in Delaborde, *Oeuvres*, I, 146f.), and more than any other pope he
personally supervised the procedure in the chancery and *curia*; R. von Heckel,
"Beiträge zur Kenntnis des Geschäftsgang der päpstlichen Kanzlei im 13.
Jahrhundert," *Festschrift Albert Brackmann*, ed. L. Santifaller, pp. 434, 447.
Thus, he probably understood that the masters constituted the corporation.

The canonists, however, most of whom studied and taught at Bologna, where
the students were the corporations of the University, could not at first cor-
rectly interpret the decretal *Quia in causis*. Johannes Teutonicus, who studied
and taught at Bologna before 1220 (Schulte, *Quellen*, I, 172), in assuming
that the students were the corporation at Paris led Denifle astray (*Universitäten*, I, 86; Denifle cites only the first part of Johannes's gloss, not the conclusion). At first doubtful, Johannes decided that even students could form a
corporation and elect procurators, ad v. *de iure communi* (*Comp. IV*, 1, t. De
procur., c. Quia in causis; *Decr. Greg. IX* 1, 38, 7): "Dubitationis causa hec
fuit, quia scolares non videntur constituere universitatem, cum causam vel ius
universitatis non sint a principe consecuti, ut ff. quod cuiuscumque univ. l. 1. ff.
de coll. l. 1 (*D*. 3, 4, 1, 1 and 47, 22, 1). Sed respondet eis quod ipsi de iure
possunt constituere procuratorem, et hoc est verum, quod secundum canones
universitas constituit procuratorem et per ipsum iurat . . . Jo.," in Bamberg
MS Can. 23, fol. 12ᵛ; Leipzig, Universitätsbibl., MS lat. 968; and MS Vat. lat.
1377, fol. 290ᵛ, where one finds "cum ius universitatis" in place of "cum
causam vel ius universitatis." Some later commentators on this decretal retain
the term *universitas scolarium*: Paris *Libellus*, BN, MS lat. 18240, fol. 9ᵛ; and
Bernard of Parma, who quotes the whole gloss of Johannes, BN, MS lat. 3949,
fol. 60.

Johannes Teutonicus probably would not have raised the question had he
known that it was the masters who received the privilege of electing procurators
of their corporation; for as Azo and Accursius said, masters engaged in a profession could form a corporation (above, n. 11). Innocent IV definitely admitted

for the appointment of judges delegate to try the case.[103] They probably gathered in assembly or congregation and elected a procurator; the act itself of petitioning the pope implies their agreement as a body on the terms of the petition. Provided with a mandate,[104] the procurator presented the written petition to a notary in the *data communis* of the papal chancery, and on the petition as a basis a papal rescript was drawn up.[105] This rescript was brought back to France and presented to the judges delegate, the bishop, the dean, and the archdeacon of Troyes.[106] By their authority the masters and the chancellor chose arbitrators (three for each party) to arrange a settlement of the matters in dispute.[107] The terms of agreement arrived at by the

---

that the *scolares* were engaged in a laudable profession and could form a *universitas; Apparatus*, 1, t. De procur., c. Quia in causis: "Causa est dubitationis, quia cum non haberent privilegium universitatis a principe, non videbatur quod constitueret universitatem, et sic non possunt constituere procur (atorem) . . . sed contra, verum est, quia cum sit laudabilis professionis congregatio, universitatem faciunt et ea possunt que universitas potest, ar. C. de. iur. omni. iu. l. ult."

103 *Chartularium*, I, no. 14. For the nature of such petitions see Bernard Dorna, *Summa Libellorum*, Wahrmund, *Quellen*, I, i, 17; von Heckel, "Der Libellus Petitionum des Kardinals Guala Bichieri," *Archiv für Urkundenforschung*, I (1908), 499-510; and Tancred, "et nota, quod, si praelatus vel syndicus seu actor ecclesiae petant rem ipsius ecclesiae, debent formulare libellum nomine ecclesiae et debent petere, sibi nomine ecclesiae ipsius rem restitui et adjudicari. Idem facere debent syndicus et actor universitatis"; Gierke, III, 339 n. 296.

104 See below, on mandates, §5. Innocent IV says that the *impetrator* should have a special mandate *ad impetrandum* even if he already had a general mandate *ad negotia et lites*; the burden of proof lay on the *contradictor* of the petition; i.e., a procurator or petitioner was accepted in the Roman Court unless the defendant proved in the *Audientia literarum contradictarum* that he had no mandate; *Apparatus*, I, t. *De rescr.*, c. Nonnulli, ad v. *mandato*.

105 On the procedure of handling petitions and issuing rescripts in the papal chancery see *Decr. Greg. IX* 1, 3, 28, and 5, 20, 4; von Heckel, "Beiträge zur Kenntnis des Geschäftsgang der päpstlichen Kanzlei," *Festschrift Albert Brackmann*, pp. 434-456; *idem, Miscel. Ehrle*, II, 291-313; and also H. Bresslau, *Handbuch der Urkundenlehre*, 2nd. ed., II, 3-7.

106 The bishop of Paris, reporting the terms of the final settlement, makes this clear: "cum contentio verteretur inter J. cancellarium Parisiensem ex una parte, et magistros et scolares Parisienses ex alia super diversis querelis, ipsi magistri et scolares ad judices delegatos litteras impetrarunt apostolicas sub hac forma"; and the bishop cites the rescript addressed to the judges; *Chartularium*, I, nos. 16 and 14; cf. no. 18.

107 *Ibid.*, no. 16. When judges delegate received a papal mandate, they should acknowledge receipt of it in their written summons to the litigants, repeat the tenor of the mandate and set the day and place for the trial; Ricardus Anglicus, *Summa*, Wahrmund, *Quellen*, II, iii, 9; cf. *Chartularium*, I, no. 18.

arbitrators were ratified by the bishop of Paris and then by the judges delegate.[108] Thus the case was settled by due legal procedure.[109] In electing a procurator and three arbitrators *ad compromissum*, the masters and students acted as a body, as a corporation.[110] Their legal competency was recognized by Innocent III when, in response to their petition, he delegated judges to try their case against the chancellor.

Again in 1218-1225 there was trouble when a new chancellor, Philip, and the bishop renewed the attack, in an effort to restrict the right of the masters to make statutes, by excommunicating the masters for not reporting misdemeanors of students,[111] by depriving them of their chairs, and by imprisoning students in violation of the terms of agreement of 1213.[112] Again the masters sent petitions to Rome, this time by their *nuntius* "ad prosecutionem appellationis."[113] In order to raise money for his expenses the masters of arts through their *procuratores* (perhaps their agents in the courts rather than the officers known later as the proctors of the Nations) obtained contributions from masters and students.[114] The chancellor riposted by

[108] *Chartularium*, I, nos. 16 and 18.

[109] Apparently, the arbitrators did not come to terms in the court of the judges delegate but at Paris. But it was under these judges that they acted; *ibid.*, 89, "cancellarius . . . contemptis statutis, que super hiis facta fuerunt per judices a sede apostolica delegatos. . . ." *Arbitri* were appointed after permission was obtained from judges delegate for a *compromissum, Decr. Greg.* IX 1, 43, 9; cf. 1, 43, 1.

[110] It would be technically wrong to call the arbitrators procurators; but a corporation could appoint several procurators for one case, cf. Tancred, *Ordo, De procur.*, "plures etiam constitui possunt procuratores simul et in solidum," Bergmann, *Pillii, etc.*, p. 115.

[111] Each master had disciplinary jurisdiction over his students; *Chartularium*, I, 79 (*an.* 1215).

[112] *Ibid.*, nos. 30 and 31.

[113] *Ibid.*, no. 30 (March 30, 1219): "Dilecti filii magistri et scolares Parisienses nobis graviter sunt conquesti. . . . Unde predicti magistri et scolares nobis humiliter supplicarunt"; no. 31, p. 89 (May 11, 1219): "Sicut enim gravis nobis eorundem doctorum querimonia patefecit. . . . Porro cum ad prosecutionem appellationis predicte foret nuntius ad sedem apostolicam destinandus. . . ."

[114] *Ibid.*, 89: "Porro cum . . . foret nuntius ad sedem apostolicam destinandus et sine collecta Universitatis non haberet expensas, magistri liberalium artium fide interposita se ac suos discipulos astrincxerunt ad servandum quod super hoc a suis procuratoribus contingeret ordinari." This money apparently did not suffice, for some time later (1222-1225) they borrowed money (*ibid.*, nos. 116, 330).

On this collection of money, M. Halphen, *Studi Medievali*, II, 136, objects that the masters could hardly have constituted a corporation because they had

excommunicating the *universitas* or members of it who were active in the matter.[115] But the *nuntius* had already set out for Rome,[116] and Honorius III appointed judges delegate to curb the chancellor and the bishop,[117] for even if the *universitas* of doctors and students was guilty of excesses it should be punished only with the consent of the Apostolic See.[118] The pope commanded that the masters and students be permitted freely to appeal to the Roman Court without fear of sentences of excommunication, and that the chancellor himself and procurators of the masters appear in Rome by Michaelmas of 1219.[119] Perhaps because of the lack of funds or because of obstacles interposed by the bishop and the chancellor, the procurators

---

"ni caisse commune ni budget; ils ne peuvent subvenir aux frais d'un procès qu'en faisant entre eux une collecte exceptionnelle." But nowhere, so far as I know, does a lawyer state that a corporation is illegal if it does not have a permanent treasury or a budget; besides, it was only at intervals that the masters needed procurators for petitioning, appealing, and litigating—1210-1213, 1218-1225, 1229-1231, 1237, 1253-1254 (*Chartularium*, I, nos. 217, 238); moreover, they could not keep a permanent procurator at Rome until near the end of the pontificate of Gregory IX (von Heckel, *Miscel. Ehrle*, II, 315-320, 316), since the rules of the papal chancery required that a procurator should not stay there more than two years (above, n. 93).

The glossators admit that procurators should be paid their reasonable expenses: Johannes Teutonicus, ad c. 1, *Comp. IV*, 1, t. De procur. (*Decr. Greg. IX* 1, 38, 6), "Quia si aliquis fuisset iturus romam, non posset petere expensas factas, nisi quatenus plus expendisset propter longiorem moram. . . . Distinguuntur tamen, quia si egit cum mandato, sive succubuit sive non, potest petere expensas. . . . Sed si non mandato egit et succubuit, non petit expensas" (BN, MS lat. 3932, fol. 209ᵛ); Henry of Susa, *Summa*, I, e.t., "dominus tenetur procuratori ad expensas moderatas quas in negocio suo iudicio fecit." Sometimes a procurator acted gratis—the procurator of the masters who carried their petition to Rome in 1210-1212 may have done so, as we see one procurator of the University doing in 1253 (*Chartularium*, I, no. 217). Hence, the masters needed no permanent *caisse* for procuration alone. That they could borrow money in 1222 or a year or two later indicates that at least one Florentine believed in the corporate responsibility of the masters; indeed, the money was borrowed in the name of the University by the four masters chosen as procurators at that time (1222, *ibid.*, no. 330, p. 379), as is evident from the litigation on the debt in 1237 and 1259 (*ibid.*, 162 and 379). Their method of borrowing is well illustrated by a model of a corporate promise to be responsible for a loan to be contracted by the procurator of a monastery, *an.* 1226; von Heckel, "Der Libellus Petitionum," *Archiv. für Urkundenforschung*, I, 509f., no. 31.

115 *Chartularium*, I, 89f. This was an attempt to prevent the masters from engaging in litigation, for excommunicated persons could not sue; *Decr. Greg. IX* 2, 1, 7 and 2, 19, 7.

116 *Chartularium*, I, 89.   117 *Ibid.*, nos. 30 and 31.

118 *Ibid.*, no. 31, p. 88.

119 *Ibid.*, no. 31, p. 90.

failed to appear within the time set to prosecute the chancellor, who did arrive at the Roman Court.[120] The disputes therefore remained in litigation. In 1221 the bishop of Paris abandoned the weak position of defendant for the stronger one of plaintiff by accusing the masters of going beyond their rights in their statutes, of encroaching on episcopal jurisdiction, and of misusing their recently made seal; and from Honorius III he obtained a rescript appointing judges delegate for the purpose of breaking the seal and examining the matters in dispute.[121] These judges, however, hampered by the stubbornness of both parties, especially of the masters as defendants, and by the multiplication of exceptions and new suits before final sentence could be pronounced,[122] accomplished nothing.[123] Unwilling to wait for a decision from a lower court, the masters sent procurators to the Roman Court.[124] The bishop sent his own procurator, but then revoked the procuratorial mandate on the ground that he would prosecute the case in person at Rome.[125] The bishop, however, failed to appear, and Honorius III refused to proceed with the litigation without him.[126] The pope therefore in 1222 appointed new judges delegate, ordering them to enforce obedience to the papal provisions for the litigants *lite pendente*: general sentences of excommunication "in universitatem magis-

[120] *Ibid.*, no. 33.

[121] *Ibid.*, nos. 41, and 45, p. 102.

[122] In legal procedure such actions *lite pendente*, that is, while one of the parties was waiting for the results of appealing to a higher judge (Henry of Susa, *Summa*, II, t. *Ut lite pendente*), were forbidden; *Decr. Greg. IX*, 2, 16, *Ut lite pendente nihil innovetur*.

[123] *Chartularium*, I, no. 45, p. 102.

[124] *Ibid.*, p. 102: "quidam ex predictis magistris [Honorius III has just mentioned the *universitas magistrorum et scolarium*] cum multitudine scolarium pro se ac aliis nec non et procurator ipsius episcopi ad nostram presentiam accessissent." It is these masters, probably, who in the name of the University borrowed money for their expenses; there were four of them (*ibid.*, nos. 116 and 330). Hence, the date of the procuration of the four masters and the loan made by a Florentine was probably 1221-1222; Denifle places it vaguely before 1227 (*ibid.*, no. 330, n. 10); Halphen places it in 1229, *Revue historique*, CLXVI, 234. The *multitudo scolarium* probably means that some masters and students went along as witnesses; or perhaps they went in order to obtain the relaxation of sentences of excommunication pronounced by the chancellor and the bishop.

[125] *Chartularium*, I, 102f.; a trial or any action initiated by a procurator whose mandate was revoked was invalid, *Decr. Greg. IX* 1, 38, 4, and 1, 38, 13.

[126] *Chartularium*, I, 103.

trorum et scolarium" and special sentences "in quosdam vero ipsorum occasione hujus discidii" were relaxed "ad cautelam"; any new action against the masters after their procurators departed for Rome was revoked; and the use of the seal of the University, except in matters pertaining to procuration in this case (the seal was therefore not broken in 1221), was forbidden until the bishop or his procurator appeared in the Roman Court.[127] The case was not, however, settled at Rome,[128] but at Paris under the Cardinal-Legate Romano in 1225,[129] when a final agreement was reached which was in effect a compromise.[130] At the same time the Legate broke the seal of the University.[131]

5. Legal Competency: Procuratorial Mandates and the Seal

Thus in 1219-1225 the masters elected procurators who were accepted in the courts and recognized by the pope. In the same period they had a common seal (1221-1225) which Honorius III emphasized in connection with procuration.[132] Could the masters have appointed procurators *ad impetrandum, ad litigandum,* or *ad appellandum,* could they have acted as a legal corporation, when they had no seal, before 1221 or after 1225? The procurator of a corporation, in presenting petitions[133] and appearing in court as plaintiff, must show a mandate from his

---

[127] *Ibid.,* no. 45, p. 103. Other provisions were the demolition of the chancellor's prison, the granting of the license to properly qualified candidates, the prohibition of actions by the masters of arts under their officers; all *lite pendente.*

[128] Perhaps because the bishop, Guillaume de Seignelay (April 28, 1220–November 23, 1223), refused to appear or to send a procurator.

[129] *Chartularium,* I, no. 45, n. 3, and no. 58.

[130] *Ibid.,* I, no. 58; the terms are lost, but they were probably similar to those in the *Parens scientarum,* 1231 (no. 79), although the settlement of 1225-1226 apparently remained in force, since Innocent IV confirmed it in 1245 (nos. 135 and 140).

[131] *Ibid.,* I, no. 45, n. 3.

[132] *Chartularium,* I, 103; until the bishop or his procurator arrived at the Roman Court the use of the seal was to be suspended "preterquam in hiis, que ad officium procurationis in hac causa pertinent."

[133] By a decree of the Fourth Lateran Council 1215: "si quis super aliqua quaestione de cetero sine speciali mandato domini literas apostolicas impetrare praesumpserit, et literae illae non valeant, et ipse tanquam falsarius puniatur, nisi forte de illis personis exstiterit, a quibus [i.e., *coniuncte persone,* as in the following note] non debet exigi de iure mandatum"; *Decr. Greg. IX* 1, 3, 28; cf. 1, 38, 1. See also Tancred's statement, above, n. 84.

dominus,[134] and the mandate was valid only if drawn up by a
public notary, or if sealed with an authentic seal.[135] As there

[134] Ricardus Anglicus, *Summa de ordine iudiciario* (1196), Wahrmund,
Quellen, II, iii, 19-20: all procurators except *coniuncte persone* (*parentes,
fratres, affines, liberti*) must have a mandate; "si vero de coniunctis personis
non fuerit nec habeat mandatum, non admittetur, etiam si offerat cautionem
de rato . . . (p. 21). Si dubitatur de mandato, cavebit de mandato aut de
rato. . . . Cautio autem ista personam vel sadisdationem desiderat . . . ; actor
civitatis nec ipse cavet nec magister universitatis nec curator bonis consensu
creditorum datus [*D.* 46, 8, 9] . . . (p. 22). Sed videtur, quod omnis procurator
repelli possit, nisi prius dominus iuret de calumpnia. . . ." Tancred, gloss to
c. 1, *Comp. I*, 1, t. De procur. (*Decr. Greg. IX* 1, 38, 1): "procurator ad agendum
datus, si de mandato constiterit, probare tenetur mandatum, vel de rato
cavere. . . . Idem est de actore universitatis . . . t."; Bamberg, MS Can. 21, fol.
17ᵛ; *idem, Ordo*, t. 6: "Mandatum enim exigitur in procuratore; alias iudicium
nullum, controversia nulla"; but *coniuncte persone* are accepted *sine mandato*
(Bergmann, p. 114); on the *syndicus* and *actor* of a *universitas*: "Et nota,
quod istorum officium eisdem modis finitur, quibus mandatum procuratoris . . ."
(p. 126). Gloss ad v. *non debere subsistere*, (*Comp. I*, 1, t. De procur., c. 1):
"quia admissi prius fuerunt sine litteris. Hoc de facto fuit, quia de iure nunquam procurator admittendus est sine cautione de rato. ff. de procur. l. i"; BN,
MS lat. 15398. But Vincentius Hispanus seems to tolerate procuration without
the mandate: "Cum quis procuratorem se dicit, aut est certum eum habere
mandatum . . . aut certum est non habere mandatum . . . aut dubitatur, quo
casu aut adversarius dicit: Non habes mandatum, aut dicit: Dubito an habeas.
In primo casu cogitur probare mandatum, in secundo sufficit satisdare rem
ratam dominum habiturum et in voluntate est adversarii, an procurator
probet mandatum an satisdet . . ."; F. Gillmann, "Johannes Galensis als
Glossator, insbesondere der Compilatio III," *Archiv für katholisches Kirchenrecht*, CV (1925), 498f.; similarly civil lawyers, for example, Placentinus: "Ego
indistincte dico, quia sive dubitetur sive negetur, in arbitrio est rei qui
convenitur, velitne cogere procuratorem ad cavendum vel ad probandum,"
Summa Codicis, BN, MS lat. 4441, fol. 28ᵛ; and Benedict of Ysernia, *Summa*, in
Meijers, *Iuris Interpretes Saeculi XIII*, pp. 63f. The *Parvus Ordinarius*
(1210-1220) and Rainerius of Perugia, *Ars Notariae*, describe the procedure of
the *cautio* of the procurator or *syndicus*; Wahrmund, *Archiv f. kath. KR.*,
LXXXI (1901), 25; *Quellen*, III, ii, 144, *De cautionibus de rato*.

The procurator of the *reus* or defendant could act without a special mandate;
"secus vero est in actore [plaintiff], quia aliquis non recipitur pro ipso, nisi
speciale habeat mandatum"; *Parvus Ordinarius*, Wahrmund, *Archiv f. kath. KR.*,
LXXXI, 25.

The mandate must contain the name of the procurator, the case for which
he is appointed, and the assurance that the *dominus* will ratify the sentence
of the court for or against the procurator; Tancred, in Bamberg MS. Can. 21,
fol. 17ᵛ; *Ordo* (Bergmann, p. 125): "Et nota, quod exprimi debet in scriptura,
de creatione syndici vel actoris confecta, quis constituatur, et ad quid, et contra
quos constituitur, nisi generaliter ad omnes lites constitueretur. . . ." See
models of procuratorial mandates for a collegiate church and of a *civitas* given
by Rainerius of Perugia, *Ars Notariae* (1226-1233), Wahrmund, *Quellen*, III,
ii, 45f.; and by the Saxon *Summa*, Rockinger, *Quellen und Erörterungen*, VII,
280.

[135] Alexander III, *Decr. Greg. IX* 2, 22, 2: "Scripta vero autentica, si testes
inscripti decesserint, nisi forte per manum publicam facta fuerint, ita, quod

[51]

were no public notaries who could give acts full authenticity in northern France in this period,[136] the mandate of the masters at Paris had to be authenticated by an authentic seal. Who could possess a *sigillum authenticum?* Petrus Hispanus held that a *universitas* could have one.[137] Tancred, his contemporary, names chapters, prelates (abbots, archdeacons, provosts), secular princes, and judges delegate as having authentic seals,[138] while the Chancery Ordinances of the time of Innocent III recognize the seals (on mandates for procurators *ad impetrandum*) of kings and nobles, of archbishops, bishops, deans, archdeacons, and other persons of this kind.[139] A statute of the Cardinal-Legate Otto for England, 1237, adds to the usual list the officials of bishops, archbishops, abbots, priors, deans, and archdeacons, and also *collegia* and *conventus* with their rectors.[140] About 1243 Geoffrey of Trani cited the decretal *Quia in causis* (Innocent III's indulgence granting the right of procuration to the masters at Paris) as proof that a *universitas* could have an

---

appareant publica, aut autenticum sigillum habuerint, per quod possint probari, non videntur nobis alicuius firmitatis robur habere." Cf. Bernard of Pavia, *Summa*, Laspeyres, p. 49; Tancred, *Ordo*, Bergmann, pp. 248f.; Ricardus Anglicus, *Summa*, Wahrmund, *Quellen*, II, iii, 51f. Cf. Bresslau, *Urkundenlehre*, I, 655-658.

136 Giry, *Manuel de Diplomatique*, pp. 828, 833; Fournier, *Les officialités*, p. 45.

137 Cited by Tancred, ad. v. *autenticum* (*Comp. I*, 2, t. *De fide instrumentorum*, c. 2, Alexander III, "Scripta vero autentica"; *Decr. Greg. IX* 2, 22, 2): "cuius erit hoc sigillum, quod dicitur autenticum? P. Yspanus dixit quod universitatis . . ."; Leipzig, Universitätsbibl., MS lat. 968, fol. 22; BN, MS lat 15398, fol. 23, where "universitas" instead of "universitatis." On Petrus Hispanus see Schulte, *Quellen*, I, 152f. For an example of a seal of a *universitas* (a chapter of canons regular), see *Decr. Greg. IX* 2, 19, 5.

138 "Michi videtur quod sigillum capituli cuiuslibet prelati, puta abbatis, vel archidiaconi, vel prepositi, vel principis secularis, vel iudicum delegatorum debet autenticum reputari"; Leipzig, MS lat. 968 fol. 22ʳ; BN, MS lat. 15398, fol. 23; this after the references to Petrus Hispanus and Laurentius: "Laurentius dixit quod episcopi vel domini pape"; BN, MS lat. 3930 (fourteenth century), fol. 11: "Mihi videtur quod sigillum capituli cuiuslibet ecclesie, et cuiuslibet prelati, etc."

139 "Nullus petitiones sublimium personarum ut regum ducum marchionum comitum vel baronum archiepiscoporum episcoporum abbatum decanorum archidiaconorum aut huiusmodi personarum, que proprium consueverunt habere sigillum, exhibeat in data communi, nisi litteras eorum propter hoc sigillatas ostendat"; Tangl, *Kanzleiordnungen*, p. 54, Constitutio II, Art. 3; Art. 7 states that the *nuntii* of such persons can present petitions.

140 Matthew Paris, *Chronica Majora*, ed. Luard, III, 438. In France, from the beginning of the thirteenth century, bishops, archdeacons, and monasteries had seals of jurisdiction in the courts of their officials; Giry, *Manuel*, p. 651.

authentic seal.[141] But this opinion, as well as later ones,[142] cannot be used without caution for the earlier period; it reflects, however, the earlier practice in the courts and the increasing use of seals by corporations.[143] Yet we can at least conclude that the seals of such ecclesiastical corporations as cathedral chapters were fully recognized by the canonists and the courts before 1220.[144]

How, then, could the masters act as a corporation through procurators before 1221 and from 1225 to 1246? We know that they sent procurators to Rome before 1221, possibly as early as the end of the twelfth century; and we know that they sent procurators to Gregory IX in 1230 "nomine Universitatis,"[145] —and this case of the University against the royal and episcopal authorities was settled in the Roman Court. Was there no legal corporation when the masters did not have a common seal?[146] It is generally admitted that the masters constituted a legal corporation in 1231, when Gregory IX promulgated statutes for the University in the *Parens scientiarum*;[147] but neither at this

[141] *Summa super rubricis decretalium*, l. II, t. *De fide instrumentorum*: "Item instrumentum sive scriptum privatum sed autenticum est, cui appensum est autenticum sigillum, id est, episcopi . . . item et aliorum prelatorum . . . item conventus . . . item universitatis, ut supra, de procur., quia in causis, item cuiuslibet corporis vel collegii"; BN, MS lat. 3974, fol. 74. On the date of the *Summa*, Schulte, *Quellen*, II, 90.

[142] For the opinions of Henry of Susa, Guillaume Durantis, and Conrad of Mure, see W. Ewald, *Siegelkunde* (Below and Meinecke, *Handbuch der Mittelalterlichen und Neuren Geschichte*), pp. 44-48; Giry, *Manuel*, pp. 649-652; Bresslau, *Urkundenlehre*, I, 719f. None of these treatises cites the opinions of Petrus Hispanus, Tancred, and Ricardus Anglicus.

[143] Giry, *Manuel*, pp. 647-648. In the time of Honorius III the seal was becoming necessary for a corporation; he appointed judges delegate to find out if a priest and some clerks had a right to a common seal without being "unum corpus, ita quod capitulum appellaretur"; they had used a seal without the consent of their superior, an abbess; *Decr. Greg. IX* 5, 31, 14. On the seals of English borough communities, see J. Tait, "The Borough Community in England," *E.H.R.*, XLV (1930), 537, 541f.; and Ch. Gross, *The Gild Merchant*, I, 24, 94f.; of French communes, A. Luchaire, *Les Communes françaises à l'époque des Capétiens directs*, pp. 103f.

[144] The canonists, when all is said, give no precise definition of the authentic seal and are indefinite on its effect and on the extent of the possession of seals, owing to the varying practice and custom; cf. Ewald, *op.cit.*, p. 42. Innocent IV himself is vague on this; cited by Bresslau, *Urkundenlehre*, I, 719, n. 1.

[145] *Chartularium*, I, no. 75, and no. 79, note, p. 139.

[146] Viollet holds that normally a corporation, to be fully legal and to have a procurator, must have a seal for its mandate; *Établissements de Saint-Louis*, IV, 229.

[147] *Chartularium*, I, no. 79.

time nor before 1221 did they have a common seal,[148] although they were acting and being recognized as a corporation in 1210-1213 and 1215. The solution of the difficulty lies in this, that it was not held absolutely necessary for a legal corporation to have its own authentic seal for procuration.[149] An authentic seal was generally held necessary, yes;[150] but the authentic seal used by a corporation might belong to a person of rank who could permit its use for procuratorial mandates.[151] Perhaps in such instances of the use of another's seal the corporation was con-

[148] Halphen emphasizes too strongly the importance of the seal of the University and apparently believes that the seal was actually destroyed in 1221 as commanded by Honorius III (*Chartularium*, I, no. 41), although it remained in use for procuration in 1222 and was not broken until 1225 (above, n. 132), *Studi Medievali*, II, 137. Nevertheless, he holds that the autonomous existence of the University was assured in 1231 by Gregory IX (p. 139), in spite of the fact that the seal was not restored until 1246.

[149] The canonists of the first quarter of the thirteenth century do not say that a corporation must have a seal; they only say that the *syndicus, actor*, or procurator must have a mandate, which, if suspect, must be examined and proved in court. But the procurator can act without a mandate, says Vincentius Hispanus, if he satisfies the court that his *dominus* will ratify his action (Gillmann, *Archiv f. kathol. KR.*, cv, 498). It might be left to the defendant to decide whether the procurator of the plaintiff should show a mandate or give satisfaction by *cautio*; so also Tancred, above, n. 84. But the Roman Court demanded a mandate under seal; Tangl, *Kanzleiordnungen*, p. 54, Constitutio II, Art. 3 and 7. Tancred asserts that "consuetudo facit aliquod instrumentum autenticum quod alias non esset"; gloss ad t. *De fide instr., Comp. III*, 2; BN, MS lat. 3931-A, fol. 168ᵛ.

[150] Vincentius, ad v. *legaliter (Comp. I*, 1, t. *De procur.*, c. 1): "Sed pone quod de mandato dubitatur, quia sigillum incognitum est, de eo fides fieri debet, ar. ff. quod cuiuscumque univ. . . . Vin.," BN, MS lat. 15398, fol. 15ᵛ, and Bamberg, MS Can. 21, fol. 17ᵛ; Chancery Ordinances, Tangl, *op.cit.*, p. 54, Art. 3; Master Arnulfus, *Summa Minorum* (1250-1254): "Item debemus videre de procuratoriis, utrum sint sigillata sigillo autentico, quoniam aliter non habent firmitatem"; ed. Wahrmund, *Quellen*, I, ii, 54; cf. J. G. C. Joosting, "Die Summa Ut nos Minores," *Zeitschrift der Savigny-Stiftung, Kan.-Abtlg.*, XVII (1928), 222. Master Arnulfus wrote at Paris and probably expresses the practice there of the recent past. But Henry of Susa seems to think that the mandate could be proved also from the names in it: "ideo forte quando est procurator universitatis inspicitur instrumentum procurationis ut appareat de nominibus . . ."; this in reference to petitions for rescripts, *Summa*, t. *De procur.*

[151] Innocent IV, *Apparatus*, 2, t. *De fide instr.*, c. Scriptura: a person who did not have a seal "poterit alieno sigillo sigillare sed tunc etiam necesse est hoc ipsum dicere, scilicet, cuius sigillo signet et quare alterius sigillo signet"; Henry of Susa, *Summa*, 2, t. *De fide instr.*: ". . . unde non debet quis alieno sigillo sigillare quin de hoc faciat mentionem . . . nam et sigillum quid ad certum usum deputatum est, ad alium verti non debet." Innocent IV emphasizes the custom of the Roman Court in recognizing seals not normally valid, e.t.

sidered a minor;[152] but more probably it was simply natural that the seals of individual members of the corporation should be accepted on mandates when it was still difficult for lawyers to think in terms of a fictitious person,[153] and when archdeacons, deans, and canons had authentic seals of their own and were members of corporations.[154] In the Faculties of Arts and Theology at Paris were masters who, as such ecclesiastic dignitaries,[155] could attach their seals to procuratorial mandates and other documents of the whole body of masters when, in conflicts with the chancellor and the bishop, the masters could hardly have used the seals of the latter.[156] In 1221 the seals of three members of the Faculty of Theology authenticated the deed of property by the University to the Dominicans.[157] It seems probable that a similar means[158] was adopted for authenticating the mandates of procurators carrying petitions to Rome in 1210-1213 and 1219.[159] In any case, the petitions obtained the ap-

[152] *Parvus Ordinarius* (1210-1220): "Si vero ille, qui citatus est, sit persona minor, debet implorare auxilium alicuius sigilli autentici"; in this case the procuratorial mandate addressed to judges delegated by the pope should terminate thus: ". . . Et quia sigillum non habeo, sigillo talis personae usus sum, datum, etc."; Wahrmund, *Archiv f. kathol. KR.*, LXXXI, 26.

[153] A seal could be used by a person with jurisdiction; it was not admitted that a corporation had jurisdiction, for "rectores assumpti ab universitatibus habent jurisdictionem et non ipsae universitates"; Innocent IV, quoted by Gierke, III, 305 n. 179, and p. 306. Hence the slowness of the recognition of seals of corporations.

[154] We have seen that such persons could have seals; for examples of their seals see Douet d'Arcq, *Collection des Sceaux*, II, nos. 8046 (seal of Magister Willelmus de Bardonay, 1211); 8051 (Magister Willelmus de Vienna, 1210); 8053, 8064, 7622, 7623 (chancellors of Paris, Pierre de Poitiers, Jean de Chandelles); 7779 (seal of Robert de Courçon, 1211, as canon of the cathedral of Paris); cf. J. Roman, *Manuel de sigillographie française*, pp. 205, 207.

[155] We find them as canons, deans, and archdeacons of Paris and other churches; *Chartularium*, I, nos. 11 (notes 8 and 13), 26, 43, 44, 46, 61, 83, 87, 116, 330 (p. 379).

[156] As late as the end of the thirteenth century, Johannes Andrea says that the "actus collegiales" can be authenticated by the subscription of the names or by the attachment of the seals of the members to the act; Gierke, III, 313, n. 205.

[157] *Chartularium*, I, no. 42; Halphen, *Studi Medievali*, II, 137, thinks that these three seals were used because Honorius III ordered the common seal of the University to be broken; but it was not broken until 1225.

[158] Seals of ecclesiastical dignitaries, who were not regent masters at Paris, were used for authenticating copies of privileges to be sent to the pope for examination in 1230 and 1244; *Chartularium*, I, nos. 75 and 132. Such seals may have been used for procuratorial mandates.

[159] There exists a model of a procuratorial mandate of an abbot and *conventus*,

pointment of judges delegate by the pope. But in 1219-1221, when the bishop and chancellor were not sparing of sentences of excommunication, the masters perhaps found it more difficult to obtain the use of seals of individuals and therefore decided to have one made for the whole body.[160] Against this, the bishop, claiming that the use of the seal was abused and that the masters were arrogating to themselves the jurisdiction of the bishop and the chancellor,[161] started suit in a petition which resulted in the appointment by the pope of judges delegate who were instructed to destroy the new seal.[162] As we have seen, the seal was not broken until 1225.[163] While it existed, it was used for procuration,[164] and also for borrowing money to pay the expenses of four procurators in 1222.[165] From 1225 to 1246 the masters had no common seal,[166] but they continued to act as a corporation in appointing procurators (1230-1231, 1233, 1237),[167] were held responsible by Gregory IX for their debts,[168]

---

which indicates the use of more than one seal (an. 1226), von Heckel, "Der Libellus Petitionum des Kardinals Guala Bichieri"; Archiv für Urkundenforschung, I, 509f.

160 Chartularium, I, no. 41, "nomine universitatis magistrorum et scolarium."

161 The seal of the bishop's official was an important source of revenue, being used to authenticate the documents drawn up for persons who could not have seals; normally it should have been used by the masters, but of course, they could not hope to use it for suits against the bishop or chancellor. Hence, they resorted to other seals and wanted one of their own; and naturally the bishop wanted to force them to be dependent on his jurisdiction alone. Cf. Fournier, Les officialités, pp. 2f., 45f.; Giry, Manuel, p. 833. Besides, the masters were not reporting misdemeanors of students (Chartularium, I, no. 20, p. 88).

162 Chartularium, I, no. 41. It should be observed that a rescript repeated the general language of the petition; the defendant could then contest the claims of the petitioner in the court of the judges delegate. From this court the masters appealed, ibid., no. 45, p. 102.

163 Ibid., no. 45, p. 103, and p. 104, n. 3. Halphen, Studi Medievali, II, 137, assumes that the seal was broken in 1221. He states that the pope, in the rescript ordering the destruction of the seal, 122 (no. 41), "ne reprend pas a son compte l'expression universitas magistrorum et scolarium." Not in this document, because it merely follows the tenor of the bishop's petition; but Honorius III does use it again in 1222 (no. 45).

164 Chartularium, I, 103: "usus sigilli scolarium preterquam in hiis, que ad officium procurationis in hac causa pertinent, suspendatur."

165 So we learn from the litigation on the debt in 1237 and 1259, ibid., nos. 116 and 330, p. 379.

166 Rashdall, Universities, I, 319, thinks that the Four Nations had seals in this period and that these seals were used for the University.

167 Chartularium, I, no. 75 ("aliquos nomine Universitatis" to be sent to Rome) and note, p. 90. To these procurators of the University the pope issued

and were treated as a legal corporation by the same pope in 1231 when he issued the famous *Parens scientiarum* for the University.[169]

A common seal, then, was not considered indispensable for a corporation. The University of Masters, acting in the courts as a legal person, had sued and been sued before 1221 and after 1225. It was awkward, the masters related in their petition for a seal in 1246,[170] to use the seal of another (*alienum sigillum*) at the expense of secrecy in their affairs; but they had managed to get along without one of their own. In 1245, in full congregation, the masters adopted new statutes;[171] in the same year Innocent IV ordered full attendance in the Congregations. It seems that the masters constituted a corporation as effectively in 1245 as in 1246, when they obtained a seal. So, in litigation, they constituted a corporation as fully in 1210-1213, 1219-1221, and in 1225-1246, as in 1221-1225, when they had a seal.[172]

6. CONCLUSION: PAPAL RECOGNITION

We have now followed the activities of the masters from the earliest indication to the full expression of their corporate will, and we have observed the attitude of canonists and ecclesiastical authorities towards the new collectivity. When can we say the corporation of masters, the University of Paris, first existed? No definite year can be given, for no charter of incorporation was granted by a superior authority—charters of incorporation belong to a later period. Holding in mind, however, the vague definitions of a corporation and the uncertain descriptions of its privileges and functions in the first half of the thirteenth cen-

---

various bulls for the protection of the University, nos. 79, 81, 82, 88, and notes to these documents; 1233 (no. 100), "Procuration de l'Université pour poursuivre un procès . . . devant les juges délégués par sa Sainteté" (the original document is lost). See also nos. 115, 121, for the litigation with the bishop of Paris in 1237. Gregory IX in 1231 and 1237 granted the procurator of the masters and students immunity from excommunication (nos. 95 and 113).

[168] *Chartularium*, I, no. 116.

[169] *Ibid.*, no. 79.

[170] *Ibid.*, no. 165; this was probably a *sigillum ad causas* alone: "petunt sigillum ad causas, non ad contrahendum mutuum sed ad tractatus negotiorum suorum. . . . Pro hiis duobus scribunt de novo magistri iiijor facultatum"; no. 113, note.

[171] *Ibid.*, no. 136. [172] *Ibid.*, no. 144.

tury, we must conclude that the University of Masters was a legal corporation, fully recognized by the highest ecclesiastical authority, by 1215 at the latest.[173] The development of the internal organization of the University was not completed until towards the middle of the century; but already, as one body with a common will and purpose, the masters elected officers, adopted statutes, enforced their authority on all the members of the society, and sued in the courts through procurators.[174] Innocent III and his legate, Robert de Courçon, both of whom had been students at Paris, confirmed these essential attributes of a corporation. Thereafter, the existence of the University was assured.[175] If in the third decade of the century the bishop of Paris tried to limit the corporate rights of the masters, particularly in the matters of statutes, the seal, and jurisdiction,[176] he did not claim that the masters had no corporation[177] but complained of their extending their activities beyond the demands of internal affairs.[178] Honorius III was perhaps not as ready to support the

173 Thus, in general my conclusion agrees with that of Denifle and Rashdall. But I am less hesitant to recognize a corporation than Denifle, who misinterpreted the privilege of procuration granted by Innocent III. On the other hand, I can no longer hold with Denifle and Rashdall that a corporation of a *de facto* sort existed as early as 1170-1200. My conviction has been fixed more definitely by the study of the Canon law and court procedure.

174 Henry of Susa, *Commentaria* to *Decretals of Greg. IX*, Venice, 1581, sums up these rights, 1, t. *De procur.*, c. Quia in causis: "Videbatur, quod eis non liceret, quasi scholares non constituant unum corpus vel universitatem. . . . Sed contrarium est verum nam et Doctores sive magistri collegium habent et statuta faciunt, ut legitur et no. supra de constitu. ex litteris [*Decr. Greg. IX* 1, 2, 11], et habent scholares universitatem . . . et secundum ius canonicum istorum causae tractari debent."

175 Halphen, *Studi Medievali*, II, 139, thinks that the "autonomous" existence of the corporation was not assured until 1231, and then by the *Parens scientarium*.

176 *Chartularium*, I, nos. 30, 31, 41, and 45.

177 The nature and extent of the rights, not the existence of the corporation itself, were in litigation.

178 The bishop complained of *conspirationes et conjurationes* (*Chartularium*, I, nos. 30, 31, 41); and he pretended that a papal legate had forbidden such illegal conspiracies of the masters but could not produce the document (*ibid.*, nos. 30 and 31). But a corporation, while it could have statutes, could not act secretly or conspire against its superior authorities; in 1257 the judges for the case of the abbot against the *universitatem et homines et scindicos universitatis ville Sancti Egidii* decided that the *universitas* could elect *syndici* and officers, but that the "homines hujus ville nunquam faciant inter se conjuracionem vel vota, . . . connexitatem vel juramentum, vel promissionem, vel convencionem suspectam"; Bligny-Bondurand, *Les coutumes de Saint-Gilles,*

masters as Innocent III had been, but he did not question the right of the University to have reasonable statutes and to elect procurators. Gregory IX did not essentially change the relations between the corporation and the church of Paris; he merely reconfirmed, while defining more precisely, the privileges and rights confirmed by Innocent III and Robert de Courçon.[179] Complete autonomy was not permitted: the bishop retained his ordinary jurisdiction over masters and students,[180] and the chancellor, even after 1231, was still formally in control of the license system. But what things the papacy confirmed were legal—"nolo disputare de plenitudine potestatis."[181] When,

---

pp. 136, 182-185, 183. Here was a corporation with limited rights. The University of Paris was given more extensive rights by Robert de Courçon in 1215: the masters and students can make "obligationes et constitutiones fide vel pena vel juramento vallatas" in certain cases, "ita tamen, quod propter hec studium non dissolvatur aut destruatur"; *Chartularium*, I, 79. But Honorius III recognized the right of *cessationes* as a remedy against abuses of the bishop and chancellor (*an.* 1222, *ibid.*, 103). A cessation was decreed by the University in 1229; *ibid.*, no. 62. In 1231 Gregory IX repeated the privilege of Robert de Courçon and expressly permitted the suspension of lectures for the redress of grievances; *ibid.*, 138.

[179] Gregory IX acknowledged that a corporation was long since in existence by requesting the masters and students to send authenticated copies of their privileges to him, above, n. 147. On the basis of these privileges he prepared the *Parens scientiarum*, incorporating their essential provisions in his statutes for the University. Henry of Susa, *Summa*, 5, t. *De privilegiis*, remarks that the *communiter corporale privilegium* is that "quod sic competit universitati quod nomine ipsius allegari potest privilegium, et quo ipsa universitas potest." This we can see clearly by comparing the statutes of Robert de Courçon (1215) with those of Gregory IX (1231) on the right of the masters to enact statutes (*Chartularium*, I, 79, 137). Moreover, the terms of the compromise of 1213 (*ibid.*, no. 16) on the *licentia docendi* are the basis of the provisions of Gregory IX (*ibid.*, p. 137), although these provisions give the chancellor slightly more authority than he was given in 1213.

[180] It should be noted that in 1257 the *universitas* and *homines* of Saint-Gilles, while constituting a corporation, remained subject in certain matters to the abbot of Saint-Gilles, Bligny-Bondurand, *op.cit.*, p. 183.

[181] Henry of Susa, *Summa*, 2, t. *De confirmatione utile vel inutile*: "Item quid non est, confirmari non potest, sicut nec collegio, quid non est, privilegium dari potest . . . nisi forte a papa fiat, qui sicut potest infectum irritare de plenitudine potestatis . . . sic et potest quid nondum est confirmare. ar. supra. de consue, cum olim . . . in quibus patet quod privilegium suum extenditur ad futura. . . . Nolo disputare de plenitudine potestatis." Above, he states that confirmation is made either tacitly through the lapse of time, "ut si a sententia infra. X. dies non fuerit appellatum," or "per litteras et privilegia superioris, et maxime domini pape." Rashdall, *Universities*, I, 302f., remarks on the importance of privileges of confirmation at a time when charters of incorporation were not customary.

therefore, in 1208-1215, the masters and students asserted their corporate will, and when Innocent III and Robert de Courçon confirmed and defined and recognized their corporate rights, the University of Paris was constituted as a legal corporation.

CHAPTER II ✦ ROMAN LAW AND EARLY REPRESENTATION IN SPAIN AND ITALY, 1150-1250[1]

EDIEVAL representation was constructed on a foundation of feudal law, local institutions (hundred and county courts, guilds and corporations, communes, boroughs, and communities of villages), new classes in society (townsmen and knights of the shire), royal curias as assemblies, ecclesiastical synods and councils, and the growth of royal and papal authority. But in the course of construction the architects were greatly aided and stimulated by the revival of Roman and Canon law, from which they obtained not only ideas but also the almost indispensable procedure of corporate representation by agents (*procuratores* or syndics) who were given full powers (*plena potestas*) by their constituents to represent the interests of the corporation in court. By granting such powers of attorney the corporation consented, before a civil suit began, to the jurisdiction of the judges and to their decision of the case. In the mandate which he carried, the proctor was considered to be "fully instructed" if *plena potestas* or its equivalent was stated; and the court generally demanded that the proctor have full powers.[2] If the case "touched" the

---

[1] This study, now slightly revised, was first printed in *Speculum*, XVIII (1943), 211-232. A complete history of all kinds of representation in the early Middle Ages would be useful. Here I merely indicate signs of the appearance of Roman agency. Recent authorities have contributed nothing new with regard to representation by proctors according to the revived Roman law. See, for example, Manuel de Bofarull y Romaña, *Las antiguas cortes*, 2nd ed., pp. 25-63; Demetrio Ramos, *Historia de las cortes tradicionales de España*, pp. 43-95; Marongiu, *L'Istituto parlamentare*, ch. II and pp. 86-101, 123-127. The work of Thomas N. Bisson, "An Early Provincial Assembly," *Speculum*, XXXVI (1961), 254-281, reveals no example of our kind of representation in France in the period treated here. On the Church and the Papal States, see below, nn. 102-114; on Italy, nn. 76-101.

[2] *Plena potestas* was taken from *C.* 2, 12, 10. It is treated fully in ch. III.

legal rights of several defendants, the court could not give a just decision unless all had been properly cited—in accordance with the principle of due process and judicial consent clearly expressed by the classical jurist Paulus: "De unoquoque negotio praesentibus omnibus, quos causa contingit, iudicari oportet," and, more sweepingly, by Justinian in the famous maxim, "Quod omnes similiter tangit, ab omnibus comprobetur."[3] When a "national" emergency involved the *status* or public welfare of a kingdom, it touched the interests and rights of all greater individuals and communities of lesser persons and corporations; and by the Roman principle of consent these must all be summoned to defend their property and other legal rights—the communities through their representatives bearing full powers to act in the name of their constituents and to accept the decision of the king's council and court in assembly. But this was made possible by the growing power of the king, who alone could declare a "national" emergency that must be met for the public and common utility, and whose prerogative, which consisted of the supreme legislative, judicial, and administrative authority, but was limited by the law, enabled him to summon all whose rights were affected and who must respond to the summons or else be declared contumacious.

This system of corporate representation by delegates given full powers flourished throughout western Europe by 1300—in provincial and general councils of the Church, in Parliament, in Cortes, and, slightly later, in States General. But when and where did it first develop? Priority has most frequently been awarded to Spain, where, it has long been said, the third estate was represented by *procuradores* as early as 1163 in Aragon and 1188 in Leon. Ernest Barker, however, was inclined to give the credit for originality to the Dominican Order in the influence of its provincial and general chapters on the rise of Parliament.[4] But such claims for this or that priority have neglected

---

[3] Paulus in *D.* 42, 1, 47, where a kind of due process is stated for the imperial *fiscus* as a court and is therefore a principle of public and private law. It is, on the side of procedure, the equivalent of the principle stated by Justinian in *C.* 5, 59, 5, 2. Both passages are connected and applied by the legists and canonists to every kind of situation where common interests or rights are involved. *Quod omnes tangit* will be the subject of ch. IV.

[4] *The Dominican Order and Convocation.* His thesis has never attracted much

the necessary presuppositions of the favorable environment, both of organized communities which had rights to defend and of the new law which provided a satisfactory means of representation.

1. The Legal Environment

Although until about the middle of the twelfth century bare references are made in legal literature to proctors representing individuals, there is little mention of proctors or syndics of corporate communities other than churches.[5] This is true of the

---

approval. Most recently, H. P. Tunmore has criticized Barker, "The Dominican Order and Parliament." *Catholic Historical Review*, XXVI (1941), 479-489. But Tunmore offers no solution, for he is unaware of the background of Romano-canonical procedure and of Innocent III's assemblies of representatives of Italian towns in the Papal States. Nor does he refer to precedents for the Dominican representation of the provinces as communities of conventual communities in the General Chapter: for example, "rural federations" or associations of villages in twelfth-century France (A. Luchaire, in Lavisse, *Histoire de France*, II, ii, 338, and III, i, 392). There is also a precedent in a papal decretal, 1185 (*Decr. Greg. IX* 3, 39, 14), which reveals that a procurator waged a suit against the Archbishop of Ravenna in the name of all the monasteries of Bologna; here is definitely an early example of the representation of a group of corporate communities. And what of the English shire as a community of hundreds and vills?

[5] I find nothing on proctors or syndics of corporations in the glosses of Irnerius published by Savigny, *Geschichte des römischen Rechts im Mittelalter*, IV, 458ff.; and by Pescatore, *Die Glossen des Irnerius*, p. 71—possession can be acquired "per procuratorem" who has a mandate; but this is not a corporate proctor. See also the glosses in Besta, *L'Opera d'Irnerio*, II, 416. The *Summa Codicis* and *Quaestiones de iuris subtilitatibus* attributed to Irnerius and edited by Fitting are later; they are, respectively, by Rogerius (an early redaction, *ca.* 1150, of his *Summa Codicis*) and Placentinus—H. Kantorowicz, *Studies in the Glossators of the Roman Law*, p. 35; Kantorowicz holds that Irnerius wrote glosses only, pp. 4, 33ff.

In the early southern French literature, notably in the *Petri Exceptiones* (*ca.* 1110), edited by Savigny, II, Anhang I. A., there are two references to proctors of churches, I, c. 61 (p. 348: "procuratores venerabilis loci [i.e., of a church or monastery] usque ad quadraginta annos rem vendicare poterunt"), and I, c. 65 (p. 350: "Res mobiles ecclesiarum . . . si a procuratoribus ecclesiarum dantur, veluti ab episcopis, ab abbatibus, et ab aliis similibus fuerint accipientium"). Since Petrus seems to have drawn frequently from the *Epitome* of the *Novellae* by Julian, he may have been influenced by Justinian's own opinion that "monachis autem liceat sive per se, sive per procuratorem monasterii causas agere," *Auth.*, Coll. IX, t. 6, c. 27 Si quando. It is significant, however, that one finds as yet no mention of a syndic, the term used by the later legists for the representative of a secular as well as ecclesiastical corporation.

See also Fitting, in *Juristische Schriften des früheren Mittelalters*, c. 67, p. 162, where proctors for individuals are briefly treated. In the slightly earlier *Brachylogus* (*ca.* 1100), ed. Böcking, I find no mention of proctor or syndic. On the *Brachylogus* and *Exceptiones Petri* see Kantorowicz, *Glossators*, pp. 112ff.

early Bolognese and Provençal legists,[6] and it is still true in Provençe about 1149.[7] At about the same time, the early work of Rogerius reveals a discussion of proctors for individuals only,[8] but his *Summa Codicis* refers to the *yconomus* as acting for a church.[9] From the middle of the century on, however, this literature flourished in Italy at Bologna, Modena, and Mantua, and in southern France at Montpellier; and discussions of syndics and corporations began to appear in the works of pupils and successors of the four great doctors or disciples of Irnerius at Bologna.[10] In Italy, Placentinus (who later taught at Montpellier, *ca.* 1166-1183 and 1189-1192),[11] and Pillius and Bencivenne were by the last quarter of the century briefly discussing the problem of the syndic as the oath-taker for a *collegium*.[12]

[6] See the preceding note for the early French school.

[7] Fitting, ed., *Lo Codi in der lateinischen Übersetzung des Ricardus Pisanus*, pp. 24ff. A fairly detailed discussion of proctors for litigation is given II, 6, "de procuratoribus" (pp. 14-18); there is nothing on the syndic or the corporation in this connection. In another place, II, 27, § 3, it is stated that if a person appoints a proctor or *nuntius*, he need not appear in court to take the *sacramentum calumpnie*; and if one of the litigants is "de aliena terra," he may plead by his *nuncius* (p. 37).

[8] Fitting, ed., *Summa Codicis des Irnerius*; it is really by Rogerius (cf. Kantorowicz, *Glossators*, p. 35); on proctors, II, 7 (pp. 31-34).

[9] II, 2; ed. by J. B. Palmieri, in *Scripta anecdota glossatorum*, I, 10f. I find nothing on the city and its syndic.

[10] As for the four doctors themselves, Bulgarus, Martinus, Jacobus, and Hugo, they do not seem to have treated corporations and syndics extensively; but I have found later references indicating that they had talked or written about the problem; see the glosses edited by Haenel, *Dissensiones dominorum . . . qui glossatores vocantur*, pp. 28, 271-273—Hugolinus—but only in connection with mandates of proctors for individuals, not with syndics of corporations, who are usually discussed in reference to the *juramentum calumniae*. Bulgarus' *Summa de judiciis*, ed. Wunderlich, *Anecdota quae ad processum civilem pertinent*, pp. 9-26, has nothing on proctors, syndics, or corporations. But in his *Ad digestorum titulum de diversis regulis juris antiqui commentarius*, ed. Beckhaus, p. 99. Bulgarus says that a *universitas* can appoint an *actor*. (No doubt the unpublished glosses—and the MSS that I have examined in recent years contain many of them—furnish additional evidence.)

[11] On Placentinus at Montpellier, see P. de Tourtillon, *Placentin*, pp. 87ff., 120f.

[12] Placentinus has nothing on corporate representatives in his *Summa "Cum essem Mantua,"* ed. Pescatore. I have not been able to consult his *Summa Codicis*; but he is quoted by Hugolinus (*ca.* 1216-1234) on the syndic and corporation, Haenel, *Glossatores*, pp. 317f., sec. 75; the same for Pillius, pp. 317f. For Pillius see also Gierke, III, 193. Bencivenne, whose *Summa de ordine judiciorum* was edited under the name of Pillius (so Kantorowicz, *Glossators*, p. 72) by Bergmann, in *Pillii, Tancredi, Gratiae Libri de iudiciorum ordine*, states that the "syndicus electus a suo collegio" can take the *iuramentum de calumnia*, pp. 52f.

Relatively full maturity among the legists was reached by Azo, who treats corporations and their representatives in greater detail than his predecessors, in his famous *Summa Codicis* (1209).[13] About 1162, the influence of the Italians spread anew to southern France (Montpellier) through Rogerius and Placentinus;[14] by 1149 Roman law had arrived—but did not take full hold—in England[15] through Vacarius, a pupil of Martinus. Perhaps Glanville could thus equate *responsales* (the later attorneys) with proctors.[16]

Far more than that of the legists and glossators, the influence of the revived Canon law on Gratian and the decretists, on the decretals from Pope Eugenius III on, and on the decretalists, and above all on the procedure in ecclesiastical courts, was bound soon to spread the ideas of Roman law into northern France and England.[17] In the so-called *Decretum* of Gratian (*ca.* 1140) there are references to proctors, and churches are treated as corporations;[18] but true corporate representatives these proctors are not—they are apparently prelates acting as agents of their churches.[19] In the flourishing French school of

13 Ed. Venice, 1610: to *Code*, ii, t. *De procuratoribus*. His glosses to *Digest*, iii, *Quod cuiusque universitatis nomine*, on syndics and corporations, need study. Azo, like most legists, holds that the syndic, not the proctor, is the representative of the secular corporation, e.g., the city.

14 Kantorowicz, *Glossators*, pp. 125f.; Rashdall, *Universities*, ed. Powicke and Emden, ii, 128. Some Roman law was taught at Orleans in the early Middle Ages (Rashdall, ii, 140f.), but it is doubtful that it was more than elementary.

15 Kantorowicz, *Glossators*, p. 88; on Vacarius see Zulueta, *The Liber Pauperum of Vacarius*, pp. xiiiff., xxiff.; but in the *Liber Pauperum* there is nothing on corporate representatives. Among his glosses, however, there are bare references to the *actor* and *syndic* of a *universitas*; Stölzel, "Glossenapparat des Vacarius Pragensis . . . ," *Festschrift für Heinrich Brunner*, pp. 7, 21. On the work of Master Guillaume de Longchamps and Roman law in Normandy see Caillemer, *Le droit civil dans las provinces anglo-normandes au XIIe siècle*, pp. 50-72, in which Guillaume's *Practica legum* (before 1189) is edited; there is a brief mention of proctors for a monastery (c. 27; pp. 6of.).

16 Pollock and Maitland, *History of English Law*, i, 213.

17 On the influence of the canonists in the twelfth century see above all S. Kuttner, "Les débuts de l'école canoniste française," *Studia et documenta historiae et juris* (1938), pp. 193-204; Kuttner and E. Rathbone, "Anglo-Norman Canonists," *Traditio*, vi, 304-336. I have found nothing in the eleventh-century decretists, notably Ivo of Chartres, on proctors.

18 Gillet, *La personalité juridique en droit ecclésiastique*, pp. 82ff., 92f.; but the proctors in the *Decretum* are not true corporate proctors but prelates themselves or their agents, the *economi*.

19 My own opinion is supported by one of the earliest *Summas* on the *Decre-*

decretists, however, at Paris, Rheims, and Amiens after 1160, one finds some striking passages on proctors as legal representatives of corporations. The *Ordo iudiciarius Bambergensis* (probably written in France, *ca.* 1182-1185) not only discusses proctors of corporations but offers perhaps the earliest example of *plena potestas* in the mandate of the proctor.[20] Still earlier, 1160-1179, the *Rhetorica ecclesiastica*, probably written in or near Rheims, mentions in a form of appeal two syndics of the canons of a church.[21]

Through the decretists, therefore, some knowledge of the Roman law on the subject began to spread in ecclesiastical circles. But it was the papacy in the twelfth century that decisively started the practical application of Roman principles to the procedure in the courts of the Church. Pope Eugenius III (1145-1153), a contemporary of Gratian and a friend of Roman law and lawyers (so St. Bernard, with much scolding!),[22] decided that the abbot and monks of Clairvaux should not be compelled to take the *iuramentum calumniae* in court (such an oath was contrary to the monastic ideal, of course) but, "sicut imperiales leges consentiunt," they should have an *oeconomus,* who could litigate and take the oath for them.[23] The *oeconomus*

---

tum, that of Rolandus Bandinellus (later Pope Alexander III), written before 1148, ed. F. Thaner; one finds mentioned only proctors for individuals, e.g., to C.5, q.3; cf. C.23, q.7, c.3.

[20] Ed. by Schulte, in Vienna *Sitzungsberichte, Philos.-Hist. Cl.,* LXX (1872), 285ff.; see pp. 298-301: "Procurator super his, quae ad ipsam procurationem spectare noscuntur, plenariam recipit potestatem" (p. 300). On the relations of this *Ordo* with the French or Anglo-Norman school, see Kuttner, "Débuts de l'école canoniste française," *Studia et documenta hist. et juris,* pp. 199f.

[21] Ed. by Wahrmund, *Quellen,* I, iv, 93: "Si unus vel duo pluribus appellare voluerint, sic scribent: 'Ego H. et P. syndici, id est defensores, canonicorum sanctae Mariae. . . .'" The corporate sense is still immature. On this *Rhetorica* see also Kuttner, *op.cit.,* p. 199. Two other works, however, probably Parisian, and written 1170-1180, offer nothing on the proctor or syndic of a corporation. C. Gross, ed., *Incerti auctoris Ordo judiciarius,* a proctor, as in the earlier literature, can take the *juramentum calumniae* for a "principalis persona," pp. 107f., C. VII; cf. Kuttner, *op.cit.,* p. 200: this *Ordo* is really an *abrégé* of procedure in Roman law for the use of the clergy. The second *Ordo* was edited by Fr. Kunstmann, "Ueber den ältesten *Ordo judiciarius,*" *Kritische Ueberschau der deutschen Gesetzgebung und Rechtswissenschaft,* II (1855), 10-29.

[22] St. Bernard: "Quotidie perstrepunt in palatio tuo leges, sed Iustiniani, non Domini," *De consideratione,* I, c.4; *MPL,* 182, 752. See also L. Genuardi, "Il Papa Eugenio III e la cultura giuridica in Roma," *Mélanges Fitting,* II, 387.

[23] *Decr. Greg. IX* 2, 7, 4; similarly the preceding decretal, c. 3, also by Eugenius.

was simply a business agent, but there is a close approach to the idea that a proctor should act for the corporation. In any event, the decretal shows how greatly the revived Roman law was influencing the developing Canon law.[24] By the time of Clement III (1187-1191) and Innocent III (1198-1216) ecclesiastical corporations with proctors (not the bishop or abbot as *ex officio procurator* of the church) were clearly recognized in the practice of the Roman Curia,[25] and the decretalists became increasingly active in defining and refining the terminology to be used for corporations and their agents in lawsuits.[26]

The last third of the twelfth century, then, is the period when the literature on corporations and their representatives in the courts began to flourish.[27] Both legists and canonists were trying to adapt the Roman procedure to the courts of secular

[24] It is probable that the advisers of Eugenius III had in mind Justinian's own decree that a monastery should have a proctor; *Auth.*, Coll. IX, t. 6, c. 27 Si quando.

[25] Clement III, *Decr.* 2, 19, 5, *procurator universitatis*, i.e., of a chapter of canons regular; Innocent III, *Decr.* 1, 38, 7—the famous decretal which, about 1210-1213, granted to the corporation of masters at Paris the right to appoint a proctor; see my article, "Parisian Masters as a Corporation," *Speculum*, IX, 431, 433f., and notes; above, ch. I, §4, nn. 99-102.

[26] Bernard of Pavia, Ricardus Anglicus, Alanus, Johannes Galensis, Silvester Hispanus, Laurentius Hispanus, Vincentius Hispanus, Johannes Teutonicus, and Tancred are the more important ones down to about 1225. They are very poorly known on the subject, for only fragments of their work have been published. See below, n. 103.

[27] A little, but very thin, influence of the Roman law in the use of proctors for prominent individuals is to be noted in the early Middle Ages through the Theodosian and Burgundian and Visigothic Codes. So the *Leges Burgundiorum* (early sixth century), tit. XXXV, §4: *procurator litis* appointed *per mandatum* (from the *Codex Theod.*, II, 12); M. G. H., *Legum Sectio I*, II, i, 153. Also the *Leges Visigothorum*, an. 654, VIII, 5; IX, 1, 8 and 21; XII, 1, 2; M. G. H., *Legum S. I.*, I, 314, 357, 364, 407.

In early formularies there are even mandates for proctors for women: *Formulae Arvernenses* (end of sixth century), M. G. H., *Legum S. V, Formulae*, I, 29; *Formulae Turonenses* (after middle of eighth century), p. 146. In Spain the *Fuero Juzgo* continued some of the principles in the *Leges Visigothorum*; and in the *Fuero Juzgo*, II, iii, 1. 1, there is the provision that high persons (princes and bishops) shall have *mandaderos* to act in lawsuits for them; Alcubilla, *Codigos antiguos de España*, pp. 19f. But in the *Usatici* of Barcelona (eleventh century), I find no trace of this procedure in a feudal court; *Cortes de los antiguos reinos de Aragón y de Valencia y Principado de Cataluña*, I, i, 10ff. (Cited hereafter as *Cortes . . . de Aragón*, etc.) A representative for an individual, then, was known before the twelfth century. In the twelfth century there is abundant evidence that the proctor is beginning to reappear in feudal society to take the oath of homage and fealty for a vassal who cannot, or will not, come to the *curia* of his lord. But in all this there is no conception of corporate proctor.

and ecclesiastical lords. But the practical acceptance of their new methods was probably slow.[28] In Italy, little evidence appears of elected proctors or syndics of municipalities or city councils until the last two decades of the twelfth century,[29] although consuls and *judices*, as administrative officers, may earlier have been a practical equivalent. In France the secular courts may have tried lawsuits of corporate representatives fairly early but not before the beginning of the thirteenth century.[30] In England we should expect the common practice only in the ecclesiastical courts (Glanville's *responsales* were not discussed as corporate agents);[31] but Henry II's courts had experience in summoning proctors of a monastery.[32] In all Spain there seems to have been no real school of law before the thirteenth century; Spanish ecclesiastics are not found as legists or canonists until the latter half of the twelfth century,[33] and very

[28] Kantorowicz, *Glossators*, p. 72.

[29] Pertile, *Storia del diritto italiano*, I, II, s.vv. *procuratore* and *sindacato*, etc., offers examples only from the thirteenth century and later. J. Ficker has found proctors acting *with* individual high persons as early as 1025-1032; but these proctors are not those of Roman procedure, for their principals stand in court with them; they are more like *advocati—Forschungen zur Reichs- und Rechtsgeschichte Italiens*, III, 107-110; cf. IV, 74f., no. 51. Ficker says, as to real proctors and syndics acting in courts for absent parties, that in the second half of the twelfth century one finds them in the practice of Italian courts (III, 101); but in his documents I find no corporate syndic until 1190—two syndics appointed by the commune of Vercelli, one syndic appointed by the commune of Novara, IV, 217, no. 175. On the other hand, a document of 1163 reveals the canons of the Church of Verona acting "in nomine ecclesie," while the adversary, a certain Adeleita, has appointed her brother as *curator*, who in turn appoints a proctor; hence, there is no corporate representation here; IV, 176f., no. 134. But obviously a great deal more evidence in documents is needed for a definite conclusion.

[30] The ecclesiastical courts almost certainly before the secular. Prof. C. H. Taylor has found no example of a corporate proctor for a city (in the south) before about 1208.

[31] *Tractatus de Legibus et Consuetudinibus Regni Angliae*, XI, i; more recently, ed. G. E. Woodbine; Glanville also mentions the proctor.

[32] A. B. White and W. Notestein, *Source Problems in English History*, p. 89. The Canon law, of course, and some Roman law, were reaching England at this time; see below, ch. IV, §3; above, n. 17.

[33] Pierre de Cardona, a Catalan, perhaps taught civil law at Montpellier before entering the service of Pope Alexander III and becoming a cardinal, fl. ca. 1160; Valls-Taberner, "Le juriste catalan Pierre de Cardona," *Mélanges Paul Fournier*, pp. 743-746. Two canonists are known: Johannes Hispanus, a decretist, fl. ca. 1186, and Petrus Hispanus, who wrote glosses to *Compilatio I*, ca. 1190ff.; Schulte, *Quellen und Literatur des canonischen Rechts*, I, 149f., 152. After the year 1200, distinguished canonists of Spanish origin were fairly

few then; but practical knowledge of the procedure must have existed in church courts. Moreover, some influence of the Roman law taught at Montpellier and Bologna spread at least into the County of Barcelona (the relations of Provençe and Genoa and Pisa with the County were close, as is well known), but it was tenuous until the thirteenth century.[34] No evidence has yet appeared that any practical use of corporate procuration was made in the secular courts of Spain before the thirteenth century. Yet before 1200 some experience in handling corporate representatives must have been gained both from local prelates, whose affairs were often treated in secular courts and who sometimes served as judges in the royal *curia*, and from Italian merchants.

Actually the history of the new procedure is yet to be written. But it seems possible to conclude that the practice of corporate representation hardly began before about 1150—and not significantly, except in the Church, until the last quarter of the century even in Italy. It is as if the lawyers and judges had suddenly realized that there were numerous communes with their institutions and officers, and numerous merchant and craft guilds, and that they must at once apply the newly discovered principles of the Roman law to them. Once more the rise of Bologna and the new Roman law are of the utmost importance in the civilization of the twelfth century. The Roman law and the lawyers, however, had first to overcome the feudal and Germanic law, in which it was difficult for any but the principal parties, the administrators in communities, or feudal lords, to appear in court. The process was slower, no doubt, in Spain, northern France, England, and Germany than in Italy. If the appointment of corporate agents for lawsuits lagged behind the

numerous. I know of no important Spanish legist before the thirteenth century, nor of the presence of Italian legists in Spain before the end of the twelfth century.

34 On Catalonia, see E. de Hinojosa, "La réception du droit romain en Catalogne," in *Mélanges Fitting*, II, 393-400. As for Castile and Aragon, the influence appeared later; see R. Altamira y Crevea, *Cuestiones de historia del derecho*, pp. 55f., 127f., 152, and 158. Conrat, *Quellen und Literatur des römischen Rechts im früheren Mittelalter*, pp. 31f., 32 n. 4, points out that Justinian's *Corpus* was not introduced into Spain until the thirteenth century. Altamira is inclined to place the introduction earlier.

theory—the appearance of city magistrates or prelates in the courts to plead for their communities or churches was the old practice, and it long continued with the new—how far behind lagged the practice of summoning to royal assemblies proctors and syndics with mandates from the towns?

2. EARLY REPRESENTATION IN SPAIN

Despite the lack of definite evidence of any practical application of the principles of corporate representation in Spanish courts, it has time and again been either implied or directly asserted that the third estate was represented by *procuradores* in the Cortes of the Spanish kingdoms by the end of the twelfth century.[35] It is quite true, of course, that citizens or members of the city councils (*concejos*) were occasionally summoned. But were they corporate representatives, empowered by mandates to carry the will of their communities to the king in his council, or simply local magistrates and prominent members of the *concejos* who had information on local custom and law, took oaths of fealty to the king in his high court, and received the royal commands issued by the king's council and court of

[35] Altamira y Crevea implies this in his *History of Spanish Civilization*, p. 105; but he is more cautious in the *Historia de España*, 3rd ed., I, 431: he states only that representatives of *municipios* or *concejos* first appeared at Leon in 1188. Colmeiro, *Cortes de los antiguos reinos de Leon y de Castilla, Introduccion*, pp. 12f. (cited hereafter as Colmeiro, *Introduccion*), does not say that *procuradores* attended the Cortes of Leon in 1188; he even admits that there is no mention of *procuradores* (but of *hombres buenos, personeros, mandaderos*, or *ciudadanos*, or *cives* as in 1188) in thirteenth-century Castilian Cortes (pp. 28f.), adding that the term *procurador del concejo* (i.e., of the city) begins to be used first in 1305; yet he thinks that the *cives electi* of 1188 were true representatives (pp. 12f.). Bofarull y Romaña, *Las antiguas Cortes*, pp. 35f., 147, 148, and notes, fully accepts the presence of *procuradores* of towns in the Cortes of Castile and Leon: at Burgos, 1169; Leon, 1188; Benevente, 1202. So also Ballesteros y Beretta, *Historia de España*, II, 507, 511, and especially 512; he thinks that the representatives in Cortes from 1188 to 1208 were *procuradores*, that these *cives* or *hombres buenos*, etc., had to present *poderes* (mandates); yet he admits that in Castile there is no evidence of *poderes* until the fourteenth century!

Of all the recent students of Spanish representation only R. B. Merriman and C. H. McIlwain are cautious. Merriman mentions representatives of municipalities at Leon in 1188, holds that they probably did not appear in Castilian Cortes until about 1250; and he refers to representatives in Aragon by 1163; "The Cortes of the Spanish Kingdoms in the Later Middle Ages," *A.H.R.*, xvi, 479, 486f.; *Rise of the Spanish Empire*, I, 219. Merriman is chiefly interested in the mature development of the fourteenth century. Cf. McIlwain, "Medieval Estates," *C. M. H.*, vii, 696.

prelates and magnates? Records of the Cortes of Leon and Castile reveal the presence of *cives electi* (Leon, 1188),[36] "many from each city" (Benevente, 1202),[37] "a multitude of citizens sent by the cities" (Leon, 1208);[38] or "good men" (Seville, 1252; Valladolid, 1258; Toledo, 1260).[39] By 1269, however, there may have been true *procuradores*, for "los de los concejos de las ciudades y villas" appeared at Burgos,[40] although it is not until 1305 that the term *procurador de concejo* is actually used.[41] We therefore have no clear evidence of corporate, proctorial representation until 1305.

Even earlier than in the Kingdom of Leon, according to the generally accepted account, *procuradores* of cities regularly were summoned to the Cortes of Aragon, notably at Saragossa, 1163 or 1164.[42] Yet for this, Zurita's *Anales de la Corona de*

---

[36] *Cortes de los antiguos reinos de Leon y de Castilla*, I, 39, no. VII; *Catálogo, Coleccion de Cortes de los antiguos reinos de España*, p. 10. (Cited hereafter as *Catálogo*.) Here it is baldly stated by the editor that "diputados o procuradores" were present; Ballesteros, *Historia*, II, 507, 511; McIlwain, *C. M. H.*, VII, 696. See the treaty, April 23, 1188, between Frederick Barbarossa and Alfonso of Castile, *M. G. H., Legum S. IV*, I, 452ff.; clauses 17 and 19 specify about fifty towns and cities, the *maiores* of which shall take oath to receive Prince Conrad.

[37] *Cortes . . . de Leon y de Castilla*, I, 43, no. VIII; Ballesteros, *Historia*, II, 512.

[38] *Ibid.*, I, 46f., no. X: "civium multitudine destinatorum a singulis civitatibus considente"; Bofarull y Romaña, *Las antiguas Cortes*, p. 148 n. 38; Ballesteros, *Historia*, II, 512.

[39] *Catálogo*, pp. 13f.; *Cortes*, I, 54f., no. XIII.

[40] *Catálogo*, p. 15; Colmeiro, *Introduccion*, I, 28f. But no *poderes* or mandates are mentioned. One source, not the original documents, states that *procuradores* of *villas* and *ciudades* attended the Cortes of Seville, 1281; *Catálogo*, p. 17.

[41] Colmeiro, *Introduccion*, I, 28; *Cortes . . . de Leon y de Castilla*, I, 173.

[42] Still earlier at Borja, 1134, according to the sixteenth-century Zurita (*Catálogo*, p. 95; Jeronimo Zurita, *Anales de la Corona de Aragon*, 2nd ed., Lib. I, cap. LIII). But there was probably no Cortes at Borja at this time; see Fuente, *Estudios criticos sobre la historia y el derecho de Aragon*, II, 55ff. Another Cortes, at Huesca, 1162, was attended by *procuradores* according to Zurita, *Anales*, II, c. XX; but no details are given; Ballesteros accepts Zurita's account, *Historia*, II, 625.

For the Cortes of Saragossa the year 1163 is given in the *Catálogo*, p. 96, and Altamira, *Historia*, I, 473. But Leicht says (p. 420) 1164, "Introduction des villes dans les assemblées d'états en Italie," in *Histoire des assemblées d'états*, IX, part IV, no. 37, pp. 419-424. Both Altamira and Leicht follow Zurita on proctors at Saragossa; also Marichalar and Manrique, *Historia de la legislacion y recitaciones del derecho civil de España*, IV, 515. Merriman is more cautious, saying that the middle class was probably not represented until 1163, and possibly not until the thirteenth century; *A. H. R.*, XVI, 486f. A document of 1157, however, shows that *burgenses* were among those present in the high court of the Count of Barcelona, but were not the *judices* who gave sentence;

Aragon (sixteenth century) is the unique source used by recent historians. Zurita relates that in addition to the usual prelates and magnates, *procuradores* of Huesca, Jaca, Tarazona, Calatayud, and Daroca were summoned by the king, and that "por la ciudad de Caragoça juraron los procuradores [fifteen of them] del concejo, que llamauan Adelantados," and similarly the *procuradores* of other cities and *lugares*.[43] But what is *his* source?[44] It is the *constitutio*, a formal *Landfried*, promulgated by the king in his *Concilium*,[45] and its provisions order the maintenance of the king's peace and justice. To the assembly itself, a feudal *curia*, the king had summoned for counsel prelates, barons, and the cities; and in the assembly, oaths of fealty and obedience to the *constitutio* were taken by all those present. Here it is that the document is of vital interest: it gives the names of sixteen "adelantados de concilio Cesarauguste" as taking the oath "asensu et voluntate et mandamento tocius concilii," seven "adelantados de concilio de Darocha," five "adelantados de concilio de Oscha," some eight *adelantados* from another city, and about twenty "alfaches de Uno Castello."[46]

In this remarkable document no use of the term *procurador* appears. But the *adelantados de concejo* of Saragossa and the other cities, were they not representatives sent by the municipal *concejo*, and consequently the same in function as the *procuradores* of the thirteenth century? To be sure, they were representatives of the municipalities, but there were so many of them from each city that they bear only a faint resemblance to the proctors or syndics of Roman and Canon law. The term *adelantados* itself seems in this instance to mean simply members of the *concejo*, or magistrates at the same time, like the Italian consuls and judges.[47] Again it is possible that taken literally the

---

Coleccion de documentos ineditos del Archivo General de la Corona de Aragón, IV, 252.

[43] *Anales*, I, 73-74, lib. II, c. XXIV. He actually names three of the *procuradores* of Saragossa.

[44] I find no mention of Zurita's source by any modern writer.

[45] *Procesos de las antiguas Cortes y Parlamentos de Cataluña, Aragon y Valencia*, in *Coleccion de documentos ineditos del Archivo General de la Corona de Aragón*, VIII, 36-41. The date of the document is 1164.

[46] *Procesos*, in *Coleccion de documentos . . . de Aragón*, VIII, 39-41.

[47] I can find no discussion of the twelfth-century *adelantado* in any history

word indicates not merely members but members sent out in the place of the whole *concejo*. Here might be an approach to thirteenth-century proctors or syndics, for in Italy and France these sometimes were sent in fairly large numbers,[48] and, significantly, the *adelantados* took the oath "asensu et voluntate et mandamento tocius concilii Cesarauguste." Nevertheless, if the feeling of community is revealed, such informal representation was hardly corporate in the legal sense of Roman and Canon law in the later twelfth and thirteenth centuries. What has been said of *adelantados* applies also to the *alfaches* of Uncastillo, some fifteen to twenty of whom are named as attending and taking the oath.[49]

After 1163 the next Cortes[50] noted for the representation of the cities was that of Lérida, 1214. This Cortes seems to have been also a legatine council, composed of both clergy and laity, for over it presided the Cardinal-Legate Peter of Benevento, by mandate of Innocent III (Pedro II had been a vassal of the Pope).[51] It resulted in a *constitucio pacis et treuge* promulgated by the papal legate in the name of the pope and of King James I,

---

of Spain or of its law and institutions. There is, of course, much said about the *adelantados* of the thirteenth century (*adelantado mayor* or *del rey*, and the *adelantados menores*: they preside over various kinds of courts); Merriman, *Rise of the Spanish Empire*, I, 230f., and references there. These *adelantados* seem to bear little resemblance to those of the *concejos* of the twelfth century; yet the latter could have been in part judges along with the alcaldes (cf. Altamira, *Historia*, I, 441, on alcaldes and *judex*, and also *jurados*); they may have resembled the Italian consuls who were sometimes judges until they delegated their judicial functions to *judices* proper. On the Italian communes, their councils, consuls, and judges, see C. W. Previté-Orton, "The Italian Cities till c. 1200," in *C. M. H.*, V, 219-221, 232ff.

[48] Professor C. H. Taylor has kindly informed me that he has found numerous examples of the informal use in France of town representatives that are not proctors, but similar to them.

[49] *Alfache* is the *alfaqui*, a theologian or doctor of law, or a man wise in the law, a *letrado*, among Moslems. Hence *alfaches* are *sapientes* from a Moorish town. One also finds *alfaquis* in an agreement between Alfonso I and the Moors of Tudela, *ca.* 1115; Muñoz y Romero, *Coleccion de Fueros Municipales*, I, 415: the *carta* of Alfonso is made with the alcaldes, *algalifos*, and *alforques*, "et afirmavit illos alcudes, et illos *alfaques*, in lures *alfaquias*, et illos alguaziles in lures alguacilias. . . ."

[50] I omit discussion of the Cortes of Cervera, 1202, although Zurita says that *sindicos* of cities were present; no reliance can be placed on this. See *Cortes . . . de Aragón, etc.*, I, i, 86; *laici* and *clerici* attended.

[51] Ballesteros, *Historia*, III, 171-188.

and with the "acclaim" of the bishops and other prelates of Aragon and Catalonia, and of many magnates "et plurium aliorum."[52] In the *constitutio* itself (really a *Landfried* in character, no doubt intended to establish law and order immediately after the tragic defeat and death of Pedro II at Muret), the Cardinal-Legate Peter speaks merely of having the *consilium* of the prelates "et aliorum prudencium virorum." But it is certainly significant that the peace and truce proclaimed must be sworn to by the nobility, knights, *cives* and *burgenses castrorum et villarum*; further, that the *cives et populi* of each *civitas*, with the advice of the bishop, were to elect two *paciarii*, one "de majoribus" and one "de populo," who with the vicar chosen from each city by the *Procurator* of Catalonia should take public oath to observe the peace and maintain the provisions of the *constitutio*; and that all the *cives* of cities and the *homines* of *loci* (*lugares*) should take the same oath.[53] Finally, there is even a provision (cap. 20) against any extraordinary financial imposition by the king on the cities, which hints at some resistance put up by the city representatives.

Were these representatives *procuradores*? The *Chronicle* of James I of Aragon tells us that the royal council summoned to Lérida ten men from each city, who were to be "furnished with powers from the rest to approve that which might be done by all"[54] (the Roman formula that was the legal equivalent of *plena potestas*), and that all those present took an oath of fealty to the king.[55] Such a delegation of ten, furnished with powers, would so strongly resemble proctors or syndics that one might well conclude at once that the meeting of the Cortes of 1214 is the earliest known example of proctorial representation in Aragon and Catalonia[56]—indeed, in all Spain. Unfortunately, since the *Chronicle* of James I—he was only six years old in

---

52 *Cortes . . . de Aragón, etc.*, I, i, 90-95.

53 *Ibid.* On the *paciarii*, frequently used in Spain to investigate ruptures of the *Paz de Dios* and used also as judicial and police officers, see Altamira, *Historia*, I, 471.

54 *Chronicle of James I*, I, 19. Cf. Marichalar and Manrique, *Legislacion*, IV, 557f.; and Smith, *Life and Times of James the First*, p. 15.

55 *Chronicle of James I*, I, 20.

56 Also that Merriman is wrong in saying that in Catalonia the third estate was first represented, probably, in 1283; *A. H. R.*, XVI, 490.

1214—was written much later, and possibly not by the king himself, we cannot be sure that conditions in the latter half of the century are not reflected here. Nevertheless, there may have been corporate representation, because the papal legate, perhaps aware of the precedent set by Innocent III in summoning mandataries of Italian cities to the Curia,[57] may have intentionally instructed the cities of Aragon to send true proctors. It is significant, certainly, that through representatives the cities were already protesting against extraordinary subsidies. If proctors were thereafter appointed as representatives in Catalonia and Aragon in the thirteenth century, there is no specific mention of them: it is *cives*, simply, who are indicated as attending Cortes. But in 1283 the two to four representatives of each town were probably real proctors.[58]

What kind of representation this was in twelfth and early thirteenth century Spain can be understood only through a thorough knowledge of town government in relation to the kings. No real history of the rising Spanish communes and informally organized towns has been written. At the moment, therefore, we can only point to the problem by stating it. By the middle of the twelfth century, some organized towns, recognized by the kings of Leon and Castile and of Aragon, had *concejos* which were composed usually of the more prominent citizens and property owners.[59] Probably the magistrates, *alcaldes* and *merinos*, or judges, and others, were sometimes elected "popularly" or in the *concejo*,[60] but the town institutions are so poorly known that we cannot be sure when the magistrates were lo-

---

[57] Below, §4.

[58] These examples among others: *Cortes . . . de Aragón, etc.*, I, i, 95f. (Villafranca, 1218; yet Altamira, *Historia*, I, 486, says that *sindicos* of municipalities attended); 102ff. (Tortosa, 1225: *cives* and prelates and nobles, to give "consilium et juvamen"); *Catálogo*, pp. 134f. (Tortosa, 1225, "los nobles ciudadanos de Cataluña"); 136f. (Barcelona, 1253, "burgensium et civium"); *Cortes . . . de Aragón, etc.*, I, i, 112 (Barcelona, 1228); 137 (Barcelona, 1251; but only the *probi homines* of Barcelona, not of other cities); 140 (Barcelona, 1283; according to McIlwain, *C. M. H.*, VII, 698, two to four representatives were summoned from many cities and towns of Catalonia).

[59] Merriman, *Spanish Empire*, I, 186-189; Altamira, *Historia*, I, 435, 472.

[60] The statements of Merriman and Altamira relate chiefly to later conditions in better organized towns. It is highly doubtful that there was much election in the early period; and "popular election" was no doubt in the hands of the leading citizens, of whom there were relatively few.

cally elected and when chosen by a local lord or by the king himself.[61] If business or lawsuits involved a town, it is likely that the magistrates and a group of leading councillors or citizens personally negotiated the affair or went to court; there are no signs of any mandate issued to agents, who were not at the same time magistrates, to conclude the business or accept the judges' sentence.[62] In the twelfth century an older, informal, representation was customary: it was individualistic rather than corporate; for if a vague conception of the corporate vassal, with the commune as the vassal, existed in Italy and Spain, in practice it was the individual, prominent citizens who were responsible, not a corporate person.[63] So we find that *omnes burgenses* of Huesca were ordered by Count Raymond of Barcelona to take the oath of fealty to King Ranimir of Aragon in 1137.[64] A few years later, about 1150, from eight to one hundred citizens of each of several Aragonese towns,[65] and in 1162 "nos omnes homines Dertose" (about one hundred names are listed), swore fealty to the Count of Barcelona and King of Aragon.[66] Obviously, it was soon inconvenient for all the citizens to come to such feudal assemblies. But since in twelfth-century Spain there was little if any conscious theory of corporate communities,[67] whatever

[61] Merriman, *Spanish Empire*, I, 186f.; Altamira, *Historia*, I, 435, 442, 472.

[62] As late as about 1255, the *Fuero Real* of Castile refers to proctors of individuals acting in the local courts of the *alcaldes*; Alcubilla, *Codigos antiguos de España*, p. 108 (I, t. vii, 1. 6). We have to wait for the *Siete Partidas* of Alfonso the Wise to find corporate proctors discussed (III, t. xvii, 1. 6; xviii, 1. 98), and they are not connected with meetings of the Cortes, unless—and this is likely—it was tacitly understood that the Cortes was the high court as far as representatives were concerned.

[63] In Leon, as late as 1177, Ferdinand II confirmed the *fueros* to "vassallis meis" of Lugo; Muñoz, *Fueros*, pp. 433f.

[64] *Coleccion de documentos . . . de Aragón*, IV, 61.

[65] One hundred from Jaca, and from eight to about thirty from smaller places (*castra*); *Coleccion de documentos . . . de Aragón*, IV, No. CLIX, 378-382. Should not this assembly be added to the list of twelfth-century Cortes?

[66] *Coleccion de documentos . . . de Aragón*, VIII, No. IX, 35f.

[67] The royal *fueros* for the towns of Leon, Castile, and Aragon reveal no use of a terminology for corporate towns in the twelfth century: such privileges are addressed to *omnes cives* or *burgenses* (in 1182, however, to the Council of Toledo; Muñoz, *Fueros*, p. 384). Contrast this with the privileges of James I of Aragon, 1255, for Barbastro, granted "vobis hominibus et toti universitati," who "possitis habere unitatem, et facere iuras, et sacramenta inter vos" and "possitis facere inter vos communitatem seu commune," Muñoz, *Fueros*, p. 359. This language of 1255 reveals an environment totally different from that of

the practical development of communes, there was no suitable machinery of representation. This situation has been observed, and it is reflected in the diversity of language used in the documents to mention the presence of townsmen in the Cortes. A rough-and-ready system of informal representation, however, was possibly adopted for the summons to the Cortes of Leon and Castile, 1188-1208, and of Aragon, 1163-1214. For example, the *Fuero* granted to Toledo (1118; confirmed in 1176) provided that "decem ex maioribus civitatis," who were probably the local judges, should come to the king to give him information about violations of the royal privilege.[68] We may suppose that if similar institutions flourished in other towns, the *cives electi*[69] at Leon in 1188 and in later Cortes of Leon and Castile were sometimes groups of ten or more summoned to give information to the king and thus help him and his councillors (the prelates and magnates) decide how to formulate the provisions of *constitutiones* for law and order. Perhaps, indeed, the number of ten, rather than the Roman legal machinery of syndics or proctors, was the real precedent for the summons to ten from each city of Catalonia and Aragon for the Cortes of Lérida in 1214.[70]

---

the twelfth century in Spain, so far as the few published documents indicate. True, in the earlier period there are Spanish communes, with their elected magistrates, *jurados*, and councils, with some rights of ownership of property. But this corporateness is imperfectly developed in the procedure of law courts.

[68] Muñoz, *Fueros*, pp. 363ff., 367, 380ff., 383. Ten of the "noblest and wisest" citizens are to be the city judges.

[69] It might be held that the word *electi* implies formal election and the conferment of definite powers on the elected delegates; but one can infer little from *eligere*: "*Eligere* is an elastic word in mediaeval documents," McIlwain, *C. M. H.*, VII, 667.

[70] It is remotely possible that, given the strong ecclesiastical element in the Cortes at Lerida in 1214 and the practice in Italy, a late twelfth-century theory deriving from the *Digest* had some influence in the choice of ten men from each city. Commenting on the *Decretum* (C. 10, q. 1, c. Si ex laicis, ad v. *ubi congregatio*), a decretist says: "Sed quot homines faciunt collegium monachorum? Respond. duo vel tres [this is the usual statement on how many make a corporation] . . . Sed decem homines faciunt populum: ut . . . ff. vi bono. rapt. l. praetor. §j. [*D.* 47, 8, 4, 3] et decem oves gregem . . ."; *Glossa ordinaria* of Johannes Teutonicus on the *Decretum*, Paris, 1561, p. 922. Similarly, about 1177-1179, Simon of Bisignano and another decretist of the late twelfth century to C. 2, q.5, c.13, ad v. *plebe*; Simon, "Id est apud bonos et graves de plebe . . . vel totam plebem, vel maiorem vel saniorem partem intelligo . . ."; the other gloss, "Nota per plebem intelli(guntur) maiores. . . . Vel per plebem X homines intelligi . . . quia ecclesia, que X habet mancipia, proprium poterit habere

(In 1175 Frederick Barbarossa was depending on ten men of each Lombard town to keep the treaty between the towns and the emperor.)[71] In Aragon the choice of citizens to appear for the rest in the Cortes of Saragossa, 1163, was perhaps indirectly based on the existence, in each of several Aragonese towns, of twenty "meliores homines," chosen, according to the royal *fueros*, to swear to uphold the royal provisions and compel their fellow citizens to take the same oath.[72] This, of course, does not explain why there were five to twenty representatives at the Cortes from each of the towns; but perhaps the differences in population, in the composition of the *concejos*, and in the number of locally and royally appointed municipal officers would help us to understand the problem if we had sufficient information. However, twenty are too many to call proctors in any technical sense.

What seems to be certain, however, is that representation of a really corporate kind (in which the agents were responsible to their constituents, even though they had to obey a superior jurisdiction in the king's court and council) did not arise as a system in Spain before the second half of the thirteenth century —with the possible exception of the Cortes of Lérida in 1214— either because the influence of the Romano-canonical procedure was not yet sufficiently felt, or because the kings were not yet powerful enough to make a logical system of centralization and local, corporate, and individual rights work effectively. But representation of a loose kind there was—as early as the middle of the twelfth century. The moment towns were granted royal

---

sacerdotem . . . "; J. Junker, "Die Summa des Simon von Bisignano und seine Glossen," *Zeitschrift der Savigny-Stiftung für Rechtsgeschichte, Kan. Abt.*, xv (1926), 411 and n. 6.

These glosses are an amusing example of distortion or adaptation by the canonists and legists; the passage in the *Decretum* relates to the number of men needed to accuse a priest; but in the law referred to, *D.* 47, 8, 4, 3, Ulpian says a *turba* is a tumult, and if two men make a *rixa*, ten to fifteen make a *turba!* All this shows how some theorists were groping for definitions not only of corporations, but also of looser aggregates of men for purposes of jurisdiction.

[71] Below, n. 101.

[72] For example, Saragossa, *ca.* 1119—the "privilege of the twenty"; and Tudela, 1127; Muñoz, *Fueros*, pp. 421, 452.

charters and rights of organization, they assumed enough prestige and responsibility to be summoned to the feudal *curia* of
the king; and members of town councils, usually as judges[73]
and magistrates, carried the "record," or information on local
conditions of law and justice, to the feudal assembly, took oaths
of fealty to the king and were placed under the obligation of
returning home to carry out the decisions of the king and his
magnates. The delegates were representatives of the king in
the cities. They did not participate directly in the council and
court of magnates and prelates who gave counsel and consent
and judged important cases. Their consent, if any, was not
"popular," rather, it was the consent involved in defending local
rights based on custom and royal franchise.[74] Furthermore, only
the town council was represented. The early Spanish Cortes,
then, was still a feudal assembly in which the decisions of matters of law and justice, taxation, and treaties were made by the
king and his *curia*.[75]

[73] Alcaldes were specially summoned to the Cortes of Zamora in 1274; *Cortes
. . . de Leon y de Castilla*, I, 87.

[74] I cannot believe that popular consent, limiting the royal prerogative, is
involved in such royal statements as "nisi, cum concilio episcoporum, nobilium
et bonorum hominum, per quorum consilium debeo regi," and "omnes etiam
episcopi promiserunt et omnes milites et cives iuramento firmaverunt, quod
fideles sint in consilio meo, ad tenendam justitiam, et suadendam pacem in toto
regno meo," *Cortes . . . de Leon y de Castilla*, I, 40; Muñoz, *Fueros*, pp. 103,
106. Likewise for the Cortes at Leon in 1208, where the king published a law
"multa deliberatione prehabita de universorum consensu"; Muñoz, *Fueros*, p.
111. Such expressions were common, but consent, at least of any citizens, has the
sense of acclaim or *laudatio*, given after the king announced the will of his
council of magnates and prelates. My conclusion is therefore contrary to that of
Carlyle, *Mediaeval Political Theory*, v, 134f. See below, chs. IV and VIII.

[75] It was still essentially the kind of *curia* described in the *Usatici* of Barcelona,
where it is stated that it is insane for anyone to resist the *iudicium curie*, for in
the *curia* are "principes, episcopi, abbates, comites et vice-comites, comitores et
vasvassores, philosophi et sapientes atque iudices"; *Cortes . . . de Aragón*, etc., I,
i, 30, no. 82.

In 1157, high court at Lerida was held by Count Berengar of Barcelona; there
were several judges who pronounced sentence "coram quamplurimis nobilibus
viris . . . comitoribus et episcopis . . . et aliis multis . . . clericis milititbus atque
burgensibus" of Barcelona, Urgel, and Aragon; *Coleccion de documentos . . .
de Aragón*, IV, 252, No. XCIX. This court is as much a cortes, even if for a province
rather than a kingdom, with "representatives" of the third estate, as royal Cortes
in the twelfth century.

3. ITALY

Logically, the origins of proctorial representation should be sought in Italy; and yet no one, not even P. S. Leicht,[76] has thought of connecting the problem with Italy as the home of the revived Roman law. This is at least moderately surprising, for much Roman law survived in Italy, and there were important contacts with the Byzantine Empire in which the law and the practice reflected a continuity of late Roman traditions. Bologna by the middle of the twelfth century was the most important center of the study of the *Corpus Juris Civilis*; by the end of the century both Roman and Canon law were receiving scientific discussion and treatment; and already middle-class notaries, lawyers, and judges were formulating rules of procedure for the practice of the new law. The flourishing communes, moreover, with their councils and consuls and judges and other elected magistrates, with their local pride and independent, almost corporate, life; and the great Frederick Barbarossa, with his aspiration to rule the cities and centralize his authority, and ready to employ loyal Bolognese doctors to formulate his imperial claims in the terminology and theory of Roman law; in short, cities and an ambitious monarch formed the political background that might logically produce representation. Certainly, then, Italy offered a more favorable environment for the early rise of proctorial representation than any other country in Europe.

As early as 1136 judges gave ear and counsel to Lothair III, but they were possibly magnates and prelates functioning as judges.[77] A later, if legendary, account of a Diet of Lothair III in Rome, "tempore Eugenii Papae" (!), at which the emperor

[76] Leicht, "Introduction des villes dans les assemblées d'états en Italie"; also Leicht, "La posizione giuridica dei parlamenti medievali italiani," in *Organisation corporative du Moyen Age*, pp. 94-109. (See now, however, Marongiu, *L'Istituto parlamentare*, pp. 39-41.)

[77] Pertile, *Storia del diritto italiano*, I, 310, n. 34: the *Constitutio* on the inalienability of fiefs was given "hortatu et consilio" of the prelates, great magnates, "simul et judicum." Also in *Libri Feudorum*, II, t. 52, c. 1; M. G. H., *Legum S. IV*, I, x. Cf. Leicht, "Posizione giuridica," *L'organisation corporative*, II, 95; and "L'introduction des villes . . . ," p. 420, where he says that these *judices* were perhaps from the cities as imperial functionaries, or perhaps were consuls, often called *judices*.

promulgated a statute "per laudamentum multorum sapientium civitatum Italiae, Papie, Mediolani, Mantue, Verone . . . necnon Parme, Pistorii, Florentiae, Lucae, Siponti," seems merely to reflect the kind of Diet that Italian lawyers of the later twelfth century thought was the ideal.[78] But Pisa sent "tres sapientes viros"[79] to Roncaglia, 1154, in response to the summons of Frederick Barbarossa to the Italian cities, asking them to send "legates."[80] And to this Diet the cities of Como, Lodi, Milan, and Genoa, as well as others, sent their consuls, *maiores*, or *legati*.[81] Hence, *sapientes*, consuls, *maiores*, and *legati* seem to be almost equivalent terms, though they may express some distinction between *judices*, consuls, leading or noble citizens, and special ambassadors or *nuntii*. Even in Bavaria in 1155 there was some kind of representation of the towns in the imperial *curia*, for at the Diet of Ratisbon (called *curia* and *publicum consistorium*) both the magnates (*proceres*) and the *cives* of Bavaria bound themselves to the emperor by homage and oath, the *cives* even furnishing surety or pledges.[82] And to the imperial *curia* at Besançon in 1157 went the usual *proceres* and many *legati*—from Rome, Apulia, Tuscany, Venice, Italy, France, England, and Spain—these *legati*, of course, representing both individual princes and lords and a few cities.[83]

Of all the assemblies or Diets held in twelfth-century Ger-

---

[78] In the fourteenth century Andrew of Isernia (†1353) accepts it as genuine and comments on it in his *In usus feudorum commentaria*, pp. 134ff. The *Constitutio* is to be found in the *Libri Feudorum*, I, t. 19, and in *M. G. H., Legum S. IV*, I, 680-683, among spurious documents: here it is described as a *summula* on the feudal law of Conrad II, a *summula* belonging to the end of the eleventh century. But the addition of the introduction and the naming of the cities belong to the twelfth century; see Karl Lehmann, *Das langobardische Lehnrecht*, p. 103 n. 2; one MS naming the cities is of the twelfth century, no. 80, p. 24.

[79] *Annales Pisani*, in *M. G. H., SS.*, XIX, 242.

[80] *Ibid.*; also Otto of Freising, *Gesta Friderici*, ed. G. Waitz; *M. G. H., SS. in Usum Scholarum*, p. 95. Leicht does not mention the Diet of 1154.

[81] Otto of Freising, *Gesta*, p. 95. The consuls of Como and Lodi made complaints in the *curia* against Milan. The *legati* of Genoa came bearing gifts of lions, ostriches, and parrots to the emperor; they were really ambassadors.

[82] Otto of Freising, *Gesta*, p. 121: "Nam et proceres Baioariae hominio et sacramento sibi obligantur, et cives non solum iuramento, sed etiam, ne ullam vacillandi potestatem haberent, vadibus obfirmantur." One should note also that the city of Verona sends its bishop and two *equites* to his *curia*; *ibid.*, p. 122. The bishop is called *legatus*.

[83] Otto of Freising, *Gesta*, p. 138.

many or Italy, however, that of Roncaglia in 1158 is the most noteworthy for an early experiment in third-estate representation. To be sure, the Diet is famous, and historians have discussed it in detail so far as its political significance is concerned. But while the presence of *cives* from Italian cities has usually been noted, the nature of the *cives* has been generally overlooked.[84] This almost unanimous presentation of the subject can be attributed to Otto of Freising's continuer, Rahewin, whose account has been accepted as sufficient. Besides the imperial army, according to Rahewin, there were from all parts of the kingdom high prelates and magnates, and "consules et civitatum iudices";[85] the "consules et missi singularum civitatum" made lengthy speeches in order to glorify the emperor;[86] and the famous doctors of Bologna (Bulgarus, Martinus, Jacobus, and Hugo), with other legal experts, helped the emperor preside over the *curia* as a high court of justice.[87]

Consuls, judges, *missi*, and legists in a fashion represented the cities, but did they sit in the Diet as a constituent part of a great deliberative assembly? Rahewin clearly states that for three days the emperor took counsel and deliberated only with the bishops and a few princes[88]—this was the great council. On the fourth day the emperor "in concionem venit,"[89] and after

---

[84] A. L. Poole does speak of the representatives of the cities but does not explain what kind of representation they constituted, nor what they did; "Frederick Barbarossa and Germany," in *C. M. H.*, v, 427. Even Leicht mentions only consuls and *primi omnium* as attending; "Introduction des villes . . . ," p. 420.

[85] Otto of Freising, *Gesta*, pp. 186-188.

[86] *Ibid.*, p. 189.

[87] *Ibid.*, p. 191; with these four doctors as judges, and with the other legal experts, Frederick "audiebat, discutiebat et terminabat negotia"—the *negotia* being the *querimoniae* and *proclamationes* of both rich and poor. Frederick, inspired by "divine counsel," appointed judges from the *curia* or from the cities to listen to the suits.

[88] *Ibid.*, p. 188: "solis episcopis cum paucis admodum principibus [secreto] consilii sui particibus iniungit, quatinus . . . de salubri consilio in Italiae rebus ordinandis ita secum deliberent, ut aecclesiae Dei pacis tranquillitate gaudeant, et ius regale decusque imperii debito provehatur honore."

[89] *Ibid.* The *concio* was perhaps the same as *parlamentum* or *colloquium* in the Italian sense. Yet Boncompagno, writing about fifty years after Roncaglia, tries to distinguish between *colloquium* and *contio*: "Colloquium est aliquorum conventus in locis et terminis constitutis, in quo communia vel privata negotia pertractantur," and it is held for negotiating marriages or for declaring war or making peace, and "pro aliis negotiis"; in the *colloquium* are assembled many persons from "diversis terris et locis pro communibus et privatis negotiis"—lib.

he spoke, the assembled Italians arose to demonstrate their devotion—first the bishops, then the *proceres*, and finally the consuls and *missi* delivered orations all day and into the night.[90] Among the orators it was the Archbishop of Milan who expressed the famous sentence of Ulpian, "Quod principi placuit, legis habet vigorem," since the people had granted to the emperor his *imperium* and power.[91] But on this day there was no manifestation of any feeling that what the people had once conferred they could now take back! During the several days following the *concio*, the Diet met in its third aspect, that of the high imperial court, to hear and settle *querimoniae*. As we have seen, the emperor presided and was assisted by the four Bolognese doctors as associate judges accompanied by other legal experts.[92] Then the members of the Diet (bishops, magnates, and cities) unanimously adjudged to the emperor his *regalia* and his right to approve the election of the city magistrates, and they all took the oath to accept and observe what had been done in the Diet and to keep the peace.[93] Finally, Frederick promulgated his *leges de iure feudorum*, "habito consilio" of the bishops and magnates and judges palatine.[94]

So far, in the account given by Rahewin, we have found no hint that the representatives of the cities consented in any fashion to the *constitutiones* decreed in the Diet. Nor is there such an indication in the *constitutio pacis*, or *Landfried*; in it one finds, besides the provisions for assuring the peace, only the statement that the magnates and lesser nobles "et omnium lo-

---

xii; a *contio* is not so general, for it takes place in a city and is addressed by a *contionator* amid shouts of "Audi! Audi!" and, if what he proposes meets approval, "Fiat! Fiat!" The *contio*, he says, reflects the great *libertas* in Italy—by which he means license, for he adds that no learned man will be a *contionator*; *Rhetorica Novissima* in *Scripta anecdota glossatorum*, ii, 294-296.

One cannot take these distinctions too seriously; and yet, we may suppose that the whole Diet of Roncaglia could be called a *colloquium*, while the day of orations was, as Rahewin terms it, a *contio*.

90 Otto of Freising, *Gesta*, p. 189. Rahewin manifests his dislike for the Italian habit of making speeches.

91 *Ibid.*, p. 190; *D.* 1, 4, 1.

92 Otto of Freising, *Gesta*, p. 191. Such legal experts perhaps included *adsessores* and *advocati*.

93 *Ibid.*, lib. iv, c. 8 and 9. For the *regalia*, see *M. G. H., Legum S. IV*, i, 244f., no. 175.

94 Otto of Freising, *Gesta*, lib. iv, c. 10. The *constitutio* is given by Rahewin; it is also in the *Libri Feudorum*, ii, 55; *M. G. H., Legum S. IV*, i, 247f., no. 177.

corum rectores *cum omnium locorum primatibus et plebeis"* bound themselves by oath to keep the peace.[95] (All this is analogous to the representation by local magistrates slightly later in Spain.) While the third important document resulting from the Diet, the well-known Authentic *Habita,* or *privilegium scholasticum,* hence not a *constitutio,* has the introductory statement, "Habita super hoc diligenti episcoporum, abbatum, ducum, comitum, iudicum et aliorum procerum sacri palacii examinacione," there is no indication that the *iudices* mentioned were other than the four doctors, who were palatine judges, not representatives of Bologna.[96] Thus the Diet of Roncaglia was a great meeting of the imperial *curia* in its three aspects of great council, parliament, and high court of the Italian kingdom—a completely feudal assembly. In the council itself, in which the decisions of general import were made, the consuls and judges of the communes had no part except that of furnishing such information as helped the council and emperor draw up the *constitutiones.* Corporate representation by proctors or syndics was not yet the practice.

From another source,[97] we learn that the *iudices* participated by furnishing under oath such information on local rights and the imperial *regalia* as to enable Frederick to assert the imperial prerogative and assess his revenues. When Frederick ordered the four doctors of Bologna to give expert information on his regalian rights in Lombardy, they replied, in the spirit of *quod omnes tangit,* that they were unwilling to do so "sine consilio aliorum judicum universarum Longobardie civitatum ibi astantium"; and Frederick thereupon chose two *iudices* of each city and commanded them all—twenty-eight in number[98]—to take

[95] Otto of Freising, *Gesta,* pp. 194f. The *iudices* and *defensores locorum* or the imperial magistrates are made responsible for seeing that the peace is kept. *M. G. H., Legum S. IV,* I, 245f., no. 176.

[96] *Ibid.,* 249, no. 178; the *Habita* has frequently been published and studied: see Rashdall-Powicke, *Universities,* I, 143-145; H. Koeppler, "Frederick Barbarossa and the Schools of Bologna," *E. H. R.,* LIV (1939), 607.

[97] F. Güterbock, ed., *Ottonis Morenae et Continuatorum Historia Frederici I* (*M.G.H., SS., N.S.,* VII). Otto Morena has been generally neglected, except by Koeppler, *op.cit.,* p. 586, and by A. Hessel, *Geschichte der Stadt Bologna,* pp. 95f.

[98] Koeppler, *op.cit.,* p. 586; fourteen towns were represented in the Diet—also Hessel, *loc.cit.*

counsel with the four doctors in order to determine the *regalia iura* and report them to him under their oath of fealty. This commission carefully discussed the *regalia* and at length submitted a written list of all that they knew. To the imperial rights thus established according to what was lawful, the prelates, nobles and consuls publicly, in the *colloquium*, renounced their claims.[99] To a slight extent, therefore, representatives (not including the four doctors)[100] of the cities contributed something to the assembly besides their mere presence for the purpose of acclaiming and applauding what was done. Yet they did not participate in the high council; they did not control legislation by effective consent. They simply were chosen as magistrates to give information that was authentic and sworn to by oath. Frederick used them as Henry II of England was using similar experts: to both rulers they were "an essential equipment of bureaucratic monarchy."[101]

4. INNOCENT III AND FREDERICK II

In the twelfth century Italian assemblies, like those in Spain, already were attended by delegates from the towns; but these delegates were, again like those in Spain, chiefly legal experts and local magistrates who brought the record to the royal authority, took oaths of fealty to the king, and to all intents and purposes represented the power of the king in the communities

99 Otto Morena, *Historia*, pp. 58-61. He continues by telling how all present swore to keep perpetual peace.

100 Shortly before, in 1156-57, they had been displaced along with the *podestà* of Bologna in favor of the government by consuls; they did not, therefore, represent Bologna; Hessel, *Geschichte*, p. 93.

101 Koeppler, *op.cit.*, p. 586. Other examples of such Italian assemblies as those described could be discussed, and one of them offers an analogy with the ten men summoned from each city in Castile and Leon to give information on the keeping of the king's privileges. A "maximum colloquium" of Lombards and Germans at Lodi in 1266 was attended by prelates, magnates, *capitanei*, and other *proceres*, and by many Lombards "tam magni quam etiam parvi." No doubt these *magni et parvi* were in part from the cities. They came to complain of the behavior of the Emperor's officers and *missi*. See Otto Morena, *Historia*, pp. 180f. In 1164 Frederick summoned the clergy and *cives* of Salzburg to his court to receive the sentence there of the archbishop and bishops in a case affecting them; *M. G. H., Legum S. IV*, 1, 314. In 1175, as specified in a treaty between Frederick and the Lombards and Venetians, ten men of each city were to take oath to observe the terms of peace and swear fealty, "vasallus sicuti vasallus et civis sicuti civis," *ibid.*, 339f.

rather than the interests and rights of their fellow citizens. Pope Innocent III, however, summoned *procuratores* with full powers from six cities of the March of Ancona to meet with his Curia.[102] If we cannot be sure that no true proctors had been sent to assemblies in the earlier period, it is at least not surprising that the papal chancery of Innocent III was fully acquainted with the Roman terminology and meaning of corporate representation.[103] In the pope's letter of 1200, addressed to the *potestas* and *populus* of each of the cities, we learn that a papal legate, sent to establish order in the March of Ancona, had been instructed to order the cities, after common deliberation, to send to the Curia *responsales idoneos*[104] provided with a *certum man-*

---

[102] A. Theiner, *Codex Diplomaticus Dominii Temporalis Sanctae Sedis*, I, nos. XLII, XLIII. Leicht has inadequately remarked on this assembly, "La posizione giuridica dei parlamenti medievali Italiani," *Organisation corporative du M. A.*, II, 96; and "Introduction des villes . . . ," p. 421. On papal assemblies G. Ermini is not satisfactory, *I parlamenti dello stato della chiesa dalle origini al periodo Albornoziano*, p. 5. But now a good treatment is available in Daniel Waley, *The Papal State in the Thirteenth Century*, pp. 91-124, but with no discussion of the powers of representatives. Marongiu, *L'Istituto parlamentare*, pp. 78-85, offers a good, if more general, treatment.

[103] Innocent III had been trained in the schools of Bologna, was a pupil of a great canonist, Huguccio, and employed several eminent decretalists in his *curia*—Bernard of Compostella, Peter of Benevento, Johannes Galensis, and Tancred, and perhaps Alanus and Vincentius Hispanus; Schulte, *Quellen*, I, 156, 189-205, 203 n. 16, 244; and G. Post, "Additional Glosses of Johannes Galensis and Silvester," *Archiv f. kathol. KR.*, CXIX (1939), 368 n.1, 374 n.3. These decretalists, and also Laurentius Hispanus and Johannes Teutonicus, helped lay the foundations of legal thought for the more famous Innocent IV, Hostiensis, Johannes Andreae, etc., and they were well acquainted with the Roman law and the glossators (notably Azo, their contemporary) on corporations and proctors; see Schulte, *Quellen*, I, and articles by F. Gillmann in the *Archiv f. kathol. KR.*, 1920ff., and his *Des Laurentius Hispanus Apparat*, pp. 100ff. Also Kuttner, *Repertorium*, on the canonists from 1140 to 1234.

Furthermore, twelfth-century popes (Eugenius III, Alexander III and Clement III) had been developing and adapting the Roman procedure for suits of ecclesiastical corporations in the courts. It was, therefore, natural that Innocent III, when he turned his attention to strengthening the papal authority over the cities in papal territory, should be readier than a completely secular prince to put to use the convenient and practical machinery of proctors of cities. The pope called such representatives proctors instead of syndics; he was establishing the principle in Canon law, as opposed to that in Roman law, that a proctor as well as a syndic could act in court for a corporation, even a secular corporation. See *Decr. Greg. IX* 1, 38, 7 and 2, 7, 6. This refers to proctors of the commune of Faenza in a lawsuit in the papal Curia, and Tancred later referred to it in stating that a *universitas* can have a proctor, although he should properly be called a syndic.

[104] A *responsalis idoneus* was technically a proctor who was *plene instructus*, i.e., was furnished with full powers. See below, ch. III, §5.

datum and *plenaria potestas.*[105] These *procuratores* and *nuntii* were to have full powers from their constituents, then, to appear at the Curia and receive the papal commands for establishing law and order, and to swear fealty,[106] so that their communes could not later refuse obedience to the pope on the pretense that they had not sanctioned what the proctors might engage them to do. And they were also to give counsel to the pope, counsel which no doubt consisted largely of the record of local exemptions or franchises, of cases of lawlessness, of matters pertaining to the municipal administration, and of petitions to the pope. In fact these "instructed" proctors came to the Curia with their counsel and information; with them, as well as with the cardinals, Innocent III "carefully treated" ("habito diligenti tractatu");[107] and "de ipsorum procuratorum consilio" the pope decided to send his own agents into the March to establish reforms—decided also that the cities should pay an annual *census.*[108]

That these proctors were at the same time consuls[109] and *podestàs* is indicated by the summons issued by the pope for an assembly in 1207. This assembly met on three different days, the first day for the taking of oaths of fealty, the second for the

---

105 One thinks immediately of the influence of this terminology, to be repeated frequently in proctorial mandates of the thirteenth century, on the *plena potestas* used in the summons of Henry III and Edward I to knights and burgesses. See below, ch. III, in general, and §§ 3 and 4, and nn. 197-204.

106 *Plenaria potestas,* "ut nobiscum super apostolice sedis justitiis convenirent, et de reformatione pacis ac terre defensione, necnon fidelitate nobis plenius exhibenda nostris exponerent se mandatis"; Theiner, *Codex Diplomaticus,* I, No. XLII.

107 The meaning of *tractare* has often been taken as implying some effective consent; but it means at this time no more than arguing a case in court and discussion or negotiation; it does not imply voting on final decisions.

108 Theiner, *Codex Diplomaticus,* I, Nos. XLII and XLIII; interesting is the revelation that recently a proctor, with "litteris de rato" (mandate), had come to the pope from Fano, promising in the name of the city that "tam vos quam omnes, qui sunt de vestro districto, nobis et successoribus nostris et ecclesie Romane *fidelitatem* curabitis universaliter exhibere, *expeditionem, parlamentum, pacem, et guerram, ad mandatum nostrum* et legatorum et nuntiorum nostrorum per totam Marchiam. . . ." The towns shall pay an annual *census.* In return, the pope confirms their corporate institutions—the consuls with jurisdiction in criminal and civil cases—and their "good customs." Cf. Leicht, "Introduction des villes . . . ," p. 421. (The italics are mine.)

109 As early as 1158 the consuls of Orvieto took the oath of *ligium hominium* and fealty to Hadrian IV; J. Seeger, *Die Reorganisation des Kirchenstaates unter Innocenz III,* p. 17.

presentation of "querelas et petitiones" to the pope, and the third for the papal promulgation of statutes for peace and justice.[110] Here, then, as in 1200 and as at Roncaglia, was a feudal assembly meeting in different aspects of the Curia. As Leicht rightly emphasizes, this representation was feudal in nature.[111] But it was something more than feudal, for it signalled the new emphasis upon the central authority, which was enhanced by the Roman corporate terminology and machinery of representation now maturely developed by Innocent III and his Curia. The essential terminology at least (the number of representatives from each city had to be fixed later) differed little from that used a century later by Edward I in his summons to Parliament. As in the case of earlier imperial and Spanish assemblies, however, there is no likelihood that the representatives of the third estate did more than give information, petition, and receive decisions. As for the consuls and *podestàs* as proctors, they were chosen because they were local judges and administrators; if the ruler could assert his authority, they were really the representatives of pope or prince in the cities. Nevertheless, the fact that they brought powers from their constituents was a long step forward in the development of a system of corporate representation; thereby some responsibility for defending, in the ruler's court and assembly, the rights of their communities was already imposed upon the delegates.

5. CONCLUSIONS

After the first decade of the thirteenth century, the system of corporate representation by agents given full powers grew steadily. By broadening the legal experience of Italian communes and accepting the formulas and procedure developed by legists and canonists, Pope Innocent III played an important if not original and decisive role in the adoption of the new method of representing communities in ecclesiastical and secular assem-

---

110 Theiner, *Codex Diplomaticus*, I, No. LI; Leicht, *op.cit.*, p. 421; Ermini, *Parlamenti*, p. 5, from Muratori, *Rerum Italicarum Scriptores*, III, c. CXXV. On consuls appearing in the papal Curia, see also a decretal of Innocent III, *an.* 1200, *Decr. Greg. IX* 2, 24, 19; the consuls are also *judices*. On this assembly at Viterbo see Waley, *Papal State*, pp. 52-56.

111 Leicht, "Introduction des villes . . . ," p. 422.

blies. He was the first pope to summon proctors to represent cathedral chapters and convents in a General Council (Fourth Lateran, 1215), and his legate in Catalonia perhaps instructed delegates of the cities to bring mandates to the Cortes of Lérida (1214). It is surely no accident that under the immediate successors of Innocent III the Dominican Order adopted a system of general chapters which, although it owed much to the experience of the monastic orders of the twelfth century, also owed to Roman and Canon law the idea of the representation of provinces (groups of convents) by priors and *diffinitores* who were given full powers.[112] Nor can it be entirely an accident that the first secular ruler definitely known to have summoned proctors with mandates or powers was Frederick II.[113] After the middle of the century, the procedure of proctorial representation continued in the Kingdom of Sicily and in the Papal States,[114] and definitely took hold in Spain, England, and France.

[112] Barker and Tunmore, cited at the beginning of this study, do not understand the Roman background; nor does G. R. Galbraith, *The Constitution of the Dominican Order, 1216-1360*. *Plenaria potestas* is specified for these representatives in 1228; H. Denifle, "Die Constitutionen des Predigerordens vom Jahre 1228," *Archiv für Litteratur- und Kirchengeschichte des Mittelalters*, I (1885), 193; Galbraith, pp. 34, 37f. The *socii* elected by the convents and sent to the provincial chapters were also given powers—to deliberate and to vote, says Galbraith (p. 38); but I have reason to think that only the conventual prior really voted, the *socius* being present merely to bring the record and defend the interests of the friars of the convent as the corporation of which the prior was the head—but a new study is needed.

[113] In 1231 Frederick ordered the cities of Tuscany to send to him *nuntii* with *plena auctoritas* to give counsel and accept his decisions; *M. G. H., Legum S. IV*, II, Nos. 151f. To a *curia* at Ravenna later in 1231 Frederick summoned the commune of Genoa to send representatives, who were to hear and receive the imperial *ordinationes*, but who also protested against an action of the Emperor and petitioned him to change his decision; *M. G. H., Legum S. IV*, II, No. 155; Huillard-Bréholles, *Historia Diplomatica*, IV, 266; Carlyle, *Med. Political Theory*, V, 137f.; and *Annales* of Bartholomaeus Scriba, *M. G. H., SS.*, XVIII, 177-179. On representation in Frederick's southern kingdom, see Calisse, *Parlamento in Sicilia*, Appendix, Nos. XLIII and XLVI; McIlwain, in *C. M. H.*, VII, 704; Marongiu, *L'Istituto parlamentare*, pp. 123-127.

[114] As late as 1278, syndics of *universitates* in Bologna and Romaniola were summoned by the famous canonist Guillaume Durantis to take the *sacramentum fidelitatis* to the pope; Sarti-Fattorini, *De claris archigymnasii bononiensis professoribus*, 2nd ed., I, 467f., 468 n. 1. But in the twelfth century, consuls frequently took the oath, as at Roncaglia, 1158; also at other times when there was no great assembly, 1155, 1162 (*M. G. H., Legum S. IV*, I, Nos. 155, 205, 211); and in the Curia of Innocent III, 1200. On the consuls see Previté-Orton, "The Italian Cities till *c.* 1200," *C. M. H.*, V, 219ff., 232f.; Ficker, *Forschungen*, IV, No. 164. By the end of the century, under the influence of the Roman law on the *iuramen-*

By 1268 Roman formulas of the proctorial mandate were adapted for the use of knights of the shire in Parliament; and soon the kings of England and France, following the precedent established by the lawyers and by cathedral chapters in provincial councils, began to express the Roman principle of due process in court, *quod omnes tangit*, etc., as an integral part of the *rationale* of the representation of individual and corporate rights before the king and his court and council in assembly.[115]

The paucity and vagueness of the sources for the early period of representation (1150-1250) permit no final conclusions either on the kind of consent which the delegates brought to the assembly or on the real meaning attached to the new formulas in the various countries. The legal thought involved in the new style of representation cannot therefore be defined with confidence, although it seems to have been approaching a logical application by 1250. But it is at least safe to conclude that corporate representation appeared in Italy earlier than in Spain, and that, whether local magistrates or true corporate agents came to the assemblies, there was no conception of popular, or sovereign, consent; if the interests of the communities were defended, nonetheless early representation was more that of the ruler in the towns than that of the towns in the royal *curia* and assembly.

---

tum calumniae, Bernard of Pavia says that "in causa civitatis vel municipii consules vel rectores iurabunt," *Summa decretalium (ca.* 1190), ed. E. A. T. Laspeyres, p. 31. But in the course of the thirteenth century legists and canonists mention syndics or proctors in this connection more frequently than consuls.

[115] On these developments see chs. III and IV.

CHAPTER III ✦ *PLENA POTESTAS*

AND CONSENT IN MEDIEVAL ASSEMBLIES

A STUDY IN ROMANO-CANONICAL PROCEDURE AND

THE RISE OF REPRESENTATION, 1150-1325[1]

B Y THE END of the thirteenth century the royal writ of summons to Parliament usually specified that communities send representatives with "full power" to consent to whatever should be ordained by the king in his court and council. This "full power" was the famous *plena potestas* which was stated in the mandates carried by knights and burgesses to Parliament and by delegates of cities and towns to Cortes and States General, and which is still current in proxies for stockholders' meetings. It has, of course, like almost every word of the terminology in documents relating to representation, challenged interpretation: on the one side is the argument that *plena potestas* implied an almost political or sovereign consent which limited the royal authority;[2] on the other, the

---

[1] Published in *Traditio*, I (1943), 355-408; now slightly revised.

[2] See J. G. Edwards, "The *Plena Potestas* of English Parliamentary Representatives," *Oxford Essays in Medieval History Presented to H. E. Salter*, pp. 141-154; this was the first attempt to interpret *plena potestas* as used in England. Edwards concludes that its origin lay in part in the king's wanting representatives with full power in order to obtain sure consent to taxation, and in part in the feudal law on consent to extraordinary aids: "Historically the legal sovereignty of Parliament sprang . . . from a double root. One root was the character of Parliament as a high court. The second root was the *plena potestas* of the representatives of the Commons" (p. 154). F. Pollock and F. W. Maitland, *History of English Law*, 2nd ed., 2 vols.; II, 228, do not interpret; they merely state how "full powers" arose in the law of agency and in procuration and representation in Parliament. C. H. McIlwain, "Medieval Estates," *C.M.H.*, VII, 679, seems to conclude that the consent expressed by *plena potestas* was more than a formality in that the representatives had some discretionary power (*ad tractandum*), which would naturally act as a brake on the king's demands. Similarly, but emphasizing more strongly the right of judgment and consent, Maude V. Clarke, *Medieval Representation and Consent*, p. 291; cf. pp. 200f. For Spain, R. B. Merriman

assumption that it was an expression of involuntary consent to the acts and decisions of the royal government.[3] In general, of course, whatever modern scholars have decided as to the right of consent has resulted either from modern conceptions of representation or from a strict interpretation of the terminology in the sources for the history of assemblies. No one has examined *plena potestas* in the light of the legal theory and procedure of the thirteenth century.[4] By studying how legists and canonists viewed the meaning of *plena potestas*, it is possible to find at least a relatively new approach to the problem of medieval consent.

1. *PLENA POTESTAS* IN ROMAN AND CANON LAW

Like nearly all the formulas in thirteenth-century mandates[5] for proctors or representatives, *plena potestas* was taken directly from the Roman law. The Emperor Alexander Severus (*an.* 227) declared that if a proctor appointed for one suit or business (*ad unam speciem = ad causam, vel negotium* in a thirteenth-century gloss)[6] exceeds or departs from his instructions (*officium mandati*), his action cannot prejudice his principal or *dominus*. But if while so acting he has *plenam potestatem agendi*, the sentence or judgment of the court need not be rescinded; for if the proctor acts fraudulently, his *dominus* can have him cited to court to obtain a remedy.[7] In other words, *plena potestas*

---

holds that the *poderes* were "one of the most important safeguards of Castilian parliamentary liberty" despite the king's right to interpret the powers of the delegates; *Rise of the Spanish Empire*, I, 222f.; and that consent limited the royal power effectively in Aragon; I, 461f.

3 For France, M. Jusselin, "Lettres de Philippe le Bel relatives à la convocation de l'assemblée de 1302," *Bibliothèque de l'École des Chartes*, LXVII (1906), 471; C. V. Langlois, in Lavisse, III, ii, 160f., 261-264; McIlwain, *C.M.H.*, VII, 686, 690. For England, T. F. T. Plucknett, "Parliament," in Morris, *English Government*, I, 101f. Lot and Fawtier, *Hist. inst. françaises*, II, Bk. VI, ch. I, on assemblies, has nothing on *plena potestas*.

4 I consider the century broadly as the period from about 1150 to 1325.

5 The *mandatum* was a contract by which an agent could act for his *dominus* in a business transaction or in lawsuits; the principal or *dominus* was so bound, if the agent honestly carried out the terms of the mandate, by the agent's conclusion of the contract or waging of the lawsuit, that he must accept the contract or the sentence of the court.

6 Accursius, *Glos. ord.*, to C. 2, 12, 10, ad v. *unam speciem*: "Id est, ad causam, vel negotium."

7 C. 2, 12, 10: " . . . quod si plenam potestatem agendi habuit, rem iudicatam

meant simply that the proctor "fully represented his principal, so that the latter's right was brought into issue."[8] This law, preserved in Justinian's *Codex*, 2, 12, 10, was known and commented upon perhaps as early as the ninth century in Italy, when a glossator said that *plena potestas* permitted the proctor to carry a matter to a conclusion.[9]

No reference to *plena potestas* in the works of the legists of the twelfth century has come to my attention. But it must have been known, for it occurs in a canonist's treatise on procedure in the 1180's.[10] Indeed, Rogerius makes *generalis et libera administratio* the equivalent of full powers, and Azo follows him.[11] In the thirteenth century Accursius decides that, since the giving of a general mandate is sufficient only for litigation proper, the addition of *plena potestas* makes the general mandate adequate also for the *transactio* (i.e., a compromise of a dispute at law,[12] for which a special mandate in addition to the general one was usually required).[13] Odofredo observes no distinction

---

rescindi non oportet, cum, si quid fraude vel dolo egit, convenire eum more iudiciorum non prohiberis." My interpretation is rather free, but it is justified by the statement in an *Epitome* of the *Codex* of the ninth century (below, n. 9) and by the legists of the thirteenth and fourteenth centuries.

8 Buckland, *Textbook of Roman Law*, p. 710.

9 Vinogradoff, *Roman Law in Medieval Europe*, p. 40; a ninth century *Epitome* of the *Codex*, to 2, 12, 10, states that "if the representative (procurator) of a person had full powers to act in the latter's behalf, a decision against him in a trial ought to stand; for in the case of a fraud, the procurator might be sued by his principal" ("nota qui habet plenam potestatem agendi posse rem sine dolo firmiter finire," p. 41). In the thirteenth century Odofredo also states that the remedy for the *dominus*, if his proctor acts collusively, is an action against the proctor; to *C.*, 2, 12, 10, below n. 14.

10 In the *Ordo iudiciarius Bambergensis* (ca. 1182-1185), ed. Schulte, *Sitzungsberichte d. Kais. Akademie der Wissenschaften zu Wien, Philos.-Hist. Cl.*, LXX (1872), 300: "Procurator super his, quae ad ipsam procurationem spectare noscuntur, plenariam recipit potestatem."

11 Azo, *Lectura*, to *C.* 2, 12, 10 (p. 159), ad vv. *convenire eum more iudic.*: "Quia conveniet eum actione mandati. . . . Si ergo [procurator] habet liberam [*literam* in this edition] et generalem administrationem, servatur quod fecit, sed tamen tenetur de dolo et fraude, et de lata culpa et levi. . . ." Rogerius, *Summa Codicis*, II, viii, *De procuratoribus*: the proctor for *administratio*, "sive habeat speciale mandatum sive generale et liberam amministrationem, potest vendere, alienare et cetera facere: si autem generale nec liberam amministrationem, nec vendere, nec alienare, nec transigere potest"; ed Palmieri, *Scripta anecdota glossatorum*, I, 27f.

12 Buckland, *Roman Law*, p. 525.

13 Accursius says, to *C.* 2, 12, 10, ad v. *plenam potestatem*: "specialiter concessam, secundum quosdam. . . . Tu dic, quod sufficit generalis cum libera

between *plena potestas* and *libera et generalis administratio;* indeed, the former is implied by the latter.[14] In the following century this opinion was taken over by Bartolus, who in addition makes it clear that anyone who has a mandate that specifies either *plena* or *libera administratio,* or contains the commonly used formula *possit facere omnia que ipse dominus possit* is thereby given *plena potestas* by the principal.[15] Baldus even more clearly expresses the same opinion.[16] Francesco Tigrini (†1360) goes so far as to say that *plena potestas* is implied by the formula *et promitto me habere firmum et ratum quicquid procurator meus fecit.*[17] Thus, the legists attach no peculiar importance to *plena potestas* alone; other formulas may have the same legal effect. All accept the general meaning of the imperial law, that if the *dominus* gives his proctor full power, he must accept the decision of the court in a suit brought by the proctor.

[administratione] ad agendum et transigendum; sed generalis sola non sufficit ad transigendum, ut ff. eo. l. procurator cui generaliter, et l. mandato generali." The second reference is to *D.* 3, 3, 60: "Mandato generali non contineri etiam transactionem decidendi causa interpositam. Et ideo si postea is, qui mandavit, transactionem ratam non habuit, non posse eum repelli ab actionibus exercendis."

[14] To *C.* 2, 12, 10: ". . . si procurator habet liberam et generalem administrationem, sententia lata contra eum nocet domino; sed si dicitur procurator collusisse cum adversario, dominus mandati poterit contra eum agere."

[15] *Commentaria*, VII, to *C.* 2, 12, 10: ". . . quero quando quis dicatur habere plenam potestatem? Quidam dicunt, quando habet speciale mandatum. Alii dicunt, et istud tenet gl. [i.e., the gloss of Accursius], quando habet liberam, et tene menti, et vide gl. (§2) Et sic no., quod idem est dicere, 'concedo tibi plenam administrationem,' et 'concedo tibi liberam administrationem.' Idem forte important illa verba, que communiter apponuntur, ut 'possit facere omnia que ipse dominus posset,' ut per hoc videatur concedi libera, ut l. (1) de offi. procu. Caesa."

[16] Baldus, *super toto Codice*, to *C.* 2, 12, 10: ". . . Quero quando quis dicitur habere plenam potestatem; et dicunt quidam quando specialiter hoc dicitur. Item quando dicitur habeas liberam, ut ff. de pecu. l. quam tuberonis.§.alia. Item si apponuntur ista verba, 'quod posset quicquid posset dominus si presens est.' Bar. allegat l. i. de offi. proc. cesar. Ego allego tex. ff. manda. l. creditor.§. lucius.—§. Conclude ergo quod tria vocabula sunt, que idem important plenam potestatem; et idem 'quod posset dominus,' idem si diceretur 'concedo tibi [*sibi* in the 1519 edition] totalem potestatem,' per d.§.lucius. Nunquam tamen in his verbis includitur donatio vel dilapidatio. . . . Item nunquam includitur delictum. . . ."

[17] Bartolus, *Commentaria*, to *C.* 2, 12, 10, 5, *Antiqua lectura*: "No. tex. cum glo. super verbo 'plenam,' quod idem est sive dicatur plena sive generalis et libera; quod si dicatur in aliquo procuratore generali, 'et promitto me habere firmum et ratum quicquid procurator meus fecerit,' nunquid ex his verbis videatur induci libera potestas et administratio?" Some say no; but "hoc satis aequipollere videtur . . . Fran. Tigr."

But, as Baldus says, such power does not give the proctor any right arbitrarily to give away the principal's property, to injure his interests, or to commit a crime.[18] Both *dominus* and *procurator* must loyally abide by the terms of the contract embodied in the mandate. *Plena potestas* simply gave the judge or judges in a court the assurance that what the proctor had done in a matter which came to trial, or what he did in the course of the trial in the interests of his *dominus*, was done under such contract with his principal that the latter was legally bound to accept any resulting sentence of the court. Naturally, an unfavorable sentence of the court could later, if reasonable grounds existed, be appealed to a higher court.

The glossators developed the law in the *Code* by bringing to bear texts from the *Digest* relating not only to the ordinary proctor, but also to the *procurator Caesaris*. Azo and Accursius made *plena potestas* almost the equivalent of *libera administratio* given in a general mandate, and refer to *Dig.* 3, 3, 58 on this.[19] But, says Accursius, such a general mandate is not valid for the *transactio* (and offers as authority *Dig.* 3, 3, 60)[20] unless it contains the additional formula *libera administratio* or *plena potestas*.[21] Bartolus and Baldus also made *libera administratio* equivalent in effect to *plena potestas*; that is, the general mandate containing the formula *libera administratio* was valid even for the *transactio*, for which no additional special mandate was needed. *Plena potestas* was inserted in the general mandate, no doubt, to give double assurance of its general validity for all kinds of legal business in a court, whether the litigant parties desired to pursue their controversy to the bitter end of judicial sentence, or to "transact" and come to an agreement before the judge but without the judge's deciding the outcome by a sen-

---

[18] Above, n. 16; Azo adds, in his *Lectura*, *C.* 2, 12, 10, ad vv. *nullum domino praeiudicium*: "Non enim debet transgredi mandatum . . . "; ad vv. *convenire eum more iudic.*: "Quia conveniet eum actione mandati. . . . Si ergo habet liberam [*literam* in printed text] et generalem administrationem, servatur quod fecit, sed tamen tenetur (procurator) de dolo et fraude, et de lata culpa et levi. . . ."

[19] Above, nn. 11, 13; *D.* 3, 3, 58: "Procurator, cui generaliter libera administratio rerum commissa est, potest exigere, novare, aliud pro alio permutare."

[20] *D.* 3, 3, 60: "Mandato generali non contineri etiam transactionem decidendi causa interpositam."

[21] See the gloss of Accursius given above, n. 13.

tence. These formulas, *libera administratio* or *plena potestas*, made the general mandate effective for other special kinds of proctorial action (e.g., selling goods for the *dominus*), for which otherwise the general proctor had to have also a special mandate, as for *transactio*.[22] In brief, where normally a special mandate was needed, if instead the proctor was given a general mandate with *libera administratio*, he could do everything that the *dominus* himself could do.[23]

The passages in *Dig.* 1, 19, *procurator Caesaris*, were all used as authority for the *libera administratio*; but as Azo says, the *procurator* of Caesar can only administer—he cannot alienate to the Caesar's injury.[24] This idea was transferred by Bartolus and Baldus to the ordinary proctor.[25] Thus, once more, if the proctor had *libera administratio* or *plena potestas*, he should not act in such a way as to damage his *dominus*;[26] if he did, however, the *dominus* would find a remedy only in another action in court. Actually, the *libera administratio* or *plena potestas*, or both, made the proctor not merely an attorney but also an administrator with a general mandate for all the business connected with a case or suit involving the principal.

Trained as they were in the Roman law, canon lawyers naturally borrowed much from the Roman theory and procedure. And from the latter half of the twelfth century on, experts on procedure, decretalists, and popes took cognizance of the importance of *plena potestas*. As early as 1182-1185 a canonist stated in his *Ordo iudiciarius* that the proctor should receive

22 *D.* 3, 3, 63; Accursius, ad v. *speciali*; cf. Bartolus to *e. l.*

23 The thirteenth century legist Vivianus, in his *Casus*, to *D.* 3, 3, 58, *Procurator cui*, says: "Si aliquem constitui procura.[torem] et concessi liberam et generalem administrationem, procur.[ator] omnia poterit facere ut dominus; novare enim poterit, et permutare, et solvere debita creditoribus."

24 Azo, as given by Accursius, *Glos. ord.*, to *D.* 1, 19, 1, ad v. *diligenter*: "Sed nonne bene potest gerere alienando? . . . quia hic habet liberam administrationem . . . unde videtur alienare; sed speciale est, ne in Caesaris praeiudicium alienet, alias contra . . . *Az.*"

25 Above, nn. 15, 16.

26 *D.* 3, 3, 49, Paulus: "Ignorantis domini conditio deterior per procuratorem fieri non debet;" to which Accursius, *Glos. ord.*, ad v. *non debet*: "nisi in tribus casibus: quando scilicet est in rem suam; et quando speciale habet mandatum; et quando generale, sed habet liberam administrationem. . . . Sed certe nec tunc quando generalem habet administrationem et liberam, potest donare. . . . Sed licet deteriorem facere non potest, tamen meliorem sic. . . ."

plenaria potestas,[27] and in 1200 Innocent III was summoning proctors of cities to come to the Curia with full powers.[28] A decretal of Gregory IX (1227-1234) specified that a suitable proctor, sent to the papal Curia for a matrimonial case, should have *plena potestas ad agendum et respondendum* (*Decr.* 1, 38, c. 10 Accedens). This meant, according to the *Glossa ordinaria*, that the proctor had such full powers that he could act as defendant as well as plaintiff in the suit if the adversary brought counter-charges and was fully responsible if the sentence went against him.[29] *Plena potestas*, moreover, according to the decretalists (who agree with the legists), was the practical equivalent of *libera administratio*: the general mandate by itself did not preclude the necessity of the special mandate for the proctor to petition for a papal rescript,[30] to transact, to alienate, or to transfer, renew, or change a debt by the *novatio*.[31] By the time of Boniface VIII, however, the general proctor could do all these things without special mandate if the general mandate contained special clauses or gave him *libera administratio*.[32] Still earlier, Guillaume Durantis (*ca.* 1271-1286)

---

[27] Above, n. 10. [28] Below, § 3; above, ch. II, § 4.

[29] To *Decr.* 1, 38, 10, ad v. *respondendum*: "Sic ergo debet constitui procurator ad agendum datus, ut possit etiam defendere et respondere adversario si eum reconveniat: alias si non defenderet, denegabitur ei actio . . . et in expensis alteri parti tamquam contumax condemnetur. . . . In qua constitutione debet satisdationem exponere . . . ; et quod tempore sententie erit in iudicio, alias omnia dabit quae in condemnatione veniunt, ut ibidem dicitur: et ita plenam habet potestatem."

[30] In the Fourth Lateran Council (1215), Innocent III decreed that without a special mandate from the *dominus* no one could ask for a papal writ for a suit (*Decr.* 1, 3, 28 Nonnulli); this was repeated by Gregory IX (c.33 Ex parte). To the latter decretal the gloss in the *Glos. ord.* ad v. *sine speciali* states that according to Roman law the general proctor who also had *libera administratio* could petition for a rescript; but the author adds, "Curia tamen non servat hoc, quod hic et in concilio dicitur, nec daret litteras propter hoc appellanti."

[31] *Glos. ord.*, to c.28 Nonnulli, § Cum autem, ad vv. *sine speciali mandato*: "Sic ergo generalis procurator non sufficit ad impetrandum litteras," for which, as for *transactio*, for *in integrum restitutio*, for *dilatio iuramenti*, and for *acceptilatio*, a special mandate is necessary; to *Decr.* 1, 38, 9 Petitio, ad v. *generales*: "Licet fuerint generales procuratores, non tamen poterant transigere . . . nec possunt alienare nisi fructus aut alia quae de facili corrumpi possunt . . . "; to c.11 Dilectus, e. t., ad v. *generalis (ad omnia eius tractanda negotia)*: "Potest ergo quis constituere generalem procuratorem ad omnia, tam ad iudicia quam ad negotia, ut hic dicit . . . ; tamen talis procurator transigere non potest, nec alienare. . . ."

[32] Boniface VIII, *VI* 1, 19, 4: "Qui ad agendum et defendendum, ac generaliter

had masterfully summed up the rules of procedure for judicial representation in church courts and had made *libera* and *plena potestas* identical with *libera administratio* in the general mandate.[33] It is probable that ecclesiastical courts themselves often accepted a proctor as fully empowered by a mandate in which the terminology was vague or in part lacking—after all, the court could interpret because of the judge's jurisdiction.[34] It was therefore not always essential that *plena potestas* be stated specifically, provided that other terms were reasonable equivalents and that the judges were willing to accept the mandate as one conveying full powers—*non obstante subtilitate legali.*[35] Such a mandate was *sufficiens* and its bearer *sufficienter instructus,*[36] if it gave *plena potestas.*

This legal meaning of *plena potestas* and its equivalents was quickly embodied in the practical treatises on judicial procedure in the courts. A canonist's *Ordo iudiciarius* as early as the 1180's emphasized the necessity of giving full powers in the mandate,[37] and by the middle of the thirteenth century treatises and formularies of civilians and canonists specified in detail what things *plena potestas* in the general mandate enabled the proctor or syndic to do. William of Drogheda's *Summa aurea*

---

ad omnia, etiamsi mandatum exigant speciale, constituitur procurator, ex vi generalitatis huiusmodi ad aliquem articulum, in quo speciale mandatum exigitur, admitti non debet. Sed si aliquis vel aliqui de articulis speciale mandatum exigentibus specificati fuissent adiecta clausula generali: tunc ad non expressos etiam admittetur. Procurator quoque absque speciali mandato iuramentum deferre, transigere vel pacisci non potest, nisi ei bonorum vel causae administratio libera* sit concessa." (* Friedberg, the editor, wrongly has *libere*; *libera*, which is given in several MSS, is better.) Zenzelinus (†*ca.* 1350) sums up the decretal thus: "Procurator generalis non agit exigentia speciale mandatum, nisi cum aliqua illorum specificatione vel libera potestate."

[33] *Speculum iudiciale*, I, iii, t. *De procuratore*, c. *Ut autem*, no. 11; below, n. 44.

[34] Honorius III (1216-1227) had declared that exception to a mandate should not be allowed if the intention of the *dominus* was to give *libera potestas* to his general proctors, even though in this instance the *dominus* failed to state whether his agents were *syndici* or *actores* (*Decr.* 1, 38, 9 Petitio).

[35] *Glos. ord.* to *Decr.* 1, 38, 9, ad v. *intentio*: "Sic patet quod quando verba generalia sive dubia, ponuntur in mandato, recurrendum est ad intentionem constituentis. . . . Unde si diceretur: 'ego do Titio potestatem agendi et defendendi in causa vel in causis, quam vel quas habeo cum tali,' sufficiens est mandatum, non obstante subtilitate legali. . . ."

[36] See below, §5, on "sufficient instructions."

[37] Above, n. 10.

(*ca.* 1240) maturely reflects Roman law and the legists on the problem: a general mandate containing clauses for *libera et generalis administratio* enables the proctor to act as if the constituent himself were present, to act in all eventualities without having to obtain special mandates from the constituent. The proctor thus has full powers and needs no further instructions.[38] Some treatises of the middle thirteenth century on procedure in ecclesiastical courts are more conservative, usually stating that the general mandate, while good for a whole suit or several suits, is not sufficient for the special acts which demand special mandates.[39] But the *Summa minorum* (1250-1254) gives a form for a general mandate which confers on the proctor for all suits, whether he acts as plaintiff or defendant, both *totalis potestas* and *mandatus speciale* for certain matters.[40] And the *Curialis* (1251-1270) offers a *procuratio ad omnia facienda* for the general proctor, which contains a clause giving him *speciale mandatum litigandi, defendendi, transigendi, componendi, etc.*, and thus provides him with *plenaria potestas* before the judges and assures him that his *dominus* will ratify whatever he does *et in curiis et extra*.[41] The Saxon *Summa prosarum dictaminum*

[38] *Summa aurea*, c. cii: the office of the proctor is to do those things "quae verus dominus faceret, si esset praesens . . . (*D.* 3, 3, 35, 3), nisi prohibeatur a iure, ut transigere et compromittere, nisi ad hoc habeat speciale mandatum . . . (*D.* 3, 3, 60 and 63)"; c. cvi: the general proctor cannot do certain things without special mandate; but, c. cvii, if the general proctor is given *libera et generalis administratio*, he can "litigare, componere, et novare"; Wahrmund, *Quellen*, ii, ii, 97, 101, 102f. William also gives a form for a general mandate so drawn up that it confers full powers on the proctor, c. cviii: "Si autem velit [dominus] ei [procuratori] dare potestatem ad transigendum et ad componendum, adiciat clausulam istam: 'Constituo etiam ipsum procuratorem ad transigendum et ad componendum' vel 'concedo ei liberam et generalem administrationem, ita quod omnia expediat, quae praesentialiter essem acturus. Ratum habiturus, quicquid iustitia mediante circa praedicta duxerit agendum; et pro eo iudicatum solvi, si necesse fuerit, promitto' . . ."; Wahrmund, ii, ii, 103f.

[39] Ordo *Scientiam* (1235-1240), ed. Wahrmund, ii, i, 49: the proctor can do only those things required to answer to the charges as given in the papal rescript which assigns the case to judges.

[40] Wahrmund, i, ii, 53f. Wahrmund has this: "Dans eidem procuratori talem potestatem et mandatum speciale, etc." But in formularies *talis* is used in place of names of actual persons, not for legal terms; and here there is no "such power . . . that," but "complete, 'total' powers . . . of" doing something. Wahrmund has probably mistaken an abbreviation in the MSS for *totalem*; cf. Saxon *Summa*, cited below, n. 42, and Baldus, above, n. 16.

[41] This form of a general mandate is worth giving in detail: "Universis prae-

(before 1241) gives a mandate by which the proctor has *libera potestas* of making special pleas, of appealing, and of *totaliter* litigating in a suit; his constituents will hold *ratum* and *gratum* whatever he does in the particular case.[42] According to Rolandinus Passagerii (*ca.* 1260), a famous professor of the notarial art at Bologna, the general mandate *ad causas et negocia* enables the proctor to act as plaintiff or defendant generally in all *lites* and *controversiae* of his *dominus*, in any *negotia*, and before secular and ecclesiastical judges. Such a proctor has *plena et libera potestas* and *generale mandatum* to offer or receive *libelli* (i.e., to act as plaintiff or as defendant), formulate the issue (*litis contestatio*), propose *exceptiones*, ask for *termini* and postponements, accept or receive witnesses, produce instruments or written evidence, choose or refuse judges, and hear the court's sentence. He can also ask, demand or receive anything owed to the *dominus*, contract and transact, borrow, sell, buy and lease, and appoint proctors in his place.[43] Finally, Guillaume Durantis sums up the meaning of *plena potestas* in Canon law: in a general mandate *ad causas et negotia* the proctor is given *plena et libera potestas . . . faciendi* all things expressed in the mandate—*libera* adds strength to *plena potestas*.[44] In his form-mandates he offers the example of a bishop and his church

---

sentes literas inspecturis officialis Belvacensis salutem. . . . Notum facimus universis, quod talis in nostra praesentia constitutus Odonem clericum, latorem praesentium, ad omnes causas motas et movendas contra quoscumque tam clericos quam laicos, coram quibuscumque iudicibus, tam delegatis quam ordinariis, suum procuratorem et* constituit generalem. Dans ei speciale mandatum litigandi, defendendi, transigendi, componendi et conveniendi debitores suos et iniuriatores, et recipiendi debita, quae sibi debentur, et iurandi in animam suam tam super principali, quam super expensis, et expensas easdem recipiendi, quotienscumque sibi fuerint adiudicatae, et constituendi alium procuratorem loco sui . . . et faciendi omnia, quacumque faceret vel facere possit, si praesens esset in causa. Eidem, tamquam procuratori legitimo plenariam concessit coram nobis potestatem, ratum et firmiter habiturus, quidquid per O. vel eius procuratores . . . fuerit actum et etiam procuratum, et in curiis et extra . . .'"; Wahrmund, I, iii, 25. *Wahrmund wrongly inserts *et*, which should be deleted.

42 Rockinger, *Briefsteller und Formelbücher*, pp. 278f.

43 *Summa totius artis notariae*, I, 214ᵛ-215ᵛ.

44 *Speculum iudiciale*, I, iii, t. *De procuratore*, c. *Ut autem*, no. 11: "Quod autem dixi 'liberam potestatem,' multum prodest: quia aliter non habet ita plenam, ff. de procu., procurator cui, et l. seq. et l. mandato, j. ver. notabiliter." He connects the *libera administratio* in the *Digest* with the *plena potestas* in the *Code*.

appointing a proctor with *specialis, plena, libera et absoluta potestas* to borrow up to 100 marks in the name of the church.[45] Other forms of general mandates give the proctor *plena et libera potestas* of acting before any judge, auditor, judge delegate, or sub-delegate; of petitioning, compromising, transacting, and so on; of acting for a corporation in the papal Curia; of petitioning, suing, responding to suits, making special pleas (exceptions) and answering pleas made by the adversary; of taking oaths, hearing the sentence, and appealing.[46]

Toward the end of the thirteenth century the *Summa notarie* of John of Bologna reflects the same practice in the English church.[47] But *plena potestas* had long since been current in ecclesiastical court procedure in England[48]—and in the common law procedure of the king's courts relating to powers of attorney. The same is true of France.[49]

In both laws the special mandate, for the special proctor, was limited to a particular day[50] or to a particular matter which required the specific consent of the proctor's constituent.[51] The general mandate for the general proctor empowered him to act in a whole suit or in all suits, contracts and business of his *dominus*, but limited that power by making it necessary for the proctor to obtain special mandates for alienating, transact-

---

[45] *Ibid.*, no. 21 (fol. 86ᵛ, c. 1).

[46] *Ibid.*, fol. 86, c. 1, nos. 11 and 16.

[47] Rockinger, *Briefsteller und Formelbücher*, p. 607: a mandate by which the prior and chapter of Christ Church, Canterbury, appoint a proctor and *nuncius* with *plena et libera potestas* of petitioning in the Roman Curia for *litterae simplices* and *legendae*.

[48] For example, a mandate of 1252 issued by St. Albans for proctors, with *plena et libera potestas*, for business in the Roman Curia; Matthew Paris, *Chronica Majora*, VI, *Additamenta*, pp. 219ff.

[49] Bracton, III, 142 (ed. Twyss, R. S., III, 408-410). See also below, §2.

[50] But in the Church, as decided by a papal legate in England, 1237, a proctor must not be appointed for one day only; William of Drogheda, in Wahrmund, *Quellen*, II, ii, 168; Matthew Paris, *Chron. Maj.*, III, 436.

[51] *Summa minorum*, c. L., *De procuratorio*: ". . . aliquando datur procurator ad unum diem vel ad unam rem et talis procurator dicitur [esse] specialis. Aliquando datur procurator in omnibus causis vel in una causa generaliter et tunc dicitur procurator generalis"; Wahrmund, I, ii, 52. The canonists follow the legists on this, e.g., *Glos. ord.* of Accursius to *D.* 3, 3, 49, ad v. *non debet* ("ignorantis domini conditio deterior per procuratorem fieri non debet"): "nisi in tribus casibus: quando scilicet est in rem suam; et quando speciale habet mandatum; et quando generale, sed habet liberam administrationem"— and in no event can a proctor *donare* if by so doing he damages his principal.

ing, petitioning, appealing or doing anything which would damage the *dominus* without his special consent. But if *plena potestas* or *libera administratio*, or both, or their equivalents, were inserted in the general mandate, the proctor could do all special acts as well as represent his principal in general litigation and business without having to get new instructions. If the proctor with full powers still must be loyal to his *dominus*, i.e., act in his real interest without fraud or collusion, nevertheless he had full powers to act as if the *dominus* himself were present. This was real representation without referendum:[52] it gave the representative such power that, under the general and special terms of his mandate or instructions, he could use his own judgment as to how best to act and respond to the acts of any opponents; it also assured him that, although technically he received in his own person the sentence of the court, his *dominus* would be responsible for him, unless he had been fraudulent, and would pay any damages or fines if the suit were lost. More important, by giving full powers to his proctor the principal thereby submitted to the jurisdiction of the court, which could not easily try a case if a litigant did not consent to the acts of his representative. Faster and more effective court action was made possible—in spite of many preliminary delays still granted to the litigants—by the elimination of "reference back" when *plena potestas* took the place of special mandates for many a contingency—agreements before the court but not in the court (e.g., *transactio*), the settlement of a case out of court, or any business that was not judicial yet might be transacted with judges as councillors or administrators. Thus *plena potestas* gave the proctor "sufficient instructions" to act as if the principal himself appeared in court, fought the legal battle and received the sentence of the judges.[53] It expressed the consent of the interested parties both to the representation and to the authority of the court to decide the issue, after judicial process, and pass sentence. Refusal of consent could come only thereafter by way of appeal to a higher court.

[52] Unless a new case or suit was brought against the principal after he had appointed and empowered his proctors for other matters; below, §5.

[53] On instructions and "reference back," see below, §5.

2. *PLENA POTESTAS*, ADMINISTRATIVE AGENTS, AND AMBASSADORS

Not only did the Roman formulas in the mandate serve for representation in courts and in ordinary business transactions, they were also adopted to express the powers both of ambassadors appointed by princes and cities to negotiate truces, treaties and other contractual agreements, and of royal procurators and papal legates as administrators. This practice began early—probably first in Italy, and perhaps under the influence of close relations in the preceding period with Byzantium, when cities sent ambassadors (or consuls and judges) to each other or to kings and emperors and when the kings and popes appointed administrative procurators and legates. The precedent and inspiration derived ultimately both from the Roman proctorial mandate and from those passages on *procuratores Caesaris* in the *Digest* and *Code* in which the legists and decretalists of the thirteenth century found formulas to justify the equivalence of *plena potestas* and *libera et generalis administratio* in general mandates.[54] It is therefore not surprising to find this terminology, along with *plena jurisdictio*, which also had its Roman background,[55] in the mandate of authority that the King of Jerusalem and his *curia* in 1176 wished to confer on Philip, Count of Flanders, as the royal *procurator*. William of Tyre, the royal chancellor and something of an expert himself in Roman and Canon law,[56] relates that the king and *curia* offered the Count *potestatem, et*

[54] See above, §1. The *Digest* furnished these opinions: 1, 19 *De officio procuratoris Caesaris*, 1; 3, 3 *De procuratoribus*, 58 (Paulus: "Procurator, cui generaliter libera administratio rerum commissa est, potest exigere, novare, aliud pro alio permutare"); 15, 1, 7, 1; 17, 1, 60, 4; *Code*, 2, 12, 10. Azo, as cited in the *Glos. ord.* by Accursius, says that the procurator of Caesar has *libera administratio*, to D. 1, 19, 1, 1, ad v. *diligenter*: "Sed nonne bene potest gerere alienando? . . . quia hic habet liberam administrationem . . . unde videtur alienare; sed speciale est, ne in Caesaris praeiudicium alienet, alia[s] contra . . . *Az.*" Azo, again, *Lectura*, to C. 2, 12, 10, ad vv. *convenire eum more iudic.*

[55] D. 1, 16 *De officio proconsulis et legati*, ll. 1, 7, 2, and 13; 1, 21 *De officio eius, cui mandata est iurisdictio*; 2, 1 *De iurisdictione*. The twelfth-century idea of the royal procurator seems to have been taken both from the Roman *procurator Caesaris* and the *jurisdictio* and *imperium* given to a proconsul or a legate, or to any magistrate on whom a *jurisdictio* and *mixtum imperium* were conferred by king or emperor or pope, who had *merum imperium*. The papal legate, who is becoming important at this time, partakes of the nature both of a procurator of Caesar and of an ambassador; below, n. 58.

[56] A. C. Krey, "William of Tyre," *Speculum*, XVI (1941), 151 n. 3.

liberam et generalem administrationem super regnum univer-sum, with *plena jurisdictio* over all, in war and in peace.[57]

By the end of the twelfth century, papal legates and *nuntii*, were somewhat like royal *procuratores* and Roman proconsuls or legates, with *plena potestas, jurisdictio,* and *imperium* conferred upon them by the pope.[58] Certainly the Cardinal-Legate Romano had full administrative and judicial authority when Gregory IX in 1228 gave him *libera ac plena potestas quaecum-que de rebus Albigensibus agendi.*[59] In the middle of the century the papal *nuntii* to England were also given *plena potestas.*[60]

An early and important usage of *plena potestas* is found in the mandates given to *nuntii* or *procuratores* as ambassadors of princes and cities. In Roman law, and also among the glossators of the thirteenth century, any kind of *pactum* or *conventio* was a contract between two or more consenting parties[61] or the agents who represented them.[62] One kind of *conventio* was a public

---

[57] *Recueil des historiens des croisades*, p. 1027, *sub an.* 1176. Philip refused the office, which was then conferred on Raymond of Antioch. *Sub an.* 1104 (p. 450) William relates how Bohemond, prince of Antioch, entrusted Tancred with *cura et administratio generalis, cum plena jurisdictione*; it is possible that William has a document before him for this statement; more likely he was putting back to 1104 a terminology that became fashionable somewhat later. Another example offered by William of Tyre is the appointment, in 1183 (p. 1116), of Guy of Lusignan as *procurator regni* with *generalis et libera administratio.*

But on the other hand, even England offers an early use of the term *procurator regni*: in 1123-1126 Roger of Salisbury, justiciar under Henry I, during the absence of the king styled himself *procurator regni Angliae*; J. E. A. Jolliffe, *Constitutional History of England*, pp. 196f.

[58] In 1195 Pope Coelestine III granted to two legates *plena potestas*, "ut evellant et destruant . . . plantent et edificent . . ."; Jaffe-Loewenfeld, *Regesta pontificum Romanorum*, no. 17274; cf. Ina Friedlaender, *Die päpstlichen Legaten in Deutschland und Italien am Ende des XII. Jahrhunderts (Historische Studien, Heft 177)*, pp. 110f. In the same year, Emperor Henry VI asked the pope to send three cardinals to his presence, *plenariam eis dantes potestatem*, who might thereby act as judges in ecclesiastical suits in place of the pope; *M. G. H., Legum S. IV*, I, 514, no. 364.

[59] *Registres de Grégoire IX*, ed. Auvray, no. 229; cited by K. Ruess, *Die rechtliche Stellung der päpstlichen Legaten bis Bonifaz VIII*, p. 70.

[60] *Annales de Burton*, p. 410, in *Annales Monastici*, ed. H. R. Luard, I.

[61] *D.* 2, 14, 1, 1-4; Accursius, *Glos. ord.*, ad v. *conventionis* (in §3): ". . . nomen *conventio* generale est ad omne pactum, nam omne pactum est conventio, et conventio est genus: et ad omnia pacta pertinet verbum conventionis; nam et in unum conveniunt, qui contrahunt, sicut scholares in scholis." *Conventiones* are "in suo nomine contractus," including special contracts, e.g., *emptio* and *venditio*.

[62] *D.* 2, 14, 2, "vel per nuntium"; or by procurator, *D.* 2, 14, 10-13.

one, treaties of peace, alliances, and truces,[63] which like private contracts could be handled by proctors.[64] In Italy, as early as the middle twelfth century, and frequently thereafter, cities were sending their *nuntii, legati,* or *ambasciatores* to emperor, pope or prince, or to each other; and throughout Europe rulers had long been familiar with ambassadorial procedure in their relations. When such *nuntii* first became, under the influence of the Roman formulas, literally plenipotentiaries cannot be determined. It must have been earlier than 1200,[65] when, as Villehardouin tells us, the crusading barons held a *parlement* at Compiègne and decided to send six ambassadors or *messages* (i.e., *nuntii*) to Venice to negotiate for transportation. These *messages,* including Villehardouin himself, were given *plain povir de faire toutes choses autretant con li seignor.*[66] They carried with them a proctorial mandate containing *plena potestas*; and Villehardouin's story shows that in Venice they acted as *nuntii* and proctors in negotiating a treaty with the Doge. But if they were proctors, they were at the same time plenipotentiaries.[67] Incidentally, they represented not the barons as a whole, but the Counts of Champagne, Flanders and Blois—it was not corporate representation.

[63] *D.* 2, 14, 5: Ulpian, ". . . publica conventio est, quae fit per pacem, quotiens inter se duces belli quaedam pasciscuntur"; *Casus* in *Glos. ord.,* ad 1. 5 *Conventionum*: ". . . [Some *pacta*] sunt publica, ut induciae et foedera, amicitiae, et treugae inter aliquos duos."

[64] Rolandinus Passagerii, *Summa totius artis notariae,* c. VI, *De compromissis,* p. 157: "Item nota quod paces seu concordiae et remissiones aliquando fieri solent per procuratores," who are appointed "specialiter ad hoc," and should be named in the *instrumentum pacis (ca.* 1260).

[65] Perhaps as early as 1162 in France, when Louis VII gave *pleins pouvoirs* to Thibaut of Champagne to negotiate with Frederick I; Luchaire, in Lavisse, III, i, 41.

[66] *Conquête de Constantinople,* ed. Edmond Faral, I, 14ff.; *Recueil des historiens des Gaules et de la France,* ed. Bouquet, XVIII, 434f. For a good account of the embassy see Donald E. Queller, "L'Evolution du rôle de l'ambassadeur: les pleins pouvoirs et le traité de 1201 entre les Croisés et les Vénétiens," in *Le Moyen Age,* No. 4 (1961), 479-501. Professor Queller has also corrected my failure to distinguish sharply enough between *nuntius* and *procurator;* the *nuntius,* he holds, was a more passive agent than the *procurator;* "Thirteenth Century Envoys: *Nuncii* and *Procuratores,*" *Speculum* XXXV (1960), 196-213. But see above, ch. I, nn. 86-89.

[67] The treaty itself refers to the six *messages* as *nuntii,* who took oath for themselves and their *domini* (the barons and counts) that the treaty would be observed; Bouquet, *Recueil,* XVIII, 436.

No doubt, the use of *plena potestas* and proctorial mandates for ambassadors spread from Italy, the seat of the revival of Roman law. It was taken up by the imperial chancery: in a letter to Innocent III, 1208, Philip of Suabia announced the sending of four *nuntii* as ambassadors to the pope, *quibus dedimus plenitudinem potestatis et auctoritatem omnimodam* for establishing peace between the Empire and the Church.[68] More fully Roman was the mandate given by Frederick II in 1244 to Raymond of Toulouse, Petrus de Vinea, and Thaddeus of Suessa for representing him before Innocent IV and the Council of Lyons, but here the plenipotentiaries were more like proctors in litigation before the papal court than ambassadors.[69]

If the papal and imperial chanceries and the barons of Flanders and Champagne were acquainted with the new usage, inevitably the English kings were exposed to it. Besides, as early as 1172 the precedent of courts ecclesiastical had resulted in Henry II's citing to his *curia* the prior and other monks of a convent who were commanded to bring "letters of the convent to the effect that the others who remained at home would regard as valid whatever he and those who came with him might do."[70] Richard I and John sent *fideles nuntii* or *procuratores* as ambassadors to monarchs and popes, but in general gave them mandates that were hardly Roman in character—the king usually asks the recipients of the letters of credentials to believe or to have faith in the bearers.[71] Toward the end of John's reign, however, the mandates began to reflect a specifically Roman influence in the clauses of the *ratihabitio*, by which the king promised to ratify, to hold *ratum* and *gratum* whatever his am-

---

68 *M. G. H., Legum S. IV*, II, 17f., no. 14.

69 Matthew Paris, *Chron. Maj.*, IV, 331: ". . . specialem et plenam concedimus potestatem jurandi in anima pro parte nostra, stare mandatis domini Papae et ecclesiae super omnibus articulis, injuriis, dampnis et offensis . . . ratum habentes et firmum, quicquid super hoc praedicti fideles nostri duxerint faciendum." Also in Huillard-Bréholles, *Historia Diplomatica Friderici II*, VI, 172.

70 A. B. White and W. Notestein, *Source Problems in English History*, p. 89.

71 Rymer, *Foedera*, I, i, 76: King John to the King and Queen of Castille, "mandamus quatinus ea, quae praedicti tres vel duo [of the *nuntii* or *fideles*] illorum dicent ex parte nostra, indubitanter credatis" (*an.* 1199); to Philip Augustus (p. 87, *an.* 1202), "fidem habeatis"; similarly (p. 101, *an.* 1208) to the Irish chiefs; and p. 114, *an.* 1213.

bassadors did[72] in establishing a truce, peace, or any kind of compromise.[73] To Innocent III, in 1215, John sent as *procuratores* his Chancellor, two archbishops, and two magnates, who were given a general mandate with *libera administratio* for all royal suits and business in the Roman Curia.[74] Thus under the influence of the two laws the English royal chancery was already using Roman formulas. But there seems to have been a temporary reaction in the early reign of Henry III, for in the 1220's the king was again sending ambassadors provided simply with *fides*. In 1229, however, if not earlier, there appeared royal writs conferring *potestas ad tractandum de pace*;[75] and in 1230 the king gave *plena potestas* to ambassadors sent to make a truce with Louis IX.[76] Thereafter, *plena potestas* and the *ratihabitio* clause were frequently, though not always, employed for mandates of plenipotentiaries.[77]

For almost every kind of agency or representation, therefore, the Roman formulas were in daily use by the middle of the thirteenth century. *Plena potestas* gave the agent *carte blanche*, within the limits set by the principal's welfare and knowledge of the issue,[78] to conclude the business; and his conclusion of it had the consent of his constituent. This consent, however, was given in the terms of the mandate before the negotiation

[72] *Ibid.*, 114; *an.* 1213, ambassadors to a Poitevin noble; p. 124; *an.* 1214, eight ambassadors to the King of France: "Sciatis quod id, quod . . . facient de firmis treugis capiendis inter Regem Franciae & nos, ratum et gratum habebimus." On *ratihabitio* see D. 46, 8; cf. Buckland, *Roman Law*, p. 712.

[73] Rymer, *Foedera*, I, i, 128: *an.* 1215, the royal *procuratores* are appointed "ad petenda . . . dampna . . . Et ad restitutionem faciendam . . .; et ad pacificandum, componendum, transigendum . . . Ratum etiam et gratum habebimus quicquid, etc."

[74] *Ibid.*, 139; the *ratum habituri et gratum* clause, where the royal proctors were the plaintiffs, and the *judicatum solvi* clause, where they were the defendants, were added. Here the proctors are not only ambassadors, but also representatives for litigation.

[75] *Ibid.*, 195.

[76] *Ibid.*, 198: "Rex omnibus, etc., salutem. Sciatis quod in omnibus, quae ad treugam pertinent, plenam potestatem dedimus" to five magnates, "ad loquendum et tractandum de treugis cum Ludovico Rege Franciae . . .; ita quod treugas, quas ipsi cum dicto Rege ceperint, gratas et ratas sumus habituri."

[77] *Ibid.*, 244f., 247, 253, 256, 264, 295, 299, etc. See also Matthew Paris, *Chron. Maj.*, VI, *Additamenta*, p. 284, no. 140 (*an.* 1254). On English ambassadors and their credentials in the fourteenth century, see H. S. Lucas, "The Machinery of Diplomatic Intercourse," in Morris, *English Government*, I, 309.

[78] See below on instructions, §5.

started.[79] If the affair was between equals (e.g., kings) or between autonomous communes and princes, the agents were ambassadors. But if it was between ruler and subjects or subject communities, the agents of the latter were clearly not ambassadors in the modern sense but proctors, representing their constituents before a superior authority. Consent to the negotiation (whether it was judicial, legislative, administrative, or merely consultative) was in the latter case quite different in quality from the consent of equals to a contract or treaty, although the procedure was strikingly similar. This distinction (overlooked by G. de Lagarde, who says that representatives in assemblies were "only ambassadors" of the different estates of the kingdom)[80] must be held in mind when we deal with the powers of proctorial representatives in Cortes, States General, and Parliament in relation to the *imperium* and prerogative of the prince who summoned them.

3. The Beginnings of *Plena Potestas* in Representative Assemblies

Long before Henry III summoned delegates with full powers to Parliament in 1268, the precedent for his writ was created not only in Romano-canonical court and ambassadorial procedure, but also in the convocation of imperial and papal assemblies in Italy. Delegates (consuls and judges) of Lombard communes had attended the Diet of Roncaglia in 1158;[81] but what their powers were is not clear, except that they were subservient to Frederick Barbarossa. Our formula emerges clearly in 1200: Pope Innocent III summoned to his Curia *responsales*

---

[79] Unless the *dominus* by another mandate dispatched in time and revealed to the opposing party and judges and accepted by them recalled his agent before the final decision was given.

[80] G. de Lagarde, "L'idée de représentaticn dans les oeuvres de Guillaume d'Ockham," in *Histoire des assemblées d'états (Bulletin of the International Committee of Historical Sciences*, IX, iv, no. 37), p. 435; but it is still possible to agree on the whole with Lagarde that in these assemblies of the fourteenth century on the Continent, not the collective person of the nation but the little cellular powers defended their interests against the royal authority. But in England the common petition (also in Aragon) indicates a unity of purpose. In any case, by the principles of public law the State, symbolized by king and crown, was the essential unity.

[81] Post, "Early Representation in Spain and Italy," *Speculum*, XVIII, 226-228; see above, ch. II, to nn. 86-101.

or *procuratores* from six cities; they must have *plenaria potestas* to meet with the pope, to consult (*tractare*), to bring *consilium* on the establishment of law and order in the Papal States, to render the services of *expeditionem, parlamentum, pacem et guerram*, and to accept the papal will in these matters and in the paying of an annual *census*.[82] These proctors, in a feudal *curia* or assembly, obviously came provided with full powers to submit to the pope's orders, not to refuse obedience and limit the papal authority. It is probable that, from 1215 on, proctors sent by cathedral chapters to general and provincial councils and by secular communities to the assemblies of Frederick II or to the Cortes of Aragon and Castille, often had "full powers" or the equivalent.[83] But since the mandates themselves have rarely survived from the first half of the thirteenth century, very few instances of the actual use of *plena potestas*, until the latter half of the century, can be given. Yet *plena potestas* must have enjoyed some popularity because of its legal importance. When the *generalissimum* Chapter of the Dominican Order met at Paris in 1228, it was attended by twelve provincial priors, each of whom was accompanied by two *diffinitores* as "deputies" of the provincial chapter, which had conferred *potestas plenaria* on them.[84] These provincial priors and *diffinitores*, however, were more than ordinary representatives; although they were elected, by the election they became administrators and judges, and as such, in the meeting of the General Chapter they constituted a high council and court rather than a representative assembly.[85]

But other representatives in ecclesiastical assemblies, such as proctors of cathedral chapters and of dioceses, and *socii* elected by the convents to attend provincial chapters of the Dominicans, had the powers of ordinary proctors for litigating, negotiating, petitioning, carrying the record and information, and

[82] A. Theiner, *Codex Diplomaticus Dominii Temporalis Sanctae Sedis*, I, nos. XLII and XLIII.

[83] Post, *Speculum*, XVIII, 229-231; above, ch. II, to nn. 102-111. Innocent III summoned proctors of chapters to the Fourth Lateran Council, 1215.

[84] H. Denifle, "Die Constitutionen des Predigerordens vom Jahre 1228," *Archiv für Literatur- und Kirchengeschichte des Mittelalters*, I (1885), 193; G. R. Galbraith, *The Constitution of the Dominican Order, 1216-1360*, pp. 37, 39.

[85] But see A. G. Little, "The Mendicant Orders," in *C.M.H.*, VI, 740; Galbraith, *loc.cit.*

accepting the decisions of bishops or of priors and *diffinitores*. These powers at first were not usually stated as *plena potestas*; but they were practically the same as the general and special mandates given by communities with the usual clause of *ratihabitio* along with the instructions.

After the middle of the thirteenth century the use of *plena potestas* was frequent. By 1300, it was normal to use it in sending representatives to assemblies, whether provincial councils, chapters of the religious (monks and friars), general councils, or high courts and councils of princes (to the English Parliament by 1268,[86] or possibly earlier;[87] to the Cortes of Aragon by 1307, and probably much earlier;[88] and to the French States General in 1302 and thereafter.[89]

4. *PLENA POTESTAS* AND THE PREROGATIVE

Plena potestas in ordinary judicial procedure signified the litigants' full acceptance of, or consent to, the court's decision of the case. However slow this procedure was because of the numerous excuses and delays granted to the litigants, the theory of judicial consent recognized the superior jurisdiction of the court. But, of course, the power, or *imperium*, of the court depended not only on legal definitions but also on the actual power of the government which claimed the right to enforce the law of the land. Thus in a well-centralized State, under a

---

[86] See the examples from 1268 on, given by Edwards, "The *Plena Potestas*," *Oxford Essays*, pp. 142ff.; G. O. Sayles, "Representation of Cities and Boroughs in 1268," *E.H.R.*, XL (1925), 580f.; Clarke, *Medieval Representation and Consent*, pp. 200, 312-314, 374; Stubbs, *S.C.*, pp. 403, 406f., 458, 476f., 480ff.; *Parliamentary Writs*, I, 21, 23, 25f.

[87] Clarke, *op.cit.*, p. 308, says that *nuncii* of the dioceses had full powers for an assembly in England, 1254; cf. Stubbs, *S.C.*, pp. 406f., for an example in 1265.

[88] *Cortes de los antiguos Reinos de Aragon y de Valencia*, I, i, 194ff.; *plena potestas* is not specified, but its equivalent is given—the delegates of Barcelona shall do all those things which their constituents could do if they were present. This is the earliest surviving mandate that I have found for representation in Spain. But *poderes* were no doubt given to representatives in Castile and in Aragon in the thirteenth century. In 1301 the king of Aragon asked the cities to send delegates with *plena et libera potestas* (*Cortes*, I, i, 183); or with *pleno posse* (an. 1311; p. 207).

[89] See, for examples, Picot, *Documents relatifs aux états généraux*, pp. 2, 27, 164, 170, 497; above all, see the important article by C. H. Taylor, "An Assembly of French Towns in March, 1318," *Speculum*, XIII (1938), 296, 299f.; and McIlwain, *C.M.H.*, VII, 686ff.

strong monarch, the royal courts had sufficient jurisdiction to enforce legal procedure, to summon accused parties, to enforce consent by inflicting penalties for contumacy or default, to interpret the powers given the agents of parties, to pass sentence, and to grant or refuse the right of appeal. These rights of jurisdiction were limited by the slowness of the procedure which was developed to guarantee due process as a protection of all private rights brought into litigation. Nevertheless, if private rights were protected by the principles of law and justice and by the theory that every legal right was accompanied by the right of consent to any change affecting it, the courts enjoyed the superior right of interpreting the legality of private rights and the quality of private consent. Judicial, procedural consent, that is consent to the decision of the court, was obviously not voluntary—it was no limitation of the *imperium* of the king and his judges. The king's judicial power in this respect was limited not by the *plena potestas* of representatives in his courts but by the law of the land according to which he must judge.[90]

Did *plena potestas*, however, mean the same kind of consent in a royal assembly? The procedure by which representatives were summoned and by which they brought powers from corporate communities, defended the "liberties" of their constituencies, and accepted the will of king and council was quite analogous to that of litigation in courts ordinary. But the assembly was no ordinary court: the king was the highest judge and administrator in the land; he presided over the assembly in the fullness of his prerogative; and the essential core of the assembly was the king's high court and council before which magnates and delegates appeared in assembly. More important, representatives were not summoned to the assembly as litigant parties in the ordinary sense; they were summoned primarily to consent to an extraordinary demand by the king for a subsidy.[91] Thus, even if the royal assembly be looked upon as a high court, analogy

[90] For the full treatment of the substance of this section see chs. v-viii. It is still useful to present this "summary" (actually it anticipated my later development of the subject) because of the close connection between prerogative and *plena potestas* and consent.

[91] But they could also bring petitions at the same time, or pursue appeals from lower courts.

alone will not explain the *plena potestas* of representatives; for the whole institution of national representation was extraordinary, even though it developed logically out of ordinary Romano-canonical court procedure as adapted to the feudal *curia* as high court, council, and assembly. Judicial procedure, therefore, is by itself insufficient to explain the formula. Any conclusive interpretation must depend on a careful estimate of the royal prerogative in the face of individual and community rights recognized by law and custom.

When the king of England, for example, needed an extraordinary subsidy, feudal law demanded that he obtain the consent of all whose rights and liberties were affected, and this consent was voluntary—witness Magna Carta, c. 12 and 14. But in the thirteenth century, under the influence particularly of Roman law, the legal experts of popes and kings were beginning to assert the doctrine that an emergency, the case of necessity, which was usually the just war of defense against an invader, touched both king and kingdom, the *status regis et regni*, the rights and welfare of the people—and not only the rights of tenants-in-chief, but also the relatively new rights of lesser free men in the communities of shires and towns,[92] which were not, strictly speaking, a part of the feudal system, but which by the very attainment of a jurisdictional status and of certain liberties granted by the king were now directly touched by the national emergency. Therefore, partly under the influence of the principle that what touches all must be approved by all, it was becoming necessary for both feudal magnates, who no longer fully represented others' specific rights except in certain feudal customs, and knights and townsmen to consent to measures which must inevitably cause some sacrifice of all liberties guaranteed by custom and law. To meet the emergency or danger, the king, who represented the kingdom, must for the common utility and public safety raise an adequate army. For this he needed more

---

[92] Serfs were not recognized as having such rights as had to be represented—except in so far as their masters represented them; as Helen M. Cam has said, the shire represented by knights was the community of all men under peers and above serfs, "L'assiette et la perception des indemnités des représentants des comtés dans l'Angleterre médiévale," *Revue historique de droit français et étranger*, 4ᵉ sér., XVIII (1939), 219ff.

money than feudal custom gave him, and consequently, for the common good he had a superior right to ask his subjects for an aid. Indeed, his prerogative "meant that reserve of undefined power necessary to any government to enable it to deal with emergencies"[93] which affected the *status* of the king and the whole community of the realm. It was the king's right to deal with the emergency: for the common good he claimed a superior jurisdiction in order to suppress disturbers of the peace within the kingdom,[94] made a new law for a new situation with the counsel and consent of his council, and of all whom the matter touched.[95] Similarly, with the common counsel and consent of all, he levied an extraordinary subsidy for the defense of all who had rights (that is, the king and the whole community of individuals and communities) in the case of necessity—which was usually a war.[96] Much of this theory, which already in the thirteenth century reflected a dawning conception of public

[93] Chrimes, *English Constitutional Ideas in the Fifteenth Century*, pp. 14-16, 38-43. What Chrimes says applies to the thirteenth as much as to the fifteenth century; see the following notes. In general, on the prerogative, see Lagarde, *Naissance de l'esprit laïque*, 1st ed., I, 140-161ff.; W. A. Morris, in Morris, *English Government*, I, 4-12. The prerogative as the *status regis* is treated below, ch. VIII.

[94] I do not mean that he was absolute in jurisdiction; as McIlwain says, in this sphere the king was limited by the law; *Constitutionalism Ancient and Modern*, pp. 79ff. But Edward I's judges gave the king's right superiority over the private rights of the Lords Marchers, for their quarrels and lawlessness endangered the public safety and utility: "Dominus Rex, pro communi utilitate, per prerogativam suam in multis casibus est supra leges et consuetudines in regno suo usitatas"; *Rotuli Parliamentorum*, I, 71; Joliffe, *Constitutional History of England*, p. 305. On Bracton's theory of royal jurisdiction and administration, see McIlwain, pp. 72ff.

[95] See G. Barraclough, "Law and Legislation in Medieval England," *L.Q.R.*, LVI (1940), 79—with emphasis on Hengham's famous words, "Ne glosez point le statut: nous [the royal justices] le savons mieuz de vous, quar nous le feimes." Also, in general, Morris, *English Government*, I, 4-12; and below, ch. XI, § 5.

[96] Carl Stephenson attached no importance to the "case of necessity"—in relation to the right of the king to meet a national danger for the common good; "Les 'aides' des villes françaises," *Le Moyen Age*, 2ᵉ sér., XXIV (1922), 308ff., 315f., 322-328. Against Stephenson I am compelled to support French scholars like A. Coville, *Les états de Normandie*, pp. 6, 32ff., 38f., 49-54, and C. V. Langlois, in Lavisse, III, ii, 250f. Unfortunately they, too, miss the connections between consent (*quod omnes tangit*), necessity, utility, and the royal prerogative. McIlwain, *C.M.H.*, VII, 685f., 691, is in fundamental agreement with Coville and Langlois, but stresses the obligation of responding to the royal summons. But the right to be summoned was also important—at least in the sense indicated in the following paragraph. For necessity and "reason of State," see below, ch. V.

right and state sovereignty as a means of defeating private or feudal rights, was derived from the Roman law.[97]

When a state of emergency existed (and it was the king and his council who had the right to declare the case of necessity, although they still must persuade the assembly that there was no pretext in the declaration),[98] the king, by his general prerogative as well as by his more specific powers of administration and jurisdiction, had the right to demand aid in order to meet the danger which touched the welfare of all—*status regis* and *status regni*. He therefore had the right to summon all to grant him the resources for defending *l'estat du roialme*.[99] If by the

[97] Ulpian, *D.* 1, 4, 2; cf. also *D.* 1, 3, 8; 1, 3, 40; 10, 16, 10; and *Inst.* 1, 1, 4. But the same theory of public utility, or the common good, is to be found in Aristotle and Cicero, and in medieval writers from St. Augustine to Thomas Aquinas, Dante, Marsiglio, and Ockham. The Roman jurisconsults added the case of "evident utility" or necessity and emergency to justify new imperial laws that might be contrary to custom and the prevailing law; cf. *D.* 1, 3, 32 and 37.

[98] This persuasion was usually in the form of the speech delivered by the king or his delegate before the assembly. In a sense the royal government had to prove its case in the assembly. Although as early as the first half of the thirteenth century the English magnates and prelates were able to refuse a subsidy to Henry III because they successfully argued that there was insufficient evidence for Henry's claim that Louis IX was about to break a truce and thus create a case of necessity, generally the king had little difficulty in proving that the enemy was the aggressor, ready to attack the kingdom. The advantage was normally on the side of the royal authority, which already could control the news and shape it for ears ready to believe that the foreigner was wicked. Thus, both Edward I and Philip IV in 1294-1295 justified the case of necessity by shouting aggression at each other—and both got their subsidies. The Church had long since accepted it as legal for a king to demand subsidies of the clergy, provided that the pope was first consulted, for the defense of the kingdom in a just war (*Decr.* 3, 49, 7). Boniface VIII discovered that the pope had no real power of consent when two national monarchies, both Christian, were determined to tax the clergy for their wars, just or unjust. See below, nn. 189-191.

[99] It is possible that the Statute of York, 1322, embodies both the idea of the case of necessity which touches the estate of the king and of the Realm, and the corresponding principle of *quod omnes tangit* in the consent of the community of the Realm to measures taken by the king to meet the emergency and defend the rights of the crown as well as of the community. The famous clause, "Mes les choses qui seront a establir, pour lestat de notre Seigneur le Roi, et de ses Heirs, et pour lestat du Roialme et du Poeple, soient tretes, accordees, establies, en parlementz, par notre Seigneur le Roi et par lassent des Prelatz, Countes, et Barouns, et la communalte du roialme; auxint come ad este acustume cea en arere" (*Statutes of the Realm*, I, 189) is no innovation; it confirms custom, as stated; and it means that when either a danger such as war, internal or external, or a new situation arises which is common to all and touches all, then all must consent to the measures taken, whether such measures be a new subsidy or a new law (statute). Therefore, the king must summon the whole

law the community had the right to be summoned (the king could do nothing of a really extraordinary nature without consulting the interested parties), nonetheless the right and power of summoning in these circumstances were greater than the privilege of being summoned.[100] The king's ordinary jurisdiction and administrative authority lay in the background; but his prerogative enhanced his power to summon and to punish for contumacy. He must summon, but those summoned must respond or suffer by default.

Perhaps, then, the analogy is not so farfetched as one might suppose: even in public matters that were not of the nature of private affairs tried in court, the assembly of the whole community met before (*coram* is the usual word) the king and his council; rather, it met before the king in his court in his council.[101] The king presided over the assembly, not as a mere presi-

---

community to give counsel and consent; and a part of the community was the representatives of boroughs and shires, or the commons. This did not mean that the commons enjoyed a sovereign right of consent; they simply had, as before, the right to hear the case of the government and to negotiate on the amount of the subsidy—but they could not legally refuse the subsidy if the king proved that it was a case of necessity and that the public safety and good were endangered. The advantage was usually on the side of the prerogative. As for a new law, the commons had, it seems, the right to bring such information about local conditions as would help the king and his council to formulate the statute; but the commons had no power to consent to legislation in the modern sense—they could only present petitions asking for a law or complaining against a law that might injure local custom and liberties. However, it may well be that it was not yet considered that law-making touched the commons; consequently, only the king, council, and magnates may have been involved. But certainly a "national emergency" which called for a national tax did touch the whole community and thus the commons within the community; and in taxation, therefore, their consent was legally necessary. But, to repeat, their consent to a subsidy was still not sovereign; the king's right was superior to individual rights in an evident case of necessity.

But these remarks are tentative; I hope to develop them in the near future and to apply the principles outlined above to the interpretations of the Statute by G. Lapsley, G. L. Haskins, J. R. Strayer, and W. A. Morris. (See now below, chs. VI and VIII, where I now hold that possibly the commons did consent to a new law that directly touched their interests.)

100 It was not merely the expense that discouraged willingness to attend the assembly; it was also the desire to delay consent to what the king would surely demand. Of course, communities might insist on the right of sending representatives in order to press their own private interests, in the form of petitions and appeals.

101 It has long been held that Parliament was largely judicial and conciliar in character and in procedure—by Maitland and McIlwain; and recently by Morris,

dent or chairman but as the highest administrator, judge, and legislator representing the public good. He and his council, before summoning representatives, decided that an emergency existed and that the whole community should help meet the danger common to all. The representatives were needed by the government to report how much their constituents could give by way of a subsidy; their constituents were interested in appointing representatives in order that their rights might be protected and that they might protest against a too burdensome tax. When it was almost a foregone conclusion that they would have to grant a subsidy, the communities might want to delay or to refuse to send delegates. But in an emergency the royal government needed the money at once and could tolerate neither delay nor refusal. Having a superior right to demand a subsidy, the king, following ordinary judicial procedure, demanded that the communities give their representatives *plena potestas*, that is, such full powers that quick action and legal consent would result. *Plena potestas*, therefore, was to an assembly what it was to a court: it was in theory an expression of consent, given before the action, to the decision of the court and council of the king. The case of necessity was, as it were, tried in the assembly, and the representatives were, in a sense, attorneys protecting the rights and interests of the communities against the royal claim of public utility and binding the communities by their consent to the decision.

In another sense the king, too, was a defendant—insofar as he had to prove the case of necessity and his honest intent to act for the public and common welfare. Yet he was no more a defendant than a modern State which, while granting a hearing to all whose property rights are touched, compels men to sell land for a public highway or an artificial lake—the right of emi-

---

"Introduction," *English Government*, I, 4ff., 11f., 13ff.; and T. F. T. Plucknett, "Parliament," *ibid.*, pp. 82-89, 112ff. Morris and Plucknett emphasize the conciliar nature of Parliament but also maintain the importance of the king's *imperium* in his presidency over the assembly. H. G. Richardson and G. O. Sayles, "The Origins of Parliament," *Transactions of the Royal Historical Society*, XI (1929), 137-183, perhaps overstress the judicial nature of Parliament; see now their *Parliaments and Councils in Medieval England*; cf. below, n. 207.

nent domain for the public good is superior to private rights.[102] And, as said above, it was relatively easy for the king and his government to make good their case. Nevertheless, the representatives could defend local and private interests by presenting petitions containing grievances, by negotiating on the amount of the subsidy demanded, by arguing against the need of a subsidy, and by trying to obtain promises of no-precedent. In turn, the king and council had the power to hear and to grant or deny the petitions, although generally promises were made to remedy the grievances presented. After such hearings and minor decisions, the king's court and council announced the decision as to the amount of the subsidy, and the assembly formally consented to the will of the government—unless, as it rarely happened, the king had been forced to withdraw his demand because of being unable to prove that a "national" emergency, such as the danger of invasion, really existed. Consent even to taxation was therefore consultative and judicial, not voluntary and democratic. Only when Parliament ceased to be a council and court, in effect, and when the king was deprived of the practical right to refuse a common petition, could *plena potestas* signify in England popular sovereignty.[103]

[102] But just as in the United States the public right of eminent domain involves the taking of private property, while taxation (also for the public utility) does not, so in the thirteenth century the power of taxing did not mean taking real property.

[103] The formulas used in the mandates along with *plena potestas* reinforce this conclusion; generally, the powers are given to the representatives to consent to what is ordained by the king and his council. In 1294 the knights are to have the power "obligandi comitatum et faciendi quod per consilium domini regis ordinaretur"; Edwards, "The *Plena Potestas*," *Oxford Essays*, p. 145, quoting Bartholomew Cotton. In 1282 Edward I's writ of summons had specified that the representatives of counties and towns should have power "ad audiendum et faciendum ea quae sibi ex parte nostra faciemus ostendi" (Stubbs, *S.C.*, p. 458); in 1290, knights from the shire shall have full powers "ad consulendum et consentiendum . . . hiis quae comites, barones et proceres praedicti tunc duxerint concordanda," and the same in 1294 (*S.C.*, pp. 472f., 476f.; the knights are to hear and do "quod eis tunc ibidem plenius injungemus," p. 477). For the famous Parliament of 1295 Edward emphasized full powers as essential in order to prevent delays—i.e., no *limited* mandates are to be given representatives by communities; when the king orders that the representatives have *plena et sufficiens potestas* to do "quod tunc de communi consilio ordinabitur," there can be little doubt that "common counsel" involves no real participation of the commons in the government, or in the king's Council (cf. Plucknett, *op.cit.*, p.

The principal kingdoms of Spain in the late thirteenth and fourteenth centuries present a complicated picture of representation in relation to the royal authority. In Castile the nobility were usually too powerful for the king to assert his authority, and the cities sometimes acted as if they were independent. The powers of consent enjoyed by the representatives of the third estate must therefore be interpreted against the background of weak kings and anarchic conditions. Nevertheless the *theory* of the royal prerogative was much the same as in England or France. The *Siete Partidas*, II, i, 8, states that the king could demand and take more than was customary when it was necessary for the common welfare of the country.[104] The king had the duty and the right to summon the towns to send representatives with *poderes*; but, at least when he was strong enough to assert his prerogative, he also had the right to interpret the *poderes* and therewith command consent.[105] In Aragon and Catalonia the same legal theory of the prerogative, the necessity of the State, and consent to taxation prevailed.[106] As in Castile, but

---

101, for the like conclusion for the years 1327-1336). As Plucknett says (pp. 101f.), "Probably all that was required of them [i.e., the representatives] was authority to do and to consent to whatever might be ordained; . . . the magnates were summoned to treat and give counsel; the commons, however, were not called to give advice, nor to treat and reach decisions." But in the sense of giving information, defending local interests, and negotiating, the commons did give advice and they did "treat"—*tractare* often means the defense of legal rights in court. See also Jolliffe, *Constitutional History of England*, p. 351.

Finally, the use of the Romano-canonical equivalent of *plena potestas* should be noted: powers to do "quae vos ipsi [i.e., the constituents] facere possetis si praesentes ibidem essetis" (*an.* 1265; Stubbs, *S.C.*, pp. 406f.).

104 One fourteenth-century commentator declares that the king can impose an aid "pro communi terrae utilitate etiam non vocatis subditis"; but no doubt the king, in practice, could obtain no subsidy without summoning representatives of the towns and the nobles; as Lucas de Penna says, "quod honestum et necessarium esset eos, quos hoc negotium tangit, ad rei examinationem evocari, ut ex consensu omnium fiat, et sic videmus etiam in Regibus de consuetudine fieri"; *Siete Partidas*, II, i, 8, ad v. *Venga.* See Merriman, *Spanish Empire*, I, 225, on a *servicio* above the customary amount.

105 Merriman, *op.cit.*, 221-223. If the king had the right to interpret the *poderes*, they were not, as Merriman maintains, "one of the most important safeguards of Castilian parliamentary liberty" (p. 223). A thorough study of the question is needed for Spain.

106 See the interesting form letters published by M. Usón y Sesé, "Un formulario latino de la cancilleria real aragonesa (siglo XIV)," *Anuario de Historia del Derecho Espanol*, VI (1929), 402f.; c. CIV, *Super subsidio postulando ratione guerre*; c. CV—because of an invasion, which concerns the honor and glory of

more effectively, the Cortes of the fourteenth century through its *Diputacion* "watched over the observance of the laws," limited the king's right to interpret necessity and public utility, and audited the royal accounts in order to be sure that a subsidy granted was actually spent for the public good.[107] In such circumstances the *plena potestas* was still no limitation of the royal power when it was honestly carried out according to law and custom; for in a real case of necessity, and in the interest of the public safety, the king still had the right to demand that the nobles and cities consent to a subsidy, though he did not always have the power to enforce consent.

What has been said about the system in Aragon and Catalonia may be illustrated by a few examples of the use of *plena potestas*. In 1301 James II ordered cathedral chapters and cities to send proctors having *plenam . . . et liberam potestatem tractandi consenciendi faciendi et firmandi ea omnia et singula que in dicta curia fuerint ordinata*.[108] In 1305-1307 the *consejo* of Barcelona elected proctors or syndics to represent the city before *(coram)* the king, and in the mandates the *consejo* gave the representatives full powers (i.e., promised to ratify whatever they did, "just as if the counsellors and *jurati* were themselves present"). But in this case, the powers are specified in illuminating fashion. As related in the mandate of 1305, the king had summoned the usual prelates, magnates and syndics to a *Curia Generalis* at Barcelona; there the assembly presented to the king *plura capitula* which he refused to accept. Another *colloquium* or assembly was held on these *capitula* in the same year at Montalban, and a Cortes was convoked to discuss the same *capitula* at Barcelona in 1307. The mandate given to its representatives for this Cortes by the city of Barcelona empowered them to renounce adherence to the said chapters presented to the king by the earlier Cortes; but they should defend insofar

---

the royal crown and of all faithful subjects, the king asks a city to support "causam nostram, que vos principaliter velut caput nostre celsitudinis tangere noscitur . . . nobis in tante necessitatis articulo quod nos et vos deceat faciatis subsidium. . . ."

107 For Castile, Merriman, *op.cit.*, 225. For Aragon, Merriman, *op.cit.*, 460f., 483; McIlwain, *C.M.H.*, VII, 699, 703.

108 *Cortes . . . de Aragon*, I, i, 183.

as possible, all corporate and individual "privileges, immunities, liberties, usages, customs, statutes, and special favors" (*gratiae*, dispensations); and they should do everything that the city councillors and *jurati* could do if they themselves were present (i.e., they should have *plena potestas*); all these acts, the *consejo* promised, would be ratified and "never revoked."[109] Following the mandate is a record of what the representatives did—they followed the instructions given in the mandate— and of the consent of the king made at Huesca in the form of a contract signed by the king, the representatives, and the witnesses.

All the above shows that the procedure was judicial and conciliar, with the king recognized as having the right to grant or refuse a petition. But essentially it is an expression of the medieval theory of the king's ruling according to law and the rights of privileged individuals and corporations, which, according to the Roman principle of consent (*quod omnes tangit*), sent representatives to defend their legal rights by petition in the king's court and council. A series of mandates for the Cortes of Gerona and Barcelona in 1358 shows that the powers given the city representatives reflect the same consensual participation of the third estate before the king's court and council, and that *plena potestas* implied initiative and capacity of judgment on the part of the representatives only for debating a common defense of liberties before the king.[110] Thus, in Aragon the judicial char-

---

109 *Ibid.*, 195f.

110 *Ibid.*, 576ff. Barcelona issued a mandate conferring full powers on its representatives for acting with others on the contents of the royal summons; the city ratified whatever should be done by all the representatives (syndics) or by the *maior pars* of them. Lerida (pp. 578ff.): two proctors (for the *negocia* of the king) to be present in the *curia*, "ad tractandum et ordinandum" with the prelates, chapters, magnates, knights, and other city representatives, "et ad concedendum firmandum laudandum approbandum consenciendum et ratificandum" all that the members of the assembly shall approve and ratify; "ad contradicendum requirendum et protestandum in animas dictorum constituencium nomine universitatis predicte quelibet juramenta necessaria vel opportuna fieri ad predicta"; and to do whatever seems expedient to the said syndics and proctors, even if a special mandate is required. Gerona (p. 581): its proctors have power to consent to the "tractatibus et ordinacionibus" in the Cortes, and even "ad dissenciendum . . . si eisdem . . . videbitur faciendum, et ad protestandum dicte curie seu in dicta curia" if expedient; and to present *capitula* and *supplicaciones* (petitions). The *villa* of Cervaria (p. 586), after giving its syndics the normal powers for Cortes, also gave them "meram liberam ac

acter of the assembly was retained even though the cities may have obtained a more effective right of consent than in Castile, or in France and England. The royal prerogative remained important, and *plena potestas* continued to mean something less than sovereignty vested in the Cortes. In reality the practical

---

generalem administrationem cum plenissima facultate" and to each syndic these powers *in solidum*. The *universitas* of Villafranca (p. 588): powers to give *consilium* and *juvamen* to the king, to treat and consent, also "ad excusandum et defendum, reverencia Regis semper salva, dictam universitatem ab eisdem que in dicta littera [the king's summons] continentur," and "ad petendum requirendum et supplicandum" (*plena et libera potestas*, and *libera et generalis administracio*). Puigcerda (p. 590): powers for doing all things "eciam si talia sint que de sui natura mandatum exhigant speciale ac maiora graviora et duriora que in presenti sindicatus instrumento contineantur vel sint nominatim expressata."

For the Cortes of Barcelona (1358) mandates detailed powers more abundantly still, and some show more clearly a strong influence of the judicial procedure, as if the proctors appear to join their colleagues in defending their rights in the king's court. The town of *Regalis* (pp. 611ff.), by the authority of the lieutenant of the royal *baiulus*, gave its proctors (12 of them) powers to appear "coram . . . Rege seu eius procuratore" or any royal deputies for any matters and discussions "tam in subveniendo et concedendo similia que per alias universitates tocius Cathalonie . . . Regi fuerint concessa, quam eciam in tractando utilitatem publicam ad reformacionem boni status" of the kingdom; for rendering fealty to the king; for renouncing the privilege of its own *forum* and of its immunity, for submitting the *universitas* and its members and their *bona* to courts whether of judges ordinary or delegate, and for appearing in such courts; for declaring and promising to pay anything contracted; for receiving warnings, requisitions, and sentences of execution and condemnation from any judge against the town, for renouncing all dispensations and privileges, and full powers for all lawsuits (excepting, replying, etc.).

Another town (*locus*, pp. 616ff.) gives powers to wage any kind of suit with any other corporations or persons in the royal *curia*, before the king or his procurator, or in any lower courts; to present complaints against royal officers; to present appeals, petitions, etc.; to renounce the right to ask for royal dispensation from the payment of the "violariorum seu censualium mortuorum" requested by the king; to grant to the king all that is granted by other towns and cities, as requested by the king, and "(ad) assecurandum illas peccunie quantitates que ad nos et ad dictam universitatem tangeant pertineant et expectent seu ad nostram partem perveniant, si casus erit quod per ipsum dominum Regem aut aliquem loco sui petantur demandentur seu exigantur illi vel illis cui vel quibus per ipsum dominum Regem vel eius venerabiles Consiliarios ordinabuntur vel mandabuntur. . . . Et ad obligandum nos et bona nostra et dicte universitatis et singularium" for any sums of money that "profentur, dentur seu promittentur" to the king for any cause or reason; "Et ad interessendum eciam in curiis generalibus domini Regis et parlamentis et consiliis generalibus vel specialibus quibuscunque et ubicunque teneantur seu per . . . Regem mandentur, et ibi per vos et per dictam universitatem concedendum atorgandum promitendum consenciendum et assenciendum omnia et singula et similia que per alios sindicos nuncios et procuratores civitatum villarum et locorum regalium Cathalonie concedantur promitantur et consenciantur de

value of *plena potestas* depended on the actual power of the third estate in alliance with the nobles.[111]

In France, in the time of Philip the Fair, the royal prerogative was even more clearly expressed in the king's power to summon to the States General and to specify the kind of powers (*plena potestas* or "sufficient instructions")[112] which he wanted the communities to give to their representatives. In 1302 Philip ordered representatives of towns and chapters to bring *plena et expressa potestas*, or *plenum et sufficiente mandatum*, of hearing, accepting, doing and consenting to what he would ordain.[113] Other examples of mandates from 1303 and later give such formulas as *plena, generalis, et libera potestas*,[114] *plena et libera*

---

quibuscunque negociis ibi tractetur seu ordinetur, et firmandum et laudandum ea omnia et singula . . . que in comodum veniant ad . . . Regem et ad totum Regnum suum, et prout per ipsum dominum Regem mandetur ordinetur seu alias voluntati sue videbitur expedire." Further, powers are given to do and ordain everything pertaining to the aforesaid "ubique in judicio et extra judicium" that true proctors can do. If any unmentioned points come up, the proctors have the power for these things understood.

These points should be emphasized. The royal *civitas* seems to have greater weight in the Cortes than the *villa* or *locus*, which appoints its proctors under the authority of royal officials for Cortes and for all royal courts, while cooperating in the common consent of all the representatives to the king's decisions. The right of consent is asserted, but it is still judicial, not political, consent to what the king and his council decide after giving all interested parties a hearing and a chance to defend their interests. Finally, it will be noted that the mandates all express full powers in varying fashion, but in such fashion generally that there is no "reference back" or referendum. If the proctors of Gerona can dissent, it is by petition in the court that they do so.

111 On the actual powers of the representatives when the king's authority was weak, see Merriman, *Spanish Empire*, I, 432-450, 460-462. The king's prerogative was not so much involved in struggles between king and Cortes as the question of forcing the king to rule according to law and in observance of individual rights. Thus, I do not believe that representation even in fourteenth-century Aragon was a democratic institution, reflecting the will of the people; it reflected the law of the land.

112 Beaumanoir, *Coutumes de Beauvaisis*, c. IV, §§ 4 and 13, had already accepted the Roman *plena potestas* for court procedure in a region of customary law; he gives an example of a mandate with *pleniere poeste* for action before any judges or officers, and emphasizes that (§13) one should answer only to a proctor who has a "sufficient mandate" (i.e., full powers), for then if one wins one is sure that the *dominus* of the proctor must be responsible.

For further discussion of "sufficient instructions," see below, § 5.

113 Picot, *Documents*, nos. I and XI (pp. 1, 27); C. H. Taylor, "Some New Texts on the Assembly of 1302," *Speculum*, XI (1936), 38-42; McIlwain, *C.M.H.*, VII, 686.

114 Picot, *Documents*, p. 164.

potestas et speciale mandatum,[115] or *generalis potestas et speciale mandatum.*[116] As Jusselin says, these representatives played a role "bien effacé," for they were summoned only to approve acts and decisions of the royal government—which they did.[117] Yet, in the matter of granting taxes, they could defend specific legal rights and custom; and the king could not raise extraordinary subsidies without obtaining the consent of the communities through their representatives; thus, the delegates with full powers did have the power of consent. But this consent was consultative and judicial, before the king and his council, or before commissioners, not a sovereign limitation of the royal prerogative.[118]

As for Germany and north Italy, while special studies are needed on the problem, it may be said that because the cities became practically independent of the imperial authority (ex-

---

[115] *Ibid.*, p. 170: Saint Marcel appoints seven proctors to appear before two royal deputies, or before any royal *curiales*, "ad omnes causas seu demandas" of the royal *curia* "contra dictam universitatem seu contra aliquem de dicta universitate"; the proctors are given full powers and special mandate "agendi, deffendendi, excipiendi, proponendi, libellum seu libellos petendi seu porrigendi, litem seu lites contestandi, etc." This mandate is not for the States General, but for responding to the demands of royal agents in a local assembly.

[116] *Ibid.*, p. 497; other examples given by McIlwain, *C.M.H.*, vii, 688f., and by Langlois, in Lavisse, iii, ii, 262.

[117] Jusselin, "Lettres de Philippe le Bel," *Bibliothèque de l'École des chartes*, LXVII, 471; cf. Langlois, in Lavisse, iii, ii, 262-264, also 160f., 261.

[118] See the important work by Strayer, *Consent to Taxation under Philip the Fair* (in Strayer and Taylor, *Studies in Early French Taxation*). Strayer admirably demonstrates the machinery by which the royal government obtained taxes and shows how the French people failed to "secure control of taxation and some voice in legislation" (p. 91) because of localism and the paradoxical weakness (p. 94) of the king; but he does not look at the other side of the question: the theoretically superior public power of the royal government and the use of the machinery of representation not only to get information (p. 21) but also to obtain the consent necessary if local rights and customs were to be respected according to the principle *quod omnes tangit*. The early use of representation was not merely for information and publicity; it was an attempt to conform to the thirteenth-century idea of getting consent in a general assembly in order to prevent later, legally justifiable, resistance to the tax. If resistance did develop in spite of the general consent given in States General, this was, when not contrary to the law, in conformity with the legal practice of dilatory procedure, of continuing litigation by appealing and making excuses to the last ditch. Courts could decide, but strongly traditional localism could delay, and obstruction override, the decision without denying the theoretical jurisdiction of the courts. Not even the royal absolutism of Louis XIV produced universal obedience to the will of the government. See below, § 5, nn. 187-206 and text. On delays caused by contumacy, or defaulting, see Picot, *Documents*, no. 137.

cept for a brief time when Frederick I held his famous Diet at Roncaglia, 1158),[119] the *plena potestas* of representatives was ambassadorial in character. There was no real State, no public law, to subordinate local liberties to the common utility; consequently the power of consent was such that there was not even a possibility of a central government capable of interpreting in its favor the representatives' power of consent. In other words, representation was that of autonomous cities sending plenipotentiaries to negotiate, as it were, with a foreign power.[120]

More clearly and logically than in the secular State, the Roman judicial-conciliar character of assemblies was developed in the Church. Popes, papal legates, and archbishops, as well as *presidentes* and *diffinitores*, according to their place in the hierarchy, presided as high executives, legislators, and judges over general and provincial councils, and over general and provincial chapters of the monastic orders. They consulted with prelates and representatives of ecclesiastical corporations, but they initiated and decided, after giving hearings and receiving information, without being controlled by the consent of the clergy. Each assembly was a court as well as council. Representatives of cathedral chapters in provincial and general councils appeared before the archbishop and the pope and their councillors (the prelates), and had only a consultative "voice" (vote). Their powers, which were drawn up as mandates, that is "sufficient instructions" with *plena potestas*, consequently expressed corporate consent to whatever the council might decide.

Yet, in the second quarter of the thirteenth century representatives of cathedral chapters tried to issue limited mandates and to refuse consent to the action of the archbishop and his provincial council.[121] Indeed, in the Council of Bourges, 1225,

[119] Post, *Speculum*, xviii, 228; above, ch. ii, nn. 86-101.

[120] McIlwain, *C.M.H.*, vii, 705f. The Kingdom of Sicily needs further study. But under Frederick II representation meant centralization under the real authority of the king; similarly in the time of Charles of Anjou. Space is lacking for any adequate treatment at this time. But see McIlwain, *C.M.H.*, vii, 704; and Marongiu, *L'istituto parlamentare*, pp. 123-127.

[121] In 1226 the Chapter of St. Osmund's, Salisbury, instructed its proctors to resist, in a "national" council held by the Archbishop of Canterbury, a royal demand for a subsidy; *The Register of S. Osmund*, ed. W. H. Rich Jones; R. S., ii, 64f.; Dorothy Bruce Weske, *Convocation of the Clergy*, pp. 42ff., 201-203;

the proctors of chapters refused consent to Honorius III's request for prebends,[122] but they were unsuccessful in resisting the demand for an extraordinary tax to finance Louis VIII's crusade in 1226.[123] In any event, such powers of consent were judicial as well as conciliar, for the council was also a court. If by the Roman principle, *quod omnes tangit*, the lower clergy had the right of consent, it was consent, after judicial and conciliar process, to what the council of prelates decided. But if the law was clearly on the side of the represented communities, the council could not legally obtain consent—though the pressure applied by an alliance of pope, king, and prelates could do what the theory of necessity could not. In any case, the ecclesiastical court and council needed to decide quickly; therefore, as in the secular assemblies, representatives were summoned to bring full powers or sufficient instructions.[124] If few mandates survive from the thirteenth century (and these in the latter half), those few and the summons express the *plena potestas* of the proctors to consent to what is enacted in the assembly by the prelates.[125]

W. E. Lunt, "The Consent of the Lower Clergy to Taxation during the Reign of Henry III," *Essays in Honor of George Lincoln Burr*, pp. 121f.; Lunt, *Financial Relations of the Papacy with England to 1327*, pp. 187f. In 1283 the clergy of the province of Canterbury asked Archbishop Peckham to grant a delay for considering a new royal request because their *potestas, quae limitata fuerit*, did not extend to this; Peckham, *Register*, II, 536. On limited powers see below, § 5.

122 Mansi, *Concilia*, XXII, 1213-1217; Matthew Paris, *Chron. Maj.*, III, 105ff.; F. M. Powicke, *Stephen Langton*, pp. 158f.; Lunt, *Financial Relations*, pp. 178-186, for the refusal of the English clergy.

123 Ch. Petit-Dutaillis, *Etude sur la vie et le regne de Louis VIII*, pp. 288-294; Berger, *Histoire de Blanche de Castille*, pp. 96-98; Auvray, ed., *Les registres de Grégoire IX*, nos. 134 and 155. Why consent could be refused to a demand for prebends and not for taxes needs further study; but it may be that there was already some distinction between taking property and taking taxes; besides, taking prebends for the necessities of the Curia was perhaps not demonstrably for the common utility of Christendom or for the *status Ecclesiae*; see above, n. 102.

124 Below, § 5.

125 Representatives of the clergy, of course, had no power of limiting the *plenitudo potestatis* of the pope in a general council. But it is interesting to show this by a mandate issued by the Benedictine prior and convent of Norwich for their proctors for the Council of Vienne, 1311; their proctors are given "generalis potestas et mandatum speciale in dicto concilio interessendi, tractandi, ac plenum et expressum consensum prebendi, una cum ceteris in dicto concilio legitime comparentibus, super omnibus et singulis dicto concilio deductis et per

All the above has been very generally stated, but the implication is that the strong king, not the communities, was the interpreter of *plena potestas* and could thereby obtain consent

---

Dei graciam deducendis . . . necnon ad omnia alia que in eodem concilio statuentur, fient, ordinabuntur, et que secundum tenorem mandati apostolici fuerint opportuna, faciendi, consenciendi, expediendi, eciam si mandatum exigant speciale, pro eisdem vero . . . rem ratam haberi et iudicatum solvi sub ypotheca rerum nostrarum promittimus et exponimus cauciones"; Pantin, ed., *Documents Illustrating the Activities of the General and Provincial Chapters of the English Black Monks, 1215-1540*, I, 171. This general mandate shows clearly the judicial character of the general council.

If a papal legate held a council, he, too, had the real authority, and representatives of the clergy were sent with full powers to consent to his decisions. This is illustrated by a mandate given by the monastery of Bec to its proctors for a legatine council at Paris in 1284; the proctors are given power "ad audienda, referenda et recipienda mandata sedis apostolice atque vestra"; *plena potestas* is not given, but its equivalent is, i.e., the clause *ratum etiam habituri et gratum quicquid, etc.*; in Brit. Mus., MS Cotton Dom. A. XI, fol. 131. Another illustration comes from the legatine Council of London, 1237: proctors shall bring mandates, "ut quicquid in concilio statueret legatus, ratum utrobique haberetur"; Matthew Paris, *Chron. Maj.*, III, 415.

Even the *diffinitores* presiding over a provincial chapter of the Dominican Order and the *abbates presidentes* of a General Chapter of the Benedictine Order act as judges in a high court; consequently, the powers of consent given to representatives of convents are procedural, not sovereign. Thus, in 1287 the prior and convent of Bec send to the "presidents" of a General Chapter of Abbots of the province of Rouen two proctors "ad proponendum et ostendendum coram vobis" the *rationes* demanded by the "presidents"; the proctors are also appointed to "hear, report back, or prosecute the *negocium*, and to appeal"; they are given *potestas plenaria* and *mandatum speciale* (MS Cot. Dom. A. XI, fol. 121). For other examples relating to General Chapters of the Black Monks in England, see Pantin, *Documents*, III, 264-275; still other examples, I, 128, 141f., 144; III, 276.

As for provincial councils of archbishops and bishops, the proctors are given powers to appear *before* the archbishop and to consent to the acts of the Council: Council of Béziers, 1280—proctors of the chapter of Elne, "ad audiendum tractatus super negotiis universalem statum totius Narbonensis provinciae tangentibus, et ad faciendum super praedictis, prout memorato concilio expedire visum fuerit, et Dominus ministrabit; ratum et firmum perpetuo habituri, quicquid super praemissis per eumdem procuratorem fuerit procuratum"; Mansi, *Concilia*, XXIV, 364f.

Likewise for the convocation of the English Clergy when the King held a Parliament. If the *communitas cleri* seems to have the power of consent in 1283 (the archbishop of Canterbury summoned proctors, "sufficienter instructi," of chapters and of dioceses to bring "plenam et expressam potestatem . . . tractandi et consentiendi quae ibidem . . . cleri communitas providebit"; *S.C.*, p. 459; Peckham, *Register*, II, 509; Clarke, *Medieval Representation*, pp. 312f.), this consent is controlled by the prelates who are the essential Convocation or Council. In 1295 Edward I ordered the clergy of the province to send proctors with *plena potestas* "ad tractandum, ordinandum et faciendum nobiscum, et cum caeteris praelatis, proceribus et aliis incolis regni nostri, qualiter hujusmodi periculis et excogitatis malitiis obviandum"; Wilkins, *Concilia*, II, 215; *S.C.*, p. 480.

to decisions which were supported by public law.[126] In this connection a question arises, however, which must be treated in some detail before we can definitely say that the consent of a community was in effect given with the mandate before the meeting of the assembly. Could a city or county limit the mandate, refuse to give full powers to its mandataries, and thereby withhold consent and cripple the prerogative? And to ask this is to ask further: after hearing the proposals of the government, could representatives who came with *plena potestas* delay their answer by claiming the right of "reference back" in order to receive fresh instructions from their constituents; and how much judgment was entrusted to representatives whose powers were not limited?

5. "SUFFICIENT INSTRUCTIONS," "REFERENCE BACK," AND LIMITED MANDATES

If representation were to develop as the means of expressing the political sovereignty of the people, not only must the king have the power to summon to his assembly, but the representatives must have a mandate from below. The mandate could not be a final transfer of responsibility from electors to representatives, for political representatives should by the mandate owe to their constituency judgment rather than mere obedience, and this judgment must be exercised in cooperation with other representatives with like powers. But if their discretion and judgment were not trusted, they must at least be able to "refer back" and obtain specific instructions from the communities that sent them.[127] Did *plena potestas* express these conditions of

---

If the king stressed the Roman principle of consent, *quod omnes tangit*, in his writ to his two archbishops in 1295, they interpreted it as procedural consent and connected it with *plena potestas*: the proctors of chapters and of the diocesan clergy shall attend the assembly, "ad tractandum, ordinandum nobiscum, et tractatibus et ordinationibusque in praemissis . . . faciendis, ac omnibus tractationes et ordinationes hujusmodi contingentibus, nomine dominorum consentiend(um) plenam et sufficientem potestatem habentes. . . . Cum commune sit periculum, et per consequens communibus, absque cujusque fori privilegio, remediis congruis devitandum, et quod omnes tangit, merito debet ab omnibus approbari"; Wilkins, *Concilia*, ii, 219f.

126 For more evidence see chs. v–ix.

127 So the argument of Clarke, *Medieval Representation*, p. 291; her contention

political representation and consent? In court procedure, we shall find, it did not deprive proctors of the right to defend with legal skill the interests of their *dominus,* and certain delays were normally permitted in order that the defense might be adequately prepared and that, if such a new situation arose without the principal's knowledge of it, the proctors could report back, inform the principal, and obtain new instructions in the form of a special mandate. But all this was determined by the court, was simply a part of the procedure and involved no limitation of the jurisdiction of the court or of the right of the judges to decide the case. Was the royal assembly, however, to return to the question discussed above, equivalent to an ordinary court except in being the highest court of the land?

Professor C. H. Taylor has studied the problem of the limited mandate and "reference back" more profoundly and challengingly than any other authority on representation.[128] After emphasizing the tautology in Philip IV's summons in 1302 (the king instructed French communities to send delegates with *plena potestas* and *absque excusatione relationis,* because he wanted both to prevent delays caused by proctors' "referring back" to get fresh instructions and to avoid the necessarily additional expense, for *plena potestas* theoretically released the proctor from the obligation of getting new instructions),[129] Taylor concludes

is not based on any study of the legal meaning of the mandate, *plena potestas,* and agency.

[128] However near the correct interpretation his may be, it is not intended as a study of the legal background. Consequently, it seems necessary to review his conclusions in the light of legal theory. See Taylor's article, "An Assembly of French Towns in March, 1318," *Speculum,* XIII (1938), 295-303; also his *Assemblies of Towns and War Subsidy,* in Strayer and Taylor, *Studies in Early French Taxation,* pp. 128ff.

[129] "An Assembly of French Towns," *Speculum,* XIII, 299, 302; M. Jusselin, "Lettres de Philippe le Bel," *Bibl. de l'École des Chartes,* LXVII, 407f., for the summons; also Langlois, in Lavisse, III, ii, 160 n. 2, 280. Cf. Viollet, *Histoire des institutions politiques et administratives de la France,* III, 98f.: a limited mandate was behind the practice of the deputies' refusing to consent to new burdens demanded by the king, because, as they alleged, they must refer back to their constituents (p. 198 n. 3: "pro eo quod asserebant se a suis communitatibus seu universitatibus nullam super hoc potestatem habere, nisi tantummodo audiendi et dictis suis communitatibus seu universitatibus referendi"; p. 199: in 1303 the Chapter of Nimes gave these powers, "comparendum, tractandum et refferendum dicto capitulo," and this mandate was judged insufficient—Picot, *Documents,* p.

that "a proctor who had full power to do anything that his constituents could do if present"[130] did not necessarily have to do anything in particular which the king asked of him. If the king could not give detailed advance knowledge of matters to be treated in an assembly, the proctors could not "commit themselves and their towns to a line of action on which they were (necessarily) not prepared and instructed by their constituencies. . . . A mandate defined the limits beyond which an agent must not go: full powers in a mandate gave the proctors apparently unlimited and discretionary range of action—but would the proctor interpret such a mandate as a blank cheque? Did towns that gave their delegates full powers expect them to act, and bind their towns, on matters whereon the town had given no advance instructions?" Answers to these questions, he ac-

---

242, no. CLXVIII). Hence, says Viollet, the king almost always insisted that the representatives have full powers and not a limited mandate.

Sometimes, however, the *referendum* stated in the mandate does not mean "reference back" in the above sense; it may mean simply the power given the proctor to "bring back" the decision of the assembly without any implication of a refusal to accept; in 1300 the proctor sent by a monastery to a royal convocation was given power *ad audiendum et referendum* what was ordained by the king, but also *ad obtemperandum* the royal commands, *si necesse fuerit, quantum justum fuerit*; Langlois, "Formulaires," *Notices et extraits*, xxxiv, 21f. The power to "obey" is an unusual expression, but the expressions *si necesse fuerit, quantum justum fuerit* show that obedience to the royal will was not questioned except in the medieval sense of obedience only if the king's will were based on justice and law (other examples are referred to by McIlwain, *C.M.H.*, vii, 688). Sometimes the proctors of ecclesiastical communities in provincial councils went with instructions in the mandate to consent and to bring, or refer or report, back the decisions and statutes made by the higher prelates; see above, n. 125. So also in the case of proctors of a group of villages in France, 1308, who were appointed *ad audiendum et reportandum mandata seu statuta* (Picot, *Documents*, p. 673, no. 998); cf. no. 996: the proctors of Autun are appointed *ad audiendum ordinationem* of the king.

For a similar use of *obtemperare*, see the request of the Chapter of St. Osmund, Salisbury, in 1226, that proctors appear before the Archbishop of Canterbury, "ut de uniformi eorum provisione et consilio, tam certa et tam uniformis procedat responsio, ut domini P. P., si viderint expedire, obtemperetur mandato et ad honorem totius ecclesiae Anglicanae et ad cleri protectionem"; this was a papal mandate to the clergy to pay an aid to the king; *Reg. S. Osmund*, ii, 61f. Again there is question only of defense of legal rights before submission to the papal authority.

130 Here Taylor cites Picot, *Documents*, pp. 148-149 and *passim*, and says that this was a common phrasing to sum up full powers. Actually, *possit facere omnia que ipse dominus possit* was an equivalent of *plena potestas*; both did not have to be stated; so Bartolus and Baldus, to *C. 2, 12, 10*, on *plena potestas*—see above, nn. 15, 16.

knowledges, must be based on a thorough study of the theory and practice of procuration. "But it is *a priori* possible that a proctor with full powers was not thereby, as institutional practice went, a free agent; possible that the government as it endeavored to get action from representative assemblies was aware of this difficulty, and tried to insure the appearance of representatives who would have, not merely formal (and formless!) *plena potestas*, but also positive *instructions*, which could be given only if the body which constituted a proctor had some knowledge of the business to be discussed."[131] Therefore, the government in 1318, 1321, and 1346-1347 obviated the difficulty of instructions by using preliminary local assemblies held in the *bailliages*, where the royal commissioners could explain the king's will. As a result, the towns could properly instruct their representatives, who would no longer need to go back to their constituents.[132]

Thus Taylor supposes that *plena potestas* did not fully obviate "reference back" for further instructions from constituencies. And G. Lapsley has observed that by 1341 the English towns attached such importance to Parliament that they instructed their representatives during sessions and received reports from them on their return—hence Parliament and the Commons were by then politically important.[133] Ernest Barker, on the other hand, has held that *plena potestas*, as given to clerical representatives to Parliament, denied any *referendum*.[134] In the one opinion, by implication, consent was not fully expressed by "full powers"; in the other, consent was absolutely given by the constituents before the assembly met. Does the legal theory of canonists and legists on procuration help us understand these problems?

In the first place, what does the royal request for "sufficiently instructed" proctors mean? In fourteenth-century France, according to Taylor, it meant that the king wanted the delegates to have, in addition to the full powers in the mandate, full instructions from fully informed constituents on how to re-

---

131 *Speculum*, XIII, 299f.
132 *Ibid.*, 300ff.
133 Maitland, *Selected Essays*, pp. 5f.
134 *Dominican Order and Convocation*, p. 73.

spond to the king's requests which were to be treated in the assembly. Such full and positive instructions were usually not specified in the mandate itself, but sent along separately with the proctors. In any case, *plena potestas* was perhaps not given to a proctor who did not also have instructions, and *plena potestas* and "sufficient instructions" were two separate matters connected with the proctor's functions.[135]

In the judicial procedure of the two laws, however, the phrase *sufficienter instructus*, which early had a technical meaning for obviating delays and subterfuges,[136] did not always mean that a proctor representing a litigant must appear in court only if fully prepared, on the basis of his principal's full knowledge and instructions, to answer every question that might come up. The plaintiff, of course, was fully informed, and should give his proctor precise knowledge of the suit. But the defendant had to be informed by the judge issuing the citation and by the *libellus* or writ of accusation submitted by the plaintiff.[137] Thus the defendant in particular could feel injured by an adverse sentence if he had not been fully informed by the court and the plaintiff as to the nature of the charges against him; from such a sentence he could appeal. In addition, both he and the plain-

---

[135] *Speculum*, XIII, 299f., 300 n. H. S. Lucas also distinguishes between the mandate or credentials and the instructions given to English ambassadors in 1327-1336; "The Machinery of Diplomatic Intercourse," in Morris, *English Government*, p. 309. As Lucas says, the letter of credence rarely stated the details of the subject of negotiations; the agent was fully "instructed" by the king either *viva voce* or in a separate instrument.

[136] Innocent III issued decretals on the subject: *Decr. Greg.* IX 1, 5, 5. "per procuratores idoneos ad omnia *sufficienter instructos*"; and *Decr.* 2, 14, 6: a certain defendant had been cited by the pope to appear in the Curia "per se vel per procuratorem sufficientem sufficienter instructum, ne postmodum per dilationes vel occasiones quaslibet subterfugere videretur examen." It appears frequently in thirteenth-century treatises on procedure. In 1226 the Archbishop of Canterbury, granting the request of the Chapter of Salisbury, permitted the bishops to ask cathedral chapters to send each an "ydoneum procuratorem . . . sufficienter instructum super negotio" of the aid asked by the king; *Reg. S. Osmund*, II, 62f.

[137] All the treatises on judicial procedure discuss the *libellus* or *petitio* submitted to the judges by the plaintiff, the court summons to the accused, and the delays granted to the latter for preparing his defense. See the collection of treatises edited by Wahrmund, *Quellen*; and Beaumanoir, *Coutumes de Beauvaisis*, cc. ii-iv, vi, vii. Bethmann-Hollweg, *Civilprozess des gemeinen Rechts*, VI, 27-53, gives only a very general discussion that is not helpful here.

Gratia, *De iudic. ord.*, ed. Bergmann, p. 324, says that the plaintiff must "sufficiently instruct" his proctor.

tiff could feel injured if new charges and counter-charges were raised in the trial without their knowledge. Technically, therefore, in both laws information in one sense was the knowledge that the litigants, especially the defendants, received of the origin and course of the suit.[138]

If the defendant had not been fully informed by the *libellus* of the plaintiff and by the citation to court, his proctor could secure a delay for further deliberation with him on how to handle the charges in court. A decretal of Pope Coelestine III states that when a defendant is cited to court by authority of a papal rescript, and if by the rescript sent to him he is fully informed (*plene potuit instrui de quo in iudicio convenitur*),[139] then he shall be given no further delays for deliberation (*induciae deliberatoriae*).[140] But a decretalist objects that papal rescripts rarely specify all matters by which the defendant is fully instructed. If, however, in addition to the rescript or citation the *libellus* of the plaintiff is sent to the defendant, the latter may then fully deliberate; and if the defendant is then fully instructed he shall have no further deliberatory delays.[141] But the judge, continues the gloss, can still give certain *dilationes* to the defendant for hiring lawyers, seeking the counsel of friends, or procuring witnesses or instruments to help him fight the charges. Such delays, however, are in the power of the judge, not of the defendant.[142] Naturally, if the citation to court does not clearly state the nature of the charges, and if the cited party

---

138 On this kind of information see the *Curialis* (1251-1270) in Wahrmund, *Quellen*, I, iii, 10f., and other treatises listed below, nn. 142f.

139 *Decr.* 2, 8, 2.

140 *Curialis*, c. VI (Wahrmund, I, iii, 17): ". . . Sicut videtur quaedam decretalis, reus inducias habere non debet, nisi in libello citatorio aliquid fuerit incertum, quia ex eo potest deliberare et instrui, super quo convenitur, ut Extra, de dilationibus, praeterea [*Decr.* 2, 8, 2]." But to this the defendant can reply, "quod etsi sciebat, super quo debeat conveniri, tamen nesciebat, qua actione, super qua causa, et ideo non potuit deliberare." The success of such cavilling depended on the will of the judge.

141 *Glos. ord.*, to e. c., ad v. *plene (potuit instrui)*: ". . . et si tunc per litteras vel libellum plene instrui potuit, non debet alias inducias deliberatorias habere. . . ." The gloss explains that the *actor* or plaintiff is not given delays because he is naturally fully instructed or informed at the start.

142 See Ricardus Anglicus, *Summa de ordine iudiciario* (ed. Wahrmund, II, iii), c. xxv.

appoints a proctor, then the proctor should be given a delay to consult with and be "certified by" his principal.[143]

One kind of information, therefore, was that which the plaintiff and the court must give to the defendant—and in time for him to deliberate on how to fight the charge and appoint and instruct his representative. (The judicial summons set a *terminus* that allowed for a delay for preparing the defense.) A different kind of information were the instructions given to the proctor by the principal. Taylor thinks that such instructions were different and separate from the mandate given the proctor by his principal; that when the prince demanded that proctors *sufficienter instructi* come to the assembly, he wanted them to have full information from the constituents on how to treat all questions that came up in the assembly, as well as full powers to handle the business and to consent to the final decision. Roman and Canon law, however, made little distinction between instructions, information, and the mandate: the proctor who was legally appointed and had a properly drawn up mandate was necessarily *sufficienter instructus* and informed.[144] A legally con-

---

[143] Innocent IV, *Apparatus*, to *Decr.* 1, 38, 11 Dilectus, ad v. *consulet*: "Ar. quod si qui citatus est, non expresso super quo, et citatus constituit procuratorem, procurator debet habere inducias ut consulat dominum."

On this whole question of delays see also Ricardus Anglicus (*ca.* 1196) *Summa*, cc. XXII, XXIV, XXV; Tancred (*ca.* 1214-1216), *Ordo Judiciarius*, P. 2, t. 17 (ed. Bergmann, pp. 180-184); William of Drogheda, *Summa aurea* (*ca.* 1239), c. CCCLVIII (Wahrmund, *Quellen*, II, ii, 292-295); the *Curialis* (1251-1270), c. XXV (Wahrmund, I, iii, 11-13). Cf. Bartolus to *D.* 3, 3, 2: "Sed procurator possit petere dilationem ut certificetur a domino quid respondeat," if proper instructions are not given the *dominus* in order that he may instruct his proctor. If the *dominus* is instructed and summoned *specialiter*, he must send "procuratorem instructum quid respondeat, et ideo non debet sibi dari dilatio; imo si non vult respondere, punietur dominus, ut contumax . . . Innoc. in c. dilectus."

[144] See the decretals of Innocent III, cited above, n. 136. Pope Gregory IX issued a decretal (1227-1234) in which he explained that a litigant should be represented "per procuratorem idoneum et sufficienter instructum ad litem contestandam et ad alia omnia negotia peragenda quae necessaria decisioni negotii videbuntur . . ." (*Decr.* 2, 14, 10 Venerabilis); *Glos. ord.*, ad v. *sufficienter instructum*: "Sufficiens dicitur qui ad agendum et defendendum et respondendum constitutus est legitime"; and in support of this, the author of the gloss refers to three decretals on proctors and their mandates (*Decr.* 1, 38, 1 Alia quidem, 10 Accedens, and 13 Mandato). From these decretals and the glosses we learn that the proctor *legitime constitutus* is one who is provided with a mandate given with the consent of the interested parties; see the following notes. Also Bartolus, *Com.*, to *D.* 3, 3, 1, no. 1: "Ille qui mittit ad iudicem procura-

stituted proctor, for example, was appointed by the mutual consent of prelate and chapter in a case that concerned both; his mandate, therefore, was valid for litigation.[145] This mandate must assure the court of its authenticity by containing at least the names of the constituents of the proctor, the nature of the *causa* or suit, and the clause of *ratihabitio* (*quod ratum habebit, etc.*).[146] In fact, the proctor for a lawsuit in the papal Curia should have in his mandate the *plena potestas ad agendum et respondendum*—so Gregory IX, *Decr.* 1, 38, 10 Accedens. In other words, as the glossator says ad v. *respondendum*, the proctor appointed as plaintiff should also have the power to act as defendant if the original defendant brought a cross-action or "reconvened" the proctor. It followed that the mandate must also contain the *satisdatio* and the *iudicatum solvi* clause by which the constituent stood as *fideiussor* for his proctor as defendant, and in addition, the clause affirming that the proctor would be in court when sentence was pronounced. By having all these clauses in the mandate *ad agendum et respondendum*, the proctor had *plena potestas*.[147] Another gloss, to *Decr.* 1, 38, 13

---

torem cum mandato non sufficienti, non est amplius citandus, tanquam vere contumax. Videtur enim declarasse se nolle venire. . . ." But Bartolus also indicates that the *procurator instructus* is instructed by his constituent on how to reply (to *D.* 3, 3, *Non solum*, no. 2: the proctor may obtain a delay, "ut certificetur a domino quid respondeat. . . . Aut fuit citatus [dominus] specialiter, et tunc debuit mittere procuratorem instructum quid respondeat et ideo non debet sibi dari dilatio . . .").

145 *Glos. ord.* to *Decr.* 1, 38, 1, ad v. *legaliter*. Of course, where a business concerned only the chapter, the consent of the prelate was not needed; and vice versa.

146 Gloss to *Decr.* 1, 38, 1, ad v. *mandato*. Authenticity was assured further by the attestation of notaries or by the seal attached to the mandate. This gloss was taken from Tancred, to *Comp. I,* 1, De procur., c. 1 Alia quidem; ad v. *mandato legaliter*: "In hoc mandato tria contineri debent, scilicet, nomen eius qui procuratorem constituit, causa ad quam constituitur, et quod ratum habebit, quod cum eo actum fuerit . . . *t*." Vincentius Hispanus adds: "Sed pone quod de mandato dubitetur, quia sigillum incognitum est: de eo fides fieri debet . . . Vinc." (Bamberg, MS Can. 20, fol. 17ᵛ, c. 1).

147 *Glos. ord.*, to *Decr.* 1, 38, 10 Accedens, ad v. *respondendum*: "Sic ergo debet constitui procurator ad agendum datus, ut possit etiam defendere et respondere adversario si eum reconveniat: alias si non defenderet, denegabitur ei actio . . . et in expensis alteri parti tanquam contumax condemnetur. . . . In qua constitutione debet satisdationem exponere, per quam ipse [dominus] fideiussor sui procuratoris existat, iudicatum solvi sub hypotheca rerum suarum . . . ; et quod tempore sententiae erit in iudicio, alias omnia dabit quae in condemnatione veniunt, ut ibidem dicitur: et ita plenam habet potestatem."

Mandato (Gregory IX), states that the mandate for the proctor as plaintiff should contain the names of the constituent and his proctor, the subject of the *causa* or suit, the *ratihabitio* clause, and the names of the judges. The mandate for the defending proctor must have, in addition, the clause of *satisdatio* or *iudicatum solvi*. This clause, however, might be omitted in the case of a proctor of a corporation, for the proctor, not the corporation, takes the oath that the action is brought or defended in good faith (*iuramentum de calumnia*).[148]

That *sufficienter instructus* meant essentially a proctor with a sufficient mandate (that is, a mandate with all the above clauses which were necessary to give the proctor full powers), rather than instructions apart from the mandate, is implied again by the canonist Aegidius de Fuscarariis, *ca.* 1262-1266. When the *dominus* as defendant promises, if he loses the suit, to pay the fine or costs (*iudicatum solvi*) for his proctor, should he say "*iudicatum solvi pro omnibus clausulis stipulationis*" in the mandate,[149] or should he merely say "*iudicatum solvi*"?[150] Aegidius decides that the mandate is *plenius* and *securius* if the whole clause with *pro omnibus clausulis stipulationis* is expressed; but if the *pro omnibus clausulis stipulationis* is not added, the mandate is nonetheless *sufficiens ad relevandum procuratorem*.[151] Indeed, the proctor is *sufficienter instructus* even if his *dominus* failed to relieve him of the burden of *satisdandi iudicatum solvi*; if the adversary claims that such a proc-

---

[148] *Glos. ord.*, ad v. *mandato procuratoris.*

[149] See Jolowicz, *Historical Introduction to the Study of Roman Law*, p. 289. The defendant should, outside court, give security (*satisdatio*) and make himself the surety (*fideiussor*) of his proctor for all the clauses of the *satisdatio* which was the *iudicatum solvi*; *Inst.* 4, 11, *de satisd.*, 4: ". . . extra iudicium satisdationem exponere, per quam ipse sui fideiussor existit pro omnibus iudicatum solvi satisdationis clausulis." See on this question Collinet, *La procédure par libelle* (*Études historiques sur le droit de Justinien*, IV), p. 140. The proctor himself furnishes the *satisdatio* or *iudicatum solvi* to the court, and for all the clauses of the *satisdatio* (to remain at the court, to conduct the suit to the end, to pay the condemnation); Collinet, pp. 190f., and in general pp. 188ff. Actually, the clause *iudicatum solvi* frequently appears in defendants' proctorial mandates of the thirteenth century and later; but it is not necessary to study this question in detail for the present purpose.

[150] Aegidius de Fuscarariis, *Ordo Iudiciarius*, c. xv (Wahrmund, *Quellen*, III, i, 28ff.).

[151] C. xv (Wahrmund, III, i, 28).

tor should not be admitted to court, and that his *dominus* should be pronounced *contumax* because the *dominus* did not send *procuratorem sufficientem,* the proctor shall nevertheless be admitted, and his *dominus* is not *contumax.*[152]

Certain formulas, however, were indispensable if the mandate and proctor were to be held "sufficient" against any contrary assertions by the adversary in court.[153] The mandate contained general clauses that stated a contract between proctor and principal and thus informed the court of the responsibility, especially of the principal. Such a mandate remained general in content even when many additional clauses were inserted to make more specific the powers of the proctor.[154] These clauses were part of the instructions given the proctor but were general nonetheless; for if the proctor really had powers, he must be able, particularly if the court were at a long distance from his constituents, to act according to his best judgment without having recourse to the constituent on every issue brought up in court. Indeed, the very fact that the defendant appointed a proctor was evidence to the judge that the proctor was *sufficienter instructus,*[155] that the defendant had given his proctor what information he had received in the *libellus* and summons and had told the proctor generally how to act to meet the charges. In fact, the courts generally demanded that the *dominus* send a *sufficienter instructus* proctor, with a "sufficient mandate," else the *dominus* would be declared *contumax;*[156] and

152 *Ibid.,* 29.

153 C. xx (Wahrmund, III, i, 34): "Contra formam [procurationis] multa possunt opponi; si constituatur [procurator] generaliter nec habeat mandatum ad agendum et defendendum, non valet. . . . Nec est sufficiens procurator, scilicet rei, constitutus ad agendum, si non contineatur: ad defendendum. . . ."

154 For example, the proctor could accept or refuse the judges delegated by papal rescript for the suit, make exceptions or pleas, offer replies (*replicationes*) to exceptions, etc.

155 Innocent IV, *Appar.,* to *Decr.* 1, 38, 11, ad v. *a iudicibus:* "Nam si ad causam, que commissa est procuratori, ut eam defendat, citetur procurator, has non debet dare iudex inducias, quia presumitur quod dominus instruxerit eum." But Innocent IV would grant delays to the defendant's general proctor in the event that a new charge, unknown to the constituent, should arise; also to a proctor for one suit if the constituent was not instructed properly by the court on the nature of the accusation.

156 Bartolus, to *D.* 3, 3, 1, no. 1: "Ille qui mittit ad iudicem procuratorem cum mandato non sufficienti, non est amplius citandus, tanquam vere contumax. Videtur enim declarasse se nolle venire. . . ."

one party could take exception to the form of the mandate given the other party's proctor, if the said proctor as defendant were not *sufficiens* because his mandate did not contain the formula *ad defendendum*.[157] It was the court, however, which had the power to decide whether, despite omissions or legal subtleties in the formulas of the mandate, the instructions given the proctor were sufficient to constitute *plena potestas*.[158]

But if the proctor *sufficienter instructus* was presumed to have a legally valid mandate giving him full powers, he was supposed to be fully informed or instructed in still another sense. He must be *idoneus*, that is to say, capable of intelligently handling the interests of his constituent because of his knowledge of the matter; and if *idoneus*, he was necessarily informed by the constituent and provided with the authentic instruments or documents or other records that were needed to establish his case in court.[159] Thus the "suitable" proctor was one who literally bore the record (*gesta*), that is, the legal instruments which would support his case, and who had sufficient legal learning and skill to use the record intelligently enough to carry

[157] Aegidius de Fuscarariis, *Ordo Iudiciarius* (Wahrmund, *Quellen*, III, i, 34): "Contra formam [*procurationis* or *mandati*] multa possunt opponi; si constituatur generaliter nec habeat mandatum ad agendum et defendendum, non valet. . . . Nec est sufficiens procurator, scilicet rei, constitutus ad agendum, si non contineatur: 'ad defendendum' ut . . . (*Decr.* 1, 38, 10 and 12, Accedens and Constitutus)."

[158] Honorius III (1216-1227) declared that if the intention of the principal was to give his proctors *libera potestas*, even though the proper terminology was lacking, then the mandate should be held valid by the judges (*Decr.* 1, 38, 9 Petitio)—on this the *Glos. ord.* ad v. *intentio*: "Sic patet quod quando verba generalia sive dubia ponuntur in mandato, recurrendum est ad intentionem constituentis. . . . Unde si diceretur: 'ego do Titio potestatem agendi et defendendi in causa vel in causis, quam vel quas habeo cum tali,' sufficiens est mandatum, non obstante subtilitate legali. . . ."

[159] *Glos. ord.*, to *Decr.* 1, 5, 5 Postulationem (Innocent III), ad v. (*per procuratores*) *idoneos* (*ad omnia sufficienter instructos*): "Quia sciant et possint reddere rationem, Dist. 17, Multis (Dist. 17, c. 5), et infra, de procura. c. 1 (*Decr.* 1, 38, 1 Alia quidem)." (This gloss derives from Laurentius Hispanus, to *Comp. III*, 1, 4, 5, ad e. v.—Bamberg, MS Can. 19, fol. 123, c. 2). To c. Alia quidem, in which Gregory I ordered a bishop to send an "instructam personam cum mandato legaliter facto . . . gestisque ex more indicto . . . ut quicquid cum ea actum fuerit iure subsistat," Innocent IV (*Appar.*, ad v. *gestisque*), says: besides *gesta* in the sense of deeds, are "gesta quedam facta in scriptis redacta vel pocius ipse scripture in quibus gesta referentur, et iste scripture apud se.[dem] ap.[osto-licam] dicuntur registra; et ista gesta si sunt bene custodita et inveniantur in archivis auctenticarum personarum, puta earum qui habent potestatem auctenti-cas scripturas faciendi, fidem faciunt hic. . . ."

conviction with the judges. Further, he was "certified" or instructed by his constituent on how to reply in a suit. Moreover, the meaning of "instruction" was connected with *instrumenta*.[160]

Yet such an unexpected point might arise that the proctor would want to "refer back" to his principal in order to inform him[161] and to get further specific instructions or additional evidence (in witnesses or instruments). Now, if the proctor was appointed for one specific suit, as plaintiff he was informed by the knowledge of his constituent in the *libellus*; as defendant, by the *libellus* and citation to court. His mandate was furnished by a constituent so informed; and by his mandate, the proctor was *sufficienter instructus*, had full powers to act. As we have seen, the proctor of the plaintiff had no need of a delay for further consultation with his *dominus*; and the defendant, if fully informed by the citation and the *libellus,* was to be granted no delay for further instructions after the trial began. The same was true when the proctor of the plaintiff answered exceptions as defendant, just as the proctor of the defendant could act as plaintiff in pleading an exception. All this applied when the proctor had a mandate with full powers for *one* case (*causa*) or suit. This was perhaps a limited mandate, but only in the sense of a mandate for one specific action, not in the sense that the powers of the proctor were limited in the particular action: for it the proctor had *plena potestas*.

Even so, the court sometimes permitted a delay to a defendant who had given full powers to his proctor for a particularly important suit (*ardua causa*). In the pontificate of Gregory IX (1227-1241) the Archbishop of Bourges was claiming the *ius primatiae* over the ecclesiastical province of Bordeaux, and he carried his case to the papal Curia. The pope, following the normal judicial procedure, issued a peremptory writ citing the Archbishop of Bordeaux, who must appear at the beginning of Lent either in person or *per procuratorem idoneum sufficienter instructum ad litem contestandam et ad alia omnia nego-*

---

[160] Bartolus, above, n. 144; William of Drogheda, *Summa aurea*, Wahrmund, *Quellen*, II, ii, 195; *D.* 22, 4; *Decr. Greg. IX* 2, 22.

[161] *D.* 3, 3, 49: "Ignorantis domini conditio deterior per procuratorem fieri non debet."

tia peragenda, quae necessaria decisioni negotii videbuntur.[162]
But after this summons was issued, the pope summoned the
same prelate to Rome in person for a quite different business,
which was *pro ecclesiae Romanae subsidio,* and therefore for
"public utility," a *causa* more important *(maior)* than the other
causa of the primacy—so the Archbishop of Bordeaux later
maintained through the proctor appointed for meeting the suit
brought by the Archbishop of Bourges.[163] The Archbishop of
Bordeaux therefore came to the Curia for the business that interested the pope and the Church; the Archbishop of Bourges
was there for the same reason. The latter seized the opportunity
of demanding that the pope proceed at once with the trial of
the question of the primacy; but the former, refusing to answer
in person, returned home, leaving a proctor at the Curia to
defend his interests in the case. This proctor was given full
powers *(omnia faceret, quae in propria erat persona facturus
[archiepiscopus]).*[164] Against the Archbishop of Bourges' demand
that he answer to the charge, the proctor countered with an
exceptio: the Archbishop of Bordeaux was not held to make
response while he was at the Curia, since he had been summoned there *pro alia maiori causa, pro publica scilicet utilitate,*
and hence must be considered as absent and as having the privilege of appealing to a judge in his own city *(revocandi domum)*;
moreover, he had not had sufficient time to deliberate with his
suffragans and the clergy of his province, whose interests or
rights were touched by the claim of primacy and whose counsel
such an *ardua causa* required[165] *(quod omnes tangit—*Bracton

162 *Decr.* 2, 14, 10 Venerabilis.
163 *Decr.* 2, 8, 4 Exposuit.
164 *Decr.* 2, 8, 4. The wording is at first glance contradictory, for the archbishop, according to the pope, reserved for himself all exceptions, otherwise
giving the proctor the power to do all that the archbishop himself would do:
"qui (procurator), salvis exceptionibus sibi compententibus in respondendo et
defendendo ac aliis, omnia faceret, quae in propria erat persona facturus." But
the proctor did present *exceptiones* against the Archbishop of Bourges and asked
for a delay in order that his principal, the Archbishop of Bordeaux, might have
more time to consult with the clergy of his province and to prepare for the suit.
165 *Decr.* 2, 8, 4. The archbishop had thus instructed his proctor to advance
the rapidly prevailing Roman principle of consent: when a case touched the
legal interests of others besides the principal party, as in a corporate community,
the head of the community (the archbishop in this instance is the head of the
province which is, by legal fiction, a corporation) was the representative of all

can likewise assert the principle for judicial process).[166] Thereupon the Archbishop of Bourges demurred, rightly asserting that the defendant had been cited by him before he had been summoned on papal business, and declared that the original *terminus* had given the defendant ample time to deliberate sufficiently to be on hand for both affairs. But the pope decided in favor of the *exceptio* presented by the proctor of the defendant: the Archbishop of Bordeaux was given a further delay, and the *terminus* was extended to Christmas.

Thus a proctor for one suit was given full powers; but because he won the point of the *exceptio* before the actual trial, he obtained a delay for his principal. He was able to "refer back," but only in the sense of reporting the pope's decision to his constituent, who was then able to complete the business of

---

the interested members. But he should obtain their consent to his action in refusing or accepting the challenge to a suit, to his appointment of proctors, and to the instructions given the proctors (the interested parties must all be responsible and accept the decision of the court). As Innocent IV says, *Apparatus*, to c. 4 Exposuit, ad v. *tenui*, the Archbishop of Bordeaux was not held to reply in person at the Curia to the Archbishop of Bourges without getting a delay, because he was in the Curia on other business; because in such an *ardua causa* he ought not to be compelled to act by proctor (thus, the proctor left at the Curia when the archbishop returned home was given full powers, but with the instruction to make good, if possible, the *exceptio* that would release him from standing trial for the archbishop and would give the archbishop time to prepare to answer in person); and because if the archbishop did not have the *ius revocandi domum*, "tamen debet procurator habere inducias ad consulendum dominum. . . . Item quia causa totam provinciam tangebat, non poterat plene deliberare an cederet vel concederet, nisi consilio habito cum eis, ff. eden. l. 1 (*D.* 2, 13, 1); non tamen dico quod necesse sit eos vocare, ff. de li. cau. si pariter (*D.* 40, 12, 9)." And *Glos. ord.*, ad v. *cum suffraganeis*: "Cum quibus, et etiam cum capitulis cathedralium ecclesiarum debet deliberare, cum eorum intersit . . .."; "*Additio.* Unde appellantur induciae ad tractandum super iure primatiae . . . et quia quod omnes tangit, ab omnibus debet comprobari, vel reprobari . . ."; and further, delays are granted "propter causam supervenientem." This plea for a delay to consult with all interested parties whose rights were at stake (the claim of primacy in this case was held to touch the bishops and cathedral chapters of the province of Bordeaux) was probably on the same legal basis as that of bishops who on occasion refused to consent to a papal subsidy until they consulted with the clergy of their dioceses—for which purpose preparatory diocesan synods were held. That the consent of the clergy of the province was in the nature of judicial process is shown by the outcome of this suit. The pope asked for the consent of the clergy of Bordeaux to his sentence that decided the case, but he ordered any chapter refusing consent to show cause in the papal court—consent was compulsory, except insofar as aided by a legal right that the pope might recognize; see *Decr.* 1, 33, 17 Humilis.

166 See below, ch. IV.

obtaining the consent of all interested parties to the instructions for the waging of the suit. It was in no sense a "reference back" after the trial began; and it was in the pope's power to deny the *exceptio* which permitted a delay for new instructions.

But let us suppose that a proctor was a general one, that is, appointed for a long term to represent his principal in all the lawsuits and affairs that touched the principal's interests. Such a *procurator generalis,* so-called because he was given a general mandate *ad omnia tam ad iudicia quam ad negotia,*[167] could not assume full responsibility in every kind of question that might come up.[168] A decretal of Gregory IX (*Decr.* 1, 38, 11 Dilectus) and the glosses on it illustrate this. If a general proctor *ad omnia eius [domini] tractanda negotia,* acting as defendant, were refused a delay for consulting his principal on whether he should yield or contend a particular suit or fact, he could appeal the sentence. For the proctor could not deliberate on whether to yield or to contest the suit; in this matter he had no judgment and must consult his *dominus principalis.* In other words, such a proctor was given an *inducia deliberatoria* (usually of twenty to twenty-five days, but the term could be lengthened if the principal were far away from the court) to consult his constituent, to get new instructions.[169] Such a delay was only one of the many

---

[167] *Glos. ord.,* to *Decr.* 1, 38, 11 Dilectus, ad v. *generalis:* "Potest ergo quis constituere generalem procuratorem ad omnia tam ad judicia quam ad negotia . . . ; tamen talis procurator transigere non potest, nec alienare," i.e., without getting a special mandate to transact or alienate. But see above, § 1, nn. 11-24, 32-38, 44, on *plena potestas* and *administratio*; the legists and canonists hold that a general and *libera administratio* or *plena potestas* permits *transactio* and *alienatio* if the constituent is not injured thereby; but *libera* must be given specifically, and then no special mandates in addition to the general are required.

[168] Hostiensis, *Summa,* II, t. *De dilationibus,* no. 4: even the plaintiff can be given *induciae* "si inopinatum quid emergat de quo non potuit divinare, puta contra rescriptum suum exceptio opponitur, in quo replicatione opus est. . . ."

[169] *Glos. ord.,* to c. 11 Dilectus, ad v. *cedere*; the quality of the *negotium* and of the parties helps the judge to decide whether to grant a delay. Hostiensis, *Summa,* I, t. De procur, no. 11: "Sed et generalis ad negocia generaliter agere et experiri potest . . . ; et dominus ita remotus sit, quod intra. xx. dies, qui dantur ad deliberandum, consuli non possit, maior dilatio danda est, que si negatur, iuste appellabitur. . . ." Guillaume Durantis, *Speculum iudiciale,* II, i, *De dilationibus* (fols. 55ᵛ-59ᵛ), no. 18 (fol. 56ᵛ, c. 2): *dilationes deliberatoriae* are given "ad deliberandum reis, utrum velint cedere vel contendere"; the *terminus* is 25 days, sometimes more, "secundum locorum distantiam, extra. de procura. dilectus"; sometimes these delays are denied. Johannes Andreae, *Novella,* to c. 11 Dilectus, ad v. *dominus principalis* in the gloss ad v. *cedere* (*Glos. ord.*): such

kinds granted to the defendant (another kind was for procuring lawyers, testimony, etc.),[170] and it was necessary to obtain it before the actual trial started.[171]

The general proctor who received a delay for "referring back" for new instructions had limited powers: he could not yield a charge without contesting it, could not "transact" and could not alienate, unless he obtained the express consent of his principal in a new and special mandate. But this meant infinite delays in justice, and even the defeat of justice. The court needed to speed matters by compelling the litigants to accept its jurisdiction; and the rules of judicial procedure increasingly emphasized that the litigants give full powers to their agents. There can be no due process unless courts can compel consent to their judicial power. So it was that by 1250 the treatises on procedure were reflecting the needs for quicker and better justice by elaborating the various formulas expressing *plena potestas* in the mandate. As we saw above, models of mandates expressed not only *plena potestas,* which should have been sufficient as "full instructions," but also most of the specific things that the proctor should have power to do in court in order to protect his constituent until he had to bow to the decision of the judges on each point. *Plena*

---

a delay was granted because the principal had not incurred blame by not "instructing" his proctor, which the principal could not do before the suit was brought against him; as Innocent IV said, if the proctor is "instructed"—i.e., given a proper mandate—for this suit, no delays are given to him ("quod speciali procuratori ad causam istam constituto non darentur induciae, de quibus hic dicitur, presumitur enim instructus"). But here Joh. Andreae cites Hostiensis, who says that whenever anything arises "super quo procurator per se respondere non potest, nec potest aliquid domino imputari, habebit inducias ad dominum consulendum, ut se sic instruat et respondeat" (i.e., he must obtain a new mandate and instructions); e.g., if a prelate is cited to court and is asked what was done in a chapter-meeting which he did not attend, he should obtain a delay to consult the chapter. But Innocent IV had held both opinions, which are in no real contradiction of each other; *Appar.,* to c. 11 Dilectus, ad vv. *a iudicibus* and *consultet*; Hostiensis and Joh. Andreae follow Innocent IV on these points: "Ar. quod si citatus est, non expresso super quo, et citatus constituit procuratorem, procurator debet habere inducias ut consultat dominum."

170 Guill. Durantis, *Spec.,* II, i, *De dilat.,* no. 22: *dilationes preparatoriae;* also Hostiensis, *Summa,* II, *e.t.*

171 Guill. Durantis, *Spec.,* II, *De exceptionibus et replicationibus,* § iii, no. 1 (p. 64): The *exceptio dilatoria* must be put forward and proved *ante litis contestationem.* The time allowed for such exceptions was set by the judge, *Decr.* 2, 25, 4.

potestas, or *libera administratio,* gave the proctor the power to petition, transact, alienate, make special pleas or exceptions, reply to exceptions, produce witnesses and instruments, refuse the judges, and to do anything for which, without full powers, the proctor would otherwise need a special mandate. As Boniface VIII decided, the general proctor could do all these things without any special mandates if the general mandate contained special clauses or specified *libera administratio.*[172] Thus such "reference back" as limited the authority of the court was obviated by a mandate which conferred full powers.

In short, in all civil matters, by legal theory and procedure, the plaintiff and court should adequately, if generally, inform the defendant as to the nature of the charges. The court should give the defendant enough time to prepare his case, to get expert advice, furnish documents and consult with all parties whose rights might be directly or indirectly touched by the outcome, and whose consent was therefore necessary. It was in the interest of speedier justice that the court grant ample time for this, since those concerned had the legal right to refuse to accept the sentence and to appeal if they had not been informed and consulted. The defendant, particularly if a corporation or a group of individuals and corporations with common rights, could then deliberate, consider the means of litigating, prepare the record, appoint a proctor or proctors, and draw up a mandate which, according to the general practice expected by the court, contained the *plena potestas* or instructions furnished to the proctor. But when the proctors of plaintiff and defendant appeared in court, they could still resort to any number of actions to delay proceedings and defend the rights of their constituents. They could, among other things, challenge the jurisdiction of the court itself, contest the wording of the *libellus* and the writ of citation, deny the capacity of the opposing proctor,[173] maintain that they had not been adequately informed

[172] Boniface VIII, *VI,* 1, 19, 4. See above, n. 32.

[173] It might be declared that the proctor of the opponent was not qualified, or that his powers were inadequate. This was particularly important, since if the plaintiff won his suit and the defendant later claimed that his proctor acted fraudulently or was not given full powers and therefore appealed the sentence, then the plaintiff must continue the battle in other courts. The reverse applied

about a new action and claim the right of "referring back" for new instructions. If the judges decided that the proctors really had full powers, they could pass on all preliminaries such as exceptions, replications, duplications, and triplications,[174] and proceed with the actual trial. The court might still grant an exception, however, which would postpone the business and give the parties time for new instructions. Yet the fact that the proctors had full powers meant that the decision of all preliminaries and of the case was accepted by the principal parties, who thereafter had no right of appeal against the decision—unless they could maintain that the judges disregarded the law and their legal rights in passing sentence.

Full powers, therefore, did not absolutely preclude possible delays in "reference back." But such "reference back" did not limit the consent of litigants to the jurisdiction of the court, did not deny the power of the court; it was not a limitation of the *plena potestas* of the representatives to accept the will of the court, for *plena potestas* acknowledged the authority of the judges to grant or deny any pleas presented by the litigants. There were still delays (justice was slow in the thirteenth century, as now) even after the defendant was legally informed and after he in turn legally instructed his agent; but all these delays were made according to the law and special circumstances as interpreted by the court. Even if the losing party had the right of appeal to a higher court, his appeal did not mean that he had limited the powers of his representative, nor that he refused consent to the sentence of the court in any manner other than that permitted by judicial process, the interpretation of which belonged to the public authority and not to private individuals.

Whatever the subtleties involved in court decisions of all these matters in a case, it is clear that, from the point of view of the court and in the interests of justice, agents of parties must have full powers, and these powers were the instructions given by the interested parties in the mandates. But from the point

---

when the defendant could prove that the proctor of the plaintiff had insufficient powers to accept the outcome of decisions of *exceptiones* or of the whole case in favor of the defendant.

174 Cf. Pollock and Maitland, II, 611-619; Bracton, III, 142 (ed. Twyss, III, 408-410), on the attorney.

of view of the litigants, a second kind of instructions were the documents and written or oral advice which were given to the proctors in order to help them act wisely in defending the constituents' interests. How much judgment was left to the proctor it is hard to say; but his judgment did not extend to injuring his principal. It was the second kind of instructions which in part led to the practice of drawing up petitions to be presented by the proctors in court; and there was nothing to prevent many different parties, all touched in common by a demand or a complaint, from instructing their representatives to cooperate, to present a common front and thus to strengthen their arguments. The jurisdiction of the court was not limited by this procedure; it had to hear the common arguments, but it could still decide against the whole body of defendants if the facts and the law so warranted. And the representatives, each of whom had full powers, lost individually even though they had either unanimously or by majority agreed upon a plea which was unsuccessful.

The essential elements of all this procedure are to be found in French and English treatises on customary law—in Beaumanoir[175] and in Bracton.[176] Indeed, the Romano-canonical rules, despite variations wrought by local custom and environment, were readily adapted to the courts of common law and to royal jurisdiction.[177] In this development the clergy, who had suits in secular courts, must have played an important role. But the direct influence of legists in England must not be undervalued.[178]

---

[175] *Coutumes de Beauvaisis*, ch. IV, §§ 4, 12, 13, 17-20, 24 (in lay courts a "sufficient mandate" without the clauses of *cautio* or surety required by ecclesiastical courts is adequate), 26; on the summons and excuses and delays, chs. II and III.

[176] *De legibus*, II, 317ff. (ed. Twyss, II, 206ff.), on the general and brief statement in the writ of the matter at issue and the claim of the plaintiff as information to the defendant; *ibid.*, III, 77ff. and IV, 245ff. (Twyss, III, 206ff. and VI, 150ff.), on exceptions; *ibid.*, IV, 52ff., 64ff. and 71ff. (Twyss, V, 92ff., 130ff. and 146ff.), on default, summonses, and excuses or essoins. The attorney, who by definiton has full powers, can transact and make all the above special pleas; *ibid.*, III, 142 (Twyss, III, 408-410).

[177] For England, see Pollock and Maitland, II, 611-619.

[178] See George L. Haskins, "Franciscus Accursius; a New Document," *Speculum*, XIII, 76; and Richardson, "The Oxford Law School under John," *L.Q.R.*, LVII, 319-338.

Certainly, the relation between the instructions carried to court and the plea for a delay because of ignorance of the law was recognized by English royal courts in 1281: the parties should be so instructed on coming to court that they could not allege ignorance of the law.[179] Moreover, the principle that all who were interested in the business must be given a hearing, that all must be summoned and informed of the business, and that they should send properly instructed attorneys to court to consent to the decision of the case—in short, the principle of *quod omnes tangit* in connection with due process and information and *plena potestas*, was a fundamental ideal of English and French law in the thirteenth century.[180]

That papal and royal requests for subsidies resulted in an application of court procedure to the summoning of representatives of all common and corporate rights can be amply illustrated. But leaving aside what is well known, namely, the history of the appearance of representatives in councils and royal assemblies, we must note how the communities were informed and how they in turn instructed their delegates and tried to limit their consent.

As stated above, the case of necessity and public utility, the dawning right of State, enhanced the royal and papal prerogative in such a way that the right to summon was greater than the right to refuse obedience to the summons. Indeed, the writ of summons was in the form of a peremptory, public citation which generally, but adequately, stated the nature of the case and of the need for a subsidy. Also, by fixing the date of the assembly, it permitted sufficient delay for electing representatives and instructing them. The summons, in other words, gen-

179 Sayles, ed., *Select Cases in the Court of King's Bench*, I, 89f.—the court refused to grant a dilatory exception: "nec poterit excusari dicendo quod nescivit si hoc esset ius vel non, cum pars debet venire ad iudicium ita instructus quod non possit inposterum allegare ignorantiam iuris."
Ignorance of the summons was treated analogously: if the citation was made publicly, then the cited could not allege that he was ignorant and therefore must not suffer injury from an adverse sentence.
180 Bracton is well acquainted with *quod omnes tangit*; see below, ch. IV. The Roman principle stated what had long been a principle in feudal law but was beneficial chiefly to the magnates; it was now being extended to cover the rights of the lesser laity and clergy, and to communities of these.

erally informed the recipients that there was an emergency which touched the *status regis* and the *status regni,* and that for the common good the king needed counsel and aid—needed, usually, a subsidy, which was required to enable the king to meet the danger common to all. Even though the precise details were lacking—the amount of money needed was not stated —the ruler intended that the summons, like a court writ, should pass for adequate information on the basis of which the communities summoned could send "sufficiently instructed" representatives, that is, representatives with full powers both to defend the rights of their constituents and to accept the final decision of the high court and council. That there existed a "national" emergency or case of necessity was information enough.[181]

Yet the royal government in France sometimes felt so strongly the need of informing, in the legal sense, the whole community of the kingdom that it sent the summons to *baillis* and seneschals who were commanded to hold preparatory, provincial assemblies. This was done not only to inform the communities but also to expedite matters in order that no community could claim lack of information and preparatory deliberation as an excuse either for limiting the powers of the representatives to be sent

[181] The theory of royal or of papal authority included the right of the monarch to interpret what constituted necessity and public utility. The pope's interpretation met little difficulty in the Church—if the pope decided that a war must be supported for the defense of the Church or the faith, naturally for the common good of Christendom, the clergy summoned to general or provincial councils could not refuse a subsidy, though they could negotiate on the amount. Yet, the clergy sometimes tried to argue that no such necessity existed except as a papal subterfuge. Of several examples, this will illustrate clerical opposition: in 1264, after a papal legate demanded a tenth from the French clergy, some of the clergy of Rheims maintained that while all things belonged to the prince *quantum ad deffentionem et tuitionem* (see below, ch. VII, nn. 75-88) the papal war against Manfred (for which the subsidy was demanded) was not a just war for the defense of the faith, and besides, Manfred was the rightful king of "Apulia." But this and other complaints made in the council and afterwards were obviously not heeded by legate or pope; see the *Summa de omni facultate,* perhaps by Drogo, in P. Varin, *Archives législatives de la ville de Reims,* 1re partie (*Documents inédits*), pp. 448-455, 449, 452f. Similarly, the English clergy had protested against contributing for earlier papal quarrels with Frederick II; Lunt, *Financial Relations,* pp. 197ff., 206-219.

In the fourteenth century, in France and in England, the magnates and representatives repeatedly tried to limit the right of the government to determine the case of necessity and what constituted public utility—in England with more success (though not complete) than in France.

to the general assembly or for later resistance.[182] Precedents had been furnished by the Church in the thirteenth century, and possibly also by the example of English county courts.[183] Thus informed, could those summoned ask for delays other than the time given before the date fixed for the assembly? Obviously, the government desired a speedy consent to its needs, and it had a good argument against delays in the plea of imminent danger to the public safety. Just as obviously, all who had vested rights and interests often failed to appreciate the need of paying extraordinary taxes, and used every legal fact or fiction in defense of their rights against new demands. On occasion, they claimed that they had been too generally informed,[184] or not informed at all about a new demand, and hence they could not give full powers to their representatives. In 1283 the proctors of the lower clergy of the province of Canterbury, asserting that their powers were for one royal request and were limited to it, and consequently did not extend to a second request, asked

182 For details see Taylor, *Speculum*, xiii, 298-302. But sometimes the local assemblies were held after the general one for the purpose of receiving the report of the royal will expressed in the general assembly and obtaining readier obedience. On speeches made by royal agents to inform provincial assemblies, see Prentout, *États de Normandie*, ii, 126.

183 By the middle of the thirteenth century, a papal request for a subsidy often was transmitted by legates who ordered archbishops to summon their suffragans to a provincial (or even "national") council; while the bishops, claiming that they could not consent for the clergy of their dioceses, in turn held diocesan synods to inform the lower clergy and obtain their consent by way of diocesan representatives chosen to go to the legatine council. The English shires, or rather the courts, were obviously convenient for the same purpose, when the king needed consent to a subsidy. Thus, king, legate, or archbishop could be sure of observing the rules of *quod omnes tangit*: through such preparatory assemblies all communities or corporations and individuals "touched" by the demand or any other "national" business were officially, publicly, legally informed (magnates and specially privileged towns were summoned individually) and given time for assenting to the representation; and therefore, no community or individual could later successfully claim that there was no proper summons and therefore that the decision of the king in the assembly was not binding.

184 In 1264 Drogo, *Summa*, complained that the legate's mandate (writ of summons) was too harsh and general, for it commanded the cathedral chapters to send proctors "qui haberent potestatem consentiendi in sua voluntate facienda precise, nulla mentione facta de sua voluntate facienda, nec aliqua certitudine super hoc expresso"; and this enslaved the churches; Varin, *Arch. législat. . . . de Reims*, 1re partie, p. 455. In this case the complaint came after the legate held the council, and no doubt the legate succeeded in overriding such pleas and compelling the delegates to consent to his will, as the summons indicated they should have full powers to do.

the archbishop for a delay to deliberate on the second for which they had no instructions.[185] The archbishop granted the delay requested, for it was legally defensible—it was no limitation of the powers given for the first request; nor for the second, since for it no powers at all had been given. Delays were similarly granted to provincial Estates in France—usually to give time for further debate.[186]

In France in the early years of the fourteenth century, when Philip the Fair was trying to obtain universal consent to an appeal to a general council against Boniface VIII, ecclesiastical communities tried to limit the mandates of proctors, and to qualify consent at the assemblies by inserting "saving" clauses. This procedure resulted from the natural feeling, based on the law of the Church, that full submission to the king's authority was impossible when royal interests were inferior to, or rather, separate from, the rights and liberties of the churches and the spiritual rights of the pope over all Christendom.[187] But there

[185] An illustration comes from England. In 1283 the proctors of the lower clergy of the Province of Canterbury asked the archbishop for a delay to consider a new royal petition for a subsidy, a petition that was separate from an earlier one for which the clergy had been summoned to convocation. They asserted that their *potestas* was *limitata* and did not extend to the second royal request; Peckham, *Registrum*, II, 536: on the last day of a council held in London (Lambeth), says the archbishop, "per procuratores cleri provinciae nostrae, post datam eorum responsionem in scriptis super petitione domini regis facta Northampton, de decima triennali, nobis et confratribus nostris extitit supplicatum, ut novas eis concederemus inducias ad tractandum et deliberandum super seconda petitione domini regis de concedendo sibi a clero pro utilitate publica aliquo subsidio liberali; praesertim, cum super ipsa petitione, quae nova fuit, prius non tractaverant, nec se ad hoc eorum potestas, quae limitata fuerit, extendebat." In this case the mandate was limited, but limited legally with respect to a second business on which neither constituents nor proctors had been informed by proper citation. But the mandate and powers of the proctors were not limited with respect to the first royal petition for a subsidy. Consequently, Archbishop Peckham granted the requested delay "ad tractandum et deliberandum super secunda petitione." It seems that this is an illustration of the use of a mandate giving full powers for one case; a new mandate was needed for a new case when the proctors had not been given a general mandate with *plena potestas* for all cases that might arise.

[186] Prentout, *États de Normandie*, II, 126f.

[187] Picot, *Documents*, no. 4 (the clergy of the province of Tours declared, 1302, that they would aid the king "ad defensionem jurium, statusque et honoris suorum et regni, salvis juribus et libertatibus ecclesiarum nostrarum, statibus nostris animarumque salute"); no. 50 (a prior gives full powers to his proctors to consent to the king's will "quantum cum Deo et salva consciencia et honore

are earlier examples of attempts among the clergy of cathedral chapters to limit the powers of their proctors in councils. In 1264 some chapters, when the cardinal-legate summoned them to send to a council at Paris "instructed" proctors with full powers to consent to a subsidy, gave their proctors only a *mandatum ad audiendum et referendum*.[188] Indeed, before it was clearly understood that the superior authority of pope or papal legate was decisive in summoning "fully instructed" representatives and in interpreting the instructions in the mandate, there must have been many instances of limited mandates.

There was, however, no legal justification for such failure to give full powers when the administrative and judicial authority demanded that communities give their delegates *plena potestas*. Even the "saving" clauses inserted by the French clergy in 1302-1303, while legally founded on the rights of the papacy and the Church, were contrary to the reviving theory of the superior right of State: the pope was, so the king alleged, endangering the common good and the rights of king and kingdom and consequently, the rights and welfare of both clergy and laity; the danger touched the *status regni* and the *status* of all, and therefore all must consent to the royal appeal to the general council against Boniface VIII. (Moreover, the legal theory of corporate appeals made it necessary for the government to appeal to a council in the name and by the consent of all members of the kingdom as the corporate community of the realm.) The king thus could demand full powers of consent, and in fact, he com-

---

Sedis Apostolice possumus et debemus et permittunt canonice sanctiones," and "salvis semper offensione divina et reverencia Romane Ecclesie universalisque Ecclesie unitate omnique conjuratione et conspiratione cessantibus"); no. 185 (the proctor of the chapter of Carcassonne adheres to the appeal to a general council, saving the honor, authority and reverence of the Apostolic See and the unity of the Church, "et in quantum secundum Deum possum et debeo, et volunt et paciuntur canonice sanxiones et sanctorum patrum statuta."—no doubt his mandate had contained, as instructions, these limiting clauses).

188 Drogo, *Summa*, Varin, *Arch. législat. . . . de Reims*, p. 448. But, as the complaint states, these proctors consented to a tenth, thereby exceeding the limits of their powers—this they could not do, says the author. The legate, it is obvious, was the interpreter of the mandates, and he compelled the proctors to consent. Complaints against his interpretation could be carried by appeal to Rome, but hardly with success.

pelled many of the recalcitrants to consent.[189] When the king wished to tax the clergy, and, as usually happened in the thirteenth century, the popes yielded to the royal declaration of the case of necessity, of a just war against the aggressor,[190] the clergy could not legally cause delays, after being informed, by asking for "reference back"; nor could they limit their consent except insofar as they could complain and reduce the amount of the subsidy or appeal to the pope because of abuses committed in the form of violence or of the violation of judicial procedure and due process. For example, it could be argued, usually after the event, that the corporate consent of a chapter bound only the chapter as corporation and its corporate property, not the individual members insofar as they had property and rights separate from those belonging to the corporation; or that those who were not summoned to be consulted did not consent; or that the lower clergy should not have to pay when the consent was ostensibly given for them by representatives of cathedral chapters—this was behind the growing practice of summoning proctors of dioceses as well as of chapters, for everyone with any kind of right was asserting the principle of consent in *quod omnes tangit*.[191] If these rules applied to the clergy, how much more to the laity!

[189] C. V. Langlois, in Lavisse, III, ii, 160f.—this in 1303, when the king obtained consent locally, not in a general assembly. But the legal theory was the same, whether applied locally or generally, or generally and locally, in succession.

[190] It was chiefly in the Church, from 1179 on, that the right to tax the clergy beyond the customary aids was based on necessity and public utility. See *Decr.* 3, 49, 4 and 7, and G. LeBras, *L'immunité réelle*, pp. 21-30, 49-148.

[191] Drogo, *Summa*, Varin, *op.cit.*, p. 448; when in 1264 the proctors of chapters consented to the tenth demanded by the papal legate, they had no right to bind the individual members of their chapters, the author claims; for if the tenth were paid the chapters must pay it "de suis bonis communibus"; the individual members should not pay, "quia nec requisite super hoc fuerunt, nec promiserunt. Unde dicit lex, quod illud quos omnes tangit, debet ab omnibus comprobari." Moreover, as in *D.* 3, 4, 7, what is owed to the *universitas* is not owed to the individual members; "etenim bona universitatis non sunt singulorum, sed ipsius universitatis vel collegii." One recognizes in this argument the corporate theory of the thirteenth century; see Gierke, III, 263; and Gillet, *La personnalité juridique*, pp. 129 n.2, 137f. We cannot pause to examine the theory in detail; nor the theory of the majority which binds the minority. Suffice to say that in the court or council the judges could interpret the consent given by proctors as binding the corporation both collectively and individually. But the subtle distinctions made by the lawyers were a source of legal resistance.

As Drogo says, pp. 448f., even if the defense of the State or of Christendom

Obviously, then, when the State was in danger, the king could not, unless too weak to enforce his will, tolerate the limited mandate, or any kind of "reference back" or reservations of consent. Delays endangered the public safety. Feudal custom[192] was here strengthened by the growth of royal power and by the procedure of Roman and Canon law: delays that had imperiled the safety of the suzerain now imperiled the safety of the king as head and representative of the kingdom, hence the safety of the State. Naturally, then, the ruler, as the highest administrator and judge, demanded that sufficiently instructed delegates, delegates bearing full powers, be sent, lest the decision be delayed by the subterfuge of "reference back."[193] He was thus assured of consent to his decisions made with the advice of his court and council, before which, not in which, the representatives appeared. No mandate, therefore, without a clause stating full powers was considered valid in the royal court and assembly.[194] So it was that, because of numerous attempts of the clergy to limit powers and consent by the claim of *referendum*, Philip the Fair specified *plena potestas absque excusatione relationis faciende*.[195] Given the circumstances and the continued efforts of

---

was involved, nevertheless a subsidy should be reasonable—and this was based on the law; whence many complaints of the English clergy in the same period.

[192] Beaumanoir, c. II, § 65: "Cil qui sont semont pour aidier leur seigneurs contre leur anemis ou pour aidier leur seigneurs a leur mesons defendre, ne doivent pas contremander ne querre nul delai." This in connection with summonses. The principle applied to corporate communities, which aided in the defense of the kingdom by paying subsidies more than by fighting, even if we should not treat them as a part of the feudal system.

[193] See the decretal of Innocent III, *an.* 1200, in *Decr.* 2, 14, 6 Cum dilecti: the pope cited *peremptorie* a litigant to appear at the Curia "per se vel per procuratorem sufficientem sufficienter instructum ne postmodum per dilationes vel occasiones quaslibet subterfugere videretur examen."

[194] As Beaumanoir had said, c. IV, § 143: "Nule procuracions ne vaut riens se cil qui fet le procureur ne s'oblige a tenir ferme et estable ce qui sera fet ou dit par son procureur." He follows the legists and canonists in this equivalent expression for *plena potestas*. In Picot, *Documents*, we find several examples of mandates of delegates refused by the royal judges or commissioners because of their insufficiency; nos. 148-152, 156, 158. These mandates were insufficient because full powers were not given; instead, power only to hear the commissioners and refer back, or to present excuses and ask for delays was given (no. 166). Sometimes, however, the excuses were heard and the delays granted; nos. 153 (permitted because of need to consult with other interested parties—*quod omnes tangit*) and 216 (same reason).

[195] Jusselin, *Bibl. de l'École des Chartes*, LXVII, 470. In Catalonia a royal statute of 1358 forbade the use of a *procuratorium* with *potestas limitata* in any court; *Cortes . . . de Aragon*, I, ii, 656.

many communities to misunderstand the royal command to send fully instructed representatives, this tautology in the royal writ of summons was necessary.

This was certainly true where the monarchy had become fairly well centralized and the king had real authority. Almost as a paradox, therefore, it was in the England of common law that the king (at least at the end of the thirteenth century) was able to apply most logically the Romano-canonical principles of necessity, public utility and *quod omnes tangit*, and the Romano-canonical procedure of corporate representation by agents bearing full powers. For England was sufficiently unified under the monarchy to enable the king to prevent the extremes of localism which in France partly resulted in the towns and ecclesiastical corporations repeatedly trying to limit the *plena potestas* in the mandate.[196] I find little evidence of limited mandates being drawn up for Parliament.[197] But on the other hand,

[196] In France there were as many local variances in procedure and in forms of mandates, even in the *pays de droit ecrit*, as there were in experiences in community spirit, enterprise, and customs. In England the procedure (like the individual participation in village, hundred, and county courts, and the responsibilities in the community) was strikingly unified as a result of the historical development of the monarchy in relation to the communities. Prof. F. M. Powicke has rightly emphasized the importance of the social position and experience in local government of the knights of the shire. It was the peculiar class of knights (i.e., peculiar to England) which facilitated the royal application of the Roman principles and procedure of representing corporate legal interests, but which at the time was an indispensable reinforcement of the power of the magnates to limit that other Roman principle of monarchy, absolutism. Thus, England, Spain, and France started in the thirteenth century with a fairly common background of Roman procedure and judicial consent which shaped the control of extreme feudal particularism and individualism. But where in England the king could go only so far toward absolutism, in Spain and France the feudal nobility, in the long run, were unable to stop the growth of absolutism because they were not strengthened sufficiently by a great body of knights. The cities proved to be an inadequate substitute for a country gentry—perhaps because the cities were too closely allied, normally, with the king—or were controlled by the royal agents.

[197] Repeatedly, however, Edward I in his writ of summons commanded that the full powers given the knights and burgesses should not have any defect that would result in unfinished business: "Et ita quod pro defectu potestatis hujusmodi idem negocium infectum non remaneat;" *Parliamentary Writs*, I, p. 26, no. 3; similarly, pp. 29f., no. 4; p. 48, no. 38; p. 84, no. 5.

On the back of the writs returned to Parliament is usually noted the statement that the knights and burgesses were chosen "ad factum quod breve exigit," or were given full powers "secundum tenorem brevis" (*Parl. Writs*, I, 21ff.). In one

the almost national feeling of community in England, along with the well-established experience of knights of the shire in local government under royal supervision, was an insuperable obstacle in the long run to a royal absolutism based on public utility and the well-known Roman theory, "Quod principi placuit, legis habet vigorem." Thus, because the king was powerful at this period, and because there was a real "community of the realm" when knights and magnates had common interests, a unified system of representation arose which resulted in the constitutional or limited monarchy of a later age.

From the point of view of the government, full instructions, or powers, meant essentially the complete acceptance of the issue and, after legal hearing in the assembly, the consent of all interested parties to the royal decision on the means of defending the community of the realm against aggression or any other threats to the common good. But since by the very theory that the king must rule according to law and justice it was essential that the government permit representatives to defend the legal interests of their constituents against any extraordinary demands, which inevitably affected all rights or liberties confirmed by custom or privilege, it was expected, and desired, that the delegates should bring all the instructions that would enable them to act intelligently and with legal proof for every step taken in protecting local interests. These instructions, which would also help the government decide its policy or the amount of the tax in relation to what burden could be reasonably borne by the communities, were analogous to the advice and means of waging suit in ordinary court procedure. They were the *gesta*, the "record," such as the originals or authenticated copies or privileges granted by the king, and statements of law and custom guaranteeing liberties; they were, in addition, information on the conditions in the communities; finally, they were frequently the complaints which the communities wished to present against royal agents and abuses of privileges

---

instance it is stated that the representatives were given *plena potestas* "ad faciendum coram domino Rege et ejus consilio quod hoc breve requirit"; *ibid.*, p. 39, no. 19. Unfortunately, the actual mandates brought with the returned writs do not survive.

as a counter-claim to challenge the king's right to ask for sacrifices. In all this the constituents probably instructed their representatives generally on how to meet the government's demands, how to proceed in the presentation of the record or of petitions supported by the record, and how to make common cause with other representatives.[198] In other words, the representatives enjoyed some discretion in their powers "to treat"—

[198] In 1226 Pope Honorius III, approving the "necessities" of Henry III of England, ordered the prelates of England to grant a subsidy, to be raised in each diocese, to the king. When the Archbishop of Canterbury urged the bishops to make the clergy of their dioceses give at least a twelfth or a fourteenth, the canons of the Chapter of Salisbury, appealing to the principle of *quod omnes tangit*, met in order to discuss whether they should agree to aid the king, whether they should give the twelfth or the fourteenth, and how the churches of England could be protected from the establishment of a precedent. The chapter then asked that the bishops persuade the archbishop to summon proctors of the clergy to an assembly where a uniform response of all the clergy could be given and thus the papal mandate be obeyed without injury to the English Church and clergy. The archbishop granted the request and through the Bishop of Salisbury summoned the chapter to send proctors who were to be *sufficienter instructi*. If the archbishop meant full powers by "sufficient instructions," the chapter gave other instructions, in addition to the technical powers, to its elected proctors in the form of a list of opinions drawn up in writing. The chief of these instructions were that the proctors of the chapter, along with the proctors of other chapters, should agree to a subsidy if it were deemed fitting to do so. If possible, they should argue for a twentieth (instead of a fourteenth or sixteenth) as a subsidy, and in no case should they consent to more than a sixth; they should try to obtain certain methods for the assessment and collection of the subsidy; they should ask (of the council of bishops) what was to be done if some canons individually refused consent to what the majority of the chapter decided (the problem of individual consent within a corporation); and they should ask for a "non-prejudice" guarantee from the king.

It is noteworthy that the chapter did not instruct its delegates to refuse consent if the subsidy was necessary—obviously, the archbishop and bishops were the essential council in the assembly, and by the papal mandate they must inevitably decide the case of necessity in favor of the king. The proctors were merely told how to negotiate, to try to reduce the amount demanded, to obtain measures in the collection that would not injure the clergy in the future. Finally, that the proctors merely had a legal hearing before the prelates is shown by the fact that the assembly granted a sixteenth, not the smaller twentieth desired by the Chapter of Salisbury. They obeyed the papal mandate but did negotiate and had a voice in the amount granted. After all, papal decrees had stated that *reasonable* subsidies should be granted in cases of necessity (*Decr.* 3, 39, 6; 3, 49, cc. 4 and 7).

On all this see W. H. Rich Jones, ed., *Reg. S. Osmund*, II, 57-67; Lunt, *Financial Relations*, pp. 187f.; *idem*, in Burr, *Essays*, pp. 121f.; Weske, *Convocation of the Clergy*, pp. 42ff., 201-203. Lunt sees the papal *plenitudo potestatis* as the compulsion which the clergy could not resist. This is true, but the pope was also applying the Lateran decrees to royal governments as well as to cities; it was the duty of the clergy to help the State in a case of necessity.

ad tractandum.[199] *Tractare* meant not only that they could negotiate with the king on the amount of a subsidy, but that they
were empowered by their constituents to bring up their own
business while attending the assembly. Towns in France and
Spain frequently gave full powers and a general mandate both
for the king's business and for all matters which they wished to
be pursued before the king or his court by way of petition. English representatives functioned in a similar fashion—whence,
no doubt, the numerous petitions in Parliament.[200]

Unfortunately, so far as I know, copies of instructions have
only exceptionally survived the thirteenth century.[201] But it is
likely that by the end of that century most of the instructions
were embodied at first in the petitions of individual communities and at last in common petitions presented by all the communities in the "community of the realm." In fourteenth-century England, at any rate, the towns did instruct their representatives even during sessions of Parliament.[202] But in the legal
theory of the age neither instructions on how to contest the
king's demands nor petitions asking for remedies of abuses
constituted a limitation of the *plena potestas.* "Full power"
was consent to the decision of king and court and council, consent given before the assembly was held. But in the assembly,
the representatives had the right to use all legal means of shaping the final decision in favor of their constituents.

It was in this sense that representatives could use their judgment. They could not deliberately injure their constituents'
rights by voluntarily yielding to the demands of the government. They must use their judgment in finding the best way
to present complaints and thus try to reduce the amount of the
subsidy requested. They might, if the atmosphere in the assembly was encouraging, especially if the magnates acted as leaders,
try to point out that the subsidy was not needed, that the government was merely pretending a case of necessity, or was plan-

---

199 McIlwain, *C.M.H.*, vii, 679.
200 *Loc.cit.*
201 See n. 198, above.
202 Lapsley, in *Maitland Selected Essays,* pp. 5f. Pollard, *Evolution of Parl.*,
p. 152, says that there was "a total absence of specific instructions." This is not
supported by Lapsley.

ning an expedition overseas when a real threat existed nearer home.[203] But individual judgment was not likely to be of much effect. By the fourteenth century, therefore, the representatives of different communities began to meet together in order to arrive at a common understanding and to present before the king and his council a common judgment. The common petition might be used in a like manner. The judgment of the whole community of communities was of far greater weight in influencing the royal judges and councillors. But this judgment, whether expressed by the speaker for all the representatives or by a common petition, was simply a carrying out or defense of the interests of the constituencies before the king's court and council. If it was well supported by the record of grievances, of universal complaints about royal demands, of abuses committed by royal agents, and of legally attested rights, and by the weakness of the position taken by the government, then it might indeed constitute a successful defense and the defeat of the king. In the legal theory, however, the king and his court and council had the power of decision; and if they judged that their case of national defense was proved, they could decide against the pleas of the representatives. To this final decision the representatives must consent in accordance with their full powers. Since they had used their best judgment, had honestly represented the interests of their constituents, these must likewise accept the decision, for they had given full powers to their delegates before the meeting of the assembly took place.[204]

---

[203] Edward I found it difficult to obtain a subsidy in 1297-1298 for his campaigns in Gascony and Flanders; the magnates argued that Scotland was the real danger, that they were not legally obliged to go to Gascony without the king, who planned to be in Flanders; Stubbs, *S.C.*, pp. 482-489. But in this case, the commons seem to have granted the subsidies demanded, leaving it to the magnates to resist the king's will and obtain a confirmation of charters. Yet, the right of consent is confirmed to the commons, just as feudal rights are confirmed to the magnates, *S.C.*, pp. 492-494. See J. G. Edwards, "*Confirmatio Cartarum* and Baronial Grievances in 1297, Part I," *E.H.R.*, LVIII (1943), 147-171.

[204] Chrimes, *English Constitutional Ideas*, p. 80 n. 2, argues that an area that failed to send representatives with *plena potestas* would not be bound by the consent of the representatives of other communities, and thus that *plena potestas* leaves unexplained the fact "that parliament came to be regarded as binding on all the king's subjects, whether they had legal representatives therein or not." But Chrimes neglects several important legal theories connected with *plena potestas*: (1) the will of the majority in a corporation determined the policy of

Instructions and judgment were related not only to the royal summons, but also to other matters which the communities thought it opportune to bring up in the king's court. Thus, if the representative was appointed for the one assembly, he was sometimes given, instead of a mandate with full powers for the main business of a subsidy, a general mandate with additional clauses constituting full powers and taking care of special matters for which a general mandate as such was not valid.[205] In that sense he was a general proctor for the assembly in which several kinds of business could come up: the proctor sent by a town or other community might be instructed not only to answer to the king's request, but also to submit petitions to the king for special favors, to sue or be sued in the king's court, or

---

defending corporate interests in court; (2) the proctor given *plena potestas* to carry out this policy and represent the corporation in court acted for the majority of the members; (3) the court's decision bound the whole corporation, even the minority of individuals who refused to consent to the representation; (4) similarly the *plena potestas* of knights of the shire and the decision in Parliament bound the whole community of the shire (i.e., except the magnates and towns in the shire, who consented for themselves); (5) when the representatives of the communities summoned to Parliament met in one body as the community of the communities, their full powers included the judgment involved in agreeing on a policy of negotiating with the government and defending the interests of the community as a whole in the king's court and council; (6) whether these representatives, the commons, agreed unanimously or by majority (cf. Chrimes, pp. 135f.; Chrimes hesitates to accept the majority-principle in the commons before the fifteenth century, but I think he misunderstands the documents), their judgment bound the dissenters and the absent, and the king's government must accept the judgment of the majority as representing the attitude of the commons; (7) but the final decision of the king, while it might be influenced by the legal force of the arguments presented by the commons as a whole, was not dictated by the commons; (8) the royal decision, however, did bind the whole body of representatives, whatever the claims or defense they had agreed upon; (9) further, the decision bound all representatives individually (even those who as a minority had not agreed on yielding to the king's demands), and through the representatives and their full powers of attorney, bound all the communities in the community of the realm; (10) finally, the decision was binding on the communities which failed to send representatives, if the whole community of the realm had been summoned properly, for such communities were in default. In brief, what bound all the king's subjects was both *plena potestas* and the king's prerogative for the public and common utility of all; *plena potestas* was the legal means of connecting the central government with the community of the realm, of giving all rights representation and a legal hearing, and of binding all the communities to any decision made for the common good. Cf. Edwards, "Taxation and Consent . . . 1338," *E.H.R.*, LVII, 473-482, where some of my conclusions are implied but not reached.

205 See above, § 2; McIlwain, *C.M.H.*, VIII, 689.

to pursue an appeal to the king. Nevertheless, so far as the king's business was concerned, the mandate was limited to that business. But it carried full powers for that business. If the king summoned representatives in order to obtain a subsidy, and if in the summons the king properly instructed the communities as to the general nature of the business of the subsidy, then the *plena potestas* of the representatives meant that there could be no delays for "reference back" after the assembly met and after the royal decision was made. The only delay possible, unless the king found it necessarily expedient to grant another delay, was that given for deliberation between the date of the summons and the date of the assembly—such a delay was normal. This delay gave the communities ample time to prepare the record, the documents and other instructions for the proctors to take to the assembly. In such circumstances *plena potestas* precluded "reference back," unless the king permitted it either by his good grace or by the necessity of bringing up unannounced business that required a new consultation with the constituencies and new mandates. But with proper instructions in the summons or citation to the assembly, and with no other business arising, the communities were fully informed; and when they sent "sufficiently instructed" delegates, whether in France, in Aragon,[206] or in England, they had no legal right to limit the full powers of their representatives by attaching a "reference back" clause.

We should not attribute too much importance to varying combinations of terms expressing instructions, powers, and "reference back." The important thing is, that if the monarch was powerful and asserted his superior rights of jurisdiction and his full prerogative, he could legally demand full powers for representatives in order to prevent the communities from enjoying *referendum* and the limitation or delay of their consent to the royal will. If he observed the rules of the law by citing to court in the correct manner, the parties cited must give such full powers to their agents that there could be no "reference back," no delay of proceedings in the assembly, nor any delay afterwards in the form of denying the legality of the royal deci-

[206] Cf. McIlwain, *C.M.H.*, VII, 700.

sion in assembly. The communities could not legally qualify their antecedent consent to the king's decision by asserting the right of *referendum*. *Plena potestas* continued, as in ordinary court procedure, to express full consent to the decisions of the king in his council and high court of Parliament, Cortes, or States General.

6. Conclusions

In this chapter the legal theory of *plena potestas* has been emphasized. The practical application of it in the assemblies, the manner in which the representatives carried out their powers, their organization and methods of agreeing among themselves on a common policy or response to the demands made of them, and the particular circumstances which an able opportunism could shape into a defeat for the government—these are a few of many problems that need further investigation if we are to understand how the practice sometimes departed from the theory: how, for example, full powers implied, at least on occasion, a more effective consent in Aragon than in England. Yet the legal theory—if properly kept in relationship with the general legal and political ideas of the time; if properly viewed against the background of feudal law and custom, individual and community rights or liberties hierarchized like medieval society itself, royal and papal authority, and the renewed conception of the superior right of State for the public utility; and if properly considered as capable of interpretation by the judges in royal and papal courts—is an indispensable aspect of representative institutions, whether it was cause, accompaniment, or result of the rise of representation, or all three at the same time.

An essential part of the legal environment was the revival of Roman law and the development of Romano-canonical procedure, which helped corporate and quasi-corporate communities become bearers of individual rights of lesser free men and stimulated the application of the procedure of representation in such a manner that local interests could be defended and obligations to the government fulfilled. Of all the terminology taken from the Roman law and accepted throughout western Europe by the middle of the thirteenth century, *plena potestas* was one of the most significant expressions of the new relationship between the communities and the central authority. It meant the acceptance of the right and power of the ruler to summon, ask for information, and demand consent to measures decided for the common good and safety. It meant the right of the communities to be summoned, to elect representatives and instruct them on how to defend local rights, to negotiate for a reasonable subsidy or beneficial statute and to consent to the decisions of the king and his council. Without precluding the right of representatives to oppose the wishes of the government by judicial means, it meant such full instructions and powers of consent that the king's prerogative could not be limited by *referendum*. If the ruler must consult with, and secure the consent of all who were touched by the business by compelling communities to give full powers to their delegates, he bound them to the central authority. *Plena potestas*, then, stood not for political, sovereign consent but for judicial-conciliar consent to the decisions of the prince and his high court and council.[207]

We must therefore neither exaggerate nor underestimate the value of *plena potestas*. It was not, as J. G. Edwards has maintained, one of the roots of the legal sovereignty of Parliament, for it was interpreted by the royal court and was subordinate to the prerogative; it could be such a root only if other forces deprived the king of his actual judicial and administrative powers. Nor was *quod omnes tangit* the second root of popular

[207] It is clear, I think, that I fundamentally agree with Richardson and Sayles, *Parliaments and Great Councils*, that the early Parliaments of which I have been speaking were essentially the king's court in his council. The procedural or judicial aspects of *plena potestas* and of *quod omnes tangit* (below, ch. IV) support their interpretation. But politics can arise in courts, and from Roman times to the feudal age a court was often at the same time a council and an assembly. Where a large number of men gather at the summons of the king as supreme judge, the business treated becomes in part political. If the representatives appeared as before the king as judge, they also indirectly engaged in the politics of the Realm, no doubt under the leadership of the magnates. If even the Supreme Court of the United States has been swayed by the political and economic and social atmosphere, it seems likely that in the time of Edward I the High Court Royal was itself subject to the influence of arguments that were as much political (e.g., on taxation) as legal and judicial. Could the king always decide purely on the basis of the law? But see the remarks of Richardson and Sayles, p. 49.

sovereignty; it was more a principle of judicial process than of political consent. On the other hand, *plena potestas* was no symbol of abject surrender to the will of the monarch. It was used partly because all interested parties had the right to be summoned, for by law and custom the government could do nothing extraordinary without consultation and consent. Even Philip IV of France summoned the third estate and the lower clergy for a better and more compelling reason than the mere desirability of propaganda and publicity: by the legal fictions of the period he could not appeal to a General Council in a case that touched king and kingdom without obtaining the consent of the community of the realm to the act of appeal. Consent was usually forthcoming, especially when the government could present a clear case of necessity and public utility—and exert real pressure. Nonetheless, absolutism was made impossible by the very theory of judicial consent and by the procedure of obtaining that consent through the full powers of representatives. Joined with the prevailing theory of rights and consent to any changes affecting them, *plena potestas* was, in favorable circumstances, a means of defending local liberties and individual rights and an essential part of a system of judicial and conciliar representation based on that law of the land by which the prince must rule.

If it be argued that *plena potestas* and accompanying terms in the documents, such as *quod omnes tangit, status regni,* and *necessitas,* were nothing more than a *flatus vocis,* the answer is that legal terminology then as now was developed by legal experts to withstand challenge in the courts, and that royal and papal judges were guided by the legal language in reaching decisions and in interpreting the law. If it be argued that the terminology was merely a matter of procedure and not of the essence of the law, the answer is that up to a certain point procedure is itself of that essence, for without a well-formulated procedure the benefit of the law is denied. *Plena potestas* was perhaps a legal fiction, but in court, fiction is often more powerful than fact.

CHAPTER IV ✦ A ROMANO-CANONICAL MAXIM, *QUOD OMNES TANGIT*, IN BRACTON AND IN EARLY PARLIAMENTS

THE REVIVAL of the Roman law furnished the principle of agency by fully empowered representatives of communities within the community of the realm. But representation involves consent. What was the nature of the consent of the representatives when they appeared in royal assemblies? The following study will show that, just as the Roman law furnished the means of effective representation, so it provided a relatively new principle of consent. As we have noted in the preceding chapter and will now illustrate in detail, consent according to the Roman law was not a democratic expression of the sovereign will of the people. Rather, it was a procedural kind of consent given in the assembly as the king's high court and council; and it was, although based on the lawful rights of all individuals represented, finally

* This study was first published in *Traditio*, IV (1946), 197-251. I have added a few references to recent scholarship.

The late G. E. Woodbine and other critics have argued that Bracton's use of the word *tangere* does not necessarily mean that he refers to the Roman maxim —so, recently Yves M.-J. Congar, "Quod omnes tangit, ab omnibus tractari et approbari debet," in *Rev. hist. dr. fr. étr.*, XXXVI, 233. They have also pointed out that I have gone to unnecessary length in support of my thesis. Precisely such criticisms challenged me at the start and cause me to persist now in offering the original study in this volume. It is valuable to treat Bracton not only according to the letter of his text and its reflection of the Roman and Canon law, but also to relate his use of the terms and principles in question to English history in the thirteenth century. As for *tangere*, let the reader look at the conclusions, particularly the parallel passages, and judge for himself whether Bracton really had in mind the Roman maxim. I remain convinced that he did—in the same way that legists and canonists did, often without quoting it literally.

When I started writing I meant the study to be a small *addendum* to a full history of the legal thought involved in *quod omnes tangit* and its equivalents. I was unable to carry out the plan. Such a history is still needed. (See below, nn. 9 and 13.) For a general interpretation, see my "A Roman Legal Theory of Consent," *Wis. Law Rev.*, 1950, pp. 66-78.

subject to the decision of the king in his capacity of supreme public authority in the realm.

In the prevailing ideal of kingship, the monarch should rule according to law and justice; he should, for the common welfare of all, protect the rights of his subjects. The twelfth and thirteenth centuries were an age not only of an increasing awareness of rights but of the rise of the legal science that provided the means of asserting rights in courts. Representation by agents with full powers was now available to all who felt, or were persuaded by their leaders to feel, that the king's business of war, taxation, and legislation so endangered their rights that they should be heard in defense of them. How could the king make the final decision if private rights prevailed over the public rights of kingship and State and if consent became dissent? It is hoped that the Roman law on consent, studied in the context of the public law which entrusted to the king the right and duty to maintain the public and common welfare, will help solve the problem—that it will explain how both public rights and private rights and consent could find expression in representative assemblies, and how the royal prerogative remained essentially intact despite the requirement that the king summon communities to send their representatives to treat (*tractare*) with him and consent to his demands.

Ideally, the whole history of consent should be presented. But not even the history of all the usages of the Roman principle, chiefly formulated in the terms *quod omnes tangit* (from a law of Justinian, *C.* 5, 59, 5, 2, as will be shown below), has been attempted. The emphasis is on the main legal concepts involved and on the reception of the principle in England—in Bracton as the greatest interpreter of English law in the thirteenth century and, more briefly, in the rise of representation in Parliament. While it is true that Bracton rationalizes and does not always reflect the practice in English courts, on the principle of procedural consent from the Roman law he reflects an environment of rights and consent that did affect courts and assemblies. It is therefore appropriate to make Bracton the chief bearer of the subject treated in this chapter. This does not mean that he is to be credited with the introduction of *quod omnes tangit* into the royal procedure of summoning knights of the shires to Parliaments. Rather, Bracton illustrates how the Roman law in this as in other respects was becoming important in England in association with the common law and with the public rights of king and crown.

Interest in the problem of Roman law in Henry de Bracton's *De legibus et consuetudinibus Angliae*[1] has recently arisen with renewed vigor—with increasing emphasis upon the European rather than insular character of his treatise and upon the necessity of studying it "within the framework of the European legal (especially legistic and canonistic) literature of his time."[2] But among the important elements of Roman law in Bracton, the familiar maxim "quod omnes similiter tangit, ab omnibus comprobetur" (the words of Justinian, *C.* 5, 59, 5, 2) has been overlooked.[3] In this chapter I wish to show how Bracton was influenced by the maxim (henceforth referred to simply as *q. o. t.*, *quod omnes tangit*) and how his acceptance of it may have some significance for its appearance in royal writs by which communities were summoned to send representatives to Parliament. Toward the end of the thirteenth century and later, the kings of England and France—when their need of extraordinary taxes or national support in quarrels with Pope Boniface VIII forced them to obtain the consent of great nobles, prelates and communities of lesser free men—sometimes stated in the preamble to summonses to an assembly that the cause of the convocation was a serious or difficult business (*ardua negotia*)

[1] Ed. by G. E. Woodbine and by Sir Travers Twyss. In this study my references are primarily to Woodbine's edition.

[2] F. Schulz, "A New Approach to Bracton," *Seminar* (Annual Extraordinary Number of *The Jurist*), II (1944), 42; and "Bracton on Kingship," *E.H.R.*, LX (1945). See also H. Kantorowicz, *Bractonian Problems*; and the answers to his criticisms of Woodbine's edition: Schulz, "Critical Studies on Bracton's Treatise," *L.Q.R.*, LIX (1943), 172-180; C. H. McIlwain, "The Present Status of the Problem of the Bracton Text," *H.L.R.*, LVII (1943) 220-237; and H. G. Richardson, "Azo, Drogheda, and Bracton," *E.H.R.*, LIX (1944) 22-47, and "Studies in Bracton," *Traditio*, VI (1948), 61-75.

[3] P. Vinogradoff, "Les Maximes dans l'ancien droit commun anglais," *Rev. hist. dr. fr. étr.*, 4ᵉ sér., II (1923), 341, does say that Bracton knew the maxim, but he does not offer a good illustration (Bracton, II, 21; below n. 98). Maude V. Clarke, stating that the maxim was widely known in England but almost invariably in an ecclesiastical context, rightly says that the passage referred to by Vinogradoff means simply a general consent to legislation; *Medieval Representation and Consent*, p. 264.

touching (*contingentia* or *tangentia*) both king and kingdom.[4] The presence of *tangere* or *contingere* in a context of the kind resulted, although students of representation have not observed it, from the influence of *q.o.t.* as an equitable principle in legal procedure. This will become apparent after the legal meaning and the terminology current in the thirteenth century are examined.

Edward I, to be sure, in his writ to the Archbishop of Canterbury in 1295, ordering him to summon representatives of the clergy, quoted Justinian's law: "Sicut lex justissima . . . hortatur et statuit ut quod omnes tangit ab omnibus approbetur, sic et nimis evidenter ut communibus periculis per remedia provisa communiter obvietur."[5] Therewith, the Roman maxim was literally inserted in a document issued by the royal chancery. But does this fact have any significance in the history of English law and institutions? Some historians have been inclined to belittle the significance of *q.o.t.* even in questions affecting the Church, asserting that it was merely a rhetorical flourish made by the king in deference to its use by the English clergy as a pious maxim, that it was pure rhetoric employed for political effect, that it meant nothing to the king and his government.[6] How could a Roman principle which reflected the imperial absolutism of Justinian have been of any practical importance in the England of common law and Magna Carta?[7]

---

[4] See the writs of Edward I, 1294 and 1295, in Stubbs, *S.C.*, pp. 476, 479; and of Philip IV, 1302, in Picot, *Documents relatifs aux états généraux et assemblées réunis sous Philippe le Bel*, nos. 1ff.; M. Jusselin, "Lettres de Philippe le Bel," *Bibliothèque de l'École des Chartes*, LXVII (1906), 470f.: "Super pluribus arduis negotiis, nos, statum et libertatem nostros, ac regni nostri, nec non ecclesiarum et ecclesiasticarum, nobilium, secularium personarum et universorum et singulorum incolarum ejusdem regni, non mediocriter tangentibus. . . ." For examples in England, from 1258 on, see below to nn. 245, 248-257.

[5] *S.C.*, p. 480.

[6] Pasquet, *Origins of the House of Commons*, pp. 25, 173f.; G. Lapsley flatly denies that *q.o.t.* had any influence on English representation, notes on Pasquet, 244, n. to 174; Petit-Dutaillis and Lefebvre, *Studies and Notes Supplementary to Stubbs' Constitutional History*, p. 345n.; White, *Making of the English Constitution*, pp. 371f.; Pollard, *Evolution of Parliament*, 2nd ed., p. 59; Jolliffe, *Constitutional History of England*, pp. 349ff.; Riess, *History of the English Electoral Law in the Middle Ages*, p. 2, and Wood-Legh, n. 4; Adams, *Constitutional History of England*, p. 186.

[7] See the review of Clarke, *Medieval Representation and Consent*, in *The Times Literary Supplement*, Jan. 2, 1937, p. 6; quoted by George L. Haskins, "Representation and Consent," *Notes and Queries*, CLXXII (1937), 258.

Bishop Stubbs and his school, however, have credited Edward with the great achievement of transforming *q.o.t.* "from a mere legal maxim into a great and constitutional principle."[8] (*Q.o.t.* has even been called a democratic principle.)[9] Modifying this view, Professor C. H. McIlwain states that in 1295 the maxim was used "in a new and political sense" insofar as it expressed the right of consent to taxation,[10] and that it was extended to consent to legislation by the Statute of York in 1322.[11] George L. Haskins in general agrees with McIlwain but restricts the political meaning of the principle to taxation in 1322 as in 1295.[12]

To understand what *q.o.t.* meant to the government of Edward I and to see whether it was important in the representation of the laity as well as the clergy, it is necessary to learn what it signified in legal theory and procedure.[13] Is it possible that *q.o.t.*,

[8] Stubbs, *Constitutional History of England*, 4th ed., II, 133f., 369; Clarke, *op.cit.*, pp. 160f., 247-316. Rightly connecting *plena potestas*, full powers, with *q.o.t.*, J. G. Edwards develops this interpretation, "The Plena Potestas of English Parliamentary Representatives," *Oxford Essays*, pp. 141-154. But Edwards does not go so far as to make *plena potestas* and *q.o.t.* stand for any sovereign consent of the commons that limited the power of the king; they signify rather the development of the sovereignty of Parliament—of king, council, magnates, and representatives together in Parliament. Hence, my statements in *Traditio*, I, 355f. need modification, for there I assumed that Edwards was speaking of the sovereignty of the commons. But I am doubtful that one can speak of the sovereignty of Parliament even in the fourteenth century. See above, ch. II, n. 2 and § 6.

[9] See, besides P. S. Leicht (below, n. 13), Antonio Marongiu, "Note federiciane," *Studi Medievali*, XVIII (1952), 305f., and also his *Istituto parlamentare*, pp. 65-78.

[10] *Growth of Political Thought in the West*, p. 302 n. 3; cf. McIlwain, "Medieval Estates," *C.M.H.*, VII, 679; and "Mediaeval Institutions in the Modern World," *Speculum*, XVI (1941), 280f.

[11] *C.M.H.*, VII, 679; for a fine discussion of *q.o.t.* in relation to the enactment of law in the fourteenth century and a sound appreciation of the problem of minorities and of the community as a whole, see McIlwain, *Constitutionalism and the Changing World*, pp. 145ff.

[12] *The Statute of York and the Interest of the Commons*, pp. 9-13, 20-30, 45-81.

[13] Heretofore, historians of law and institutions have been content to observe that the maxim was familiar to legists and canonists and was well recognized in ecclesiastical court procedure by the middle of the century. See P. S. Leicht, "Un principio politico medioevale," *Rendiconti della Reale Accademia Nazionale dei Lincei* (Cl. di Scienze morali, storiche), XXIX (1921), 232-245; P. Vinogradoff, "Les maximes . . ." (n. 3 above), pp. 333-343, and *Collected Papers*, II, 245f. These studies are general and inadequate, for the legal meaning of *q.o.t.* is not examined.

But recently (this study appeared in 1946) more attention has been devoted to the legal meaning, and a greater number of examples of usage have been found; see besides Marongiu (above, n. 9), Congar, "Quod omnes tangit," *Rev.*

or rather an analogous principle which an interpreter could explain in Romano-canonical terminology, existed in the law of England during the time it was becoming customary to summon knights of the shire and burgesses to Parliament? I think it is possible that an analogous principle was practiced in English secular courts and that Bracton, the great interpreter of the common law, explained the practice in the terminology used for *q.o.t.* in the two laws, and that he thus made the maxim important in the realm of private law. If this is so, perhaps we can understand why this principle, like the *plena potestas* of representatives, which also originated in private law, entered the public law and was stated essentially in the formulas of writs for Parliament in the second half of the thirteenth century. Perhaps, too, we shall begin to understand what *q.o.t.* meant to Edward I and the community of the realm after we see how the Romano-canonical principle was easily and naturally adaptable to common-law procedure and was readily grasped by Bracton. But to appreciate how naturally Bracton accepted the maxim we must first explain the legal theory of *q.o.t.* in the Roman and Canon law of the thirteenth century and observe how something analogous to it had long existed in Germanic and feudal law and custom.

1. *Q.O.T.* in Romano-Canonical Procedure

From the Roman law of the *Corpus iuris civilis* the legists and canonists of the thirteenth century selected and combined certain passages in such a way as to develop a consistent theory of procedural consent, *q.o.t.* What these passages were I shall indicate briefly without pretending to make a historical study of consent in Roman law and institutions and without assuming that the classical jurists had in mind any logical connection between the laws and opinions that stated various kinds of consent. I intend to illustrate merely how the medieval jurists proceeded.

---

hist. dr. fr. étr., XXXVI, 210-259. One more work deserves mention, that of Orio Giacchi, "La regola 'quod omnes tangit' nel dirito canonico," in *Studi in onore di Vicenzo del Giudice*, I, 343-372. The author calls attention above all to the importance of the principle in connection with consent by the *maior pars* and in connection with the Church and the papal authority.

As stated by Justinian (*C.* 5, 59, 5, 2), *q.o.t.* laid down the rule that when several *tutores* had an undivided *tutela*, their joint administration could not be ended without the consent of all.[14] This, however, was merely an extension and restatement of the classical law on common consent in defense of joint rights in court. If a suit touched co-*tutores* in common, all must be summoned. But if only one of them was solvent and therefore he alone was sued, he could request that the others be summoned; then all were sent before the same judge.[15] When several persons had common rights, such as a servitude (easement), their consent was necessary for any change that affected their use—for example, the use of water from a stream.[16] If several plaintiffs or defendants appeared together as parties interested in a case, one judgment operated equally for or against all—this was a procedural *consortium*.[17] But the same object could be attained without procedural *consortium*: the judgment affected equally all the owners of land adjoining a disputed boundary whether only one sued or all were coparties to the suit. If land owned by several persons was subject to a praedial servitude, each co-owner could sue, and his victory profited the others.[18] All could bring suit as interested parties, just as suit could be brought against several co-owners of land subject to a servitude; but it was "more convenient to let *one* be sued."[19] In cases in which several were equally interested in a

14 Buckland, *Textbook of Roman Law*, pp. 161-166.

15 Wenger, *Institutes of the Roman Law of Civil Procedure*, p. 85; *D.* 11, 2, 2: "Cum ex pluribus tutoribus unus, quod ceteri non sint idonei, convenitur, postulante eo omnes ad eundem iudicem mittuntur: et hoc rescriptis principum continetur." The judgment need not affect all the *tutores* equally, although all must be summoned. This is consent under compulsion by the decision of the case in court. See Buckland, *Textbook*, pp. 162f., 166.

16 *D.* 39, 3, 8 (Ulpian): "In concedendo iure aquae ducendae non tantum eorum, in quorum loco aqua oritur, verum eorum etiam, ad quos eius aquae usus pertinet, voluntas exquiritur, id est eorum, quibus servitus aquae debebatur, nec immerito: cum enim minuitur ius eorum, consequens fuit exquiri, an consentiant. . . ."

17 *D.* 3, 3, 31, 1; 3, 5, 30, 7; *C.* 3, 40; Wenger, *Institutes*, p. 83. As Buckland says, in the earlier Roman law each *consors* was entitled to the whole, subject to the claims of the others; but all the *consortes* might arrange that one should act for them; "Alienation and Manumission by One of *Consortes*," *L.Q.R.*, LVIII (1942), 483-486.

18 *D.* 8, 5, 4, 3; 10, 1, 4, 5; Wenger, *Institutes*, p. 84.

19 Wenger, p. 84; *D.* 8, 5, 4, 4. As Wenger says, "the Roman legal order aims rather at attaining the same effect of a judgment for several interested persons,

common thing, either all should appear to accept the judgment or they should appoint a *procurator*.[20] But when there were several cases connected by subject matter or by interested persons, they were "to be handled before the same judge upon occasion in one whole or partly united proceeding. The judgments therein need not result conformably in the different united cases —one *tutor* can be exonerated, another condemned."[21]

In all this, the principle which medieval jurists stated as *q.o.t.* expressed in varying degree, according to the nature of the action and the validity of the rights, both a voluntary consent, implicit in joint and common or several property rights, and a fictitious, constructive (*praesumptio iuris*), procedural consent (the latter increasingly in the later Empire as the *cognitio* process developed), whether all of several interested parties or one of them in the name of the others were sued. "What touches all must be approved of all" did not always mean that no action could take place without the consent of all individually.[22] It meant, rather, that all must be given a hearing and defense of their rights. A passage which was to be connected with *q.o.t.* in the thirteenth century stated one of the obvious reasons for the necessity of summoning the parties: no one should suffer injury because of ignorance of the business that concerns him ("Ideo autem voluntas exigitur, ne dominus ignorans iniuriam accipiat"; *D*. 39, 3, 9, 1). But the most important passage that was to be related to *q.o.t.*, and even made the procedural basis of it, was Paulus's statement about several parties touched by a case before the praetor in charge of the imperial *fiscus*: "De unoquoque negotio praesentibus omnibus, quos causa contingit, iudicari oportet: aliter enim iudicatum

---

by ascribing to a suit conducted between two persons effect also for or against other persons not parties to the suit but interested in the juristic relationship, instead of the actual, here also possible but more inconvenient, requirement of several persons as plaintiffs or defendants."

20 *D*. 10, 2, 48 Si familiae erciscundae; *D*. 10, 2, 27; cf. Buckland, *Textbook*, pp. 314f. on coheirs and one of them acting as procurator.

21 Wenger, *Institutes*, p. 85; cf. *D*. 11, 2, 2; *C*. 5, 51, 5.

22 Of course, in some cases relating to the common ownership of property, the court must judge only on the basis of individual and unanimous consent, e.g., to a division, unless the parties could not arrive at a unanimous agreement; Buckland, *Textbook*, pp. 252, 536.

tantum inter praesentes tenet" (*D.* 42, 1, 47).[23] That is to say, a judgment affected only those who were present in court; but if all the parties had been summoned, the judgment equally affected those who were absent by default and who thereby forfeited the right to a legal defense, or to consent or dissent.[24]

It was, to repeat, the legists and canonists of the twelfth to fourteenth centuries who connected these and other passages in the Roman law and achieved a synthesis of voluntary and procedural consent. This they did whether the situations to which they applied the law were identical with, or simply analogous to, the Roman ones; and they frequently stated the synthesis in paraphrases rather than in literal quotations of the sources. If at first it seems astonishing that they felt the need of repeating a principle which we take so much for granted that we are almost unconscious of it in our theory of due process of law, these experts in the two laws appreciated the importance of *q.o.t.* in that vital period of the rise of new interests, new communities, new rights, and new or more efficient governments and jurisdictions.

Q.o.t. was already current among decretists, decretalists, and legists at Bologna when Pope Innocent III recognized the importance of the maxim both for good government in the Church and for the legal rights of the clergy and stressed it in terms of procedural consent. *Ratio iuris,* he said, demands that nothing be ordained to the prejudice of those who were neither summoned nor convicted (by legal process, of course) nor absent by default.[25] He quoted Justinian's maxim when settling the matter of the consent of bishop and archdeacon in the appointment of a rural dean.[26] Such decretals aroused the decretalists to a display of their knowledge of the Roman law. To a decretal of Innocent III relating to a case in which the Archbishop of York

[23] *Q.o.t.* is here associated with public law, since the imperial *fiscus* was the state treasury in spite of its belonging to the emperor. See C. H. McIlwain, *Constitutionalism Ancient and Modern,* pp. 48f.; *Inst.* 1, 2; and Hugh Last, *C.A.H.,* XI, 422f.

[24] *D.* 42, 1, 47, 1, and 53; *C.* 7, 44.

[25] *Decr. Greg. IX* 1, 33, 8: "Iuris namque ratio postulat, ut in eorum praeiudicium, quibus eaedem ecclesiae sunt subiectae nihil ordinemus de ipsis quum nec citati sunt, nec convicti, nec per contumaciam se absentent."

[26] *Decr.* 1, 23, 7 Ad haec.

and the rector of a hospital were codefendants, a gloss of 1210-1214 stated the maxim in a form which became recurrent: "omnes enim vocari debent quos causa tangit"; and the author referred to *C.* 5, 59, 52 and *D.* 39, 3, 8 as sources.[27] About 1217 Johannes Teutonicus, to another decretal of Innocent III, said: "omnes illi quos res tangit vocandi sunt," and supported this with a reference to Paulus *D.* 42, 1, 47, on the summoning of all interested parties.[28] But in this gloss, *C.* 5, 59, 5 and *D.* 39, 3, 8 are not mentioned! A century later Johannes Andreae connected the maxim with an *enquête* or investigation of rights: "tamen quando inquiritur de iuribus, debent vocari omnes quos res tangit, et nisi vocentur, vel etiam si ignorent, subvenitur eis de facili."[29]

The point I wish to make by these illustrations is that Justinian's maxim is often stated as *omnes quos causa tangit vocandi sunt*. The emphasis is on the summoning of all parties interested because of their rights, and *D.* 42, 1, 47 (Paulus) is ultimately in mind when the decretalists say that all whom the case touches must be summoned. Frequently, therefore, the canonists do not quote the words, "ab omnibus comprobetur," in *C.* 5, 59, 5, 2. *Similiter* ("quod omnes similiter tangit") is nearly always omitted. When it is considered, there is some dif-

---

27 *Decr.* 2, 28, 48 Significavit; the gloss occurs in an *Apparatus* to *Compilatio III*, 2, 19 (De appellat.), c. 6, ad v. (tam) *archiepiscopum* (quam rectorem): "Ut defenderet . . . Omnes enim . . . tangit; ar. III. Q. VI Hec quippe [c. 10], ff. de aqua plu. ar. in concedendo [*D.* 39, 3, 8], C. de aut. tu. veter. [5, 59, 5], C. de servit. aquam [3, 34, 4]"; in Paris, Bibl. Nat., MS lat. 15398 fol. 152ᵛ, and Bamberg, MS Can. 19 fol. 169. On the MSS and the *Apparatus* see G. Post, *The Jurist*, II (1942), 5-31; and Kuttner, *Repertorium*, p. 356.

28 To *Compilatio IV*, 2, 11 [De sent. et re iud.] c. 3 Cum in presentia, ad vv. (quia cum inter te et episcopum fuisset) *causa commissa* (ipso episcopo non citato contra ipsos monachos): "Tantum [*al.* Tamen] hec causa fuit commissa, quod episcopus nolebat confirmare eius electionem, et occasione huius mandati fuerunt vocati contradictores omnes, quia etsi non fiat mentio de ipsis in litteris, tamen omnes illi quos res tangit vocandi sunt . . . ff. de re iudi. de uno quoque, et l. sepe [*D.* 42, 1, 47 and 63]. . . . Item quia episcopus non fuit citatus [*al.* accusatus], de quo principaliter mandatum receperunt, cassatur id quod factum est. . . . Sed si episcopus esset vocatus et non monachi, quorum interest, tenet sententia lata contra episcopum. . . . Preiudicatur autem [*al.* tamen] illi qui scit causam agi, cuius defensio principaliter ad ipsum spectet . . . ff. de re iudi. sepe. *Jo.*"; in MS Vat. lat. 1377, fol. 296ʳ. The variants included above in brackets are those of the edition by Antonius Augustinus, *Antiquae collectiones decretalium*, Ilerdae, 1576, fol. ccc3ᵛ.

29 To *Decr. Greg. IX* 2, 27, 25 Quamvis, in *Novella Commentaria*.

ference in opinion as to whether it should be interpreted literally: Accursius gives *equaliter* as the meaning; while Innocent IV, discussing the joint consent of bishop and archdeacon to the appointment of a rural dean (on which Innocent III quoted *C.* 5, 59, 5, 2), declares that the consent of the bishop is superior to that of the archdeacon.[30] No doubt *similiter* meant *equaliter* when several who had equal shares or rights in common were touched, for example, co-*tutores* or members of a corporation; but it meant a hierarchy, rather than an equality, of rights and consent when princes, prelates, heads of corporations, and nobles were interested in a thing in common with lesser free men who had rights and consent of a subordinate nature. These omissions reflected both the need of emphasizing a sufficiently strong jurisdiction to enable men to challenge or defend rights and the process by which rights could be brought into court.

The underlying voluntary element, however, was not forgotten. The canon lawyers continued to assert it by quoting either *C.* 5, 59, 5, 2, or *D.* 39, 3, 8, or both at the same time. Before the end of the twelfth century, Bernard of Pavia stated both passages to express the principle: "Sciendum est igitur, quod in his quae a capitulo fieri vel ordinari debent omnium consensus est requirendus, ut quod omnes tangit ab omnibus comprobetur."[31] A half century later Innocent IV fused them into a loose paraphrase: "Nam in transactione voluntaria sicut in compositione necessarius est consensus omnium quos res tangit."[32] A decretist could paraphrase *D.* 39, 3, 8 ("cum enim minuitur ius eorum, consequens fuit exquiri, an consentiant") and refer not to it but to *C.* 5, 59, 5, 2: "Argu. quod omnium consensus est requirendus quorum iuri in aliquo detrahitur: ut hic, et . . . C. de auctor. praest. l. ulti."[33] In slightly different

---

[30] Accur., *Glos. ord.* to *C.* 5, 59, 5 ad v. *similiter*; Innocent IV, *Apparatus* to *Decr. Greg. IX* 1, 23, 7; cf. to n. 26.

[31] *Summa decretalium*, ed. Laspeyres, p. 75. Bernard, of course, refers specifically to the two laws mentioned.

[32] *Apparatus* to *Decr. Greg. IX* 1, 36, 2 Statuimus (decretal of Alexander III, who states that a *compositio* over a tithe is valid when the two clerks making it do so with the consent of the bishop or archbishop).

[33] To *Decretum*, Dist. 54, c. 1 Nullus, that no bishop shall promote the *servus* of another to clerical office "nisi forte eorum peticio aut voluntas accesserit, qui

fashion this mention of rights along with consent and summoning all who have rights was emphasized by Bernard of Parma, who in one place combined *D.* 39, 3, 8 and *C.* 5, 59, 5, 2, and in another quoted or paraphrased them separately but as equivalent in meaning: "Nota quod omnes vel aliquos tangit, eorum consensus requirendus est"; and, because the prelates and chapters of the ecclesiastical province of Bordeaux were affected by Gregory IX's decision of a suit brought by the Archbishop of Bourges against the Archbishop of Bordeaux (to the Archbishop of Bourges the pope awarded the right of procuration or visitation in the province of Bordeaux), "ita eorum intererat consentire vel contradicere: quia quod omnes tangit, ab omnibus est approbandum . . . , et in concedendo haustum aquae omnes vocandi sunt qui ius habent, ff. de aqua plu. arc. in concedendo, et ideo requiruntur ut consentiant vel dissentiant."[34] Moreover, "omnes debent venire ad quos ius aquae spectat."[35]

It is the canon lawyers who say *omnes quos causa tangit vocandi sunt* as readily as *quod omnes tangit, ab omnibus comprobetur* or *necessarius* (or *requirendus* or *exigendus*)[36] *est consensus (voluntas) omnium illorum quos res tangit*. As for the civilians, Azo gives no cross references when he comments literally on *C.* 5, 59, 5, or when he refers to it in his discussion of the consent of members of a corporation.[37] But Accursius

---

aliquid sibi in eo vendicant potestatis," ad v. *qui aliquid*; from the *Glossa ord.* by Johannes Teutonicus. The gloss refers to Dist. 85, c. 1, and to *extra. de off. deleg. super eo* (*Decr. Greg. IX* 1, 29, 15). Cf. Joh. Andreae, above, to n. 29: "Tamen quando inquiritur de iuribus, debent vocari omnes, etc."

34 *Glos. ord.* to *Decr. Greg. IX* 1, 33, 17 Humilis. The glossator adds, on the pope's command that those who were unwilling to consent should be summoned before the papal court to prosecute "ius, si quod habere contendunt, et satisfacturi parti alteri, si succubuerint, in expensis," ad v. *noluerint*: "No. quod ille cuius interest, impedit provisionem papae: sicut aliquis retardat executionem sententiae. . . . Arg. quod non intendit papa alicui praeiudicare suas litteras." True, the pope does not mean to prejudice anyone's legal rights; but such rights are subject to the final decision by the pope. Here is a good illustration of procedural consent; the voluntary element is subject to the court's decision of the case. On this see also above, ch. III, nn. 162-165.

35 To *Decr.* 1, 11, 6 ad v. *ab omnibus*: "Not. quod omnes tangit, ab omnibus comprobari debet, quia in concedendo haustum aquae omnes debent venire ad quos ius aquae spectat"; other references to *D.* 39, 3, 9 and *C.* 5, 59, 5, 2.

36 We shall see how William of Drogheda brings in *exigere* from *D.* 39, 3, 9: below, n. 110.

37 Below, nn. 100, 101.

gives a variety of references: to *D.* 42, 1, 47 (Paulus on the summoning of all interested parties before the *fiscus*) he adds the familiar *C.* 5, 59, 5, 2; and he does the same thing when commenting on *D.* 39, 3, 8 (Ulpian on consent in the law of servitudes). Other references include *D.* 21, 1, 31, 5, on the consent of several heirs of the buyer to the return of a slave and their appointment of a *procurator* for the purpose; *D.* 40, 9, 30, 4, on the consent of several *patroni* when one of them accuses a freedman; *C.* 11, 59, 7, 2, on the consent of all to what will profit all ("ut id consensu omnium fiat, quod omnibus profuturum est"); *D.* 42, 1, 36-39, on the consent of judges who jointly try a case; and *D.* 50, 1, 19 and 160, 1, on the consent of the majority as expressing the consent of all the members of a corporation.[38]

Legists and canonists, in sum, brought the *q.o.t.* of Justinian's maxim into relationship with all kinds of several and joint or common rights in a thing. The rights were individual rights, with individual consent indispensable if any change were to be made, when the thing pertained to all severally, as when several persons had an easement, when two or more prelates or administrators had administrative rights in common,[39] or when several individuals or several corporations (or individuals and corporations jointly) had the right of patronage or presentation.[40] But when the business pertained either to a corporation or to any community as a whole, and its transaction was held to be for the common utility, individual rights were subordinated to the will of the majority and to the common good of all; then *q.o.t.* was interpreted by the theory of the *maior* (and sometimes *sanior*) *pars* and no longer protected individual

[38] See the *Glos. ord.* to these laws; the glosses confirm those already quoted.

[39] Innocent III, *Decr. Greg.* IX 1, 23, 7 Ad haec; and on this Johannes Teutonicus, *Appar.*, to *Comp. IV*, 1, 11 (De off. archid.), c. 1, ad v. *imperialis*: "lxv[i] di. archiepiscopus [Dist. 66, c. 1], et C. de auct. pres. 1. ult. [*C* 5, 59, 5, 2]. Jo.," in MS Vat. lat. 1377, fol. 287ᵛ (ed. Ant. Aug., fol. aaa6). *Decretum*, Dist. 66, c. 1, to which Joh. refers, is on the common interest of the suffragan bishops in the ordination of the archbishop; and to this a gloss (in the *Glos. ord.* of Joh. Teut. to the *Decretum*) says, ad v. *ab omnibus*: "Argum. quod omnes tangit, ab omnibus debet approbari . . ."; See also *Glos. ord.* to *Decr. Greg.* IX 1, 11, 6, ad v. *ab omnibus*.

[40] *Decr. Greg.* IX 3, 10, 6 Ea noscitur (*an.* 1191-1198); and on this the comments of Innocent IV, Hostiensis, and Johannes Andreae.

rights in absolute fashion.[41] Whether consent was voluntary or compulsory, or something in between, depended on the nature of the rights in question. Were the rights founded upon law and custom? What was their relationship with each other in the persons of the holders, and what was the *status* of the persons? Were private rights affected by public rights and the public law? The nature of the consent depended in addition on the actual ability of kings and other princes to exercise their prerogative, enforce the law and develop some practical concept of the State.

Normally, nothing that changed established rights could be done without the consent of the possessors. If such rights were challenged by complainants who claimed to be the true lawful possessors, the tenants or defendants must all be summoned to court, where the issue could be debated and the validity of the consent or dissent and of the rights could be determined by the judges. The plaintiff could hope that the court would decide for him by compelling the defendants to consent to a change in the possession of the right or rights. It was to his interest that the defendants be compelled to attend. And it was normally to the interest of defendants that they be informed and summoned lest they be injured in their absence. But how could justice ensue if those summoned refused to appear in court? How could their refusal to consent to a change be overcome even if their rights were not legally established?

The legists and canonists based their discussion of the summons and attendance essentially on *D.* 42, 1, 47, which we have repeatedly encountered, and on *D.* 42, 1, 53, which speaks of the necessity of three separate summonses, or of a single, peremptory summons, before the summoned could be penalized for default and the sentence given in favor of the plaintiff. Whether there were three summonses, or a peremptory one, or a final summons in addition to the three, depended on the nature of the action as well as on local custom and the will of the judicial

41 The glosses are too numerous and lengthy to give here. But see Accursius to *D.* 50, 17, 160; Bartolus to *D.* 50, 1, 19; and Innocent IV, Bernard of Parma (*Glos. ord.*). and Joh. Andreae to *Decr. Greg. IX* 1, 2, 6, and 1, 11, 6. On the *maior pars* see below, n. 180.

[176]

authority. (In the English law of real actions the single summons had, by the time of Bracton, replaced the three summonses described by Glanville.)[42] If the summoned presented no valid excuses for absence, he lost the right of defense, that is, of consent; he lost by default. But the sentence by default was not always final: in some actions the defaulter was given the opportunity of appearing within a certain term and reestablishing his claim and carrying on his defense.[43] Moreover, there were degrees of contumacy or default. Accursius, to *D.* 42, 1, 47, ad v. *praesentibus* ("praesentibus omnibus, quos causa contingit"), says: "Praesentibus vere vel interpretative, quia contumaces, ut infra, eodem, contumacia [*D.* 42, 1, 53]."[44] He means that those summoned are present by fiction (*interpretative*) if contumacious after being summoned either three times or peremptorily; the court can decide the case as if all the parties were present, and the decision thus binds all, including the absent. William of Drogheda arrives at the same point by stating it conversely. If a party is *vere* absent because he refused to appear after being summoned, his contumacy is real and final; but if his failure to appear is not explained and it is not certain that he was wilfully absent (he might have been in foreign parts and therefore ignorant of the summons), he is absent *interpretative* and his contumacy is *praesumpta.*[45] Aegidius de Fuscarariis says that they are *praesumptive contumaces* who are summoned three times publicly at home but are absent, that is, are not at hand to hear the summons.[46] Presumptive contumacy was, of course, less serious than wilful contumacy; and the person absent by interpretation and presumptively at default was given some later opportunity to defend his interests. But generally speaking, as William of Drogheda says, the peremptory sum-

---

[42] Pollock and Maitland, *History of English Law,* II, 592; but it is not necessary to speak of Germanic custom in relation to the three summonses, for they were in the classical Roman as well as in the Canon law.

[43] See the decretal of Innocent III, *Decr. Greg. IX* 2, 6, 5, 6; it laid down the essential rules for real actions and was frequently cited by canonists and even by legists. See also the title *De dolo et contumacia* (*Decr. Greg. IX* 2, 14) in general; and the corresponding rubric in the *ordines iudiciorum.*

[44] *Glos. ord.* to *D.* 42, 1, 47.

[45] *Summa aurea,* ed. Wahrmund, *Quellen,* II, ii, 161f.; below, nn. 105, 108, 111.

[46] *Ordo iudic.,* ed. Wahrmund, III, i, 165; Aegidius refers to *Decr. Greg. IX* 2, 14, 10, and 3, 4, 11.

mons was final; thereafter, the defaulter was to suffer somehow for his refusal to consent to the litigation, for otherwise his condition would be better than that of the *non contumax*: "nemo enim ex delicto suo meliorem facit suam conditionem, sed deteriorem."[47] On the procedural side, then, *q.o.t.* meant that all interested parties must be summoned and informed of the issue; it did not mean that all the parties had to be present for the court to come to a decision. Those who failed to present valid excuses—and thus defaulted—were *interpretative* present and consented to the decision.

In still another fashion *q.o.t.* was connected with the problem of getting into court all parties interested in the thing sought by the plaintiff. In certain real actions, says Innocent III, the plaintiff is given possession until the defendant appears. If the defendant comes within a year he recovers possession upon giving security. But if he does not appear in that time, the plaintiff obtains possession—though even thereafter the defendant can offer a legal defense.[48] But if anyone is summoned who possesses immovables in another's name (*in nomine alieno*), that other, as *dominus*, must be named at once. The judge should then summon the owner or *dominus* to appear in person or by proctor. Should this second party fail to appear within the time set, the judge should summon him three times. Failure to respond to these summonses resulted in the judgment of the *dominus* by default and in the court's putting the plaintiff in possession of the property in question, but with the defense of the principal issue still reserved for the original defendant.[49] The pope here uses the language of the *Code*, 3, 19, 2. The clue to the decretal lies in the difference between possessory and petitory actions: if the original defendant is a possessor *nomine alieno* and the suit touches the property rights, the need of summoning the *dominus* follows from the nature of real rights rather than from *q.o.t.* itself. But if the Roman device in these cases (*laudatio auctoris*) is not primarily concerned with *q.o.t.*, William of Drogheda associates with this decretal and C. 3, 19,

---

[47] *Summa aurea*, ed. Wahrmund, II, ii, 29; he refers to *D*. 43, 24, 4; 50, 17, 121 and 134 and 173; 9, 4, 13; 22, 6, 6.
[48] *Decr. Greg. IX* 2, 6, 5, 6.
[49] *Ibid.*, 2, 6, 5, 7.

2 the important passages on *q.o.t.* and procedural consent, namely, *C.* 5, 59, 5, *D.* 39, 3, 8 and 9, and *D.* 42, 1, 47.[50]

In certain real actions, then, according to the nature of real rights (to which *q.o.t.* and related rules perhaps with some artificiality were applied by jurists such as Drogheda), all parties to the defense, whether primarily or secondarily concerned, were to be summoned. Lacking the presence, real or interpretative, of any one of the codefendants, the plaintiff had no case. The presence of the party named by the first defendant was necessary for the court to determine whether his interests were really involved and whether the action could proceed without him. Of course, as in the roughly similar feudal and English vouching to warranty,[51] so in the Canon law, the defendant might intentionally claim that others had interests involved in the case and by having them summoned obtain delays that made it difficult for the plaintiff ever to get a decision; for in some actions all the defendants had delays in succession, delays based on lawful excuses, before judgment could be given. Hence, a defendant frequently offered pleas or exceptions to the effect that he could not answer because the business touched another, or others, without whom the suit should not proceed. If this procedure was abused, nonetheless it developed as a protection of all legal rights in property.

The effect of contumacy upon the theory of the presence of all may be seen in the procedure of the canonical *inquisitio*. A decree of the fourth Lateran Council prescribed that when an *inquisitio* was to be made against a prelate, the accused must be present in court unless he absented himself by contumacy; and he must be informed not only of what he was accused but also of the names of the accusers.[52] Having in mind *fama* and *clamor*, directed at the clergy, Aegidius de Fuscarariis says in his discussion of this procedure that a prelate investigating the accusations should go to the place where the reports originated, summon all the accused before him, explain the purpose of his visit and the items of accusations, and receive explanations se-

---

50 See below, to nn. 113-116.

51 Below, to nn. 146, 148.

52 *Decr. Greg. IX* 5, 1, 24 Qualiter et quando: "Debet igitur esse praesens is, contra quem facienda est inquisitio, nisi se per contumaciam absentaverit."

cretly and individually: "et sic ille, contra quem inquiritur, debet esse praesens et omnes, contra quos proceditur, nisi prop- ter contumaciam se absentent."[53] Although this procedure was more summary and secretive than in civil suits, it was intended as fair trial according to the medieval conception of due process.

We are interested, however, in civil suits, in real and personal actions. In those actions the procedure, according to the two laws in the thirteenth century, was based definitely on the prin- ciple of *q.o.t.*: all interested parties, whatever their relationship in the thing sued for, must be summoned, sometimes thrice, sometimes peremptorily, depending on the nature of the action. Usually, allowance was made for excuses and delays before the summoned ever appeared in court, and usually the procedure was slow, especially when there were several defendants in real actions. The delays were the more numerous because it was felt that the party who did not ask for them seemed to approve the decision—to admit that he had no legal right. "Non petendo indutias videtur approbasse sententiam," says a decretalist of the early thirteenth century.[54] Similarly, it was probably felt that defendants who failed to obtain all possible delays at the beginning of the trial seemed to admit that their rights were of too doubtful legality to defend. In any event, the general meaning of our maxim was that all whose rights were touched by an issue should have every opportunity to prepare the de- fense of their rights, to take advantage of all means within the law and to consent to the court's decision of the legality of the rights only after a full defense and "treatise" or discussion and debate (*tractare*) had taken place. "Nemo privatur iure suo sine culpa."[55] But property rights and the consent attached to them were subject in the long run to the interpretation, by the courts, of the law by which rights existed and were enjoyed.

[53] *Ordo iudic.*, ed. Wahrmund, III, i, 156-158.

[54] Gloss to *Comp. III* 2, 18, 5 (*Decr. Greg. IX* 2, 27, 15); in Paris, BN, MS lat. 15398, fol. 149, c. 2. The decretal relates to delays between sentence and appeal.

[55] *Glos. ord.* to *Decr. Greg. IX* 1, 2, 2 Cognoscentes, ad v. *culpa caret*; the gloss continues: "Vel dicas, quod licet quandoque quis privetur iure suo sine culpa, non tamen fit illud sine causa. . . . In sex casibus privatur aliquis iure suo sine culpa sua. Unde versus:

Paupertas, odium, vitium, favor, et scelus, ordo,
Personas spoliant et loca iure suo."

2. Rights and Consent in Feudal and English Law

In certain respects, the principle of consent in association with rights in a thing was as natural to a primitive society as to the Roman Empire. It was stated in an early Frankish law: the consent of all of several occupiers of a piece of land was required for the admission of a new settler to share the land.[56] In the feudal and manorial period law and custom protected joint and common rights of many kinds. While the heritage of Roman and German law may have been of importance in the continuity of the principle, more important was the environment of joint and common (at times communal) holdings and uses of the land. In the communal system of agriculture the lord of the manor, the serfs or villeins, and the freeholders of the village community all had rights, though not equal rights, in the common.[57] Custom prepared the way for expressing the situation in the terms of *q.o.t.*: what touched the right of lord, freeholder, or villein often touched the rights of all. Many varieties of rights to profits *a prendre in alieno solo* were known to the English law, and "most of them may be subjects of common rights, which were a necessary part of the common or open field system. Rights of common of pasture are many."[58] Moreover, in the pastoral areas of England sometimes "the sheep and cattle of adjacent manors shared the wide pastures, intercommoning on the waste . . . ; and village councils regulated the rights of all."[59] And in feudal tenure "both lord and tenant have rights in the land, in the tenement, the subject of the tenure."[60]

[56] Richard Kuebner, "The Settlement and Colonisation of Europe," *Cambridge Economic History*, I, 34—on the Salic Law, *Titulus de migrantibus* (45). The veto of a single proprietor should decide against the new settler, even if "one or several want to admit him." No big village community is involved, for some three or four neighbors are not agreed about the admission of another. This was not a question of the communal disposal of shares in the land by the tribal assembly. It was the individual settlers who had to agree to the division. But Clovis declared that the *migrans* must be admitted if he came recommended by the king (34).

[57] Holdsworth, *History of English Law*, III⁴, 143-146; Pollock and Maitland, *History of English Law*, I, 360-376, 620-630. For France, see M. Bloch, *Cambr. Econ. Hist.* I, 264-271. For English local custom and villagers' rights and common consent or action, see also Nellie Neilson, "The Early Pattern of the Common Law," *A.H.R.*, XLIX (1944), 204.

[58] Holdsworth, III⁴, 143.

[59] Eileen Power, *The Wool Trade in English Medieval History*, p. 7.

[60] Pollock and Maitland, I, 236.

The Church was compelled to submit to a similar regime of common interests in what was originally an indivisible thing, the local church. As a result of the rise of the *Eigenkirche* in the Carolingian period, lay domination lent support to the local churches and clergy against the bishop and taught them "to become the independent upholders of their own rights. . . . The Germanic races transformed the episcopal church into a *Rechtskirche*, built up on a careful partition of rights, just as they transformed the state into a *Rechtsstaat*, the basis of which again was a balance of rights."[61] From the lay control of the churches also sprang the right of patronage, or advowson, which became the subject of plural rights when it was enjoyed by several persons.[62] The tithe, too, which pertained to the private church, fell under the principle of divided rights. "The undivided right over the proprietary church broke up into as many particular rights as there were possibilities and means of exploiting the church. . . ."[63] Naturally, both in legal theory and practice, such rights were the source of the claim to the right of consent of all to any change affecting the holding and division of the thing and hence affecting particular rights.

All these developments of common and several rights and consent (many additional illustrations could be given by the expert on feudal and ecclesiastical institutions) had taken place by the twelfth century, both on the Continent and in England. From this time on, the great revival of Roman and Canon law began to affect the expression of consent not only in relation to joint and common rights but also in relation to corporate and community rights. In the Church the corporate organization and rights of the cathedral chapter were recognized, and the bishop and his chapter possessed both divided or joint and common rights in certain things; and by the thirteenth century *q.o.t.* was being quoted as a statement of the theory of the consent of both when such rights were at stake. Within the corporation of the chapter, the theory of corporate consent by the

---

61 U. Stutz, "The Proprietary Church as an Element of Mediaeval Germanic-Ecclesiastical Law," *Mediaeval Germany 911-1250. Essays by German Historians* (transl. G. Barraclough), II, 51.

62 Stutz, *op.cit.*, p. 52; Holdsworth, *op.cit.*, III4, 138-142.

63 Stutz, *op.cit.*, p. 68.

maior et sanior pars was modifying the implication of individualism and unanimity in *q.o.t.*[64] Similar was the rise of the theory
of consent in the Italian communes and their corporate councils. In England, long before tangible Romano-canonical influences appeared, the tradition of participation in the communities of vills, hundreds, and shires, and in their courts,
made all free men conscious of individual and common rights
in the land, in common of pasture, in the welfare of the community as a whole,[65] and in keeping the peace.[66]

It is clear, then, that the English law embodied the earlier
system of several and common rights and consent. Englishmen
understood the importance of an adequate procedure if the
rights of free men were to be defended according to due process
—witness Magna Carta, c. 39, which reflected what was being
asserted still earlier on the continent.[67] But the invasion of

[64] See below, n. 180.

[65] Neilson, *A.H.R.*, XLIX, 204, 208; on the common interest in the maintenance
of walls, dykes, and ditches, lest "the negligence of one might endanger all."

[66] Holdsworth, *Hist. Eng. Law*, II[3], 57f., 377f.; *ibid.*, III[4], 143. In any society,
primitive or modern, there must be some practical, if unconscious, observance of
the same principle as that of *q.o.t.*; for all the members of a community are
touched by any individual who tries by force or fraud to usurp the rights of others,
just as all are touched by a brigand or murderer; and all are therefore interested
in measures for law and order. Bracton, in fact, hints at *q.o.t.* in connection with
the common interest in the king's peace: some crimes touch both the king and
those who are injured (II, 298). In saying that "though there are romanesque
phrases in this section, it consists in the main of pure English law," Maitland
fails to note Bracton's application of the maxim to royal jurisdiction and the
king's peace; *Select Passages from the Works of Bracton and Azo*, pp. 186f. On
the Germanic essence of the development of the king's peace see Lear,
"The Public Law of the Ripuarian, Alemannic, and Bavarian Codes,"
Medievalia et Humanistica, II (1944), 5, 25ff.: "It is a 'king's peace' because
the king has identified his rights with the rights of all and to that extent
the royal peace, conceived in the Germanic personal sense, becomes a general
peace of the land and a basis of public order, if one may speak of *public* in an
order where rights remain personal" (p. 26); *idem*, on the contractual element
in the king's peace, "Contractual Allegiance vs. Deferential Allegiance in Visigothic Law," *Illinois Law Review*, XXXIV (1940), 557-566, and "The Idea of
Majesty in Roman Political Thought," *Essays in History and Political Theory in
Honor of Charles Howard McIlwain*, pp. 168-198. But in the thirteenth century
the king's peace for the public utility begins to control contractual individualism,
and *q.o.t.* begins to be limited by the royal prerogative and the right of State—
the revival of Roman law is of great importance in this development; see my
remarks and references in *Traditio*, I, 372, and below, chs. v-ix.

[67] C. 39: "Nullus liber homo capiatur, vel imprisonetur, aut dissaisiatur . . .
nisi per legale judicium parium suorum vel per legem terrae." McIlwain, *Constitutionalism and the Changing World*, ch. v, concludes that c. 39 meant legal

England by the two laws resulted in a greater, more logical, consciousness of the principle and in a more abundant expression of it in practice than would probably have been the case otherwise.[68]

3. THE TWO LAWS IN ENGLAND

Roman and Canon law were beginning to play an important role in the growth of common-law procedure by the end of the twelfth century. Before Bracton wrote the *De legibus,* the chancery of Henry III was using Roman terminology in drawing up mandates for ambassadors;[69] and, through ecclesiastical suits brought before them, the royal justices were learning something about the Roman proctorial procedure for the representation of corporations.[70] In 1225 and following years the lower clergy of cathedral and conventual chapters were beginning to proclaim *q.o.t.* as the basis of their right to representation in Church councils for any business, such as a subsidy commanded by the pope for the king, which touched not only the prelates but also members of ecclesiastical corporations.[71] Finally, ecclesiastics who were trained in both laws, or at least in the Canon law, were appointed as royal justices and clerks; and in the decision of cases in the king's courts they applied some of the Romano-

---

judgment by peers or "by the justices of the king in cases in which this has become the common procedure, 'the law of the land in effect everywhere and accepted as such,'" p. 124; but the *lex terrae* also meant "the substantive principles of the customary law," p. 125; it meant the "law of the land" both in the procedural and in the substantive sense of the law, pp. 114, 116. Max Radin, *Handbook of Anglo-American Legal History,* pp. 166f. emphasizes too much, I think, the "local and special and—in England—very exceptional custom" as the meaning of *per legem terrae*. It does mean local and special custom, but it also means the general law of the land and procedure which embrace and recognize local custom. In the Church the same theory prevailed among the canonists. As to due process, Plucknett, *Concise History of the Common Law,* 2nd ed., pp. 25, 41: "Could anything be more mediaeval than the ideal of due process . . . ?" —and p. 338; also, McIlwain, *Constitutionalism and the Changing World,* p. 114, on *per legem terrae* as "par due proces de lei" in 1354.

[68] Cf. Holdsworth, *op.cit.,* II[3], 57f.; and III[4], 143-151.

[69] See "Plena Potestas," *Traditio,* I, 367f.; above, ch. III, § 2.

[70] *Loc.cit.*

[71] Matthew Paris, *Chron. Maj.,* III, 97, 103, and IV, 37, 375; Powicke, *Stephen Langton,* pp. 158f.; Lunt, *Financial Relations of the Papacy with England to 1327,* pp. 178ff. For Pope Honorius III's recognition of *q.o.t.* in provincial councils, see *Decr. Greg. IX* 3, 10, 10; below, nn. 218, 220, 252.

canonical procedure which the lawyers, too, used in defense of their clients' rights.[72]

Some slight Roman influence, of course, had begun to appear in Anglo-Saxon and Norman England.[73] But the study of Roman law really began about the middle of the twelfth century with Vacarius at Oxford.[74] There the school and traditions thus established were carried into the thirteenth century by Thomas of Marlborough, who had had close relations with Bolognese canonists in 1205 and 1215,[75] and by the more famous William of Drogheda.[76] At the same time, the dissemination of the new law was helped by ecclesiastics who brought Roman law manuscripts to Exeter and other churches. Bracton, like William de Raleigh, a royal justice on whose decisions Bracton liked to draw, was connected with Exeter[77]—but it is more likely that he learned his Roman law at Oxford by 1239.[78] Not only the *Corpus juris civilis* but Romano-canonical treatises on judicial

---

[72] On Englishmen who were canonists and decretalists in the early thirteenth century, see Schulte, *Quellen*, I, 183, 188, 189; Kuttner, *Repertorium*, Index, *s.v.* Anglo-normannische Schule; idem, "Bernardus Compostellanus Antiquus," *Traditio*, I, 284 n. 25, 285, 289, 301, 311, 321, 326 n. 32; J. C. Russell, *Dictionary of Writers of Thirteenth Century England*, p. 111. On churchmen as royal judges and their training and influence, Pollock and Maitland, I, 132f.; Holdsworth, *op.cit.*, II⁴, 177, 227; Richardson, "The Oxford Law School under John," *L.Q.R.*, LVII, 322f.; and on a clerk who was employed by Henry III in ecclesiastical business, Powicke, "Master Simon the Norman," *E.H.R.*, LVIII, 330-343.

[73] Pollock and Maitland I, xxxiif.; Holdsworth, *op.cit.*, II⁴, 7-28; Senior, "Roman Law in England before Vacarius," *L.Q.R.*, XLVI, 191-206; Scrutton, *Influence of the Roman Law on the Law of England*, Part I; H. Levy-Ullman, *The English Legal Tradition*, pp. 173-175.

[74] Zulueta, ed., *The Liber Pauperum of Vacarius*, pp. xiii-xxiii. But Vacarius omits *C.* 5, 59, 5, 2, and has no gloss either on it or on *D.* 42, 1, 47.

[75] Kuttner, *Traditio*, I, 301f.; *Dictionary of National Biography*, art. on Thomas; below, n. 186. Thomas taught Roman law at Oxford (and at Exeter?), was a monk at Evesham, 1199-1229, and was made abbot of the monastery in 1229.

[76] Pollock and Maitland, I, 118-121; Holdsworth, *op.cit.*, II⁴, 147f.; Richardson, *L.Q.R.*, LVII, 324ff.; Plucknett, "The Relations between Roman Law and English Common Law down to the Sixteenth Century," *Univ. of Toronto Law Jour.*, III, 24-50. But Plucknett is grudging about accepting any important influence of the Roman law except in the rationalization of the common law by Bracton. It scarcely penetrated English court practice; *q.o.t.* itself meant nothing when Edward I stated it.

[77] Senior, "Roman Law MSS. in England," *L.Q.R.*, XLVII, 337-344; Scrutton, *op.cit.*, 79f.; Plucknett, *Concise History of the Common Law*, pp. 210f.; cf. below, ch. VII, n. 17, and ch. IX, n. 30.

[78] Richardson, "Azo, Drogheda, and Bracton," *E.H.R.*, LIX, 40-43.

procedure were used at Oxford; and, along with formularies and works on the notarial art, they were studied by young men who obtained employment from great lords to write letters, keep accounts, draw up legal instruments, and help hold court. These men might even be sheriffs' clerks.[79] Through Oxford, then, the Roman legal terminology (and the theories) crept into the usage of local courts and probably into the county courts —if only to a slight extent and in civil rather than criminal procedure.[80] From the decretalist, Hostiensis, who served Henry III as ambassador to Pope Innocent IV in 1244 and perhaps taught Canon law in England,[81] and from the legist, Francis Accursius, who was employed by Edward I as councillor and secretary (1273-1281),[82] may have come at least an accentuation of the new forms in the royal chancery, courts, and council. In the early fourteenth century the work of drafting a statute in the royal council "would be done by men of whom, or whose like, it has been said that they were trained in English and Roman (or at least Canon) law, men who, when they gave a judgment or advised upon a decision, appreciated its legal or administrative consequences."[83] In fact, a century earlier, the

[79] Richardson, *L.Q.R.*, LVII, 324-335; *idem*, "An Oxford Teacher of the Fifteenth Century," *Bulletin of the John Rylands Library*, XXIII, 2 (1939), 18.

[80] G. Barraclough, "Praxis Beneficiorum," *Zeitschrift der Savigny-Stiftung, Kanon. Abt.*, XXVII (1937), 96f., thinks that few of the officials in English episcopal courts and few of the many notaries, proctors, advocates and syndics attended a university or received a degree in Canon or Roman law. But this does not mean that the Roman law was not a vital part of the procedure in church courts, for it formed the background of the treatises on procedure and the notarial art which were used by those who had little formal education in the two laws. Of course, the province of the common law was barred to these notaries in England; they could practice only in ecclesiastical courts (Richardson, *L.Q.R.*, LVII, 333). But the notarial art perhaps had some influence outside.

[81] Schulte, *Quellen*, II, 124; Pollock and Maitland, I, 122; H. Kantorowicz, *Studies in the Glossators*, p. 91.

[82] G. L. Haskins, "Three English Documents Relating to Francis Accursius," *L.Q.R.*, LIV (1938), 87-94; *idem*, "Francis Accursius: A New Document," *Speculum*, XIII (1938), 76: "The presence of a civil lawyer among the councillors and close advisers of Edward I, in a period of one of the great advances of English law, is a matter of no slight importance for legal history." Without contradicting this statement, I would remind the reader that the Roman terminology and procedure for corporate representation were familiar to English secular institutions and law before Accursius was employed by Edward; see *Traditio*, I, 367, 369; above, ch. III, nn. 70-77, 86.

[83] H. G. Richardson and G. O. Sayles, "The King's Ministers in Parliament," *E.H.R.*, XLVI (1931), 550; quoted by G. L. Haskins, *Statute of York*, p. 30 n. 1.

writs and statutes of John and Henry III had begun to reflect a Roman terminology in such expressions as common utility, necessity, *status regni* (for *status Reipublicae*), and "business touching the king and kingdom."[84]

Elements of the two laws came to England from many sources: the Canon law and procedure in church courts, the ecclesiastics trained in both laws and employed by the king, the cases involving churches and brought before the royal courts, the continuity of the study of Roman law at Oxford, the contacts (in diplomacy and legal business) with the Continent (particularly with France and Louis IX and with the papacy), the sojourn of continental canonists and legists in England, and the work of the justices in the king's courts. These elements ranged all the way from the rules of procedure (royal writs, summonses, exceptions, delays, default)[85] to the fundamental theories of law and justice—and to legal maxims.[86] And they continued to be expressed in the English courts and in royal writs and statutes despite Henry III's prohibition of the teaching of the civil law in London.[87]

But how deeply did the Roman terminology and thought penetrate? "As to Roman law," say Pollock and Maitland, "it led to nothing"; but they admit that the English law of procedure was rationalized under the influence of Roman and Canon law.[88] "Civil law," says Vinogradoff, "did not become

[84] *S.C.*, pp. 277, 325, 358, 403, 406f.; and Bracton, IV, 295f. (Tw. VI, 288): "generaliter tractatum esset de communi utilitate totius regni super pluribus articulis regem et regnum tangentibus"—on the Provisions of Merton, 1236; the words "regem et regnum tangentibus" do not appear in the document (*Statutes of the Realm*, I, 1; *Close Rolls H. III, 1234-1237*, p. 337), but Bracton violates no tradition in adding these words as a reflection of *q.o.t.* In 1258 one encounters similar words that relate to the summons and the consent of the magnates as the community of the realm in Henry III's consent to a plan for reforming the *status regni*: "Cum pro negotiis nostris arduis nos et regnum nostrum contingentibus, proceres et fideles regni nostri . . . faceremus convocari"; *S.C.*, p. 371. See below, nn. 123, 246, 248; and ch. VIII, § 1.

[85] Pollock and Maitland, I, 134; Holdsworth, *op.cit.*, II[4], 283.

[86] Pollock and Maitland, I, 217f. On the maxims see James Williams (*q.o.t.*, however is not mentioned), "Latin Maxims in English Law," *Law Magazine and Review*, XX (1895), 283-295; and Vinogradoff, *Rev. hist. dr. fr. étr.*, II, 333-343 (*Coll. Papers*, II, 245f.).

[87] Vinogradoff, *Roman Law in Medieval Europe*, p. 98. Henry III's prohibition indicates no hostility to Roman law; it was probably issued to protect the monopoly of Roman law at Oxford; Richardson, *E.H.R.*, LIX, 40.

[88] I, 122, 134.

a constituent element of English common law acknowledged and enforced by the courts, but it exercised a potent influence on the formation of legal doctrines during the critical twelfth and thirteenth centuries."[89] Holdsworth, with Vinogradoff, emphasizes the importance of the Roman influence particularly on the side of juridical ideas, the statement of which, in the form of maxims, was more important than precise references to laws in *Digest* and *Code*.[90] Plucknett, however, asserts that "the contributions of continental jurists must be sought not in the deliberate reception of rules and doctrines, but in the more general stimulus of a lawyerly approach to the law."[91]

The following pages will show, I hope, that at least one of the continental, Romano-canonical maxims of the thirteenth century, *q.o.t.*, was of more than doctrinal importance in the development of legal procedure as interpreted by Bracton and practiced in English courts. For procedure is as much the essence of the law as the ideal and theory; without an adequate, logical procedure the fundamental principles of any body of law are so much ideological wind. The very development of a carefully defined procedure with elaborate rules on informing the defendant, summoning all parties concerned, granting delays that protect challenged rights in certain circumstances, permitting appeals from the decision of lower courts, and, in short, guaranteeing a fair trial and a just sentence, is nothing less than a real and essential expression of the ideal of law and justice—justice according to the famous Roman definition: "Iustitia est constans et perpetua voluntas ius suum cuique tribuendi." All this was especially true in the thirteenth century, when, under the influence of the two laws and the feudal emphasis on individual rights, the ideal of due process, as it is understood in the United States, was virtually stated in the rules on procedure.[92] At the same time, however, a government must find a way of preventing a joint defense from defeating justice by causing infinite de-

89 *Roman Law*, p. 97.
90 Holdsworth, *op.cit.*, II[4], 117; Vinogradoff, *Roman Law*, p. 118.
91 *Univ. Toronto Law Jour.*, III, 44.
92 Plucknett, *Com. Law*, pp. 338-340; above, n. 67.

lays.[93] But those who alleged that they had legal rights in something for which others were summoned finally won recognition and obtained the right of consenting for themselves, in the judicial or procedural sense, to a decision that affected the rights of all. This development was no doubt hastened by royal justices who were trained in the principles of the two laws and could perceive the importance of *q.o.t.* as a part of the procedure of summoning interested parties and enforcing the jurisdiction of the courts. The justices "brought to the task of declaring the custom of the king's court some knowledge of a body of law the rules of which were logically coherent, the expression of which was precise and clear. This training in method and principle enabled them to construct a rational, a general, a definite system of law out of the vague and conflicting mass of custom, half tribal, half feudal, of which the English law consisted."[94]

4. SOURCES OF *Q.O.T.* IN BRACTON

The evidence comes in part from the treatises on the common law and from Bracton's *De legibus*. Many aspects of the influence of Roman and Canon law on Glanville and Bracton have been recognized;[95] and it has been amply noted that Bracton (above all, in the introduction and in the first parts of his treatise on persons, things, and *De adquirendo rerum dominio*), referred only occasionally to the *Code* and *Digest*, but was familiar with the *Institutes* and with Azo on *Institutes* and *Code*. He knew the *Glossa ordinaria* of Accursius (1228) and was acquainted with the work of several decretalists, possibly Bernard of Pavia, certainly Tancred and Raymond of Peñafort, and, possibly, Bernard of Parma's *Glossa ordinaria* to the *Decretals*

[93] Plucknett, p. 364 n. 1, on the meaning of the Statute *de conjunctim feoffatis*, 34 Ed. 1 (1306), which was intended to prevent delays by the use of "an old rule that all joint-tenants must be made defendants (or 'tenants') in a real action." The old rule, of course, is similar to that of *q.o.t.* strictly applied; see below for a solution known in Roman law and also in Bracton and in the Statutes, nn. 142-149.

[94] Holdsworth, *op.cit.*, II⁴, 177f.

[95] Pollock and Maitland, I, 122, 165f.; Holdsworth, *op.cit.*, II⁴, 202f., 228, 232ff., 253f., 267ff.; Woodbine, ed., Glanville, *De legibus*, p. 187. On the Roman part of the "constitutionalism" in Bracton, see McIlwain, *Constitutionalism Ancient and Modern*, pp. 69-94; and Fr. Schulz, "Bracton on Kingship," *E.H.R.*, LX, 136-176.

of Gregory IX.[96] Vinogradoff believes that while Bracton was relatively ignorant of the letter and purity of the *Digest*, he understood it in the popular forms of continental customs.[97] But apparently no one, except Vinogradoff, who gives an inadequate illustration,[98] has either observed or interpreted the presence of *q.o.t.* in Bracton. This is all the more surprising because the maxim is referred to, if briefly, in well-known sources of Romano-canonical influences in Bracton. In Bernard of Pavia's *Summa decretalium*, even if it was outmoded, Bracton may have noted the application of *q.o.t.* to the consent of the members of a corporation to corporate acts and to the consent of all parties enjoying a servitude or easement: "Sciendum est igitur quod in his quae a capitulo fieri vel ordinari debent omnium consensus est requirendus, ut quod omnes tangit ab omnibus comprobetur, ut ar. Dig. de aqua pluv. arc. In concedendo (*D.* 39, 3, 8), et Cod. de auctor. praest. L. ult. (*C.* 5, 59, 5, 2)."[99] Azo is an obvious source: he quotes *C.* 5, 59, 5, 2,[100]

[96] Güterbock, *Bracton and His Relation to the Roman Law*, in general; Maitland, *Bracton and Azo*, pp. xivff., 84, 130f., 221-225, and *passim*; Holdsworth, *op.cit.*, II⁴, 267-286, 356, and III⁴, 154ff., VII, 323f.; G. E. Woodbine, "The Roman Element in Bracton's *De adquirendo rerum dominio*," *Yale Law Jour.*, XXXI (1921-1922), 827-847; P. Vinogradoff, "The Roman Element in Bracton's Treatise," *Coll. Papers*, I, 237-244; Levy-Ullmann, *Engl. Legal Tradition*, pp. 137, 177ff.; Kantorowicz, *Bractonian Problems*, pp. 17f., 58-61; Fr. Schulz, "Critical Studies," *L.Q.R.*, LIX, 172-180; *idem*, "A New Approach to Bracton," *Seminar*, II, 42-50; *idem*, "Bracton on Kingship," *E.H.R.*, LX, 136-176; *idem*, "Bracton and Raymond de Penafort," *L.Q.R.*, LXI (1945), 286-292; Richardson, "Azo, Drogheda, and Bracton," *E.H.R.*, LIX, 22-47; *idem*, "Tancred, Raymond, and Bracton," *E.H.R.*, LIX, 376-384; Schulz, "Bracton as a Computist," *Traditio*, III (1945), 267. See n. 104, below. Professor Stephan Kuttner has recently written me that he does not believe that Bracton read Bernard of Pavia, whose work was outmoded by his time.

[97] *Roman Law*, pp. 117f., and *Coll. Papers* I, 237-244; cf. Plucknett, *Com. Law²*, p. 233.

[98] *Rev. hist. dr. fr. étr.*, II, 341. Remarking on the importance of *q.o.t.* as stated by Edward I in 1295, Vinogradoff refers (n. 3) to Bracton, fol. 1 (Woodbine, II, 21): "Quae quidem [leges], cum fuerint approbatae consensu utentium et sacramento regum confirmatae, mutari non poterunt nec destrui sine communi consensu eorum omnium quorum consilio et consensu fuerunt promulgatae." But Bracton is not here stating *q.o.t.*; he is merely giving the theory of consent by magnates and prelates in the king's council as it was expressed in the familiar medieval fashion. Of course, *q.o.t.* expressed the same theory for like circumstances.

[99] Ed. Laspeyres, p. 75.

[100] *Summa Codicis*, Venice, 1610, to *C.* 5, 59, 5: if several *tutores* act in the interest of a ward, "tunc necesse est omnes tutores authoritatem suam prestare, ut quod omnes simpliciter tangit, ab omnibus comprobetur" (551). *Similiter* should no doubt be read for *simpliciter*.

and he associates *q.o.t.* with the consent of the members of a college to the election of a new member;[101] when a corporation as a whole consents, consent by majority is sufficient; otherwise *q.o.t.* in *C.* 5, 59, 5 and *D.* 39, 3, 8 demands that all individually consent.[102]

It is possible, of course, that Bracton read these passages in the *Digest* and *Code*,[103] but it is more likely that his attention was called to them by the legists and canonists of the late twelfth and the first half of the thirteenth century—by those mentioned above, by decretists like Johannes Teutonicus, and by Bernard of Parma's *Glossa ordinaria* (*ca.* 1234-1253 in the first three redactions—Bracton probably wrote his treatise 1250-1259).[104]

---

[101] *Summa Codicis*, XL, 27, no. 3 (979), to *C.* 11, 18 (17), 1, 1: "Eliguntur autem in collegiis in locum mortuorum, vel eorum, qui removentur, praedicto muneri sufficientes, cum iudicio primatum eius qui surrogatur. Hoc (inquam) sic intelligo, i.e., iudicio primatum illius muneris, in quo surrogatur, caeteris forsan collegiatis consentientibus vel non contradicentibus electioni, ut quod omnes tangit, etc., ut *C.* de autho. prestan. 1. ult. Vel primatum [*privatum* in ed. of 1610] obtinebit iudicium, si non veniant ceteri, ut ff. de pac. 1. maiorem [*D.* 2, 14, 8]." (Placentinus, not Azo, is the author of this gloss.)

[102] *Lectura*, Lyon, 1596, to *C.* 5, 59, 5, 2-3, ad vv. *ut quod omnes tangit* and *plures*.

[103] He may have read other relevant passages, e.g., *D.* 42, 1, 47, and the passages noted above, nn. 14-23. On Bracton's use of the *Corpus juris civilis* see H. Kantorowicz, *Bractonian Problems*, pp. 58f., and Güterbock, *Bracton*, p. 50n. But neither Güterbock nor Kantorowicz seems to think of the possibility of Bracton's having read passages which he neither refers to nor quotes literally.

[104] Bracton was acquainted with Tancred's *Ordo Iudiciarius* (ed. Bergmann), as Schulz points out, *Seminar*, II, 42-50, and *L.Q.R.*, LIX, 172ff. But in the *Ordo* I have found no references to or quotations of *q.o.t.* as stated in *C.* 5, 59, 5 or *D.* 39, 3, 8 and 42, 1, 47. However, Tancred's *Apparatus* of glosses of such decretalists as Silvester, Laurentius, Vincentius, Joh. Galensis, Alanus, and Joh. Teutonicus, on the *Compilationes I, II, III*; and the several *Appar.* of Joh. Teut., Laur. and Vinc. to *Comp. III*; of Joh. Teut. to *Comp. IV*, and of Jacobus de Albenga to *Comp. V*; such commentaries as these on the decretals of popes from the middle of the twelfth century to Honorius III (1216-1227) circulated among the prelates and canonists of England—but in how many MSS, and where they were circulated needs study. Moreover, glosses of the decretists on the *Decretum*, especially in the *Glos. ord.* by Joh. Teut., were available in some ecclesiastical libraries, or were in the possession of prelates. Here and there, we have seen, these sets of glosses contained references to and paraphrases of the Roman laws on *q.o.t.* (above, nn. 24-28, 31). On the work of the canonists to 1234 see Kuttner, *Repertorium*; Schulte, *Quellen*, I; on the decretalists who glossed *Comp. III*, Post, *Jurist*, II, 3-29 and references. We must remember that in each of *Comp. IV* and *V* there is a papal decretal which quotes or paraphrases *q.o.t.*: *Decr. Greg. IX* 1, 23, 7 and 3, 10, 10. Much of the work of the earlier decretalists was incorporated in Bernard of Parma's *Glos. ord.* to the Gregorian *Decretals*. On the respective dates of the *Glos. ord.* and of Bracton's treatise see S. Kuttner and

Moreover, he may have obtained the maxim from William of Drogheda, who carried on the tradition of Roman law at Oxford and whose famous treatise on procedure, the *Summa aurea*, and, possibly, lectures had some influence on Bracton.[105]

If, asks William of Drogheda, an abbot who is appointed by the pope as a judge signs his commission with his own seal (*signum*) and not with that of his convent, is the *commissio* valid? It may be argued that it is valid, for the pope appointed the abbot, not the convent. But on the other hand "illud generale, quod omnes tangit, ab omnibus debet approbari" must be recalled: the convent might be interested "pecunialiter," for if the abbot made a bad decision the convent would be jointly liable with the abbot. The solution, however, is this: the *signum* of the abbot is sufficient; "nec obstat lex de auctoritate praestanda (*C.* 5, 59, 5) cum suis similibus,"—the pope delegated authority not to the convent but to the abbot or prior. In any case, if the abbot or prior judges badly and is condemned, no execution can be brought against him when the property of the abbot and the convent is held in common and is not the abbot's alone. Moreover, no one can start a proceeding in court against the judge. Nevertheless, in the appointment of proctors and in corporate business, the seals of the prior and the convent must be attached, but with this distinction: the goods of the abbot or prior and the convent are either common or separate; if common, the seals of both are used according to the legal rule of *q.o.t.* in *C.* 5, 59, 5 and similar laws; if separate, the seal of the prior or abbot suffices for actions involving his property,

---

Beryl Smalley, "The 'Glossa ordinaria' to the Gregorian Decretals," *E.H.R.*, LX (1945), 97-105 (first redaction 1234-*ca.* 1241; second 1243-1245; third 1245-*ca.* 1253; final 1263-1266); and n. 105 below.

105 The *Summa* was written about 1239; ed. Wahrmund, *Quellen*, II, ii. Recently H. Kantorowicz has argued that at least the first pages of Bracton were written as early as 1239, and that Drogheda borrowed citations of the *Institutes* from Bracton; *Bractonian Problems*, pp. 29-32. But G. E. Woodbine in a review of Kantorowicz, *Yale Law Jour.*, LII (1943), 428, adheres to Maitland's dating of Bracton's treatise, 1250-1259. So does C. H. McIlwain, "The Present Status of the Bracton Text," *H.L.R.*, LVII, 230. H. G. Richardson likewise refutes Kantorowicz, and adds important information about Bracton's studying at Oxford just before 1239; he concludes that Bracton got at least a little from the *Summa aurea* and possibly, earlier, from Drogheda's teaching at Oxford; "Bracton, Azo, and Drogheda," *E.H.R.*, LIX, 22-47.

the seal of the convent for actions involving only the *bona* of the convent.[106]

Here William of Drogheda is involved in the problem of the rights of the corporation and its head—whether their rights are common or separate, whether the consent of corporation and head is common or separate. Such rights may pertain either to property or to administration and jurisdiction. The mutual rights and consent of all interested parties in the appointment of a proctor (the consent of the judge, in whose presence the appointment is made, and the consent of the litigants) are stressed with a reference to *D.* 39, 3, 8: "cum enim minuitur ius eorum, consequens est requiri, an consentiant."[107]

In still another place, in connection with a judgment made with one party absent, William brings *q.o.t.* to bear. He asks whether in such a case a *reformatio* or *restitutio* can be claimed in the absence or ignorance of the party. If the reinstatement is made for the good of the absent person, absence is no obstacle. He who was absent and ignorant of the summons did not consent to the judgment; therefore, the judgment can be altered for the better with the said party still absent, since it contains no injury in itself. But on the contrary it is argued, among other things, "quod omnes tangit, ab omnibus debet approbari. . . ." When the case is reopened and the *reformatio* or *restitutio* affects a person who is absent, it must be heard in his presence unless he persists in default.[108] This is particularly essential if the *reformatio* or *restitutio* should injure the said party.[109] As in *D.* 39, 3, 8, where it is said that when anyone's right is diminished his consent is necessary, in this case, "exigitur voluntas, ne ignorans iniuriam accipiat."[110] Thus the *causa*

---

[106] Wahrmund, II, ii, 305-307.

[107] *Ibid.*, p. 115. The consent of the judge is needed because he might suffer from the appointment, "unde eius est requirendus consensus," as in *D.* 39, 3, 8.

[108] "Cum igitur per partem absentem possit negotium aperire et reformatio tangat eum, in ipsius praesentia vel per contumaciam absentia est restitutio sive reformatio agitanda"; II, ii, 161.

[109] Wahrmund, II, ii, 161: "Sic adhibita praesentia partis adversae, quae contradiceret reformationi, tractabitur ea."

[110] II, ii, 161: "ff. de aqua pluvia arcenda, l. in concedendo (*D.* 39, 3, 8), ubi dicitur, quod ubi minuitur ius alicuius, eius voluntas exigitur, igitur exigitur voluntas, ne ignorans iniuriam accipiat." Here Drogheda is referring also to *D.* 39, 3, 9, 1: "Ideo autem voluntas exigitur, ne dominus ignorans iniuriam accipiat."

reformationis must be tried in the presence of the party who had been absent when the judgment was given, lest his rights suffer in his absence. William of Drogheda's solution is that no *restitutio* or *reformatio* can be made in the absence of one of the parties unless that party is by contumacy *vere* or *interpretative* absent.[111]

In these passages William of Drogheda stresses *C.* 5, 59, 5, 2 and *D.* 39, 3, 8 and 9 as having the same import. If a suit touched several who had rights in the thing sued for, they must all be informed and summoned in order that their consent or dissent might be heard and judged. If any of the parties wilfully defaulted, the sentence could be given by the court in his absence. But if it was later established that the default was committed involuntarily or in ignorance of the summons, the said party was given the opportunity to reinstate himself, obtain a hearing and possibly win a reversal of the sentence and a *restitutio*. Although William of Drogheda in all this reflects the legal theory of legists and canonists on the procedural aspect of voluntary consent,[112] he does not refer to *D.* 42, 1, 47 ("De unoquoque negotio praesentibus omnibus, quos causa contingit, iudicari oportet"). But elsewhere he does, and in a context that includes *C.* 5, 59, 5 and *D.* 39, 3, 8 and 9. Among the exceptions allowed the defendant was that of *nominandi dominum in iudicio*—the Roman *laudatio auctoris*. He might claim that the plaintiff was a monk and hence could not wage suit without the consent of his abbot, or that the plaintiff was not a sufficient or lawful opponent (*iustus contradictor*) and thus no valid sentence of the court could be given. To this plea the plaintiff could reply that he was a *iustus contradictor* and was suing by a right which belonged to himself and to no other.[113] The defendant's *exceptio* was peremptory when the plaintiff had no right to bring his *ius* into court because it was a "ius utendi fruendi in rebus alienis

---

111 II, ii, 161f.: "Ad hoc dico, quod restitutio sive reformatio non potest fieri in alterius absentia, nisi per contumaciam fuerit absens vere vel interpretative. Vere, quando constat, eum vocatum fuisse et nolle venire ad iudicium. Interpretative, quando constat, quod vocatus fuit, non autem comparet impeditus forte alia ex causa, nec constat, eum nolle venire. In eo casu est contumacia praesumpta." See above, nn. 44-47.

112 See above, nn. 14-35.

113 Wahrmund, II, ii, 403.

(s)alva rerum substantia" (*D.* 33, 2, 1; 40, 16, 3; and the like). That is, he could not bring suit without naming the owner as the principal party. If, on the other hand, the plaintiff had a *ius in re* of his own, as a "superficiarius, usufructuarius, ratione sui fructus" in emphyteusis, he was a *iustus contradictor* (*D.* 7, 6, 5; *D.* 43, 18, 1, 3-9).[114] In that case, the defendant's exception was dilatory since the suit interested the lessor of the emphyteusis as well as the lessee, but interested the lessor or proprietor "non principaliter, sed secundario," as in *C.* 7, 16, 13; *C.* 5, 59, 5, 2; and *D.* 39, 3, 8 and 9. Therefore, when the defendant's exception, that the *dominus* or lessor was interested with the plaintiff (the lessee), was made good, the *dominus* should then be summoned. If he and any other parties interested *secundario* failed to respond to the summons, their default resulted in the continuation of the process without the original plaintiff; and the defendant waged the suit to its conclusion, for the defaulting parties, having been summoned, were *interpretative* present and sentence could be given without them.[115]

This discussion leads to another question: whether the *nominatio* (the naming of all parties interested in one way or another with the plaintiff or with the defendant, for in replying to a counter-claim the plaintiff became defendant) must be made in every case of the kind. The *nominatio* was not necessary in all cases; but it was necessary when, for example, the prior of a convent was summoned, for then the abbot must be named. When a vicar was summoned, the rector (of the church actively served by the vicar) should be named. But since the vicar possessed a legal right that could be touched, he could bring his right into court after having advised the rector of his action, "ut ff. de re iudicata, l. unoquoque" (*D.* 42, 1, 47).[116] Thus if a

---

114 The nature of these various rights in property owned or possessed by another is a subject too complex to treat here.

115 Wahrmund, II, ii, 403f. Drogheda refers, on the last, to *C.* 3, 19, 2; 2, 4, 23; and *Decr. Greg. IX* 2, 6, 5. On all this see above, nn. 44-47.

116 Here the text is not clear; perhaps Wahrmund has kept a corrupt text and misunderstood it. As it stands it reads (II, ii, 406): "Hoc tamen adiecto, quod vicaria nomen iuris, quatinus tangit ius suum, potest deducere (ratio) in iudicium . . . rectore tamen prius ammonito, ut ff. de re iudicata, l. unoquoque (*D.* 42, 1, 47)." But if one reads *vicarius* for *vicaria* and omits *ratio*, which Wahrmund adds, the passage makes sense thus: "quod vicarius nomen iuris, quatinus tangit ius suum, potest deducere in iudicium . . . rectore tamen prius ammonito. . . ."

vicar sued or was sued, both his right and the rector's were involved, and the rector must consent or be in a measure a coparty to the suit;[117] both in consequence were to be summoned, for all must be present whom the business touched, as Paulus says, *D.* 42, 1, 47. This does not mean that the rector as well as the vicar had to be present in person; in this case it was sufficient if the vicar had advised, or taken counsel with, the rector. If this had not been done before the action was brought into court, the defendant had a valid exception, and the trial could not proceed until the rector had been advised or summoned.[118]

William of Drogheda does not, so far as I have read him, use the same expressions for *q.o.t.* as the decretalists, who for similar situations said, *omnes quos res tangit vocandi sunt,* or a variant of these words. Perhaps because he was as much a civilian as a canonist, he was rather inclined to quote, or simply refer to, *C.* 5, 59, 5, 2; *D.* 39, 3, 8 and 9; and *D.* 42, 1, 47. Nonetheless, Drogheda was familiar with the Roman laws that were cited in the thirteenth century as authorities for *q.o.t.,* and from him Bracton may have learned something about the procedural meaning of the maxim.

5. *Q.O.T.* IN BRACTON'S TREATMENT OF THE SUMMONS

Bracton was influenced by such elements of the Roman and canon law as he learned from the sources outlined above. Was one of these elements the maxim *quod omnes tangit?*

Rights, of course, as we have observed, whether individual, several, joint, or common, amount to nothing unless they can be maintained in a court of law by means of the procedure of fair trial according to the law. Bracton, therefore, agrees with Paulus, even if unconsciously, that if a case touches several parties as plaintiffs or defendants all must appear in court before judgment can be given, unless they persist in absence or default. The plaintiffs must all, either individually or by representatives, participate in the writ of summons and be present

---

117 Drogheda adds that if the vicar alone has the *potestas restituendi* he alone need be summoned.

118 Wahrmund, II, ii, 404-406.

on the day set for trial. The defendants or tenants must also be properly summoned, informed, and thus given the opportunity to defend their rights in court.

In discussing the citation or summons, Bracton states the maxim in its procedural sense for the summoning of *omnes* of the county for any business which touches (*tangit*) the *universitas* or community of the shire. Such a summons is general and is made publicly in order that no one may plead ignorance as an excuse for having refused to attend the county court; as a result of the publication, what all the members of the community know can be denied by no one to avoid the penalty of default or to plead that a decision was unjust.[119] It is this kind of summons which is made before the circuit of the justices in eyre (and, we may add, although Bracton does not discuss it, before the meeting of a parliament to which not merely one county but all the communities of the community of the realm are sum-

[119] Publication had a legal significance likewise in the two laws. When a business touched the whole community and it was difficult to send individual summonses, or when a case touched individuals who might be hard to find, publication in public places by crier or by posting on the church door was considered sufficient information and summons to prevent pleas of ignorance of the fact as an excuse for not responding and not accepting the decision of court or assembly. Ignorance of the fact excused no one who was legally and properly summoned. Those thus summoned and thereafter absent were in default; in other words they were *interpretative* present and the business of the court could proceed.

Similarly the promulgation of a statute was followed by the publication of it in open (not necessarily full) county and hundred courts, and in cities and boroughs and market places, in order to prevent excuses based on the plea of ignorance of the law. See, among many examples, *Statutes of the Realm*, I, 4, 39; *Close Rolls H. III, 1234-1237*, 338. At first, it may have been held that only those who were actually present in the county court and heard the proclamation were bound by the statute. But it was more practical to accept the theory, borrowed from the procedure of summoning parties to court, that if all who ought to hear, because they were affected by the law or had to administer it, had been properly summoned, then all heard—even the absent heard because present *interpretative*. Still later, with the rise of representation, in part under the influence of Romano-canonical theories of the corporation, it was held that a statute made in Parliament was binding if promulgated and published in Parliament, since the whole community of the realm was there present in the magnates and the representatives of the communities, and therefore all heard and were thus informed. See G. O. Sayles, *Select Cases*, p. xvii; Plucknett, *Com. Law*, p. 292. Publication, however, was still necessary and practiced because, in my opinion, the common people were not represented in Parliament and they could be informed only through local publication. Besides, the legal tradition called for it.

moned).[120] Of course, not every member of the community was touched by the general summons, which was directed to magnates, prelates, knights, and other free men who by custom or by the sheriff's designation regularly attended the county court as the leading men of the community or as representatives of vills and boroughs. (Those who, as possessors of rights affected by cases to be tried, were directly interested as plaintiffs and defendants, were individually summoned.) Not all those who were summoned as members of the county court attended: excuses for absence were accepted, and unexcused absences were penalized.[121] Nonetheless, the county court and assembly represented the county and was the essential corporate community of the county insofar as the corporate fiction was used for the convenience of jurisdiction and administration. Thus the magnates, knights, and other free men who were generally summoned were the representatives of the whole community of the shire, and hence by fiction *omnes de comitatu* were touched by the summons. But what in theory touched the *universitas* in practice touched only the free men, who were the community. "The county, through its court, had some of the qualities of a juristic person."[122] Similarly, Bracton associates the corporate fiction with the whole kingdom in the case of business that touched king and kingdom; the *maior pars* of the magnates and

---

[120] Bracton, IV, 61 (Tw. v, 118-120): "Item summonitionum alia generalis alia specialis. Generalis autem sive communis est quae tangit aliquam universitatem, sicut omnes de comitatu vel omnes alicuius civitatis, burgi vel villae pro aliquo quod tangat* universitatem, sicut generalis summonitio quae fit ante iter iustitiariorum et huiusmodi, quae semper fieri debet in loco magis publico, et ideo dedici non poterit nec defendi, quia quod omnes de comitatu vel civitate sciverint vel cognoverint, unus vel plures hoc dedicere non possunt." But certain excuses for absence without default are permitted "si ad primum diem communis summonitionis non venerit, dum tamen veniat ad diem sibi datum ad warantizandum essonium et ita quod inde postmodum sine licentia non recedat." *Tangit* is so customary, even where the subjunctive would be better, that it should have been retained, especially since in several of the manuscripts the reading is *tangit* (61, n. 23).

[121] See Pollock and Maitland, I, 545.

[122] Holdsworth, *op.cit.*, I[5], 69; II[3], 377f. On the county court see Holdsworth, I, 69f.; Jolliffe, *Const. Hist. of England*, pp. 305-312; White, *Making of the English Const.*, pp. 9-63, 76-79, 184, 197-201; Pollock and Maitland, I, 411, 532-560; and H. Ke Chin Wang, "The Corporate Entity Concept (or Fiction Theory) in the Year Book Period," *L.Q.R.*, LVIII (1942), 498-511.

prelates represent the community of the realm.[123] To this kind of general representation Bracton does not add that of the counties. But already, partly as a result of the growth of the theory of the right of judicial or procedural consent for all legal rights, the magnates could not completely represent the community of the realm by themselves, at least not in the matter of extraordinary taxation. Lesser feudal tenants and free men, knights of the shire and burgesses, were acquiring the right to represent their own interests insofar as their rights were distinguishable from those specifically pertaining to the great lords. The non-free members of the kingdom were to remain without direct representation and consent.[124]

Bracton does not make the community of vill, hundred, or county sufficiently corporate for it to own property or to sue as a corporation apart from the individuals constituting it. (That capacity he confers upon cities; here he is academic, citing the familiar passage, *Inst.* 2, 1, 6.)[125] But for all that, the community was becoming quasi-corporate for some purposes of jurisdiction, taxation, and administration.[126] In the case of

[123] In his discussion of the Provisions, or Statute, of Merton, 1236 (IV, 295f.; Tw. VI, 288): "coram . . . Cantuariensi archiepiscopo, et coram suffraganeis suis omnibus, et coram maiore parte comitum et baronum Angliae tunc ibi existentium pro coronatione regis et reginae pro quo omnes vocati fuerunt, generaliter tractatum esset de communi utilitate totius regni super pluribus articulis regem et regnum tangentibus. . . ." The reflection of *q.o.t.* is Bracton's; it does not appear in the Statute: "cum tractatum esset de communi utilitate regni super articulis subscriptis"; *Statutes of the Realm*, I, 1; in *C. R. H. III, 1234-1237*, p. 337, "pro communi utilitate totius regni nostri provisum fuit, etc."

[124] Bracton nowhere discusses taxation as something apart from feudal aids. But, as is evident from the king's writ for the collection of the thirtieth, 1237, the prelates, magnates, and "milites et liberi homines," who were summoned to a parliament, represented both themselves and the villeins of the kingdom—"pro se et suis villanis"—in granting the subsidy; *S. C.*, p. 358. See Cam, "L'Assiette et la perception des indemnités des représentants des comtés dans l'Angleterre médiévale," *Rev. hist. dr. fr. étr.*, XVIII, 219ff.

[125] Bracton, II, 40; III, 128, 130 (Tw. I, 58; III, 368, 372); cf. *D.* 1, 8, 6, 1. Nor does the kingdom exist as a corporation in the technical, strictly legal, sense; yet, by fiction, with the king acting as the head and representative, it acts as a corporation when the king and council in the name and with the consent of the community of the realm take common action for the public and common utility.

[126] Pollock and Maitland, I, 627ff., object to the terms "corporate" and "quasi-corporate" for the English community. And certainly, so far as the community of county or hundred's owning property is concerned, there is no corporateness. Nor is there a Fiction Theory involved, for "the English community has not yet been detached from individual members" (Ke Chin Wang, *L.Q.R.*, LVIII, 511); it

a suit over common rights in pasture, the office of the sheriff, upon receiving the king's writ, was to convene the hundred— "et omnes quos admensuratio illa tangit."[127] "It was a familiar occurrence for every hundred, vill and borough to send representatives to the county court, where a general investigation would be made into local government, and apparently a vote of taxes might occasionally be made."[128] In a strictly procedural sense four knights of the shire represented the county court when they bore the record of cases to the king's court.[129] Hence, Bracton mentions[130] how four knights were sent "pro comitatu cum recordo ad audiendum iudicium suum" as "quasi partes in iudicio."[131] This was not corporate representation; but as a part of the administrative machinery of the English government, representation by knights of the shire began as early as the reign of John. In the second half of the century, if not as early as 1227,[132] the system acquired a new significance, that of the representation of the rights of the community of knights of the shire before the king's court.

Similarly, for several individuals who had rights in a thing common to them, or whose separate rights were made common

---

is an aggregate with group liability; "the capacity to act as a unit could be claimed by incorporate as well as unincorporate bodies" (*i.e.* 500, 506). Cf. Pollock and Maitland, I, 529f., 558f., 615-632; Plucknett, *Com. Law*, pp. 84f. But it must be remembered that even in the Fiction Theory of Innocent IV there was still some aggregateness, some collectivity and joint liability in the corporation; that individual members were after all made responsible for corporate obligations; that the corporation was a fictive person precisely because it was not a real person that could be treated in some matters apart from the individual members. In any case, I use the term corporate in a restricted sense as applied to the county and its duties and obligations. There is, after all, something corporate about the county when through the sheriff the county court, as the essential corporation of the county, is commanded by the king to send to him representatives provided with *plena potestas*; this is corporate representation; see *Traditio*, I, 355-408, and above, ch. III.

127 Bracton, III, 183; Tw. III, 538.

128 Plucknett, *Com. Law*, p. 140.

129 Pollock and Maitland, I, 534-537, 547f., 554f.; Plucknett, *op.cit.*, p. 345.

130 IV, 79; Tw. V, 172.

131 This belongs to the discussion of legitimate excuses for not responding to a summons: the knights are excused and granted delays if summoned by a lower court while they are appearing before the higher court of the king, for the king's business was more important than that in any lower court.

132 See A. B. White, "Some Early Instances of Concentration of Representatives in England," *A.H.R.*, XIX (1913), 738. But White thinks that in 1227 it is merely "bearing the record," not litigation by the knights in their own interest.

by one suit, but who constituted neither corporation nor community, Bracton follows the principles of Romano-canonical
procedure in specifying that all such parties, either as plaintiffs
or as defendants, must be properly summoned. In his treatise on
exceptions or pleas, which became numerous as a result of the influence of Roman law,[133] he shows how dilatory exceptions can
be made on the basis of common consent and *q.o.t.*: a defendant
may plead that the *ius* is common, that he cannot answer without the other interested parties, "vel quia in parte tangit alios
sine quibus, etc."[134] In such a case all must be summoned (just
as in the Roman law on co-*tutores*).[135] There can be several
plaintiffs and several defendants as parceners, one plaintiff and
several defendants, or one defendant and several plaintiffs, and
so on.[136] Whether the plaintiffs as parceners are coheirs or not,
"oportet quod omnes qui petunt et qui capere debeant de re
petita nominentur in breve."[137] Because of exceptions, replications, and triplications relating to the failure to name in the
writ and summons some of the parties deemed interested either
by the plaintiff or by the defendant, whether it be proved or
not that other parties are *participes* in the thing sued for, all

---

[133] Holdsworth, *op.cit.*, II⁴, 251, 282; Pollock and Maitland, I, 134.

[134] Bracton, IV, 330f. (Tw. VI, 378-382): "Competit etiam tenenti exceptio pe-
remptoria et quandoque dilatoria tam ex persona alterius quam petentis, quia
sine alio agere non poterit per se qui tantundem iuris habet quam ipse qui petit,
ut sunt plures participes." For example, where interests are common, a man
cannot sue without his wife's being consulted; nor a chapter of canons or a
convent without the consent of the dean, abbot, or prior; nor a dean and chapter
without the consent of the bishop (see also p. 335; Tw. VI, 390-392). This reflects
the Canon law. Coparceners who have "tantundem iuris" in a thing must all be
named in the writ whether as plaintiffs or defendants (on coparceners see Pollock
and Maitland, II, 274f., 306, 313), for they are "quasi unum corpus in eo quod
unum ius habent, et oportet quod corpus sit integrum, et quod in aliqua parte
non sit defectus"; IV, 330; cf. IV, 83f. If an inheritance is divided among several
and only one of the heirs is sued for his part, he is permitted one delay, and in
his person the case is terminated so far as his part is concerned. But if he claims
that "sine particibus suis non debeat responderi," in that event "summonendi
sunt participes quod sint ad respondendum cum eo et sine quibus etcetera"; IV,
83; Tw. V, 184. Cf. below, nn. 155, 156.

[135] When one *tutor* was the defendant but demanded that the others be
summoned (*D.* 11, 2, 2: "Cum ex pluribus tutoribus unus, quod ceteri non sint
idonei, convenitur, postulante eo omnes ad eundem iudicem mittuntur; et hoc
rescriptis principum continetur"); cf. *C.* 5, 59, 5, 2; *C.* 7, 56, 2 and 4; *C.* 7, 60,
1 and 2.

[136] On the problem of joint tenancy and tenancy in common see Holdsworth,
op.cit., III⁴, 126f.

[137] IV, 331f.; Tw. VI, 382.

such parties should be named in the writ.[138] There are cases, however, in which there is such a division of interest among several heirs or coparceners that not all need be named in one writ; rather, separate writs for the individual suits are issued.[139] But in general, no defendant is held to reply without his *participes*; for if he should do so and lose the case, he would have no legal means of compelling the other interested parties to share in the damages.[140] Thus all the defendant's *participes* must be summoned to court even if they are not named in the plaintiff's writ.[141] Naturally, if several parties have separate, individual rights in a thing, all must individually be summoned.

Such pleas or exceptions, of course, had a foundation in the common law. In real actions particularly, when several persons had rights in the same piece of land, "all joint-tenants must be made defendants."[142] To obtain delays, a defendant could make "hasty enfeoffments to a friend who reenfeoffed the tenant (defendant) jointly with others"; and as a result of a situation in which several were touched by a suit which at first touched only one, delays and pleas became numerous, and the original defendant might succeed in postponing a decision almost indefinitely. No decision by default was possible when the defendants in succession were excused, or rather, obtained delays.[143] This fraudulent method was partially checked by statutes beginning shortly after Bracton's time.[144] But if several persons were already interested in the piece of land or in the right sued for, a plea by a defendant that others were touched and should be summoned was in that case well founded and was upheld by the court. Still other pleas resulted "in the joinder or substitution of new parties to the action," for example, the reversioners

138 IV, 332f. (Tw. VI, 386): "Sed omnes nominandi sunt de quibus certum est vel dubium utrum capere possint vel non, quia in dubio in benignam partem erit interpretandum, videlicet quod capere possint donec probetur in contrarium."

139 IV, 334 (Tw. VI, 390): "si plures petant [as plaintiffs] non est necesse omnes nominari in uno brevi quia diversae sunt actiones, quia quilibet petat partem suam propriam quae eum contingit sine alio participe. . . ."

140 IV, 336f.; Tw. VI, 394-398.

141 *Loc. cit.*

142 Plucknett, *Com. Law*, p. 364.

143 *Loc. cit.*

144 See below, nn. 146-149, 160-162.

if a tenant for life was the defendant,[145] or warrantors. As to warrantors and the naming of the warrantor by the defendant—"vouching to warranty," which was feudal in nature—the plaintiff was often able to make the plea that the tenant could not respond by himself and that his warrantor must be summoned or vouched to warranty. To complicate matters, the vouchee, upon coming to court, might plead that he was not bound to warrant. It is easy to see that the system of vouching to warranty was often used for purposes of fraud or delay—but not in the summary procedure of novel disseizin, for in actions of novel disseizin vouching to warranty was apparently not permitted, although pleas that other parties were directly interested might be allowed.[146]

It will be remembered that in the two laws, exceptions based on the principle of *q.o.t.* reflected situations analogous, even though anything but feudal, to those in the English law. Land or other property often belonged in some fashion to one person and might be held or used in some form of rental or tenancy by others. If the lessee was the defendant, he might plead that his was not the sole right and that the owner or lessor was involved and should be summoned; and the plaintiff might be without sufficient right to wage the action unless others were named as coplaintiffs. We have seen that William of Drogheda, following the procedure laid down in the *Code* and in a decretal of Innocent III, associated *q.o.t.* with such situations.[147] It is not surprising that Bracton does the same for analogous situations in the English law. Indeed, a plea might be offered by a baron as defendant that the king was his voucher to warranty, for since he was a tenant-in-chief he could not reply without the king, whom the case touched.[148] But, of course, the king acknowl-

145 Plucknett, *op.cit.*, p. 364.

146 See in general Pollock and Maitland, II, 48f., 158, 163, 611-613, 662; Plucknett, *op.cit.*, p. 364; Sayles, *Select Cases*, III, xxxiv. Several statutes, 1275, 1292, 1340, established special procedures in certain cases in the attempt to remedy abuses; *Statutes of the Realm*, I, 36, 108; below, nn. 186-189.

147 Above, nn. 48, 49, 113-118.

148 II, 301, on *placita de baroniis*, which are terminated before the royal justices or before the king: "ubi ipse petens tenere clamat immediate de domino rege in capite per breve de recto, quod vocatur praecipe in capite, et hoc ideo, quia hoc tangit ipsum regem in toto vel in parte."

edged no superior and could not be made to respond; by his grace, however, he might choose to do so. The judges, according to the Statute *de bigamis*, 1276, must proceed without delay and simply notify the king when he was vouched to warranty.[149]

In another sense, however, the practice of making pleas that other parties were interested may have led to its application to situations in which the king, as well as the parties to a suit, was concerned because of his jurisdiction or because of his being the feudal suzerain, whose tenants-in-chief persisted in maintaining that in certain cases he was under obligation. This practice bore fruit in the development of Parliament as a high court of justice as well as an assembly for the business of subsidies. There is no hint of this in Bracton; but his statement about the exception made by a defendant, that he should not answer without the king, seems as it were to anticipate a wide extension of the plea in 1311. In that year the Lords Ordainers declared that the king should hold a parliament at least once a year, twice if necessary, in a convenient place; for "many folk are delayed in the king's court because the defendants allege that the plaintiffs ought not to be answered in the absence of the king, and many also are wronged by the ministers of the king, which wrongs they cannot get redressed without common parliament."[150] Broadly speaking, many kinds of business that touched tenants and subjects touched the king—touched, that

149 *Statutes of the Realm*, I, 42; Sayles, *Select Cases*, III, xliii-xlvi. Sayles points out how litigants tried to protract the action and avoid amercements and damages by making the king a party to the proceedings; but the king tried to suppress this practice.

150 Pollard, *Evolution of Parliament*, pp. 35f.; *Statutes of the Realm*, I, 165, c. 29. Pollard believes that the main business of Parliament was to deal out justice and that (42ff.) the financial necessities of the king were secondary to justice in causing the rise of Parliament, for "the frequent summons of parliaments was a measure required not by the crown so much as by its subjects." But in my opinion, the king's business of administration and taxation was equally important, and perhaps prior to justice, in that the summoning of representatives of the communities for taxes and the like, or for bearing the record, gave the communities the opportunity, or rather acquainted them with the means, to pursue their own interests in Parliament. See also to n. 132, above. The magnates had long had the opportunity to go to the king's *curia* in the feudal sense to obtain justice; in 1311 they were trying to go back to the good old days when access to the king's person was easier than in Edward I's time, perhaps because of the development of the king's courts in which he was not always present in person; in reality, they intended to limit the prerogative. See below, ch. VIII, §2.

is, the king's obligation to rule according to the law, to make his justice available, or to prove as it were in court that his right to a subsidy was legally founded. Parliament was therefore not possible without the king or his fully empowered delegate (the magnates wanted the king in person), nor without representatives of the community of the realm—the king's business touched the community, and the business of the community or of portions thereof touched the king. In the development of the theory, which may not have been consciously held by everyone but which was implicit in representation in Parliament, the procedural aspect of *q.o.t.* may through Bracton have had an imponderable influence.

Q.o.t. was also applied by Bracton to the procedure of granting delays on the basis of legal excuses before the summoned could be judged guilty of contumacy or default.[151] If all parties interested either directly or indirectly in a suit must be summoned, all, as defendants, must be given the usual delays that were considered legal (delays because of a more important business in a higher court; because of a higher necessity or utility; because of natural obstacles impeding the journey to court, such as floods or highwaymen; because of distance from court, overseas or in the Holy Land; and because of serious illness).[152] The system was, as in Romano-canonical procedure, complicated; in many kinds of real and personal actions, delays were numerous even when there was but one defendant. Justice was normally slow, although by the time of Bracton the Roman and Germanic triple summons (before default could be declared) had been dropped in real actions.[153] Except in the summary procedure of novel disseizin, in which there was little or no patience with defaulters and delays were not granted before default was declared,[154] the procedure was still more dila-

[151] Cf. Pollock and Maitland, II, 562f., 577, 592-595; Plucknett, *Com. Law*, p. 343.

[152] IV, 61-190, 82f.; Tw. v. 118-491, 178ff.

[153] On the triple summons see Glanville, I, 7 (ed. Woodbine, pp. 43f.); Pollock and Maitland, I, 592, where it is wrongly assumed that the triple summons is Germanic in origin—it is Roman, too.

[154] Pollock and Maitland, II, 48f.; but sometimes the unavoidable absence of a party who could not be reached by the summons because of being abroad resulted in a postponement of a case to a future assize; see below, n. 186.

tory when several parties who held in common were defendants, or when pleas were made that warrantors should be summoned; for then each defendant was given a delay, but not,
says Bracton, for every step in the proceedings—lest "ita fierent
dilationes immortales."[155] If one of several heirs was sued for
his part, he might obtain a delay for himself and the business
could be terminated in his person so far as his part was concerned. But by the principle of *q.o.t.* he might plead that since
the other parceners or coheirs had rights that were touched,
they should be summoned to respond with him. In that case
all must be summoned to answer along with the original defendant.[156] Then the defendants might each be given a delay—but
neither as one heir nor as several, until it was established that
they were all *participes*. When they were all present and this
had been established, from that point on they waged the suit
as one heir. For the division of the inheritance made plural
the unity of the *ius* and created plural heirs; but the common
defense of all reestablished the unity of the *ius* and made the
defendants "unum corpus et unum heredem propter iuris unio-
nem"; for if one of the defendants should lose, the others
would be held to contribute.[157] As for determining the validity
of the excuses offered for delays, *q.o.t.* was once more applicable:
in returning an essoin, all whom the case touches shall be re-

[155] IV, 83ff. 162; Tw. V, 184ff. 410ff. If one of the several defaults, his portion
of the thing sued for is seized as a penalty. If all the interested parties appoint
an attorney and he defaults, then all lose. In his words on "dilationes immortales" Bracton reminds one of *C*. 3, 1, 13: "ne lites fiant paene immortales et
vitae hominum modum excedant." Tw. V, 184, reads *innumerabiles*; Woodbine
IV, 83, *immortales*, which is justified not only by some of the manuscripts but
also by *C*. 3, 1, 13. It is interesting to note that in 1227-1234 Gregory IX follows
C. 3, 1, 13: "Volentes finem imponi litibus, ne immortales exsistant"; *Decr. Greg.*
IX 2, 14, 10.

[156] See the decision of the royal court in the case of the division of the County
of Chester among sisters, 1238-1239, Bracton's *Notebook* (ed. Maitland), III, 283:
". . . et preterea cum omnes sint quasi unus heres et nulla earum potest sine aliis
petere vel respondere." But according to the *Statutum hibernie de coheredibus*
(1236), if several daughters inherit from a tenant of a lord other than the king,
the eldest shall do homage for herself and her sisters; the sisters are "quasi unus
heres de unica hereditate"; *Statutes of the Realm*, I, 5. Cf. above, n. 134. Thus a
kind of representation was permitted for feudal obligations such as homage and
suit-service (below, nn. 159, 160)—but not for litigation when a case touched
coheirs in common.

[157] IV, 83, 162.

quired or summoned—those who are interested as litigants (the parcener and the warrantor of the essoiner and others) and those who have to attend as jurors, recognitors, or *inquisitores,* and knights as members of the county court, either as electors or as participants in great assizes.[158]

This was Bracton's theory, that the unity of the right and the common defense should obviate such delays as would, if used by each parcener in turn, defeat the efforts of a plaintiff to obtain justice. For this reason he would modify, as the Roman law did, the extreme individualism implicit in *q.o.t.* by subordinating the maxim to the needs of a speedy process.[159] But the practice in the courts was otherwise: a decision in a case involving coheirs or parceners might be seriously delayed if one of them claimed that the others were equally touched, if the codefendants were now compelled to appear jointly, and if each of them could in turn obtain a delay and make it difficult for all to appear at the same time—a subterfuge that no doubt was sometimes resorted to deliberately. Moreover, as we have noted above, still others might be vouched to warranty. As a result, royal provisions and statutes provided for some unity in feudal obligations and tried to develop a speedier procedure for cases affecting common rights. In order to facilitate suit-service of coheirs or parceners of a fief in magnates' courts and to limit the jurisdiction of these courts while increasing that of the king's court, the Provisions of the King and Barons, 1259, c. 2, and the Statute of Marlborough, 1267, c. 9, stated that when an inheritance that owed one suit-service passed to several

---

[158] IV, 109f. (Tw. v, 264-266): "exigendi sunt omnes quos loquela tangit;" and again: "In essonio reddendo . . . exigantur omnes illi quos causa tetigerit, sicut particeps, warantus et alii ut supra, etc."

[159] *D.* 11, 2, 2; 8, 5, 4, 4; 10, 2, 27 and 28; 21, 1, 31, 5. The Roman classical law tried to solve the problem not only by prescribing that in certain cases the coheirs should appoint a procurator, but also by limiting the number of summonses and delays (*D.* 42, 1, 47 and 53). Note also *D.* 10, 2, 48, quoted below, n. 173. The English solution was to be that of limiting the right of successive delays and making the coheirs, or several defendants who had no rights in common but were touched by the same suit, appear on the same day; see nn. 156, 161. But in matters of feudal obligations like homage and suit-service, representation of coheirs by the eldest was permitted; nn. 156, 160, 172. On several rights challenged by several complaints connected with the same case, see Provisions of King and Barons, 1259, c. 3 (*S.C.,* p. 390), and Stat. of Marlborough, 1267.

heirs, the eldest should do the suit for the others. However, they still must contribute according to their shares and were therefore responsible in the procedural sense.[160] In 1275 the Statute of Westminster I, c. 43, stated that the plaintiff was often "delayed of his right" because when several parceners were defendants, none of whom could be compelled to answer without the others, they sometimes appeared separately and on different days (*fourcher*), and each had his own essoin and delay. Accordingly, henceforth such codefendants should have essoin for one day only, and no more than a sole defendant should have.[161] Further remedy was the intent of the Statute *de conjunctim feoffatis* (1306), which aimed at preventing a defendant from "delaying the plaintiff of his right" by making a fraudulent plea that the plaintiff's writ failed to name a joint tenant; but if it were found that there was in fact a joint tenancy before the plaintiff purchased his writ, then the plea was valid.[162] Other statutes were designed to remedy abuses of fraud and endless delays in vouching to warranty.[163]

Such delays were sometimes a serious handicap to speedy justice and could indeed cause justice to miscarry.[164] Nonetheless, they reflected the same principle as that in *q.o.t.* and were a part of the due process which safeguarded rights. In fact, the procedure was still based on the principle when it was speeded up by the use of the single, peremptory, general summons for the assize of novel disseizin and for public business either in county court or in Parliament—for the serious business of a case of necessity and dire emergency which touched king and

160 *Statutes of the Realm*, I, 8 and 21f.; *S. C.*, p. 390. In the fourteenth century the royal courts decided that the Statute of Marlborough, c. 9, applied only in seignorial courts; in the royal courts all the coheirs still owed individual suit-service; Plucknett, *Statutes and Their Interpretation*, p. 154. Note the analogy with homage, above, n. 156.

161 *Statutes of the Realm*, I, 37. On *fourcher* and how in 1346 this statute was interpreted as affecting tenants, but not codefendants in the action of Debt, see Plucknett, *Statutes*, p. 126 n. 3, and *Com. Law*, p. 342. *Fourcher* was especially common in actions of Debt; Sayles, *Select Cases*, III, xxxiv; Holdsworth, *op.cit.*, III, 625.

162 *Statutes of the Realm*, I, 145f.—this for the assize of novel disseizin. Cf. Plucknett, *Com. Law*, p. 356 n. 1.

163 See above to n. 146.

164 See the example in an action of Debt, 1346; Plucknett, *Statutes*, p. 126.

kingdom and the common good and safety. The king's command that each community send to a parliament representatives with full powers (this began as early as the 1260's) meant that no delay beyond the date set for the assembly need be given. The community that failed without adequate excuse to be present through its representatives was guilty of default,[165] althought it was not, apparently, always penalized, since the grant of a subsidy could not be refused by defaulting boroughs—they were present, as it were, *interpretative,* their silence being interpreted as consent.[166]

Bracton had the principle of *q.o.t.* in mind when he discussed the summoning of all parties to a suit. He stated it, moreover, in connection with the summoning of those who assisted as recognitors, witnesses, and jurors, and who as lawful men of the community regularly attended the county court. One more illustration may be given. In case a memorandum of earlier proceedings was needed for a higher court, both the litigants and the recognitors, witnesses, jurors, and the like must be named; for otherwise a writ of error might be sought by one of the parties: "Et eodem modo de omnibus fiat mentio quos tangit negotium et quorum praesentia fuerit necessaria."[167]

But above all, those whose rights were in question must be summoned; and to avoid the penalty of default they must obey the summons either in person or by attorney or by simple bailiff unless given a delay.[168] This balancing of the right and power of the jurisdiction of the government with individual rights and consent must be held in mind as the natural dualism in-

[165] See *Traditio,* I, 386-402; above, ch. III, nn. 135-195. By his prerogative the king could grant delays or excuses for absence, and he could postpone an assembly.

[166] This subject needs treatment that cannot be given here; but see Pollard, *Evolution of Parliament,* pp. 139, 154f. 316-319, 387-444; and McKisack, *Parliamentary Representation of the English Boroughs,* pp. 8-43, 66-99. The *Modus tenendi Parl.* says that it is a *plenum parliamentum* when, even if some are absent, all were informed by reasonable summonses; *S.C.,* p. 503.

[167] IV, 102; Tw. v, 240.

[168] In Bracton the attorney corresponds to the Romano-canonical proctor with a general mandate and full powers, the bailiff to the proctor with a special mandate for one particular act and powers limited to that act; see *Traditio,* I, 356-364, and above, ch. III, § 1; Holdsworth, II³, 316; and Cohen, *History of the English Bar and Attornatus to 1450,* pp. 141f.

herent in the principle of judicial process; on the one side, coercion, ultimately justified by the king's right to maintain law and order for the common good and safety of people and kingdom; on the other, private rights under the law, including the right to defend rights, the right of fair hearing and trial, the right of consent or refusal of consent to any loss of rights, except according to the law as interpreted by the courts. As in Paulus and in William of Drogheda,[169] so in Bracton the power of the courts to compel defendants to appear and consent to the lawful decision of a case and the judicial or procedural consent of all whose rights were touched were necessary concomitants of a civilized judicial procedure—of due process in accordance with the law and customs of the land.[170]

6. Rights and *Q.O.T.* in Bracton

The procedure outlined above was largely determined by the nature of the thing in which a plurality of rights existed, just as the relationship of joint or common rights was in part affected in the same way. We have already seen that several persons could have rights in an inheritance. In that case one heir could be sued for his part without the other heirs being concerned. But *q.o.t.* came into its own when the said heir declared that he should not have to answer alone to the suit, since the coheirs were equally touched. When all the heirs were consequently summoned and appeared in court and were unable to prove that they were not parceners, from that point on they were considered, as it were, one heir. In other words, the division of the inheritance resulted in plural rights and plural heirs; but the common defense of all restored the unity of the rights and thus constituted of the several one body and one heir, for if the

---

169 *Summa aurea* (Wahrmund, II, ii, 14-36): in his long discussion of the three summonses and the peremptory summons, William shows how slow justice could be because of the many delays and excuses granted before a party could be judged contumacious. He then quotes passages on how rights must be protected (the law must not be too severe—"rigor et aequitas solvunt contrarietates," 32), and therefore, delays and extra summonses are to be approved. Nevertheless, the court must have the power to declare a defendant to be at default: "frustra essent iura in civitate, nisi esset aliquis, qui ea regeret" (36; *D.* 1, 2, 2, 13)—cf. *Glos. ord.* to *D.* 1, 1, 1, 2, on the public law and magistrates; below, ch. VII.

170 IV, 63, on *coertio*, the summons, and contumacy.

original defendant should lose, all would be held to contribute.[171] The Provisions of Westminster, 1259, and the Statute of Marlborough, 1267, in the case of a fief divided among several heirs or coparceners, placed the undivided suit-service in the hands of the eldest of the heirs; he was to do one suit for himself and his coparceners, who should contribute to the suit according to their portions.[172] The business still touched all the interested parties, but through a kind of representation. This method, if not the feudal situation, resembles what was prescribed for coheirs by the Roman law, though here representation by a proctor was permitted and the situation was that of litigation.[173]

The rules on procedural consent affected several persons who held in common an indivisible right. Such a right was an incorporeal thing, a *ius*, a franchise (*libertas*).[174] So the right of advowson[175] or presentation to a church: the advowson cannot be divided, but it can be held jointly by coheirs who thus constitute "unum corpus propter unitatem iuris," and who must all individually and simultaneously consent to the presentation unless they have consented to a method of presentation called *successive*. When a right is held in common and cannot be divided even with the consent of the interested parties, all must consent (consent by majority is not permitted)[176] to a change in the exercise of the right.[177] A gift, too, is indivisible, but several may be interested in it; a donation, consequently, requires the consent not only of the donor and donee but also of all others who have rights either in the

---

[171] IV, 83 (Tw. v, 184); cf. Holdsworth, *op.cit.* III⁴, 126-128; Pollock and Maitland, II, 274f. 306, 313.

[172] *Statutes of the Realm*, I, 8, 21f.; *S.C.*, p. 390; above, nn. 156, 159, 160.

[173] Wenger, *Institutes*, p. 84; *D.* 10, 2, 48: "Si familiae erciscundae vel communi dividundo vel finium regundorum actum sit et unus ex litigatoribus decesserit pluribus heredibus relictis, non potest in partes iudicium scindi, sed aut omnes heredes id debent aut dare unum procuratorem, in quem omnium nomine iudicium agatur." Cf. *D.* 10, 2, 27, and 8, 5, 4, 3-4; Buckland, *Textbook*, pp. 535f.

[174] II, 158-160; Tw. I, 416ff.

[175] Cf. Holdsworth, *op.cit.*, III⁴, 138-143.

[176] Nor in the Roman law on common ownership; Buckland, *The Main Institutions of Roman Private Law*, p. 288.

[177] II, 222; III, 205, 214, 225, 235, 239.

persons or in the property (or in both) involved in the transaction. Thus archbishops, bishops, abbots, and priors of churches in the royal advowson can make no gift of property pertaining to their churches without the consent of their chapters or convents; nor they and their chapters together without the consent of the royal or other patron or patrons to whom the advowson belongs: "quia omnium illorum consensus quos res tangit erit necessarius et requirendus."[178] Similarly, a rector who possesses nothing except in the name of his church can neither give, alienate, nor exchange without the consent of the bishop or patron, unless the condition of the church be improved by the act.[179] In the case of a gift or alienation affecting the common rights of prelate and ecclesiastical corporation Bracton, of course, reflects the two laws on consent.[180] But nowhere does he

---

[178] II, 52, 63: "Item in quibusdam donationibus oportet quod aliorum consensus interveniat quam donatoris et donatarii: ut si archiepiscopus, episcopus, abbas vel prior, rector ecclesiarum, sindicus vel procurator donationem fecerint, omnium eorum quorum interfuerit requirendus erit consensus, sicut regis, et capituli vel conventus." See also II, 158ff. In these cases *q.o.t.* reflects the canonical principle which forbids the alienation of church goods. The consent of the chapter is required not so much in the corporate or common interest as to put a check on the prelate. Perhaps here *q.o.t.* is an artificial façade, but it was expressed in this connection by the canonists as well as by Bracton.

[179] II, 52; Tw. I, 94, 96.

[180] Legists and canonists frequently referred to passages in *Digest* and *Code* on consent and *q.o.t.* in this connection. The prelate or head and the corporation as a fictive person each had the right of consent, and both must consent if an act involving their rights in a common thing were to be valid. But how did the corporation consent as a person? Literally interpreted, *q.o.t.* meant that all the members had the right to consent to an act of the corporate body, and the dissent of one member was enough to make an action impossible. And this was the interpretation if the individual rights of the members were touched but not the corporate right of the whole body. But when something touched the rights of the corporation as a whole, the lawyers applied the theory of the *maior pars* to corporate consent: what was approved by the majority (sometimes of at least two thirds of the members present in assembly) was approved, as it were, by all; a dissenting minority could not prevent action and had no legal right to maintain, after the decision was made, that the act did not bind them. On this for general accounts, but with no references to *q.o.t.*, see Gierke, III, 202-231, 312-330, 353-415; *idem*, "Über die Geschichte des Majoritätsprinzips," *Essays in Legal History*, ed. P. Vinogradoff, pp. 312-327; Gillet, *La personnalité juridique en droit canonique*, pp. 137-140; and Esmein, "L'unanimité et la majorité dans les élections canoniques," *Mélanges H. Fitting*, I, 355-382. See also Giacchi, "La regola 'quod omnes tangit'," *Studi . . . del Giudice*, I, 343-372.

Bracton has nothing to say about the *maior pars* in the community of shire or kingdom. But in connection with joint and common consent in advowsons, where there is no corporate interest, he says that neither *maioritas* nor *pluralitas*

more than mention the theory of consent in matters pertaining solely to the corporation, and then he refers to *Inst.* 2, 1, 6.[181] He does not discuss consent among the members of the corporation.[182]

Consent in relation to common and joint rights is illustrated further in the sections on novel disseizin;[183] and the procedural aspects of consent in terms of *q.o.t.* may be seen in Bracton's treatment.[184] True, the action was intended to be a summary one; consequently, there was at first no toleration of essoins and delays, nor of pleas or exceptions and vouching to warranty.[185] But from the second and third decades of the thirteenth century on, pleas were increasingly allowed; and on occasion a plea was successfully offered by a defendant that he should not have to answer in the absence of one of the plaintiffs.[186] Moreover,

---

shall apply (III, 129f.; Tw. III, 370-374). Naturally, the doctrine of the *maior pars* could develop in a corporation or corporate community but not in communities of men having joint or common rights but no "personality." The group of coheirs can act only in common with the consent of all individually; a personified corporation need not—hence Bracton's statement.

181 A tenement may be held in common by several who are not coparceners for some use and is neither the property of one person nor common to several, but is held by a city as a corporation; II, 40; III, 128, 130 (Tw. I, 58; III, 368, 372). See *D.* 1, 8, 6, 1.

182 See n. 180.

183 Bracton illustrates it also in similar fashion, with allowances for differences pertaining to the relative speediness of the procedure, in his treatment of other kinds of assizes, e.g., *mort d'ancestor*, III, 247-317; Tw. IV, 115-331.

184 The influence of Roman law on this assize, which corresponds to the Roman interdicts *unde vi* and *uti possidetis,* of Canon law, has been adequately discussed by Güterbock, *Bracton,* pp. 159ff.; Scrutton, *Influence of Rom. Law,* pp. 112-115; Maitland, *Bracton and Azo,* pp. 184f.; Pollock and Maitland, II, 48; Holdsworth, *op.cit.,* II⁴, 204f. Cf. Plucknett, *Com. Law,* pp. 233, 321.

185 Holdsworth, *op.cit.,* III⁴, 8f.

186 Holdsworth, *op.cit.,* III⁴, 9, acknowledges that *exceptiones* were allowed in the fourteenth century (also p. 11). But the Rolls of the Justices in Eyre reveal pleas made in actions of novel disseizin in 1221-1222; see *Selden Soc. Publ.,* LIX, nos. 20, 29, 540, 603, 1044. An interesting example is that of the case in which the Abbot of Evesham was accused of disseizing three men of their common pasture. When it was testified that one of the three plaintiffs was "in partibus Jerosolimitanis," the abbot "petit judicium si debeat sine eo respondere." As a result of this plea, which—since an abbot of Evesham probably was careful to take advantage of the rules of procedure in the Canon law—may have been a conscious application of *q.o.t.* as a procedural maxim, the assize was put in respite (no. 86). (Is it possible that Thomas of Marlborough's legal science was behind this plea? He was a monk at Evesham and had already served the abbot in a legal capacity; above, n. 75.) Hence we find the royal justices recognizing

one case in 1221-1222 shows that one of the plaintiffs essoined himself and the other pleaded that he did not wish to act without the first; and a postponement was granted.[187] To what extent pleas that warrantors should be summoned were permitted in the assize is not clear. In any event, all codefendants must be summoned, and all coplaintiffs must be present to wage the suit before the jurors could bring in a verdict. If one of the defendants defaulted, the verdict and judgment were given in his absence. In certain other real actions, however, the court was reluctant to judge by default.[188] But in novel disseizin, although there was no patience with defaulters, those who appeared could make pleas some of which were based on the legal necessity for the presence of all parties except those wilfully rather than unavoidably absent.

Bracton explains why such pleas had to be recognized. Several, he says, can be disseized of a common thing, and they may seek their remedy in the assize. This is because a tenement can be held in common in several ways.[189] It can be held by man and wife, neither of whom can sue or be sued without the other, for they are as it were one body with one right.[190] It may be held by two or more persons if the tenement is the boundary and boundary marks and ridges or balks separating the holdings of neighbors; for such a tenement is possessed not by one tenant by himself, but by him in common with others.[191] It may be common between several as coheirs and coparceners when the inheritance is undivided—joint heirship. It may be common

---

the validity of the principle. For similar pleas see Bracton's *Notebook*, Index, under Assize of N. D., *s. v.* Pleas; and nos. 1195, 1197, 1242, 1284. Plucknett, *Com. Law*, p. 362, discusses pleas made in novel disseizin; also Pollock and Maitland, II, 612f.

[187] *Selden Soc. Publ.*, LIX, no. 416.

[188] Plucknett, *op.cit.*, p. 343.

[189] See Holdsworth, *op.cit.*, III⁴, 126-128, 143-151, on the meaning of the law on tenancy in common, joint tenancy, and common rights in field or pasture; Pollock and Maitland, I, 620ff., 673, 685, and II, 245f.; and K. E. Digby, *Introduction to the History of the Law of Real Property* (3rd ed.), 155-166.

[190] Cf. Radin, *Handbook*, p. 517.

[191] III, 30f.; Tw. III, 51-58. Bracton adds that some think that if anyone plows the boundary ridges or removes a boundary stone or tree, this act constitutes a *transgressio*, trespass, rather than a disseizin, because the *divisae* are not "per partes divisae, sed iacent in communi, quia nullus scit nec scire poterit partem suam"; but he thinks that the act is really a disseizin of a tenement in common.

among neighbors as a tenement put to joint use; and if one of the coparceners disseizes one of the others, the disseized will have an assize against him.[192] To all such several rights in a common thing Bracton applies the procedure of pleas or exceptions.[193] An exception is valid if made to a writ of novel disseizin that, contrary to the common law, contained the names of several plaintiffs when actually the complaints, persons and disseizins were separate. But it is not valid if the *ius* is *unicum* and held by different persons who are coheirs and coparceners and hold in common.[194] In this case, all who are touched because of their joint rights in a thing must be named in the writ whether they are plaintiffs or defendants.

This procedure is made clearer by the discussion of how tenements may be divided or held in common.[195] As we have noted in connection with advowson, incorporeal things such as rights and liberties may be held by several in common, but for all that are indivisible. Similarly, a corporeal thing that is by nature divisible among coheirs and coparceners becomes indivisible when by their common consent it is converted to a common use, for example, of pasture or digging; and such a use is a tenement that is indivisible and yet common to all coparceners.[196] Consent is necessary for the conversion of a piece of land to the common use; and, of course, this kind of joint tenancy can neither be dissolved nor divided without the consent of all, "for nothing is so agreeable to natural equity" (as this principle of consent based upon property rights).[197] The same rule is valid

---

[192] III, 31. Bracton now offers several distinctions on common interests, which, of course, are subjected to many legal subtleties in the attempt to define common rights.

[193] See, for a general explanation, Plucknett, *Com. Law*, pp. 353-367.

[194] III, 79; Tw. III, 210.

[195] III, 128ff.; Tw. III, 368-374.

[196] III, 128f., and IV, 335 (Tw. VI, 390): "Sunt etiam qui tenent in communi rem aliquam de communi consensu sicut participes et capaces, sed non tamen ut heredes, ut si de communi consensu aliquam vastitatem pro communi commodo reliquerint ad pasturam vel aliud commodum vel alium usum. . . ." None of the interested parties can sue or be sued without the consent of the others.

[197] III, 129: "et unde quod de communi consensu semel inter partes contrahitur quod tenementum remaneat in communi, sine contrario consensu omnium dissolvi vel dividi non potest, quia nihil adeo tam conveniens est naturali aequitati et cetera." Here Bracton has in mind *Inst.* 2, 1, 40: by natural law property is acquired; and nothing is more agreeable to natural equity than that the consent of the owner to the transfer of his property to another should be held valid.

for common rights in the undivided right of presentation: although here the thing itself, because incorporeal, cannot be divided even with the consent of all who jointly participate in it, nonetheless the holding, sharing, and transmission of it, all changes in the joint rights in it, are subject to the necessity of common consent. In all these cases none of the interested parties can sue or be sued without the consent of all the coparceners.[198]

Still another kind of tenement may be a certain use which is common to several who are not coparceners in the thing subject to the use—for example, a *stadium* or theatre, which belongs to a corporation (the city) and not to any particular person or persons.[199] By analogy, or by extension (one cannot be sure of Bracton's awareness of this), among tenements held in common may be reckoned as a quasi-tenement one that pertains neither to several in common nor to a corporation in the technical sense, but to the kingdom as a whole and consequently to all members of the kingdom, members, that is, both individual and corporate. Thus, a royal highway and the seashore belong to king and kingdom, to the whole community of the realm.[200] Like the public and common welfare that was dependent upon the maintenance of law and order and touched both king and kingdom, so other things were held in common by all free men and their communities; so likewise (though Bracton does not take the logical step that had already been taken by the royal government) the defense of the realm in a case of neces-

[198] III, 130, where Bracton adds that the joint consent connected with an indivisible right must be given by all the interested parties individually and equally, not by a majority, plurality, or seniority of them; IV, 335.

[199] II, 40; III, 128, 130; cf. *Inst.* 2, 1, 6. Bracton fails to discuss the problem of the consent of the members of a corporation to any change made in the tenement belonging to the corporation itself.

[200] III, 130: "sed commune omnium, sicut est via regia, litus maris. . . ." By implication Bracton approaches the idea—which was already understood on the Continent, and at least in practice in England, in the sense that the kingdom was composed of communities of shires and the shires of communities of hundreds and vills—that just as several individuals could be commonly interested in one thing, so could several corporations or communities, and several corporations and several individuals apart from the corporations. This was the practice of the thirteenth century, and it was vital to the rise of national representation, in that a "national" business could touch not only all important individuals who had rights (and with them the right to consent to any sacrifice that was necessary for the common good) but also all communities of lesser free men and all legal corporations which had special franchises or liberties.

sity touched all, since all had a common interest in the public safety, and all must consent to such extraordinary taxes as were justified by the emergency.

A more tangible use common to several was the easement, and to it Bracton applied the law of procedural consent. The right of all persons who had rights in a thing to consent to any change or diminution of their rights, and the compulsion of all such to sue or be sued in common and thus to submit to the jurisdiction of the courts—these two aspects of *q.o.t.* were an essential part of the Roman law on servitudes, particularly as interpreted by thirteenth-century legists, and of the common law on easements.

In the classical law of the Roman Empire praedial servitudes "were rights vested in a person as owner of one piece of land over another piece";[201] it was a right "exercisable over another's property."[202] To be specific, a rustic servitude might be the right to draw water, to burn lime, to dig sand, or to pasture cattle.[203] Such a servitude, called an easement in modern law,[204] could be enjoyed by several parties all of whom, therefore, had common rights in a thing that belonged to someone else. If the right of drawing water, for example, were to be granted, the consent of all who owned the property on which the water originated and of all to whom the use of the water belonged must be obtained (Ulpian, *D.* 39, 3, 8): "In concedendo iure aquae ducendae non tantum eorum, in quorum loco aqua oritur, verum eorum etiam, ad quos eius aquae usus pertinet, voluntas exquiritur, id est eorum, quibus servitus aquae debebatur." The consent of all is required whose rights will be diminished by the concession (Ulpian, *l.c.*): "cum enim minuitur ius eorum, consequens fuit exquiri, an consentiant." As Paulus says, *D.* 39, 3, 9, 1 and 2, those who have rights either as owners of the land or as users of the water must be informed and their consent obtained: "Ideo autem voluntas exigitur, ne dominus ignorans iniuriam accipiat: nullam enim potest videri iniuriam

---

[201] Buckland, *Textbook*, pp. 261, 259-268.
[202] Roby, *Roman Private Law in the Times of Cicero and the Antonines*, I, 484.
[203] Buckland, *op.cit.*, pp. 259-268; Roby, *Roman Private Law*, I, 482-502.
[204] Holdsworth, *op.cit.*, III⁴, 153.

accipere, qui semel voluit."[205] (We cannot be sure that in Paulus *exigere* implies the compulsion inevitably present in the necessity of summoning, of informing, the interested parties. But in William of Drogheda, who borrows *exigere* from this passage, there is an element of compulsion in the procedure of obtaining consent.[206] As we have seen, Bracton used the word in its compulsory, procedural sense in context with *q.o.t.*)[207]

In his treatise on novel disseizin Bracton discusses the same principle in relation to easements, although here, strangely, he quotes *Inst.* 2, 1, 40, where consent is justified, like the property rights on which the right of consent is based, by natural equity; while in connection with gifts and advowsons, he states the principle of consent in a terminology drawn from *C.* 5, 59, 5, 2 and *D.* 39, 3, 8.[208] But he does state *q.o.t.* for a case involving rights of common pasture.[209] There is no need of a detailed examination of his treatment of easements and the closely related rights in common.[210] It is sufficient for the present purpose to emphasize his theory of joint consent in the creation of an easement.[211] Just as an easement can be established "de mutua voluntate contrahentium per communem consensum," so can it be dissolved by common consent. But this consent is valid only if all the interested parties agree. By common consent the easement can be converted into a different use, or be

---

[205] He continues, § 2: "Non autem solius eius, ad quem ius aquae pertinebit, voluntas exigitur in aquae cessione, sed etiam domini locorum, etsi dominus uti ea aqua non possit, quia reccidere ius solidum ad eum potest."

[206] Above, n. 110.

[207] Above, n. 158.

[208] On *Inst.* 2, 1, 40 see below, n. 213. On gifts and advowsons, above, nn. 175-178. The influence of the Roman law on Bracton's treatment of easements has been pointed out by Maitland, *Bracton and Azo*, pp. 84, 130f.; Holdsworth, *op.cit.*, II⁴, 281-284, 356; III⁴, 154ff.; VII², 323f.; Güterbock, p. 122; Digby, *Real Property*, pp. 147-154. But these authorities do not mention *q.o.t.* in connection with easements in Bracton and in the legists and canonists. Perhaps, as Holdsworth says, Bracton's acceptance of Roman rules on easements does not mean that these rules were a part of English law, which they were only long afterwards (III, 356, 154, 157; VII, 323). Yet, as stated above, early English law deals with common consent and common rights in common or pasture; and it was easy for Bracton to state the common law in terms of *q.o.t.* Besides, in 1236 the Statute of Merton recognized the existence of the rights of lord and tenants in the common; below, n. 214.

[209] Below to n. 215.

[210] II, 158-160, and III, 162-190; Tw. I, 416ff., III, 472-563.

[211] III, 163; Tw. III, 474-476.

increased or diminished.[212] The same rules are valid for common rights in pasture: if one of the parties wishes to dissolve the use, all must consent, "quia nihil tam conveniens est etcetera";[213] and just as the use is acquired by common consent, so is it lost. If, against the will of the interested parties, anyone restricts, changes, increases, or otherwise affects common rights in pasture or in an easement, the remedy for those injured is the assize of novel disseizin. The lord of the land which is the subject of the servitude or use enjoys the remedy if the users act *per vim*; that is to say, his consent is necessary to any change in the nature of the rights of use or easement. But, says Bracton, by the Statute of Merton the common can be restricted by the lord even if the holders of the easement or use are unwilling. Thus, while common consent remained necessary, it was limited in 1236 in favor of the lord of the tenement and was made less individualistic.[214]

Finally, in an example of a royal writ Bracton in specific words associates *q.o.t.* with the procedure of obtaining a remedy against a party who, it is alleged, runs more livestock on the common pasture than is his customary right. In the writ the king orders the sheriff to have the pasture admeasured for the purpose of restricting the defendant's use of the common to the number of animals that he ought to have, according to his free tenement in the vill. On receiving the writ the sheriff shall go to the place in which the common is sued for, "et ibi conveniri faciat hundredum et omnes quos admensuratio illa tangit."[215]

212 III, 178; Tw. III, 520-522. Bracton adds a discussion of the problem of consent in relation to the holding of an easement by coparceners, heirs, neighboring tenants, or outsiders (*extranei*); and in relation to the division of the tenement subject to the easement. Consent thus becomes very complicated and must be considered in connection with the rules of procedure on summoning all interested parties.

213 III, 167f.; Tw. III, 484-502. See above, n. 208: ". . . quia nihil adeo tam conveniens est naturali aequitati etcetera," from *Inst.* 2, 1, 40.

214 III, 179; Tw. III, 524. On the effect of the Provisions of Merton and the Statute of Westminster II (1285) on rights of common, see Holdsworth, III4, 147ff.; and Pollock and Maitland, I, 620ff.: before 1236 the consent of the individual freeholder was necessary for the lord to subtract from his right "any part of the land over which it had been exercisable. That Statute gave the lord a right to 'approve,' that is, to make his profit of, and hence to enclose, to subtract, the waste land, provided that he left sufficient pasture for the commoners" (622f.); Plucknett, *Statutes*, n. 151.

215 III, 183; Tw. III, 538.

It is obvious, in sum, that the essence of *q.o.t.* is, for Bracton, an important principle of procedural consent in the assize of novel disseizin.[216]

7. CONCLUSIONS: THE SIGNIFICANCE OF *Q.O.T.* IN BRACTON AND IN ENGLAND

It seems evident, now, that Bracton sometimes paraphrased or used the decisive words of a few of the Roman laws on joint and common consent expressed in terms of *q.o.t.* Perhaps because he neither quoted these laws literally nor gave any references, modern authorities have not listed them among his Roman sources. Nor have they noted them among the passages stated in the "popular form in which it [the Roman law] was then current, rather than the academic purity of the *Digest.*"[217] But if we place pertinent passages from Bracton and the Roman law side by side, we can see at a glance that Bracton used some of the terminology that came ultimately from the *Corpus iuris civilis*:

216 The same use of the maxim could be traced in Bracton's discussion of other assizes such as that of *mort d'ancestor*, whether he states it explicitly or implicitly. Once more he brings in a trace of *q.o.t.* in showing how a defendant might plead that the assize touched the king and he should not have to respond without the king. This was an attempt to vouch the king to warranty; as we have seen, the king refused to submit to such a procedure; above, nn. 148f. Bracton says: "Si assisa tangat regem et dicat tenens quod sine rege non possit respondere, capiatur nihilominus assisa, sed ponatur iudicium in respectum quousque dominus rex inde praeceperit voluntatem suam"; III, 247-317, 250, 267f. (Tw. IV, 115-331, 128, 180). Again, on *placita de baroniis*: "ubi ipse petens tenere clamat immediate de domino rege in capite per breve de recto, quod vocatur praecipe in capite, et hoc ideo, quia hoc tangit ipsum regem in toto vel in parte"; II, 301.

217 Plucknett, *Com. Law*, p. 233: "We may probably assume, therefore, that when Bracton used foreign law he had a fairly good idea of what he was about." Similarly, Vinogradoff, *Rom. Law*, pp. 117f.: "If we want definite traces of it (Roman Law) we have to look out not for references but for maxims, some of which, besides, had passed through the medium of Canon law. The only real test of its character and extent is afforded by the development of juridical ideas, and in this respect the initial influence of Roman teaching on English doctrines will be found to be considerable. On many subjects the judges and legal writers of England were, so to speak, prompted by their Roman predecessors, and this intercourse of ideas is nowhere as conspicuous as in the frequent cases when English lawyers did not simply copy their Roman models, but borrowed suggestions from them in their own way." My study of *q.o.t.* in Bracton confirms these remarks but goes farther: the juridical meaning of *q.o.t.* in procedural consent is more tangible than a suggestion.

| BRACTON | ROMAN LAW |

1. CONSENT PRIMARILY IN RELATION TO RIGHTS
(voluntary consent):

II, 52: "quia omnium illorum consensus quos res tangit erit necessarius et requirendus."

C. 5, 59, 5, 2: "ut quod omnes similiter tangit, ab omnibus comprobetur."

II, 63: "Item in quibusdam donationibus oportet quod aliorum consensus interveniat quam donatoris et donatarii . . . omnium eorum quorum interfuerit requirendus erit consensus."

D. 39, 3, 8: ". . . verum eorum etiam ad quos eius aquae usus pertinet, voluntas exquiritur . . . ; cum enim minuitur ius eorum, consequens est requiri, an consentiant." Cf. D. 39, 3, 9, 1.

(Cf. gloss to *Decretum*, Dist. 54, c.1 Nullus, ad v. *qui aliquid*: "omnium consensus est requirendus quorum iuri in aliquo detrahitur.")

C. 11, 59, 7, 2: "ut id consensu omnium fiat quod omnibus profuturum est."

2. PROCEDURAL CONSENT
(the result of the possession of rights):

IV, 109f.: "Exigendi sunt omnes quos loquela tangit"; "exigantur omnes quos causa tetigerit." (Cf. D. 39, 3, 9, 1, for *exigere*.)

D. 42, 1, 47 (Paulus): "De unoquoque negotio praesentibus omnibus, quos causa contingit, iudicari oportet: aliter enim iudicatum inter praesentes tenet."

IV, 330f.: An exception made by a defendant "quia in parte tangit alios sine quibus, etc."

D. 11, 2, 1: "Si inter plures familiae erciscundae agetur et inter eosdem communi dividundo . . . eundem iudicem sumendum: praeterea, quo facilius coire coheredes vel socii possunt, in eundem locum omnium praesentiam fieri oportet."

IV, 102: "Et eodem modo de omnibus fiat mentio quos tangit negotium et quorum praesentia fuerit necessaria."

III, 183: ". . . et ibi conveniri faciat hundredum et omnes quos admensuratio illa tangit."

D. 11, 2, 2: "Cum ex pluribus tutoribus unus, quod ceteri non sint idonei, convenitur, postulante eo omnes ad eundem iudicem mittuntur."

IV, 61: The general summons "est quae tangit aliquam universitatem, sicut omnes de comitatu vel omnes alicuius civitatis, burgi vel villae pro aliquo quod tangat universitatem. . . ."

A comparison of these passages shows that, apart from some almost literal statements of *quod omnes tangit,* the spirit rather than the letter of *C.* 5, 59, 5, 2 (Justinian) is emphasized by Bracton. But the important words used by Ulpian on servitudes and consent (*D.* 39, 3, 8) and by Paulus on the presence in court of all who are touched by a case (*D.* 42, 1, 47) are among Bracton's favorite expressions. And on the subject of one of several coparceners pleading that the others are concerned and must be summoned, Bracton perhaps has in mind the roughly similar rules (*D.* 11, 2, 1 and 2, for example) on all coheirs and co-*tutores* appearing before the same judge in cases affecting all. It is in procedural consent, therefore, that the Roman maxim is most applicable and most recognizable.

But since Bracton does not quote literally or make references, is it possible that the Romano-canonical *q.o.t.* was in fact unknown to him and had no influence on his work? Was he merely using words similar to those in the Roman law because, writing in Latin, his choice of words was so limited that he could not avoid using the same terminology for analogous situations? "Anyone writing in Latin," is the caution urged upon me, "be he Englishman or Roman, would be obliged to state similar concepts or principles in practically identical language." This caution certainly must be heeded, and particularly in the realm of the history of ideas, to which this study belongs. Yet I cannot believe that the explanation is as simple as that of chance or analogy. In the thirteenth century, surely, writers in Latin had some choice of words and could use synonyms. The legal language was already wordy, and it is not likely that Bracton was such a simple Englishman, uncorrupted by continental sophistication, that he had in his Latin vocabulary only one word, *tangere,* to express the idea that something may interest, affect, concern, touch, or pertain to several persons. Indeed, the legal Latin of the thirteenth century had several words for the situation—*pertinere* and *interesse.* In one place, William of Drogheda, discussing the publication of the papal rescript which initiated proceedings, says: "ante publicationem faciendam *vocandi sunt omnes, ad quos pertinet publicatio*; vel qui possunt laedi illa publicatione vel gravari"; and on this he refers *inter alia* to

C. 5, 59, 5, 2.[218] Similarly, *omnes quorum interest* occurs in the glosses of the decretalists,[219] as it does in Bracton ("omnium eorum quorum interfuerit requirendus erit consensus" [II, 63]), in a context of terminology deriving from *D.* 39, 3, 8 and from the canonists. Usually, however, Bracton uses *omnes quos causa tangit* in slightly varying forms.

It may be objected that analogy is still a better explanation since Bracton never says that a business touches several *similiter* and never adds *ab omnibus comprobetur*. How then could he have been influenced by Justinian's statement of the maxim, "ut quod omnes similiter tangit, ab omnibus comprobetur"? This objection at once loses its apparent force when we recall that these omissions were customary. *Similiter* was omitted by Innocent III, *Decr. Greg. IX* 1, 23, 7: "quod cum iuxta imperialis auctoritatis sanctiones quod omnes tangit ab omnibus comprobari debet." It was omitted by Edward I nearly a century later: "quod omnes tangit ab omnibus approbetur." Honorius III's paraphrase of the maxim implied no *similiter* or *equaliter* when he legalized the right of cathedral chapters to attend provincial councils.[220] Nor did the legists and decretalists like to remember the word when they were quoting or paraphrasing the maxim, for many a business that touched all did not do so *similiter* or *equaliter*.[221] In like fashion, probably because he was chiefly interested in the procedure of obtaining consent, Bracton neglected to add *ab omnibus comprobetur* whenever he said that all who were touched by a case must be summoned (*exigantur, conveniri faciat*, or *consensus requirendus*). Here he was probably influenced by the decretalists, who frequently stated the principle of procedural consent in such words as *omnes quos causa tangit vocandi sunt* and referred to Justinian without saying *ab omnibus comprobetur*. But even where those summoned were defendants who had valid rights

218 *Summa aurea*, Wahrmund, II, ii, 353; also *Decr. Greg. IX* 3, 10, 10, in which we find *pertinere* and *contingere*.

219 See Joh. Teutonicus, above, n. 28; and *Glos. ord.* to *Decr. Greg. IX* 1, 33, 17—above, n. 34 and text.

220 *Decr. Greg. IX* 3, 10, 10; below, n. 253. On this the decretalists are careful to state that the prelates (bishops) had the decisive, the chapters only a consultative, vote.

221 On Accursius and Innocent IV and *similiter* see above to n. 30.

and whose consent was therefore needed, where, in other words, the voluntary aspect of procedural consent was evident, Bracton still did not use *ab omnibus comprobetur*. Instead, he combined *q.o.t.* with words that came from *D.* 39, 3, 8: *omnium illorum consensus quos res tangit erit necessarius et requirendus,* or *omnium eorum quorum interfuerit requirendus erit consensus.* Here again we have what the decretalists contributed to the development of the maxim from about 1190 to 1250. Perhaps from William of Drogheda Bracton acquired, in addition to references to the familiar passages in the Roman law, the occasional use of the verbs *requirere* and *exigere.*

It was therefore the habit of the commentators on the two laws, in the fifty to seventy years preceding Bracton's treatise, to combine *quod omnes tangit, necessarius* or *requirendus est consensus,* and *omnes vocandi* or *exigendi sunt,* in a variety of ways—but with the famous Roman laws and opinions constantly in mind as the authority for the maxim. These expressions they applied to all kinds of situations that affected common and several rights. The situations were frequently merely analogous to those envisaged by the Roman law, but the statements of the maxim came from the Roman law. The continental lawyers simply gave the maxim a Procrustean treatment. Can we not say the same of Bracton's method? The English law presented situations that were feudal and sometimes not even analogous (vouching to warranty, for example) to those in the Roman law. But he couched English law in "Roman" language; and this was natural, since after all, if the situations were different, there was something in common—rights in property, whether the property was owned, used, held in fief, leased, or rented, and whether it was held severally or in common. Hence, we need not worry about the complex problem of the differences between the Roman and the English law of property. The point is that there were in both laws certain kinds of joint and common rights, and the Roman maxim of voluntary and procedural consent was as readily applicable to English, feudal, situations as to Roman—or modern.

Finally, one more objection may be made. When Bracton is discussing gifts in connection with the clergy he says, "quia om-

nium illorum consensus quos res tangit erit necessarius et requirendus" and "omnium eorum quorum interfuerit requirendus est consensus." But when, in his treatment of novel disseizin,
he turns his attention to mutual consent in common rights in
land or pasture, he quotes literally the first words of *Inst.* 2, 1,
40, which bases consent on property rights and natural law and
equity. If he was influenced by the Roman *q.o.t.* why does he
quote literally the passage in the *Institutes* but not *C.* 5, 59, 5,
2? It would seem that Bracton would have quoted more accurately the passages on *q.o.t.* had he known them, just as he quoted
Inst. 2, 1, 40—a work familiar to him.

But we have seen that he followed the legists and canonists
in his habit of stating *q.o.t.* If he sometimes justified consent by
Inst. 2, 1, 40, the reason may be that he was connecting it with
things strictly English, and that he applied *q.o.t.* and words from
D. 39, 3, 8 and 9 to matters in which the clergy were interested,
hence turning to the language of the decretalists. Yet, this
reason will not survive a critical examination. For property
rights were as much at stake in gifts and advowson, to which
Bracton applied *q.o.t.* and *omnium consensus requirendus*, etc.,
as in purely English situations. Moreover, one recalls that while
he cited *Inst.* 2, 1, 40 on the dissolution of a common use of
pasture, he also said that the sheriff should summon "omnes
quos admensuratio illa tangit" when a party was accused of
injuring the rights of others in the common.

We may advance still another reason to explain why he did
not state *q.o.t.* for every situation where it was suitable. Perhaps
he called upon the *Institutes* for an adequate justification of
rights in property in natural law and equity but upon *q.o.t.*
for a situation in which rights were challenged and the case
could be settled only in court after judicial process. Yet again
the evidence does not support a distinction between the one use
and the other.

My conclusion is that Bracton had no distinctions in mind,
that, like the canonists and legists, he simply drew on any of
several versions of the Roman maxim whenever he felt the need.
But, as we have said, he particularly liked *q.o.t.* because he was
more interested in the judicial process than in the pure theory

of consent. In one sense, of course, no real distinctions were necessary: both procedural and voluntary consent rest on the belief that property rights exist according to the law, and that the equitable interpretation of the law demands that no one be deprived of his rights without due process according to the law of the land. The maxim was, moreover, simply an extension to several persons and interests and rights of still another maxim which was current among canonists and which Bracton quoted: "Nulli autem iuris beneficium denegent" (already it had been stated in other words in c. 39 of Magna Carta)[222]—and of such maxims as "Scienti et consentienti non fit iniuria,"[223] which Bracton knew, and "Cuius effectus omnibus prodest, eius et partes ad omnes pertinent."[224]

For certain situations in the common law, then, Bracton expressed *q.o.t.* The situations might be more or less analogous to those in the two laws in England and on the Continent. But the language used by Bracton was more than analogous; it was language borrowed from the two laws, language that came from the Roman law. How Bracton learned *q.o.t.* is uncertain. He did not learn it from reading the *Institutes*, which so far as I can discover does not contain a theory of consent stated in the terms of the maxim. Did he read the portions of the *Digest* in which the civilians and canonists found either *q.o.t.* or its equivalent, namely, *D.* 39, 3, 8 and 9, and *D.* 42, 1, 47? It is not likely that he did, for these passages occur in the *Dig. novum*, which the student who spent only a year or two in law at Oxford probably did not study. But the teachers of Roman law sometimes referred to such passages when they were commenting on the *Dig. vetus*, and thus Bracton may have learned of *q.o.t.* in the *Digest* from William of Drogheda's lectures. Again, he may have read *C.* 5, 59, 5, since he was familiar with the *Code* and with Azo's commentary. Yet, not only for the passage

222 Bracton, II, 307 (Tw. II, 178); cf. *Liber Sextus* (ed. Friedberg, *Corpus iuris canonici*, II), tit. *De regulis iuris*, no. 17: "Indultum a iure beneficium non est alicui auferendum"; this rule was stated by canonists as early as the twelfth century. It will be recalled that Justinian's expression of *q.o.t.* is also among the maxims (no. 29) in this part of the *Liber Sextus*.

223 *Liber Sextus*, tit. *De reg. iur.* 27, from *D.* 42, 8, 6, 9, and 50, 17, 116; Vinogradoff, *Rev. hist. dr. fr. étr.*, 2, 342.

224 *D.* 50, 17, 148. Did Bracton know this maxim?

in the *Code* but also for the passages in the *Digest*, the probability is that Bracton acquired his method of expressing and using *q.o.t.* from the glosses, treatises, and commentaries of Azo, Accursius, Drogheda and the decretalists, whose cross references, application of *q.o.t.* to a variety of situations, and paraphrases as well as literal quotations furnished the immediate background and made the maxim both popular and useful. But we must not forget that *q.o.t.* was in the ecclesiastical atmosphere of England as early as 1213.[225] Indeed, the same principle had been used as the basis of a plea made by the abbot of Evesham in 1219-1221 before royal justices,[226] and *q.o.t.* was commonly asserted by the clergy from 1225 on, when they wanted to send representatives to councils. Who could say that Bracton, himself an ecclesiastic, was blind to all that went on in ecclesiastical procedure?

It is perfectly obvious, of course, that procedural consent did not mean the same thing in the classical Roman law and in Bracton. It had several different meanings in the course of the development of Roman law from the Republic to the late Empire. Consent in its procedural meaning became more and more compulsory as the voluntary element faded before the rise of the *imperium* of the judges as the emperor's delegates.[227] In the common law, too, because of the growth of the law of property and of the development of the royal jurisdiction, procedural consent underwent a changing interpretation. The twelfth and thirteenth centuries were a period of transition from the voluntary consent of the feudal age to the more or less compulsory consent, according to the rules of procedure, gradually, but not completely, made effective by the royal courts. This period corresponds, as it were, to the classical age of Roman law, to the time of Gaius, Paulus, and Ulpian. "In both systems of law

---

225 See the report of the papal legate in 1213 on the negotiations between the English prelates and King John; Angelo Mercati, "La prima relazione del Cardinale Nicolò de Romanis sulla sua legazione in Inghilterra," *Essays in History Presented to Reginald Lane Poole*, ed. H. W. C. Davis, pp. 279, 280, 286; for example, the bishops replied, said the legate, "quod inde mihi respondere non poterant sine consensu et consilio aliorum quos predictum negotium contingebat."

226 Above, n. 186.

227 See Buckland and McNair, *Roman Law and Common Law*, pp. 316f.

there was a great reluctance, more than a reluctance, to give judgment against a defendant who had not appeared. . . . But in fact," continue Buckland and McNair, with the classical and later law in mind, "ways were found of putting pressure on a recalcitrant defendant, ways based on the *imperium* of the magistrate. . . . Thus in classical law the consent, though nominally necessary, was very unreal, and in the procedure of later law, when cases were tried by a iudex who was a public official, or a person deputed by him, it had disappeared altogether." In the later Roman law, when the consent of the defendant was no longer necessary, "judgment could be given against an absent defendant, though only after long delays."[228] Of course, this was the history of procedural consent; but the consent based upon lawful rights was itself subjected by the new procedure to the decision of the court and henceforth was less voluntary than before, although the defendant who did appear and proved his right was not forced to consent to an adverse sentence.

Similarly, a summary procedure for certain actions was instituted by Henry II (novel disseizin); and the consent of the parties became compulsory, but with an element of voluntary consent surviving when pleas were increasingly allowed before judgment was given. The important fact is that the English law in the thirteenth century contained something of a balance between voluntary consent and an effective royal jurisdiction which tried to subject consent to a speedier procedure. Much of this had been achieved when Bracton studied the records of some of the royal justices. But Bracton's treatise probably had some influence on the continuation of this development in the hundred years that followed.[229] His contemporaries, the civilians and canonists, were not handicapped and confused by the historical method of distinguishing between the periods of the Roman law; from the *Corpus juris civilis* they simply selected and put together those passages which seemed to fit the practical needs of rights and jurisdiction in their own time. Bracton naturally reflected their achievement. The result was that con-

228 *Loc.cit.*
229 Cf. Maitland, *Bracton and Azo*, p. xxxiii; Holdsworth, *op.cit.*, II, 237f., 286f.; Woodbine, I, 1-20.

sent based on rights and liberties, when these were the subject of litigation, came to mean something that was surprisingly similar to the procedural consent of Paulus and Ulpian.[230] There were differences between the Roman and the common law in the treatment of common ownership or possession on which common rights and consent were based.[231] But all the same, in the ways in which Bracton tried to express and explain joint and common rights and apply procedural consent to them, the essence of the common law of the middle thirteenth century was not fundamentally different from that of the Roman law, despite the different conception of common and joint and corporate rights in English law.

Surely, then, it is no forced conclusion that to the procedure of the common law pertaining to a civil suit which touched the rights of several parties Bracton adapted *quod omnes tangit* in its varied applications and meanings.[232] Common and several rights in administration, jurisdiction, advowsons, donations, elections, easements, contracts, and in property of all kinds, all such rights, both tangible and intangible, and the corollary procedural consent, were brought into harmony with the Roman principle of consent. Or, rather, that principle was brought into harmony with the various kinds of several and common rights that were customary in England, but it influenced and

---

[230] Buckland and McNair, *Roman Law* . . . , p. 316, think that the underlying principles are not the same, that in the common law the "reluctance to give judgment against a defendant who had not appeared" does not rest on the need for the consent of the parties, as in the early and classical Roman law, but on this basis, that "the law wants to be exceedingly fair, but is irritated by contumacy" (quoting Pollock and Maitland, II, 595). But it seems to me that the desire to be "exceedingly fair" was quite important likewise in the Roman law—even in the late imperial law, as is clearly shown by the rules on summoning all interested parties and on obtaining consent and by the cherished maxims on fair trial, *q.o.t.* and the like. There is compulsion, but fairness in judicial process—at least for free men in civil suits. Moreover, one must not forget that consent was important in the common law on real actions.

[231] Buckland and McNair, *Roman Law* . . . , pp. 80-86.

[232] Yet Güterbock asserts: "Procedure offers but little for our purposes in Bracton. In its main features the development of that branch of the law had been so much upon the basis of peculiarly English views and principles, and, as far as actions in rem were concerned, so much in the forms and spirit of the feudal system, that the Roman law had not been able to exercise the same influence there as elsewhere, and has left in it few and detached traces"; *Bracton and Roman Law*, p. 154.

shaped their development under the control of the royal jurisdiction. Bracton was indeed rationalizing the English law in
Roman terms; but in his use of *q.o.t.* he was not supplanting
English rules with the Roman, although on occasion he was
ahead of the English rules of procedure and anticipated the acceptance of a speedier process in the English law. He was applying the Romano-canonical rules to what by its nature could
in part be explained by them.[233] *Q.o.t.* in his treatise illustrates
his use of "Roman terms, Roman maxims, and Roman doctrines to construct upon native foundations a reasonable system
out of comparatively meagre authorities."[234] If he did not always
truthfully state the law of his own day, it is certain that in most
instances his statement of it in terms of *q.o.t.* was no misinter-
pretation of the current legal practice in the royal courts, however unconscious the English law may have been of maxims.

We have been discussing *q.o.t.* chiefly as a principle of private law, for Bracton does not reveal much awareness of its
significance in public affairs that were the concern of the king
and the community of the realm. He does, it is true, approach
the interpretation of *q.o.t.* in relation to what we think of as
public business when he speaks of the general summons of all
of the county for any business which touches the *universitas*
or community of the shire.[235] In his discussion of the Provisions
of Merton we find an important change in wording that suggests
q.o.t. in association with the common utility of the kingdom:
"generaliter tractatum esset de communi utilitate totius regni
super pluribus articulis regem et regnum tangentibus."[236] Moreover, in his famous theory that laws can be changed only with
the counsel and consent of those who had consented to them,
there is a consciousness of the importance of consent in public
matters, but not in terms of *q.o.t.*[237] Generally speaking, how-

[233] On this I agree with Maitland, *Bracton and Azo*, p. 221, and Holdsworth,
op.cit., II⁴, 268.

[234] *Ibid.*   [235] Above, n. 120.

[236] Above, n. 123.

[237] See n. 98; II, 21: "Quae quidem [leges], cum fuerint approbatae consensu
utentium et sacramento regum confirmatae, mutari non poterunt nec destrui sine
communi consensu eorum omnium quorum consilio et consensu fuerunt promulgatae." This is the traditional theory of law-finding, but with a suggestion
of Roman terminology.

ever, Bracton's emphasis of *q.o.t.* was in the realm of private law. But a rule of procedure pertaining to the private could become useful in the public law. *Plena potestas*, the full powers of representatives, became important in the public business of representation in assemblies, although it was first used in ordinary courts.[238] *Q.o.t.* entered the realm of public law, insofar as a business such as a national tax was of public concern, touching king and kingdom, the *status regis et regni*, and the common welfare. At the same time, naturally, *q.o.t.* remained a principle of private law, since a general subsidy touched individual rights. Were Bracton and his treatise, therefore, despite the concentration on private law, of any importance in the appearance of *q.o.t.* in the public law of England? A tentative answer may be given by indicating when *q.o.t.* began to appear in royal writs issued for assemblies of magnates, prelates, and representatives.[239]

In Magna Carta there is no suggestion of representation of communities of knights of the shire or of citizens and burgesses when the king asked for an extraordinary aid. Nor does *q.o.t.* appear either in the voluntary or procedural sense. But there is a suggestion of compulsion, implying procedural consent, in c. 14, where it is provided that, when the common counsel of the kingdom is needed "de auxilio assidendo aliter quam in tribus casibus praedictis vel de scutagio assidendo," the king shall summon individually the prelates, earls, and greater barons. For, the summons having been properly made in order to inform the summoned of the nature of the business, the *negocium* shall proceed on the day set "secundum consilium illorum qui praesentes fuerint, quamvis non omnes summoniti venerint." Were the absent presumed to consent by default and did they have to accept what was done by those present? Such may have been the presumption in the minds of those who drew up the terms of Magna Carta.[240] In 1237, however, a case shows that absence did not yet necessarily mean consent—here knowledge of the

---

[238] *Traditio*, I, 355-408; above, ch. III.

[239] Since I am dealing chiefly with Bracton in this paper I do not pretend to exhaust the subject of *q.o.t.* in English assemblies.

[240] See McIlwain, *C.M.H.*, VII, 673-675. Of course, those not summoned were not bound.

law proclaimed in open county court.[241] It was only later, beginning with Bracton, that the principle was well established that those present bound the absent.[242] At least it was tentatively stated in Magna Carta, and we thus find a hint of procedural consent in connection with voluntary consent. Perhaps it was implied more strongly in that part of c. 14 which indicates a general summons, through sheriffs and bailiffs, of the king's tenants-in-chief: "et praeterea faciemus summoneri in generali . . . omnes illos qui de nobis tenent in capite." This language expresses the same principle as that which was later stated as *q.o.t.*, although we cannot say that *q.o.t.* was already of influence.

There is no suggestion of *q.o.t.* in summonses to members of the county court in the first half of the century,[243] nor in the writ of summons to knights of the shire to a parliament in 1254.[244] But in the king's consent to the project of reform, 1258, one finds the terminology that was soon to become customary in England and on the Continent in documents relating to the convocation of the community of the realm, including knights of the shires, for a national business: "Cum pro negotiis nostris arduis nos et regnum nostrum contingentibus, proceres et fideles regni nostri . . . faceremus convocari."[245] *Q.o.t.*, despite the fact that it is not quoted, thus appears in the summons to national assemblies for an important business that touches king and kingdom. In the form just given and in its variants it reflects the language of Paulus in *D.* 42, 1, 47 ("De unoquoque negotio praesentibus omnibus, quos causa contingit"), and of the legists and canonists who had popularized *C.* 5, 59, 5 and its

241 Sayles, *Select Cases,* III, xvii. John de Baiuse made the plea that he had not been present at any shire or hundred court where the charter of liberties was read or proclaimed. As a result, the question was postponed for jury trial even though the sheriff produced seven men who swore that John was not absent when the reading took place.

242 See above, n. 119.

243 For example, in 1231 the sheriff was to summon to meet before the justices in eyre prelates, earls, barons, knights, and "omnes libere tenentes"; and four "legales homines et praepositum" from each vill, two burgesses from each borough, and "omnes alios qui coram justitiariis itinerantibus venire solent et debent"; *S.C.,* p. 354. See Bracton, II, 310; Pollock and Maitland, I, 545.

244 *S.C.,* pp. 365f.

245 *S.C.,* p. 371; and below, n. 248.

equivalents, and who used *contingere* and *tangere* interchange-
ably along with *negotium* (or *causa* or *res*) and *vocare*. If *contingere* does not appear in writs of general summonses or in
preambles to provisions and statutes before 1258 (Bracton, however, supplied *tangere* to the Statute of Merton, 1236),[246] it
occurs fairly often thereafter. It helped express what was already
practiced: if the king's business touched the kingdom, it touched
all who represented the community and communities of the
realm, and all these must be summoned.[247] This does not mean
that *contingere*, or *tangere*, was always used for the same thing.
In 1272 Edward I speaks of his readiness to make his justice
available to all "in omnibus juribus et rebus ipsos tangentibus."[248] Nor was it always used after 1258 in the summons to a
parliament—chancery clerks could use circumlocutions whether
the terminology of a preamble was determined by the purpose
of the royal document or not.

But if it did not become customary, it was stated in the summons to knights of the shires in 1258; in the summons to cities
and boroughs in 1268 to send representatives "ad tractandum
de negociis domini regis et regni et ipsos tangentibus";[249] in
the writ *Circumspecte agatis* in 1285: "Circumspecte agatis de
negotio tangente dominum episcopum Norwicensem et ejus
clerum"; in the summons to the clergy, 1294: "sicut et cetero-

246 IV, 295f.: "de communi utilitate totius regni super pluribus articulis regem
et regnum tangentibus."

247 I agree with Professor Joseph R. Strayer that the community of the realm
is not the same as the communities of shires and towns, for it is the whole
realm, including king, prelates, magnates, and the communities or commons.
See below ch. VI, nn. 45, 46.

248 *S.C.*, p. 439.

249 Probably knights of the shire were summoned in 1258, for although the
writ does not survive, later it is said that the knights attended "pro quibusdam
negociis communitatem tocius comitatus praedicti tangentibus"; Wilkinson,
*Studies in the Constitutional History of the Thirteenth and Fourteenth Cen-
turies*, p. 38. From the year 1268, G. O. Sayles has published a memorandum for
the issue of writs of summons; the king is to write to the mayor and citizens of
York and to other cities and boroughs in this fashion: "Quia super arduissimis
negociis nos et* regnum nostrum* statum et communitatem regni nostri* et vos*
tangentibus . . . vobiscum ac aliis fidelibus regni nostri quos ad hoc fecimus
convocari [et sine quibus negocia ipsa nequiunt expediri] tractatum et colloquium habere volumus speciale . . ."; Sayles, "Representation of Cities and
Boroughs in 1268," *E.H.R.*, XL (1925), 584f.; Wilkinson, *Studies*, p. 39. (The
asterisk indicates words struck out; the brackets, interlineations.)

rum praelatorum ac cleri de regno nostro quos communiter negotium istud tangit" (the business was that of a subsidy for the war in Gascony); in the summons of knights of the shires: "super quibusdam negotiis arduis nos et idem regnum nostrum contingentibus"; and in the summons of the Archbishop to a great council, 1295: "quia super quibusdam arduis negotiis nos et regnum nostrum ac vos ceterosque praelatos de eodem regno tangentibus."[250] Whoever planned or drew up the terms of the general summons of the clergy in 1295 was simply saying the same thing in full when he inserted the almost literal quotation of *C.* 5, 59, 5, 2: "ut quod omnes tangit ab omnibus approbetur." It is surely more than a coincidence that the official acceptance of this terminology began about 1258 (perhaps as early as the 1230's), when the representation of the knights of the shire in parliaments was becoming necessary in any kind of national business that touched their rights.[251]

The new style, it seems, resulted in part from the popularity of the maxim among the English clergy: in 1213 it was asserted by the prelates;[252] in 1225 and later, the lower clergy sometimes based upon it their claims to the right of the representation of cathedral and conventual chapters when royal and papal subsidies were demanded. (Decrees of the Lateran Councils of 1179 and 1215 had established the principle that no lay authority should tax the clergy in extraordinary manner without the consent of the bishops and their clergy and of the pope.) Pope Honorius III, probably in 1217, had recognized this right as one legally justified by *q.o.t.*: "ut capitula . . . debeant invitari . . .

---

[250] *S.C.*, pp. 469, 476, 479.

[251] Knights of the shire had occasionally been summoned to the king's court and council still earlier, and for business that concerned their rights and interests rather than for the customary duty of bearing the record or bringing information. John summoned knights of the shire in 1213; Henry III summoned them in 1226-1237 to represent the interests of all the knights of the shire (above, n. 132; below, n. 257); and knights were probably in an assembly of 1237, for they are mentioned among those who granted a subsidy to the king (*S.C.*, p. 358). Possibly *q.o.t.* was stated in this connection in the writs of 1237, for Matthew Paris says that the king summoned prelates, earls and barons, "ut omnes sine omissione . . . convenirent, regia negotia tractaturi totum regnum contingentia"; *S.C.*, p. 326. Matthew fails to mention knights of the shire, but it is possible that they, too, were summoned, since the king relates that they along with the prelates and magnates consented to the tax.

[252] Above, n. 225.

maxime super illis, quae ipsa capitula contingere dignoscuntur."[253] Matthew Paris reports that in 1240 the bishops assembled at Northampton refused to answer the papal legate's request for a subsidy until their archdeacons could be consulted. The archdeacons were needed to furnish information about the value of benefices held by the clergy, and thus the business concerned them as administrators and experts: "Omnes tangit hoc negotium, omnes igitur sunt conveniendi, sine ipsis nec decet nec expedit respondere."[254] Is it not possible that Bracton—who was trained in the two laws, was an ecclesiastic, and was one of the royal justices in the period of attempted baronial reform— helped introduce the new style into the administrative, judicial, and legislative business of the royal government? In any case q.o.t. was in the legal atmosphere and quite naturally it slipped into the style of the royal chancery.

In the later years of Henry III and in the reign of Edward I, q.o.t. became a rule of procedure in the "public law" of England. The circumstances prepared the way; the two laws, the Church, and, perhaps, Bracton furnished the maxim. However much the younger Accursius may have contributed to the formulation of administrative policies in the early years of Edward, q.o.t. was already of some importance in the government of Henry III, partly because men like Bracton were stating it as a principle of procedure in the courts. Q.o.t. was no mere rhetorical flourish of scribes in the royal chancery; nor was it a maxim that occurred only in connection with the clergy. It was not alien to England and the spirit of the common law. It was, as Bracton was intelligent enough to see, a principle that was easily applicable to the voluntary and procedural consent al-

---

[253] *Decr. Greg.* IX 3, 10, 10. The decretal is directed to the Archbishop of Sens. There can be little doubt that the pope had the Roman maxim in mind even if he did not quote it; the decretalists were soon connecting *C.* 5, 59, 5 with this decretal. See above, n. 220. On the date, 1217, see Eric Kemp, "The Origins of the Canterbury Convocation," *Jour. of Eccles. Hist.*, III (1952), 133. (I owe this reference to Dr. Richard Kay of Knox College.)

[254] *Chron. Maj.*, IV, 37. Note how in England Innocent III's decretal, *Ad haec* (*Decr. Greg.* IX 1, 23, 7), which applied to the administrative rights of bishop and archdeacon, and in which the pope quoted *C.* 5, 59, 5, 2, was extended to a national business touching all the bishops and their archdeacons. Note, too, that here the bishops led in making a plea, based on *q.o.t.*, for lesser prelates.

ready practiced in the English private law, but practiced more fully when it was consciously used as a basis of pleas in court.[255]

In the business of a national tax the practice of *q.o.t.* developed at first, perhaps, more as a result of the assertion of legal rights by magnates and knights of the shire than as a result of the king's desire to secure a more general and effective consent to taxation. The great lords and tenants-in-chief of the king already had the right to consent to an extraordinary subsidy. But when the king asked for such a subsidy, it is possible that the magnates, like the prelates for the lower clergy,[256] made the plea that the business touched the class of knights and other free men as well as themselves and that they should not have to make answer unless the knights were summoned.[257] This they could have done according to the rules of procedure outlined by Bracton and practiced in the royal courts, either because they wanted to obtain delays and defeat the king, or because they wanted a wider public opinion represented in royal or baronial assemblies to help them resist the king in his court and council. But the plea was as likely to come directly from the knights and burgesses when they felt that the magnates had no right to consent for others than themselves: the business of a subsidy touched

[255] Clarke, *Med. Representation*, p. 264, though accepting the importance of the maxim for the laity in 1295, says that before then it occurred almost invariably "in an ecclesiastical context," with the one exception of Bracton. But Clarke has in mind Bracton's statement of the consent of all to legislation in terms that do not express *q.o.t.* See above, nn. 3, 98. In the late thirteenth century Gilbert de Thornton reflects the *q.o.t.* of Bracton; see S. E. Thorne, "Gilbert de Thornton's Summa de Legibus," *Univ. Toronto Law Journal*, VII (1947), 5.

[256] Above, nn. 225, 253.

[257] In 1290 we find the magnates granting a customary aid for the marriage of the king's daughter, and this "pro se et communitate totius regni quantum in ipsis est." This seems to indicate that they felt they could consent only for their class, not for the knights of the shire, who were separately summoned; see *S.C.*, pp. 471f. There were, no doubt, precedents in such cases: in 1226, Henry III issued a writ for the summoning of four knights of the shire, not to bring the record (a purely administrative representation), but to represent the knights of the shire in complaints against the sheriffs arising from the interpretation of certain articles in Magna Carta (*S.C.*, p. 353; above, n. 132). The king states that this summons was the result of a petition of the magnates, in an assembly at Winchester, that he hold an assembly at Lincoln "ad terminandum contentiones ortas inter quosdam vicecomites nostros et homines comitatuum suorum super quibusdam articulis, etc." It seems that already the magnates find that they cannot represent the interests and rights of the class of knights. See below, ch. VI, n. 49.

the rights of all free men, and all should therefore have the right to consent, to defend their interests, at least, before consenting.[258] If the administrative experience of the knights of the shire was important in the rise of representation in Parliament, so was their judicial experience either as parties to suits or as jurors in the county court, where they surely learned how pleas could be based on the same principle as *q.o.t.* Consequently, they may have initiated similar pleas when their rights were affected by subsidies or by any business of national concern. The period of Henry III, when opposition to his policy culminated in the baronial reform movement (1258-1267), was particularly favorable to an active participation of the knights in public affairs.[259] Later, if not at the same time, the royal government perceived the usefulness of the procedure of representation and judicial or procedural consent as a means of binding all to what was done in an assembly of the community of the realm.

Did Edward I transform *q.o.t.* into a "constitutional principle" and give it a "new and political sense"? Broadly speaking, he did; but strictly speaking, in the legal sense his statement of *q.o.t.* was simply an embodiment of a constant medieval theory of consent, without constitutional and political implications. What he did was to complete the transition from private to public law insofar as private and public were distinguished in his time. But in the system of representation in England the royal prerogative and the "right of State" for the public welfare had a distinct advantage over individual rights. In the public as in the private law, therefore, a large measure of compulsory, procedural, judicial consent remained as the real essence of *q.o.t.*[260]

It is possible that Bracton was partly responsible for the ap-

---

[258] Perhaps there is some analogy here with the way in which the English courts permitted third parties "to intervene in the proceedings, and even make good their claim to the property which was the subject of the action"; Holdsworth, *op.cit.*, II⁴, 249f., referring to Bracton's *Notebook*, cases 5, 525, 688. This principle was emphasized in Roman law, *C.* 7, 56, 2 and 4; 7, 60, 1 and 2; *D.* 42, 1, 63; and was frequently discussed by the canonists and legists of the thirteenth century.

[259] See R. F. Treharne, "The Significance of the Baronial Reform Movement," *Transactions of the Royal Historical Soc.*, xxv (1943), 49-53.

[260] *Traditio*, I, 370-375, 397-408; above, ch. III, § 4 and to nn. 181-206, and § 6.

pearance of *q.o.t.* in royal writs issued to summon all interested parties to treat the business of king and kingdom. If this is conjecture, it is not conjecture that Bracton stressed the procedural nature of consent in English courts and made use of the Romano-canonical *q.o.t.* as an equitable principle of private law.

PART II
PUBLIC LAW AND
THE STATE

CHAPTER V ✦ *RATIO PUBLICAE*

UTILITATIS, RATIO STATUS, AND

"REASON OF STATE," 1100-1300[1]

EPRESENTATION and consent in royal assemblies developed in response both to the rights of free men in their corporate or quasi-corporate communities and to the public rights and necessities of king and realm. But the prerogative, or public right, of the king to maintain the peace and welfare of the realm was, if exercised properly by an able monarch, superior to all private rights of individual subjects. The following series of studies are devoted, therefore, to the role of those theories of public law and the State which, although not unknown or even altogether unfelt in the early Middle Ages, from the twelfth century on found abundant expression in the literature of the Roman and Canon law and in the documents drawn up for the business of government. We have already encountered some of the terms and concepts—*utilitas publica, status regni,* and *status regis.* Now we shall examine them chiefly for their own sake.

The remarkable achievements of such kings as Henry II and Edward I of England, of Philip Augustus, Louis IX, and Philip the Fair of France, and of Roger II and Frederick II of Naples and Sicily are themselves an indication that they and their advisers had some understanding of public law and how its rules pertained to a central government. If, like architects of Gothic churches, they sometimes proceeded by trial and error, like the architects they were capable of reasoned planning. This is not

[1] This study was first published in *Die Welt als Geschichte,* xxi (1961), 8-28, 71-99. I wish to thank the editor, Prof. Dr. Fritz Ernst, for his careful attention and suggestions, and also to thank the translators into German, Dr. Fritz Trautz and Mr. Peter Moraw. The present English version is a slight revision of the original article sent to *Die Welt als Geschichte.*

said in order to compare the new structure of the State either with a Gothic cathedral or with the *Summa Theologiae* of Thomas Aquinas. It is said in order to stress the fact that intelligent kings and their jurists employed reason, sometimes Roman reason, as well as political opportunism, in practicing the skill or art of building States. Part II, therefore, begins with a study of medieval "reason of State."

Historians of modern Europe have not liked to believe that the State, as they define it, existed in the Middle Ages. They admit that some elements, some attributes, of the State were appearing in the thirteenth and fourteenth centuries; but the real fact and substance of it are a modern creation. Logically, if there was no State, there was no *ragione di stato* before the sixteenth century.

The late Friedrich Meinecke, the most profound authority on the history of the concept,[2] contended that "reason of State" is the "fundamental principle of national conduct, the State's first Law of Motion"; it "tells the statesman what he must do to preserve the health and strength of the State," and often "takes on the profound and serious character of national necessity"; and it presupposes a supreme, independent State that is in no wise subject to a universal religion and its moral commands. The Greek city-state and the Roman Empire were independent States, and the classical authors could and did attribute "reason of State" to them. In the Middle Ages, however, Christian ethics and Germanic jurisprudence were obstacles to the growth of the State and its "reason."[3] If in a fashion the State existed, "it did not rank supreme. Law was set above it." As Fritz Kern said, "politics and *raison d'état* were not recognized at all in the Middle Ages."[4] Yet, Meinecke did concede that Frederick II

---

[2] *Idee der Staatsräson*, 4th ed. by W. Hofer in Friedrich Meinecke, *Werke*, vol. I. Here I refer to the 4th ed. and also to the English translation by Douglas Scott, *Machiavellism. The Doctrine of Raison d'État and Its Place in Modern History*.

[3] *Staatsräson*, pp. 1f., 29-31; *Machiavellism*, pp. 1f., 25-27.

[4] *Staatsräson*, p. 31; *Machiavellism*, p. 27. Meinecke refers to Fritz Kern, "Recht und Verfassung im Mittelalter," *Hist. Zeitschr.*, cxx (1919), 57; transl. by S. B. Chrimes in Kern, *Kingship and Law in the Middle Ages*; new printing of German version by E. Anrich. Kern argues that there was no State and no true public law in the Middle Ages, and no distinction between law, equity, *raison d'état,*

and Philip IV practiced some "reason of State," and that in the later Middle Ages there were "a few basic admissions of the new conception of necessity of State." In the later fourteenth century Philip of Leyden thought that the ruler should revoke any privilege that was injurious to the *publica utilitas*; and a little later Jean Gerson and Jean Petit recognized that since *necessitas legem non habet*, no law should be in conflict with the peace and safety of the State. But it was Machiavelli who, although he did not use the words, first stated and "thought through" the modern "reason of State" in its essential nature. This Machiavelli could do because he was completely secular in his political thought; he was not handicapped by any theory of an inviolable moral law.[5]

Having a high ideal of the State, Meinecke could not approve a cynical "reason of State" either in Machiavelli or in statesmen of the twentieth century. Perhaps this explains why he was convinced that the principle is ancient-modern: medieval Christianity and the constant belief in the supremacy of law and justice were not a favorable environment for its full expression. Cicero's *ratio reipublicae* and Florus' *ratio et utilitas reipublicae* had to wait for the modern age for fulfillment.[6]

Quite different is Carl J. Friedrich's definition of "reason of State." He argues that Machiavelli did not "discover" the problem precisely because he had no thought of an end outside the State and saw no need "for 'justifying' the means which were required for building or maintaining a state." He thought only in terms of that *necessità* which knows no law of a normative kind. Giovanni da Botero, the first author of a treatise on the principle, is credited with inventing the terms, *ratio status, ra-*

---

and ethics; law was sovereign, not the State; there was no constitutional law; and there was no place for necessity of State or *Staatsräson, Kingship*, pp. 125, 154, 185, 198f.; *Recht und Verfassung*, pp. 21, 72, 93f.; and Kern, *Gottesgnadentum und Widerstandsrecht im früheren Mittelalter*, 2nd ed., pp. 227-229, 4th ed., pp. 111f., 124f., 142-146. Like Meinecke, Otto Brunner has accepted Kern's generalizations, *Land und Herrschaft*, pp. 124f., 138f., 160-164. I am deeply indebted to Professor Dr. Fritz Ernst for this and other references and for his criticism.

5 *Staatsräson*, pp. 34f., *Machiavellism*, pp. 28f., and the whole section on Machiavelli.

6 *Staatsräson*, pp. 1f., 29-31; *Machiavellism*, pp. 25-28.

gione di stato; and he first understood it as a problem of how the security of the State could be maintained and justified "within the context of Christian morality." Altogether Friedrich himself believes that where there is no reasoning about political actions in relation to a moral sanction or end (or in our day in relation to "constitutionalism"), that where there is no ideal of a constitutional law, there is no "reason of State."[7] (He might well, therefore, have wondered whether such a reason could have been understood in the Middle Ages, when king and kingdom were under God and the law). With respect to Machiavelli, J. H. Hexter offers a compromise between Meinecke and Friedrich. He says that in the *Discorsi* Machiavelli approached the idea of a body politic or State as a transcendent good and held that the end justifies the means of saving the State in time of danger; and he thus began to understand "reason of State" as an ethical doctrine. But in *The Prince* he viewed *lo stato* as the government or principality; there was no State outside the prince himself. Hence, Machiavelli developed no consistent theory of "reason of State." Hexter, like Friedrich, finds little medieval "reason of State" as a background.[8]

Thus, on the one hand, one group of authorities is sure that "reason of State" could not be medieval because it is a principle which presupposes the amoral, secular, independent, and sovereign State. On the other hand, those who, like Friedrich, believe that it is a moral, constitutional principle in itself, related to the limitation of the State by law, find the beginning of it neither in the Middle Ages nor altogether in Machiavelli, but in the sixteenth and following centuries. Ernest Barker, associating a part of it with Althusius, thinks that true *raison d'état* was a still later development.[9] One great authority on the Italian Renaissance, Federico Chabod, baldly asserts that no

[7] Friedrich, *Constitutional Reason of State*, pp. 15-30.

[8] "*Il principe* and *lo stato*," *Studies in the Renaissance*, IV (1957), 113-138, esp. 130-133. But Hexter does have some understanding of how the *status regis* was closely associated with the rights and powers of government, that in this sense the *status* was the ruler; and how *status regni* approached our "state of the nation"; p. 118.

[9] Barker in a footnote, p. 230, to n. 7, in his translation of Otto Gierke, *Natural Law and the Theory of Society, 1500-1800*—vol. IV of *Das deutsche Genossenschaftsrecht*.

one has even ventured "to put forward the thesis that the political ideas of a Machiavelli . . . are already implicit in the writings of the twelfth and thirteenth centuries." And only two or three years ago another distinguished scholar, Felix Gilbert, announced that *ragione* was the key to understanding Florentine foreign policy in the time of Savonarola, Soderini, and Machiavelli, as if reasoning about politics and public policy had been foreign to medieval thought and action. The old thesis of Burckhardt, that the science or art of the State was an invention of the Italian Renaissance, that "the deliberate adaptation of means to ends, of which no prince out of Italy had at that time a conception," was the essence of "the State as a Work of Art," still prevails.[10]

Medievalists themselves have been slow to recognize a conscious theory of the State and public law before the late thirteenth century, and only a few elements then and in the fourteenth century—so Otto Gierke, Fritz Kern, and Otto Brunner. A. O. Meyer, despite his good history of the word *Staat* (*status*), finds *ragione di stato* no earlier than the sixteenth century.[11] F. A. Freiherr von der Heydte, while describing the development of important aspects of the sovereign State and its public law in the thirteenth century, still refuses to attach any sense of modern *Staatsräson* to medieval ideas of the common or public utility and necessity.[12]

[10] Federico Chabod, *Machiavelli and the Renaissance*; transl. by David Moore, p. 238. He continues: "Recent attempts to discover Machiavelli's sources (A. H. Gilbert and the commentary by Father L. J. Walker) merely serve to emphasize the gulf that divides the thought of Machiavelli from that of the various writers of the Middle Ages"—see A. H. Gilbert, *Machiavelli's Prince and Its Forerunners*, and L. J. Walker, *The Discourses of Niccolo Machiavelli*.
Professor Felix Gilbert in his quite recent essay has not referred to any medieval sources, "Florentine Political Assumptions in the Period of Savonarola and Soderini," *Jour. of the Warburg and Courtauld Institutes*, xx (1957), 187-214. For more on this see below, n. 141. For Jacob Burckhardt, see *Die Kultur der Renaissance in Italien*, vol. v of the *Gesamtansgabe*, ed. by Werner Kaegi, p. 4.

[11] A. O. Meyer, "Zur Geschichte des Wortes Staat," *Die Welt als Geschichte*, x (1950), 229-239. Gierke's *Deutsche Genossenschaftsrecht* (vol. iii on the Middle Ages) is so well known that there is no need of giving specific references to it, nor to the English translation of the section on political theories, Maitland, *Political Theories of the Middle Age*.

[12] *Die Geburtsstunde des souveränen Staates*, p. 187 n. 20a; on the rise of sovereign States, esp. ch. ii. My own opinion is that the theory of independent States outside the Empire was already strongly represented in the twelfth and early thirteenth century, even by John of Salisbury (cf. pp. 46-48); see below, n.

But a few historians have begun to attribute "reason of State" to the policies of Frederick II and Philip IV. More than twenty years ago Sir Maurice Powicke perceived it in terms of responsible kingship in the interest of the State and showed its importance in the reign of Edward I; and E. F. Jacob has also pointed to its importance for the fourteenth century.[13] Quite recently Ernst Kantorowicz has indicated how it was implied in ideas about the king's public office.[14] Others, too, have noted it, chiefly in terms of defense of the realm and of utility and necessity, whether in the law of expropriation, in the policies of Frederick II and of the French monarchy, or in the thought of William of Ockham.[15] Professor Charles C. Bayley, in his fine study of Ockham's political thought, posed the problem of the

17, for references. As for the statement that *necessitas*, etc., bore no meaning of the modern "reason of State," my "presumptions" in the following paragraphs will indicate how I accept Meinecke's emphasis on *necessitas* as the very essence of Staatsräson (but not always amoral or immoral); and how I believe that it was quite modern in the sense of being associated with the corporate entity of the independent *regnum*. Von der Heydte should have remarked on the equivalent of our "reason" when discussing the powers of the king in time of war and in legislation (pp. 293-313); limitations on the royal authority do not mean that the king could not act *ratione status regni*.

On Kern and Brunner, see above, n. 4.

13 Powicke, "Reflections on the Medieval State," *Transactions of the Royal Historical Society*, XIX, 1-19 (chiefly on the policy of Edward I; it should be remarked that St. Louis is another good example of a king who practiced a Christian reason of State that worked to the advantage of the centralization of the royal authority; Buisson, *König Ludwig IX*, chs. 5 and 6); Jacob, "Changing Views of the Renaissance," *Trans. Roy. Hist. Soc.*, XVI (1931), 228f.

Strangely, the general historians of medieval political theories have not dealt specifically with the subject; e.g., Gierke, Carlyle, McIlwain, and d'Entrèves. Otto Gierke mentions "reason of State" in passing, but offers no illustrations except possibly for the late thirteenth century.

14 *King's Two Bodies*, p. 257; see also the Index, sub vv. *public, reason*, and *necessity*.

15 Besides C. V. Langlois in Lavisse, III, ii, 250f., and standard works on French law and institutions, e.g., Déclareuil, *Histoire gén. du droit français*, pp. 517, 701-709, see also J. R. Strayer, "Laicization of French and English Society in the Thirteenth Century," *Speculum*, XV (1940), 75-86, and again Strayer, "Defense of the Realm and Royal Power in France," in *Studi in onore di Gino Luzzato*, I, 289-296. Important also is Wilhelm Berges, *Die Fürstenspiegel des hohen und späten Mittelalters*, p. 78, on Philip the Fair as *minister publicae utilitatis*, which is Staatsräson, and on John of Salisbury, 43-46. For the frequent use of the terms *utilitas communis* and *publica* in Germany, see v. d. Heydte, *Geburtstunde*, p. 187 n. 20a, and the references there.

The standard work on the law of expropriation, with many references to *justa causa* and *necessitas*, is G. Meyer, *Das Recht der Expropriation*, pp. 76-115.

contribution of medieval necessity·and utility to the theory of *ragione di stato* in the early seventeenth century.[16] Unfortunately, some historians have found the origin of the concept of public *necessitas* in the new Aristotelian secularism or naturalism in the mid-thirteenth century, whereas actually both necessity and the literal *ratio utilitatis publicae*, we shall see, were current in the twelfth century, if not earlier.[17]

In the circumstances, then, a detailed study of medieval concepts of "reason of State" as a principle of public law may be useful. This chapter is therefore an attempt to set forth some of the evidence and to demonstrate what kinds of "reason of State" appeared in the intellectual history of the period (*ca.* 1100-1300), in which the modern age began perhaps as much as in the Italian Renaissance.

1. PRESUMPTIONS

This attempt would be useless, however, without presenting my presumptions or premises. (Definitions are worthless, since experts disagree on the meaning both of the State and of "reason of State.") The first presumption is that in the twelfth and thirteenth centuries the kingdoms of France, England, and Spain were in fact, and sometimes in legal theory, independent and sovereign communities, each one a *Respublica, corpus,* or *universitas,* with its own public law and sovereign government of the king.[18] The kingdom was a *communis patria* like the Ro-

[16] On Ockham, and *necessitas* also in the preceding two centuries, Professor Bayley has remarked how necessity and the general welfare were the "*ratio* and final sanction of legitimate public authority," "Pivotal Concepts in the Political Philosophy of William Ockham," *Journal of the History of Ideas,* x (1949), 199-218, 200, 217.

[17] Wieruszowski, *Vom Imperium zum nationalen Königtum,* pp. 166-173: J. Hashagen, *Staat und Kirche vor der Reformation,* pp. 433ff.; and Alois Dempf, *Sacrum Imperium,* chs. 8 and 9. Others, too, have steadily associated the "naturalness" of the State and secularism with the revival of the *Politics* in the Latin version made by William of Moerbeke, *ca.* 1260. I shall indicate how in fact a full century earlier John of Salisbury, and to some degree the legists and canonists, believed that nature and the natural law sanctioned the State, though of course nature was an instrument of God; below, ch. XI.

[18] I have already presented some preliminary studies of a few of these problems of public law and the State: "The Theory of Public Law and the State in the Thirteenth Century," *Seminar* (Annual Extraordinary Number of *The Jurist*), VI, 42-59; "Two Notes on Nationalism," *Traditio,* IX, 281-320; "The Two Laws and the Statute of York," *Speculum,* XXIX, 417-432; "*Plena potestas* and

man Empire, and the king was "emperor in his own realm," recognizing no superior secular authority. The king of England, said Bracton, was under no man (either in or outside England); he was under God and the law. Patriotic loyalty was the ideal: every subject of the king should be willing not only to pay taxes but to fight and die for the safety of the fatherland. Surely such a *regnum*, or *Respublica* or *civitas*, was a State in the modern meaning of sovereign independence. But the word "State" itself, from the Latin *status* in the sense of the public welfare of kingdom or city-state, was only beginning to separate itself from its object in such expressions as *status regni, status Reipublicae, status civitatis,* and *status imperii.* The usual terms for "State" in the thirteenth century were *Imperium* and *Respublica* (when they did not mean the government or any public office or property), *regnum,* and *civitas*—sometimes *Anglia* or *Francia* in place of *regnum Angliae* or *regnum Franciae.* The lack of a word to define something common to kingdoms and cities is no indication that there was no State. It is, in fact, remarkable that today men can apply the word "State" to such different political entities as Britain, the United States, the Soviet Union, India, and Ghana.

The objection is often raised, however, that medieval kingdoms were not States because (1) they accepted the spiritual authority of the pope and the universal Church, (2) king and realm were under God and the law of nature, and (3) the royal government was poorly centralized. As for the first argument, it might be raised against the use of the term "State" for Eire and Spain today. Yet we assume that these two countries are States even though they are essentially Catholic and in some fashion recognize the spiritual authority of the Roman Church.

Consent in Medieval Assemblies," *Traditio,* i, 355-408. See above, Introduction and ch. iii, and below, chs. vi and x; for new studies, below, chs. vii-ix.

As for the sovereignty of England, France, and Spain and their independence from the Empire, I have disagreed (*Traditio,* ix, 296-320) with Francesco Calasso, *I glossatori e la teoria della sovranità* (2nd ed.), whose general argument is that the theory that the king was emperor in his own realm meant only that each kingdom enjoyed autonomy within the Empire. (Von der Heydte is influenced by Calasso; above, n. 12.) Calasso has not changed his opinion in the 3rd ed. of *I glossatori.* See below, ch. x, § 2.

With respect to other ideals of universalism, the United States and Italy, not to mention other nations, are sovereign States while belonging to the United Nations. As for the second argument, on subjection to God and a moral law, it must be replied that the official motto of the United States is "In God We Trust," and Americans take an oath of loyalty to "one nation indivisible under God." Furthermore, the sovereignty of the American people and their State is surely limited in fact by a moral law that belongs to the Judaeo-Christian tradition: it is not likely that the representatives of the people in Congress will ever think of making laws that violate the Ten Commandments, nor that the Supreme Court will approve them. It is therefore not absurd to call medieval kingdoms States despite limitations within which derived from the ideal of law and justice, and despite limitations from without (also within) from the universalism of Christianity and the Church. Papal arbitration of "international" disputes in the thirteenth century interfered with the sovereign right of kings to go to war (always the "just war" in defense of the *patria* and the *status regni*) no more and no less than international organizations do in the twentieth century. And "world opinion" was respected as much or as little.

In reply to the third argument, regarding the amount of centralization, one must ask, what degree of centralization is necessary for a State to exist? If the central government must be absolute in power, then the United States might not qualify, since a great many powers remain in the fifty states within. And did France become a State only with the more thorough centralization that resulted from the Revolution? Logically we might conclude that only a totalitarian State is a true State. Within the history of one country, France, for example, it is clear that if this attribute of the State is taken seriously, it would be difficult to call France a State whether in the 1930's and 1940-1945 or in the period of the religious wars. The lack of a perfectly centralized government, then, should not prevent our calling the *regnum Angliae* a State, the *status* of which Henry III and Edward I claimed they should maintain.

The third presumption is related to the theory that the State is a juristic person, a corporate entity. We say that the State does this or that, that it acts, not merely that it is something for which the government acts. This capacity has been denied to the medieval realm or city. Without going into the problem of the corporate theories of the thirteenth century and their application to a *regnum*, let it be said here that in the legal theory the *Respublica, Ecclesia* (the Church), or *universitas* was sometimes the subject of a transitive verb, not always the object. Naturally, the legists and canonists knew, and frequently said, that the king or other magistrates acted as the agent or representative of the corporate body of the community. This was common sense, for the State can do nothing; the magistrates, the men who have public authority, act in the name of the State. Today, so often do we say that the State, or the Nation, does something, we forget that the State is only a legal fiction, or fictive person, and can do and suffer nothing at all. We should therefore not worry about the State as a person in the thirteenth century. How much of a person is it now? We may presume that a State, whether medieval or modern, has only a fictive reality. But in all ages the fiction is important.

These three presumptions can now be summarized: however much the *regnum* of the thirteenth century differed from the State of France or of the United States of our time (and, of course, there were important differences), it was, in the legal and official thought about its purpose and its reason for existence, very similar to the modern State.

The fourth presumption naturally follows, that if one cannot define the State so as to make it logically dependent on certain fixed conditions, one must be hesitant so to define "reason of State" that it can be said to originate and become logically complete only in one kind of environment and in one time and place. In the period to be examined "reason of State" was most frequently expressed as the just cause, necessity, or evident utility of making law, doing justice, or fighting a war for the public and common utility, the *status*, of the kingdom. If it was usually related to new situations or emergencies, it was not necessarily non-moral, for it was sanctioned by God as well as the public law. Sir Maurice Powicke has justly observed how kings and popes used the argument of public utility and necessity of

State and Church in the thirteenth century without divorcing this plea from equity and moral responsibility.[19] Philip the Fair skillfully employed these elements of "reason of State" against Boniface VIII, without, of course, intending to attack the universal Church. Edward I and Philip IV alleged the necessity of the safety of their kingdoms in order to prove that each was fighting a just war of defense against the other. At the same time, in both States, the royal governments and the courts, in theory and practice alike, usually acted and judged cases according to fundamental and positive laws which protected the rights of subjects. To be sure, there were abundant violations of the ideal of fair trial and due process of law, not only in ordinary cases but in the case of the Templars. Nonetheless, the pretension was that the public law of the safety of people and realm and the maintenance of the true faith for the salvation of souls, which also pertained to the *status regni*, justified extraordinary measures that were not in reality contrary to law and justice. As we shall see, the highest "reason of State and Church," cynical though it seem, was often sincerely believed to be in conformity with that reason which comes from God, participates in the law of nature, and approves the moral entity of the State.

In our own time, however non-moral and immoral "reason of State" and necessity may be in the totalitarian State, they are not always a completely secular principle in States which have "constitutional" governments and call upon the law of nature and God. The late Franklin Delano Roosevelt was accused of employing a cynical "reason of State" in order to persuade the American people to plunge into the Second World War, of being a super-Machiavelli in enticing the Japanese into the overt act of aggression at Pearl Harbor in order to give the United States a just *casus belli* or war of defense. No doubt, however, while using the end of the *salus populi* to justify the means employed in his speeches and acts, Roosevelt was sincere in believing that all this was in accordance with the God-given right of every State to use right reason to maintain its interests and safety. Herein most Americans were agreed; and by and

[19] "Reflections," *Trans. Roy. Hist. Soc.*, XIX, 6-11.

large they remain convinced, if they ever think of it, that American "reason of State" is related to a State which was founded and exists by God's will, and the government of which, though limited by the law of God and nature and by the Constitution, has with God's approval the right to use doubtful means to defend and assure the common welfare and safety of the people.[20]

One can, of course, interpret the whole matter in a completely skeptical fashion. But the point is that when people sincerely believe in a moral or fundamental law as a norm of government, sometimes the government itself is limited along with "Statism." At the same time, however, the moral right to defend the State and maintain the public welfare in times of emergency or necessity steadily enhances the power of the public authority in every kind of State. In any case, if the use of "reason of State" can be a moral, constitutional principle of government today, possibly it was so also in the thirteenth century. Nor is "right" or "good" "reason of State" completely devoid of Machiavellian compromising with the devil, either now or then.

Common sense, finally, should remind the historian that "reason of State" has always been—however unconsciously, or expressed in whatever terms—a rule of conduct for every kind of community, at least in times of emergency and danger. Accepting Meinecke's definition insofar as it holds that "reason of State" is the rational understanding of what must necessarily be done "to preserve the health and strength of the State," we find it in primitive, ancient, medieval, and modern communi-

[20] Yet, one encounters, among Americans of learning and experience in public affairs, some cynicism about morality in the State—so Senator J. William Fulbright, who according to a reporter (*Wisconsin State Journal*, on the editorial page, August 27, 1959), said: "To infuse moral concepts into a political discussion is simply to confuse it. . . . Morality is not involved in achieving a policy." Thus the State, as Paine, Ortega y Gasset, Spencer and others have held (add Machiavelli and Hobbes), is amoral. As for the author of the present study, he holds that one cannot properly speak of the morality (or of the mind or soul) of an abstract juridical, corporate entity. But what is important is that the men who govern a State can be conscious of moral principles in public matters even when they are *casualiter*, in cases of necessity or emergency, compromising or violating the principles. Insofar as the State is really the magistracy, it can be subject to concepts of a higher moral law—or it can, as in the totalitarian system, be cynically and normally amoral, or non-moral.

ties alike. As a principle which sanctions the general welfare above private interests in cases of conflict, which approves extraordinary measures to meet emergencies, which justifies compromises with moral laws to assure a higher moral end, which tolerates a lesser to prevent the triumph of a greater evil, which justifies the means by the end, it has always existed. Carried to the extreme of normal practice in the norm-less kind of State, it is "Machiavellian" in the bad sense of the word. Used only rarely, for cases of dire necessity and the natural right of defense, it is approved by every great religion and by every "constitutional" State; and it is indeed here a serious problem of political philosophy and ethics, not to speak of religious faith, precisely because it must be judged according to the law. Whether non-moral or moral, whether the one or the other kind has prevailed, whether both kinds can live together, "reason of State" has no doubt been a universally accepted principle since men became by nature social and political animals. The Athenians did not invent it when, Thucydides tells us, they made the plea of necessity to justify aggressive attacks on neutral cities. The power of the pope was greater, St. Bernard told Eugenius III, in cases of that necessity which knows no law. In 1914 Bethmann-Hollweg made the same excuse for Germany's violation of the neutrality of Belgium. The principle, if not the wording, is ageless.

2. The Roman Tradition, John of Salisbury, and the Canonists

For the Middle Ages the evidence comes not only from the legists and canonists who did much to create modern legal science by adapting the revived Roman law to their environment, but also from political theorists like John of Salisbury, Thomas Aquinas, and Henry of Ghent. Their sources were, of course, the *Corpus iuris civilis*, the Latin classical writers (chiefly Cicero), the Latin Fathers, and, after about 1260, Aristotle's *Politics*. Consequently, the legal and political thought of our period is replete with appeals to the maxim, "Necessitas legem non habet," to the *iusta causa*, and to *utilitas* (*evidens, publica,* and *communis*) and the common good.[21] These terms will be noted only in connection with the more rarely appearing literal statements of *ratio*; *ratio utilitatis publicae, ratio reipublicae, ratio status,* and *ratio civitatis,* which are related to the *status Reipublicae, imperii, regni, civitatis, ecclesiae,* will be emphasized. Since *status* in the context meant generally the public welfare (*utilitas publica*), *ratio publicae utilitatis* was often the same as *ratio status regni,* etc. Naturally, the public *ratio* included necessity and utility, as we shall see. By and large, the meaning of these expressions will be treated from the point of view of the presumptions given above and in comparison with the definitions of "reason of State" by Meinecke (the reasoning about the means necessary for preserving the health and strength of the State) and Friedrich (reasoning about the State under the control of a normative kind of law or a moral end). In essence, *ratio* will be understood (1) as the *raison d'être* of the magistracy or government and its public authority, (2) as the reasoning used by the ruler to the end of preserving the *status* or public and common welfare of State and people, and (3) as the *raison d'être* of the State itself.

In the Roman Empire, in the thought of the jurisconsults and the emperors, *Respublica* came to mean, apart from the public business of government or public property, the *Imperium* (and this apart from *imperium* as the power of the prince). The Republic or Empire enjoyed a public welfare or *status* which was the *ratio* for the imperial office and the activities of the emperor as the supreme public magistrate. The *ratio reipublicae* was also the *ratio status reipublicae* and the *ratio status imperii.*[22] Cicero, *De oratore,* I, xlvi, 201, had already said that to the *Respublica* belonged those public *iura* which were concerned with the city and *imperium* and which pertained to the "reason and science" of ruling the Republic. Hence, the public law in dealing with all problems of government expressed the method or "reason" of government.[23] But elsewhere Cicero

21 See above, Introduction; *D.* 1, 4, 2 (Ulpian); on *necessitas,* Kuttner, *Kanonistische Schuldlehre,* pp. 291-298, 336ff.

22 F. Crosara, "Respublica e respublicae," in *Atti del Congresso Internazionale di Diritto Romano e di Storia del Diritto,* IV, 241f.

23 Quoted in part by Eugen Ehrlich, *Beiträge zur Theorie der Rechtsquellen.* I.

referred to "reason of State" in a modern way when he said that utility was often an excuse for evil in the republic, and mentioned a *ratio reipublicae*, or *ratio et utilitas reipublicae*. He was against any expediency in the name of the State which resulted in acts of cruelty, holding that history offered splendid examples of the superiority of *honestas* over the specious plea of public utility (*publicae utilitatis species*).[24] "Reason of State" in Cicero, then, was related to a higher moral law and was essentially the whole method of good government of the State according to public law. It was practically the same in Ulpian's famous statement, that the public law deals with the *status rei Romanae* and with those public authorities (priests and magistrates) and *sacra* (religion, temples, ritual, and the like) which are necessary for the public welfare (*D*. 1, 1, 1, 2: "publicum ius est quod ad statum rei Romanae spectat . . . sunt enim quaedam publice utilia . . . publicum ius in sacris, in sacerdotibus, in magistratibus consistit").[25] In the Roman law, indeed, whether expressed by the jurisconsults or by imperial laws, the *status rei Romanae* (*reipublicae*) was the common or public utility and necessity of the Empire and of all the citizens in the Empire.[26] So, for example, Diocletian and Maximian decreed

---

Das jus civile, jus publicum, jus privatum, p. 168; see all of ch. XII. The main part of the passage deals with the duty of the orator, who must know "publica quoque iura, quae sunt propria civitatis atque imperii," and understand "et publici iuris auctoritas et regendae reipublicae ratio ac scientia." *Ratio*, of course, is not perhaps here literally "reason," but can be so interpreted, i.e., the general rationale of government.

24 *De officiis*, III, xi: "Sed utilitatis specie in re publica saepissime peccatur"; e.g., the Roman destruction of Corinth and various crimes committed by the Athenians against other cities; cited by Meinecke, *Machiavellism*, pp. 25f.

25 J. Gaudemet, " 'Utilitas publica,' " *Rev. hist. dr. fr. étr.*, XXIX (1951), 477, suspects a part of Ulpian's words as post-classical. Francesco Calasso flatly states that in *D*. 1, 1, 1, 2 the words, "sunt enim quaedam publice utilia, quaedam privatim," are not Ulpian's but an interpolation by the compilers in the sixth century; he thinks that *publice utilia* is different from the concept in *status rei Romanae*; *Ordinamenti giuridici del rinascimento medievale*, p. 279. I am no expert on interpolations in the *Digest*, but since Cicero and other writers before Ulpian used *status* in this sense, I see no reason to doubt that Ulpian could talk both of *status* as the public *utility* and of things that are publicly *utilia*; see the following n. 26. Ehrlich supports my interpretation of the passage, that Ulpian meant that the public law pertains not only to the *status rei Romanae*, but also to the public magistrates (*Behördenrecht*), *Beiträge*, I, 189.

26 Gaudemet, *op.cit.*, pp. 465-499. But Gaudemet distinguishes too much between an earlier prevalence of *utilitas communis* and a later prevalence of

that when a judge had to leave one province and go to another *publicae utilitatis ratione,* another judge should be appointed in his place (*C.* 3, 3, 4 Placuit). This was *ratio status* with respect to the public office of judges in the necessary administration of jurisdiction in the Empire. The same emperors (*C.* 8, 50 [51], 6 Cum et postliminii) declared that since both the *postliminii ius* and the *communis utilitatis ratio* demanded the redemption of men captured by the enemy, it should be at the accepted price, and the men should be restored to the security of their former condition. Again this was a statement of *ratio status* with respect to the public welfare of the Empire and its people. Further, if necessity and public utility sanctioned marriage, they also made the provisioning of troops come before the rights of dower—but here the supreme necessity of defending the Empire "knew no law" which protected marriage and doweries for the public utility.[27] One kind of public necessity could be superior to another.

If there was no literally expressed "reason of Empire" or of abstract State, there was a strong consciousness of "reason" of the public utility or *status* of the Republic. In the Roman law on the imperial authority, as in Cicero, this reason was normally subordinated to principles of law and justice. Exceptionally, it could mean, for the defense of the emperor and the Empire, the necessity that justified a compromise. But in the age of absolutism itself, there persisted some of the theory of Stoicism and Christianity, that the government in acting for the public

---

util. publica; and he fails in general to relate the public utility to the *status Reipublicae.* On *status* and *utilitas* in the public sense, in Cicero, Pliny, Tertullian, and Orosius, see E. Köstermann, "Status als politischer Terminus in der Antike," *Rheinisches Museum für Philologie,* N.F., LXXXVI (1937), 231ff., and Joseph Svennung, *Orosiana,* pp. 127-132. But Köstermann tends to make *status* mean the abstract entity of the *Respublica,* in spite of showing that in Cicero and others it referred usually to the condition and stability, even to the form of government, of the Republic. Svennung believes that *status* in Orosius was almost the Roman State. *Status urbis* no doubt meant the general welfare of the city of Rome in a law of Valentinian and Valens, *C.* 1, 28, 1. Finally, on the *status Reipublicae* from the time of Cicero to the sixth century, see Crosara, "Respublica e respublicae," *Atti,* IV, 234-247. For *status* in the later period see Meyer, *Welt als Gesch.,* x, 229-239.

27 Gaudemet, *op.cit.,* pp. 478 and 481f., referring to *D.* 49, 15, 12, 3, and *C.* 12, 62, 3. But necessity was well known in the Roman law. See also below, nn. 90f.

interest was subject to the law of nature, divine reason, and the principles of fair trial.

Some of the ideal participated, no doubt, in the Latin Fathers who helped transmit the idea of Rome to the Middle Ages. Thus St. Ambrose, precisely in the work most influenced by Cicero, the *De officiis,* says that the very *ratio societatis,* the "reason" of human society, is justice and kindness; and public justice is for public matters, private for individuals.[28] No doubt he associated the *ratio societatis* or justice with the public law that pertains to the duties of magistrates, whether priests or laymen, in administering the community for the public welfare of all. In like manner, St. Augustine believed in the supremacy of justice as the *ratio societatis* for the achievement of order and peace. But quite within the tradition of Roman legal thought Gregory the Great declared that *ratio nulla* permits the private use of what is known to be given for the common utility. In effect, he was saying that the *ratio utilitatis communis* must prevail over private interests and was perhaps reflecting the Roman maxim that the public must be preferred to private utility.[29]

The end of the Roman Empire in the West meant the decline of the ideas and practice of public law in the barbarian kingdoms. The State itself became weak, public law was submerged in private law, and in the ninth to eleventh centuries feudalism reflected the triumph of private rights over the public interest. Yet, Roman ideas of public law and the State persisted, and with them some expression of "reason of State," in the terms *status regni* or *status Reipublicae,* necessity, defense of the *patria, utilitas regis* and *regni,* and the like.[30] Even in the feudal system one can find traces of the old theory of public law, in that originally fiefs were granted by king to vassals as a means of

[28] *De off.,* I, c. 28, 130 (*M.P.L.,* 16:61): after saying that justice is related to the society and community of human kind, he adds, "Societatis enim ratio dividitur in duas partes, justitiam et beneficentiam. . ." (132); the public form of justice "pro publicis habeat, privata pro suis." See also Gaudemet, *L'Église dans l'empire romain,* vol. III of G. Le Bras, ed., *Histoire du droit et des institutions de l'Église en occident,* pp. 468f. Cf. Lagarde, *Naissance de l'esprit laique,* II, 2nd ed., 24; Lagarde translates *ratio societatis* "l'âme même de la société."

[29] The words of Gregory the Great are in a decretal letter, *Decr. Greg. IX* 3, 5, 3 Ratio; cf. *D.* 2, 14, 38.

[30] Powicke, "Reflections," *Trans. Roy. Hist. Soc.,* XIX, 5, 9f.; and Crosara, "Respublica e respublicae," *Atti,* IV, 249-261.

defending the kingdom; and the king himself was the highest authority even when he had no public power to command the public services of the great lords. But of course there was no State and no effective "reason of State."

In the great revival of political life, learning, and law in the Renaissance of the twelfth century the classical and patristic ideas again flourished. Before 1150 mystical, but nonetheless practical, theologians understood how the power of kings and popes was the greater in cases of necessity. Hugo of St. Victor, influenced perhaps by the revived Canon and Roman law, directly associated *ratio* and *necessitas*. If reason and necessity demanded it, he said, churches and their property owed obedience to the royal *potestas*. If this was in part the "reason" of the royal authority—and Hugo in support says, " 'Reddite quae sunt Caesari Caesari' "—it was also the "reason" of the safety of the kingdom. A century and a half later Aegidius Romanus, repeating Hugo's *ratio* and *necessitas*, observed that when both reason and necessity concurred, the king did not have to wait for the pope's consent to tax the clergy in his realm. Obviously, taxation for the necessity of war in defense of the realm is what Hugo and Aegidius had in mind. St. Bernard of Clairvaux quoted the already well-known maxim, "necessity knows no law," and told Pope Eugenius III that the papal powers of dispensation were lawful when the necessity was urgent. So early, then, and probably in the eleventh century, too (I have not studied the literature; above all, the compilations of Canon law should be examined), *ratio* and *necessitas* were that "reason of State" which a government must use in cases of emergency when the safety of State or of Church was at stake. Henry I of England in 1100 was pleading the necessity of defense.[31]

---

[31] Hugo, *De sacramentis*, II, ii, 6, *De potestate terrena* (*M.P.L.*, 176:420): ". . . quando si ratio postulaverit et necessitas . . . et illi ipse possessiones debeant in necessitate obsequium . . ."; St. Bernard on necessity, *M.P.L.*, 184:433, no. 281, and 182:769. For Aegidius Rom., see below, n. 136. "Necessitas legem non habet" and *necessitas* were almost a commonplace in Gratian's *Decretum*, and, of course, came from antiquity and the early Middle Ages. On dispensation see in general Brys, *De dispensatione in iure canonico*; *necessitas* appears repeatedly. See below, n. 51.

As for *necessitas* in the time of Henry I of England, in a letter to Anselm the king excused his hurrying his coronation without waiting for the arch-

The Ambrosian-Augustinian theory of justice as the normal *ratio societatis*, combined with the Roman law on the power of the prince and the common or public utility, inspired John of Salisbury almost to write a small treatise on "reason of State." This great Christian humanist of the twelfth century says, first, that each State, the *Respublica*, is a certain kind of *corpus* animated by the grace of God and ruled "by a certain control of reason." *Lex* in the Republic is a gift of God (cf. *D.* 1, 3, 1 and 2);[32] and all who are engaged in the "university of political business," that is, all magistrates or rulers, should live according to the law. If the prince is *absolutus*, not bound by the law (the famous words of Ulpian in *D.* 1, 3, 31: "Princeps legibus solutus est"), nonetheless, he will love and cultivate justice and equity, and follow the *Digna vox* and acknowledge that he is as a public person *legibus alligatus* (*C.* 1, 14, 4) and the *servus aequitatis*.[33] Therefore, he will care for the "rei publicae utilitatem" and prefer the good of others to his private will.[34] But how can any-

bishop, because "necessitas fuit talis quia inimici insurgere volebant contra me et populum quem habeo ad gubernandum"; *S.C.*, p. 120. In the *Leges Henrici* (*ca.* 1109-1118) the *necessitas regis* is associated with the *commune regni commodum*; *S.C.*, p. 123. "Urgent and evident necessity" appears in Ralph de Diceto, *an.* 1176; *S.C.*, p. 154. Of course, *necessitas* was also appearing in the documents of princes in Germany and elsewhere.

[32] *Policraticus*, v, 2 (ed. Webb); also IV, 2. John definitely refers to *D.* 1, 3, 2, where Demosthenes is quoted by Marcianus on how "omnis lex inventum est et donum dei." On this see G. Post, "Philosophantes and Philosophi in Roman and Canon Law," *Arch. d'hist. doctr. et litt. du moyen-âge* (1954), p. 137; but there I overlooked John of Salisbury. On John's *moderamen rationis* see also Anton-H. Chroust, "The Corporate Idea and the Body Politic in the Middle Ages," *Review of Politics*, IX (1947), 436. In general, for the classical influence on John, see Liebeschütz, *Mediaeval Humanism in the Life and Writings of John of Salisbury*.

[33] Kantorowicz, *King's Two Bodies*, pp. 94-97, offers a good treatment of John; see also pp. 104-106 on the *Digna vox*, *C.* 1, 14, 4. Cf. Berges, *Fürstenspiegel*, pp. 43-46, 138f., and Liebeschütz, *op.cit.*, pp. 23-33, 45-55, 56f., 61f., 69, and 74, on such matters as John's use of the Roman law in his political thought and his theories of the prince as the head of the corporate body of the State, of the royal government, of tyranny, and of natural law; also John Dickenson, "The Mediaeval Conception of Kingship and Some of Its Limitations, as Developed in the Policraticus of John of Salisbury," *Speculum*, I (1926), 308-337.

[34] I think that John has in mind *C.* 6, 51, 1, 14-14a, the famous words of Justinian, that in certain claims of the imperial fisc the emperor will not use imperial privilege, "sed quod communiter omnibus prodest, hoc rei privatae nostrae utilitati praeferendum esse censemus, nostrum esse proprium subiectorum commodum imperialiter existimantes." This is related to the public law insofar as it holds that the prince should rule for the welfare of subjects and their

one speak of the (arbitrary, private) will of the prince? For in public affairs, he has no right to want anything for himself except what law or equity sanctions or the "reason of the common utility" (*ratio communis utilitatis*) demands. In public affairs his will is not private but the (public) "force of judgment" (*vis iudicii*) and the "vigor of law" (*legis vigor*).[35] He is the *minister* of the public utility, the servant of equity.[36] Even his own property, e.g., in horses, servants, and baggage, should not be more than is demanded by "reason of necessity or utility" (*ratio necessitatis aut utilitatis*); and this is the reason in essence of the good of the people.[37] Finally, in cases of treason, *laesa majestas*, the "reason of necessity or utility" justifies the use of torture.[38]

John of Salisbury understood "reason of State" as the reason of the public welfare administered by a king or prince according to the law of God and man. It was a moral reason, related both to divine reason and to the end of the common good of all men in the community. Presumably John would, if challenged, have argued that the tyrant was a ruler who was cynical, amoral, and immoral in practicing "reason of State"; for how could he act for his private, selfish interests without violating true "reason of State" as the "reason of the public utility" for which the law itself exists as the gift of God? The tyrant might claim that in

---

property rights; here again the prince is not above that positive law which protects private rights, although by public law his power is above private law for the protection of private rights in his courts. It is related also to the maxim *quod omnes tangit*: what touches the private interests of all demands the procedures of law and justice, procedural hearing, before the ruler can take rights away or modify them. At any rate, the public interest of all singly or collectively is superior to the private interest of the prince. On *q.o.t.* in legal procedure see my study, "A Romano-Canonical Maxim, *quod omnes tangit*, in Bracton," *Traditio*, IV, 197-251; ch. IV above; and now for more details Yves M. J. Congar, "Quod omnes tangit ab omnibus tractari et approbari debet," *Rev. hist. dr. fr. étr.*, XXXVI (1958), 210-259.

[35] Here John of Salisbury is interpreting the famous so-called *lex regia*, *Inst.* 1, 2, 6, and *D.* 1, 4, 1: "Quod principi placuit, legis habet vigorem: utpote cum lege regia, quae de imperio eius lata est, populus ei et in eum omne suum imperium et potestatem conferat ['concessit' in *Inst.*]." *Vis iudicii* might be translated as the "power of the courts" in which the judicial authority of the prince is present.

[36] *Policraticus*, IV, 2; also Berges, *Fürstenspiegel*, pp. 138f., 139 n. 1.

[37] *Policraticus*, IV, 4.

[38] *Policraticus*, VI, 25 (*M.P.L.*, 199:627): "Tormentis quidem subdendi sunt, si hoc ratio necessitatis, aut utilitatis inducat." He means also the necessity of the prince and of the *patria*.

violating law and justice in cases of necessity he was doing so not for himself but for the safety of the State; but he could not be sincere. The safety of the State, the public welfare, should not be an excuse for illegal measures. But John did not go into this problem of apparent contradiction. The full development of the legal theory of public law and the State in the following century was necessary before Bartolus of Sassoferrato and Coluccio de'Salutati could hold, as did Innocent IV, that a good prince could *casualiter*, in a real case of necessity, in a real emergency, lawfully recognize no law if his act was for the safety of the State. He became a tyrant, using "reason of State" selfishly and thus immorally and illegally, when regularly or normally, with no dire necessity existing, he practiced expedience (Cicero's "publicae utilitatis species").[39]

A Christian-Roman "reason of State," then, was stated by John of Salisbury; and John's influence in this direction was important in the following period. Not to mention others who read John's work, the great Neapolitan jurist of the fourteenth century, Lucas de Penna, quoted his words on the will of the prince, law, equity, and *ratio communis utilitatis*, agreeing with him completely on "reason of State."[40] But the influence of Stoic-Roman-Christian ideas about a fundamental law of God and nature which limited the government was universal. This is so well known that it can be understood without further discussion. It explains why Frederick II, secular in spirit though he was in pleading necessity and the public welfare, could declare that his absolute power and *impetus* of will were controlled by nature and by that all-powerful reason which rules over kings, and that his imperial *majestas* was subject to that "judgment of reason" which is the mother of law.[41] If this reason was not precisely "reason of State," it was much the same thing, in that the natural reason from God tells men that law and justice are necessary for the sake of society and the common welfare and com-

[39] Above, n. 24; below, n. 57.
[40] *Commentaria in Tres Libros Codicis*, pp. 119f. n. 3.
[41] E. Kantorowicz, *Kaiser Friedrich der Zweite*, p. 232, and *Ergänzungsband*, p. 106, n. to p. 232 in the text. See also his *King's Two Bodies*, p. 106 n. 55, and his discussion of the theory of Frederick II and of the idea that reason is the mother of law, etc., pp. 105-107.

pels the prince to act accordingly. Ernst Kantorowicz says that "a century later this semi-divine *Ratio* will become a *ratio regis et patriae,* synonymous with Reason of State . . . a mere instrument of statecraft."[42] It was, however, simply another way of attaching the Stoic-Roman-Christian "reason of State" to God on the one side and to the imperial authority and the natural end of the State on the other. Clearly, it belonged to the whole set of ideas about the direct moral sanction of the State by the law of God and nature. In fact, the "semi-divine Ratio" already participated in the *ratio patriae* and the *ratio gubernationis regis* that were in the intellectual atmosphere well before the reign of Frederick II. This will now be shown.

More down to earth, more practical, and certainly more influential in the courts of princes than John of Salisbury and other writers on the science of governing were the canonists and legists. Although they, of course, accepted the supremacy of God and the law of nature, they were more specific about *ratio* and necessity and the just cause in matters of State and Church. A century before the appearance of Aristotle's *Politics,* the decretists and the glossators were assuming that *societas* in general and the State were approved by God either directly through nature and the natural law or indirectly through the participation of the natural law in the *ius gentium* and the *ius civile. Naturalis ratio,* Gaius had said (*D.* 9, 2, 4), made it lawful for every man to defend himself against an aggressive attack; and what *naturalis ratio* established among men was the *ius gentium* (*D.* 1, 1, 9). The Roman legal theory, rather than Aristotle, was the more immediate source of those appeals to "natural reason" which were already in the legal atmosphere of the late twelfth century and which became common in the thirteenth.[43] Thus either directly or indirectly private natural law, "international" law, and, because the natural law according to some legists was one of the sources of the *ius publicum* of every *Respublica* or State, the public law sanctioned the right of every

---

[42] *King's Two Bodies,* p. 107.

[43] On nature and the State see below, ch. XI; on *ratio naturalis* in the time of Philip the Fair see Kantorowicz, *King's Two Bodies,* p. 255 n. 193, and p. 256; from Wieruszowski, *Vom Imperium zum nationalen Königtum,* pp. 173, 186, 198, 243f.

State to wage just wars of defense. It was indeed a fundamental "reason" of kingship and human association, that the king and his subjects should fight in defense of the *patria communis* of the independent kingdom. *Pugna pro patria!* "For the defense of the fatherland," said Laurentius Hispanus, a canonist of the early thirteenth century, "many things are lawful which otherwise are unlawful." For example, a man who unavoidably kills his father while defending the *patria* should be rewarded, not punished. The legists approved—and so did Henry of Ghent, a secular theologian at Paris in the last quarter of the century.[44]

Already in the late twelfth century a decretist, Johannes Faventinus, associated the idea of the just war in defense of the *patria* with *ratio*. *Ratione rei*, he said, that is, by reason of or because of the *defensio patriae* or because of *causa* or necessity, a war is just.[45] He really summed up the current doctrine, that when the State was in danger the reason of its safety was the supreme necessity that justified war against the aggressor. The king was, of course, compelled by his office to practice "reason of State" when violent attack on his realm had to be repulsed: "vim vi repellere" was approved by every kind of law, by the *ius naturale* as well as the *ius gentium* and the public law of the State.[46] Hugo of St. Victor had put it succinctly in equating *ratio* and *necessitas*. As Gregory VII still earlier had declared—

[44] See below, ch. x, § 1, and my article "Two Notes on Nationalism in the Middle Ages," *Traditio*, IX, 281-320, esp. 281-296, "Pugna pro patria"; Laurentius to *Decretum*, C. 23, q. 8, c. 8, ad v. *patriae*—quoted in *Trad.*, IX, 283, n. 10. For the legists, see *Trad.*, IX, 285ff.; Henry of Ghent below, n. 113.

[45] To *Decretum* C. 23, q. 2, on words by Gratian himself, beginning "Quod autem," Joh. Fav. says that *ratione rei* a war is unjust "si non est de repetendis rebus, vel pro defensione patriae"; if not *propter causam* but "propter voluntatem, et non propter necessitatem pugnatur"; and if not waged by the authority of the prince (in the *Glos. ord.* of Joh. Teutonicus).

Another decretist of the early thirteenth century also uses this argument in the *Apparatus* "Ius naturale" to the *Decretum*, to C. 23, q. 2: circumstances and the *ratio rei* justify war, also the *ratio personarum*, when it is for necessity against enemies; Paris, BN, MS lat. 15393, fol. 181ᵛ, c. 1. A later gloss on this says: "Causa," quia nunquam nisi necessitate, scilicet, pro contumacia adversarii." On the *iusta causa*, necessity, and war in Huguccio and others, see *Trad.*, IX, 282 nn. 8 and 9; below, ch. x, nn. 9f.

[46] See on *vim vi repellere* and its source in *D.* 9, 2, 44, 4 and *D.* 43, 16, 1, 27, and in general on necessity, the just war, and natural law, Kuttner, *Kanonistische Schuldlehre*, pp. 336, 334-379; also my "Two Notes on Nationalism," *Trad.*, IX, 296f.; below, ch. x, nn. 62f.

and the decretists quoted him—the king who did not fight for the *regnum* was useless and should be deposed in favor of a prince who would defend the common safety.[47]

"Reason of State" was also a principle well understood in the Church. The canonists attributed to the pope the supreme public *auctoritas*, with the fullness of power to legislate, judge and administer for the *status Ecclesiae*, that is, for the public welfare of the Church and for the security of the faith. They constantly subordinated this authority to the "state of the Church" and to law and justice, but gave the pope extraordinary powers of dispensation, sometimes even from the natural law, in cases of the *justa causa* and necessity. These cases could involve the acceptance of a lesser evil to avoid a greater (or a lesser good to achieve a higher end), or to prevent public scandal from endangering the welfare of the faith and the Church.[48] The just war in defense of the faith and of the "state of the Church" was lawful whether it was a crusade against the infidel or against a Hohenstaufen. But all these matters were generally repeated in the usual terms of necessity, common or public utility, and *status Ecclesiae*,[49] rather than in the literal "reason of State" or "reason of the Church." Nonetheless, occasionally decretists said the same thing in the words *ratio publicae utilitatis* or *ratio utilitatis Ecclesiae.*

[47] *Trad.*, IX, 283f.; above, n. 31; below, ch. x, to nn. 15f.

[48] *Decretum*, Dist. 13, Item (Gratian) and c.1; Dist. 4, c.6; C. 1, q. 7, c. 4, Nisi rigor, and cc. 5, 6; cf. below, n. 138. The glosses in the *Glos. ord.* of Joh. Teutonicus to these passages in the *Decretum* are illuminating.

[49] In general see Tierney, *Foundations of the Conciliar Theory*, pp. 50-53, 89. But Professor Tierney speaks of the maintenance of the *status Ecclesiae* as if it were always a limitation on the authority of the pope. Since I am convinced that the papal government in cases of *justa causa* and necessity could do things not normally permitted, all for the faith and for the *status Ecclesiae*, the legal theory of the necessity of the *status Ecclesiae* greatly enhanced the papal prerogative. Therefore, I plan to treat the *status Ecclesiae* in a special study.

Alois Dempf was too eager to see a deep significance (the complete separation of the Church as a State, or *Respublica christianorum*, from the Empire) in Gérard d'Abbeville's *status totius ecclesiae* (*Sacrum Imperium*, 353f.); and v. d. Heydte, *Geburtsstunde*, 43 n. 5, accepts this and says that *status Ecclesiae* had in Gérard almost the sense of the modern word *Staat*. This is nonsense. As I remarked, *status Ecclesiae* appears steadily from the fifth century on (see *Decretum*, Dist. 97, c. 1 Ecclesiae—the Emperor Honorius should always protect the faith and the rights of the Church, and be mindful of the *status universalis Ecclesiae*) to the time of Gérard (*ca.* 1250-1271); it means, above all, the welfare of the faith and of the Church. Actually, the Church had long since been a kind of State.

Two examples from the late twelfth and early thirteenth century can be given. The proper ordination of priests, said Gratian, is for the utility of others; therefore, a decretist commented, priests are ordained "ratione publice utilitatis." and laws on ordination are public laws—and he refers to *D.* 1, 1, 1, 2 (Ulpian on how the public law that pertains to the *status rei Romanae* and deals with *sacra*, priests, and magistrates).[50] In a word, the "reason of the public utility" was the "reason of the *status*" of the Church, for without priests the Church and the faith could not be maintained. This fits in with the abundantly held theory that the *status Ecclesiae* was above all the faith, for the maintenance of which the *ordo ecclesiasticus*, from pope to parish priests, was necessary, *ratione publicae utilitatis*.

The second example comes from Stephen of Tournai (*ca.* 1160-1170). In the *Decretum* one finds a famous opinion of Pope Leo I, that no change could be made of those things that had been ordained for the perpetual utility or common good (of the Church and the faith). This inspired the decretists to discuss the problem of the papal power of dispensation. They generally agreed that the pope could not do anything that was contrary to general statutes and the *status* of the Church, or contrary to the articles of the faith. Papal dispensations, however, were lawful for just cause or necessity; but the just cause and necessity, after all, made dispensations necessary for the "state of the Church."[51] But Stephen of Tournai stated this theory in a most interesting fashion. General ecclesiastical laws for the perpetual utility (Leo I's "quae ad perpetuam generaliter ordinata sunt utilitatem"), he said, cannot be subject to changes (by dispensation or privilege), "unless the reason of the utility of the Church having been perceived," it is evident that the change can be made for the better; nor can privileges or other statutes of the Roman Church be granted for any private utility.[52] His

---

[50] Vat. MS Ross. 595, fol. 86, gloss to *Decretum*, C. 1, q. 1, c. 44 Si qui § Ecce, ad v. *ad quorum utilitatem*: "Sacerdotes enim ratione publice utilitatis institui debent. Unde et iura de his constituta dicuntur publica, ff. de iustitia et i.j. publicum." The author of the gloss is uncertain; see Kuttner, *Repertorium*, pp. 57f., 77 n. 4, 84 n. 2. See also below, n. 56.

[51] Tierney, *Conciliar Theory*, pp. 50-53. On papal dispensation see also Stephan Kuttner, "Pope Lucius III and the Bigamous Archbishop of Palermo," in *Medieval Studies Presented to Aubrey Gwynn, S.J.*, pp. 409-430.

[52] *Summa*, to C. 25, q. 1, c. 3, ad v. *varientur*: "Nisi perspecta ratione utilitatis

"reason of the utility of the Church" is virtually the "reason of the state of the Church." Further, his thought is related to the theory in the Roman law that privileges and dispensations are justified by the public law itself, since it is good for the public welfare to confer special favors on those who, so to speak, have merit in the service of the State.[53] Perhaps this explains why later canonists, e.g., Johannes Andreae, could explain that *ratio*, in the granting of dispensations, is *triplex*, "necessitas, utilitas, et evidens prerogativa meritorum," that papal dispensations are justified by the merits of learned men and nobles when *ratio* is used.[54]

Secular theologians as well as canonists understood the papal power of dispensing as a practice of "reason of State" in the Church. Gérard d'Abbeville (fl. 1254-1271) was not always obedient to the papacy during the famous quarrel between the secular masters of theology and the Friars at Paris. Nevertheless, in a *Quodlibet* he argued strongly for the *plenitudo potestatis*. He saw clearly that the papal authority in dispensing from the general laws of the Church belonged to the principle of public necessity and the public and common utility of the Church and the faith. If he did not actually say *ratio publicae utilitatis* or *ratio status Ecclesiae,* he almost said it—certainly he stated it in equivalent terms. Asking whether the pope could release a nun from the solemn vow of chastity, Gérard discusses a special *casus.* Suppose the emperor were a Saracen and a tyrant who planned to destroy the Christian faith and all the faithful, but the Church by giving him a girl in marriage could stop him and convert him to the faith. Could the pope in this case, if the girl had taken the solemn vow and assumed the habit and pro-

---

ecclesie, tunc in melius fieri posse perpenditur"; ad v. *quae ad bonum*: "Sicut privilegia vel alia romane ecclesie statuta"—the pope should not grant privileges that are against the public utility or *status* of the Church. I have taken these glosses from Vat. MS Borghes. 287, fol. 89; the edition by Schulte is not at the moment available to me.

53 Below, to nn. 78-84.

54 Joh. Andreae, *Novella Com.*, III, 35ᵛ to *Decr. Greg. IX* 3, 5, 28, ad v. *ratio* (no. 14). It was accepted by the jurists that learned men as well as nobles were publicly useful, and schools were subjects of the public law. Joh. de Deo also emphasized *ratio*; Kuttner, "Pope Lucius III," *Med. Studies . . . Aubrey Gwynn,* p. 430 n. 90.

fession of a nun, release her and give her to the emperor? Gérard refers to arguments against and then for dispensation, thus revealing that a *casus* of this kind had long since become a part of casuistry. For example, he quotes a certain Bernardus, *De dispensatione et poenitentia*, that it is a greater *caritas* to protect the faith and the faithful than to protect the chastity of any single person. His own answer is completely affirmative. Since the vow of virginity is voluntary and does not belong to necessity, while the faith is an absolutely necessary vow ("fides vero votum necessitatis absolutum"), in this case the vow of chastity can be relaxed to prevent the fury of the tyrant who occupies the monarchy of the whole world from jeopardizing the faith. Here the words of St. Bernard apply: "Whenever necessity is urgent, dispensation is excusable; whenever utility demands it, dispensation is praiseworthy. The common utility, I say, not one's own." In the aforesaid case, Gérard continues, the dispensation would be a change for the better, not by reason of the loss of chastity by an individual, but by reason of the utility of the *Respublica*, that is, by reason of the passionate and zealous love of the common utility and the general *salus* of the faithful. The pope, therefore, because of his *plenitudo potestatis*, can grant dispensation for such a marriage and absolve the girl from her vow of chastity and from the religious life of a nun. Especially can he do so because in this the *maxima utilitas* of the universal Church is evident, and urgent and evident necessity demands it—the public utility of the Church is preferred to any private welfare. Those who deny that the pope can do this, *causa necessitatis vel utilitatis*, do not understand the Canon law![55]

[55] This discussion is in a *Quodlibet* of Gérard; since so far as I know it has not been published, I present the main passages here, from the Paris, BN, MS lat. 16405, fols. 51 c. 2-51ᵛ c. 1: (*Questio* 13, *De voti sollempnis dispensatione*—can the pope grant dispensation to a nun from the vow of chastity?) "Si imperator esset sarracenus et tyrannus, et vellet fidem totaliter evertere, et fideles omnes perimere, nisi ecclesia sibi puellam matrimonialiter copularet, ac per hoc a premissis cessaret et ad fidem converteretur, utrum papa in hoc casu cum puella, que votum sollempnizavit per habitus regularis susceptionem et factam professionem, posset dispensare? . . . Ber., de dispensatione et penit., '. . . sed maior caritas est totius ecclesie servare fidelis et fidem, quam alicuius persone singularis servare castitatem. . . .' Respondeo: dic quod cum votum virginitatis sit votum voluntatis non necessitatis, fides vero votum necessitatis absolutum, unde si tota fides periclitaretur ob furorem unius tiranni monarchiam totius

Gérard d'Abbeville, in sum, did not need to say *ratio status Ecclesiae* or *ratio Ecclesiae*. Even if his *casus* belonged to academic debate and hardly responded to any possible actuality, he was consciously and intelligently presenting a logical "reason of the Church" and "reason of the faith" which the pope must understand as a fundamental principle of action in governing the Church. Again we see that "necessity knows no law" when the State and what it stands for are in danger. This was no nonmoral or cynical "reason," for God approved the defense of Church and faith; it was, therefore, in the mind of Gérard and his contemporaries, no violation of the moral law of God. But the papal authority was the greater for the practice of the "reason" of necessity and common utility of the Church and the faith and the salvation of the faithful.

Some twenty years later, Henry of Ghent confirmed this association of *ratio* and the papal authority as a constitutional principle of government. For, he said, necessity, reason, and utility permit the pope to modify details, but not the essential ecclesiastical *ordo*. The pope can create new dioceses but cannot destroy the episcopal system or change the established hierarchy of pope, prelates, and priests. *Ratio*, furthermore, in case of necessity, for the utility of the Church, permits the pope to transfer bishops.[56] In a word, the pope could not change the *status Ecclesiae*, but could make changes in detail that were

---

mundi occupantis, redimi posset in hoc casu. Et locum haberet illud Bernardi ad Eugenium .iii.⁰ li.⁰ [*De consideratione*, III, 4; *M.P.L.*, 182.769]: 'Ubi necessitas urget, excusabilis est dispensacio; ubi utilitas provocat, laudabilis est dispensacio. Utilitas, dico, communis, non propria. . . .' In predicto enim casu fieret commutacio in melius, non quidem singularis persone ratione amisse castitatis, sed utilitate rei publice ex fervore caritatis zelantis utilitatem communem et fidelium generalem salutem. Potest ergo papa dispensare cum tali coniugio de plenitudine potestatis et eam absolvere a voto et ab habitu, presertim unde eminet universalis ecclesie maxima utilitas et urgens ac evidens postulat necessitas . . . quia publica utilitas preferenda est private. . . . Non ergo bene intelligunt regulas ecclesiasticas, qui hoc negant causa necessitatis vel utilitatis fieri posse, quociens communis necessitas aut utilitas persuaserit." (These last words are from the *Decretum*, C. 7, q. 1, c. 35 Scias. See also the gloss of Joh. Teutonicus to this, ad v. *praeferenda est*.)

56 Lagarde, *Naissance de l'esprit laïque*, II, 206. In a separate study of the meaning of *status Ecclesiae*, I plan to show that the *ordo* ecclesiasticus was an essential part of the *status*. The sources are abundant. See above, n. 50, for an early source; and below, ch. IX, n. 26, on *status Ecclesiae illaesus*.

necessary for maintaining the "state of the Church." In cases of necessity, *casualiter* (so Innocent III and Innocent IV, meaning much more than incidentally or casually, for the *casus* was a vital concern of the pope and the Church), the *ratio status ecclesiae* was a part of and enhanced the *plenitudo potestatis*. No wonder that Huguccio had said that *ratione prelationis*, by reason of jurisdiction, the authority of the pope was greater than that of the Apostle.[57]

3. The Legists

We must now turn our attention to the legists—the glossators and commentators who wrote chiefly before the time of Bartolus, Baldus, and Lucas de Penna, for these great jurists of the fourteenth century generally accepted the "reason of State" developed by their predecessors. However much they owed to the older tradition, to John of Salisbury and to the canonists, the glossators naturally started with Ulpian's definition of the *ius publicum* as that law which regulates the *status rei Romanae*. This *status* they normally defined as the public welfare or utility of the *Respublica*, sometimes as the magistracy or supreme public authority necessary for administering the State for the common good, peace, and safety. Indeed, they so strongly emphasized the necessity of the prince and lesser magistrates for the end of the State that at times they anticipated the idea that the *status* is the *magistratus*, "L'état, c'est moi." "The power of the prince," said a decretist for them, "is a mundane necessity."[58] The result was that the public *status* or estate of the prince was becoming confused with the "state of the community," and finally with the State—another anticipation of some of the thought of Machiavelli and the modern age.

One kind of "reason of State" was the *ratio status* of the supreme public authority, the *ratio status regis* or *principis*. The

[57] On *casualiter* see McIlwain, *Growth of Political Thought*, pp. 232-234; Tierney, *Conciliar Theory*, p. 89; Brys, *De dispensatione*, p. 191 n. 4; Pacaut, *La théocratie*, pp. 146, 161f. (*casualiter* means "occasionellement"!); Wilks, *Problem of Sovereignty* (see Index, *s.v.* casual jurisdiction). For *ratio prelationis* see Kuttner, "Pope Lucius III," *Med. Studies . . . Gwynn*, pp. 424f.

[58] See below, ch. VII. For the quotation see the *Summa Parisiensis*, McLaughlin, to Dist. 10, c. 1: "Vis enim principis mundana necessitas est."

most important early example of it, to my knowledge, is in Richard Fitzneale's exaltation of the royal power of Henry II of England. Richard, treasurer under Henry II and Richard I, and author of the famous *Dialogus de scaccario* (*ca.* 1177), was the son of a bishop who also had been important in the royal government. If he was acquainted with the Canon law, he obviously knew a good deal of Roman law too—his treatise on the Exchequer echoes some ideas of the glossators about the imperial fisc and the powers of the emperor. His theory of kingship is therefore particularly interesting. Since the power of kings comes from God, he says, ecclesiastics should assist them above all in that abundance of worldly goods which is the concern of kings "by reason of their state"—*sui status ratione. Dignitates* make kings shine illustriously, but wealth adds to their power. Surely by "reason of state" (not State) Richard means the "reason" of the royal power or authority. The thought is similar, except for the addition of *ratio*, to that of a glossator of the same century who explained the *status* of the Roman Republic as the *magistratus* or *potencia*.[59] We shall now see how the same principle was stated as the *ratio jurisdictionis et gubernationis*, or *ratio principatus*—or, as the canonist Huguccio said, the *ratio prelationis* of the pope.

It appears in Johannes Bassianus, an important glossator at

[59] The text in *S.C.*, p. 200: "Oportet autem hiis [regibus] servire, non in conservandis tantum dignitatibus, per quas gloria regiae potestatis elucet, verum in mundanarum facultatum copiis, quae eos sui status ratione contingunt; illae enim illustrant, haec subveniunt. Porro mobilium copia, vel defectus, principum potestates humiliat vel exaltat." Now Richard praises Henry II. In Bk. I, ch. iv, on the powers of the Exchequer, Richard compares them with those of the Royal Curia; these powers derive not only from the great seal of the king, but also from those who preside in the Exchequer, because it is by their *solertia* that the "totius regni status indemnis servatur." And there (*illic*) sits the *capitalis Justicia* of the king, "primus post regem in regno ratione fori. . . ."

Equally important is this passage (II, x; *S.C.*, p. 234): the king, or his fisc (Exchequer), can seize the property of a creditor or usurer (*foenerator*) who has become rich by "enormously" injuring one of the king's vassals; this the fisc can do, even if the creditor had held the property for two years and more, "ratione publicae potestatis."

As for the glosses, they are the following, to *D.* 1, 1, 1, 2 ad v. *statum* (rei Romanae): "Veluti magistratus in civitate" (in MS Vat. lat. 2511, fol. 3); "Id est, ad similitudinem, veluti magistratus in civitate" (Paris, BN, MS lat. 4458-A, fol. 1ᵛ); and "Id est, potencia" (London, Brit. Museum, MS Royal 11 C. III, fol. 1). See below, ch. VII, nn. 9-14.

Bologna in the late twelfth century. In his treatise on judicial procedure, he says that *ratione divini iuris* the pope while engaged in *sacra* cannot be summoned or sued—on the spiritual side divine law coincides with public law, the spiritual function of the pope with his public *status*. The *ratio humani iuris* includes both the "reason of the public *honor*," or "public necessity," and the "reason of private (utility or law)." Now, it is by "reason of the public honor" and "public necessity," hence by reason of the public law and the government (*honor*), that no one can summon (to court to respond to suits) a magistrate who has *imperium*, with powers of coercion. Johannes lists consuls, prefects, praetors, and the like, that is, *illustres*, as magistrates who cannot be sued while in office. In another place he says that "superior magistrates cannot be brought to judgment for any cause," and refers to Ulpian, *D.* 2, 4, 2. He repeats that because of the public law pertaining to their office, magistrates who have *imperium*, the emperor and other high dignitaries (prefect, consul, and praetor), cannot be summoned. Nor can these and others be brought to court while engaged in any business that is for "common necessity" (the harvest and the vintage), for "public necessity" (war, solemn and unexpected or extraordinary holidays), or for private necessity (marriages and funerals; here public and private rights are joined, for marriage and the burial of the dead are also for the public welfare).[60] For

---

[60] *Libellus de ordine iudiciorum*, in *Scripta anecdota Glossatorum*, II, 222, 227, 230: (97) "Ratione divine iuris" the pope cannot be summoned "dum sacra facit"; (98) "Ratione humani iuris, alias *ratione honoris publici vel publice necessitatis*, alias ratione privati . . ."; (99) "*Honoris publice ratione* non vocas magistratum qui habet imperium et qui potest cohercere aliquem et iubere in carcerem deduci, ut consulem, prefectum, pretorem, et consimiles, idest illustres . . ."; (178) "Item magistratus superiores non sunt in iudicio pro aliqua causa vocandi. . ." *D.* 2, 4, 2; 47, 10, 32. Certain persons, finally, are not to be summoned "causa humani sive publici iuris, ut in magistratibus habentibus imperium ut imperator, prefectus, consul et pretor, dum sunt in magistratu . . . aut gratia negotiorum sive necessitatis communis, ut messim et vindemmiarum; sive causa publice necessitatis ut belli et feriarum solemnium vel repentinarum, sive private necessitatis, ut nuptiarum et funeris. . . ." (Italics are mine.)

On these *necessitates*, both public and common, see for an elaboration, but without the word *ratio*, Azo, *Summa Codicis*, Lyons, 1564, to *C.* 3, 12 De feriis; cf. *D.* 2, 12.

On *honor* as the *administratio*, magistracy, or government, see *D.* 50, 4, 14, and below, ch. VIII, nn. 28, 69-75.

Johannes Bassianus, then, "reason of State" included the "reason" of the public authority.

The mention of the emperor was hardly necessary. The legists assumed that he was *legibus solutus* (*D.* 1, 3, 31) with respect to any judicial process. Bracton agreed, for the king (like the emperor) was under no man, and no writ ran against him.[61] Canonists, too, concluded that no one could bring suit against prince or pope. Some held, however, that if the pope erred against the faith he could be brought before a general council; and the advisers of Philip the Fair made clever use of the idea of appeal in the name of France from pope to council. In secular States another kind of appeal was beginning to appear, the appeal from king poorly informed to king better informed. But this kind of appeal was extra-judicial. As for regular procedures, it was sacrilege to dispute or challenge the decisions or sentences of the prince as supreme judge and lawgiver.[62] Any "transgression of the public law," said a decretist, "is sacrilege"; and it is sacrilegious and therefore contrary to the public law either to dispute the judgment of the prince or to fail in reverence for laws and canons.[63] After all, the power of the prince was for the "state of the realm," the public welfare, and this included justice for all his subjects; and the lawyers were developing the theory that according to the public law he must give every man a fair hearing or trial.[64] How could he be the final source of justice if he were justiciable in his own court?

If no one could bring suit against him, how could any unjust

61 *De legibus* (ed. Woodbine), II, 3.

62 See in general Kantorowicz, *King's Two Bodies*, pp. 143-172 on Bracton; p. 158 n. 209 on the sacrilege of disputing the royal power; also Fritz Schulz, "Bracton on Kingship," *E.H.R.*, LX (1945), 136-176. The source is *C.* 9, 29, 2: "Disputare de principali iudicio non oportet: sacrilegii enim instar est dubitare, an is dignus sit, quem elegerit imperator." The canonists naturally said the same about the power of the pope: "Nolo disputare de plenitudine potestatis"— so Hostiensis; above, ch. I, n. 181.

63 *Glos. ord.* of Joh. Teutonicus to *Decretum*, C. 17, q. 4, c. 3 Sacrilegium. He refers to Dist. 1, c. 11 Ius publicum, which is the old statement that public law deals with *sacra*, magistrates, and priests.

64 A separate study should be devoted to fair trial in relation to *quod omnes tangit* as a principle both of the public law and of the natural law which here participates in the public; already partly done in my "Romano-Canonical Maxim," *Traditio*, IV, 197-251; cf. above, n. 34, and ch. IV; Congar, "Quod omnes tangit," *Rev. hist. dr. fr. étr.*, XXXVI, 210-259, does not treat this subject.

decision of the king be remedied? By and large, the remedy lay in the king's grace, his duty to be kind and just of his own free will (though by God's command), and in the right of petitioning him for his gracious help—an extra-judicial procedure which developed everywhere. As Bracton said, reflecting an age-old idea about kingship as well as the Roman law on the duty of the emperor, the king must be ready to give justice whenever it was sought from him. Since no writ ran against him, the procedure of seeking justice was that of the petition asking him to correct his judgment, decision, or act.[65] The Neapolitan jurist, Andrew of Isernia (†1316), specifically included the right of petitioning in the public law and its *ratio*. On the *constitutio* of Roger II, which declared that it was sacrilege "disputare de Regis judicio," he held that if the king did anything "minus bene," one could, "by reason of the common good," supplicate him to amend it. Petitioning was the proper procedure whenever the business was of interest to the public utility—appeals from the judgment of the king were out of the question.[66] The public law, then, gave the king his supreme authority, his public *status*; but it also protected his subjects in their private rights, for the reason of the common good was a part of a general reason of the public welfare of the State.

But as we observed in connection with John of Salisbury's theory of the royal authority and "reason of State," the question still remained: if the king persisted in acts of tyranny by refusing justice to his subjects, if he used expediency rather than good "reason of State," what was the remedy? Tyrannicide, the right of rebellion, or punishment ultimately inflicted by God? This is not the place to discuss the problem. But one steady remedy, according to the Roman as well as Germanic and feudal

---

[65] *De legibus* (ed. Woodbine), II, 3.

[66] *Peregrina lectura super Constitutionibus et Glossis Regni Siciliae* (in *Liber Augustalis*, or *Const. Regni Sicil.*, ed. Ant. Cervone; Naples, 1773), p. 15, to I, 4 *Disputare*: ". . . Sed si Rex faceret aliquid minus bene: ratione communis boni posset supplicari Regi, ut emendet, vel si sua hoc interesset, et publicae utilitati, sic possent agere. . . . Ubi non potest appellari, potest supplicari Regi. . . ." I have not examined other jurists of the thirteenth century on the petition with respect to the *ratio* of the common good or public welfare. See the text of Roger II's *constitutio* in Huillard-Bréholles, *Hist. Dipl. Frid. II*, IV, i (*Const. Regni Siciliae*), 9; it is also sacrilege to dispute the kings *consilia, institutiones,* and appointments. Cf. above, n. 62.

law and custom, was the theory and practice of counsel. Every prince should, on all important matters, consult with his counsellors and ask for their *consilium*. This was the principle whether the counsellors were the Roman *proceres sacri palatii*, feudal barons and prelates, or royal judges and jurists, or all these and more in an assembly. Whether the king received counsel in his own council or in a parliament, his interpretation of a case of necessity and his decision as to what was the "right reason" to employ *ratione publicae utilitatis* was normally limited by his duty to seek advice. To be sure, the king who ably asserted his authority could usually obtain the counsel he desired. Nonetheless, royal counsellors sometimes participated intelligently in discussions involving the use of "reason of State"— and sometimes they were learned in principles of the Roman public law. But if the king was suspected of accepting the evil or wrong counsel of favorites, the great men of the realm on occasion tried to gain control of the royal council in order to make the king accept their own reasoning about public affairs. In any event, unlike Machiavelli's prince, the medieval ruler found it difficult to interpret the public law by himself and to decide arbitrarily what was necessary for the security of people and realm.[67]

Returning now to the legists, let us look at another part of their theory of a public *ratio*. The Roman public law, of course, protected soldiers and the whole military establishment. Quite

[67] On counsel in the Roman Empire see Crook, *Consilium principis. Imperial Councils and Counsellors from Augustus to Diocletian*; and *C.* 1, 14, 2 and 8 for the late Roman Empire. Of course, Tacitus on Germanic consultation of the *principes* and of *omnes* is well known; well known, too, is the fact of counsel in Anglo-Saxon England and in other early medieval kingdoms, and in the feudal *curia* of great lords and kings. Odofredo, the great Bolognese legist of the mid-thirteenth century, well illustrates the legal theory of counsel that prevailed not only for the emperor but for kings and popes. In his *Lectura* on the *Codex* (Lyons, 1552), II, 39f., to *C.* 6, 23, 21 Hac consultissima, he says: ". . . 'Hac consultissima,' id est, hac lege facta cum magna deliberatione, et animo pensato. . . . Unde colligitur hic, quod imperator debet omnia facere cum magna deliberatione, et ad hoc facit supra, de le. et con. l. humanum [*C.* 1, 14, 8]. Sic et alia omnia debent fieri cum consilio. . . ." Cf. below, ch. VIII, § 2.

Moreover, even if emperor, pope, or king was said "omnia iura in scrinio pectoris sui habere," it was understood that he must consult with his expert counsellors in order really to know the law in detail and interpret it. See below, ch. VII, nn. 64, 71.

naturally, the legists, like the canonists, assumed that a principal responsibility of king or prince was the use of the army for the defense of realm or Empire. Consequently, said Johannes Bassianus, a military *expeditio* led by the prince is for the *ratio utilitatis publicae*; and for the same *ratio* a soldier who "necessarily" goes on a campaign cannot be summoned to court to respond to a suit.[68]

If the public law dealt with the military establishment, it was because it was concerned with the defense of the *patria*. Now the local *patria* within the *patria communis* of the sovereign State enjoyed its own if subordinate public welfare (just as today within the United States there is a public welfare of every local community from incorporated town to any of the fifty states in the Union). Each local *patria* should therefore be able to maintain itself. But normally, the Roman emperors declared, no new tax could be levied by a local *patria*, whether city or province (*C.* 4, 62, 1-3). If, however, the locality became so poor that it needed an extraordinary *auxilium*, and the *praeses* after deciding that the tax was for the common utility wrote to the emperor, the emperor should finally decide whether the alleged *ratio* was sufficient (*C.* 4, 62, 1). Thus, no new local tax was lawful without the consent of the prince or sovereign ruler. (So also in the Canon law of the thirteenth century—the clergy of a city or kingdom could not grant an extraordinary aid to the secular government, even for a just war of defense, without first obtaining the consent of the pope.)[69] Azo, commenting on these imperial laws, said that the prince, on receiving the report of the head of the province on the *ratio tenuitatis et paupertatis patriae*, should decide whether the *ratio patriae* should be accepted. While *ratio* can mean an accounting or reckoning, in the context it comes to the same thing as "reason" or "necessity."

"Reason" of local *patria* was, of course, subordinate to "rea-

---

[68] *Libellus*, in *Scripta Anec. Glos.*, II, 222, 108: "Ratione utilitatis publice non est vocandus qui necesse habet in expeditionem proficisci vel esse. . . ." On the legists and the defense of the *patria*, again my "Two Notes on Nationalism," *Trad.*, IX, 284-296; below, ch. X, nn. 17-63.

[69] This is well known, but see my "Plena potestas, etc.," *Trad.*, I, 400; also "Two Notes on Nationalism," *Trad.*, IX, 285; above, ch. III, n. 190, and below, ch. X, n. 18.

son" of *patria communis*. The necessity of the sovereign king-dom, when the king could declare a just war of defense, was a higher "reason" than that of any locality or individual. By the late twelfth century decretists were saying that *ratio rei*, that is, the "reason" of the defense of the *patria* (= *regnum*), made a war just if the prince authorized it. Azo and other legists, of course, accepted this theory and held that the just war was a case of necessity that permitted the prince to levy extraordinary taxes and expropriate private property.[70] But how soon did they speak of *ratio necessitatis* or *ratio publicae utilitatis*? Johannes Bassianus virtually did so in equating the *expeditio* and *ratio utilitatis publicae*; yet, I have found no example of the usage for this purpose in the *Glossa ordinaria* of Accursius. At the end of the thirteenth century, however, Pierre Dubois and Pierre de Belleperche no doubt were not the first to talk about the right of the king of France to demand extraordinary subsidies and expropriate *ratione necessitatis defensionis*, or for a proved (*probabilis*) *ratio* and *causa*.[71]

In a case involving feudal law and custom, Azo stated the equivalent in presenting arguments for a king's use of the "rea-son of the public welfare" to secure peace. In 1199 King Philip Augustus had become the guardian of the young Arthur of Brit-tany; he became the liege-lord of Arthur, who thus was to be his immediate vassal and hold Brittany as a fief directly from the French monarch. But in 1200, because of his own difficul-ties, Philip concluded the treaty of Goulet with King John of England. By this treaty Philip agreed that John should be the liege-lord of Arthur and Brittany. Arthur therefore became merely a sub-vassal of the king of France, who retained only his general suzerainty over Brittany. In a word, Arthur was to be John's *homo*, not Philip's. This was contrary to what Arthur and his mother, Constance, wanted; and indeed the rights of

---

[70] *Summa Codicis*, 122ᵛ c. 2, no. 2: "Decreto autem principis posset institui novum vectigal . . . maxime ratione tenuitatis et paupertatis patrie, que debet vectigalia: et hoc ipsum debet allegare pauper patria praesidi provinciae, qui re diligenter inspecta, et utilitatem communem intuitus, scribat principi, quae reperit: et princeps aestimabit an et quatenus ratio patriae sit habenda . . ."; for canonists on this, *Trad.*, IX, 282-285, and below, ch. X, nn. 9-18.

[71] Below, nn. 96-98.

Arthur were sacrificed. The treaty, then, presented a legal question to Azo—a question related to the feudal law in the *Libri Feudorum*, which probably had little influence in England and France. (Whether someone in France or England sent a copy of the treaty to Azo for his opinion, I cannot say.) The question was whether a king can indeed alienate his liege-lordship over a vassal and transfer it to another. On the affirmative side, Azo says, "today every king seems to have the same power in his land as the emperor; therefore, he can do as he pleases" (the king is emperor in his own realm, and what pleases him has the force of law!).[72] *Item*, he can do this *ratione publicae utilitatis*, because perhaps he surrendered his rights over the vassal in order to make peace with King John. "Many things are lawful by reason of the public utility!" (As in the Roman law, waging war to win peace and making treaties to secure it were a part of the public law of the State as well as "international" law.)[73]

On the negative side, Azo argues that the king cannot alienate the fief of any vassal who does not consent, for such an act would injure the vassal's dignity and "fame," not to mention his rights in the fief itself. Indeed, he accepts this as his *solutio* and thus shows that the feudal law protecting the private rights of vassals was in this case, at least, more important than the new claims of "reason of State."[74] But fundamentally Azo holds that here the king of France was injuring his vassals' rights without of-

[72] On Azo and the theory of the king as emperor see also below, ch. x, n. 70; of course, Azo has in mind, besides the *rex imperator* argument, the *lex regia*, *D*. 1, 4, 1 and *Inst*. 1, 2, 6. On the historical background and the Treaty of Goulet see Powicke, *The Loss of Normandy*, p. 200.

[73] *D*. 2, 14 De pactis 5 Conventionum—that public *conventiones* are made for peace, as Ulpian says, "quotiens inter se duces belli quaedam paciscuntur." Here the meaning is more that of truces made by generals according to the *ius gentium*. But the glossators related the passage also to treaties of peace and public law: an early gl. to *D*. 2, 14, 5, 1 ad v. *pacem*: "Quasi ad publicam utilitatem"; in MS Vat. lat. 1405, fol. 17. As Odofredo said, "cum pax sit utilitas publica," and refers to *D*. 2, 14, 5; *Glossa super pace Constantie*, in Paris, BN, MS lat. 5414.A, fol. 11ᵛ.

[74] The *quaestio* is edited by E. Landsberg, *Die Quaestiones des Azo*, p. 86f.; I quote from the Paris, BN, MS lat. 4609, fol. 131ᵛ: "Item quilibet rex hodie videtur eandem potestatem habere in terra sua quam imperator; ergo potest facere quod sibi placet. . . . Item ratione publice utilitatis potuit, quia forte hoc fecit, ut faceret pacem cum alio. Multa autem licita sunt ratione publice utilitatis. . . ."

fering compensation in equal rights, since the vassal could claim that King John was not as illustrious a lord as Philip. Philip, therefore, had no right to transfer his suzerain right in the fief to John, because such a transfer was injurious to the right of Arthur to be the vassal of the king of France.[75] The "reason of public utility" in peace between the two kings was not above the "reason of the public utility" in the maintenance of the rights of vassals. Perhaps Azo had in mind the idea that in this case the agreement of the kings, though necessary for peace, could have been made without injuring private rights. Whatever he meant, he understood the theory that kings had the right to use the "reason" of peace and the public welfare of the State. But "reason of State" should not unnecessarily injure private rights without the consent of the interested parties. At least, his very discussion of the question reveals that the king of France and his counsellors may have advanced the plea of the *ratio publicae utilitatis* of the realm in order to excuse the injury to Arthur and give satisfaction to John of England.

Still other aspects of the *ratio publicae utilitatis* are to be found in the *Glossa ordinaria* of Accursius to the *Corpus juris civilis* (*ca.* 1230). On the claim of the imperial fisc to half of any treasure found in public or "fiscal" places (*D.* 49, 14, 3, 10), a glossator remarks that although this is contrary to common equity, it is lawful by reason of the authority of the emperor and by reason of the public utility, "cuius ratione quandoque derogatur aequitate communi." (Besides, Caesar is the fisc and all things belong to Caesar!)[76] So, too, an imperial rescript, even when it is contrary to natural law or natural right, is valid *ratione publicae utilitatis.*[77]

---

[75] "Queritur an dominus rex Franciae possit vassallum suum alii minori vel pari ipsi vassallo delegare vel in vassallum dare vel permutare . . . Contra. Pro vassallo faciunt, quia interest eius habere illustratiorem dominum. . . . Ergo eius non debet diminui. . . . Item diminutio dignitatum est dominutio fame. . . . Item interest suam dignitatem non diminui. . . . Item non licet semper alicui ius suum transferre in alium. . . "; MS lat. 4609, fol. 131ᵛ.

[76] *Glos. ord.* to *D.* 49, 14, 3, 10, ad v. *fisco vindicaretur.* All things belong to Caesar not only in this sense, but also *ratione jurisdictionis*; see below, n. 87.

[77] *Glos. ord.* to *C.* 1, 22, 6: the emperor declares that no rescript, and no *pragmatica sanctio*, is valid if it is contrary to *ius generale* or to the *utilitas publica*. On the words *generali iuri*, the glossator says first that this means that no rescript can go against the "ius Dei vel evangeliorum." But if it is contrary

Related to this is the justification of privileges in terms of the reason of the public welfare. Ulpian, after stating that the people had conferred upon the prince his *imperium, potestas,* and legislative authority, explained that an imperial *lex* or *constitutio* which was a special privilege for a meritorious person, did not extend to any other person or case; it was not a general law applicable in similar cases (*D.* 1, 4, 1). On this, a glossator comments that no privilege is valid if it violates natural, human, and "international" law; that is, a privilege granted to one man is not lawful if it injures the legal rights of others, or if it authorizes what is contrary to fundamental laws. Nonetheless, if the privilege is given *ratione publicae utilitatis,* it is valid even if it violates those laws which protect private rights in property! How could this be possible? The glossator refers to *D.* 11, 7, 12, an opinion of Ulpian, that a man had the right by public law to go through a neighbor's property or land in order to have access to the tomb where he could bury his dead. (Cemeteries and tombs were "religious" places, *sacra,* and therefore subjects of public law; *D.* 1, 1, 1, 2 and *D.* 11, 7, 43.) If passage was refused, he could bring an extraordinary action against his neighbor by asking the local judge to give him an easement or right of way that would not seriously damage the property, and by paying a just price. The reason for this reference, therefore, is that the legist was making the point that a special right that was given to one man and not to all was lawful for the reason of the public utility of burying the dead, even when it was apparently a violation of the law which protected rights in property. Moreover, a special privilege for one person, if it was for the public welfare, was lawful if it did not seriously injure the private rights of others.[78]

The special privilege, immunity, or franchise is always a prob-

---

to that *ius humanum* which reflects the *ius naturale* or the *ius gentium* (e.g., laws which protect property rights), again it is not valid. Yet, it is none the less valid, even if against private rights in property, *ratione publicae utilitatis.* This opinion is similar to that on privileges, below, n. 78.

[78] *Glos. ord.* to *D.* 1, 4, 1, 1 ad v. *non egreditur:* the law that a *lex* for one person is not valid when it is applied to a different person "fallit . . . ratione publicae utilitatis, ut infra de reli. et sumpt. fu. l. si quis sepulchrum. non tamen [*D.* 11, 7, 12]." (For decretists' opinions, see above, n. 52.)

lem for the public welfare and the right of State. This was particularly true in the age of feudalism and the beginnings of modern States. How could a feudal kingdom be a State when great lords enjoyed special immunities from the ordinary powers of the central government? This again is not the place to discuss the problem. But the glossator was approaching the solution of other legists and canonists. The general theory was that privileges for individuals were useful to all when they were granted to men who merited them because they used them in the service of the common and public welfare of the State.[79] Thus, a great franchise or liberty in England, such as the palatine earldom of Chester, was in theory no longer a feudal immunity in the old sense; rather, it was a delegation of the royal jurisdiction for the administration of justice in a part of the realm, and the earl remained subject ultimately to the king's power and right to do justice and maintain the peace.[80] The supreme public rights of jurisdiction and securing peace, Bracton said, "belong to no man save only the crown and the royal dignity."[81] In fact, according to the Roman law, privileges carried no immunity from public necessities. As a canonist said, not even the *privilegium dignitatis* should weaken the public utility.[82] And the legists held that no liberties, privileges, or favors should injure the State. If by "reason of office and the public welfare" (so a glossator, recalling perhaps Johannes Bassianus' *ratio honoris* or "reason" of the magistracy) certain men

---

[79] E.g., the *Summa Parisiensis* (*ca.* 1160) to *Decretum*, Dist. 4, c. 2, ad v. *nullo privato*: ". . . Vel possumus dicere quod privilegia singulorum omnibus sunt utilia quia ibi aliquis remuneratur merito quod utile est omnibus exemplo"; ed. McLaughlin, p. 4.

[80] Helen N. Cam, "The Evolution of the Mediaeval English Franchise," *Speculum*, XXXII (1957), 427-442; Constance M. Fraser has reached a similar conclusion, that the bishops of Durham were subordinate to royal policy and authority, "Prerogative and the Bishops of Durham, 1267-1376," *E.H.R.*, LXXIV (1959), 467-476. In France the apanage, too, in theory was no immunity; see Jean Le Foyer, "Deux problèmes de la formation de la théorie de l'apanage en France," *Tijdschrift v. Rechtsgeschiedenis*, XIII (1934), 1-17.

[81] Cam, *Speculum*, XXXII, 440.

[82] *Glos. ord.* of Joh. Teutonicus, to *Decretum* C. 25, q. 1, c. 14 (cf. *Codex*, 1, 19, 3 and 7): "Nec damnosa fisco, ut si aliquis per privilegium velit se excusare ab eo, quod est damnosum iuri communi. Nam dicit lex, quod omnes necessitatibus publicis debent obedire sine dignitatis privilegio ut C. lib. xi. de navi. non excu. l. multi [*C.* 11, 4, 1]. Nec praetextu privilegii publica debet vacillare utilitas . . . C. de sacrosan. eccle. l. iubemus nulli [*C.* 1, 2, 10]."

were excused from labor on such public works as aqueducts and the repair of city walls, this was no doubt because their official duties as well as *dignitas* were necessary for the higher public welfare of the State as a whole.[83] But of course, such great privileges as franchises did continue to obstruct the formation of the State, and increasingly so from the fourteenth century on. Nonetheless, the theory was already current in the public law that the public authority of the king and the *status regni* should not be harmed by the privileged.[84]

In theory, again, delegation was replacing immunity because by public law the sovereign authority should be wholly in the hands of the prince or king who was "emperor in his own realm." The king could delegate, but not alienate, those *iura regis et regni* which were considered to be indispensable for the public welfare; no alienation of the royal powers of legislation and jurisdiction was lawful. In other words the king should hold and keep in his hands all those powers that were essential to the maintenance of the *status regni*.[85] If he was not the State, the public business of governing it with justice for all and of defending it and preserving law and order, belonged to him. He was not the State, but the State belonged to him to govern. Justinian had said that the *Respublica* was the emperor's, that God gave him the *Imperium* to rule by waging war successfully,

[83] *Glos. ord.* to *C.* 8, 12, 6 Ad portus, ad v. *privilegiis*: ". . . Solu. illi non excusantur ratione dignitatis, sed officii et publicae utilitatis."

[84] The literature on the subject is abundant, esp. the *Glos. ord.* and the Commentators on *C.* 11, 4, 1.

[85] On the inalienability of the king's public powers of jurisdiction the best treatment is now that in Riesenberg, *Inalienability of Sovereignty.* Cf. below, ch. IX. Bracton, *De legibus* (Woodbine, II, 166), put it very well: the king "habet enim omnia iura in manu sua quae ad coronam et laicalem pertinent potestatem et materialem gladium qui pertinet ad regni gubernaculum"—all public *iura*, that is, for maintaining law and order and defending the realm.

About 1245, the canonist, Johannes de Deo had already said almost the same thing for any independent prince or king: "Item de dispensatione principum qui non habent alium principem super se, nisi papam loco dei. Et licet omnia sunt principis, quia per principes et reges deus distribuit humano generi omnia . . . tamen sic est intelligendum, scilicet, quod sint omnia in manu eius quo ad tuitionem et defensionem, ut xxiii. q.v. regum officium [c. 22]"; *Libellus dispensationum*, in MS Casanatense 108, fol. 297. On the origin of *omnia in manu* see Kantorowicz, *King's Two Bodies*, p. 153 n. 192; on Joh. de Deo, Schulte, *Quellen*, II, 94-107, and A. D. de Sousa Costa, *Um mestre portugues em Bolonha no seculo XIII, Joao de Deus: Vida e obras*, pp. 101-103; and Kuttner, "Pope Lucius III," *Med. Studies . . . Gwynn*, p. 429 n. 27, p. 430 n. 90.

by decorating it with peace, and by maintaining the *status Reipublicae*.[86] The emperor was the *dominus mundi*, said a classical jurisconsult (*D.* 14, 2, 9). Was the prince, then, or the king in his realm, literally the owner of the State and everything in it as his private property? Not at all, said the glossators (except Martinus) and commentators. In one sense only did the empire belong to the prince: it was his by reason of his public authority, which should be exercised for all subjects and for the public welfare by means of his jurisdiction and government. According to an early gloss to *C.* 7, 37, 3 Bene a Zenone, all things belonged to the prince by way of his jurisdiction, for his *jurisdictio* existed *ratione delicti* and *ratione publicae utilitatis*. In other words, as Jacobus de Arena put it, the prince possessed the *Respublica* because the *ratio gubernationis* was his; all private property was his *ratione jurisdictionis* (not by reason of any actual ownership); he was the "lord of the world" *ratione jurisdictionis et gubernationis*. This "reason of jurisdiction" gave the prince no right to anyone's property except by judicial process, when the public utility gave him just cause for taking it (but with compensation to the owner).[87]

Bracton used different words to express the same idea: to the king and crown belonged the supreme powers of jurisdiction

[86] Introductory *constitutiones* to the *Digest*, "Omnem rei publicae nostrae" and "Deo Auctore," in Mommsen-Krueger, eds., *Corpus Iuris Civilis*, I, 10 and 8.

[87] MS Vat. Pal. lat. 763, fol. 113: ". . . vel omnia sunt iurisdictione . . . vel ratione delicti. . . . Item ratione publice utilitatis. . . ." See also the *Glos ord.* to *C.* 1, 22, 6 (cf. above, n. 77), *C.* 7, 37, 3 and *D.* 14, 2, 9. To the words of Justinian, above, to n. 86, Accursius says: "Et quod hic dicit 'Omnem totius reipublicae nostrae,' id est totius imperii, quod est suum, et res in eo contentae, ratione iurisdictionis vel protectionis. . . ." To *D.* 40, 11, 5, a gloss reads: "Non ergo potest princeps rem privati vendere eo invito . . . nisi ob publicam utilitatem." Obviously, Jacobus develops the idea in these glosses, *Commentarii in universum ius civile* (Lyons, 1541), 61, to *Dig. Vet.*, Justinian's "Omnem rei publicae": "gubernande: vel id est nostre gubernationi commisse, et sic nostre ratione gubernationis . . ."; the emperor does not own the *res singulae* of individuals: "Sunt autem eius ratione iurisdictionis, et sic loquitur C. de quadri. prescrip. l. fin. [*D.* 7, 37, 3] . . . ; et quod dicitur C. ad le. rho. de iactu. l. deprecatio [*D.* (not *C.*) 14, 2, 9], dicitur 'ego quidem dominus mundi,' scilicet ratione iurisdictionis et gubernationis"; Jacobus now discusses jurisdiction and taking private owners' property. Cf. above, n. 76.

Later, Matthaeus de Afflictis spoke of Frederick II's words on giving security to his subjects as a part of the power of the emperor, who is called "Deus totius mundi, scilicet ratione iurisdictionis et protectionis"; E. Kantorowicz, "Invocatio nominis imperatoris," *Boll. Centro Studi Filol. Ling. Sicil.*, III (1955), 6.

and government.[88] He might well have said that the king held in his hands not only *omnia iura* but the kingdom itself *ratione jurisdictionis et gubernationis*. The king, aided by counsel, possessed the supreme public right and power to decide and to do what was for the public welfare of the realm in administering law and justice and in defending the *patria*. Jacobus de Arena saw clearly that the essence of "reason of State" was the "reason" of government. This *ratio* belonged to the constituted authority. Again we can see the connection between the *ratio gubernationis*, the *ratio status regis*, and the *ratio status regni*. Thomas Aquinas saw it too.[89]

The *ratio publicae utilitatis* that was in the hands of the government naturally included the normal protection of private law and private rights, particularly those that were also of public interest. We have noted that although the classical jurisconsults and the Roman emperors treated marriage and dowries as principally a subject of private law, they held that the public law was concerned. For marriage was, of course, recognized as an institution that was necessary for the existence of the State. The dowry was of public interest because it was important in the law on marriage. As Pomponius said, "it is above all necessary that women be dowered for the procreation of offspring and filling the city with children"; and it was a function of public law to protect rights in dowry.[90] A glossator stated the principle more concisely: the dowry interested the Republic as well as women. Here, in fact, the *ratio* of private utility, he added, was in concordance with the *ratio publicae (utilitatis)*; but when they did not coincide, the reason of the public utility was preferred.[91] In some instances, then, public and private "reason," like public and private law, complemented each other. It was a commonplace among the glossators (on *D.* 1, 1, 1, 2) that what di-

---

[88] *De legibus* (ed. Woodbine), II, 32, 166f.

[89] See below, to nn. 103-108.

[90] *D.* 24, 3, 1: ". . . nam et publice interest dotes mulieribus conservari, cum dotatas esse feminas ad subolem procreandam replendamque liberis civitatem maxime sit necessarium." The editors think that the words "ad subolem . . . civitatem" are Justinian's. See above, to n. 27.

[91] To *D.* 24, 3, 1 Dotium, ad v. *publice interest*: "quasi dicat, non solum mulierum, sed etiam rei publicae. . . . Item nota quod ratio privatae utilitatis concordat hic cum ratione publice, que etiam si discordent, praefertur publica."

rectly pertained to the public law and the public welfare pertained secondarily to private law and the interest of individuals; and what the private law dealt with pertained, if indirectly, to the public law and the State. Naturally, since the ruler by the public law had the power to make as well as interpret the private law, the public "reason of State" was superior to private law and private rights.

These developments raised the problem of the Church and the public interest of the State. How did the "reason of the public utility" affect the "reason of State" of the Church, which in its churches, ecclesiastics, and property was partly within the State? Already ancient, the rivalry of the claims of Church and State was now finding expression in the relatively new theories of public law. We must recall that legists and canonists agreed that in times of dire emergency or necessity Italian *civitates* and independent kingdoms had the right to demand extraordinary taxes (*auxilia*) of the clergy and churches in their territory. From 1215 on, the Canon law prescribed that the pope must approve before the clergy could consent. Boniface VIII, however, was forced to accept the supremacy of France and England in this, that if the danger to the State was so imminent and urgent that the king must act at once, the clergy should submit without waiting for authorization. Apart from emergencies, Italian communes had long expected churches to contribute toward the construction or repair of public works (e.g., roads and bridges) that were for the public health and safety. To what extent a commune legislated or made statutes in other ways that might affect ecclesiastics and their property rights demands a detailed study, but undoubtedly there was no intention of intervening in or changing fundamental rights, nor of interpreting the faith, unless heretics actually for a moment seized control of the community. No more than in a Catholic nation today, and no more than in the United States, where Church and State are separated, would *regnum* or commune in the thirteenth century plan to regulate doctrine or purely spiritual matters. Not even Marsiglio thought of the sovereignty of the State in terms of doctrinal change. Nonetheless, while not going so far, the communes and kingdoms were anticipating some of Marsiglio's secular spirit in their demand that churches serve the State. As Edward I said, in words that came from the Roman law, a serious danger that touched the *regnum* was common to all—clergy and laity alike; and the business of defense that touched all in common must be treated and approved in common—*quod omnes tangit*. Canonists and legists also stressed *communiter* for a business that concerned a corporate body as a whole and demanded action and measures in common when the danger to the State threatened king, community, and all members of the community, including the clergy. Philip the Fair, not only against Edward but against Boniface VIII, skillfully brought the same principle into play, all for the corporate *regnum* of France. Marsiglio knew and understood the maxim; and so did William of Ockham, who declared that the necessity of State in times of danger demanded the *caritas* of churchmen even if the poor were neglected. Love of the State was more demanding than love of one's brother and neighbor.[92]

Well before the fourteenth century, "reason of State," in terms of imminent and urgent danger (almost national emergency) and necessity, was adding additional threat to the universalism of the Church. Moreover, in the late Roman Empire the emperors had legislated for the protection or regulation of the clergy, churches, and their property. The Church did not object so long as such legislation was approved by the pope; and, of course, the papacy and the canonists held that those parts of the Roman law which were acceptable to the Church were a part of the Canon law. In brief, the prince as the defender and protector of the Church could make laws that were, according to papal interpretation, for the common good of the Church. For example, it was but natural that the Canon law should accept imperial laws against the alienation of properties belonging to churches. Over and over again, in discussing in what circumstances a bishop could alienate anything belonging to his church, the canonists referred to the Roman law. The legists

92 See in general Congar, "Quod omnes tangit," *Rev. hist. dr. fr. étr.*, XXXVI, 210-259; and my "Romano-Canonical Maxim," *Traditio*, IV, 197-251—also my "*Plena potestas*," *Traditio*, I, 397-403. As for *caritas* and the State, see my "Two Notes on Nationalism," *Traditio*, IX, 294f. See above, ch. III, nn. 181-198; IV in general, and below, ch. X, nn. 59, 63.

were well acquainted with these passages, as they were with the theory that *sacra* and priests were subjects of the public law and that churches and their properties were *respublicae*. Religion and religious institutions, indeed, were necessary for the public welfare of the Republic, for the *status Reipublicae*.

It was on this kind of legislation by the secular prince in favor of the Church that Jacobus de Belvisio (Giacomo Belviso, †1335) spoke of a *maior ratio pro re publica*. On the words of Justinian (*Auth.*, Coll. 2, 1, 9 Quia verosimile, 1 Oportet = *Nov.* 7, 9, 1, 1), that general laws for the common utility must prevail over special laws and privileges, Jacobus says that the emperor has jurisdiction in those property rights which are for the common utility of the Church. Since the Church and churches are *respublicae* and subjects of the public law, legislation and jurisdiction in their interest are for the common welfare. The public *iura* of the Church thus protected are superior to all private rights, for public rights must prevail when the *maior ratio* is *pro re publica*.[93] Now certainly, Jacobus did not envisage the use of the *maior ratio* of the public welfare against the Church, for priests and the faith were a public good that

---

[93] *Nov.* 7, 9, 1, 1: "Oportet enim ea quae communiter et generaliter et in omnium utilitatem sanciuntur, potius valere quam ea, quae circa aliquos studentur ad corruptionem communium agi legum." For legislation for the common utility of the republic, see, of course, *D.* 1, 1, 2; 1, 7; 3, 1; 4, 1 and 2. From Irnerius on, the glossators and commentators spoke of legislation for the common or public utility.

Jacobus says, *Summa Authenticarum*, p. 17, c. 2: "Et nota hic quod princeps iurisdi[c]tionem exercet etiam in spiritualibus communiter ut sunt pro communi utilitate ecclesie invente. sanciuntur ut prohibitio alienationis rerum immobilium ecclesiarum. . . . Nota secundo quod communis et publica utilitas preferenda est private. . . . Aut iura sunt varia et tunc prefertur publica, ut hic; aut sunt paria: et tunc etiam prefertur publica si maior est ratio pro re publica, alias secus. . . . Concurrunt publicum et privatum: et tunc prefertur utilitas privata si principaliter vult quis consulere ut sibi prosit et nulli noceat; . . . et est ratio, quia ordinata caritas a se ipso incipit. . . ." *Ordinata caritas*, love of oneself and one's children, which ordinarily comes before love of neighbor and of State, is naturally subordinate to the love of the State or common fatherland in times of danger. Love of self and children must then be a part of society and yield to the sacrifice of one's life if necessary in fighting for the *patria*. This is an accepted theory of *caritas* in legists, canonists, and scholastic philosophers; G. Post, "Two Notes on Nationalism," *Traditio*, IX, 283, 287f., 290, 294, 296; Lagarde, *Naissance de l'esprit laique*, II², 174-185; also on Thomas Aquinas, p. 78 n. 65; and Kantorowicz, *King's Two Bodies*, pp. 241-249. Besides the references in these places, see the *Glos. ord.* to *Decretum*, C. 7, q. 1, c. 35 Scias, ad v. *praeferenda est*; also above, nn. 78-82. See also below, ch. x, nn. 11, 26-38, 42, 54-58, 63.

coincided in part with that of the State. Nonetheless, this idea of secular legislation for the welfare of the Church within the State, when cities and realms were demanding that the property of churches and ecclesiastics serve their interests, contributed its influence to the extreme theory of Marsiglio, that except in purely spiritual matters the State should directly regulate and control the clergy in its territory. *Ratione Reipublicae* the king of a sovereign realm might decide not only to tax churches but demand complete obedience from the clergy and even interpret the faith—as Henry VIII was to do.

But the logical outcome of what was developing in the theory and practice of public law in the thirteenth century (of what Henry II had tried to do in the twelfth), is not our concern in this study. In the thirteenth century the doctrine of "reason of State" affected the universalism of the Church only with respect to those material possessions which owed something to the royal government in return for protection against a common enemy.

We have now seen that the early canonists and legists thought of "reason of government" and "reason of the public welfare" of the State as normal principles of the public law, but principles most obviously applicable to the necessity of extraordinary measures, such as levying taxes, in times of dire emergencies or dangers that threatened the *status regni*. It was largely from these theories of the public law that princes of the twelfth and thirteenth centuries acquired the habit of alleging the necessity of defending the State in order to justify war and extraordinary subsidies. In other ways, too, the necessity of the defense of the realm weakened feudal law and custom. Not only did the "reason of the public welfare" support the efforts of kings to overcome feudal immunities; some jurists held that it permitted a violation of the custom that only a knight could create knights. So in the *Siete Partidas* there is a reference to those who said that a king who is not a knight can nonetheless create knights for the defense of the realm, "per razon del reyno." But the Spanish jurists decided that in Castille only a knight could create knights.[94]

[94] Quoted by Berges, *Fürstenspiegel*, p. 92, from the *Siete Partidas*, ii, xxi, 11 and 2—"por razon del Reyno" in *Los codigos españoles*, ii, xxi, 11.

There is no need to continue to list the many instances of appeals to public necessity, the defense of the realm, and the public welfare. But a few examples of the use of *ratio* in this context in the late thirteenth and early fourteenth century will show how important it remained among the jurists. In England itself, if Bracton did not speak of *ratio* in relation to the public powers of the king, the author of *Fleta* asserted that the king should govern his people "perpetua racione."[95] In France, not only *ratio naturalis* but *ratio* and *necessitas* continued to sanction the right of the king to make extraordinary demands on his subjects, both lay and clerical. As Pierre Dubois said, the necessity of the defense of the realm knew no law. When, he continued, the king's normal income was insufficient, the king could in such a case of necessity levy extraordinary taxes on church property and ecclesiastics. Normally any lay taxation of the clergy was a mortal sin, for it was contrary to the "common canon and civil law." But when the *ius speciale* and *ratio* of the *evidens necessitas defensionis* demanded it, the king could, without sin, ask for a subsidy.[96]

Pierre de Belleperche, famous both as a legist and as one of the counsellors of Philip the Fair, unfortunately has left no report of what was said in meetings of the royal council.[97] Hence, we have no way of knowing whether king and counsellors talked about *ratio* and *necessitas* while planning how to deal with Edward I, Flanders, or Boniface VIII; nor can we ever know whether the king and his legal advisers were sincere or cynical in using arguments from the public law of the Church as well as the State. In his commentaries on the Roman law, however, Belleperche did understand *ratio* as a principle of public law.

---

95 *Fleta*, ed. H. G. Richardson and G. O. Sayles, ii, 2, in the *Prologus*.

96 *De recuperatione* (ed. Langlois, p. 116): ". . . tunc in casu necessitatis defensionis regni, que legem non habet, dominus rex, quatinus sibi deest ad commodam defensionem, exigere et capere poterit de bonis ecclesiasticarum personarum. . . ." This is contrary to the common civil and Canon law and is a mortal sin, "nisi subsit jus speciale cujus virtute et ratione capi potest." But the "evidens necessitas defensionis" is the *jus speciale* and *ratio*. The government of Louis IX understood *ratio* both in this sense and as the reason used in law and justice; Buisson, *König Ludwig IX*, pp. 242-248.

On "natural reason" see above to n. 43.

97 On the royal council and Philip IV's leadership, see the excellent study by Joseph R. Strayer, "Philip the Fair—A 'Constitutional' King," *A. H. R.*, LXII (1956), 18-32.

For *ratio probabilis* (demonstrable or evident "reason") and *causa* (necessity and utility) permit the king to violate the natural law itself if he needs to seize private property for his hungry soldiers. Furthermore, a *consuetudo* that is contrary to the natural law can be valid. For example, the custom of primogeniture in England and in Picardy is lawful because the *causa et ratio probabilis* of the defense of the country demands inheritance by the eldest son. Thus "reason of State," the right of the State to defend itself, was in effect a natural right which was superior to other natural rights.[98] We can sense in Pierre de Belleperche the influence of the theory that by the law of nature the safety of the State was a right which took precedence over private rights sanctioned by the same law. "Reason of State," then, in a dire emergency, was not a violation of the laws of nature and God.

Aegidius Romanus was no champion of the State in its relations with the Church. Yet he, too, believed that when *ratio* and *necessitas* concurred, a king, without waiting for the consent of the pope, could tax the clergy in his realm. The old combination of reason and necessity in Hugo of St. Victor, whom Aegidius quotes, had become an indispensable part of that general "reason of State" which kings and their counsellors were no doubt consciously using for the *status regis et regni*.[99]

[98] Pierre de Belleperche thus relates "reason of State" to the fundamental law of nature; his discussion is in his *Lectura aurea . . . super librum Institutionum*, fol. 42ᵛ-43, to *Inst.* 1, 2 Ius naturale: ". . . Iura naturalia immutabilia sunt. . . . Sed contraria naturalia mutari non possunt sine probabili ratione"; nor can the natural law be changed "sine causa." Therefore, "princeps non potest michi rem aufferre sine causa . . . sed cum causa probabili potest . . . : puta princeps ducit exercitum suum, milites esuriunt, in casu isto potest rem meam michi aufferre et militibus assignare . . ."; cf. above, n. 87. Furthermore, *consuetudo*, which is *ius civile* (Bracton had held that English customs were *leges*), can "beneficium iuris naturalis tollere" but not "sine causa." For example, the custom of primogeniture in England and Picardy, that the "primogenitus totum habeat," is valid "si fuerit introducta ex causa et ratione probabile, ut cum guerra moveretur expedit ut terra uni remaneat, ut terram defendat." For the *ius naturale, pub. utilitas*, and the right of expropriation, see also Odofredo to *C.* 1, 22, 6 (Lyons, 1552), p. 49, nos. 5-8. Pierre did not need to apply the right of primogeniture to the French monarchy; apanages took care of younger brothers and sons and in theory kept the *regnum* united (above, n. 80).

[99] *Tractatus quomodo reges et principes possunt possessiones et bona regni peculiaria ecclesiis elargiri* (*Opera*, I, 37ff.). I have consulted the work in the Paris, BN, MS lat. 6786, fols. 22-41ᵛ, esp. 35ᵛ-36. See also below, n. 136, and above, n. 31.

Of the many instances of such ideas in the jurists of the fourteenth century, whose works should be examined more carefully than I have done to appreciate their influence on Renaissance political thought, I offer two that I have noted in passing. If the "reason of the common and public good" is demonstrable (or evident: *probatur*), says Albericus de Rosciate, it is preferred to private reason. Indeed, the private reason or interest of private wealth is subordinate to, and finds its justification in, the public "reason of State": a statute which orders subjects to maintain their real property (*res immobiles*) is founded "super ratione publici et communis boni," for rich subjects can the better fulfill their obligations to the *civitas*. This was simply another way of putting the older theory, that by the public law the prince should always protect the wealth of his subjects for the common interest of the people and the Empire and should prevent the abuse of private property by the owners.[100] The great Neapolitan jurist, Lucas de Penna, who was influenced by John of Salisbury as well as the earlier legists, while naturally admitting that a prince is not bound by the law, held that he must always love equity and justice and take care of the *utilitas Reipublicae*. "But who can speak of the (arbitrary) will of the prince in public affairs, since in them he can not desire anything except what *lex* and equity and the *ratio communis utilitatis* demand?" *Iusta ratio* should be in all his statutes. If the king seems to be harsh or unjust in seizing private property, the *malum* must be endured when he so acts since it is *pro utilitate publica, ratione connexi boni*.[101]

4. THE SCHOLASTIC PHILOSOPHERS

So far, we have concentrated on the theories of "reason of State" which derived in large part from the revival of Canon and Roman law and from interpretations of the work of princes in bringing some order into feudalism. What was the contribu-

---

100 *Com. de statutis* (in *Tract. Univ. Juris*, II), 29ᵛ, no. 41.

101 *Com.*, p. 120, to *C.* 10, 26, 4 Nulli, no. 3: "Sed quis in negociis publicis loquetur de principis voluntate, cum in eis nil sibi velle liceat, nisi quod lex aut aequitas persuadet; aut ratio communis utilitatis inducit"; *iusta ratio*, etc.; also p. 622 to *C.* 11, 71, 5 Praedia, no. xxiiii; below, n. 138. The influence of John of Salisbury is evident.

tion of Aristotle? We must now turn our attention to the scholastic philosophers and theologians who after 1260 studied and commented on the *Politics*. The surprising fact is that despite the great contribution of the *Politics* to later medieval political theories, the Aristotelians, whether moderate or extreme, still owed much to the older tradition. In the twelfth century the State was already partly natural, in many respects approved by the law of nature.[102] The naturalness of the State, then, was not a sudden discovery made by Thomas Aquinas in Aristotle's statement that man is by nature a social and political animal. Nor was the "secularizing" of politics an invention of the extreme Aristotelians. In general, however, the Aristotelians added emphasis to the theory of the State as a natural, moral entity, and they made it the supreme end of human life on earth. "Reason of State," therefore, was strengthened as the principle of political action. Yet the ultimate authority of God and the fundamental law of nature remained as powerful restraints. Perhaps not even the extreme Aristotelians completely abandoned the ideal of a fundamental moral law; and if Marsiglio declared that he was interested only in the public law of the *civitas*, he did not say that the *pars principans* or even the sovereign body of citizens could violate either the eternal or the natural law.

But this is not the place to discuss the general trend. What doctrines of "reason of State" appear in a few leading scholastic philosophers and theologians who tried to combine the older tradition with Aristotle? Thomas Aquinas in his *Commentary* on the *Politics* shows at once that Renaissance "reason of State" may have owed something to him as well as to the canonists and legists and Hugo of St. Victor and John of Salisbury. For, Thomas says, the end or purpose of the perfect community (*civitas*) and its organization in order that men may have the necessities of life, is the *ratio civitatis*. Hence "reason of State" includes the public welfare of the citizens in enough material and other necessities sufficient for the good life. Naturally the *politia*, the *communicatio civium*, the government itself, as the

102 On nature and the State in the twelfth and early thirteenth century, see below, ch. XI. On "right reason" in Thomas' disciple, Ptolemy of Lucca, see Chroust, "Corporate Idea," *Rev. of Politics*, IX, 428; in Henry of Ghent, below, to nn. 118 and 121.

principal means to this end, exists *ratione civitatis*. "Reason of State," therefore, is not only the *raison d'être* of the State and its constitutional order but also the "reason of the city" or "reason" of its well being and safety. It is also the "reason" of good government, which should rule according to "diligent reason."[103] Since Thomas frequently equates the *politia* and the *status* (that is, the government is *lo stato*), one can say that his "reason of State," or "reason of the city," is the "reason" of the good life and safety of the community and its members.[104]

In other works of Thomas Aquinas "reason of State" is fundamentally the same as in the *Commentary* on the *Politics*. It is the reason, first, of the end of the natural community in the utility, the common good, safety, and peace of all in unity, the reason of the whole.[105] In the second place, it is the reason prudently used by the magistracy, "regulated reason" in legislation, jurisdiction, and the defense of the community; it is the *perfecta ratio regiminis*. This reason is, as Professor Alessandro Passerin d'Entrèves says, subject to the "assoluta supremazia dell'ordine naturale e razionale di giustizia, che pone un limite in-

---

103 Thomas Aquinas, *In libros Politicorum expositio*, ed. Spiazzi, p. 10, no. 31: "Est enim de ratione civitatis, quod in ea inveniantur omnia quae sufficiunt ad vitam humanam," including the *bene vivere*; p. 126, no. 364: "Cum enim communicatio civium, quae politia dicitur, sit de ratione civitatis"; p. 49, no. 160, I, 10: the prince should have a perfect moral virtue in directing his subjects, "et ideo habet officium rationis. . . . Et oportet quod ille qui principatur habeat rationem perfectam"; p. 129, no. 366, III 3: "Ad propriam enim virtutem uniuscuiusque pertinet, quod habeat diligentem rationem et curam de proprio officio, sicut gubernator de gubernatione . . ." and the good citizen is one "qui bene operatur ad conservationem politiae" for the "salus communitatis"—his proper political virtue is perfect "secundum prudentiam"; no. 369: this virtue is not in all good citizens, but in the prudent "rector politiae" (no. 370) for the "regimen civitatis"; p. 130, no. 376: "Nam proprie virtus principis est prudentia, quae est regitiva et gubernativa"; p. 137, no. 390: "rectae politiae" are those in which the "principes intendunt communem utilitatem . . . secundum iustitiam absolutam."

104 *Status* as the kind of polity or government and its public authority is treated below, ch. VII.

105 *De regimine principum*, I, 2, 15; no matter that the word *ratio* is not used here. In the *De regimine Judaeorum* (in A. P. d'Entrèves, *San Tommaso d'Aquino, Scritti Politici*, p. 47), Thomas says that the prince, in fighting for the common utility, can levy special taxes; he then adds that "similis ratio" justifies this in case of a new emergency, "vel pro honesto statu principis conservando," e.g., when an enemy invades the land. Here "reason of the common welfare" of the State may coincide with the *ratio status principis*, since the safety of prince and community is common to both. See also *Summa Theol.*, II^a 2^ae q. 58 art. 7.

valicabile alla sovranità dello stato."[106] Needless to say, then, "reason of State" in the "reason of government" is under the control of the eternal reason and law of God; it derives from the *ratio gubernationis rerum* by which God rules the universe.[107] Thomas does not seem to be as alert as succeeding scholastics to the problem of the possible victory of absolute sovereignty, in the hands of the prince who claims that he and his advisers can interpret and decide what is "right reason," over moral principles. He is familiar with the maxim, "Necessity knows no law," but assumes that it applies only in a dire emergency, when there is no time for consultation and interpretation. For example, the law ordering the closing of city gates in time of danger must be violated if citizens closely pursued by the enemy need to enter. Here, however, necessity that knows no letter of the law violates neither a moral law nor the public law, for the safety of the city is not endangered—unless, of course, the opening of the gates for refugees should let in the pursuers.[108]

Toward the end of the thirteenth century Pierre d'Auvergne, in his continuation of Thomas Aquinas' *Commentary* on the *Politics*, held that a citizen exists not for himself alone but for himself and the city and is subordinate to the good of the city. The very "reason of the part" derives from the "reason of the whole"; therefore, the "reason of the part" is to be sought in the "reason of the Republic." The end of the Republic is safety (*salus*) and survival (*permanentia*). (One recalls Accursius' statement, that the public law pertains to the "status rei publicae, ne pereat.")[109] This end is the good of the parts but is superior to them. He does not literally say "reason of State," but

---

[106] *San Tommaso d'Aquino, Scritti Politici*, p. xxxi. On *ratio regulata*, see *Summa Theol.*, 1ª 2ᵃᵉ q. 90 art. 1: reason is the rule and measure of human arts, aimed at achieving the end; the will of the prince in making law must be "aliqua ratione regulata"—only in this way does his will have the force of law. Again, art. 4, *lex* "is nothing other than a certain *rationis ordinatio* for the common good," promulgated by him who has the care of the community; and (q. 91 art. 1) *lex* is a certain "dictamen practicae rationis" in the prince who governs the perfect community. Finally, the "perfecta ratio regiminis" is the reason used by the prince in ruling the "perfect community of the city or kingdom," and this reason is controlled by prudence; IIª 2ᵃᵉ q. 50 art. 1.

[107] Chroust, "Corporate Idea," *Rev. of Politics*, IX, 429.

[108] *Summa Theol.*, 1ª 2ᵃᵉ q. 96 art. 6.

[109] *Glos. ord.* to *D.* 1, 1, 1, 2, on the famous definition of public law by Ulpian.

it is the same thing in different words, "reason of the republic," or reason of the public welfare of all citizens in common. It is also the "reason" of the existence of the State as a corporate entity. Furthermore, the *raison d'être* of the government, of the *principatus*, of a good *politia*, derives from the end, the happy life of the city. To achieve this end the prince must possess "perfect virtue," must indeed use *ratio perfecta* in exercising his powers of coercing and punishing.[110] Since the word *ratio* in this context does not seem to appear in William of Moerbeke's Latin translation of the *Politics*, it is reasonable to think that the legal terminology of the Roman lawyers influenced Pierre as it did Thomas Aquinas.

Pierre d'Auriole offers variations on the theme. In part, he follows in the tradition of John of Salisbury and Thomas Aquinas, holding that the "ordo rationis" demands a principate or government among men for the achievement of the end of the community, which is to live and work well according to "right reason," an end that is unattainable without a prince. Naturally, the prince must be subject to law and rule by "right reason." Pierre is also Aristotelian and Thomistic in saying that the *ratio boni* is the *ratio finis*; but he places this reason of the good, the end, of the community chiefly in the prince or *dux*. Indeed, the very *ratio boni* is essentially the necessary *ratio dominii* of the prince, whose power is lawful even when deriving from force rather than from the consent of the people.[111] In fact, Pierre d'Auriole approaches the idea that the State is primarily the prince; at least its "reason" is that of the prince, although ideally his reason is limited by law and "right reason."

110 On the thought of Pierre d'Auvergne see Lagarde, *Naissance*, II², 106-111, esp. 111 n. 14: ". . . Ratio partis per se consideranda est ex ratione totius": "ideo ratio partium per se civitatis quaerenda est ex ratione reipublicae"; "finis autem reipublicae est salus et permanentia eius; et ergo bonum partium reipublicae intenditur in ordine ad finem istum. . . ."

The following passages are from Pierre's continuation of Thomas Aquinas on the *Politics* (ed. Spiazzi), p. 161, no. 455: "Manifestum est enim quod ratio principatus ex fine sumitur. Finis vero politiae rectae est feliciter vivere; ideo ex hoc debet sumi ratio principatus"; p. 182, no. 520: "quod ratio principis sumitur a ratione; et ideo bonum principis est in ordine ad principatus"; p. 153, no. 438: "quia duo exiguntur in regimine politiae. Unum est ratio recta. . . . Aliud est potentia, ut possit coercere et punire malos." On "right reason" see above, n. 102 and below, to nn. 118 and 121.

111 Lagarde, II, 284, n. 49, 298 nn. 101 and 103; and 299.

A more complete and literal theory of "reason of State" was achieved by a secular theologian at Paris, Henry of Ghent. His principal thoughts on the subject belong to the years 1276-1292, in his *Quodlibeta* and *Quaestiones*.[112] It will become obvious that he is as much at home with the legists and canonists as with the Aristotelians. For him, as for Thomas Aquinas, the State (*civitas* or community) is a natural end in itself, and in it the common good or utility is more divine than any individual good. Even the right to save one's soul is sometimes in doubt when the *patria* demands individual sacrifices for its safety. He repeats the classical ideal of fighting and dying for the fatherland and understands the legal concept of the public welfare. Naturally, a prince or king is necessary, as the head and representative of the body of the community, to achieve the end of public welfare in law and order and in the safety and existence of the State. His power in the name of the common good is supreme and cannot be challenged. As for the Church, the pope cannot change its *status* or *ordo ecclesiasticus*, which is the hierarchy of pope, prelates, and priests. But if necessity, reason, and utility concur, the pope can modify details, such as creating new bishoprics.[113]

All this is well known. But Henry's arguments for the power of the king in legislation, *ratione status*, need elaboration, for they have not been emphasized. In a *Quodlibet* he debates the question of whether subjects of a king are bound to obey a statute which is allegedly made for the common utility, when in fact the common utility is not *evidens*. (We must remember that *utilitas evidens* goes back to the ancient Roman theory of legislation, that when the emperor makes a new law that marks a change of older law, it must be for "*evident* utility"—so Ulpian, *D.* 1, 4, 2, a passage cited over and over again by legists and canonists.)[114] It can be argued, he says, that subjects are not bound to their superior in those things which do not pertain to

---

[112] The best treatment of Henry's political ideas is in Lagarde, II, 161-213.

[113] Lagarde, II, 179-185; 190-195; 206. See also Kantorowicz, *King's Two Bodies*, pp. 243-245; and above, to nn. 49-56; below, ch. IX, n. 26.

[114] Besides the *Glos. ord.* see Odofredo, *Lectura* or *Com.* on the *Dig. Vetus*; above, to n. 21.

their special wish (*votum*), unless they are necessary for safety ("de necessitate salutis"). A statute which is not for evident utility or necessity is therefore not binding.[115]

But if a statute or new law that is not evidently useful orders the payment by laymen of a tenth of all goods (as a tax), must they obey? To understand Henry's answer we must recall once more that according to the Roman and Canon law of the thirteenth century no prince or city could levy an extraordinary tax except for "evident utility," "just cause," "evident necessity," or dire emergency in a time of great peril to the State. Accordingly, he says that an unnecessary tax is an arbitrary confiscation of property rights.[116] For the power of the prince is subordinate to the end of the State, namely, the public welfare and safety, including private rights in property. On this point Henry is particularly interesting: "I say that the goal (*finis*) of superior princes and prelates ought to be the safety and peace of the Republic; that tranquility (*quiecia*) should be the end of individual subjects insofar as they are parts of the community. This (twofold) end they along with the prince should strive for," as that end in which the prince and every subject finds his own good.[117] And now, Henry brings in Aristotle's good of the city that is more divine than any particular good, and Cicero's words about being born for the Republic and about the glory of death for it. "But because this end," he continues, "imposes a neces-

---

115 The *Quodlibeta* of Henry of Ghent were published in the sixteenth century (e.g., Paris, 1518); but I have used, because I had access to it more readily than to a printed text, the Paris, BN, MS lat. 15350, fols. 251-290ᵛ. This *quodlibet* begins fol. 262ʳ c. 2, ends fol. 263 c. 1; inc.: "Arguitur quod subditi tenentur servare statutum superioris in omnibus eis que sunt ad communem utilitatem, licet non sit evidens." Then Henry says: Yes, for such statutes are *opera virtutis* and in all such *opera virtutis* subjects are bound to obey their superior; "Contra: subditi non tenentur superiori in eis que non pertinent ad speciale votum eorum, nisi sunt de necessitate salutis. . . . Talia autem statuta [which are not for "evident utility"] non pertinent ad aliquod speciale votum subditorum, nec sunt de necessitate salutis, ergo etc."

116 Fol. 262ᵛ c. 1; after asking about statutes and taxation, and saying that the pope likewise made the clergy pay tenths, he says, against: "Item. Si talia [statuta] possent statuere, tunc per superiorum statuta laycis auferretur potestas disponendi de rebus suis pro voluntate, quod similiter videtur inconveniens, ergo, etc."

117 Fol. 262ᵛ c. 1: "Dico quod finis superiorum principum vel prelatorum debet esse salus et pax reipublice; quieciam debet esse finis singulorum subditorum in quantum sunt partes communitatis, quem etiam tenentur intendere una cum principe. . . ."

sity on those things which belong to it, therefore just as they (prince and subjects) are bound to strive for that end, so they are bound to work for the things that are for the end, to effect their ordering to it."[118] It is the function of the prince to have an architectonic science in doing those things, in the proper manner and at the right time, that are necessary for the end (as in *Ethics*, 1), and every subject is bound to obey statutes made by superiors on things necessary for the end.[119]

So far, Henry seems to be arriving at the conclusion that subjects need not obey the prince if his laws and acts are not for the evident utility of the State. But instead, he turns to arguments for the supreme authority of the ruler as the bearer and sole interpreter of the public welfare. Every subject, he says, must obey statutes necessary for the end of the community, even "if it is not evident to everyone that that statute (levying a tenth) is necessary to the end or to anything arranged for it."[120] Why? It is because the prince should be so superior in all virtues that in a certain manner the good of the whole community is in him; and his good is the good of each and everyone in the city. The prince is useful to all. Moreover, the subjects are useful to the prince, by a utility which is almost a "slavery" (*servitus*), except that the subject is a free man while being useful to others. As free men, therefore, subjects should obey the statutes of superiors even when they do not know or are doubtful whether the statutes are intended for "the common utility." They should, because of confidence in the prudence and goodness of the prince and his counsellors, believe and suppose that statutes are made for "the public utility." (Of course, it was the common theory that the prince should always legislate and judge and decide with the advice of his counsellors, and that what he did was presumed to be for the public welfare.)[121]

118 Fol. 262ᵛ c. 1: "Nunc autem quia finis imponit necessitatem eis que sunt ad finem, sicut ergo tenentur intendere finem illum, sic eciam tenentur intendere ea que sunt ad finem illum, et operam exhibere ut in finem ordinentur. . . ."

119 Fol. 262ᵛ c. 1.

120 *Ibid.*: ". . . etiam si non sit evidens cuilibet, quod statutum illud sit necessarium ad finem vel ad aliquid ordinatorum ad ipsum."

121 Fols. 262ᵛ c. 1-262ᵛ c. 2, especially these words: ". . . Propter quod subditi debent tenere superiorum statuta in predictis, etiam si ignorent quod aut quomodo vergant in com[m]unem utilitatem propter dubium de hoc, quia ex con-

But suppose the contrary is true, that because of several similar bad acts of the same prince, it cannot be assumed that this particular statute is for evident utility. In that case, before doing anything else, the subjects should petition ("supplicate") the prince to revoke the statute.[122] If the prince refuses, they should depose him rather than tolerate and obey him.[123] Nonetheless, Henry concludes, the supposition is that the prince is prudent and industrious in legislating for the public welfare. His prudence and industriousness, then, must be presumed *ratione status!*[124] As Aristotle says, *Politics* I, every house is ruled by an elder ("senissimo"); the prince or king, as head of city or kingdom, which includes houses and villages, should be an "elder in mind" ("de senio mentis").[125] Once more, then, it should be presumed that the prince, like his progenitors and successors, is mentally superior from the start. If his statutes are not *evidenter* contrary to virtue, obedience to them is the rule.

---

fidencia de prudentia ac bonitate principis ac suorum consiliariorum [*consiliariorum* in the MS] debent ei in hoc credere et supponere, quod talia sunt quod vergant in publicam utilitatem. . . ."

Similarly Pierre de Belleperche, *Lectura*, to *Inst.* 1, 2: after saying that *ex ratione et causa probabile* the prince could do things that are contrary to the natural law (above, n. 98), he concludes that the prince cannot change the benefit of natural law *sine causa*, "sed semper presumam causam donec probatur contrarium"; fol. 43. And Lucas de Penna (*Com.*, p. 747), to *C.* 12, 20, 1 Nullus, no. 7, says that the prince should take counsel, but "quod princeps agit, praesumitur ad utilitatem publicam redundare. . . . Cor enim eius in manu Dei est."

Elsewhere, however, Lucas argues that the king should in no event levy extraordinary taxes, even those necessary for the common utility, without getting the consent of all touched by them; *Com.*, 82f., to *C.* 10, 18, 1. Others too, like Godefroid de Fontaines (Lagarde, *Naissance*, II, 197), believed that consent was necessary. And indeed, by the principle of *quod omnes tangit*, kings did have to ask for consent to extraordinary subsidies. But was the consent given truly voluntarily, thus limiting the prerogative of the prince? Not so long as the king had the ultimate right, *ratione jurisdictionis et gubernationis*, *ratione status regis*, *ratione necessitatis*, and *ratione status regni* to interpret the case of necessity for the defense of the State. See my "Plena potestas," *Traditio*, I, 370-383, 397-408; and "A Romano-Canonical Maxim, *Quod omnes tangit*," *Traditio*, IV, 197-251; above, ch. III, § 4 and nn. 180-206; ch. IV in general.

122 Above, to nn. 65f., on the petition as the remedy.

123 In two separate passages, fol. 262ᵛ c. 2, Henry speaks of the procedure of deposition and thus reflects old feudal ideas about the right of rebellion; cf. Lagarde, *Naissance*, II, 324f.—this *droit de résistance* is also in Thomas Aquinas and others.

124 Fol. 262ᵛ c. 2: ". . . supponenda de prudencia et industria principis, quod vere presumendum est ratione status."

125 Ed. Spiazzi, *Politics*, I, 7-10, 107; also the *Com.* of Thomas Aquinas, nos. 19, 24, 160.

As for the argument that a statute is invalid if not approved by the subjects as individual parts of the community, consent was really given when the people accepted the prince as their superior, whether he was elected by a group of electors, was chosen by his predecessor, or succeeded to the office by hereditary right. The people consented to his legislative power even though they made no verbal promise of obedience! Henry of Ghent means, obviously, that consent given originally to the authority of the prince cannot be withdrawn thereafter and remains as a tacit consent to all laws promulgated during his reign. (His thought here may reflect the attitude of those legists who maintained that the consent of the people in the *Lex regia* was permanently valid.) Hence, it is a great error on the part of members of public councils to believe that they are not obligated to obey the public edicts promulgated by their superiors for the utility of the community.[126]

It is clear that Henry is convinced that unless the evidence to the contrary is certain and well known, the presumption must always be that the ruler is acting for the public welfare, with the approval of the community as a whole. This presumption is based in part on a *ratio status*. But what is this *ratio status*? Is it the same as the *ratio publicae utilitatis* of the State? The context of the whole discussion of statutes for the common or public utility, and the statement that the purpose or end of superior princes ought to be the "salus et pax Reipublicae" at first seem to indicate that it is. Probably, however, Henry means only that the presumption is that by reason of the public office, or of the public *status* of supreme authority and power, the prince and his statutes must be obeyed. Like the *ratio status* of Henry II of England in the *Dialogus de Scaccario*, it is perhaps the *ratio status regis*, the "reason" of the public office and crown, rather than the *ratio status regni*, or public welfare of the realm. But the one *status* is virtually the same as the other.

In fact, Henry is very near the idea that the public *status* is the *magistratus* of prince or king, a *status* necessary for the maintenance of the *status civitatis, reipublicae, regni*, that is,

---

126 Fols. 262ᵛ c. 2-263 c. 1. I have summarized here, for the passage is too long to quote, given my purpose.

the public utility or safety and peace of the community.[127] This is evident in his final argument for the supreme authority. "Are lay subjects, then," he asks, "compelled to pay tenths to the prince, like the clergy to the pope? I say that this is true, if it is necessary for the said end, and not only a tenth, nay a half, even the whole, even themselves!" (No sacrifice of property or life is too great for the safety of the community!) "But the superiors should indeed beware of decreeing or exacting anything when it is not at all evident to them that it is for the common or public utility, and not for their private utility alone." They should promulgate statutes and edicts that are so "reasonable" that they proceed not from the power (*potentia*) of fact but from the power of law. This *potentia* is itself not absolute. It is controlled by the deliberation of reason which does not err!—"potentia regulata pensa rationis non errante." Reason that does not err, however, is obviously for Henry of Ghent the right reason with respect to the end, the public welfare of the Republic.[128] It is the "reason" of the *status* of the State, rightly interpreted by the supreme authority by reason of his public *status*. Again, essentially, the *ratio status Reipublicae* and the *ratio status magistratus* are in harmony as two aspects of "reason of State." It may be, after all, that Henry's *ratio status* was the "reason" of the public welfare and peace; certainly it anticipates *ragione di stato*.[129] In any case, his "reason of State" in the hands of the prince and his wise counsellors was the art or science of government em-

127 See below, ch. VII; cf. above, n. 104.

128 MS lat. 15350, fol. 262 c. 1: "Ad secundum, quod tunc subditi laici tenerentur solvere decimas principi sicut clerici pape? Dico quod verum est, si necesse sit ad dictum finem, et non solum decimam, immo medietatem, immo totum, immo se ipsos. Sed bene debent cavere sibi superiores, quod nichil talium statuant aut exigant, quin saltem evidens sit ipsis quod sit ad communem utilitatem seu publicam, non tantum ad privatam. Et ponant statuta et edicta tam rationabilia ut procedit ab ipsis non de potentia facti sed iuris, nec de potentia absolute, sed de potentia regulata pensa rationis non errante." Henry ends this long discussion with a statement about how laymen are more in command of their property than the clergy, whose surplus property must be shared with the poor. The last sentence, a final answer to the early argument that a tax which is not for "evident utility" deprives laymen of control of their property, states that their property rights are limited by ("evidently useful") statutes of superiors, otherwise not (fol. 263 c. 1). On evident utility and new taxes see also Odofredo, to D. 1, 4, 2, no. 2.

129 As I concluded in my "Two Laws and the Statute of York," *Speculum*, XXIX (1954), 421, n. 16; below, ch. VI, n. 16.

ployed for the *evident,* not the pretended or specious, public utility.

5. CONCLUSIONS: *RATIO STATUS REGIS ET REGNI*

No doubt, additional literal statements of the doctrine of "reason of State" can be found in the jurists and other writers of the fourteenth century. For example, Marsiglio of Padua was familiar with the principle of the use of "right reason" by the *pars principans* in the city; and William of Ockham, not to mention the great legists, Bartolus and Baldus, abundantly refers to necessity and the common utility.[130] But there is no need of going on. My purpose has been to show how *ratio publicae utilitatis* and *ratio status,* how the terms and substance of the modern doctrine, go back chiefly to the revival of Roman public law in the twelfth and thirteenth centuries. Enough evidence has been presented to justify the following conclusions.

The medieval *raison d'état* was no more clearly defined than is the modern one. In general, however, it was "right reason"— primarily the right reasoning by the highest authority about the means used in domestic and foreign affairs in order to assure the protection of the people and their society in the State. Reasoning was "right" when it was related to the fundamental laws of God and nature on the one side, and to law and justice for the people on the other. It was right reason, in accordance with the universal reason in the higher law of nature, to do everything necessary for the defense and survival of the State, to coerce and punish wicked men for the protection of the innocent and obedient, and to crush any disorders that disturbed the peace, which was the common utility of all, laity and clergy alike. "Reason of State" was the "reason" of the public and common welfare, including all the ways and means of maintaining the common good, the commonweal, the *respublica,* and the "state" of Empire, Republic, Realm, or City. It included all necessary measures taken for the material and spiritual *bene vivere* of the people—at least of those people who had

---

[130] Chroust, "Corporate Idea," *Rev. of Politics,* IX, 439f.; *Defensor pacis,* I, 2, 15; on Ockham, above, n. 16.

rights that were touched by what might endanger their lawful possession of them.

On the one hand, then, "reason of State" pertained to the public welfare of the community and the common welfare of all law-abiding people within it. On the other, it pertained to the magistracy. It was the "reason" of the necessity of a public authority, the *ratio gubernationis et jurisdictionis*. For as the glossators said, if the public law dealt with the *status Reipublicae* it necessarily dealt with the magistracy. How futile law and justice would be if there were no one to interpret and enforce it and do justice according to it![131] Besides, many held, the power of the prince as the head of the magistracy and of the State came from God. Therefore, "so great is the power of the prince," a decretalist said, "that his will is (taken) for reason." No one, he continued, can dispute what he does. His power must be "informed for" and "conformed to" the public utility. The *digna vox* of majesty demands that he use his reason for the public welfare.[132] (Here, probably, is one of the sources of the theory that in his legislation the king presumably always subjected his will to "right reason." The superiority of reason over will does not have to wait for Thomism.) "Right reason" was therefore

[131] *Glos. ord.* to *D.* 1, 1, 1, 2; Accursius here sums up what had often been said; and like other glossators, he connects the public law, the *status Reipublicae*, and the magistracy with a famous passage in *D.* 1, 2, 2, 13: "quantum est enim ius in civitate esse, nisi sint, qui iura regere possint?" But the glossators use the word *parum* for *quantum*; the meaning is essentially the same.

[132] *Apparatus* (after 1234; before 1249) on the *Decretals of Gregory IX*, in Paris, BN, MS lat. 3967, fol. 1 c. 1, to Prooem. of Gregory IX, ad v. *servus*: the pope's power as the vicar of God is great, "sed debet eam conformare publice utilitatis . . . ; et imperator ducit noctes insompnes pro re publica . . . *Vinc.*"; and fol. 30ᵛ to 1, 6, c. Quanto, ad v. *vicem*: "No. quanta est potestas principis, ut in eo sit voluntas pro ratione, inst. de iure naturali. §. sed quod principi. Nec etiam est aliquis qui dicat contra hoc. . . . Hanc tamen potestatem tenetur ipse informare utilitati publice, C. de legibus, digna [*C.* 1, 14, 4]. . . . In hoc gerit vicem dei, quia de nichilo facit aliquid . . . *Jo.*" But in the earlier *Appar.* of Vinc. to *Comp. III* (Decretals of Inn. III), the second gloss lacks the final words, "In hoc gerit . . . aliquid . . . *Jo.*" and has "voluntas principis" and "reformare utilitati publice," thus: "Nota, quanta est voluntas principis ut in eo voluntas pro ratione. . . . Nec est aliquis qui dicat contra hoc fac[tum]. . . . Hanc tamen potestatem tenetur ipse reformare utilitati publice, C. de legibus. digna; infra, de cen. cum instantia"; in Bamberg MS. Can. 20 [P. II. 7], fol. 104ᵛ, to *Comp. III*, 1, 5, 3, ad vv. sed veri dei vicem gerit *in terris*.

Obviously Vinc. and Joh. are speaking chiefly about the power of the pope, but this power is the same for the Church as that of the emperor for the Empire.

the "reason" of the public welfare of king and Realm, of the *status regis et regni*.[133] Indeed, the public *status* was already frequently treated as the royal or any legitimate government—so by some legists and by Thomas Aquinas. It was becoming *lo stato*, just as the *status* of the Republic or Realm was anticipating the *Stato*, the State, as a territorial yet abstract juridical entity. Quite often, at any rate, the *status regis* was the public *potestas* and *iura coronae*, the royal *honor* and *dignitas*. It is not absurd to say that in one sense "reason of State" was, as in the Renaissance and today, the "reason of government." (In fact, it is possible that not only in Machiavelli but in the full sixteenth century, by *lo stato* Italian writers sometimes meant the government rather than the State.) But if the "reason of State" was also the "reason of the public welfare," the "reason of jurisdiction and government" exclusively in the hands of the prince was tending toward the confusion not only of king and *status* but also of king and State. There is certainly a suggestion of this in the developing theory that *ratione jurisdictionis et protectionis* the king as *lex animata* was omnipresent—in all his courts throughout his realm. He was everywhere; and if he was everywhere, he was pantheistically, so to speak, the State itself. The head was tending to absorb the corporate body.[134]

Both the *ratio status regis* and the *ratio status regni*, however, were subordinate to a higher "reason of State." This was the reason of the community as a naturally existing entity that was approved by God and the law of nature for the social and political end of man on earth. From the twelfth century on, the *regnum* was treated as a corporate body including the head, who represented the whole, and the members. It was achieving a fictive personality. Thus, when lawyers and philosophers spoke either of a *ratio publicae utilitatis* (*status*) or of a *ratio Reipublicae* and *ratio civitatis*, they were actually very near our "reason of State" as the ultimate "reason" of an abstraction, of a corporate *universitas regni* that is and yet can do nothing except through its leading members, the head and his magistracy

---

[133] Cf. Kantorowicz, *King's Two Bodies*, p. 7, quoting Edmund Plowden.
[134] See the excellent study of this by Kantorowicz, "Invocatio nominis imperatoris," *Boll. Centro Studi. filol. ling. Sicil.*, III, 1-16. See below, ch. VII.

and the greater men. As Aegidius Romanus said, *ratio* and *necessitas* justified a king's taxing the clergy without waiting for papal authorization. For the "reason" and necessity of the corporate State, the *ratio status regni*, made it the duty of the head to act speedily; delay would be dangerous to the community as a whole as well as its head and members.[135]

To be sure, the abstraction of corporate State from *status regni* was not as complete as in the modern age. But already the Realm was the object of governmental action. Although generally kings said that they were maintaining or defending the *status regni* instead of the *regnum*, in fact they had in mind something similar to the concept of the State. But was the community or *universitas regni* so personified that it, rather than its head and agent, was said to do or act? We do find that the corporate body of Republic, Kingdom, *civitas*, or *patria* was the subject as well as the object of actions. The community existed and demanded sacrifices for its well-being; and the members should if need be fight and die for it. In a word, the legal theory that a corporation was a responsible if fictive person, although normally only the officers were in fact made liable, was to a remarkable degree applied to *civitas* and *regnum*. Naturally, it was difficult to punish a kingdom, not to mention its head, for any alleged crime against the *ius gentium*. Yet in essence there was a personification of the community, whether it was independent or autonomous, and therefore the *regnum Franciae* or *Angliae*, and the greater Italian communes, were not unlike States in the ideas of the age. But the emphasis was on the king and his public *status* as the head and agent of the Realm.

Superior to "reason of State" as the *rationes* of the public welfare, magistracy, and the corporate community, was that highest *ratio* in law and justice, John of Salisbury's *moderamen* of all the "reasons," skills, art, and methods employed for the end of the State. It was that *ratio* which coming from God participates in men. But again, since the State existed naturally and

---

[135] *An et quomodo principes*, Paris, BN, MS lat. 6786, fol. 35ᵛ–36 (see above, n. 99): papal consent is necessary "nisi forte tanta est necessitas et tam evidens quod sine dispendio regni non posset haberi recursus ad capud ecclesie"—as Hugo said, *ratio* and *necessitas* must both be present. This reference is to Hugo of St. Victor, above, n. 31.

was approved by God, the necessity of its safety and welfare "knew" no ordinary restraint of law. The public law and, partly directly and partly indirectly, even the natural law gave to the prince the right (and duty) to defend the State and its *status*. There was no novelty in the idea of Ptolemy of Lucca that the *ius naturale* approved royal taxation for just wars of defense. Hence, the highest "reason" of the safety of the State was itself a moral end. In the later thirteenth century a philosopher actually argued that adultery committed by a private citizen in order to save the *civitas* from a tyrant was a lesser evil and might even be licit.[136] The commands of God for private morality could thus be compromised for the sake of a higher moral end, that of the State. Furthermore, the just cause, necessity, and "reason" of the public welfare (the three *causae* were practically synonymous) were excusing *dolus bonus*, good or useful deceit, the lesser good or evil for the greater good of all in the community. The "Holy Pretence" of the modern age was well known in the twelfth and thirteenth centuries. Some crimes, a decretist said, should be tolerated "by reason of public scandal or schism," or "by reason of the multitude."[137] Apparently unjust acts of a government must be endured if they were necessary for the public welfare. Lucas de Penna, reflecting the legal thought of the preceding centuries, held that when a king seized private property it was a *malum* despite the owner's receiving com-

---

[136] In anon. *Questiones in libros Ethicorum* (Paris, BN, MS lat. 14698, fols. 132-164^v). The author asks whether adultery can ever be lawful (fol. 146). Arguing pro and con the hypothetical case of a citizen's committing adultery with the wife of a man who is planning to be a tyrant and destroy the "bonum communitatis," he concludes that it is a lesser evil if the result is the discovery of the secret plans of the would-be tyrant, and is thus the safety of the city.

For Ptol. of Lucca see Gierke, *Polit. Theories*, pp. 190f. n. 323.

[137] For the importance of *dolus bonus* in the early modern age, along with casuistry, see George L. Mosse, *The Holy Pretence*, p. 51 and *passim*. But *dolus bonus* was discussed in the decretists of the late twelfth and early thirteenth century; see the *Glos. ord.* of Johannes Teutonicus to *Decretum*, Dist. 43, c. 2 In mandatis, ad v. *eludere*: "Nota dolum esse bonum contra hostem"; also see glosses to C. 22, q. 2, c. 21 Utilem; and, of course, the Roman law is a source, *D.* 4, 3, 1, 3, that *dolus is bonus* when committed against public enemies; the *Glos. ord.* of Accursius approves.

As for the avoidance of scandal in order to protect the common welfare, see *Decretum*, Dist. 4, c. 6 Denique, gloss ad v. *venia*: "Sustinenda enim sunt crimina ratione scandali, vel schismatis . . . vel ratione multitudinis." Several other examples could be given; cf. above, n. 48.

pensation. But the evil should be tolerated first because of the *ratio connexi boni*, that is, the *ratio publicae utilitatis*, and second because of the *honor principis* "qui est res publica et res publica est in eo." And all decrees of the prince, unless they were contrary to the faith, should be obeyed bad as they might seem to be.[138] It was therefore in accordance with the highest *ratio* in law and in justice that the prince had the ultimate right, if good counsellors agreed, to practice the *rationes* of the *utilitas publica* and the *status magistratus-regis*, and to do all that was necessary to maintain the State by assuring the *status regis* and the *status regni*.

Whether it was the *ratio gubernationis et jurisdictionis* or the *ratio publicae utilitatis*, the *ratio status regis* or the *ratio status regni*, and whether it was the normal art and science of good government or the abnormal, "casual," use by a good prince of extraordinary means to meet emergencies and necessities and assure the safety of people and realm, "reason of State" in the twelfth and thirteenth centuries was a rational principle of "constitutionalism." It was similar, perhaps, to the "public welfare clause" and rules concerning national emergencies in the American Constitution. An act needed to defend the State in a *casus necessitatis* was neither illegal nor immoral. Both the law of nature and the public law of the State approved it; in taking care of a national emergency, the king, if he could show *ratio* and *causa probabilis*, violated neither the law of God nor positive laws. Unnecessary, specious pleas of reason and necessity, however, were arbitrary and unlawful—the excuses of a tyrant. Unlawful also was the continued plea of necessity after the emergency ended; the *casus necessitatis* was indeed a *casus* and therefore could be adduced only *casualiter*, not *normaliter*.[139] What made a prince a tyrant was the needless, normal, and arbitrary proclamation of necessity in order to maintain his selfish interests and power. As we remarked above, the problem

138 *Com.*, to *C.* 11, 71, 5 Praedia, p. 622, no. xxiiii; for Henry of Ghent and Pierre de Belleperche, above, n. 121.

139 But Ernst Kantorowicz has shown that from the time of Frederick II on, in taxation and in the administrative needs of the government, the case of necessity was becoming annual and regular—the fiction of *perpetua necessitas* was appearing; *King's Two Bodies*, pp. 285-288.

was how far the authority of the prince could go in compelling his subjects to accept his own interpretation of *ratio* and *necessitas*. Much depended on the king's ability as a statesman. But in legal theory the ruler was not "Machiavellian" when he could demonstrate (*probare*) a genuine case of necessity and thus persuade, as in England, all those who would be touched by a tax that they must consent to this policy. The king by his prerogative, by his royal *status*, had the advantage. For as the glossators said, to *D.* 1, 1, 1, 2, the *ius publicum* that dealt with magistrates made it their duty and right to maintain (*conservare*) the *utilitas publica*, the *status Reipublicae*, "ne pereat." Altogether, then, medieval "reason of State" was on the one side the steady art or science of governing justly for the protection of all subjects and their rights, and on the other, the reasoning about meeting emergencies when the State and the common welfare were in danger.

The medieval State at its strongest was, to be sure, lacking in the centralization of the modern State. Kings had neither sufficient revenues nor the power to resort to universal conscription for their wars. Their police force was inefficient. The very slowness of communications prevented their being nearly so powerful as a democratic government in the twentieth century. Private rights made it more difficult than today to apply the principles of eminent domain and the "public welfare clause." After the thirteenth century the private rights of the nobility of the orders and estates of the privileged frequently triumphed over the public law and the ideal of the State as the natural end of all members in common. Not even absolute monarchs could always make the *status regni* superior to the *status privilegiatorum*. Perhaps the French Revolution resulted in part from the hardening of special privileges enjoyed by nobles and members of the *Parlements* and by provinces, privileges that constituted a kind of modern feudalism and were a serious obstacle to the king's effective practice of "reason of State." It is a paradox that in the early modern age, just when treatises on *ragione di stato* began to appear, "reason of State" was sometimes a more futile principle than it had been in the governments of Henry II, Innocent III, Frederick II, Edward I, and Philip IV.[140]

It is wrong to exaggerate in order to magnify "reason of State" in the twelfth and thirteenth centuries. Nonetheless, whatever the nature of the medieval State, kings and their legal advisers were more intelligent and mature in public affairs than is generally supposed. They understood and practiced their own kind of science or art of the State. There was a conscious and intelligent *Staatsräson*, however ineffectually applied. Legists, canonists, theologians, and philosophers were in their fashion as alert to the importance of the use of reason in the business of the State as the government of Florence was in the time of Savonarola, Soderini, and Machiavelli. And the Florentines, as readily as their medieval ancestors, assumed that human, political *ragione* needed God's help.[141] Machiavelli himself, al-

[140] These remarks about privileges from the fourteenth to the eighteenth century apply chiefly to France and are inspired largely by the excellent book by Palmer, *Age of the Democratic Revolution*; see above, Introduction, n. 12.

[141] Yet, quite recently, without any reference to medieval sources, Professor Felix Gilbert has concluded that Burckhardt was right in saying that it was first in Italy (from the fourteenth century on) that "an objective treatment and consideration of the state and all things of this world became possible"; "Florentine Political Assumptions in the Period of Savonarola and Soderini," *Jour. Warburg and Courtauld Inst.*, xx, 202, 187-214. Gilbert proceeds to show that in the *Consulte e pratiche* of the Grand Council, *ragione* is the key to understanding Florentine thought on foreign affairs; *ragione* was the means of reaching right political reasons. "The problem of the use of *ragione* in politics consisted in subordinating an individual case to the appropriate general rule of behaviour." So in using *ragione*, the Florentines understood how times and conditions change; how "gli animi delli huomini sono vari" (205). At the same time they often felt that *necessità* compelled them to modify *ragione*, for "necessità non ha legge"; they appealed to God as superior to necessity, fortune, and reason; indeed, they appealed to moral *ragione*. "To maintain the power of Florence was a service to God" (209). All this helps one understand Machiavelli and his "true originality"!

No comment is really necessary. But I must point out once more that this kind of *ragione*, the *ratio publicae utilitatis*, etc., as we have abundantly seen, was as medieval as modern; *necessitas legem non habet* was a commonplace in the twelfth century; the legists and canonists often said that the prince could make new laws because situations, circumstances, and the times are constantly changing (see below, ch. XI, §§ 3-5); and Terence was frequently quoted (*Phormio*, II, iv, 454): "quot homines tot sententiae." And why were the Florentines more "rational" about politics than medieval men in subjecting *ragione* to the moral law and God? Who was more sincere, who more cynical, in calling upon God? Finally, why say that the idea of *necessità* is opposed to or limits the use of *ragione*? After all, *necessitas* is a part of and enhances the force of "reason of State." Even the maxim, "Dove necessità caccia non bisogna consiglio" (206),

though completely secular and sometimes amoral in his doctrine of *necessità*, was not altogether un-medieval. If he did not appeal to God and the law of nature, he related the prince's use of unlawful means to the achievement of a good State, ruled according to law and justice for the common welfare. Giovanni da Botero, however, the first writer of a treatise on *ragione di stato*, was quite medieval in emphasizing "reason of State" both as the means of developing and maintaining the government and as the duty of the prince to rule with justice and preserve *lo stato* in peace and tranquillity.[142] Did Machiavelli and Botero get their *necessità* and *ragione di stato* from medieval sources? I cannot answer the question. Yet, while they owed much to the direct influence of the ancient classics, they no doubt owed much also to the continued use of the medieval legal terminology that persisted in the public business and documents of Italian States in the Renaissance.[143] No matter: medieval lawyers and kings were familiar with principles derived from the Roman law; they needed little instruction from Machiavelli. Indeed, they may have instructed him. At any rate, medieval monarchs and their counsellors were trying to build their States upon the *ratio status regis et regni*.

---

represents the medieval doctrine, that by reason of the safety of the State, when the necessity or danger was so urgent and imminent that delay in taking action could not be risked, there was no need of waiting for lengthy debate or the consent of all interested parties. Not only was this understood when Edward I and Philip IV taxed the clergy without waiting for the consent of Boniface VIII, but Thomas Aquinas stated it for a more ordinary immediate danger (above, to n. 106).

As for objectivity, can one really demonstrate that the Florentine concept of *ragione* was free from subjectivity, from irrationality, and piety? And who can maintain that *ragione di stato* today is objective or scientific? "Reason of State" has always been under the influence of all kinds of emotions of patriotism and religion, as well as the practical considerations of the self-interest of the government or the genuine safety of people and State.

[142] *Della ragione di stato*, in *Scrittori politici*, 449-454.

[143] See Baron, *Crisis of the Early Italian Renaissance*, I, 151f., for *ragione* in Gregorio Dati's *Istoria*, *ca.* 1406.

CHAPTER VI ✦ *STATUS REGNI:*

LESTAT DU ROIALME IN THE STATUTE

OF YORK, 1322

T HAS ALREADY become evident that the *status* of an organized community was preeminently the public and common welfare of the corporate body and its members. The "state" of the State was the principal subject of public law, and the maintenance and preservation of the *status regni* was the supreme right and duty of the king. "Reason of State" was therefore the art of reasoning about what should be done to establish law and order and defend the State in times of danger. Consequently the *status* of the king, the "estate royal," became increasingly public, indicating those powers of government that were necessary for maintaining the *status regni*.

This has been treated quite generally, however, in connection with representation and consent and with "reason of State." Much more needs to be said, and in detail, if only because it is interesting to observe how *status* began to stand by itself and become the equivalent of *Respublica, Civitas,* and *Regnum,* and how it could also mean the governing body rather than the territorial State. More important, further study of the legal thought embodied in *status,* it is hoped, will contribute to our understanding the development of public law in England from the time of Henry II to that of Edward II and the Statute of York. For, as will be emphasized in the next three chapters, the terms *status regni* and *status regis* frequently appear in English sources, and yet they have not inspired historians of English law and institutions to study them from the point of view of Roman principles of public law. It is true that a great deal of attention has been paid to their meaning in the French *lestat du roialme* and *lestat du roi* of the Statute of York. But the necessary interpretation based on the history of *status regis* and *status regni* in English usage, and on the legal concepts involved, has not appeared. Perhaps a comparative study, bringing the continental Roman law into English situations, will furnish a satisfactory explanation of what the "state of the realm" meant to the king, and what the "state of the king" meant to the realm —rather, how the *status-estat* of the realm was connected with the *communitas* and *universitas* on the one side and with the *status-estat* of the king on the other. Let us look first at *lestat du roialme*.

The Statute of York (1322) has long attracted the attention of scholars in the field of English legal and constitutional history, and yet to this day its wording arouses controversy.[1] The method of approach used has naturally and rightly been the study of the terminology largely within the English legal and constitutional tradition. But since it has not resulted in a "concordance of discordant" opinions, an interpretation based on the method of observing the meaning of the same or similar terminology in Roman and Canon law and applying the equivalent meaning to an English document is now offered.

The difficulties involved are serious. In the two laws and in the legists and canonists one finds little direct discussion of representation in national assemblies and no attempt to explain the constitution of England in the time of Edward I and Edward II. But much of the terminology, occurring ever more abundantly from the late twelfth century on in English royal documents pertaining to assemblies, came from the Roman law, partly through the Canon law, and was defined and discussed by the experts on the Continent. It has seemed logical, therefore, to

[1] This part is a revision of an article that appeared under the title, "The Two Laws and the Statute of York," in *Speculum*, XXIX (1954), 417-432; and the article grew out of a paper read at the meeting of the American Historical Association in Boston in 1949. The reader will therefore understand why there remains a good deal of repetition of ideas developed in my earlier studies. In any case, some repetition is necessary in order constantly to keep in mind the legal environment that helps explain developments in England. See above, Introduction and chs. III and IV, and the original articles, "*Plena Potestas* and Consent in Medieval Assemblies," *Traditio*, I (1943), 355-408; "A Romano-Canonical Maxim, *Quod Omnes Tangit*, in Bracton," *Traditio*, IV (1946), 197-251; "The Theory of Public Law and the State in the Thirteenth Century," *Seminar* (Annual Extraordinary Number of *The Jurist*), VI (1948), 42-59.

study the legists and canonists in relation to the corporateness of representation and to the problem of the royal authority. Yet there is obvious danger in transferring legal definitions and practices: the meaning of full powers of attorney in mandates for agents of corporations was not necessarily the same as in the instructions of knights of shires; an English shire was not the same kind of corporation as a guild, an Italian *civitas*, a cathedral chapter, or an ecclesiastical province; the Romano-canonical theory of consent in the maxim *quod omnes tangit* was of doubtful application in a *pays du droit coutumier*; and the theory of consent in the realm of private law was not necessarily the same in public law.

Critics of the history of ideas remind us of another difficulty. It is almost a maxim that theory follows the event. How can one apply later theory to what has meanwhile been changing in fact? Sometimes, indeed, the practice contradicts the current theory, and it is tempting to force the facts into conformity with the idea, or even to deplore the fact as an unfortunate deviation or exception. Naturally, we are prone to trust apparently reliable public records, royal charters, statutes, writs of summons, judgments of courts, and the like, rather than legal opinions which are presumed to be "uncontrolled."

This very study results from ideas in the Statute of York. From Stubbs to our own day, authorities on representation have disagreed on the meaning of consent in Edward I's summons to the clergy in 1295. If royal justices disagreed when interpreting statutes, we can hardly ignore some knowledge of the legal theories that they used—or indeed failed to use. Since the documents contain many expressions that derive from the two laws, we must study the legal meaning of the terminology, despite the dangers of analogy, indirect approach, and the cutting of the cloth woven by the lawyers to fit English, French, and Spanish institutions. Lawyers then, as now, loved subtle distinctions and disagreed in their interpretations. Nonetheless, their opinions help us understand the constitutional developments. Ideas do have some influence on the making of institutions, just as the things established result in ideas.

In fact, we have already observed that the developing English

law and institutions of the twelfth to fourteenth centuries were
not in isolation from the Continent, that legal theories and
practices in the two laws pertaining to corporate communities,
representation, consent, the public authority of the prince, and
the State played no mean role in the rise of Parliament. In the
early Middle Ages kings asserted, if they could not practice, the
theory of public powers in part derived from the late Roman
Empire. But it is important that the revival of the two laws, in
which England shared through participating in the traditions
of the common ancient Mediterranean and medieval European
civilization, coincided with the rise of national monarchies and
furnished many a convenient legal term and idea for the fixing,
shaping, and further developing of extant institutions and concepts in public and private law alike. For example, it is more
than coincidental that the representation of shires, towns, and
ecclesiastical corporations in assemblies arose after the Romano-
canonical principles of the case of necessity, *status Reipublicae*
(*status regni*), public welfare, and *quod omnes tangit* became
well known, and after the feeling of local and general community was subjected to the influence of the two laws on corporations and agency.[2]

Now let us turn to the terminology of the Statute of York,
and see whether it reflects, in more than accidental manner,

[2] On the community of the vill and its corporate responsibility in the thirteenth century, see Helen M. Cam, "The Community of the Vill," in *Medieval
Studies presented to Rose Graham*, eds. V. Ruffer and A. J. Taylor, pp. 1-14.
Professor Cam says that this is evidence that "representation in England was not
a device introduced in the thirteenth century by canon lawyers" (p. 13). But no
one, except possibly Ernest Barker, has implied that representation was literally
introduced into England by the canon lawyers. What I hold is simply that the
very corporateness of the vill, as shown by the documents, and the representation
of it in the courts, reveal the influence of the two laws on the corporate community and agency. In the twelfth century, possibly earlier, monasteries and
chapters were already acting as corporations and so appearing in courts ecclesiastical and royal, and often enough ecclesiastics sat as royal justices who
heard cases from the communities. The influence of the two laws and the
increasing recognition of the corporate character of vill, hundred, and shire, had
a relationship that is more than coincidental. I agree that Maitland did not do
justice to the corporateness of the vill, hundred, and shire—see my comment and
references in *Traditio*, IV, 221-224, and above, ch. IV, nn. 119-124. Of course, the
community came first; but the corporate theory and procedure from the Roman
and Canon law helped give it a legal capacity that was helpful to central
government and community alike.

the meanings in the two laws. These are the important words: "Mes les choses que serount a establir pur lestat de nostre seignur le roi et de ses heirs, et pur lestat du roialme et du poeple, soient tretes, accordees, establies en parlementz par nostre seignur le roi et par lassent des prelatz, countes et barouns et la communalte du roialme, auxint come ad este acustume cea enarere"[3]—literally translated, "But the things which shall be established for the estate of our lord the king and his heirs, and for the estate of the realm and the people, shall be treated, granted and established in parliament by the king, with the assent of the prelates, earls, and barons and the community of the realm, as has been the custom heretofore."

What is the "estate" of the realm? And what is the community of the realm that assents? Does the estate imply the most important affairs of the kingdom, including some kinds of general legislation, and demand the consent of a community of knights and burgesses, the commons (G. T. Lapsley and B. Wilkinson)?[4] Is it the public welfare connected with fiscal matters and taxation and treated with the consent of the commons (George L. Haskins, C. H. McIlwain, and S. B. Chrimes)?[5] Or, if the estate means matters of public concern, is "community of the realm" a mere tautology for prelates and magnates, who alone have a real right of assent, as Professor Strayer believes?[6] On the contrary, did the community not mean the representatives or commons (W. A. Morris)?[7] Finally, shall we rest content with the literal definitions of "estate" given by Dowdall and

3 *Statutes of the Realm*, p. 189.

4 Wilkinson, "The Coronation Oath of Edward II and the Statute of York," *Speculum*, XIX, 445-469; Lapsley, "The Interpretation of the Statute of York, 1322," *E.H.R.*, LVI, 22-51, 411-446, and now in *Crown, Community and Parliament in the Later Middle Ages*, eds. Helen M. Cam and G. Barraclough, pp. 153-230.

5 Haskins, *Statute of York*, pp. 93-110; Chrimes, *English Constitutional Ideas in the Fifteenth Century*, pp. 91-93; McIlwain, in *C.M.H.*, VII, pp. 678-681, and *Growth of Political Thought in the West*, p. 378.

6 Strayer, "The Statute of York and the Community of the Realm," *A.H.R.*, XLVII, 1-22. H. G. Richardson also objects to the idea that the commons could consent to legislation, "The English Coronation Oath," *Speculum*, XXIV, 70.

7 W. A. Morris, "Magnates and Community of the Realm in Parliament, 1264-1327," *Medievalia et Humanistica*, I (1943), 83-94, esp. 85. For other interpretations see Strayer, *A.H.R.*, XLVII, 2f.

Plucknett? (The word, they say, can be defined variously as the condition or rank of persons, as office, power, the governing body of a city, classes, or as the territory in which persons have power. Not until after Machiavelli—he has the idea, but does not use the word—does it mean the State of a sovereign prince, that is, the territory and the government of the prince.[8] And, Meinecke holds, reason of State begins with Machiavelli, even if there is a late medieval background.)[9]

Perhaps a better understanding will result if we consider "estate," the Latin *status*, in the context of the clause, as a principle of public law derived in large part from the Roman law; and if we consider "community of the realm" in relation to the corporate theory of the legists and canonists. This method is not absurd: England in the period especially from about 1100 to 1322 was influenced in many ways by the two laws, and experts in the Roman and canon law were employed at times by the kings—we find them active in the government of Edward II in helping draft important documents.[10] Nor is it altogether novel: elements of the theory of public law and the State, such as the "public welfare clause," the case of necessity and evident utility found in the just war of defense, have been noted in general by Sir Maurice Powicke, and in particular for Frederick II by Ernst Kantorowicz and Helene Wieruszowski, for France by Joseph R. Strayer, and for England, on the side of military service and

8 H. C. Dowdall, "The Word 'State,'" *L.Q.R.*, xxxix (1923), 98-125; T. F. T. Plucknett, "Words," *Cornell Law Quarterly*, xiv (1928-1929), 263-273. Cf. Holdsworth, *History of English Law*, III[4], 457.

9 Meinecke, *Die Idee der Staatsräson*, pp. 31-58; see also E. F. Jacob, "Changing Views of the Renaissance," *History*, xvi (1931), 214-229; and above, ch. v, nn. 2-15.

10 For some examples of the earlier influence of the two laws in England, see above, ch. iv, nn. 69-91, for bibliography; and now Stephan Kuttner and Eleanor Rathbone, "Anglo-Norman Canonists of the Twelfth Century: An Introductory Study," *Traditio*, vii (1949-51), 279-339. As for French legists in England in the time of Edward II, see Richardson, *Speculum*, xxiv, 69. It is well known that the great canonist, Hostiensis, had on occasion advised Henry III, and that the legist, the younger Accursius, had come to England for a while with Edward I. Richardson, *loc.cit.*, n. 124, says that it is "not evident why the king should have employed French legists." But it is probable that it was because the king needed legal arguments from the Roman law to support his royal rights; see the opinions of "duo legistae Francigeni" in *Ann. Lond.*, R.S. 76, pp. 211f. On Francis Accursius in England, G. L. Haskins, "Francis Accursius: A New Document," *Speculum*, xiii (1938), 76f.

claims to the throne of Scotland in the reign of Edward I, by Barnaby Keeney.[11]

Cicero, St. Augustine, and St. Thomas Aquinas had much to say about the common good or utility as something superior, normally, to the private good.[12] And there was Biblical sanction for the idea that in case of necessity the letter of the law is to be interpreted equitably.[13] But the main source of the legal theory was the Roman law. "Public law," said Ulpian, "pertains to the *status rei Romanae*, private law to the utility of individuals"; and the public law deals with religion, priests, and magistrates.[14] The glossators developed this and many other passages in the *Digest* and *Code* into a fairly consistent theory. By 1228 they were saying that the public law exists to preserve the *status* of the *Respublica* lest it perish.[15] A philosopher-theologian of the late thirteenth century, in the context of the public welfare, speaks literally of the *ratio status*.[16] But *status* is not personified as the State. It is either the public powers of the government or the public and common welfare, as glosses preserved by Accursius and as Odofredo and the Commentators

11 Powicke, "Reflections on the Medieval State," *Trans. Roy. Hist. Soc.*, 4th ser., XIX (1936), 1-18; Kantorowicz, *Kaiser Friedrich der Zweite*, I, 96ff., II, 99f. n. 223, and *King's Two Bodies*, ch. v; Wieruszowski, *Von Imperium zum nationalen Königtum*, pp. 40, 167-173; Strayer, "Laicization of French and English Society in the Thirteenth Century," *Speculum*, xv (1940), 76-86, and "Defense of the Realm and Royal Power in France," *Studi in onore di Gino Luzzato*, pp. 289-296; Keeney, "Military Service and the Development of Nationalism in England, 1272-1327," *Speculum*, XXII (1947), 534-549; and "The Medieval Idea of the State: the Great Cause, 1291-2," *Univ. Toronto Law Journal*, VIII (1949), 48-71.

12 See I. Th. Eschmann, "A Thomistic Glossary on the Principle of the Preëminence of a Common Good," *Mediaeval Studies*, v (1943), 123-165; Ewart Lewis, "Organic Tendencies in Medieval Political Thought," *American Political Science Review*, XXXII (1938), 849-867.

13 Matthew, XII, 3-4; Luke, VI, 3-4, and XIII, 14-16.

14 D. 1, 1, 1, 2: "Publicum ius est quod ad statum rei Romanae spectat. . . . Publicum ius in sacris, in sacerdotibus, in magistratibus consistat."

15 In the *Glossa ordinaria* of Accursius, which was finished by 1228; H. Kantorowicz, "Accursio e la sua biblioteca," *Rivista di Storia del Diritto Italiano*, II (1929), 43; Rashdall, *Universities*, eds. Powicke and Emden, I, 256 n. 4. The gloss reads, to *D.* 1, 1, 1, 2, ad v. *Publicum*, "ad statum conservandum, ne pereat." See below, ch. VII, n. 7.

16 In the *Quodlibeta* of Henry of Ghent, late thirteenth century, in Paris, BN, MS lat. 15350, fol. 262ᵛ c. 2-263ᵛ c. 1: Henry discusses the duty of subjects to observe the statutes of their rulers when they are made for the *utilitas communis*, for princes and prelates are presumed to have in view the *salus et pax reipublice*; (fol. 262ᵛ c. 2) "supponendo de prudencia et industria principis, quod vere presumendum est *ratione status*." See also above, ch. v, nn. 112-129.

clearly show.[17] (*Status Reipublicae* is in a sense the State of the Commonweal, or the public welfare of the commonwealth.) Private law itself is indirectly a concern of the public, since it interests the *Respublica* and its *status* to prevent anyone from misusing his property. And what is public pertains secondarily to the utility of private individuals. For the common utility, priests forgive men their sins and save souls; and magistrates interpret the laws, render justice, and maintain law and order, for otherwise laws would be useless. They and their office are therefore subjects of public law.[18] The *fiscus*, too, is public, for it is the treasury of the Empire, not the patrimony of the emperor; and criminal jurisdiction and the fines imposed by the courts and the confiscations made by the *fiscus* are treated by the public law because they are for the common welfare.[19]

The supreme head and magistrate of the Empire, the prince, rules in order to maintain the public and common welfare. He legislates, administers, and judges for the *status Reipublicae*. His prerogative, belonging to public law, is a public right, superior to private rights. Normally, however, his government for the common welfare is limited by private law and private rights. But in an emergency, when the *status* is threatened by rebellion or by an aggressive foreign enemy, he has, by public law, the right to take extraordinary measures to meet the danger and as-

[17] Again the material is too abundant to give here. Let the reader consult the glossators and commentators on *D.* 1, 1, 1, 2, and pursue the references given by them to other passages in the *Corpus Iuris Civilis*. For many opinions from the late thirteenth and the fourteenth century, see Gierke, III, 198-210, 356-360. Gierke refuses to admit that a kingdom could have its public law in the same sense as the Empire. On the distinction and confusion of *utilitas publica* and *communis* see below, ch. VIII, n. 24. See also ch. VII.

[18] *Glos. ord.* to *D.* 1, 1, 1, 2, ad v. *in sacris*: "Patet ergo quod tit. de sa. sanct. eccl. vel de epis. et cle. [*C.* 1, 2], ubicumque sunt, et similes sunt de iure publico; et idem de iure fiscali, ubicumque sit; et idem de officio magistratuum." That is, the titles in *Digest, Code, Institutes*, etc., on these subjects concerning priests, churches, magistrates, and the fisc, belong to public law.

[19] See the gloss above, n. 18; also Azo, *Summa Codicis*, introduction to 10, 1; Accursius, *Glos. ord.*, to *C.* 10, 1: "Occasione criminum, de quibus superiori libro dixit, augetur fiscus: ideo de eius iure dicit: vel dixit de iure publico circa crimina: nunc circa bona fisco quaerenda et conservanda: quod et ipsum est publicum alio respectu quam supra, ut ff. de iustitia et iur., l. j § publicum [*D.* 1, 1, 1, 2]. Item fiscus dicitur ipsa imperialis, vel imperii camera, non dico patrimonii Imperatoris. . . . Quicquid tamen specialitatis habet fiscus: et Caesaris, et Augustae ratio solet habere . . . quae fiscalis loco rei Romanae successit . . . Accur." See Kantorowicz, *King's Two Bodies*, pp. 164-192, 342-347.

sure the common safety. The defense of the common *patria* and the maintenance of peace, which itself is sometimes called the public utility, are the supreme duties of the prince.[20] If the emergency is dire, that is, a case of evident necessity, the prince can compel private rights in the form of special privileges to yield for the sake of the common welfare. "Necessity knows no law!"[21] It knows, that is, no private law that stands in the way of the state of the Empire.

In an emergency, then, the right of the *status*, the public and common welfare, is supreme. But *status* is not yet separated as an entity in itself from the common welfare. Not yet, moreover, is the supreme right of the *status* amoral, as in Machiavelli and in the totalitarian state. Not yet in its name can the prince rule arbitrarily without regard for the moral and material rights of his subjects. Even in a dire emergency the prince must give fair compensation in cases of expropriation;[22] and he must obtain the consent of all whose rights are affected by an act for the common good—"what touches all must be approved of all"— *quod omnes tangit*. All the same, this *status* is the origin of the idea of the State as something different from the government and the people, indeed, as a corporate, juristic person.

Does this theory of public law and the State apply to a kingdom? It does, for canonists and legists who became advisers to kings were, long before 1300, declaring that the king was emperor in his own realm, implying and even saying that a kingdom, independent of the Empire, had its own public law and was sovereign.[23] The kingdom is treated as a great corporate

[20] On the *patria*, see the excellent study by E. Kantorowicz "*Pro patria mori* in Medieval Political Thought," *A.H.R.*, LVI (1951), 472-492, and now his *King's Two Bodies*, pp. 232-272; also my study below, ch. x, § 1.

[21] "Necessitas legem non habet"—this maxim, for public as well as for private law, was stated so frequently from the twelfth century on that it would be superfluous to give references here. Suffice it that St. Bernard used it, Azo includes it in his *Brocardica*, and canonists and legists refer to it for almost every special case of interpreting the letter of the law; it is a principle of equity and casuistry.

[22] See in general Meyer, *Das Recht der Expropriation*, pp. 76-115; for Lucas de Penna, Walter Ullmann, *The Medieval Idea of Law*, pp. 185-187.

[23] On the formulas, *rex imperator in regno suo*, and *superiorem non recognoscens*, the literature is abundant. F. Calasso, *I Glossatori e la teoria della sovranità*, 2nd ed., is the most recent work of importance on the side of Gierke's interpretation, that the formulas did not imply independence from the Empire

community the head of which, the king, knows no superior but God and the law.[24] The members are the subjects who have certain legal rights, and are both individuals considered as such and communities or lesser corporations of individuals. As head, the king has the public right of his prerogative to govern the corporate body of the realm for the common welfare and safety of all the members including himself. This is the superior right of his office or *dignitas* and is distinct from his private rights as a person. It is stated as a part of the coronation oath; it is the inalienable right of the crown.[25] It is indicated by the separation of the *fiscus* from the person of the king, as Ernst Kantorowicz has recently shown for England.[26] In short, the king by his office represents the realm and exercises a right of State, that is, the right to legislate, administer, judge, raise armies and tax for the *status regni, l'estat du roialme,* the common profit, utility, or welfare and safety of all; and he has the right to interpret the case of necessity and the "public welfare clause."

Are English illustrations needed? One recalls numerous examples of the terminology in the writs of John, Henry III, and

---

and a true public law for each kingdom. Sergio Mochi Onory, *Fonti canonistiche dell'idea moderna dello stato,* champions the opposite view. Calasso and Mochi Onory offer sufficient bibliography. I am convinced that while there remained a strong tradition of the inferiority of kingdoms among canonists and legists of Italian and German origin, on the other hand, some of those of English, Spanish, French, and Neapolitan connections stressed complete independence. For all this see below, ch. x, § 2.

[24] Bracton: "Si autem princeps vel rex vel alius qui superiorem non habuerit nisi deum," ed. Woodbine, III, 43; also II, 3: "Parem autem non habet rex in regno suo. . . . Item nec multo fortius superiorem. . . . Ipse autem rex non debet esse sub homine sed sub deo et sub lege. . . ." See also F. Schulz, "Bracton on Kingship," *E.H.R.,* LX (1945), 149-151. In using the word *corporate,* I do not mean that the kingdom is like an ordinary corporation and the subject of private law. (Today the State as a corporate entity is the subject of private as well as public law, for it owns property.) But the medieval realm was now treated as a corporate body of which the king was the head.

[25] On the crown, see Richardson, "The English Coronation Oath," *Speculum,* XXIV, 44-75; Wilkinson, "The 'Political Revolution' of the Thirteenth and Fourteenth Centuries in England," *Speculum,* XXIV, 505; also Bracton, ed. Woodbine, II, 167, 297f., 337-339—167: "Est enim corona facere iusticiam et iudicium et tenere pacem et sine quibus corona consistere non poterit nec tenere." More references will be given in ch. x, below.

[26] E. Kantorowicz, "Christus-Fiscus," in *Synopsis, Festgabe für Alfred Weber,* pp. 225-235, esp. 232f., for Bracton, quoted p. 233 n. 1: "Est etiam res quasi sacra res fiscalis, quae dari non potest . . . a principe vel a regi regnante, et quae coronam et communem respiciunt utilitatem."

Edward I. By the time of Edward I, general legislation in statutes was for the common profit, and one source holds that the king was deemed emperor when he made a new law. In 1291 the royal justices asserted that for the common utility and maintenance of the peace the king's jurisdiction was superior to the private right of the Earls Marchers to fight each other.[27] In 1297 Edward claimed that his plan of campaigning on the Continent to wage a war of defense of king and realm against the aggressor was justified by the necessity or danger that threatened the common welfare; at the same time he justified his plan to obtain a more universal military service from £20 men and knights of the shire, for the danger touched all.[28] Such, again, was the justification whenever general subsidies were demanded. The *status regni*, moreover, was a principle used, as in the Roman law, to help the king obtain an extraordinary tax from ecclesiastical corporations such as convents that had received special exemptions from the king himself.[29] I know of no case from the thirteenth century of a church or monastery's resisting a tax on this basis of a royal franchise, but a famous case of 1441, discussed by Plucknett, is a good illustration. Then Chief Baron Fray argued that the exemption of a convent was not valid in a time of great necessity when the subsidy was for the common safety, and that a subsidy was as one of the revenues of the king's courts (so Parliament) an inheritance of the king. Plucknett argues that this case illustrates the persistence of the idea of private law in public matters. But it is possible that the chief justice, not knowing the Roman law as it had been known in the time of Edward I and II, was trying to express the idea that a subsidy as a revenue of a court belonged to a public office under the king, to the *fiscus*.[30] In theory, *non obstante* special privilege

---

[27] *Rotuli Parliamentorum*, I, 70-75; Vickers, *England in the Later Middle Ages*, 4th ed., p. 33; see also below, n. 46. On the king as emperor, see Keeney, "The Medieval Idea of the State," *Univ. Toronto Law Jour.*, VIII, 60-61.

[28] Keeney, "Military Service in England," *Speculum*, XXII, 541-543. He notes the importance of *quod omnes tangit* here as well as in 1295.

[29] Even the Church admitted that, with the consent of the pope, the clergy should assent to subsidies in times of evident necessity touching the common welfare; see G. Le Bras, *L'Immunité réelle*, pp. 21-30, 49-148; cf. above, ch. III, n. 190.

[30] T. F. T. Plucknett, "The Lancastrian Constitution," in *Tudor Studies Presented to . . . Albert Frederick Pollard*, pp. 161-181.

belonging to private law, the public right of the state of the realm generally triumphed.

Of course, the baronage sometimes offered opposition to the king's sole right to interpret these principles of public law and rule with unlimited prerogative. So in 1215, 1258, 1297, and 1311.[31] In 1242 and again in 1297 the magnates argued that the king was wrong about his alleged case of necessity, or that in any event fighting abroad could not be called a just war of defense.[32] (They did not believe that the defense of England began on the Rhine!) St. Louis decided in favor of the royal prerogative in 1264; and Clement V similarly supported the king in 1305, referring to the coronation oath.[33] The royal government itself reasserted the rights of the crown in the Statute of York. The general theory, stated essentially by Bracton, was that the public right of the king as head of the realm, his "government," was the full, absolute right and power to judge and keep the peace of the realm. If his jurisdiction was normally limited by that law which protected the rights of subjects, according to the public law it was unlimited in case of emergencies. His supreme authority, we shall see below, belonged to his public *status*.[34]

[31] In 1215 the magnates, in Magna Carta, were chiefly interested in protecting their rights from the royal absolutism of John by forcing him to acknowledge that he must rule according to the law. In 1258 and 1311 the aim of the magnates was to supervise the king and thus limit the royal prerogative—which was contrary to the law that gave the king his power of administration and jurisdiction for the common good of the realm. See below, VIII, § 2.

[32] In 1242 Henry III asked for a subsidy for possible war with Louis IX; the magnates and prelates declared that the French monarch had not broken the truce and hence, there was no case of necessity or just war and no reason for a subsidy. See Matthew Paris, *Chron. Maj.*, IV, 185-187; *S.C.*, pp. 360-362. On the episode of 1297-98, when Edward I planned a campaign in Flanders, see *S.C.*, pp. 482-494; Keeney, "Military Service in England," *Speculum*, XXII, 541, 547; J. G. Edwards, "*Confirmatio Cartarum* and Baronial Grievances in 1297, Part I," *E.H.R.*, LVIII (1943), 147-171; Wilkinson, *The Constitutional History of England 1216-1399*, I, ch. v.

[33] *S.C.*, pp. 395-397; Wilkinson, *op.cit.*, I, 175-177; and Richardson, "English Coronation Oath," *Speculum*, XXIV, 50.

[34] Bracton, *De legibus*, ed. Woodbine, II, 166 (f. 556): the king has "ordinariam jurisdictionem et dignitatem et potestatem super omnes" in the kingdom; "habet enim omnia iura in manu sua, quae ad coronam et laicalem pertinent potestatem et materialem gladium, qui pertinet ad regni gubernaculum. Habet etiam iustitiam et iudicium quae sunt iurisdictionis. . . . Habet etiam ea quae sunt pacis"; (167) "Est enim corona facere iustitiam et iudicium, et tenere pacem." See the fine discussion of the distinction between the *gubernaculum* (the above absolute power) and *jurisdictio* by McIlwain, *Constitutionalism Ancient and Modern*,

But the king's business of governing, when it affected the lawfully established rights of subjects and their common welfare, became in part the business of the *universitas regni*, the community of the realm. The whole medieval tradition, Roman and feudal alike, called for the king's seeking counsel and, if specific rights were in question, obtaining consent. Inevitably, in important affairs the *status regni* and the *status regis* were each involved in the other. A matter that touched both the estate of the realm and the estate of the king must be considered by the *universitas regni* and the head (the king) in common, the king having the right of making the final decision. Above all, the public and common welfare of realm and people was at stake in whatever might endanger it. The *estat du roialme*, then, in the Statute of York, surely meant the *utilitas publica* and *communis* (the French *commun profit*) of the realm as a whole and of its members, king and subjects alike. The public *estat* of the king, that is, the powers of authority vested in king and crown, was mentioned separately because of the custom, based on the law of corporations, of mentioning both head and members when their interests and rights were held in common as well as when their rights were viewed separately in relation to office and membership.[35]

To repeat, as head, the king had the public right, in his "estate royal," to maintain both his estate and the estate of the realm. But if what he planned to do for the estate of the realm

---

pp. 69-94, esp. 73-84; cf. Schulz, *E.H.R.*, LX, 144, 165-169. See below, ch. VII, nn. 27, 64, 71; ch. VIII.

[35] On common and separate rights, and representation of them, in ecclesiastical corporations, consult the *Glos. ord.* of Bernard of Parma, to *Decr. Greg. IX* 1, 3, 21 Edoceri, ad v. *debeant*: if a business touches the head principally, the prelate in person or by his representative acts with the consent of the corporation; if it touches the corporation principally, the corporation acts through an agent with the consent of the head; if it touches both equally, being common to both, then both with mutual consent appoint a syndic or proctor. See to the same decretal Inn. IV, *Appar.*, ad v. *teneantur* and ad v. *congregationum*. See also Ber. of Parma in *Glos. ord.*, Hostiensis, Joh. Andreae, and other decretalists to *Decr. Greg. IX* 3, tit. 10, "De hiis quae fiunt ab episcopo (a praelatis) sine consensu capituli." Certainly, a case of lay taxation of the clergy affected both separate and common rights, and hence demanded the separate representation of prelates and chapters, and also of the lower clergy of the diocese. See also above, ch. III, n. 165.

and of himself was extraordinary, it touched the legal rights of all the members in common;[36] and by the prevailing theory of consent, *quod omnes tangit,* he must obtain the consent of all in common assembly, in Parliament.[37] (This theory of consent in common assembly of the members of a corporate body was not always perfectly practiced in the Church and in France; local assemblies, provincial in nature, were either substituted

[36] Examples in royal writs are common, e.g., *S.C.*, p. 406, No. v (1265); p. 457, No. III (1282); p. 459, No. IV; pp. 479f. (1295). French examples are numerous for 1302. The legists and canonists insist repeatedly, that when an important business arises that concerns any corporate community and all its members in common, all the members whose rights are touched must be summoned to a general assembly to treat the matter—the legists above all to D. 3, 4, 3-4; D. 50, 1, 14; D. 50, 17, 16, 1; the canonists to *Decr. Greg. IX* 1, 2, 6; 3, 10, 10; 3, 11, 1. The legal thought is too complicated to repeat here; the problem of common consent needs a detailed study.

[37] Strayer (in Strayer and Taylor, *Studies in Early French Taxation*), p. 21, speaking of the necessity of the king's consulting the people who were taxed, in the time of Philip the Fair, thinks this was because medieval governments had no other method of getting information on the wealth of the subjects. It is true that this is a part of the picture (and it may be related to the idea of the legists, that taxation should be proportional to individual wealth) as it was when the English prelates declared that they could not consent to a subsidy without consulting their archdeacons, for the business touched them too. But a government that does not need to get the assent of those taxed does not need to consult them, for it need not be careful about the amount demanded in relation to the means of the subjects. I repeat that consent was important—it was accepted by most lawyers that not even the emperor could obtain extraordinary aids without getting consent. For examples of the use of *quod omnes tangit,* in England, see above, ch. IV, nn. 240-254: also Wilkinson, *Constitutional History,* I, 45, 122, 127, 228.

As for the argument that the king summoned representatives largely to persuade more people by making the assembly a means of propaganda, again this is an important factor, but surely not more important than the principle of consent related to rights protected by private law. The need of persuasion is not sufficient to account for an elaborate procedure of summoning in order to obtain consent, even if the king by demonstrating successfully his case of necessity or defense of the realm had by public law the right to such consent. The documents either quote or imply the principle, *quod omnes tangit,* and the writs of summons state that the representatives are to have full power to consent to what the king and his government decide. Surely, then, the legal necessity of summoning all who were touched by the business was more important than propaganda and the convenience of obtaining information. See my article, *"Plena potestas," Traditio,* I, 375 n. 14, for the terms of the writs of summons; and now above, ch. III, n. 103.

Chrimes, *English Constitutional Ideas,* p. 60, puts it well: "But all his [the king's] legislation and his taxation must necessarily prejudice someone's rights; and to do that lawfully, the assent of those whose rights were to be infringed must be secured. That assent could be conveniently got in parliament, and it had to be so obtained." I would add to the word "conveniently" that, as I said elsewhere, an assembly was legally necessary in a business that was common to many.

for or made preliminary to a general assembly. But the consent must still be given in common in relation to the membership of a province. Consent obtained separately from individuals and at different times was illegal, since unfair pressure was possible and the members should have the right to prepare a common defense of rights held in common.) In England as on the Continent, as a result of the influence of the two laws, all concerned by a national business must be properly summoned, informed about the general nature of the business, and given a right to a hearing, a right that included "treating" or debating the issue before consenting to the decision of the king. Consent might be refused if the king's case of necessity and utility could be shown to be false or ill-founded. More often a compromise on the amount of a subsidy would result. But normally, the king had the advantage, for his prerogative included the final right to interpret the public welfare or state of the realm. Consequently, the consent of the members of the realm was not that of the sovereign people; it was a procedural consent in high court as assembly and was based on law and justice. Consent could not be democratic because by public law the king, in the name of evident utility and necessity, could normally expect knights and burgesses to assent to what was for the common good and safety.[38]

If the "estate of the realm" was the public and common welfare of all, including the king, how was it related to the "community of the realm"? Was the community the same as the whole membership of the realm that was to consent to acts of government for the estate of the realm? According to the theory of corporations in the two laws, the community was the membership, including that member who was also the head. The estate of the realm, like the *status* of a corporation, concerned head and members, the head in his office and in his personal rights. But the membership of a great community included magnates and prelates as heads of lesser communities or as possessors of special rights, as it included many smaller men as members of communities within the realm. Hence, the greater men were

---

[38] See, for a fuller statement of my argument, *"Plena potestas," Traditio*, I, 370-375; above, ch. III, § 4; also Introduction.

summoned individually by the supreme head, the king, while the general membership was summoned as communities to send representatives.[39] For the business in the assembly would touch the rights of heads as persons having jurisdiction, and at the same time the rights of all the members apart from the heads and the rights of the heads as members.

Was this not the practice in England? Since about 1250 (on occasion earlier) the general business of a subsidy that touched the kingdom and its welfare had resulted in such summonses to Parliament. Magnates and prelates, as men of greater jurisdiction and dignity, were summoned individually; communities of the lower clergy and of knights and citizens and burgesses collectively, to send representatives with full powers. Were they not all members of the corporate body of the realm, the estate of which was to be treated and decided? Usually in the thirteenth century the magnates had considered themselves to be the essential corporation or *universitas regni*. (The canonists held that the *universitas regni*, apart from the king, was the great men, the *populus*.)[40] In the second half of the century, however, when in fact knights and townsmen had rights of lesser jurisdiction and at the same time rights touched by an extraordinary tax, it was increasingly necessary to include their communities in the community of the realm. Certainly Edward I did so. *Quod omnes tangit* made this procedure, that of summoning knights and burgesses, legally necessary. It was not ex-

[39] When the archbishop of Canterbury called a council at London in 1257 to treat the common business (royal aids among other things) of the English Church, the summons went to the archdeacons, deans, priors, and abbots of each diocese; and all these as heads of churches or administrators of the lower clergy had to bring mandates from churches and subjects; *Ann. Mon.* (R. S.), I, 401f. For the case of 1255, see Lunt, *Financial Relations of the Papacy with England to 1327*, p. 139; in 1258 the bishop, deans, abbots and greater priors, and the archdeacons (with mandates from their subjects) of each diocese, *S.C.*, p. 446. In 1273 the archbishop summoned the bishops and three or four representatives of each diocese; *S.C.*, pp. 446f. Representation of all the clergy of provinces and kingdoms became common before the end of the century. On the summons of all parties interested either directly or indirectly and their right of consent, see *D.* 42, 1, 47 and 63, *D.* 44, 1, 10; *D.* 44, 2, 1; *C.* 7, 56, 4, and glosses; also *Traditio*, IV, 200-209; above ch. IV, § I. See below for the summoning to Parliament and Estates General, n. 45.

[40] See below, ch. VIII, n. 16. On the *universitas regni* of England see also Powicke, *Thirteenth Century*, pp. 131-169, and Wilkinson, *Constitutional History*, III, 48-51.

clusively a matter of the king's desire to make propaganda and publicize his business that caused the participation of the representatives of the communities or commons.[41]

The magnates continued to lead and influence lesser nobles and townsmen. But even for their private right to protest or to propose something to the king, if their action interested (in the legal sense of the word) the knights, the new legal procedure compelled them to obtain the consent of the body of knights of the shires. A petition initiated by the earls, for example, in the name of the greater and the lesser nobility, needed the adherence of the knights. No real corporation acted, but the fiction of corporate action, to which all interested parties had consented, was maintained. It is possible that on occasion, perhaps in such cases as grievances over the merchants' being alone consulted by the king about a new tax on wool, the knights, who were experienced in legal and administrative affairs, were as responsible as the magnates for complaints offered the king.[42] At any rate there was a legal as well as an expedient basis for the magnates' enlisting the support of the knights of the shires during periods of baronial reform movements—in 1258 and following years, in 1297, and in 1311. The knights were interested in the *maltote*, in the confirmation of the Charters, and in the troubles of the reign of Edward II.[43]

[41] Above, n. 37.

[42] As to the consent to the custom on wool, etc., in 1275, of representatives of cities, boroughs, and merchant vills, and the assent of the merchants, see Morris, *Med. et Human.*, I, 71, and Wilkinson, "Coronation Oath of Edward II," *Speculum*, XIX, 465. Eileen Power, *The Wool Trade in English Medieval History*, shows how wool and taxes on wool affected magnates and knights as well as merchants (pp. 64-67), for "if the king raised a tax on wool . . . it was the merchants who directly paid it, though its true incidence might be elsewhere"; also pp. 71-75. The documents need further study to determine whether magnates and knights actually stated that the business of a wool-tax touched them as well as the merchants. But according to the legal meaning of *quod omnes tangit* they could maintain that what touched others directly, touched them secondarily, and therefore, they had the right to be consulted, too; cf. *D.* 42, 1, 63, and glosses; also *C.* 7, 56, 2 and 4; *C.* 7, 60, 1-2.

[43] On the actual appearance of the knights of the shires in Parliament to consent to subsidies and their interest in other matters before 1322, and on occasions when the magnates seem still to represent the whole community of the realm, see Morris, "Magnates and Community of the Realm in Parliament, 1264-1327," *Med. et Human.*, I, 58-94. Morris shows much appreciation of the problem of varying degrees of consent of knights, burgesses, and merchants, in relation to their capacity to pay taxes, p. 73. According to the legists, all should

To return to the king's government. By the end of the century Edward I, in order to raise a subsidy for the defense of the realm, was summoning the whole community of the realm. That is to say, he summoned all subjects who because of recognized legal rights in jurisdiction, property, and franchises were members of the fictively corporate body of the kingdom. The membership did not include a million or so small freeholders, nor, it seems, the well-to-do £20 men. Probably the knights in a fashion represented them. Nor, as Helen M. Cam has shown, were villeins and serfs members; and they had no representation except in a sense by their lords whose lands they cultivated; and these lords were knights, magnates, prelates, and ecclesiastical corporations.[44] But the membership did include the prelates and lower clergy, who met in separate convocation, and the great nobles, the knights of the shires, and burgesses and citizens of en-franchised towns, who met in Parliament. The king must summon all these members, the greater ones individually, the lesser ones in their communities by way of representation.[45]

---

contribute to a subsidy in time of necessity, but in proportion to wealth. Morris holds that especially after 1311 it became customary to summon representatives, and that they were certainly included in the *communitas regni*, pp. 73ff. See also Wilkinson, "Coronation Oath of Edward II," *Speculum*, xix, 465-467.

[44] Helen M. Cam, "L'Assiette et la perception des indemnités des représentants des comtés dans l'Angleterre médiévale," *Rev. hist. dr. fr. étr.*, xviii (1939), 219ff.; *S.C.*, p. 358.

[45] The situation in France, for the Estates General of the early fourteenth century, is analogous. The general assembly did not include representatives of all the people; to it were summoned the nobles and the clergy (prelates and representatives of ecclesiastical corporations), and representatives of the *bonnes villes*, i.e., of privileged towns. The lords represented the *roturiers* of the country-side and unincorporated villages. The legist, Jean Faure, asks if all individuals from a region or an Order should be summoned when the business "tangat multos." On the one hand, it seems that they should all be summoned, "quia omnes tangit." But on the other hand (obviously because summoning all individually is difficult, if not impossible—also in the Roman law), if they are members of corporate communities, it is sufficient to summon the administrators (as representatives—this was often done, although more frequently syndics or proctors were elected). If they do not have corporations, the prelates and barons who have jurisdiction over the rural communities and villages are summoned (A. Esmein, *Cours élémentaire d'histoire du droit français*, p. 475 n. 2). But see now, for local assemblies and collectivities representing them, F. Cheyette, "Procurations by Large Scale Communities in Fourteenth Century France," *Speculum*, xxxvii (1962), 18-31.

Jean Faure, in his *Commentary* on the *Inst.*, discussing the summons (*citatio, monitio, conventio*, etc.), reflects the principles of Roman law. But, he continues,

In short, the king, the prelates and magnates, and the communities of shires and towns were all members of and constituted the "community of the realm" when the "estate of the realm," the common welfare of all, was the business of Parliament. In the Statute of York, then, the community of the realm, although mentioned in addition to king, prelates, and magnates, means neither the commons alone nor the great nobles alone. But just as in the two laws head and general membership were named, the latter to emphasize the ensemble of members below the head, it is likely that "community of the realm," thus added to the greater members, stressed the presence of the communities of lesser members, or the commons, without, however, excluding the great from the general community. The expression is not, I am convinced, completely redundant—added, that is, to indicate the magnates and prelates as still the *universitas regni* which they had been a century earlier, although in some matters they continued to represent the community because of their prestige and influence.[46]

The "estate of the realm," then, was the concern of the whole community including knights and burgesses when the king asked for a general subsidy for the common defense. Was there any other business that was for the common utility and touched the community of the realm and required the assent of magnates, prelates and commons? The royal jurisdiction existed

---

the French *curia* observes a different practice in law-suits concerning a *terra* or *villa*, for it summons the inhabitants and gives them permission to elect a proctor. When, however, the *curia* of France wants a subsidy, "it practices what I have said, for it summons only the prelates, barons, and notable towns" (p. 621).

46 My disagreement with Professor Strayer on this point (he argues that "community of the realm" is redundant, for he believes that the magnates were still the real community) stems both from the background of the two laws on individual rights and the communities, and from the increasing appearance of representatives in matters of general national concern or of legislation concerning them. See Strayer, "Statute of York," *A.H.R.*, XLVII, 21, 22 n. 79. The fact that in a writ to the judges the king said the pardon was revoked only by the prelates, earls, barons, and other *proceres* does not prove that the statement in the statute revoking the pardon is wrong in saying that knights of the counties also assented. Perhaps the clerk who drew up the writ to the judges felt it was not important to mention the knights in a writ.

But Strayer is certainly right in holding that the community of the realm is not the commons. The commons are the communities of shires and towns, not *la communalte* of the realm. See also my remarks below, ch. VIII, n. 115.

for the public and common welfare,[47] but it was normally exercised by the king as a part of his prerogative for maintaining peace within the realm, and it required no consent other than the purely procedural consent in the acceptance of the power of the courts and in the right to be summoned and have fair trial according to the law of the land. But legislation could touch legal rights and require consent that was more voluntary in nature, though subordinate again to the public right of the king to make and interpret law for the common good. In general, a statute that was primarily feudal in content needed the assent only of the magnates and prelates as tenants-in-chief and as men of jurisdiction, which may explain why the knights of the shires apparently were not asked to consent to famous statutes of the thirteenth century. Nonetheless, a proposed law might touch the rights of the knights either directly or indirectly, and on the basis of *quod omnes tangit* they could claim that they should be consulted. (If only we had reports of what went on in the shire courts as assemblies!) It is even possible, though generally denied by scholars, that the knights participated in the making of the Statute of Westminster I, 1275, for the community of the realm is mentioned as well as the prelates and magnates, knights of the shires had been summoned to the assembly, and knights' fees were among the things treated.[48] Everyone says that the magnates and prelates consented to an aid of forty shillings on the knight's fee in 1290 both for themselves and for the knights. But I am bold enough to interpret otherwise the words *"pro se et communitate totius regni quantum in ipsis est"*:[49] the great

---

[47] See *Rot. Parl.*, I, 71ff., for the famous case of the Earls Marchers, 1291; also Lodge and Thornton, *English Constitutional Documents*, p. 9; above, n. 27—also below, ch. VIII, n. 66.

[48] C. H. Jenkinson, "The First Parliament of Edward I," *E.H.R.*, xxv (1910), 236; the knights and other representatives were summoned "ad faciendum quod tunc . . . ordinabitur," and "ad tractandum una cum magnatibus" (pp. 232f.); Morris, in *Med. et Human.*, I, 71.

[49] Morris, *Med. et Human.*, I, 65 and 73, says that this grant of a "feudal aid of 40 shillings on the knight's fee 'quantum in ipsis est' seems designed to raise the question whether . . . so heavy a burden should fall on knights' fees." Yet a letter patent of Edward I, *an.* 30, states that the prelates and magnates in Parliament granted 40 shillings from every knight's fee as an aid for the marriage of the king's daughter (*Rot. Parl.*, I, 266). It is possible that the inconsistency lies in this, that at times the magnates represented knights as well, at other times felt that the knights of the shire should be consulted; or that the knights claimed

nobles consented for themselves and the community of the realm insofar as the right to do so was in them, but, by implication, not for others who had rights concerned here and were also a part of the community! Otherwise, why the qualifying phrase, "*quantum in ipsis est*"? At any rate, the Statute of Carlisle, 1307, which forbade the taxation of monasteries by alien abbots and priors, was in the interest of lesser as well as greater nobles, and the communities assented.[50] Wilkinson and Morris have given other examples of probable participation of the commons in legislation before 1322.[51] Toward the end of the fourteenth century it was stated for the king that he wished to have the advice and consent of the commons when statutes and subsidies were for the "common profit" of the realm.[52] But the "common profit" is the estate of the realm. If, then, proposed legislation was general enough to be for the estate of the realm and also to affect the rights of knights, the assenting community of the realm in the Statute of York included the commons.[53] The commons, however, would hardly be called upon to give counsel and consent as often in legislation as in taxation. Moreover, the Statute did not imply the consent of the commons to statutes which were for the common welfare but did not clearly touch the rights of knights and burgesses. Nor did it as yet imply the consent of the communities of the shires to a tax or law (taxation was a kind of legislation as well as a kind of jurisdiction) which the king could lawfully interpret as one concerning the merchant towns exclusively; nor, again, the consent of the towns to what affected

---

that their rights were at stake and they should be summoned; for the legal principle, see above, nn. 39, 41.

[50] *Statutes of the Realm*, I, 150-152: "de consilio Comitum, Baronum, Magnatum, procerum, et aliorum nobilium, et regni sui communitatum"; also, with full deliberation or *tractatus*, and with the unanimous consent of all these. See also Morris, in *Med. et Human.*, I, 71f.

[51] See above, to n. 42.

[52] McIlwain, *Constitutionalism*, p. 159; Chrimes, *English Constitutional Ideas*, pp. 93, 161f., for claims of the commons in 1407 and 1414.

[53] On consent of knights of the shire to legislation, e.g., the first Statute of Westminster, see Morris, *Med. et Human.*, I, 71. At least the representative knights were probably consulted, because some of the provisions certainly interested them and touched their rights. I agree with Wilkinson that participation of the commons is implied in 1306, *Speculum*, XIX, 467. But I feel that what is meant is that the communities can participate only if new laws directly touch their interests; so likewise Morris in *The English Government at Work*, I, 22, for 1328.

only the rights of the magnates and knights. This broader theory of the consent of the commons was to develop later when the king's sole right to interpret both the common welfare and the scope of rights involved could be limited, and not fully until the seventeenth century with the triumph of parliamentary sovereignty.

If analogy with the theories of public law and the State in the two laws has any value, and if the appearance of the Romano-canonical terminology in English documents permits a similar interpretation in relation to the actual growth of the royal power and the rise of the commons in Parliament, I feel certain that "estate of the realm" in the Statute of York means both the public welfare of the realm as a whole and the common welfare of all in the kingdom who have specific rights that may be touched by any act necessary to preserve the *status regni* or the State. The king has the public right, by public law, to preserve the State and to do what is necessary to that end. But he must do it in Parliament with the consent of the members of the corporate body of the realm. For the assurance of the estate of the realm will usually involve an extraordinary act that is not permitted by the law of the land unless the consent of all whose rights are touched is obtained. In a word, what is for the estate of the realm is to be done by the king with the assent of the community of the realm. A general subsidy for the common defense and safety requires the consent of magnates and commons alike. And the consent of the commons, although not democratic or sovereign, is necessary to a general statute for the common profit, but is rarely called for, since legislation rarely affects both the state of the realm and their rights. I come to agreement, therefore, with Haskins and McIlwain with regard to the estate of the realm, taxation, and the consent of the commons; and qualifiedly with Wilkinson, with regard to the consent of the commons to legislation. But, to repeat, while consent has become necessary according to the law, it is not the consent of a sovereign body, but consent to what the king and his government want or are willing to concede.[54]

[54] See above, to n. 38; I agree at this point with Richardson, "English Coronation Oath," *Speculum*, xxiv, 73: "The statutes [of 1322 and earlier] were . . .

Finally, the theory of public law and the State is thus expressed in the Statute of York, in the joint action in Parliament of king as head and of the members of the body of the realm to assure the common welfare of all and preserve the State. Here is an anticipation of the words of Henry VIII addressed to the commons: "At no time do we stand so highly in our estate royal as in the time of parliament, wherein we as head and you as members are conjoined and knit together in one body politic."[55] In Parliament, in the fourteenth century, as in the time of Edward I, the king and lords and commons are the community of the realm for the purpose of treating the estate of the realm whenever the common welfare is the concern of all in common. The Statute of York is of some importance for its confirmation of what had been developing but had been challenged by the baronage. The magnates should not again try to limit the prerogative and pretend to be the sole representatives of the community and the common welfare; they must recognize the king as the head of the community, and as members cooperate with the other members, king and commons, of the whole community of the realm. In this sense, and by stating what had become the practice according to the legal procedure embodied in the maxim, *quod omnes tangit*, the Statute reaffirmed, but did not create, a constitutional as well as political principle of royal government.

---

prepared by the council on behalf of the king and brought before the 'people' for their assent." But, I disagree with his effort to belittle the presence of representatives and the necessity of getting their consent, especially to general taxation.

[55] Quoted by G. L. Haskins, *Growth of English Representative Government*, p. 124; for Kantorowicz and myself on Henry VIII, below, ch. VIII, nn. 5-7.

CHAPTER VII ✦ *STATUS, ID EST,*

*MAGISTRATUS: L'ETAT, C'EST MOI**

I N THE Statute of York the *estat* of the realm was the traditional *status regni*, that is, the public and common welfare, or common profit, of the *universitas* or *communitas regni* and of king and people. The king was the head and it was his right and duty to use his public authority so as to defend and maintain the state of the realm. But according to the Statute, the king possessed an *estat* of his own. What was the estate royal? Again we turn to the legal tradition of the preceding centuries in order to determine whether this *estat* was a kind of private estate or the public estate or public authority and powers of the king. In this chapter the legal thought on the *status magistratus* will be examined as a background for understanding the *status regis*, which will be treated more specifically in the following chapter. In both sections we shall be dealing essentially with one kind of terminology expressing the nature of the royal prerogative and sovereignty within the State.

* The following chs. VII-IX of this section were recently published in *Studies in Medieval and Renaissance History*, I (1963). The editor, Professor William M. Bowsky, and the University of Nebraska Press, kindly permit their use here—with some revision.

A few words about *l'Etat, c'est moi* in the title. I had already been reflecting on it and using it, e.g., in my "*Ratio publicae utilitatis, ratio status* und 'Staatsräson' (1100-1300)" in *Die Welt als Geschichte*, XXI (1961), 71 n. 54 (written in 1959), when I received in July, 1961, a reprint of an excellent article by Professor Michael J. Wilks of the University of London, "The Idea of the Church as 'Unus homo perfectus' and its Bearing on the Medieval Theory of Sovereignty," in *Miscellanea Historiae Ecclesiasticae*, pp. 32-49. Wilks, on the pope as the Church in theories of the late thirteenth century, says (p. 43) that this meant that the ruler "acts as the state itself: *l'Etat, c'est moi*." He adds that "the term 'State' itself gradually evolved from the proposition that the pope, on behalf of the mystical personality, contains within himself . . . the complete good of the society." But in this study it will become clear that the origin of the essence of *l'Etat, c'est moi* is to be found rather in the glossators of the Roman law in the twelfth century. But it is interesting that Professor Wilks and I have been thinking in similar ways about the rise of elements of the modern State in the Middle Ages. See below, to nn. 55-69, on *status papae* and *status ecclesiae*.

Since the State—whether it is a reality or a fiction as a legal or juristic person—can do and suffer nothing except through the men who act in its name, it is sometimes defined as the government.[1] The most extreme statement of the definition is of course the famous "L'Etat, c'est moi" formerly attributed to Louis XIV. We know that while *le roi soleil* often acted as if he were in fact the State, he really thought of himself as the *dépositaire* of the public good, ruling with justice for its achievement.[2] Perhaps Napoleon was the first ruler to say in effect that he was the State: "La chose publique, l'Etat, ce fut moi."[3] Yet did he have the State in mind? "La chose publique" may have connoted the old *respublica*, which in earlier times meant the public business of government, even the constitutional order itself, almost as often as it stood for the Republic, the State. Further, as will be shown, *status* in its public meaning was used at times for *respublica (chose publique)*, *utilitas publica*, and the powers of the magistracy—for the government itself. Thus, the French emperor may have reflected the ancient and medieval idea that the *status* was in one of its usages the magistracy and the fullness of powers of the prince.

Whatever "L'Etat, c'est moi" meant to the first man who said it, historians assume that the idea is modern. And if it means "I am the State," it no doubt is chiefly modern. But if it means "I am the state," that is, "I am the final authority and therefore the real government," then we can no longer say that it is modern. Indeed, we shall find the idea in medieval sources, long before *lo stato* in Machiavelli was usually the prince or the prince's authority.[4] But again, the idea that the head of the government and his appointed officials were the essence of the public *status* could easily persuade a king that he was not only

1 Snyder, *Meaning of Nationalism*, p. 19, quoting Benedetto Croce and Harold Laski.

2 For a standard discussion of the statement attributed to Louis XIV see Lavisse, in Lavisse, *Histoire de France*, VII, i, 131, 147. The best treatment, however, is by Fritz Hartung, "L'Etat c'est moi," *Historische Zeitschrift*, CLXIX (1949), 1-30. See also Herbert A. Rowen, " 'L'Etat c'est à moi': Louis XIV and the State," in *French Historical Studies*, II (1961), 83-98.

3 Hartung, *H.Z.*, CLXIX, 17-23, 27, on Napoleon.

4 See above, ch. v, in general, and nn. 2-10, 140; and also G. H. R. Parkinson, "Ethics and Politics in Machiavelli," *Philosophical Quarterly*, v (1955), 37-44.

the indispensable ruler but also the essence of the territorial State which he ruled; and this may have contributed to the later absolutism implied in "L'Etat, c'est moi." After all, it is not only in monarchies that the chief executive, after enjoying great prestige and authority for a number of years, can yield to the corruption of power and feel that he is the State because he alone knows what is essential to the welfare of State and people alike.

Now, in the Middle Ages no prince was likely to say that he was the *status Reipublicae*, the *status publicus*, or the *regimen*, *imperium*, or *magistratus*; nor that he was the *respublica (chose publique)*, much less the Republic, Realm, or State. Legists, canonists, and scholastic philosophers, however, sometimes came near saying it for the prince in speaking of his *status* as if it were far more than his well-being and private estate, as if, indeed, it were the fullness of public power invested in him and his magistracy or government. How could they not do so? For they studied and were inspired by Roman sources.

Status defined as the form of government or the constitution of the State occurs in Cicero and other classical Latin authors.[5] But it was Ulpian's use of the word (*D.* 1, 1, 1, 2) which chiefly inspired the legists of Bologna, who in turn influenced drafters of the public documents of princes and cities, and writers on government and politics. Ulpian defined the public law as that law which deals with the *status rei Romanae* and with those things that are necessary for this *status*, namely, with all *sacra* pertaining to religion and the cult, and with priests and magistrates—with all things that are "publicly useful."[6] Evidently, because of the emphasis on religion, the priesthood, and the magistracy (religion and priests being as essential as magistrates to the public and common welfare and the Empire), the *ius publicum* was the constitutional law.

---

[5] For this meaning of *status* in the Latin classics, one needs only to consult a good Latin dictionary, e.g., Lewis and Short, s.v. *status*.

[6] *D.* 1, 1, 1, 2: ". . . publicum ius est quod ad statum rei Romanae spectat . . . ; sunt enim quaedam publice utilia, quaedam privatim. publicum ius in sacris, in sacerdotibus, in magistratibus consistit. . . ." For our purpose here it hardly matters that the words on public and private utility may be an interpolation of the sixth century. The glossators accepted them as Roman and not Byzantine.

In commenting on this passage, the glossators and commentators most frequently defined the *status rei Romanae* as the public utility or welfare, which included the general common welfare of the people and the safety and peace of the whole State. It was sometimes the *Respublica* itself, almost the State. For they explained that the public law dealt also with all the means needed for maintaining the *status*—"ad statum conservandum, ne pereat."[7] At any rate the public law pertained *inter alia* to the magistracy and its powers, for the prince and his subordinates were indispensable for interpreting and enforcing law and justice and defending the *status Reipublicae*. As remarked above, "reason of State" was in part the "reason" or art of government for the end of preserving the common welfare and the State.

The early legists, in fact, began to identify this *status* with the *magistratus*. One glossator of the twelfth century equated the *ius publicum* itself with the magistrates: the public law is "the consuls or others."[8] Perhaps in this there is a suggestion of the modern Italian *diritto publico*, that is, the constitution and constitutional law of a State. But according to another gloss the *magistratus* simply has the "public right" (*ius publicum*) to command or execute court decisions.[9] More important are two or three early glosses which interpret Ulpian's *status rei Romanae* as the magistracy or public authority. One glossator says

[7] Accursius in the *Glos. ord.* to *D.* 1, 1, 1, 2, ad v. *Publicum ius*. Azo had already, ad v. *statum*, said: "Id est, existentiam, ne pereat. *Az*."; gloss in the Paris, BN, MS lat. 4451, fol. 9; and also Hugolinus, ad v. *statum*: ". . . ne pereat"; MS lat. 4461, to *D.* 1, 1, 1, 2. Important, too, is a fuller statement made by Accursius on the same words of Ulpian in *Inst.* 1, 1, 4, ad vv. *Publicum ius est quod ad statum rei Romanae spectat*: "Scilicet, principaliter, nam et singulorum est utilitas rempublicam salvam conservari. *Accursius*." This indicates that he thinks of the *status* as not only the public welfare of the Republic, but as practically the same thing as the Republic. In the whole context of the *Glos. ord.*, no doubt, *status* as the object of public law does not yet mean the State; but it is clear that the early glossators and Accursius were approaching the idea of *status* as something over and beyond the welfare of the community and its members; it is almost an abstract or juridical person in itself.

[8] To *D.* 4, 2, 23 Non est verosimile, ad vv. *ius publicum invocare*: "Id est, consules vel alios"; MS Vat. lat. 2511, fol. 33.

[9] To *D.* 9, 2, 37 Liber homo, ad vv. *si homo ius imperandi habuit*: "Scilicet, publicum, ut magistratus in executiones"; MS Vat. lat. 2511, fol. 78ᵛ. The passage in *D.* states that if a free man inflicts a physical injury on another as a result of a command by one who has the *ius imperandi* he is not guilty of a crime.

that the *status* is as it were the *magistratus* in the city. In another version of this opinion the words, "Id est, ad similitudinem," indicate that the *status* has only a similitude, as it were, to the magistracy.[10]

In one MS a gloss of the twelfth century adds words which are difficult to interpret, for it is not clear whether they apply to *publicum ius* and *ad statum* or to the succeeding clause attributed to Ulpian, *D.* 1, 1, 1, 2, "privatum ius quod ad singulorum utilitatem." The gloss reads: "Nam hoc est ius est hoc confirmat et retinet civitatem."[11] The difficulty of interpretation is threefold. First, there is, no doubt, a needless repetition of *hoc* and *est*; and therefore, I make the conjecture that the reading should be, "Nam hoc ius confirmat et retinet civitatem." Second, the words are interlinear in the line immediately following "Id est, ad similitudinem, etc.," and thus may very well refer to the definition of *ius publicum* as that law which pertains to the *status rei Romanae*. Third, if the gloss is intended to explain *privatum ius*, which pertains to the utility of individuals, it may instead refer not only to private law but also to Ulpian's opinion, that private law derives from precepts from the natural law, the *ius gentium*, and the civil law.[12]

What, then, is the meaning? Literally, the author of the gloss says that "this law establishes and preserves the city (State)." Perhaps he meant that it was the public law that maintained the State in dealing with the *status*, that is, the public welfare and the magistracy—but especially the magistracy, since without a government there could be neither State nor its public welfare. On the other hand, perhaps he meant that the private law, although it directly pertained to the private welfare of individu-

---

[10] MS Vat. lat. 2511, fol. 3, to *D.* 1, 1, 1, 2, ad v. *statum*: "Veluti magistratus in civitate"; and in the Paris, BN, MS lat. 4458-A, fol. 1ᵛ, ad v. *statum*: "Id est, ad similitudinem veluti magistratus in civitate." Both glosses are interlinear and refer to *statum* in Ulpian's definition, "publicum ius est quod ad statum rei Romanae spectat." They stand in sets of glosses of the twelfth century on the *Dig. Vetus*.

[11] Paris, BN, MS lat. 4458-A, fol. 1ᵛ. The gloss is interlinear, and while its position is just above the words of Ulpian, "Privatum quod ad singulorum utilitatem," it could easily be a continuation of the gloss to *statum* in the preceding line—the gloss quoted above, n. 10. ,

[12] *D.* 1, 1, 1, 2: "privatum ius tripertitum est: collectum etenim est ex naturalibus praeceptis aut gentium aut civilibus."

als, indirectly pertained to the public welfare that depends in part on the enforcement of private law by the public authority, and is as important as the public law for the strength and the survival of the community. Perhaps he had vaguely in mind the general thought expressed by the glossators, that the public law primarily treated the things that were for the public welfare, but secondarily interested individuals, both in maintaining the general public utility and the security of all in peace, and in regulating the government needed to interpret the private law in courts. The private law, in turn, primarily pertained to private rights and the private welfare of the individual members of the community; but secondarily it was of public interest to the community that private rights be used justly; and, of course, it interested the government to enforce the private law, and to make new private law for new situations. "Private law," said Azo and others, "is public by authority."[13] On the whole, however, I conclude that the words "hoc ius confirmat et retinet civitatem" seem logically to refer to *ius publicum* and *status rei Romanae*. That is, the public law in dealing with the magistracy and religion and priesthood pertains to the maintenance of the *status* of the Republic. But above all it regulates the *status*, and hence *magistratus* and *status* are in part equivalent terms.

In a sense, therefore, already in the twelfth century the idea had appeared that the public welfare, the *status*, of the Republic or city, of the State, was essentially the public authority, the magistracy or government. But at the same time, *status* in its public meaning was being associated with the idea of the powers of the head of the State and his magistracy. One glossator made *status* and *potentia* (that is, the *status* or *potentia rei Romanae*) mean the same thing; and he defined the *res Romana* as *dicio*, that is, sovereignty, rule, power, and the like. In other words, he was trying to explain Ulpian's *status rei Romanae* as

[13] See the *Glos. ord.* of Accursius to *D.* 1, 1, 1, 2. Azo says, ad v. *privatum ius* "utilitate, sed pub[licum] autoritate"; in the Paris, BN, MS lat. 4451, fol. 9. Thus, the private law is itself public because its interpretation and enforcement, for the common welfare of the people in the State, depends on the supreme public authority; and, of course, new laws in the realm of private law are made and promulgated by the public authority. This theory was repeated in detail by the legists and canonists of the thirteenth century.

[338]

the public power of the Roman government.[14] This was a stronger way of saying that the "state of the Republic" was the magistracy and its powers to preserve it—"lest it perish," said Hugolinus, Azo, and Accursius.[15] The public law was the law of the constitutional order and the public authority, and it demanded obedience to them.[16]

The gloss defining *status* as *potentia* stands in a late twelfth or early thirteenth century manuscript of the *Dig. Vetus* preserved in the British Museum, and the glosses of the later twelfth century in this manuscript are frequently different from those in other manuscripts containing the *Dig. Vetus*. Although the manuscript belonged to a monastic library at Reading in the thirteenth century, this is no indication of any English authorship of early glosses not specifically attributed to Irnerius, Hugolinus, and Azo. The script for text and glosses alike indicates a Bolognese provenance.[17] Nevertheless, it is interesting that in his *Dialogus de Scaccario* (*ca.* 1177) Richard Fitzneale, treasurer of the Exchequer under Henry II, and educated in some elements of Roman law, indicates a close relationship between the king's *status* and *potestas*.[18] Perhaps this usage was more common than might be supposed. At least, it is hinted in a document of Lothair III: since, the emperor said, monasteries strengthen the *potencia regalis*, privileges for them profit both the *status regni* and the king's eternal reward; they are "pro nostro et totius imperii statu."[19] In 1212–1213 Frederick II declared that his public *status* was the powers of office which

[14] Brit. Mus., MS Royal 11 C. III, fol. 1, to *D.* 1, 1, 1, 2, ad v. *statum*: "Id est, potencia"; and ad v. *rei romane*: "Id est, dicionis." These glosses are interlinear and clearly belong to the words indicated. In effect, therefore, the glossator was saying: "Id est, ad potenciam dicionis," or "Id est, ad potenciam dicionis rei publicae," or even "Id est, ad potenciam magistratus," since sometimes *respublica* and government were equivalent in our period. See on the MS below, n. 17.

[15] See above, n. 7.

[16] Gloss to *D.* 1, 1, 1, 2, ad v. *magistratibus*: "obediendis"; in MS lat. 4451, fol. 9.

[17] A careful study of the MS is needed; but I am inclined to place the copying of the text of the *Dig. Vetus* and of the earlier glosses in the late twelfth century rather than the early thirteenth, as in the *Catal.* of the Royal MSS. The earliest record of the MS in England shows that the MS was not in the monastic library of Reading before the thirteenth century—it is not listed in a late twelfth-century catalogue. See N. P. Ker, *Medieval Libraries of Great Britain*, p. 87.

[18] *S.C.*, p. 200; see below, ch. VIII, n. 9.

[19] *M.G.H.*, *Dipl. Reg. et Imp. Ger.*, VIII, 25, no. 19; p. 58, no. 35; see below, § II, nn. 25-27.

he wished to exercise for the *bonus status*, peace, and tranquility of the Empire. The *status* of the king, also of the pope, will reappear as the *potestas* in the theologians.[20]

In the thirteenth century, as in the twelfth, the *status* of the State was most frequently defined as the public welfare, *utilitas publica*—sometimes as the common welfare and common good, although there was a technical, legal distinction between the public and the common utility.[21] But one also finds, as in the preceding period, the definition of *status* as the magistracy and constitutional order or accepted system of government. Thus Jacques de Révigny, a great French jurist of the second half of the century, made the *status Reipublicae* and the *regimen imperii* equivalent. Both are subjects of the public law, which includes laws on churches, priests, and judges—judges specifically, since laws would be to no purpose unless there were magistrates to interpret and enforce them.[22] Further, the public law indirectly includes private law; for that law which pertains to private utility pertains to the public *imperium*, for the Roman law says that the *imperium* will prosper if it has wealthy subjects.[23] Here is a kind of confusion of *status*, government, and Empire and Republic.

Jacques de Révigny, again, stated almost the same thing in a farfetched definition of *majestas*, in a gloss on *D.* 48, 4 Ad legem Iuliam majestatis, 1 (Ulpian on the crime of treason against the Roman people, republic, and the magistrates). *Majestas*, he says, is as it were the *maior status*, whence magistrates can be so

---

[20] *M.G.H., Legum S. IV, Const.*, II, 54-56, nos. 43 and 45; below, nn. 43, 47, 61, 67.

[21] See below, ch. VIII, n. 24, for a brief explanation.

[22] This kind of statement about the need of magistrates was long since a common one among the legists—its origin is in *D.* 1, 2, 2, 13: "Quantum est enim ius in civitate esse, nisi sint qui iura regere possint?"

[23] *Com.* or *Lectura* on *Inst.*, in Paris, BN, MS lat. 14350, fol. 144ᵛ-145, to *Inst.* 1, 1, 4, ad vv. *publicum ius est, quod ad statum rei Romanae spectat*: "id est, ad statum rei publice. Unde ius quod pertinet ad regimen imperii ius publicum dicitur. . . . Unde iura que loquuntur de ecclesiis, de sacerdotibus, de iudicibus pertinent ad ius publicum. . . . Item iudices, quia frustra essent iura nisi essent magistratus qui iura redderent. . . ." The public law indirectly includes private law: "Sed videtur quod ius quod pertinet ad utilitatem privatam sit publicum, quia pertinet ad imperium, et tale est publicum. Dicit lex habundabit imperium, si locupletes habeat subiectos. . . ." Jacques repeats, on the Empire and rich subjects, what had frequently been said by earlier legists.

called because they dwell in a greater and higher place.[24] Thus the *maior status*, the majesty of the prince, is in effect the *magistratus*, magistracy, of the head of the State.

He was able even to associate the crown with the common fatherland of the kingdom of France. King Philip Augustus in 1197 had already spoken of the defense of the *caput* and of the *corona regni*. A French legist, Jean de Blanot, had connected the defense of the crown of France with the good of the *patria* and the public good or public utility of the kingdom.[25] Jacques de Révigny, obviously having in mind the problem treated by Jean, did not go so far as to say that the king of France was emperor in his own realm and that France was a sovereign state. Yet he judged that like Rome and the Empire, the kingdom of France was the *patria communis*, the independent common fatherland, of all subjects of the king. Therefore, in case of simultaneous, aggressive attacks, one on the local *patria* of Burgundy and the other on the common *patria* of France, should a vassal of the duke of Burgundy respond to the summons of the duke or to that of the king to fight the enemy? Jacques is in doubt and is inclined to favor the local *patria*. But significantly, he furnishes these strong arguments, made by certain legists ("doctores legum"), for the king, crown, and the *patria communis*: the *tuitio Reipublicae*, that is, of France and the crown, is a public utility that is to be preferred to the lower utility of a province; and the "corona regni est communis patria, quia caput." Because it is the head, the crown of the realm is the common fatherland.[26]

[24] Gloss to *D.* 48, 4, 1: "Maiestas dicitur quasi maior status; inde et magistratus dici possunt, quia in maiori loco at altiori morantur . . . Iac. R." It is in the Vatican MS Pal. lat. 753, fol. 151. Cf. Isidore of Seville, *Etymol.*, x: "Magister, major in statione."

[25] G. Post, "Two Notes on Nationalism," *Traditio*, IX, 289; below, ch. x, n. 40. On Philip Augustus, see J. R. Strayer, "Defense of the Realm and Royal Power in France," *Studi in onore di Gino Luzzato*, p. 292; also Kantorowicz, *King's Two Bodies*, p. 340.

[26] This comment is in the Paris, BN, MS lat. 14350, fols. 185-185ᵛ, to *Inst.* 4, 6, 13: "Sed pone Carses ingrediuntur Burgundiam. . . . Ipsi [doctores legum] dicunt contrarium [to the first duty of the vassal to fight for the local *patria*] . . . quia Roma est communis patria, sic corona regni est communis patria, quia caput. . . ." Almost he implies that Paris, seat of the royal government, is both crown and common fatherland. See below, ch. x, n. 41.

Perhaps Jacques de Révigny was hesitant about choosing between the defense of the local *patria* and the defense of the *patria communis* because in the Roman

It is also the *Respublica,* which no doubt is the royal government as well as the kingdom.

Meanwhile, in England, Bracton was associating with the crown all the king's rights of jurisdiction and power in the realm, rights that pertained to the government and the defense of the *patria.* For, like Johannes de Deo, a distinguished canonist, who had *(ca.* 1245) explained that all things belonged to the prince in the sense that *omnia* are "in manu eius quo ad tuitionem et defensionem," Bracton held that the king in his *iurisdictio, dignitas,* and *potestas* possessed "omnia iura in manu sua quae ad coronam et laicalem pertinent potestatem et materialem gladium qui pertinet ad regni gubernaculum"; that in brief, all businesses relating to justice and peace in the realm belonged solely to the *corona* and *dignitas regia.* His concept of the crown was thus in the tradition of the equation of the royal *dignitas, status, potestas,* and *corona.*[27] French legists, however, were go-

---

law the necessity (or defense) of a province might be so urgent that the provincials should at once furnish supplies to the army defending it. In such a case it was presumed that the main duty fell on the people of the region immediately in danger, and not directly on the Empire as a whole or the *patria communis.* The provincial governor himself was duty-bound to act speedily and wage a defensive war without waiting for the approval of the emperor. In this situation of dire, urgent, immediate danger or necessity, then, the local *patria* demanded loyalty first to itself rather than to the common *patria.* Obviously, however, in the long run, since the danger to a province also threatened the Empire as a whole, local loyalty or patriotism was ultimately subordinate to the emperor and the Empire. In other words, local patriotism came first only momentarily, in cases of emergency and necessity; the interests of the Empire and of the common fatherland were thus served. There was in theory no sacrifice of the superior patriotic loyalty to the State.

Perhaps, however, Jacques did not fully accept this. But he does refer to legists who did, who understood how, when enemies threatened a local and the common *patria* at the same time, defense of the common *patria* came first, for only thus was the safety of the province or local *patria* assured. In such a case, the common *patria* of the State as a whole demanded a loyalty that superseded local loyalties. Cf. below, ch. x, nn. 41-44.

27 It is interesting that before Bracton wrote his treatise, Johannes de Deo connected the *omnia in manu principis* with the Roman law and the glossators (that all things belong to the prince not as his property but as subject to his *iurisdictio, protectio,* and *gubernatio;* see below, nn. 80f.); like Bracton, he also reflected the early medieval tradition in Sacramentaries and in a Frankish coronation *ordo—* on this see Kantorowicz, *King's Two Bodies,* p. 153 n. 192. Since the passage from Joh. de Deo is apparently unknown, I now give it from his *Libellus dispensationum* (in the MS Casanatense 108, fol. 297 c. 2): *"De dispensatione principum vel regum qui non habent maiorem super se, nisi papam loco dei. Et licet omnia sunt principis, quia per principes et reges deus distribuit humano generi omnia,*

ing farther: the crown stood for more than the king's public authority: it was not only the symbol of it, it *was* the *patria communis* of the realm; and thus also the king, by way of the concept in *corona-caput regni*, was the State. The *pater patriae* was becoming confused with the *patria*. But we must not exaggerate. No doubt Jacques de Révigny was merely emphasizing the majesty of the king's power over the realm. Nevertheless, the tendency that became more manifest in the jurists of the late thirteenth and the fourteenth century was already appearing in France. If the king and crown existed for the *status regni*, they were, as the head, the common fatherland of the realm.

In England itself, in the late thirteenth century, one finds a reflection of the tendency to identify the royal magistracy with the realm. In the case of the dispute between John Baliol and Robert Bruce over the succession to the kingdom of Scotland, the argument was made in court that the "right of a realm is principally royal dignity and government of people."[28] At the same time, and in the following century, Neapolitan and Bolognese jurists were being more explicit. Andrew of Isernia held that the king and the *respublica regni* were identical: the king is in the kingdom and the *respublica* is in him as in the head.[29] The glossators and others had a century earlier noted that the prince was not only the *caput regni* but was also a *corpus* (the "body politic" of the sixteenth century?), which in-

---

ut testatur Aug. viii. di. quo iure [St. Augustine, quoted in the *Decretum*, Dist. 8, c. 2]; C. de quadrien. prescrip. bene a Zenone [*C.* 7, 37, 3] . . . ; tamen sic est intelligendum, scilicet, quod sint omnia in manu eius quo ad tuitionem et defensionem. . . ." Cf. below, nn. 81-88.

See Bracton, *De legibus*, ed. Woodbine, II, 160; and on Bracton Kantorowicz, *op.cit.*, IV, 3. (Of course, one recalls C. H. McIlwain's famous treatment of the meaning of Bracton's *iurisdictio* and *gubernaculum*; but there is no need of discussing the distinction here.) The crown is not the realm, but it includes the royal power necessary for the "defensio regni et patriae" (Woodbine, II, 28, 32). On the crown and the coronation oath see below, ch. VIII, to nn. 12, 25-33, 67-94, and ch. IX.

28 Barnaby C. Keeney, "The Medieval Idea of the State: the Great Cause," *Univ. Toronto Law Journal*, VIII (1949), 62f., 63 n. 42, from the *Annales regni Scotiae*: "Kar dreit de reaume principaument est reale dignite e governement de pople." I gave above Keeney's translation. For crown as *regnum*, see Richardson, "The English Coronation Oath," *Speculum*, XXIV, 50.

29 Quoted by E. Kantorowicz, "Mysteries of State: an Absolutist Concept and Its Late Medieval Origins," *Harvard Theological Review*, XLVIII (1955), 80; also below, n. 68.

cluded the lesser magistrates and senate as members.[30] The prince was both the head of the State and the head of the governing body of the State. It is therefore possible that Andrew of Isernia thought that the king was the *respublica* (*chose publique*) in the sense of the government rather than the Republic. This seems the more likely because he also said that where the prince is, there is the whole law.[31]

Lucas de Penna, too, avoided the danger of calling the king the State. In one place he does say that "the prince is the head of the realm, and the realm the body of the Prince";[32] in another, that the prince is in the *respublica* and the *respublica* is in the prince.[33] But even when he says that the prince is in the *respublica*, and the *respublica* is in him, he probably means only that the king is the *chose publique*, the "body politic," the government; for the king is not the *utilitas publica*, rather his *honor* (office) exists for the public welfare.[34] Nor can we at-

---

[30] Azo, *Summa Codicis*, p. 40, to C. 1, 26: "Dictum est supra de principe, qui caput est omnium magistratuum: nunc audiamus de aliis magistratibus qui sunt principis tanquam capitis membra. . . ." This kind of thought was expressed by other legists and also by John of Salisbury; Kantorowicz, *King's Two Bodies*, 207, 208 n. 42. Thus, the *princeps* was not only the *caput* of the State; he was a *corpus*, a corporation sole, so to speak, including the lesser magistracy and the senators who were all a *pars corporis principis*—see C. 9, 8, 5 and C. 12, 1, 5 and the *Glos. ord.* to these imperial laws.

Late twelfth-century glossators had already noticed this; so Placentinus (in his *Lectura* or *Com.*, published as Azo's to the *Tres Libri*, in the ed. Paris, 1577), to C. 12, 1, 5: the *senatores* are "magna pars corporis imperii" (*imperium* here meaning no doubt the imperial government or powers); Pillius (Paris, BN, MS lat. 4429, fol. 170ᵛ), to C. 12, 1, 5, ad v. *curiam nostram*: "Ergo nec senatores, qui sunt magna pars corporis . . . p."; and Johannes Bassianus, in his *Summa* on the *Authenticae* (MS lat. 4542, fol. 185ᵛ): "*De senatoribus* . . . Ideo de officiis singulorum magistratuum tracta[tu]rus, premittit de senatoribus tanquam maioribus, qui pars corporis principis esse dicuntur. . . ."

It was not difficult, therefore, for legists to think in terms of the *curia regis* and king as a "body politic" and identify the corporate body of king and government with the State. See below, to nn. 67 and 71, on the pope as a corporate body and even the Church.

[31] Francesco Calasso, *Gli ordinamenti giuridici del rinascimento medioevale*, 2nd ed., p. 268, and nn. 1 and 2.

[32] Quoted by Kantorowicz, *King's Two Bodies*, p. 216 n. 66.

[33] *Op. cit.*, p. 214 n. 60.

[34] *Com. on the Tres Libri*, to C. 11, 71, 5 (p. 622 c. 1, no. XXIII): when the king is acting for the public utility, his apparent harshness must be endured "propter honorem principis, qui est res publica, et res publica est in eo." Cf. Kantorowicz, *op.cit.*, pp. 215f.; also Walter Ullmann, *The Medieval Idea of Law as Represented by Lucas de Penna*, p. 170. On *honor* see the following study, ch. VIII, nn. 28, 69-75.

tribute the identification of the State with the prince to the great jurists of Bologna and northern Italy. If Alberico da Rosciate said that in obeying the *patria* one obeyed the magistrates who preside over the *regimen patriae*, this is not quite the same thing as saying that the *patria* is the government.[35] Bartolus reverted to the old literal way of defining the *status* of the Roman Republic as the *magistratus*—which, however, he calls the *regimen*.[36] And Baldus emphasized the familiar idea that the prince represents the people; and the prince is the *imperium* and the *fiscus*, because only in him does the Empire live, will, and act.[37] Again the prince is the government rather than the State.

Meanwhile, it is important to note, the scholastic theologians, partly inspired by Aristotle's *Politics* but partly continuing the legal tradition, identified *status* and *magistratus* perhaps as frequently as the legists did. Thomas Aquinas is above all important. To understand his treatment of *status* it is well first to recall that his *raison d'état* was the "reason" of the natural end of the city in the common good of the citizens and in its own welfare and safety; and it was the "right reason" used by the government for the attainment of the *ratio civitatis*.[38] So far as I know, he did not literally speak of the "reason of the public welfare" as the lawyers did (*ratio publicae utilitatis*), nor of the equivalent "reason" of the *status civitatis, regni, Respublicae*— but his *ratio civitatis* is close to the same meaning. Nor did he often distinguish literally between the *status regis* or *principis* and the *status regni*. Once or twice, however, he treated the government as the *respublica*. That is, the public business of ruling the State is the government. The whole *impositio ordinis* is in him who rules the city, and this is the *respublica* itself, the *ordinatio civitatis*.[39] But in one instance, in the Latin text of the

---

[35] *Com.* on the *Dig. Vetus*, I, 12, no. 18, to *D.* 1, 1, 2 (Pomponius, on obedience to parents and the *patria*): ". . . dicit ergo hic parendum patrie: idest magistratibus qui presunt regimine patrie. . . ."

[36] Bartolus, to *Inst.*, 1, 1, 4.

[37] Gierke, *Political Theories of the Middle Age*, p. 163 n. 216, quoting Baldus to *C.* 10, 1; also *Glos. ord.* to *D.* 49, 14, 3, 10: Caesar "pro fisco accipitur: cuius Cesaris omnia sunt."

[38] See my study, "Ratio publicae utilitatis, etc.," *Welt als Geschichte*, XXI, 86f.; above, ch. v, nn. 89, 102-110.

[39] *Com.* or *Expositio* on the *Politics*, ed. Spiazzi, p. 136 (III, lectio 5, no. 385): "Et dicit [Arist.] quod respublica nihil est aliud quam ordinatio civitatis quantum

Politics, the *communitas* itself is the *politia,* or form of government;[40] and therefore, the citizen should have the virtue proper for participating in the *politia.* Thomas, however, in general subordinates citizens and government alike to the community, since the necessity common to all is the *salus communitatis.* Yet at the same time, the community "consists in the order of the *politia,*" and every good citizen works for the "conservatio politiae."[41] There is a certain assumption that the community, good government, and *respublica* are for practical purposes public aspects of the same thing, the State. Roughly, therefore, Thomas's thought, although largely in Aristotelian terms, is close to that expressed in the *status Reipublicae* and *status regis et regni* of the lawyers and royal documents. Indeed, at least once, he advocates extraordinary taxation, in case of the necessity of defense against an enemy, either for the common utility, or "pro honesto statu principis conservando."[42] The *status communitatis* and the public *status principis* are closely related.

When he uses the word *status* in its public sense, only rarely is it the *status* of the State or city. If he does say once that a king is useful to the city in using his power so as to "conserve the state of the city" (*statum civitatis*), and thus may recall the words of the glossators, that the public law deals with the maintenance of the "state of the Republic lest it perish,"[43] normally he prefers to say "the good" and the "safety" (*salus*) of the city. Usually, therefore, the public *status* is not the common good or public welfare; it is the government itself, or the kind of *politia* in a State. It is the public magistracy of prince, aristocracy, or

ad omnes principatus qui sunt in civitate, sed praecipue quantum ad maximum principatum, qui dominatur aliis principatibus. Et hoc ideo, quia impositio ordinis in civitate, tota consistit in eo qui dominatur civitati; et talis impositio ordinis est ipsa respublica." See Thomas Gilby, *Between Community and Society,* p. 276 n. 1, where the first part of this passage is quoted. In another place Thomas says that *Respublica* "est nomen commune omnibus politiis"—ed. Spiazzi, p. 139, III, lect. 6, no. 393.

40 Ed. Spiazzi, p. 127, Arist. (Bekker 1276b 16f.), no. 233: the need of individual citizens is the "salus communitatis," but the *communitas* "est politia."

41 *Op.cit.,* p. 129, no. 366.

42 *De regimine Judaeorum;* in A. P. d'Entrèves, *San Tommaso d'Aquino, Scritti Politici,* p. 47.

43 To *D.* 1, 1, 1, 2; see above, nn. 7, 15. Thomas Aquinas says (*Com. on Politics,* ed. Spiazzi, p. 104, no. 316): "quia rex est utilis civitati ut sua potestate efficaciter conservet statum civitatis."

people, necessary for achieving the end of the city. Examples of this usage are numerous. In one case, the "totus status civitatis" might be altered by a change made by a new law; in the context it seems that here *status* means *politia*, although Thomas is close to making the *status civitatis* equivalent to the common and public good of the State.[44] Clearly, however, the *status* is the form of government in the following: the *status plebeius*, when the whole multitude of the people wishes to rule;[45] the good *status popularis*, the kind of mixed polity which Solon established in his *patria* in place of the *status paucorum* (oligarchy);[46] the *regius status*, or *regia potestas*, the good kind of monarchy that governs for the common utility;[47] the *status optimatum*, or *politia* of the few when they "principantur propter bonum commune."[48] Finally, not to give more examples, Thomas speaks of the *status politici gubernatio*. Perhaps in this instance, since he is referring to Aristotle and Plato on the Spartan military virtues and remarks that the Spartans were not apt in those things "which pertain to the government of the political state," he means the government or "principate" in a good *politia*; hence *status politicus* may be translated "constitutional order."[49]

44 *Com.* on *Pol.*, ed. Spiazzi, p. 94, II, lect. 12, no. 289: "Habebit enim transmutationem politiarum. Una enim lege transmutata, quandoque totus status civitatis mutatur." Such a statute, permitting innovations, might even lead to the annulment of good earlier laws (*patrias leges*). This would mean the dissolution of *leges* and of the whole *politia* "sub specie communis boni." In other words, specious "reason of State" cannot justify new laws that nullify good law and fundamentally change the constitutional order.

45 *Ibid.*, p. 80, II, lect. 7, no. 242; also nos. 246-249. Here the *status plebeius* is a bad kind, for plebeians are the lowest of the people, without virtues.

46 *Ibid.*, p. 115 (II, lect. 17, no. 342); also p. 122, no. 350 (III, lect. 1): "qui est civis in statu populari secundum quem populus principatur" is not a *civis* "in statu paucorum" (the oligarchy); p. 139 (lect. 6, no. 393): the rule of the multitude when it is for the common utility "vocatur respublica, quod est nomen commune omnibus politiis."

47 *Com.*, p. 139, III, lect. 6, no. 393: the *principatus* of one is called "regia potestas . . . si intendat communem utilitatem"; Pierre d'Auvergne, in his continuation of Aquinas's *Com.*, says (p. 184, III, lect. 16, no. 524): "regius status est cui subiicitur multitudo quae nata est subiici secundum inclinationem naturalem alicui superexcellenti in virtute ad principatum politicum vel regalem."

48 *Com.*, p. 139, no. 393.

49 *Com.*, p. 105, no. 319 (II, lect. 14): "Et ideo, quia bene se habebant in his, quae pertinent ad bellum, male autem in his quae pertinent ad status politici gubernationem." But the last words together seem to be equivalent to the principatus or government, for Thomas says that when the Spartans finally had a principate, many dangers threatened, since they did not know how to live in peace.

Ernst Kantorowicz is right, therefore, in saying that Thomas Aquinas "uses *status* in a descriptive fashion without any connotation of abstractness."[50] In this usage, apart from the word *politia*, Thomas carried on the tradition of the legists. For the State itself, he preferred such terms as *communitas, civitas*, and *regnum*—sometimes *Respublica* in the sense of Republic rather than the best kind of government.[51]

Some other scholastic theologians and philosophers accepted *status* in the same sense. Kantorowicz notes that Guillaume d'Auvergne equated *status* and *status publicus* with the form of government.[52] Georges de Lagarde has found another example in Pierre d'Auriole, who stresses the necessity of the prince for the good of the community. But subjects should obey the law even more than the prince and magistrates. For since, as Aristotle says, as few things as possible should be entrusted to the prince, because men are prone to evil, "in omni statu pauciora sunt committenda arbitrio judicis et omnia deberent committi legi."[53] Tempting as it is to exclaim that already in the late thirteenth century the word *status* meant the State, probably Pierre's words should be translated, "in every kind of government." Again the *status* is the magistracy. In particular it is the order that cannot exist except in the authority of the head, the *Dux*, for the *Dux* is a greater good than that of the city and its order, which is the discipline that unites the city with its head. The unity of the community is in the unity of command. Nonetheless, the "reason of government" of this head is subordinate to the "right reason" of justice and the reason of the good of the city and its parts.[54]

The canonists naturally accepted much of the language of the Roman law and the legists. But if on this point, with respect to the papal government and the *status Ecclesiae*, they do not talk in the same way, a near equivalent appears in decretists and decretalists from the late twelfth century on. The author, perhaps French, of the *Summa* "Antiquitate et tempore" on the *Decretum* of Gratian, had Ulpian's definition of public law in

---

[50] *King's Two Bodies*, p. 271 n. 235.
[51] *De regimine principum*, I, 4 (d'Entrèves, p. 12), and I, 15 (p. 40).
[52] *King's Two Bodies*, p. 271 n. 235.
[53] *Naissance de l'esprit laique*, II, 2nd ed., p. 299 n. 106.
[54] *Op.cit.*, pp. 284 n. 74; 296-299.

mind when he said that the *ius publicum* pertains to the *respublica*. What is called *publicum* is derived not from the *populus* but from the *respublica,* and the public law is concerned with the prerogative of the emperor, priests, and others whose function is to protect the *Respublica* and provide for it in *sacra,* priests, and magistrates.[55] He seems, therefore, to equate *respublica* with the *status rei Romanae* of Ulpian (that is, the *status* or public welfare is the *respublica*), with the magistracy, and with the Republic. The magistracy is not quite, but almost, the *status Reipublicae.* It is interesting, moreover, that this decretist hints at the thought that the public law is the magistracy. Another decretist stated it better (late twelfth century): since the public law is for the public utility (again Ulpian's *status*), whoever injures magistrates or other public persons is said to injure the *ius publicum.*[56] The famous Huguccio had said much the same thing, adding that sacred things (churches, altars, *vasa,* vestments, etc.), magistrates, and priests pertain to all (in State and Church) and that by the public law these three subjects of it enjoy immunity and reverence. Further, it is a violation of the public law to damage or injure any *sacra,* priests, or magistrates, or to prevent, by any means, appeals to pope, king, or judge. For the public law protects the public utility or *status rei Romanae* and all men or things that exist for the public welfare.[57] Still another decretist came even closer to *status-mag-*

---

55 Vatican MS Pal. lat. 678, fol. 37, c. 2 (to Dist. 1, c. 11): "Sed ius publicum dicitur quod pertinet [ad] rem publicam; et sic non a populo sed a re publica dicitur publicum. Hoc autem est, quod est de prerogativa imperatoris et sacerdotum et aliorum, quorum precipue est tueri enim rempublicam et ei providere in sacris . . . et sacerdotibus . . . et magistratibus." Further, "magistri dicuntur, quibus precipua cura incumbit, et qui maiorem diligentiam et sollicitudinem debent rebus quibus presunt." On this *Summa* see Kuttner, *Repertorium,* pp. 178f.

56 Vat. MS Reg. lat. 1061, fol. 1-1ᵛ: "est publicum quoque ad puplicam respiciat utilitatem. Unde si quod [read *quis*] ledat magistratus vel alias puplicas personas, dicitur ledere ius puplicum." On the *Summa Reginensis* see Kuttner, *Repertorium,* pp. 160-166.

57 *Summa,* to Dist. 1, c. 11: ". . . Est publicum quod ad publicam principaliter respicit utilitatem, vel ad statum rei romane: et consistit in sacris, etc. . . . Unde si quis ledat sacra vel sacerdotes vel magistratus, vel alias publicas personas, dicitur ledere ius publicum . . . ; nam sacra, sacerdotia et magistratus ad omnes pertinent. . . . Ius ergo quo ista tria gaudent immunitate et reverencia dicitur publicum. Et contra hoc ius facit quicumque aliquod istorum trium ledit; contra hoc ius facit quicumque appellantem ad papem vel iudicem vel regem quoquo

istratus. The public law, he says, pertains to the *status*, that is, the *dignitas* of the Roman *Res (publica).* Since he says elsewhere that the *dignitas* of the apostolic See is in part the papal authority in dispensing and legislating, and is one of the means of exalting the *majestas* of the Roman Church, he implies that the public *status* of the whole Church is practically the same as the papal government.[58]

No doubt Henry of Susa (Hostiensis) was reflecting this tradition when, in his *Lectura* or *Commentary* on the *Decretals* of Gregory IX, discussing the renunciation of his right as a cardinal to vote in a conclave of 1270 (in the long process of electing a pope in 1268-1271), he debated the legality of such a renunciation. The *ius eligendi papam* is a divine and public law, he says, public because it pertains "ad statum rei Romanae," for (as in *D.* 1, 1, 1, 2) the public law consists in *sacra*, magistrates, and priests. But insofar as the papacy is the highest (public office), the *ius eligendi* is "summe publicum." Since the public law cannot be changed by private agreements (as in *D.* 2, 14, 38), since renunciations must be approved by a superior, and since the *ius eligendi* belongs to the cardinalate, a cardinal cannot renounce his right (and duty) to vote. Again, a cardinal cannot renounce his office nor any right pertaining to the office, "maxime in his, quae publicum statum respiciunt." But in the election of the supreme pontiff "omnia sunt de iure publico"!

Actually, the good Cardinal Bishop of Ostia was permitted (perhaps by the college of cardinals as a corporate body of the magistracy acting as the *caput Ecclesiae* when there was no pope) to retire from this particular conclave and thus renounce his

---

modo impedierit, scilicet, vel verberando vel necando vel alio modo." There are many MSS of the *Summa* of Huguccio; here I have taken the text from the Paris, BN, MS lat. 3892, fol. 3ᵛ.

Related to this thought is a passage from the *Summa Parisiensis, ca.* 1160, ed. McLaughlin, p. 3: "*Jus publicum:* i.e. personarum publicae utilitatis curam habentium."

58 *Summa*, wrongly attributed to Rufinus, in ed. by Schulte, p. 9, to Dist. 1, c. 11: "Ius publicum est, quod ad statum, i.e. dignitatem rei romanae principaliter spectat . . ."; and p. 375, to Causa 25: "Duo sunt maxime, in quibus romanae ecclesiae maiestas inaltatur [*exaltatur* in the MS]: potestas ligandi et solvendi, et ecclesias dispensandi, nunc autem subiungit, quantam sedes apostolica dignitatem habeat ecclesias dispensandi, ostendens, quomodo sua auctoritate quas voluerit potest ecclesias specialibus privilegiis munire et novos canones condere. . . ."

right—after all he was old and ill, and the citizens of Viterbo were virtually imprisoning the cardinals and depriving them of proper shelter and food in order to make them hasten to elect a pope.[59] Nevertheless, Hostiensis here shows that the *ius publicum* and *status publicus* were the constitutional law and *ordo* of the Church, regulating *inter alia* the election of popes. The cardinalate and the papacy, essential for maintaining the *status Ecclesiae*, were in another sense the highest *status publicus* in the Church.

One finds this meaning of *status Ecclesiae* in at least two renowned scholastic philosophers and theologians of the late thirteenth and early fourteenth century. Henry of Ghent understood the "state of the Church" as the *ordo ecclesiasticus*—the ecclesiastical hierarchy, of which the pope was the head.[60] John of Paris still more specifically attributed to the pope a *status* that was public and meant the *plenitudo potestatis*. For, he says, the pope, because he is the vicar of Christ, is the *dominus omnium*. The pope is the universal *dispositor* and *dispensator bonorum*; and, according to the "needs of his state" ("secundum exigentiam sui status"), he can make his own more of the revenues of churches than inferior prelates can, for only he has the *plenitudo potestatis*. Alexander de S. Elpidio held that the papal *potestas* belonged to the *status*, not the person.[61]

However, so far as I know, *status papae* is not a frequently used term; and no matter how great the *plenitudo potestatis*

---

[59] *Lectura* or *Com.*, I, 91ᵛ-92, nos. 32-34, 42, 50; the comment is to *Decr. Greg.* IX 1, 9, 10 Nisi cum pridem, ad vv. *humiliter obedire*. There is no need here to discuss the whole problem of renunciation in relation to public law; it was often debated by the canonists. For one treatment of it see Riesenberg, *Inalienability of Sovereignty*, pp. 59-80, on Hostiensis and the *publicum statum* of the Church. On the papal election of 1268-71 and the date of Hostiensis' *Lectura* see Ch. Lefebvre, "Hostiensis," in *Dict. de droit canonique*, v, col. 1220-1221; also H. K. Mann, *Lives of the Popes*, xv, p. 339. On the cardinals as a corporate body and *caput Ecclesiae* see Brian Tierney, *Foundations of the Conciliar Theory*, pp. 74f.

[60] Quoted by de Lagarde, *Naissance de l'esprit laique*, II, 206.

[61] Dom Jean Leclerq, *Jean de Paris et l'ecclésiologie du XIIIᵉ siècle*, pp. 174, 186f.; Tierney, *Conciliar Theory*, pp. 157-178, 167, for a good discussion of John of Paris, but without specific reference to the papal *status*. This argument, that the pope is *dominus omnium* and can make full use of the revenues of churches (naturally in accordance with the law, but also for the defense of the faith and the Church), is similar to the doctrine of the legists on the powers of the emperor; on this, see below, nn. 77-82. On Alexander, see Wilks, *Problem of Sovereignty*, p. 362, n. 2.

and *dignitas* and *majestas* of the pope, no canonist fully equated the pope with the *status Ecclesiae*. The "state of the Church," which cannot be fully treated at present, was largely the public welfare of the Church and the faith. Yet, the exalted position of the pope inevitably led to those statements which were close to holding that he was the Church, or the "state of the Church," in the sense that he was the law itself, and his magistracy was the public *status* for interpreting the law and the public welfare of the Church. Herein the pope was like the prince in the secular State. In the late twelfth century a decretalist, Honorius, said that the pope was the *magister* and *custos* of the canons of the Church, that he was the *canon* (*lex*), and that it was sacrilege to dispute what he did.[62] Another decretalist (on Innocent III's declaration that the pope is the vicar of God, exercising a divine authority when for necessity or utility he makes changes in the lands of churches) said that the papal power was beneath God but above man. If the secular prince had a "celestial power," so much the more had the vicar of Jesus Christ. Nor was the law (*lex*) made for him: he was the *lex*, and what was pleasing to him was *lex*.[63]

To be sure, no canonist meant this literally: in the general theory of the papal authority, the pope could not be the law to the extent of being completely unlimited and arbitrary in legislating and interpreting and judging. And if, like the em-

---

[62] *Summa decretalium quaestionum*, in the Paris, BN, MS lat. 14591, fol. 50. Treating the subject of papal rescripts, Honorius says: "Item ipse [papa] est magister et custos canonum, ut xxiii.Q.iii. cum quibus (c. 36). Item ipse est canon, ut ix.Q.iii. ipsi sunt. Item sacrilegii instar habet de facto pape disputare. . . ." If a rescript is contrary to natural law, "non est secundum illud procedendum"; "si vero iuri positivo . . ." the rescript is valid "ut causa necessitatis, id est . . . publico. . . ." (Here the text is not clear.)

On this work see Stephan Kuttner and Eleanor Rathbone, "Anglo-Norman Canonists of the Twelfth Century," *Traditio*, VII (1949-51), 304-336.

[63] Paris, BN, MS lat. 15398, fol. 112ᵛ, to *Comp. III* 3, 1, c. Quanto (*Decr. Greg. IX* 1, 7, 3), ad vv. *romanus pontifex, qui non puri hominis sed veri dei vicem gerit*: "Unde potestas eius ultra hominem et citra deum. Celeste enim dicitur arbitrium habere princeps secularis, nedum vicarius iesu christi. . . . Nec ei lex posita est . . . ; ipse est lex . . . ; et quod placet ei lex est. . . ."

On the theory of the papal monarchy see in general Walter Ullmann, *Medieval Papalism*, who exaggerates the absolutism of the papacy; Tierney, *Conciliar Theory*, esp. pp. 23-36, 47-84; and Tierney, "Grosseteste and the Theory of Papal Sovereignty," *Jour. Eccles. Hist.*, VI (1955), 1-17. Of course, the literature on this subject is too abundant to refer to here, but L. Buisson, *Potestas und Caritas*, should be consulted.

peror, the pope was presumed to have "omnia iura in scrinio pectoris sui," this again did not mean that he did not need to consult with the cardinals and legal experts in important matters.[64] No doubt, however, the theories of the pope as the supreme *auctoritas* in his *plenitudo potestatis*, and as the head of the corporate body of the Church, had their connection with the idea that in his being the head of the sacerdotal magistracy, of the *ordo ecclesiasticus*, the pope was the essential *status Ecclesiae* in the sense of his being the *status, id est, magistratus*. St. Cyprian, in a well-known passage quoted by Gratian in the *Decretum*, had said: "The bishop is in the church and the church in the bishop."[65] On this, before 1220, a decretist remarked that "here the Church is called the bishop," and that the Church is the clergy (*ecclesiastici viri*). But he preferred to say that the Church is the *congregatio fidelium*.[66] In general, however, if the Church was treated as the mystical body of Christ and the corporate body of all the faithful, the definition of the Church as the clergy, particularly the prelates, surely led to the extreme statement of Aegidius Romanus, that the pope as the head can be called the Church. Or, as Alvarus Pelagius was to say, "the mystical body of Christ is where the head is, namely, the pope." Indeed, St. Jerome had declared that the *salus Ecclesiae* depended on the *dignitas* of the pope. The logical conclusion was drawn by Augustinus Triumphus, that the good of the pope was greater than that of the Church, since the good of the Church could not exist without that of the pope. Such ideas, of course, were analogous to the theory of the glossators, that the magistracy, as a *status* subject to public law, was a necessity, for otherwise there could be no administration of law and justice for the sake of the *status Reipublicae* (to D. 1, 1, 1, 2). In one sense, then, the pope was the Church; he was a "corporation sole" and

[64] On *iura omnia*, see Fr. Gillmann, "Romanus pontifex iura omnia in scrinio pectoris sui censetur habere," in *Archiv f. kathol. KR.*, xcii (1912), 3-17, and cvi (1926), 156-174. See below, n. 71; above, n. 27.

[65] Quoted by Ernst Kantorowicz, "Mysteries of State," *Harvard Theol. Rev.*, xlviii, 79; *King's Two Bodies*, p. 215; referring to *Decretum*, C. 7, q. 1, c. 7 Scire.

[66] *Glos. ord.*, to C. 7, q. 1, c. 7: ". . . Hic dicitur ecclesia episcopus: alibi est idem quod ecclesiastici viri, ut supra .lxiii. dist. ca. 1." To Dist. 63, c. 1 one finds this gl. ad v. *ecclesia*: "Ecclesiam hic vocat viros ecclesiasticos. Quandoque vocatur congregatio fidelium. . . . De hoc dixi vii. q. 1. scire."

was absorbing into it the corporate body of the Church. At least, he was the *status Ecclesiae* in the sense that the lawyers had long been speaking of the king's *status* as the public *potestas* and authority.[67]

This development resulted, too, no doubt, from the frequent claim that the local Roman Church, the pope and cardinals, was the universal Church. *Urbs et orbis* in reality were often absorbed into the one *Urbs*—the analogy to ancient Rome is clear. Thus, one cannot but think of the fact that, apart from the prevailing theories of the papal government and the Church, the supreme magistrate acted at times as if his authority was indeed the Church, or at any rate the public *status Ecclesiae*. Let it be emphasized again, however, that the thought was rarely expressed, and never outside the context of the doctrine that the pope was subordinate to the faith and the law of God. But again, as the final interpreter of all laws, even under the limitations of tradition and the faith and the necessity of acting with the counsel of the cardinals, in practicing the reason of the necessity of the faith and the Church, the *ratio status Ecclesiae*, the pope in substance was both the head and in his office the public welfare of the Church.[68] The *iusta causa* and the *casus necessitatis* increased the powers inherent in the *status papae*, which was deemed necessary for preserving the *status Ecclesiae*. The *ratio status papae* must be exercised *ratione status Ecclesiae*. We can now understand how Pope Clement VI could denounce Cola di Rienzo for trying "primatum ecclesie prefate [Romane] subvertere ac tocius orbis statum . . . conturbare."[69] The primacy of the Roman Church and the pope was practically equivalent to

[67] Kantorowicz, *King's Two Bodies*, pp. 194-206, 204 n. 32; Wilks, "The Idea of the Church as 'Unus homo perfectus,' " *Miscel. Hist. Eccles.*, pp. 41-43; *idem*, *Problem of Sovereignty*, pp. 157-159, 364, n. 1.

[68] See also my study, "*Ratio publicae utilitatis*, etc.," *Welt als Gesch.*, XXI, 24-28; above, ch. v, nn. 48-57.

[69] Quoted by Eugenio Dupré-Theseider, *L'idea imperiale di Roma nella tradizione del medioevo*, p. 335. Clement VI goes on to say (p. 336) that Rienzo unlawfully pretended to have rights in the election of the emperor "et de statu Romani imperii ordinare." In a word, the pope was making *status* equivalent to the government according to the constitutional *ordo* of the Empire. This strengthens my interpretation of *tocius orbis status* as essentially the papal authority, which, of course, the pope held was superior to the *status Romani imperii*. Besides, the pope was, according to many canonists, the true emperor.

the state of the World, another way of expressing the state of the Church, *urbe et orbi*.

A development similar to that in the Church had long been going on in theories of the *status* of secular princes. Professor Ernst Kantorowicz has treated it so well that I need only call attention to how the prince was the soul, the *lex animata*, of the State, and the *vigor iustitiae* and *pater legum*. As Lucas de Penna said, quoting Seneca, the emperor is the soul of the *Respublica*, and the *Respublica* is his body; and, in his own words, "the Prince is the head of the realm, and the realm the body of the Prince."[70] But in the theory of the State as a corporate body, the head was likely to coincide with or absorb the whole. "The estate of the king (*status regalis*)," said Ptolemy of Lucca, "has by nature a certain universality, because it is common to the people subject to him." Moreover, as remarked above, the prince, like the pope, was in a general sense, the law, having "omnia iura in scrinio pectoris sui."[71]

John of Salisbury and the glossators, however, generally avoided such identification by resorting to the theory of representation. John held that the prince was neither the public utility (*status*) nor the State, but its minister, the bearer of the "public person" and of the whole body (*universitas*) of his subjects and their community. He was the *potestas publica* whose duty it was to reason and act for the public and common wel-

---

[70] *King's Two Bodies*, pp. 214f., 99; see Index s.v. *Lex animata*. Interesting also are *Auth.* Coll. 6, 2 (Nov. 73), and Coll. 8, 6, 1, 4, and the *Glos. ord.* thereto: ". . . Nec mirum si imperator novit, ut dicit: quia omnia sunt in pectore suo. . . . Item est pater legum. . . . Item est anima legum"; and "No. principem esse ipsam legem animatam in terris . . . Acc." Cf. Calasso, *Ordinamenti giuridici*, pp. 267f.

[71] Ptolemy (Tholemy) of Lucca quoted by Wilks, "Idea of the Church," *Miscel. Hist. Eccles.*, p. 43 n. 41, from the *De regimine principum*, II, 7. On *omnia iura*, see above, n. 64. The maxim came from the Roman law and was often repeated for the powers of sovereign princes in the thirteenth century. The legists, like the canonists, held that the prince had only a presumptive general knowledge of the law. He must consult with his counsellors and legal experts before making new laws and interpreting the law, for only the experts could know the law in detail. And if they did not know the law for a particular case, they should go to the documents in the archives—the *scrinium* is occasionally called the *registrum* or archives. Hence, we can say that the prince's possession of *omnia iura in scrinio pectoris sui* really meant that he was the final authority in deciding cases and interpreting the law on the basis of research and consultation. Besides n. 64 above, see the *Glos. ord.* to C. 12, 20, 3, and Lucas de Penna to C. 12, 19 (p. 715, no. 2), where the *scrinia legum* are *iurisperiti*.

fare. In the legists, too, one finds that the prince represented the State. Yet, by changing the theory of consent in an ordinary corporation into a theory of *ex officio* representation, without any active consent of the members, in the corporate State, Azo helped prepare the way for identifying ruler and community. The *universitas*, he says, cannot consent, either because of its multitude (it was a common saying that a corporation could not easily consent), or "quod est verius," because the members conferred "consensum suum omneque ius et potestatem in magistratus"; and therefore, "quod faciunt magistratus videtur ipsa universitas facere."[72] But this is agency in private law applied to the representation, without recall of the representatives and without consent to new ones, of the State by the magistracy, by the prince himself; for Azo has in mind the *Lex regia* (*D.* 1, 4, 1) and the *universitas* of the people in the State. Perhaps this explains why at this point he departs from the standard theory of consent in the ordinary corporation, that while it is difficult for the members to consent, consent is possible by means of the *maior pars*. As for the State, Azo apparently holds that the membership is too great for any effective practice of consent; hence, all consent along with powers that had belonged to the people was surrendered to the government—whether council in the Italian commune, emperor and his magistracy in the Empire, or king in a realm. As a result, it was easy to speak of the *magistratus* as the *universitas* of the State itself, or at least to think in similar terms, and to forget that the magistracy represented people and State while acting for the common safety and public welfare. If, therefore, the idea that the prince was the law and the soul of the body of the State was not an actual identification of State

72 *Policraticus*, iv, ii, iii; quoted by Jolliffe, *Angevin Kingship*, p. 16; also in Antonio Rota, "L'Influsso civilistico nella concezione dello stato di Giovanni Salisberiense," *Revista di storia del diritto italiano*, XXVI-XXVII (1953-54), 220.

Azo's theory is expressed in a gloss to *C.* 1, 53 De contract. iudicum (in the Paris, BN, MS lat. 4536, fol. 26—this MS contains many glosses of the twelfth century): ". . . Hic nota ipsa universitas consentire non potest, et propter sui multitudinem, ut ff. de libertis uni. l. i [*D.* 48, 3, 1]; aut, quod est verius, quia consensum suum omneque ius et potestatem in magistratus contulerunt; et ita quod faciunt magistratus videtur ipsa universitas facere, nec potest ut supra media persona intervenire. *Az.*" But Accursius, *Glos. ord.*, to *C.* 1, 53, 1, ad v. *Provincias*, says: "Ipse magistratus universitatem repraesentat;" however, the whole gloss shows that he has in mind lower magistrates only.

and magistracy, it encouraged, along with the theory of *ex officio* representation, the ultimate appearance of the concept that the head of the corporate body of the State was in a sense the State itself, and not merely the representative and minister of it and its *status*.

Moreover, still another trace of this kind of identification appeared in the late thirteenth and early fourteenth century. As we noted above, the legists sometimes thought of the ruler as the *imperium, respublica, fiscus,* or even the *regnum*. In all probability they understood these terms in the sense of government or *regimen*, the public *status* in his magistracy. The prince was the *status-respublica*. So, to repeat, Andrew of Isernia said that the king and the *respublica regni* were the same; for whoever was the head in the kingdom, the *respublica* was in him as in the head; and where the prince was, there was *totum ius*.[73] Lucas de Penna essentially agreed, holding that any apparent harshness of the king, if he was acting for the public utility, must be borne "propter honorem principis, qui est res publica, et res publica est in eo."[74] These legists, then, understood what we might express in the words "l'état, c'est le roi," meaning that the "state," *respublica*, was the public welfare and also the magistracy of the king. But the State was not the king, nor the king the State. They did not say that the *rex* or *princeps* was the *regnum*. Even when they identified prince and *imperium*, as Baldus did, probably *imperium* meant the supreme power or authority, not the Empire.

Status est magistratus, then, was seldom expressed literally. But in some legists and canonists, and in Thomas Aquinas, in varying degree, the word *status* bore the meaning both of the

---

[73] Kantorowicz, *op.cit.*, 215f.; "Mysteries of the State," *Harvard Theol. Rev.*, XLVIII, 78-80; Andrew of Isernia, *Lectura* on the *Const. Regni Siciliae*, xxvi, col. 2: ". . . quia fiscus et respublica Romanorum idem sunt, sicut Imperator et respublica, ut ff. de bon. poss. non est ambigendum [*D*. 37, 1, 12]. Rex ergo et respublica regni sui idem sunt, sicut Imperator et respublica Romanorum, qui est in regno, sicut caput, respublica in eo [*ea* here], sicut in capite, dicit Seneca. I. de clementia, hoc modo. . . ." Calasso, *Ordinamenti guiridici*, 268, quotes Andrew thus: "princeps et respublica idem sunt," and "ubi est princeps, est totum ius." See also above, nn. 26-37.

[74] *Com., Tres Libri*, to *C*. 11, 71, 5 (p. 622 c. 1, no. XXIII); cf. Kantorowicz, *King's Two Bodies*, 215f.

public welfare of the community and of the necessary government. Perhaps this meaning was derived in part from an age-old
habit of princes and other chief magistrates who often said "my
administration," "my authority," "my government," and indeed, "my *imperium*" (either as power or as Empire), or "my
kingdom." Such expressions were often casual, as unimportant
as "my country," "my fatherland," "my State," whether said
by a public official or by a private citizen. As remarked earlier,
however, a head of State accustomed to great prestige and power
might succumb to the thought that both government and
State were his personal property. By an easy transition he might
identify his private person both with his public office and with
that entity called the State. This kind of confusion of public
and private in the supreme authority has perhaps been more a
part of kingship in the modern age than in the feudal—at least
in the monarchy of such princes as Louis XIV and Napoleon.

No doubt, a medieval emperor or king, if he thought about it
at all, was conscious only of his duty when declaring that the
State and its government were his. Political and legal theorists,
too, generally intended only to say that the State and its administration belonged to the prince *ratione publicae et communis utilitatis, ratione status regis et regni.* But in this feeling
of ownership, which was not the same thing as feudal proprietor-
ship, and in the very failure to separate his public and private
"bodies," the ruler's identification of himself with the State was
at least possible. In any case possessiveness was present. Thus,
Frederick Barbarossa was surely claiming that the essence of the
Empire was his when, replying to Arnold of Brescia and the
citizens of Rome, he exclaimed: "Behold our republic!"—"Nostram intuere rem publicam!" In his power, he continued, was
the glory of Rome, the senatorial dignity and the consuls (members of his "body politic"?), and the *imperium*. Then, after telling how he prescribed laws for the people, not the people for
him, and how he protected the rights of possessors of property,
he declared that he was not obligated to take oaths to confirm
old laws and customs or to defend at the risk of life the *patria*.
For how could he not defend the *patria*, and especially the "See

of my imperium"?[75] Frederick was virtually saying this is *my* Republic, *my* Empire, *my* Fatherland; neither Arnold of Brescia nor the pope could tell him what his duties were! In fact, his *respublica* and *imperium* were more than his powers of government; they were the whole territorial extent of the Empire: *reipublicae curam gerere*,[76] *Romani imperii gubernacula* (at Roncaglia, 1158—but also *legitimum imperium*, i.e., lawful power),[77] *bonus status imperii nostri* (1177), and "Ex debito imperialis officii tenemur per universum imperium nostrum pro necessitate et statu provinciarum pacem ordinare" (1179).[78]

This kind of royal or imperial possessiveness, however old and customary, was, of course, the more vigorous in the twelfth century because of the revival of the Roman law. Frederick Barbarossa's advisers, some of whom had been disciples of Irnerius at Bologna, were familiar with Justinian's usage of the terms *respublica nostra* and *nostrum imperium*.[79] As is well known, Martinus took Justinian at his word and therefore asserted that the Empire and everything in it were the emperor's property. Bulgarus, however, made the important distinction which all the legists of note were to follow, and which made possible the steadfast theoretical separation of the public office from the personal property of the prince.[80] Against Martinus he

[75] Otto of Freising, *Gesta Friderici, M.G.H., SS. Scholarum*, pp. 109f. Does this mean that Frederick maintained that only kings took coronation oaths, as he did at Aachen in 1152, but that as emperor he was above taking oaths? See below, ch. IX, to nn. 7, 14, 21.

[76] *M.G.H., Legum S. IV, Constitutiones*, I, 207, no. 148, *an.* 1154: "Imperialem decet solertiam ita rei publicae curam gerere et subiectorum commoda investigare, ut regni utilitas incorrupta persistat et singulorum status iugiter servetur illesus." This is in the famous *constitutio* against the alienation of fiefs, confirmed at Roncaglia in 1158. Compare with Richard Fitzneale's words on the *sollertia* of the king's officials in the Exchequer; *S.C.*, p. 205; cf. below, ch. VIII, n. 9.

Is it possible that, besides the Roman law, Macrobius, *Saturnalia*, I, 11, was of influence in such a formulation?—"Alii putant eundem Priscum cum statum ciuium sollertia providi principis ordinaret. . . ."

[77] Speech reported by Otto of Freising, *Gesta*, p. 188.

[78] *M.G.H., Legum S. IV, Const.*, I, nos. 263 and 277.

[79] Mommsen and Krüger, eds., *Digest*, pp. 8 ("Deo auctore nostrum gubernantes imperium"), 10 ("Omnem rei publicae nostrae sanctionem"), 13 ("Tanta circa nos . . . usque ad nostri imperii tempora . . ."). In the second and third examples the meaning is government and power, or administration.

[80] An early gloss states this, in Vat. MS Pal. lat. 763, fol. 113, to *C. 7, 37, 3 Bene a Zenone*, 1, ad vv. *omnia principis esse intelligantur*: "Quantum ad iuris-

argued that the Empire belonged to the emperor only with respect to jurisdiction and protection. It was the emperor's, other glossators said, solely *ratione jurisdictionis et gubernationis*.[81] Since according to this theory the prince enjoyed no proprietary right either to the State or to the highest public office, except insofar as they were his for governing justly and defending against enemies, a weakening of the feudal emphasis on the private, personal character of kingship was to result. Yet, the very exemption of the royal government from private law may have brought about the danger that the king could claim that if the *status* of his public powers and the *status* of the realm were his in a purely public sense, he really was the State. So in the Church, as we have observed, the pope did not own the properties of churches and the clergy, nor the Church. But since the supreme authority was his, *ratione status Ecclesiae*, it was

dictionem; vel dic omnia quantum ad proprietatem secundum ea, scilicet, que procedunt [tam] ex suis rebus quam ex fiscali substantia. . . ." Of course, the fisc is treated by the legists sometimes as completely public (treasury of the State), sometimes as quasi-public (the treasury that belongs to the prince but normally is used for all expenses of his position and government). Rowen, "L'Etat c'est à moi," *French Hist. Studies*, II, 83-98, does not refer to this kind of "property-kingship."

81 The gloss in Accursius' *Glos. ord.* to Justinian's introduction to the *Digest* (above, n. 79) sums up the conflicting opinions; also to *C.* 7, 37, 3 Bene a Zenone, 1, ad v. *omnia principis*. I quote the first gloss, ad vv. *Omnem reipublicae nostrae sanctionem*: ". . . Et quod hic dicit, 'omnem totius* rei publicae nostrae,' id est totius imperii, quod est suum, et res in eo contentae, ratione iurisdictionis vel protectionis, ut hic; non proprietatis, secundum Bul. Sed M. etiam proprietatis. . . ." (* *Totius* is an interpolation made by the glossator in the text of Justinian's introduction.) See also my *"Ratio publicae utilitatis," Welt als Gesch.*, XXI, 79; and above, ch. v, n. 79.

Odofredo, one of the first great Commentators (mid-thirteenth century), offers an interesting discussion to *D.* 50, 17, 66. On the argument that the emperor "potest absorbere ius meum in totum," because "omnia sunt principis," and that St. Paul said that every soul is subject to "potestatibus sublimioribus" (*Rom.* XIII, 1), Odofredo replies that "quod competit mihi naturali ratione, et equitate, ut dominium rei mei, et exceptione competenti, pacto non potest tollere: quia iura naturalia sunt immutabilia. . . ." Nor can the emperor issue a rescript to one man which injures another. *Omnia* belong to the prince "quo ad protectionem." *Fiscalia* do belong to him; but if all things did, no one could claim anything as his own. As for St. Paul, that every soul is subject to the higher powers, this is true only "quantum ad obtemperandum in his, que sunt iurisdictionis." The prince can punish only for *iusta causa* (in the *Lectura* on the *Dig. Novum*, p. 193, no. 2.)

the easier for extremists to declare that in effect he was the Church.[82]

Possessiveness and some identification with the State, then, could and did develop. Another aspect of the development resulted from a pious statement made by Justinian. On the claims of the fisc to property of persons dying intestate and without heirs, he said that he would not exercise this imperial privilege to the injury of his subjects. For *"imperialiter* we judge that the welfare (*commodum*) of subjects is our own," and "what profits all in common, this we think should be preferred to the utility of our private affairs."[83] The glossators quickly made the connection between the emperor's possession of the public welfare and his possession of the jurisdiction for maintaining it.[84] In other words, "what profits all" was public and above the prince's private utility. But the common welfare itself belonged to the prince. It was another way of saying *quod omnes tangit*: "what touches all" in effect touched the prince, too, as the head of the State; and thus the maxim became a principle of public law. (We shall note, in the following chapter, how the business of the *status regni* was the king's business, touching the royal *status*.)[85]

Azo, on Justinian's words about the *commodum* of subjects as his own, briefly referred to a *novella* in which the emperor condemned the exploitation of subjects in the provinces by any magistrates and ordered his agents and governors to collect no more than was owed to the fisc. Immoderate exactions, said

82 Above, nn. 58-64, 61; Tierney, *Conciliar Theory*, pp. 167f., and *passim* on the *plenitudo potestatis* (see Index); Guido de Baysio, *Rosarium*, to *Decretum*, C. 23, q. 8, c. Tributum, nos. 6 and 7, where the theory is applied to the French monarchy.

83 *C*. 6, 51 (50), 1, 14a: "Tantum et enim nobis superest clementia, quod scientes etiam fiscum nostrum ultimum ad caducorum vindicationem vocari, tamen nec illi pepercimus nec Augustum privilegium exercemus, sed quod communiter omnibus prodest, hoc rei privatae nostrae utilitati praeferendum esse censemus, nostrum esse proprium subiectorum commodum imperialiter existimantes."

84 For example, a pre-Accursian gloss to *C*. 6, 51 (50), 1, 14a, ad v. *subiectorum commodum*: "Et cum omnia imperatoris esse censentur, ut j. de quadri. prescrip. bene a ze[none]"; MS Vat. lat. 11152, fol. 141ᵛ c. 1. The reference is to *C*. 7, 37, 3, 1; cf. above, nn. 80-81. A later gloss adds, fol. 141ᵛ c. 1: "Nota imperatorem extimare subiectorum utilitatem suam propriam."

85 See below, ch. VIII, in general.

Justinian, diminish the *imperium* and injure subjects.[86] Lucas de Penna, more than a century after the time of Azo, also directly connected these two laws of Justinian with his own statement that the emperor thought of the *commoda provincialium* as his own, and that Cicero held that the property and wealth of individuals belonged to the *civitas*.[87] Writing with the same passages in mind, Albericus de Rosciate said that the *novella* of Justinian meant also that if a man tried to purchase high office that carried with it both *dignitas* and *iurisdictio*, he was burdening the *Respublica*. Indeed, the prince should appoint only worthy and virtuous men to "dignitates et honores," "judging imperially that the public utility is his own."[88]

Thus, in their different ways both Justinian and the legists held that not only the State (*Respublica* or *Imperium*) and its government (*respublica* and *imperium*) were the prince's, but also the public welfare and *commodum* and common utility of his subjects were his to maintain. This obviously was connected with the public duty of the magistracy to be just to all private persons in exercising *iurisdictio*, and with the right of subjects to receive protection and justice. And it was connected with the frequent association of these principles with the *status* both as the public welfare and as the government, and with *quod omnes tangit* as a principle of public law: the *status regis* and *status regni* touched the welfare of all; and what touched the common interest and utility of all touched the public welfare of king and realm. But first such a public business touched and demanded the exercise of the *potestas* or *status* of the king.

---

[86] To *C.* 6, 51 (50), 1, 14a ad v. *existimantes*: "I. (nfra) aut. ut iud. sine quoquo suf. § cogito. *Az.*" The reference is to *Auth.*, Coll. 2, t. Ut iudices, etc., § cogitatio, or Nov. 8 Praef., §1 cogitatio. See the *Glos. ord.* also to these passages.

[87] *Com.*, p. 866, no. 1: "Provincialium, quorum commoda propria reputat imperator, supra. de cadu. toll. 1. i. prope fi. Nam tunc et imperium et fiscus abundabit, cum subiecti locupletes sunt, ut iudi. sine quoquo suffra. § 1. unde Tullius 3. de offi. Singulorum facultates et copiae divitiae sunt civitatis [Cicero De off., III, 15 (63)]." This is to *C.* 12, 37, 8.

[88] *Com. on the Code*, II, 195ᵛ c. 1, to *C.* 9, 26, 1 Nullus; no purchase of office, "quia lex presumit quod rempublicam gravaret, in aut. ut iudices sine quoquo suffra. §. j. et. §. cogitandum"; and "princeps cessante pecunia et precibus solum dignis et virtuosis daret dignitates et honores utilitatem publicam imperialiter estimans propriam, ut supra. de cadu. tol. 1. unica circa fin. . . ." He adds that, alas! the prince today often yields to money and entreaties; he is *legibus solutus*.

Some of this was expressed by German emperors of the eleventh and twelfth centuries, some of it by Philip Augustus,[89] much more of it increasingly by kings of France and England in the following century, and by the lawyers. John of Salisbury already understood the essence of it when he said that the prince is the public power, an image of the divine majesty on earth, obeying the law and accepting all the burdens of ruling. Hence, the power over all subjects was conferred on him in order that he might be able to achieve the utility of all individually and in common, and maintain the "state of the human Republic." For each is a member of the others; they are members of each other. Herein, John continues, *natura* leads; nature placed in the head of the community the universal *sensus*; thus, all members are subject to the head, and the people must carry out and obey the needs of the prince.[90] If John thought of the Republic or State as a body, a *universitas*, like the glossators he also viewed the prince and other magistrates or judges as the public head, possessing the real public mind or "reason" of the State in the public and common welfare of all—of all as one body and of all as individuals.[91] Naturally—by the sanction of nature—the

[89] Examples in H. Fichtenau, *Arenga. Spätantike und Mittelalter im Spiegel von Urkundenformeln*, in *Mitteilungen des Instituts für österreichische Geschichtsforschung*, Ergänzungsband, XVIII (1957), 80, no. 154: Conrad II, *an.* 1030, "Publice rei et communi hominum utilitati in omnibus et per omnia consulendum fore censemus . . ."; no. 155, Lothair III, *an.* 1136: "Imperialis benevolentie proprium iudicamus commoda subiectorum investigare et eorum diligenti cura mederi calamitatibus simulque publicum bonum statum ac dignitatem imperii omnibus privatis commodis preponere"—this in the famous feudal law promulgated by Lothair. Philip Augustus, in his provision for the government of the realm while he was crusading (Fichtenau, "Arenga," p. 80 no. 156; also in H. F. Delaborde, *Recueil des actes de Philippe Auguste*, I, 416, no. 345): (*an.* 1190) "Officium regium est subiectorum commodis modis omnibus providere et sue utilitati private publicam anteferre." This obviously reflects the words of Justinian in C. 6, 51 (50), 1, 14a, and the maxim that the public welfare must always be preferred to any private welfare.

[90] *Policraticus*, IV, 1, ed. Webb, I, 235: "Est ergo . . . princeps potestas publica et in terris quaedam divinae maiestatis imago. . . . Unde merito in eum omnium subditorum potestas confertur, ut in utilitate singulorum et omnium exquirenda et facienda sibi ipse sufficiat, et humanae rei publice status optime disponatur, dum sunt alter alterius membra. In quo quidem optimam uiuendi ducem naturam sequimur, quae microcosmi sui, id est, mundi minoris, hominis scilicet, sensus universos in capiti collocavit, et ei sic universa membra subiecit, ut omnia recte moveantur. . . ."

[91] Cf. Kantorowicz, *King's Two Bodies*, pp. 207, 208 n. 42; also Rota, "L'Influsso civilistico," *Riv. stor. dir. ital.*, XXVI-XXVII, 213-226.

prince as head possessed the magistracy and the supreme authority over the body. The common opinion was that as the head he represented the community. Almost, however, he was the community, for practically speaking it was in him more than he was in it.

Now we can sum up. Professor Percy Ernst Schramm has remarked that in the Middle Ages the king was the *Zeichen* of the State, and that consequently scepter, crown, and other symbols of monarchy are better sources for understanding medieval kingship than chronicles, documents, and treatises. But in this study it has become clear that the legal ideas are by no means unimportant.[92] Perhaps the doctrine of the *status* as the magistracy, and as the rights and duties of the crown, is as important as a symbol; the concept of the *corona* as the *ensemble* of those rights which pertained to and were the royal estate and dignity is as important as the material and symbolic crown. Perhaps the *status regis* is as positive an indication of the royal majesty as any other expression. To be sure, the "state" of the king was not the State; but it was not only the royal *potestas*, it was also the whole magistracy, the government. For as early as the latter half of the twelfth century, the glossators were beginning to revive the ancient Roman understanding of the *ius publicum* as the constitutional law that was concerned both with the *status* (public welfare) of the State and with the indispensable *magistratus*. Without the magistracy of prince and lesser administrators and judges, how could the state of the Republic be maintained? So it was that, as in antiquity, the public *status* became in one sense the *magistratus*, the constitutional order. Furthermore, *status* and *magistratus* were at times equivalents of the *respublica*, in the sense of the *regimen, gubernatio,* or *politia*— "la chose publique."[93] And the scholastic theologians agreed: the *status* of the State was, as it were, the *magistratus* of prince, king, or any sovereign government.

Almost, but not quite, the jurists of the later thirteenth and the fourteenth century made the transition from "state" to

---

[92] *Herrschaftszeichen und Staatssymbolik*, III, 1067; Kantorowicz, "Kingship," *Twelfth Century Europe*, pp. 89-111, on the importance of "scientific jurisprudence."

[93] This has been noted occasionally, above, nn. 31, 34, 39, 55-58.

"State." They were approaching the identification of the State (Republic or Realm) with the supreme authority vested in the government of the prince. Yet, neither they nor those who equated *magistratus* and *status* really had in mind the kind of absolutism attributed to *L'Etat, c'est moi*. The prince might be the public *status*, but he was not the State. As the public *status* he was included in the whole body of his realm, and, therefore, the prince as the *status* was subordinate to the end of the public welfare or commonweal of the community as a whole, to the *status* which finally became the "State." If he was subordinate to the State and the public and common welfare, nonetheless, he had the right to interpret and practice that *ratio status* (*ratio publicae utilitatis*) which was the necessary reasoning for the achievement of the end of the State, its well-being and safety, and the common welfare of its members. *Ratio status magistratus* and *ratio status Reipublicae* became inseparable. Quite naturally, though never saying it, a powerful king might think to himself that he was not only the *status* or government, not only the head of the State, but the State itself.

In this chapter the main emphasis has been placed on the theme of *status, id est, magistratus*. But in passing, we have noted that in the glossators, in the *Dialogus de scaccario*, and in the theologians the word *status* occasionally meant the public authority and powers (*potestas* and *potentia*) of the chief magistrate, the head of the State. Most frequently, in fact, we find that the ruler, rather than being the *status*, possessed a *status—status regis* was a frequent term in royal documents, chronicles, and the writings of the jurists. In the following chapter, therefore, we shall examine the importance and meaning of the "state" of the king. The *status regis* no doubt became the more important because of the assumption that the "state" of the king was also in essence the government of the realm, and because the *status regis* was necessary "ad statum (regni) conservandum, ne pereat."

Once more, it is clear, the twelfth and thirteenth centuries contributed important political ideas to the Italian Renaissance and the modern age. Even if he did not study them, Machiavelli perhaps owed his emphasis on *lo stato* as the Prince not only to

Cicero but also to the glossators and to Thomas Aquinas. No doubt, he got this definition more directly from current usage in the Italy of the fourteenth and fifteenth centuries. A few examples have come to my attention. When in 1315 the people of Mantua made a Gonzaga the head of the city, it was because the care of the "status rei publice" belonged "especially to those whom the *status* itself touched."[94] That is to say, in effect, in public law *quod omnes tangit* meant that the public welfare chiefly touched or was the chief concern of the Gonzaga, and the care of this *status* belonged to him. In consequence, as the *magistratus*, the Gonzaga held the *status* and was the substance of it if not completely identical with it. Another example comes from Ludovico de Corthosiis (de Padua), 1418. In his *De principibus*, if in one instance *status* is almost our State, it is in other instances the "state" of the prince perhaps in the sense of public office or government.[95] About the same time the famous Coluccio de' Salutati, writing on the subject of the tyrant, seems clearly to have used *status* for the magistracy.[96] The medieval background is evident.

Perhaps the medieval background, or at least the continuing terminology and the meaning which became current in the Middle Ages, is also evident in the sixteenth century in England as well as Italy. These words of Sir Philip Sidney remind one both of *status-magistratus* and Justinian's identification of the emperor and the public welfare of his subjects: "The Princes persons . . . in all monarchall governmentes are the very knot

---

[94] Marongiu, *L'Istituto parlamentare in Italia*, p. 78 n. 42, quoting from V. Vitale, *Il dominio di parte guelfa in Bologna, 1280-1327*, pp. 237f.: ". . . illis status rei publice cura spetialior comitatur quos tangit sinipse status."

[95] The *De principibus* seems to be unedited; I consulted it in the Paris, BN, MS lat. 4612, fols. 229-268: (fol. 229ᵛ) the pope cannot depose a prince for burdening his subjects if the prince is acting "cum causa, puto pro iusta deffensione status"; (fol. 243ᵛ) on the confiscation of the property of those who are guilty of treasonable acts "contra statum suum. . . . Barones facientes contra statum principis debent magis puniri quam alii cives. . . ." Even the first example could mean that the prince, acting for the security of his public power, could, e.g., collect extraordinary taxes. The second example indicates that treason against the "state" of the prince is treason against the State—as in the Roman law, D. 48, 3, 1.

[96] *De tyranno*, ed. F. Ercole; c. 2, art. 21, "statum . . . ordinavit"; c. 3, art. 7, the *status reipublicae* in Caesar, c. 4, art. 6, on recovering the *status* and *dignitas*. Coluccio also speaks of the *status civitatis* (c. 4, art. 8).

of the peoples welfare, and light of all their doinges to which they are not only in conscience but in necessitie bounde to be loyall."[97] Plowden, the Tudor jurist, surely had the medieval royal *status* in mind when he said: "But his Body politic is a Body that cannot be seen or handled, consisting of Policy and Government, and constituted for the Direction of the People and the Management of the public weal"; and to the "natural Body" of the king "is conjoined his Body politic, which contains his royal Estate and Dignity."[98]

Perhaps, finally, had Louis XIV actually said, "L'Etat, c'est moi," he might possibly have intended that a small *e* (*l'état*) be understood, meaning that he was the supreme *potestas* and magistracy, existing for the *commun profit*. And when Napoleon declared that he had been *la chose publique, l'Etat*, was he departing radically from the old tradition of the *status-magistratus-respublica-potentia-potestas* of the prince as the *lex animata* and the soul of the *Respublica*?[99] The classical-medieval Roman legal thought on the public law and the State was not unknown in the new Empire, and Napoleon had possibly absorbed some of its spirit with respect to the *status principis*.

[97] In the *Arcadia*, quoted by A. H. Gilbert, *Machiavelli's Prince and Its Forerunners*, p. 3.

[98] Quoted by Kantorowicz, *King's Two Bodies*, pp. 7 and 9; cf. n. 29 above.

[99] See above, to nn. 54-58. In the fifteenth century Jean-Juvenal des Ursins wrote of the king as the soul and principle of life of the *chose publique*; Gilbert., *op.cit.*, p. 3, from Ch. Petit-Dutaillis in Lavisse, *Histoire de France*, IV, ii, 207—where one also finds that Jean-Juvenal said that the king's own soul is the soul of, or belongs to, the crown. Therefore, in effect, whereas in the Canon law the salvation of one's soul was a right more important than the common welfare, here the king's private soul is so identified with the life of the *chose publique*, the State in this case, that its eternal salvation is less important than the salvation on earth of the public soul of king-crown-realm-people. Moreover, the State is the king and the king is the State. Perhaps this idea resulted from another principle stressed by the canonists and popes: ordinarily, the right of the private soul was superior to the common welfare; but in the case of great prelates, who were subjects of the public law and in turn administered their churches in the public and common interest, they must remain in office, even at the risk of their personal immortality, for the sake of the public and common welfare in the work of saving souls.

CHAPTER VIII ✧ *STATUS REGIS:*

LESTAT DU ROI IN THE STATUTE OF YORK

I
N THE thought of the legists and canonists the *status* of the Republic or State was the public welfare. But quite early it meant also the magistracy or government and its public authority. At times, indeed, the *status regis* was the royal *potestas*. If the *status regis* bore this meaning, does it help us understand *lestat du roi* in the Statute of York? Again we turn to the famous Statute, for as in the case of *lestat du roialme*, historians have variously interpreted *lestat du roi* and *lestat de la coronne*. Again the method of a Romano-canonical commentary on *status* and other terms connected with the public authority of the prince—*majestas, honor, dignitas,* and *corona*—will be employed, with deliberate repetition of concepts already encountered, in order to interpret the nature of public law and kingship in England.

1. *STATUS REGIS;* THE ESTATE ROYAL

Influenced perhaps by the assumption that medieval kingship belonged to feudal and private more than to public law,[1] G. T. Lapsley decided that the king's estate was largely personal, closely related to the royal household and its revenues and administration, while the estate of the crown was public, signifying the inalienable public powers of the king in his courts. Quite recently John H. Trueman has supported this interpretation.[2] George L. Haskins, whose conclusions were criticized by

[1] For example, Pollock and Maitland, *History of English Law*, I, 512-518, and II, 2-5; and recently, J. E. A. Jolliffe, *Angevin Kingship*, ch. IV, and R. S. Hoyt, "Royal Taxation and the Growth of the Realm in Mediaeval England," *Speculum*, XXV (1950), 40. Professor Hoyt also believes that *status regni* came to have the sense of "state of the realm" only in the late thirteenth or early fourteenth century.

[2] See the summary of various interpretations given by Trueman, "The Statute of York and the Ordinances of 1311," *Med. et Human.*, X (1956), 64-69, and Trueman's own conclusions, 75-81. For Lapsley, whose interpretation is defended by Trueman, see his article, "The Interpretation of the Statute of York, 1322," *E.H.R.*, LVI (1941), 22-51, 411-466—reprinted in *Crown, Community and Parliament in the Later Middle Ages* (eds. H. M. Cam and G. Barraclough),

Lapsley, held that the king's estate was principally his properties and revenues and was the same as the estate of the crown. S. B. Chrimes assumed that the estate of the king was the mass of rights and duties and attributes which constituted the kingship, the royal sovereignty or prerogative; the estate of the realm was probably the "state or good condition" of the kingdom as a whole, and it involved taxation more than legislation.[3] Joseph R. Strayer, however, has emphasized legislation as the main concern of king and Parliament in dealing with both estates.[4]

Ernst H. Kantorowicz, in *The King's Two Bodies*, has given us quotations from English sources of the sixteenth century which set the theme of this study. Let Henry VIII begin the interpretation of the Statute of York. "We be informed by our judges," he said, like a medieval king advised by his counsellors and judges, "that we at no time stand so highly in our estate royal as in the time of parliament, wherein we as head and you as members are conjoined and knit together in one body politic." Moreover, he declared that England was an Empire "governed by one supreme head and king, and having the dignity and royal estate of the imperial crown of the same."[5] In the later sixteenth century, we learn from Edmund Plowden's *Reports*, the "body politic" consisted of policy and government and was "constituted for the Direction of the People and the management of the public weal." To the natural body of the king was "conjoined his Body politic which contains his royal Estate and dignity"; the "body natural" was "adorned and invested with the Estate and Dignity royal"; and the "body natural" and the "body politic" were indivisible and incorporated in one person.[6]

---

pp. 153–230. My references are to the older printing in the *E.H.R.* Wilkinson, *Constitutional History of Medieval England*, II, ch. III, does not discuss the problem of *status regis*.

[3] Haskins, *Statute of York and the Interest of the Commons*, pp. 98–104; Chrimes, *Constitutional Ideas of the Fifteenth Century*, pp. 91-93.

[4] "The Statute of York and the Community of the Realm," *A.H.R.*, XLVII, 1–22—but Strayer's study, excellent though it is, does not treat the meaning of *estat*, for his emphasis is on the "community of the realm" and on consent.

[5] The first passage is quoted also by Haskins, *Growth of English Representative Government*, p. 124; by Kantorowicz, *King's Two Bodies*, p. 228. The second passage is quoted by Kantorowicz, *loc. cit.* Cf. above, ch. VI to n. 58.

[6] *King's Two Bodies*, pp. 7 and 9.

What Henry VIII thought of the royal estate is not clear, but in the first statement it was certainly an attribute of his headship in Parliament. Presumably he was describing the supreme authority which he most fully exercised when he and Parliament constituted the governing body of the realm. He was not the "body politic" itself, but he as head and the members of Parliament constituted it; and thus, in a way his words remind one of the glossators' *corpus principis*, a body which included the emperor, his greater magistrates, and the senate.[7] At any rate the "estate royal" was no private aspect of kingship, for in the second statement Henry attributed to the head the "dignity and royal estate" of the crown; and indeed, the royal estate was assimilated to the crown. Plowden seems to identify the king and his estate and his dignity still more closely with the "body politic," as if the king and his *status* were the whole government, not including Parliament. But again the estate or dignity of the king was public, standing for the royal authority. The "estate royal" belonged to the "body politic," not to the "body natural."

Yet the "body politic," consisting of policy and government, and containing the royal estate, dignity, and office, could not be separated from the "body natural." They were two aspects of one public person. How this may be analogous to the Chalcedonian doctrine of the two natures of Christ has been shown by Ernst Kantorowicz. What is significant for the present purpose is that while the public body was essentially the royal estate and dignity, or contained these, it was manifestly impossible to separate this estate completely from the "body natural." But it was different, for it was a public estate related to the royal office and dignity and to the crown.

In Shakespeare, too, as Kantorowicz reminds us, the king's "state" was his public office. Richard II says (IV, i, 192f.):

> You may my glories and my state depose,
> But not my griefs, still am I king of those.[8]

The royal "sacred state," moreover, was virtually the crown

[7] Above, ch. VII, n. 30.
[8] Quoted by Kantorowicz, *King's Two Bodies*, p. 37.

and was closely tied to the king's "pomp and majesty," his "manors, rents, revenues," and his powers of legislating and administering (IV, i, 208-213):

> With mine own hands I give away my crown,
> With mine own tongue deny my sacred state.
>
> ....
>
> All pomp and majesty I do forswear;
> My manors, rents, revenues I forgo;
> My acts, decrees, and statutes I deny.

Both in Shakespeare and in the crown lawyers, indeed, and in Henry VIII, the concept of the royal *status* as something connoting the public authority, crown, power, dignity, and majesty and glory of the king, an estate supported by "manors, rents, revenues," strongly reminds us not only of the early legists and canonists, but also of Richard Fitzneale's words in the *Dialogus de Scaccario*. We have encountered the *Dialogue* already, but it is so significant as the work of a great public officer who long served Henry II that we must again examine it for the meaning of the royal estate. For Richard speaks of those *dignitates* by which the *gloria regiae potestatis* shines forth; even ecclesiastics should serve kings and their *iura*, above all in maintaining the material wealth which belongs to or touches kings *ratione sui status*; and the *potestates principum* are measured by the *mobilium copia*. In a word, the royal estate is the king's power, not his revenues; it is supported, however, by his wealth in revenues. Furthermore, the *status regis* participates in the Exchequer, where royal officers administer and judge in fiscal matters both for the *utilitas* and *status regis* and for the *status regni*.[9] In the Exchequer as in the royal government in general,

---

[9] S.C., pp. 200, 205. See the text also in the ed. by Charles Johnson, *Dialogus de Scaccario* (Nelson's Medieval Classics), pp. 1, 14. Johnson's translation of "sui status ratione" is not satisfactory, given Richard's reflection of the Roman law and the glossators. The text reads (ed. Johnson, p. 1): "Oportet autem hiis servire non in conseruandis tantum dignitatibus per quas gloria regie potestatis elucet, uerum in mundanarum facultatum copiis que eos sui status ratione contingunt. Ille enim illustrant, hec subueniunt. Porro mobilium copia uel defectus principum potestates humiliat uel exaltat." His translation reads: "And we ought to serve them by upholding not only those excellencies in which the glory of kingship displays itself but also the worldly wealth which accrues to kings by virtue of their position. Those confer distinction, this gives power.

therefore, the *ratio publicae utilitatis (status) regni* is the principal *ratio potestatis (status) regis*.[10] Thus, Richard Fitzneale was in fact reflecting the legal thought of contemporary glossators, that the public powers of the supreme magistrate and his judges were the *status* that existed to maintain (*conservare*) the *status Reipublicae*, "lest it perish."[11] Obviously, as Shakespeare said, the king must have his public property and revenues in order to exercise the powers that belonged to and were the royal estate.

If a twelfth-century authority on English kingship presents a concept of the public estate of the king which fundamentally

---

Their power indeed rises and falls as their portable wealth flows and ebbs." (It is interesting that Cicero, *De off.*, III, 15 [63], quotes Hecaton of Rhodes thus: "Singulorum enim facultates et copiae divitiae sunt civitatis.")

In my opinion the words *potestas* and *status* are here virtually equivalent in meaning; therefore *status* is weakened by the translation "position." And "by virtue of their position" weakens too much the literal "by reason of their state" or "power." "Portable" wealth suggests to me the wealth in revenues (which the Exchequer collects) that is necessary if the king's "state" or power is to be sufficient for defense against enemies, as the next sentence suggests: "Quibus enim hec desunt hostibus preda fiunt. . . ."

And the passage in Bk. II, c. 10 (ed. Johnson, p. 100; *S.C.*, p. 234), on how "ratione publice potestatis" the king can confiscate the property of a usurer who has injured a loyal subject, illustrates again how the translation is weakened by the lack of regard for the current legal thought and terminology. Johnson has for the key words: "because as head of the executive he (the king) is to receive all the goods of the creditor, or rather usurer, who has enriched himself by ruining one of them (i.e., one of the king's faithful subjects)." Obviously a literal translation is better: "by reason of his public power," or "by reason of his *status* or estate" the king receives the goods of the usurer. To be sure, the "reason" of the king's public *status* or power is related to his being the "head of the executive"; but why not put it in the sense of the words in the twelfth century?

Finally, in the edition of the *Dialogus* by A. Hughes, C. G. Crump, and C. Johnson, the editors (p. 163), say that Hugh of Fleury, *De regia potestate* (ca. 1100) uses almost the same language. This is only partly true. I find nothing like *ratione status sui* and the words about kings' powers and wealth in Hugh, although in general Hugh stresses the royal power, which comes from God, and the duty of ecclesiastics to be obedient to the king. See Hugh's *De regia potestate* in *M.G.H.*, *Libelli de lite*, II, 466-494.

R. L. Poole, *The Exchequer in the Twelfth Century*, does not discuss the problem of the influence of Roman law.

10 *S.C.*, p. 234: if a usurer has enormously injured a subject, the king "ratione publicae potestatis" can confiscate the usurer's property. As for the Exchequer, the king's revenues, and the demesne, and problems connected with the king's private as opposed to his public revenues and expenditures, see in general R. S. Hoyt, *The Royal Demesne*. On the public character of the imperial and royal fiscs see Kantorowicz, *King's Two Bodies*, pp. 164-191, 342-346.

11 Above, ch. VII, nn. 7, 15.

agrees with that of the sixteenth century, many sources between the two periods show that the tradition was continuous. To be sure, Bracton says only that the public *iura* of the king, the royal powers of jurisdiction and government for the protection of private rights and for keeping the peace, pertain to the crown and the royal dignity. These powers belong to the *iurisdictio ordinaria* and cannot be alienated by the king.[12] Bracton does not mention the *status regis*. Nonetheless, his doctrine of the rights of king and crown puts in different words Richard Fitz-neale's description of the royal authority or powers as the *status regis*. And because his theory of kingship belongs in substance to the context of the main current of thought in the legists, one can say that he, too, was really talking about the public estate of the king.

The legists and canonists, however, and the scholastic theologians, from about 1150 carried on a steady, continuous theory of the public *status* of prince or king and, indeed, if later, of the *status* and *ratio status* of the pope. We need recall now only the opinion of the legists, that the public law dealt both with the *status principis et magistratus* and with the *status Reipublicae*. By reason of his public *status*, by reason of his jurisdiction and government, the prince could say that the Republic or Empire belonged to him. The *status Reipublicae* was indeed his own; the common and public welfare of his subjects and of the State was his; and his welfare, his *status*, in the powers of governing, was itself necessary for the "state" of the Republic. The *ratio status principis* was also the *ratio status Reipublicae*. Both estates, the public authority and the common welfare, were public, complementing each other—sometimes, indeed, the confusion of both resulted in the prince's being the public *status* if not the State.[13]

[12] *S.C.*, p. 413; *De legibus*, ed. Woodbine, II, 166f. (fol. 55b); Kantorowicz, *King's Two Bodies*, p. 149. In general on Bracton's idea of kingship, see McIlwain, *Constitutionalism Ancient and Modern*, pp. 71-94; Kantorowicz, pp. 143-164; and, for the influence of Roman law, Fritz Schultz, "Bracton on Kingship," *E.H.R.*, LX, 136-176. Cf. above, ch. VII, n. 27.

[13] See my *"Ratio publicae utilitatis,"* *Welt als Gesch.*, XXI, 8-28, 71-99; and above, chs. V and VII, esp. to nn. 67, 73. For the "impact of scientific jurisprudence" in the twelfth century, see Kantorowicz, "Kingship," *Twelfth Century Europe*, pp. 89-111.

Obviously, since the prince needed revenues in order to govern and defend the Republic, his fisc or treasury was public; it was necessary to and a part of the *status Reipublicae*. Therefore, as Justinian said, the imperial fisc should act not against but for the common profit ("quod communiter omnibus prodest"; C. 6, 51, 1, 14a); and the *proprium commodum subiectorum* was also the emperor's good or profit. It follows that the revenues of the prince in his fisc were both for the public state of his office and for the state (public and common welfare) of his subjects and of the State.[14] The prince, of course, enjoyed a private patrimony that was his private estate, but the revenues that came into the fisc were certainly not his private estate but a part of his public estate. Rather, these public revenues supported his public estate. Both the estate of the prince and the means to support it, therefore, were businesses that concerned the prince and the people's welfare in common.

It has been argued, however, that the business of the king of England was different from that of the realm.[15] But in fact, just as in Justinian's ideal, any important *negotium* that touched the state of the realm touched the king and was his business; and the public business of the king in his public estate was sometimes the business of the *populus* (i.e., the greater men) or of the *universitas regni*. So, for example, Innocent IV held that a king could not debase the coinage "sine consensu populi" or of the *maior pars regni*, "for the business of the king is the business of the *universitas*."[16] Normally, of course, the king's estate

14 Above, ch. VII, nn. 83-90; also Kantorowicz, *King's Two Bodies*, pp. 173-230.

15 Trueman, "Statute of York," *Med. et Human.*, x, 69; cf. below, n. 36. But Ullmann, *Principles of Government and Politics in the Middle Ages*, pp. 175-178, notices that some *negotia* are common to king and realm. So does Wilkinson, *Constitutional History of England*, III, 51-53, and *passim*.

16 *Com. on Decr. Greg. IX*, p. 118, to 2, 24, 18 Quanto. This decretal was the basis of the standard theory developed by the canonists, that any debasement of the coinage, or any change in its value, required the consent of the people (the *populus* usually meaning the greater men of the realm). It is well known that Nicholas of Oresme was to emphasize the theory of consent to changes in the coinage of the realm.

On the meaning of *populus*, while sometimes it meant all the people, including the *plebs* as well as the nobility, generally it was assumed that the greater men were the effective *populus*. So a decretist of the early thirteenth century expresses quite well the difference between *populus* and *plebs*, in the

as the supreme power and magistracy for maintaining law and order, although it vitally touched the *status regni*, required no consent except what was often presumed to be the original consent of the people to the transfer of the *imperium* to him and his heirs. With regard to his normal powers of ruling, however, the *populus* which counted, e.g., chiefly the great lords of England, sometimes questioned the wisdom of the king and his advisers and tried to control the powers that properly belonged to the royal *status* and crown. Indeed, the Statute of York was the royal government's reply to such an attempt in the early fourteenth century. But any *negotium* that required the king's action because of his public estate and at the same time touched the rights and well-being of his subjects, and therefore the *status regni*, was a business that was common to king and "people" (including the commons in case taxation or legislation touched them). In such matters *quod omnes tangit* was sometimes consciously applied as a principle of public law, although the king had a greater right to demand and get consent to any action necessary for the safety of the realm and "people" than the "people" had to refuse it. What touched the *status regni* was, then, definitely the king's business; and as we shall observe, it touched his public *status* too. Head and members were interested in any important business that touched both and affected the all-embracing *status regni*.

There were two businesses of the greatest importance (*ardua negotia*) that were of vital interest and concern to king and realm in common—the defense of the public and common welfare (the *status* of the realm) against enemies threatening the safety of the State, and the maintenance of justice and law and order, *ratione communis et publicae utilitatis*, again *ratione status regni*. "Regis namque officium pugnare est bella populi sui, et eos rectissime iudicare" (I Kings, 8). Justinian declared

---

Summa "Antiquitate et tempore" on the *Decretum* (in Vat. MS Palat. lat., fol. 37ᵛ), Dist. 2, c. Lex est: ". . . Nota quod ea[dem] differentia est inter populum et plebem, que est inter animalem et hominem, inter genus et speciem. Nobiles enim, et in nobiles simul collectum, sunt populus. Ple[b]s est ubi non sunt senatores et viri consulares. . . ; id est, universus populus maiores natu tribus modis dicuntur, nobilitate, dignitate, antiquitate." Cf. *Inst.* 1, 2, 3, 4.

in well-known words that the imperial majesty should be decorated with arms and armed with laws in order to vanquish enemies in battle and do justice in the courts. As an early glossator
said, the office of the emperor was twofold, that of peace and
war, of "expelling the iniquities of false accusers" and of fighting enemies and conquering and triumphing—in time of peace
fighting with laws was to hold trial and give sentence.[17] The war
of defense and the system of justice, of course, concerned subjects also, the subjects in varying degree as fighters and taxpayers and as interested parties in the courts. Each was a business
common to the *status regis* and the *status regni*. Legists and
theologians held that extraordinary subsidies levied for the defense of the realm were levied also for the maintenance of the
status regis—so, for example, Thomas Aquinas and Lucas de
Penna.[18] The royal estate must be the stronger for waging war
and providing justice for subjects.

This development had its roots not only in the early history
of kingship but in the Canon and Roman law of the twelfth
century. Popes and decretists agreed that a king who refused
or was too *fainéant* to defend the *patria* should lose his royal
status and *dignitas*. As a decretist said, *ca.* 1169, if the *status* of
a king changed for the worse because he would no longer fight
in defense of the realm, the pope had the right to absolve the
king's vassals from the oath of fealty. Hence, Pope Zachariah
released the Franks from their oath taken to the king "intuitu
regie dignitatis," and deposed the last of the Merovingians because he was *inutilis* in the exercise of the royal *potestas*.[19] The

---

17 *Inst.*, Prooem., "Imperatoriam maiestatem"; and gloss to this in MS Vat.
lat. 8782, fol. 49: "Officium imperatoris duplex est diversarium, id est, pacis
et belli. . . ." There is no need of quoting the whole gloss; the idea also is in the
Glos. ord. of Accursius—also in English sources, e.g., Glanville and *Fleta*.

18 Above, ch. VII, to n. 42, for Thomas Aquinas; Lucas de Penna says, *Com.*,
to *C.* 10, 18, 1 (p. 83, c. 1, no. 10): ". . . si aliquis casus de novo emergat in
quo oporteat multa expendere pro utilitate communi, vel pro honesto statu
principis conservando, ad quae non sufficiunt redditus proprii, vel exactiones
consuetae, puta si hostes terram invadunt. . . ." Clearly, Lucas holds that the
status regis is the royal, public power, directly serving the *status regni*.

19 Paris, BN, MS lat. 14997, fol. 109, *Summa Coloniensis* ("Elegantius in iure
divino"), to *Decretum*, C. 15, q. 6, c. 3 Alius item: "Status quoque mutatione
interveniente, a iuramento fidelitatis absolvere ecclesia consuevit. Unde Gelasius
[actually Gregory VII, in a letter of 1080]: Zacharias papa regem francorum,
non tam pro suis iniquitatibus quam quod tante potestati inutilis esset, a regno

French (*Francigenae*), said a decretist, were absolved from their oaths of fealty "ratione dignitatis . . . non ratione personae." Another decretist associated the *corona* with the royal estate and dignity: the *corona regni* should go to that man who was successfully waging war *pro communi salute.*[20] The French king and legists, indeed, were soon making the war of defense a business so important to king and realm alike, that they tended to confuse *rex, regnum, corona* and *patria*; the *defensio patriae et coronae* was also the defense of the *bonum commune* or *bonum publicum regni.*[21] The royal estate, dignity, and crown, therefore, existed chiefly for the defense of the kingdom and the public welfare.

Because of the vital necessity of the king's *status* for defending the realm, clearly his estate included the public right to meet necessities or emergencies. Since such necessities touched or concerned both king and subjects, the king of England frequently claimed that every necessity of defending even an overseas possession that was not in the territory of the kingdom touched the *status regni* and the crown as well as his own feudal rights. The defense of the realm of England was involved in the defense of Normandy or other fiefs in France, even though such fiefs really pertained to the king as a feudal lord and not to the realm of England proper. In fact, these overseas possessions, in spite of being the king's private, feudal rights of lordship or *dominium*, belonged also to the *imperium* of the king and were

---

deposuit, omnesque francigenas a iuramento fidelitatis absolvit. Hoc intelligendum est de iuramento quod prestitum fuit intuitu regie dignitatis. Nam quod intuitu persone fit, relaxari nequit, nisi is, cui factum est, ab ecclesia separetur. . . ." (On this *Summa* see Kuttner, *Repertorium*, pp. 170-172.) The papal letter and a gloss to the above gloss show that the Merovingian king was accused of failure to fight in defense of the *patria*; see my "Two Notes on Nationalism," *Traditio*, IX, 283f.; below, ch. x, nn. 15f.

[20] Johannes Faventinus, in *Glos. ord.* of Joh. Teutonicus, to *C.* 15, q. 6, c. 3; MS lat. 14997, fol. 109; *Traditio*, IX, 284 n. 15; below, ch. x, n. 16.

[21] Jean de Blanot and Jacques de Révigny, quoted in my "Two Notes on Nationalism," *Traditio*, IX, 289f. (below, ch. x, nn. 39-44); also Guillaume Durantis, *Speculum Iuris*, IV, Part. iii, 2, no. 31, as quoted by Kantorowicz, *King's Two Bodies*, p. 251 n. 180—on king and crown, pp. 340f. See Strayer, "Defense of the Realm and Royal Power in France," *Studi in onore di Gino Luzzato*, p. 292. On the crown, see also Hartung, "Krone als Symbol," *Abhandlungen d. preus. Akad. d. Wissenschaften, Philos.-histor. Kl.*, no. 13, 3-46.

subject to the royal jurisdiction and administration in the Chancery and the Exchequer. They were a part of a feudal empire, and they were subjects of the crown.[22] By the time of Edward I, Wales, like Ireland under Henry II, was also treated as a part of the empire that belonged to the crown.[23] It is therefore not surprising that the king's *status* was public even for the defense of territories that properly had nothing to do with the *status regni*. The *universitas regni Angliae* itself, the community of the realm represented chiefly by the magnates, admitted in 1294-1295 that Edward I in fighting a just war in defense of Gascony was also defending the *regnum* and the *status regni*.

Thus, the king's business of defending both the kingdom and his feudal empire was also the business of the people in the community of the realm. Whether stated as *necessitas regis et regni* or *negotia regis et regni*, in time of war—which the king on his side naturally said was a just war of defense—the necessity or business that touched the king touched the kingdom; what touched the head touched the members; what touched the *status regis* touched the *status regni*. Conversely, the necessity of preserving the *status regni* was a public business that directly concerned the public *status* or duties and powers of the king, powers exercised for the "common profit" (*publica* and *communis utilitas*) of the realm. In other words, we see again that the *ratio status* of the king, the reason and necessity of his public *potestas*, existed *ratione utilitatis publicae et communis regni*, or *ratione status regni*.[24]

22 See Julius Goebel, Jr., "The Matrix of Empire," Introductory Essay to Joseph Henry Smith, *Appeals to the Privy Council from the American Plantations*, pp. xiv-xxii, xliii-liii; Powicke, *Thirteenth Century*, p. 108; also Barnaby Keeney, "Military Service and the Development of Nationalism in England, 1272-1327," *Speculum*, XXII (1947), 542f. On an early thirteenth-century claim that England was an Empire, see Kantorowicz, *King's Two Bodies*, pp. 345f.

23 Goebel, "The Matrix of Empire," in Smith, *Appeals*, pp. xliii-lii. It is particularly interesting that in 1278 counsel for Llewellyn, while arguing that every province "sub imperio Regis" should have its own laws and customs in its own language, admitted that each province and its customs existed for the *ampliacio corone* rather than the *diminucio corone*; p. xliv n. 131. It is interesting too that here is a possible reflection of the contemporary theory of provinces or kingdoms within the Roman Empire, a theory transferred to the "Empire" under the king of England.

24 I cannot treat the subject here, but it should be remarked that some

I have anticipated the final conclusion, which is based on the presentation of much more evidence. But before turning again to English sources, it is interesting and useful to notice briefly some indications of the equivalence in meaning, on the Continent, of the terms *status, dignitas, honor,* and *corona,* in connection with the authority of the prince and with the *status regni.* Lothair III declared that the *regalis potencia* was strengthened by monasteries; privileges for them profited both the *regni status* and the eternal reward of the king, and they were "pro nostro et totius imperii statu." Louis VII associated the *honor regis* with the protection of all subjects, including monasteries. In the documents of Philip Augustus one finds that any injury done to the rights of the metropolitan of Tours was an injury to the *status coronae* and the realm, and that Pope Innocent III should be favorable to "nos et regnum nostrum et negocia honorem nostrum contingentia" and to "regni nostri proficuum."[25]

---

glossators tried to explain that the *utilitas publica* was the *status* of the whole Republic or State as a corporate entity, *universitas,* including the head and the members; that the *utilitas communis* was the common welfare of the members viewed individually. In a fashion the public welfare was the subject primarily of public law, the common welfare the subject of the private law that was made for private rights. But since private law depended on the authority of the government for its enforcement, it was subordinate to public law; it was "public by authority," private in its application to the private rights and welfare of individuals. Hence, the common welfare of the individual members of the State depended on the public welfare of the State and its government, else private law and rights could not exist. No matter—the glossators could be inconsistent, and frequently *public* and *common welfare* were used without distinction, although the *public* looked more to the State as a whole than to the members viewed either individually or collectively. In the French of English royal documents *commun profit* stands for *public* and *common welfare* alike, and for *status regni et populi.*

[25] Lothair III, in *M.G.H., Dipl.,* VIII, 25, no. 19, and 58, no. 35; Louis VII, letter quoted by Fichtenau, *Arenga,* in *Mitteilungen d. Inst. f. österreichische Geschichtsforsch.,* Ergsbd., XVIII, 44; for Philip Augustus, see Delaborde, *Recueil des actes de Philippe Auguste,* I, pp. 179f. (to Pope Lucius III, against the papal injury to the Church of Tours, the *regnum,* and the *corona*), and 165f. (letter composed by Stephen of Tournai, to Lucius III, on the peril to the *status corone*); and Phil. Aug. in letter to Innocent III, *Recueil,* II, 144 and 246, nos. 593 and 685, against the Pope's favoring Otto of Brunswick as emperor; again Philip speaks of the *corona* as if it were the "crown of the realm," not simply the royal crown: the invasion of *terra nostra* by the Count of Flanders is "in damnum corone," and the king asks for aid "tum pro capite nostro, tum pro corona regni defendenda," and "pro defensione capitis nostri et corone regni" (*Recueil,* II, 115f., no. 566). On the French crown in this period, see

To be sure, the king's salvation was a private matter; but just as in the Roman law, so in the twelfth century *sacra* (*inter alia* monasteries, churches, and religion) were subjects of the public law, and it was the duty of the prince to aid religion and churches for the public and common welfare in the salvation of souls—so the *Glos. ord.* to *D.* 1, 1, 1, 2. (As late as the seventeenth century, Oxenstierna, justifying Gustavus Adolphus's invasion of Germany, said that "it was a question not so much of religion, as of the *status publicus*, in which religion is comprehended.")[26] Privileges and gifts to monasteries and churches, therefore, enhanced the public and royal power because they also increased the *utilitas publica, status regni*. So the jurists sometimes argued in the thirteenth century: royal gifts and privileges to churches were no alienation that injured the rights of king, crown, and realm and thus violated the coronation oath. Donations to God, said Johannes de Deo (*ca.* 1243), do not injure the Empire, because the Empire is better defended by the prayers of the Church than by arms and physical labor. But a donation can be revoked, he admitted, if by it the Empire or a kingdom, duchy, or county is "enormously injured—unless, however, prescriptive right defends the gift and the donee."[27]

Frederick Barbarossa's advisers and his chancery understood quite well the public nature of the imperial *status, dignitas, honor*, and *majestas*, and how the *status* of the prince existed to prevent injury to the rights and *status* of people and Empire.

---

also Strayer, "Defense of the Realm and Royal Power in France," in *Studi in onore di Gino Luzzato*, I, 289-296.

More examples could be given from our period. But let one from 1034 suffice: Conrad II and Henry III, in a privilege for the bishopric of Bamberg, that it belongs "ad imperialem nostram maiestatem . . . totius regni curas statumque imperii precipueque omnium sanctarum dei ecclesiarum commoda considerare . . ."; Fichtenau, *Arenga*, p. 118, no. 238. See also n. 28 below.

26 See the glosses in the *Glos. ord.* to *D.* 1, 1, 1, 2. Legists and canonists constantly stated that religion and the Church, and the maintenance of the faith, belonged to the public law and vitally interested the State. Of course, this theory was not forgotten in the modern age. For Oxenstierna and Sweden, see M. Roberts, "The Political Objectives of Gustavus Adolphus in Germany, 1630-1632," *Trans. Roy. Hist. Soc.*, 5th ser., VII (1957), 22. Stuart Hoyt, therefore, on the same problem in England, needs correction, *Speculum*, XXV, 40 (see n. 1, above).

27 *Questiones de facto*, in the Vat. MS Borghes. 260, fols. 132-161; this *questio* fols. 132-132ᵛ.

At the Diet of Roncaglia (1158) Frederick asserted that his powers of jurisdiction and coercion belonged "ad statum eius dignitatis" and to the office of the imperial majesty. Perhaps the *bonus status imperii nostri* was the "good state" of his *imperium* or authority as well as that of his Empire.[28] Moreover, the *status Romani Imperii* and the *status* of the illustrious princes who maintained the glory of the Empire should be "preserved unharmed"; and in 1162 the emperor declared that he was the *defensor ecclesiarum Dei*, "ut eas et earum iura integra et illesa sub nostro imperiali protectione defendamus."[29] So the imperial chancery was recalling laws of late Roman emperors on the oath of judges and magistrates and on the rights of the public fisc and the rights of subjects and churches, using famous words derived therefrom ("publicum illaesum," "privilegia . . . illibata," "ita eius patrimonium iugiter servetur illaesum"), and connecting them with the *status principis* and *status Reipublicae*. Particularly important is the wording of the famous feudal law promulgated by Frederick in 1154: "Imperialem decet solertiam ita reipublicae curam gerere, et subiectorum commoda investigare, ut regni utilitas incorrupta persistat, et singulorum status iugiter servetur illaesus."[30] If this law directly prohibited the alienation of fiefs, indirectly it prohibited the alienation of the *iura regis et regni (imperii)*, since it aimed at preventing the loss of *debita servitia* and the consequent injury of the *honor imperii* and of the military power of the emperor.

We shall encounter this terminology again when we consider the English coronation oath and observe how, like the rights

[28] *Gesta Friderici, M.G.H., SS. Scholarum*, p. 188; *M.G.H., Legum S. IV, Const.* I, nos. 161, 205, 211, 263, and 277. The documents of Conrad III are also interesting: *an.* 1152, the *dignitas imperii nostri* adorned by works of piety, and to cultivate justice and engage in piety "sic nostro convenit honori" (Fichtenau, *Arenga*, pp. 39f.); *an.* 1139, "ad nostre dignitatis spectat coronam, boni operis dare et relinquere posteris suis exemplum" (Fichtenau, p. 52). Such formulas were already ancient; for example, in the *Formulae imperiales* of the Carolingian age one finds the *regia et imperatoria dignitas* associated with doing justice; Fichtenau, pp. 41f., from *M.G.H., Formulae*, p. 291. On *honor* see Peter Rassow, *Honor imperii. Die neue Politik Friedrich Barbarossas 1152-59*; but Rassow neglects the Roman public law. See below, nn. 69-75.

[29] *M.G.H., Legum Sectio IV, Const.*, I, nos. 231 and 217.

[30] *Ibid.*, no. 148 (also in the *Libri Feudorum*, 2, 55).

of the fisc and of subjects in the Roman law, the rights of king and crown, subsumed in the *status* and *dignitas regis* and in the *status coronae*, should be maintained *illibata* or *illaesa*. Indeed, the so-called inalienability clause, which may have been added to the English coronation oath as early as 1154, originated in part in the wording of the oaths of Roman magistrates in the time of Justinian.[31]

Now we must return to the terminology in imperial documents on the powers of the prince. Two more examples will be sufficient to our purpose. In 1212 and 1213 Frederick II piously subordinated his public *status* to the *decor et potestas imperii* and the *bonus status pacis* throughout the Empire.[32] This was another way of saying what his grandfather had said in 1165: "The *dignitas* of the Empire and the imperial *honor* demand that the emperor should always have before his eyes and in his hands the *necessitates Reipublicae*; the *honor* (*imperii*) uses the right method, and its *status* is made the stronger, when the *salus totius patriae* and the *necessitates* of the poor are usefully and mercifully provided for."[33] Here, surely, the *status* of the emperor was the *honor imperii*, or powers of office.

In the two laws, then, and in the documents of emperors and kings on the Continent, *status, honor, dignitas*, and *corona* often stood for the public authority, or for those powers of the prince which were deemed necessary for the maintenance of the *status* of the realm. Therefore, such important businesses as defending the State and doing justice for the protection of the lawful rights of subjects were common to, or interested in common, the *status regis* and the *status regni*. But, of course, the conduct of such *negotia* belonged primarily to the "estate royal," to the crown. How they were conducted sometimes touched the *status populi et regni*; but the *negotia* themselves always touched, because they were for, the *status* of the realm and all its members. Altogether, in the twelfth century, kings and their administrators and judges were advancing, if slowly in the midst

---

31 See below, ch. IX, for a full treatment of the subject.

32 *M.G.H., Legum S. IV, Const.*, II, nos. 43 and 45.

33 *Op.cit.*, I, no. 228; cf. Rassow, *Honor imperii*, in general, for the background in the twelfth century; cf. below, nn. 69-74.

of feudal habits and concepts, toward the theory and ideal stated in an edict of Louis XV in 1717: "Notre couronne n'est à nous que pour le bien et salut de l'Etat."[34]

We can now understand how in England, as early as the twelfth century, there was a similar appreciation of the *status regis et regni*. In the so-called *Leges Henrici* (*ca.* 1109-1118) we find the idea that the *imperium* of the king was strengthened by the establishment of courts at certain times and places. *Placita* were not to be held more often unless the "propria regis necessitas vel commune regni commodum" demanded them.[35] The king's own necessity, no doubt, could be different from the common good of the realm, but in this case it was the necessity and common good of the realm, too.[36] Again, just as the Emperor Lothair III felt that privileges for monasteries strengthened the *status* of the Empire, so King Henry II granted lands to churches not only for the salvation of his own soul and the souls of his grandfather, Henry I, and of his sons, but also *pro statu regni mei*.[37] Unlike Lothair, Henry did not stress the strengthening of the royal *potencia*, but no doubt that aspect of the *status regis* was closely related to the king's spiritual welfare. Ralph de Diceto says that Henry II was acting as the *pater Anglorum* when, solicitous for the common safety, he used the *publica potestas* in the shires to reform the sheriffs, who had not been doing justice and had abused the fiscal rights of the king and injured (*laedere* is the verb) the *majestas principis*.[38] In the assize of Northampton, c. 7, if justice belonged "ad dominum regem et ad coronam suam" and "ad commodum domini regis," it also belonged, in the context of the ideas and terminology of

[34] Quoted by Fichtenau, *Arenga*, p. 202, no. 448—from A. Babeau, "Les préambules des ordonnances royales et l'opinion publique," *Séances et Travaux de l'Académie des Sciences Morales et Politiques*, Compte Rendu, 56ᵉ année, NS, part 46 (1896), 853.

[35] *S. C.*, p. 123.

[36] Trueman thinks that this is evidence for a distinction between *negotia regis* and *negotia regni*; "Statute of York," *Med. et Human.*, x, 69; above, n. 15. But of course *vel* can mean "or" in the sense of "and" and "what is the same thing," or "or rather." In any case, the business of the common welfare of the realm was the king's business, and it belonged to his office, crown, dignity, and estate to conduct it.

[37] Quoted by Hoyt, *Speculum*, xxv, 40; above, nn. 1 and 26.

[38] *S. C.*, p. 155. On *majestatem laedere*, see below, ch. IX, nn. 6, 7, 38, 39.

the century, to the public *status regis* and to the crown alike.[39] Justice belonged to the estate of the king for the maintenance of the estate of the realm; and it was as profitable and useful for the king's *status* as it was for the public and common welfare.

The *Dialogue of the Exchequer* shows that the important public business of war was common to king and realm. A knight's horses and armor, says the author, should normally be left to him if he is an insolvent debtor, so that in case of necessity he can serve in the *negotia regis et regni*. But if he fails, when summoned, to heed the *necessitas regis vel regni*, his creditors shall leave him one horse so that he can retain his knightly dignity and fight in the king's service.[40] The necessity common to king and kingdom, then, was above all the necessity of the king's authority both for good government and for war in defense of the realm.

We find increasingly abundant evidence of this in the thirteenth century. King John identified his own *magna et ardua negotia* of the war against Philip Augustus with the *utilitas communis* of the kingdom. Further, he declared that it was just that all the members (of the realm) should hasten with their aid to the *defensio capitis*. Thus, quite early the corporate theory of the realm appears in a royal document (of course, John of Salisbury had already fully stated the old doctrine of the body of the Republic and its head and members). If the *status regis* is not mentioned, it is implied, in that it was the public business of the king as head to defend the *status regni*.[41]

To judge from a few examples of usage from the reign of Henry III, just as in the twelfth century so in the thirteenth, the royal *status* was concerned in any public business that was common to king and realm; rather, a business common to king and realm touched the *status regis et status regni*. In the reissue of Magna Carta in 1216 it was stated for the young Henry that he

---

[39] S. C., p. 180. On the early development of the concept of the crown in England in relation to the public law and kingship, see Kantorowicz, *King's Two Bodies*, pp. 342-346; also Ullmann, *Principles of Government and Politics*, pp. 178-180. For other examples of *status regni* and Henry II, see Wilkinson, *Constitutional History*, II, 51f.

[40] S. C., p. 239; *Dial.*, II, 14, p. 111. Note again how *et* and *vel* are used.

[41] S. C., p. 277; Rymer, *Foedera*, I, 87; Wilkinson, *Constitutional History*, II, 52.

and his council (*consilium*) would fully take care of those things which suggested themselves for correction, all those things, that is, which pertained to the *communis omnium utilitas* and the *pax et status noster et regni nostri*.[42] In 1237 the *status noster et regni nostri* was concerned with the common business of a subsidy that was debated in a Parliament held at Westminster. Obviously, the *status regis* was the public right or authority which the king held for the defense of the realm and of the rights of the crown in France. The demand for extraordinary taxes could not in theory be made for any private interest of the king (although he was capable of misusing the proceeds of a subsidy), but only for a business that concerned the public interest of king and kingdom.[43] A report of a debate in Parliament in 1242 confirms this. Summoned by Henry to give him a subsidy for defending his *iura* in France, in those parts which pertained "ad regnum suum Angliae," the prelates and barons protested, arguing that they should not give an aid unless Louis IX broke the truce (that is, unless Henry could show that he actually faced the necessity of fighting a just war of defense). They complained that the king had not respected their wishes about an earlier subsidy, which they had intended should be spent only if necessary for the utility of the king and the realm.[44] *Utilitas* in the legists was often equivalent to *status*. Clearly, the public "state" of the king, his powers or prerogative for meeting emergencies and defending the "state"of the realm, is indicated.

In 1258, according to the Burton *Annals*, the king and his son Edward submitted to the ordinances of the twenty-four on the correction of their *status* and of the *status totius Angliae*.[45] Again the sources show that the estate of the king and his heir was public. For in the provisions of Oxford, the twenty-four prescribed three Parliaments each year for treating "les communs besoingnes del reaume e del rei ensement." From the contents of the Petition of the Barons, the Provisions of Oxford, and the Provisions of the Barons, it seems evident that the

[42] *S. C.*, p. 339.
[43] *Ibid.*, p. 358.
[44] *Ibid.*, p. 360f.; cf. Sir Maurice Powicke, *The Thirteenth Century*, p. 78.
[45] *S. C.*, pp. 330f.

business common to king and realm was largely that public authority of the king which Richard Fitzneale had related to the royal *status*, but which also pertained to the crown—for example, matters connected with the Exchequer.[46] This becomes clear also in the Award of St. Louis. After saying that the Provisions of Oxford had injured or detracted from the *ius et honor regius* (*honor*, again, often meant the public honor, dignity, or office),[47] the Award ordered that the royal castles be returned to the king, and that the king have the right freely to choose all the greater and lesser officials "regni sui ac domus suae." Most significantly, the French monarch ordered that the king of England should have *plena potestas et liberum regimen* in his realm and its pertinencies and that he should be in *eo statu et in ea plenaria potestate* in which he had been in the past.[48]

But what was the royal *domus* mentioned in the Award? What had the provisors of 1258 thought it was when they had urged the "amendment" of the *hostel* of the king and the queen? In neither case was the term *status* used to qualify the *domus* or *hostel*. Nevertheless, did St. Louis and the framers of the Provisions have in mind the household as the more private estate of the king —which Lapsley thought was the meaning of *lestat del hostel* in the Statute of York?[49] Although it is difficult to say whether in the minds of the provisors the royal household was the private or public estate of the king, it is probable that to St. Louis it was at least an essential part and center of the public estate, which was above all the *plena* (*plenaria*) *potestas et liberum regimen* of a sovereign monarch. Perhaps the household enjoyed a similar public *status*, derived from the *status regis*, in the later thirteenth and the early fourteenth century. Since the king was the active head and no mere symbol of the State, the government was in some important ways centered in the household. In it the king consulted in his council with his *proceres*, counsellors and officials, and formulated policies; it was an important center of the administration of the whole realm.[50] In some respects, possibly,

46 *Ibid.*, pp. 373-394; p. 382 for *communs bosoingnes*.
47 See below, to nn. 68-75, on *honor*.   48 *S. C.*, pp. 395-397.
49 "Statute of York," *E.H.R.*, LVI, 43-49.
50 On the confusion between public and private in the royal household, see Jolliffe, *Angevin Kingship*, ch. ix. Powicke, *Thirteenth Century*, pp. 323f., 545f.,

members of the royal family partook of the public estate of *hostel* and king. Certainly, the heir to the throne was treated as a subject of the public law. The Young Edward was deeply involved in the *negotia regis et regni* from 1258 on, and the estate of the heir along with the estate of the king was to be stressed in the Statute of York.

There was, to be sure, much that was private in the royal household. But at the same time, just as in his office the king was a *persona publica,* just as he enjoyed a public as well as private *status,* so the royal *domus, hostel,* household, shared in the public aspects of kingship. Perhaps, indeed, the very joining of *status* to *hostel, lestat del hostel,* resulted from the concept of *palatium* in the Roman and Canon law and in the legists and canonists. The imperial palace was "sacred" and like all *sacra* was a subject of public law. Further, according to the legists, city halls (*palazzi communali*), which housed the communal councils of priors and courts of justice were called *palatia* and *domus;* and like royal *palatia* they were *sacra* and public. The *domus fiscalis,* too, was *sacra.*[51] In the *Glossa ordinaria* of Johannes Teutonicus on the

---

stresses the public nature of the household in the time of Edward I; Davies, *Baronial Opposition to Edward II,* chs. 2 and 3, treats the personal and private aspects of the reign of Edward II, along with the confusion of public and private in household activities, in that the king did not draw "any distinction between his household and the administration" (p. 63); but on the whole, he shows that the public nature of the household was more important than the private. Chrimes, *Introduction to the Administrative History of Medieval England,* agrees with Davies and adds good comments, pp. 156-160. Of course, Tout, *Chapters in the Administrative History of Mediaeval England,* is invaluable—see for the twelfth and thirteenth centuries I, 18-31, 181-183, 313-317, and II, 10-59; for Edward II, II, ch. viii. Tout's emphasis is on the Wardrobe, but here and there he discusses the problem of the public vs. private nature of the household.

Wilkinson, *Constitutional History,* II, 113f., also stresses the fact that in the time of Edward II the household and royal council were at the center of the government, that even the officers of state, like the chancellor, treasurer, and justices, in carrying out the king's commands were subject to the household system.

[51] For the Roman law see *D.* 1, 1, 1, 2 and *C.* 11, 77, 1; and a gloss to *C.* 11, 76, (77), 1, ad v. *excipimus:* ". . . nam cum palatia vel domus in civitatibus deputantur ad usum publicum principis, vel ad reponendas species publicas, vel ad redditionem iuris, non debent privati eas impedire nec suis usibus occupare"; Lucas de Penna says that palaces and all things which belong to the prince are *sacra,* because the power of the prince is from God (*Com.,* to *C.* 10, 6, 2, ad v. *sacris,* p. 37, no. 3). Elsewhere he says that the *curia,* as the

Decretum we find that the bishop's *domus* was in one sense his *familia* (administrative household), in another his church.[52] We must not go too far afield on a subject that needs much study, but as early as the time of Henry II, Gilbert Foliot, Bishop of London after 1161, described the *palatium* as the center and place of the exercise of the authority of the king in judicial matters.[53] At the same time, the concept of the *civitas regia* as the

---

locus where *decuriones* assemble, is a palace, like the palaces of cities in Tuscany, "ubi morantur regimina [*regina* in the text I have used] seu priores" (to *C.* 10, 31, 41, p. 166, no. 5). He adds here his remarks about the *curia principis, curia ecclesiastica praelatorum, curia iudicum maximorum,* and the *curia* as the *fiscus*. In the *curiae* of magnates and kings, he continues, ambition and vice, informing and prying, and detraction and jealousy prevail. See Lucas also to *C.* 11, 76, (77), 1; p. 646, nos. 4-6. The *Glos. ord.*, to *C.* 4, 44, 18, had already spoken of the *palatini* as the *proceres palatii*, "quorum consilio regitur respublica"; and to *D.* 43, 6, 1, ad v. *aedes sacras*: "Id est Deo consecratas . . .; sed et domus fiscalis dicitur sacra."

Baldus implies that the royal palace is where the king and his government are, that the king as *caput regni* is in his palace, just as the *regia civitas* is called the *caput regni* (to *D.* 1, 18, 1, no. 26; quoted by Kantorowicz, *King's Two Bodies*, p. 204 n. 35). This is related to such ideas as those of the thirteenth century which equated *corona, patria communis, caput regni,* and king and capital city; see my "Two Notes on Nationalism," *Traditio*, IX, 289-296; below, ch. x, nn. 39-63. See also n. 53 below. It is related also to the idea that where the emperor is, there is Rome (Kantorowicz, pp. 204f.). To be sure, this means in one sense that the king is the realm wherever he may go. But there is also, perhaps, the meaning that the king's government and the king are present everywhere in the realm, even though the king remains in the *regia civitas* (and in his palace); see Kantorowicz, "Invocatio nominis imperatoris," *Boll. del Centro di Studi Filologici e Linguistici Siciliani,* III (1955), 1-16.

The *dignitas gloriosa* of the royal *palatium* is related to the *maximum splendor regiae potestatis* in a Frankish coronation *Ordo* of 768-816; Schramm, "Ordines," *Archiv f. Urkundenforschung,* XI, 369f. Cf. below, ch. IX, n. 1. On the public nature of the royal palace at Pavia in the eleventh century see Kantorowicz, *King's Two Bodies,* p. 58 n. 34, and p. 188 n. 306. The idea of the *sacrum palatium,* so far as it concerned the legists in our period, goes back to the classical Roman law; H. Fichtenau wrongly starts it with Byzantine theologizing, whence it came to the West in the time of Charlemagne, "Byzanz und die Pfalz zu Aachen," *Mitteilungen d. Inst. f. österreichische Geschichtsforsch.,* LIX (1951), 1-54, esp. 13f. But, of course, the Byzantine influence may have stimulated the revival of the classical idea in the West.

On the architectural symbolism of the *sacrum palatium* as the seat of government in the late Empire, see E. Baldwin Smith, *Architectural Symbolism of Imperial Rome and the Middle Ages,* p. 10.

[52] *Decretum,* Dist. 47, c. 8 Sicut § Necesse (Gratian), and Dist. 89 "Domui" (Gratian), and the glosses to these.

[53] Giles, ed., *Gilberti Foliot Ep.,* I, 277: to Thomas Becket, Gilbert Foliot writes that it is the duty of bishops to serve the king, for the Church thereby enjoys a greater *potestas* on earth, a *potestas* "qua magnum in palatio obtinet ecclesia principatum, cum in omnibus regni judiciis, praeterquam si de vitae

caput regni was anticipating the identification of the capital city
and the *patria communis*—at least in France in the later thirteenth century, when Paris was, like Rome with respect to the
Empire, becoming if not *urbs* and *orbis*, the *caput regni* and
common fatherland of the kingdom of France. For any city in
which a king had his *sedes* became the capital, because of the
regis potentia or the powers of the king as head of the realm.[54]
Similarly, the *status regis* gave the *hostel, domus,* or *palatium*
its "estate public." At any rate, the royal *hostel* in England may
have enjoyed an estate that was as public as the estate of the
king. No doubt, it was very different from the ancient *sacrum
palatium*, but it was more the center of the public authority
and government than Buckingham Palace is today.

It is thus probable that St. Louis had in mind the public nature of the *domus* of Henry III. The royal *domus* was the very
core of the king's public powers of government; and surely,
given the prevailing theory of kingship, Henry III should have
the full right to choose the officers of his household, including
the members of his council. And the old Roman term, *proceres
sacri palatii (C.* 1, 14, 2, and 8), was still in use for royal coun-

---

periculo tractatur aut sanguine, locum habeat ipsa praecipuum; haec regi nos
obligat . . . ut ab ipso citati debeamus assistere, et singulorum causas universi
discutere, et judicare."

[54] So the great decretist Huguccio, *Summa*, to Dist. 96, c. 13 Sicut, ad vv.
parva civitas praerogativam praesentis regni non minuit: "Comparata regno,
vel habens sedem regiam, nam in quacumque civitate sit sedes regia, non
diminuitur regis potentia" (MS Vat. lat. 2280, fol. 87ᵛ); also in the *Summa
Reginensis:* "Nam in quacumque civitate sit sedes regia, non imminuitur
potentia" (Vat. MS Reg. lat. 1061, fol. 28ᵛ). In the context the *praerogativa
regni*, the *sedes regia*, and the *potentia regis*, are thus closely related. See also
n. 51, above.

As for London as capital as early as the time of Henry II, Alexander III in
1161 called London the *regia civitas* where the king frequently sojourns, "et
ibi frequentes baronum et procerum de toto regno soleant esse conventus"; and
"quanto autem praedicta regia civitas inter alias regni civitates magis est
nobilis et famosa," so much the more does the king want the church of London
to be administered by a man who is worthy and wise in divine and human
law (Giles, ed., *Gilberti Foliot Ep.*, I, 192f.). In another letter the pope, again
to Gilbert, says that Henry II had asked that Gilbert be bishop of London
"ut in ea civitate quae quasi caput regni est" (II, 85f.). But so far as I know,
no one in this or the following century went so far as to identify London with
the *patria communis* of England, as Pierre de Belleperche did for Paris and the
communis patria of France in the time of Philip the Fair; see my "Two Notes
on Nationalism," *Traditio*, IX, 291, 293; below, ch. x, to nn. 45, 54.

cillors, counsellors, judges, and administrative officers, and sometimes also for the great men of the realm who were summoned to Parliament as a greater council and court.[55] Private and personal though medieval kingship was, it was also public. If Louis XIV constantly combined and displayed his private and public persons in the palace at Versailles and yet is treated as a modern king, it is not illogical to claim a similar treatment for Henry III and Edward I.

Altogether, then, in the Award of St. Louis, the *status* of the king is virtually the same thing as the *status* of the crown; both estates are aspects of the same thing, the fullness of the king's public *potestas*. Had Bracton drafted the document for the French king, he would perhaps have spoken about the rights of jurisdiction and government, about those things which, connected with justice and peace, belong to no one except the crown and the royal dignity. But he would have meant what the Award declared was the lawful *status* of Henry III.

The language of other sources for the reign of Henry III does not contradict the general sense of what has been said. In the Form of Peace, 1264, it was provided that the king, advised by nine counsellors, should appoint greater and lesser officials to the "regimen curiae et regni," and these officers should swear to conduct themselves in office "ad utilitatem domini regis et regni."[56] The nine *consiliarii* were to be chosen "ad reformationem status regni Angliae"—and here the *status regni* could as easily mean the royal government as the state of the realm. In the Confirmation of Charters of 1265, the king referred to the earlier settlement "pro regni pacis et securitate," and to the *ordinatio* "super nostro et regni nostri statu."[57] Once more, since the business treated had been the public authority of the king, the probability is that the *status regis* was again the king's lawful public rights and powers. Those who drew up the *Dictum*

---

[55] *Proceres* appears over and over again in English as well as continental royal documents; in the legists the word sometimes means the members of the government of an Italian commune. See above, n. 51, and the *Glos. ord.* to C. 4, 44, 18—*palatini* are *proceres* by whose *consilium* the *Respublica* is governed. On legislation by the emperor and his *proceres*, who give counsel, see C. 1, 14, 8.

[56] *S. C.*, p. 401.

[57] *Ibid.*, p. 404.

of Kenilworth emphasized the *honor* and *bonus et pacificus status* of the king; and the commission given delegated powers provided that the king should fully hold and freely exercise his *dominium, auctoritas,* and *regia potestas.* The *dignitas regia,* as defined by the approved *iura, leges,* and *consuetudines* of the realm, must not suffer damage. The king should pardon all who in the civil war had inflicted any injury "in ipsum vel in coronam regiam"; but all places, rights, property and other things belonging to the *corona regia* should be restored "ipsi coronae et domino regi."[58] In the *Dictum,* then, the *honor* and *status* of the king included the public powers of the royal jurisdiction (justice was a true reflection of the *regia majestas*),[59] and were equivalent to the royal *dominium, potestas,* and *dignitas.* Possibly, in fact, in this instance *status regis* signified the public office of kingship better than *corona.* But since the royal estate could not function without the rights and properties that belonged to the crown, it is likely that *corona* and *status,* along with *dignitas* and the like, were not fundamentally different in meaning.

Henry III did not have the ability to govern his realm according to the developing concepts of the public law. Edward I had the ability; and he and his advisers seem to have been intellectually and politically aware of the importance of the *status regis* and the *status regni* to each other. That the public "estate royal" was the king's power, which it was his duty as well as right to use, to maintain the *status Reipublicae, ratione status regis et regni,* Edward understood well enough. He realized, as Sir Maurice Powicke has said so well, "that the state of the king was in the end identical with the well-being of the community of the realm."[60] Justinian, we noted above, had long since expressed the same ideal for the imperial government, if in terms of "what profits all in common" and "the welfare of subjects is our own."[61] No matter that the terminology varied

---

[58] *Ibid.,* pp. 407f.

[59] *Ibid.,* p. 408, § 2.

[60] *Thirteenth Century,* p. 37; Sir Maurice long ago observed how Edward was practicing "reason of State," "Reflections on the Medieval State," *Trans. Roy. Hist. Soc.,* XIX (1936), 1-19.

[61] Above, to n. 14.

—royal policies and acts *pro re publica, pro utilitate regni, pour le profit commun* belonged to the *status regis* and the crown, and were for the maintenance or defense of the *status regni* and of the royal estate in common. A few examples will indicate, along with the well-known appeal to *quod omnes tangit*, why Edward was long ago called the English Justinian.

In 1274 Edward, ordering the great inquest, indicated that the royal rights and liberties (such as wreck of the sea) which pertained to the crown, as well as common justice and the *regia potestas*, touched both his *status* and the *status* of the community of shires.[62] In 1275 Parliament granted him a subsidy—"causa suae novitatis," said some; "ad relevationem status nostri," said the king. To the king and his heirs the same Parliament granted the custom on wool, woolfells, and leather.[63] These examples point first, to the royal estate in its fiscal and judicial rights and powers; second, to extraordinary taxation for the new king as he is beginning his reign, hence for the proper maintenance of his public estate because perhaps of the increasing costs of government and household; and third, to additional regular income for the estate of the king and his heirs, that is, probably, for Edward and his successors.

If the Statute of Gloucester, 1278, held that the "profit de office regal" (*utilitas regalis officii*, 1267, in the Statute of Marlborough) demanded that the king provide for the "amendment" of the realm and the fullest exhibition of justice (*dreit*) but did not mention the "profit" of the crown, the terms were equivalent to *status regis* and *status coronae*.[64] The business *pro re publica* for which in 1282 Edward summoned the clergy to Parliament, was a *negotium* (war in Wales) to be finished for the praise and honor of God, the *magnificentia nostrae famae*, and the peace and tranquillity of the whole realm and people. And in 1294-1295 the king's war in Gascony touched king and kingdom.[65]

---

[62] *S. C.*, pp. 421f.

[63] *Ibid.* pp. 422, 443. A subsidy *ad relevationem status regis* reminds one of the idea expressed by Thomas Aquinas; above, to n. 18.

[64] *Ibid.*, pp. 449, 333.

[65] *Ibid.*, pp. 459, 430, 476-480. For another emphasis on war as a business common to king and realm, see Keeney, "Military Service and the Development

Disturbance of the peace, or of the common utility of the realm, was naturally another business that touched king and realm in common. In 1291 Edward appointed commissioners to investigate the private war between the Marcher Earls of Gloucester and Hereford, because the matter "dominum regem et coronam et dignitatem suam tangit." The commissioners pointed out that the king by his prerogative was above the laws and customs of the realm when he was acting for the common utility.[66] Maintaining peace for the *status regni* certainly belonged to the king and his crown and dignity; it also belonged to his supreme authority and the public powers in his prerogative. Thus, if the *status regis* was not mentioned in this case in 1291, the equivalent words implying the public status of the king were used. The same is true of the king's claim that the custody of the temporalities of the bishopric of Llandaff, *sede vacante*, belonged "ad nos et nostre corone dignitatem," just as in all cathedral churches of England.[67] The king could hardly claim that temporalities during vacancies of episcopal sees were his private possession as well as the possession of the *dignitas coronae*. Such rights were the king's as a "body politic," by reason of his public *status*. The implication once more is that *nos* and *dignitas coronae* could not be separated, that they meant the same thing as *status regis* and *status coronae*, two ways of describing the public office and its fiscal powers.

That the highest estate of the king was essentially the same as the estate of the crown in the thirteenth century can be shown again in sources relating to the coronation oath, or to the so-called inalienability clause.[68] According to Pope Honorius III,

---

of Nationalism," *Speculum*, XXII, 534-549. For the background in legal thought, see above, to nn. 16-20.

[66] On this episode see now A. J. Otway-Ruthwen, "The Constitutional Position of the Great Lordships of South Wales," *Trans. Roy. Hist. Soc.*, Ser. 5, VIII (1958), 1-20, esp. 16; also Powicke, *Thirteenth Century*, pp. 329f.; and J. E. A. Jolliffe, *Constitutional History of England*, p. 305. Of course, many other scholars have observed the significance of the case.

[67] Otway-Ruthwen, *Trans. Roy. Hist. Soc.*, VIII, 17f. On the great franchises and the king's public authority, see my remarks and references in my "*Ratio publicae utilitatis*," *Welt als Gesch.*, XXI, 78 n. 73—above, ch. v, n. 80.

[68] The scholarly literature has become abundant; I refer chiefly to H. G. Richardson, "English Coronation Oath," *Speculum*, XXIV, 44-75, Riesenberg, *Inalienability of Sovereignty*, chs. IV and V; and Kantorowicz, "Inalienability,"

in the decretal *Intellecto* (*Decr. Greg. IX* 2, 24, 33), the king of Hungary had alienated certain things to the injury of his realm and of his *honor*; but the king in his coronation oath had sworn "iura regni sui et honorem coronae illibata servare." In 1215 Innocent III had already equated the rights and honor "ius pariter et honor") of King John of England.[69] Now *honor* in the Roman law was office and *administratio*; and in a legist of the late twelfth century, Johannes Bassianus, the *ratio honoris publici* was the "reason" of the public necessity of the magistracy and the *imperium* (powers of jurisdiction and coercion).[70] In the early Middle Ages, too, the royal *honor* could mean the public office and power of the king.[71] An Anglo-Saxon coronation *Ordo*, in a version of the late eleventh century, states that the *regalis status* was the *honoris et regni solium*.[72] This tradition gained strength, we noted above, among the legists of the twelfth and thirteenth centuries and in the usage in imperial and royal chanceries.[73] *Honor* certainly refers to the king's duty

---

Speculum, XXIX, 488-502. See below, ch. IX, for other references and the background in Roman law.

[69] Richardson, *Speculum*, XXIV, 48f.

[70] *D.* 50, 4, 15: "Honor municipalis est administratio rei publicae cum dignitatis gradu"; for Joh. Bassianus see my "*Ratio publicae utilitatis*," *Welt als Gesch.*, XXI, 72; above, ch. V, nn. 59f. About 1228 John of Viterbo, in his *De regimine civitatum*, identified *honor* with *regimen* or *administratio*: "Dicitur regimen administratio seu ille honor municipalis qui est administratio rei publicae cum dignitatis gradu . . .": quoted by Berges, *Fürstenspiegel*, p. 71 n. 3.

[71] Kantorowicz, *King's Two Bodies*, p. 58 n. 34, referring to a law of King Recceswinth in the Pseudo-Isidorean Decretals; Scheyhing, *Eide Amtsgewalt und Bannleihe*, p. 55.

[72] Schramm, "Die Krönung bei den Westfranken u. Angelsachsen von 878 bis um 1000," *Zeitschr. d. Sav.-Stift. f. Rechtsgesch.*, XXIII (1934), 168f.: "Sta et retine regalem statum, honoris videlicet et regni solium. . . ." Interesting also is the *Anonymous of York*, Tract. IV: ". . . quia claves regni, id est potestas et regimen regni et regnum ipsum honor est proprium regum," and the *regimen* is the *honor* or *officium regis*; M.G.H., *Libelli de lite*, III, 672 and 678.

[73] Besides the glosses in the *Glos. ord.* to *D.* 1, 4, 1 (the famous *lex regia*, "Quod principi placuit, etc.," because the people "ei et in eum omne suum imperium et potestatem conferat"), earlier glosses of the twelfth century are of interest: to the word *ei* a glossator says, "ad honorem"; to *in eum*, "curam et solicitudinem" (Bamberg, Staatsbibl., MS Iur. 12, fol. 5). Another gloss, ad vv. *ei et in eum*, reads, "Scilicet, ad eius honorem" (MS Vat. lat. 1408, fol. 7). In the thirteenth century Odofredo, *Com.* on the *Dig. Vetus*, p. 17, to *D.* 1, 4, 1, says: "nam lex ortensia lata de imperio principis cavetur quod populus romanus principi omnem suam potestatem quantum ad honorem ei et in eum quantum ad onus concessit. . . . Scilicet animo condendi legum: ut subditi servent . . .";

and powers of public office in relation to the safety of the realm in the thought of a French legist, Bernardus de Deutio (?), in the early fourteenth century. In time of war, he says in his *Quaestiones* (1318), not only vassals but all subjects are bound to follow the king "ad exercitum." For every subject, even if he is not a vassal, "iurat honori domini." But the "honor regis est regni protectio, et quod fortem et potentem habeat exercitum." Therefore, not only for the *honor regis* and the *regni protectio* but also "ad utilitatem reipublice" the king's subjects can be compelled to fight in defense of the realm.[74] And Lucas de Penna stresses the *honor principis* as the supreme authority: even if a king's *rigor* seems unjust, when it is for the public welfare (*status regni*) it must be endured "propter honorem principis qui est res publica, et res publica est in eo."[75]

No doubt, then, in the letters of Innocent III and Honorius III on the inalienability clause in the coronation oath, the *honor* of a king was more than feudal *honour*; it was the public office and powers of the king, stated also as the *honor coronae*. We must remember, therefore, when we encounter *honur* in the Statute of York, that the royal honor was sometimes either a part of or the same as the public *status regis*.

---

and ad v. *ei*: "scilicet, quantum ad onus: quia sicut ipse debet habere honorem: ita onera imperii debet sustinere, scilicet, condendi legem. . . ." Thus, the *imperium* and *potestas* of the prince belong to him as to his office, *honor*, along with its duties and burdens. See above, nn. 25, 28-31.

[74] MS Vat. lat. 2642, fol. 117-117ᵛ: ". . . quia quicumque subditus iurat honori [honorare in the MS] domini, licet non sit vassallus . . . ; sed honor regis est regni protectio . . ."; no one can excuse himself from military service, because the royal army "vadit et ordinatur ad utilitatem rei publice. . . ." As for the author, I cannot find a Bernardus de Deutio; but E. M. Meijers, *Etudes d'histoire de droit* (eds. R. Feenstra and H. F. W. D. Fischer; 3 vols.), III, 168, 191f., discusses the work of an important French legist and cardinal, Bertrand de Déaux (Bertrandus de Deocio). Although Meijers mentions no *Quaestiones* among his works, nor the Vatican MS, it is possible that this Bertrand is the author of the gloss I have quoted.

Another gloss of the early fourteenth century closely associates *dignitas, status,* and *honor publicus* (Vat. MS Borghes. 374, fol. 262ᵛ), to C. 12, 1 De dignitatibus: "Aliquociens dignitas sumitur pro nobiliori et pleniori statu . . . ; aliquociens ponitur pro honore publico, et ita accipitur hic, et infra e.l.ii. cunh." (No doubt *cunh.* stands for Guillaume de Cunh; Meijers, *Etudes*, III, 122f.) In fact, C. 12, 1 and 2 deals with *dignitates* as offices, occasionally as *honores*. Cf. Azo, *Com.*, to C. 12, 1; below, n. 78.

[75] To C. 11, 71, 5 Praedia (*Com.*, p. 622, no. XXIIII).

Several times we have mentioned the *dignitas regis* as comparable to the royal *status, potestas,* and *honor.*[76] Let us now see more fully what it means in sources relating to the coronation oath. *Dignitas* was often treated as office. John of Salisbury likened *publica dignitas* to *publica potestas.*[77] Azo held that the *ius publicum* itself could not be applied (for the public welfare) except by those elected or chosen "in dignitate"—that is, by magistrates who were themselves subjects of the public law. Innocent IV said that *iurisdictio* is "penes loca et dignitates, et non penes personas."[78] A decretist made the *status rei Romanae* (in *D.* 1, 1, 1, 2) virtually identical with the *dignitas* of the State and its government; and he covered *iudices* and kings with the mantle of the public *status-dignitas.*[79] Another decretist associated the *potestas* and *dignitas* of the pope with the *majestas* of the Roman Church; and he, too, defined the *ius publicum* as that law which pertains principally "ad statum, i.e., dignitatem rei romane."[80] These decretists do not mention the *status papae;* but their use of *majestas* and *status* and *dignitas* refers to the papal power and dignity and the dignity of the Church,[81] and thus helps prepare the way for the extremists' identification of pope and Church, or of the "estate papal" and the *status Ecclesiae,* in the late thirteenth and early fourteenth century. *Majestas* itself, so Jacques de Révigny said, referring to the secular State, was, so to speak, the *maior status* of magistrates.[82]

[76] Above to nn. 5, 6, 9, 11, 17, 18, 26, 30, 54, 63, 64, 70, 73. See also Kantorowicz, *King's Two Bodies,* p. 78 n. 34; p. 219 n. 76 (consult Index sub. v. *dignitas*); and Riesenberg, *Inalienability,* pp. 98-112 (without any mention of *status*).

[77] *Policraticus,* IV, vii.

[78] *Glos. ord.* to C. 8, 12, 6, ad v. *privilegiis;* Azo, *Com.,* Paris, 1577, p. 791, to *C.* 12, 1 De Dignitatibus; Inn. IV, *Com.* on *Decr. Greg. IX,* Frankfurt, 1570, to 1, 29, 14. Of course, it was a commonplace that *dignitas non moritur* (as in *Glos. ord.* to *Decr. Greg. IX* 1, 3, 36, ad v. *viveret*), which is a part of the doctrine so well treated by Kantorowicz, *King's Two Bodies,* that the king in his public body is immortal.

[79] Paucapalea, *Summa,* ed. J. F. von Schulte, p. 7: "Ius publicum est, quod ad statum i.e. dignitatem rei romanae principaliter spectat. . . . Iure publico tenetur, si qui civem publicum iudicem vel regem appellantem necaverit, aut terruerit sive verberavit aut vixerit"; the same in Brit. Mus., MS Royal 11 B. II, fol. 2ᵛ.

[80] The author of a *Summa* wrongly attributed to Rufinus, ed. Schulte, p. 375—see above, ch. VII, n. 58.

[81] Above, n. 54, Huguccio was quoted on how the *potentia regis* and the

Dignitas, too, in the context of the public law on the magistracy, was a higher estate. According to a French legist of the early fourteenth century, Guillaume de Cunh, "at times *dignitas* is understood for a more noble and complete *status.*" Since this follows the definition of *dignitas* as a *potentia* given to man by nature, which made him the "dignicima creaturarum," and precedes the statement that sometimes *dignitas* "ponitur pro honore publico," he apparently thought that the dignity and power of public office were the same as the public *status* of a magistrate. Lucas de Penna said that the *corona* was the *insignia* of the *dignitas* of the king.[83] The logical implication of these passages, therefore, is that the dignity of a king was the highest in the realm; associated with *status, honor,* and *majestas,* it was the public estate of the supreme authority.

No wonder, then, that in papal decretals and letters on the coronation oath, and in the decretalists, the royal dignity amounted to the same thing as the royal estate and the crown. In 1235 Pope Gregory IX, without speaking of *honor* or *corona,* said that Henry III had sworn to preserve the *iura, libertates,* and *dignitates regales.*[84] Honorius III in the *Intellecto* had specified the *iura regni* and *honor coronae.* Johannes de Deo, one of the first decretalists to comment on this decretal after it was incorporated in the *Decretales Gregorii IX,* simply speaks of the "iura corone regni."[85] But others, Innocent IV, Hostiensis, and Bernard of Parma, fail to mention the crown, returning

---

sedes regia could not be lessened by being in a *parva civitas*—to *Decretum,* Dist. 97, c. 13 Sicut. On the same passage Simon of Bisignano says, ad vv. *praerogativam praesentis regni . . . non minuit:* "Id est, sicut parva civitas non mutare dignitatem tocius regni, sic imperator non potest mutare dignitatem vel constitutionem ecclesie, id est, canones"; Brit. Mus., MS Royal 10 A. iii; also in the Bibl. Angelica (Rome), MS 1270.

82 Above, ch. vii, to nn. 57-69 (on the *status papae*); and n. 24 (on Jacques de Révigny).

83 Vat. MS Borghes. 374, fol. 262ᵛ, a gloss to *C.* 12, 1: after saying that in one sense *dignitas* is a *potencia* given to man by nature, and hence "homo est dignicima creaturarum," he adds: "Aliquociens dignitas sumitur pro nobiliori et pleniori statu . . . ; aliquociens ponitur pro honore pub[lico] . . . Cunh." See above, n. 73. See also Lucas de Penna, *Com.,* p. 388, no. 2, to *C.* 11, 7, 11.

84 Richardson, "English Coronation Oath," *Speculum,* xxiv, 51; and on this and on Honorius III's decretal "Intellecto," etc., Riesenberg, *Inalienability,* ch. v. See also below, ch. ix.

85 In his *Casus,* which I consulted in the MS Vat. lat. 2343, fol. 24.

to the *dignitas regalis,* which the king must not gravely injure by alienations. They agree, however, that moderate alienations do not hurt the royal dignity.[86] On the other hand, we observed above that the canonists were bound to argue that alienations of a more serious kind were not injurious when they benefited the Church, for what profited the Church profited the State and the secular authority. The public law was interested in the salvation of souls as well as the *status Reipublicae* on earth.[87] Furthermore, important alienations of royal rights in property that pertained to the crown and was not the king's private property were lawful if thereby peace was secured, the faith defended, and the *magna utilitas regni* achieved.[88] But this was no injury to the *dignitas regis,* for the maintenance of the *status regni* belonged to the king's dignity—and to his public powers or estate and to the crown. On the whole, therefore, in the decretalists the *iura coronae* and *status coronae* were understood as the *dignitas regalis*—as they had been by Gregory IX, and in the late twelfth-century version of the Laws of Edward the Confessor in the words "omnes dignitates et iura et libertates corone regni." These terms were simply other ways of speaking about the

[86] *Glos. ord.* of Bernard of Parma, ad v. *regni sui;* Innocent IV, *Com.,* Venice, 1578, p. 348, c. 2: "Haec decr. intelligitur quoniam facit alienationes propter quas graviter leditur dignitas regalis . . ."; Host., *Com.,* Venice, 1581, II, 137ᵛ c. 2: "Haec decr. intelligitur quando facit alienationes, per quas graviter leditur regalis dignitas." On moderate alienations see the whole comment of Inn. IV; also Baldus, *Margarita* to the *Com.* of Inn. IV, p. 348, c. 2: "Rex potest donare et etiam alienare moderate, non ita immoderate ut laedatur dignitas regalis." Abbas Antiquus (Bernard de Montmirat) was more specific: the coronation oath prohibits the alienation of property that belongs to the royal dignity, but not the property that is the king's own (as private property)—*Com.* to *Decr. Greg. IX,* Venice, 1588, fol. 24, to 2, 24, 33 Intellecto. On this decretalist see Stephan Kuttner, "Wer war der Dekretalist 'Abbas Antiquus,'" *Zeitschr. d. Sav. Stift., Kan. Abt.,* XXVI (1937), 471-487.

[87] See above, to n. 26.

[88] Oldradus, *Consilia,* 37ᵛ-38, No. XCV, discusses the problem of how a king can give important real properties to the queen without injuring the *iura regis et regni* and also the *iura* of his heirs. A king of Leon, for example, had lawfully given *castra* to a princess of Castille when he married her, because the marriage was for the *magna utilitas regis et regni,* for securing peace for his subjects, and for the *expugnatio infidelium* (to *Decr. Greg. IX* 4, 20, 5). Further, gifts to the queen are lawful because marriage and dowry are for the procreation of children and certainly royal children are for the public utility (cf. *D.* 24, 3, 1; and my "*Ratio publicae utilitatis,*" *Welt als Gesch.,* XXI, 80). Hence, if such alienations violate the letter of the coronation oath, it turns out that in reality they are no violation at all, for they profit the *status regis et regni.*

estate royal—so Pope Clement IV put it in 1265 on the injury to the *libertas, dignitas, honor,* and *status* and *iura* of Henry III and Edward and of the realm.[89] They were the source of the assertion made by Edward I, that the magnates and *proceres* of the realm were bound by homage and fealty to defend "his dignity and the crown"; that nothing could be done "to the disinheritance or injury of the crown or otherwise to the king's royal dignity."[90]

As we observed earlier in another connection, the background of the inalienability clause was chiefly the terminology and theory in the Roman law and in documents of the twelfth century. In the first place, the authority of the prince and the public welfare were enhanced by privileges granted to churches. Such privileges, indeed, should be, like the *iura regni (Angliae)* in 1235, maintained *illibata;* the patrimony of the Church must be kept *illaesum.*[91] It was the duty of the emperor, said Frederick Barbarossa (1162), as the *advocatus* and *defensor* of churches, to maintain their "iura integra et illesa." Otto of Brunswick (1198) explained to Innocent III that he wished to strengthen the *status ecclesiae,* and that he had accepted his election, consecration, and coronation "cum plenitudine regie dignitatis" and taken an oath to maintain *illibata* the possessions and *iura* of the Roman Church and other churches. The *regia dignitas,* the *status regis,* thus existed also for the protection and defense of the *status Ecclesiae.*[92] In the second place, it was also the duty of the prince and lesser magistrates, by reason of their office, again for the public welfare of all and of the State, to protect the rights of the public fisc while at the same time protecting the rights of all subjects. All judges, said Justinian, should take the oath of office that they would practice equity, protect the fisc, be impartial, and keep "subditos . . . illaesos undique." If the emperor wanted to aid private persons who suffered in-

[89] Richardson, "Coronation Oath," *Speculum,* XXIV, 52—p. 49 on the *status coronae* in the documents of Edward I; *idem,* in *Traditio,* XVI, 167f; also Riesenberg, *Inalienability,* p. 122, quoting Clement IV, from Rymer, *Foedera,* I, i, 459.

[90] Trueman, "Statute of York," *Med. et Human.,* X, 70 and n. 6. Still other passages cited here by Trueman indicate that there was no real distinction between the royal dignity and the crown.

[91] *C.* 1, 2, 12 and 1, 2, 14, 2; above, nn. 26-31; see below, ch. IX, for details.

[92] Frederick, *M.G.H., Legum S. IV, Const.,* I, no. 217; Otto, *Const.,* II, no. 18.

justice, he also wished the "publicum (fiscum) illaesum manere."[93] Let us repeat how Frederick Barbarossa put it: it be-
hooved the imperial *sollertia* so to govern the Republic and
investigate the *commoda* of subjects, that the *regni utilitas* persist *incorrupta* and the "singulorum status iugiter servetur illaesus." Hence, the *status principis* included the powers necessary for taking care of the *status* of all subjects and the *status
regni*.[94] The officers of the fisc or Exchequer in the kingdom of
England, said Richard Fitzneale (obviously reflecting the Roman law if not the words of Frederick), exercised a *sollertia* by
which "totius regni status indemnis servatur." Naturally the
ratio status regis, about which he had spoken earlier, included
the *sollertia* of the royal officers—*ad statum conservandum*, as
the glossators put it.[95] In 1231 the Constitutions of Frederick II
prescribed that the royal *bajuli* and *camerarii* should swear to
maintain *illaesa* the *demania* and *iura* of the *curia regis*.[96]

These passages indicate, in the full context of ideas about
kingship, justice, and the *status regni*, that the office, dignity,
honor, sollertia, duty, and powers of the king were the *status
regis et coronae*. This royal estate was in substance the king's
authority, the rights of the crown; and it was based on the king's
iura and *libertates*, and on the royal demesne and on customary
revenues that came into the fisc. It was the king's public *status*,
his fullness of power; and it existed for maintaining unharmed
the *status* of churches and of all subjects, that is, the public
welfare or *status* of the whole body of the realm. In other words,
whatever the actual history of the clause in the coronation oath
on the preservation of the rights of the crown, the main purpose
and *ratio* of the public *status regis*, in terms of the royal honor,
dignity, skill, and the like, was the preservation or maintenance
of the *status Reipublicae*—"ne pereat." Therefore, the king had
no right to give away, except by way of delegation, either the
powers of kingship or the essential revenues and rights on which
his public estate or authority was based. If alienation was per-

93 See below, ch. IX, to nn. 3-9.
94 *M.G.H., Legum S. IV, Const.*, I, no. 148; *Libri Feudorum*, 2, 55; above, n.
30, and ch. VII, n. 76.
95 *S.C.*, p. 205; above, n. 9, and ch. VII, n. 76.
96 Huillard-Bréholles, *Hist. Dipl. Frid. II*, IV, i, 41f., Tit. LXII.

mitted with respect to property-rights (but then not to the extent of weakening seriously the king's capacity to govern for the *status regni*), no alienation of the substance of the *status regis* or *status coronae* was lawful. The public law of the State forbade any fundamental change of the accepted constitutional *ordo magistratus regis*.

In the twelfth and thirteenth centuries, therefore, in England and on the Continent, the estate of the king was his public office and powers, and it was the same as the estate of the crown. Was the *status regis* substantially different from the *status coronae* in the reign of Edward II? Edward II himself, or those who framed the wording of a writ of 1312 to the sheriffs, used a terminology that reflected the older idea of the public authority embodied in the royal *dignitas, regimen,* and *majestas,* without indicating any real distinction between these and the *corona.* All rights of the crown, he said, the royal dignity, the *regimen* of the people, the peace and tranquillity of the Church, and in sum, the royal majesty, must be maintained *integra et illaesa.*[97] In 1314 Edward used the expression, "ad iura nostra regia . . . manutenda," as equivalent to rights of the crown and the royal dignity.[98] At other times, we find, the "state" of the king implied the meaning of *dignitas* as well as the *status regis* in the sense of royal rights and powers. Judicial processes should not prejudice the "state of the king and of his crown." Piers Gaveston was accused of damaging "the state of the king and his crown" by alienating lands and tenures of the crown. The royal estate in Gascony was certainly the king's rights in revenues and in jurisdiction. The "king's state" and right of the crown included his rights in a church; and the "state of king and kingdom" was concerned in the war against Scotland.[99]

No doubt, occasionally the estate or state of the king was related to the household, e.g., in 1309-1310.[100] At times, proba-

[97] For the whole passage, Richardson, *Speculum,* xxiv, 62.

[98] Richardson, *Speculum,* xxiv, 62.

[99] These examples are given by Trueman, "Statute of York," *Med. et Human.,* x, 72f. Trueman admits that the king's estate might on occasion mean powers of jurisdiction, or the "well-being of the government." On Piers Gaveston and the general situation in 1311-1322 see May McKisack, *The Fourteenth Century,* pp. 21ff.

[100] Trueman, *op.cit.,* pp. 71f.

bly, it might refer chiefly to the material or financial support of the king and household. But was this estate in revenues and in the household kept distinct from the estate of king and crown? The *Dialogue of the Exchequer,* we must constantly remember, had measured the *status regis* or royal *potestas* by the wealth of the king that came not only from the demesne, but also from all kinds of rights of patronage, from his feudal empire overseas, and from extraordinary taxation. The fisc or Exchequer was public. In taking care of the revenues of the king it provided him with the normal income of his public office (the Exchequer and the Wardrobe in the household remained closely connected in the reign of Edward II).[101] Quite properly, then, Richard Fitzneale had held that by its work "totius regni status indemnis servatur." The financial estate of the king, apart from purely private property, was evidently the main support of his public estate, dignity, honor, powers, or authority. It supported but was not the same as that *status regis.* The *utilitas* or *status regis* was surely the public welfare of the royal magistracy, and it was at the same time the *potestas* or *dignitas* or *majestas* of the king; it was the *status coronae.*

Against Lapsley and Trueman, then, I must argue that still in the time of Edward II the estate or *bene esse* of the king looked to the rights of the crown as well as the household administration. His rights of public jurisdiction in his realm and in his feudal Empire could hardly as yet be fully separated from the household and the financial and military resources which it held at his disposal.[102] It seems strange, at any rate, that the *status regis* in 1322 should be quite different from what it was in the twelfth, the thirteenth and in the sixteenth century—or in the fourteenth after the death of Edward II.[103] At times, as we have seen, the *ratio status regis* not only existed for but was the same as the *ratio status regni.* Further, quite often

---

[101] See above, n. 9; on the Wardrobe and the finances, Davies, *Baronial Opposition,* pp. 178-199, 181.

[102] Lapsley, "Interpretation," *E.H.R.,* LVI, 43.

[103] Trueman gives examples from the later fourteenth century, *op.cit.,* pp. 8of. Also for the late fourteenth century Jean Gerson is interesting: the king's "second life," his *vita civilis et politica,* is the *status regalis aut dignitas;* Kantorowicz, *King's Two Bodies,* pp. 219 n. 76 and 402 n. 299—Kantorowicz supports my identification of *dignitas* with *status,* also pp. 383-450.

the *status*, whether of king or communal magistracy, was defined as government.[104] So, too, at least for the French legist Jacques de Révigny, the crown was not only the king's jurisdiction over the whole realm but was also the *corona regni* and *communis patria*.[105] For the crown was the *caput regni*. The *bonus status regis* was the healthy strength, dignity, and power of the king in his public office, and surely meant the same thing as the *bonus status coronae*.[106]

So often did the king say that the business of war and justice, not to mention revenues for himself and his government, touched himself, his *honor, profit, utilitas*, and *dignitas*, as well as the crown, that evidently he was speaking of his own public *status* as the head *(caput)* of the community of the realm. We have noted that King John held that the members of the realm should aid the *caput* in his war in France. In 1321 the Canon of Bridlington was astonished that the magnates or *membra* in Parliament were acting without the assent of the king and were thus separating themselves from the *caput*.[107] This kind of thinking reappeared in the words which Henry VIII addressed to Parliament. If it was present only occasionally in English legal thought on the king and the realm, it reflected the abundantly expressed doctrine in corporate theories applied to the State by canonists and legists and by political theorists.[108] It therefore has its importance for the meaning of the *status regis*. Above all, the king as head of the realm had a public estate—an estate that was based on the normal revenues of the fisc and on the household, but an estate which was the ensemble of his powers

[104] Above, ch. VII, in general.

[105] Above, nn. 20, 21; for similar expressions, see Kantorowicz, *King's Two Bodies*, pp. 339f.

[106] Kantorowicz, *op.cit.*, pp. 368f., tends to draw some distinction between *status regis* and *status coronae* for 1322.

[107] Quoted by Wilkinson, "The Coronation Oath of Edward II and the Statute of York," *Speculum*, XIX, 460.

[108] See my "Statute of York," *Speculum*, XXIX, 425f. (above, ch. VI, nn. 38-49), for general remarks. Of course, Gierke, *Polit. Theories*, devotes himself largely to the corporateness (or degree of corporateness) of the State. There is a great deal on the subject in Lagarde, *Naissance*, II², in every chapter on the scholastic philosophers, and in the conclusion, ch. XI, iii. Kantorowicz, *op.cit.*, p. 208 n. 42, and ch. V, shows how important the concept was that the king or prince was *caput* both of the magistracy and of the *Respublica*. Cf. above, ch. VII, to nn. 28-37, 70-74, 91.

as the supreme authority. His real public *status*, again, was also the *status coronae*. As head of the State, by reason of his "state," the prince enjoyed the fullness of public power to use right rea-son for all reasons of the public welfare (*status regni*). His dig-nity, public office, *honor, potestas, majestas*, and rights of the crown were the "estate royal."

2. *LESTAT DU ROI* IN THE STATUTE OF YORK

The conclusions reached can now be applied to the inter-pretation of the Statute of York with respect to the terms *lestat del hostel, lestat du roi*, and *lestat de la coronne*.[109]

Lestat del hostel. In §1 the Statute refers to the Ordinances of 1311 and the committee chosen by the magnates and prelates to "ordener et establir lestat del hostel nostre dit seignur le roi et de son roialme," and to do so "al honur de Dieu et al honur et profit de saint eglise et al honur du dit roi et a son profit et au profit de son poeple." Here the estates of the royal household and of the realm are as closely related as the old *status regis* and *status regni*. Like the *status regis*, the *estat del hostel* exists for the *honur* of God, Church, and king, and for the *profit* of king and people. Except for the insertion of the "honor of God," the language used is simply a French version of the traditional ideas about the *status regis*, including his officers and counsellors, that was necessary for the maintenance of the royal office (*honor*) and powers (*profit* or *status regis*), the *status Ecclesiae*, and the *status regni* (public and common welfare or *profit* of people and realm). Even if the *lestat del hostel* is not quite the same as the *status regis*, it logically implies the same thing, since the baronial ordainers were chiefly interested in controlling the king's choice of advisers, who were members of his "body poli-tic." At any rate, the estate of the household was as essential to the public office of the king and to his *status* as it was to the *status regni*.

In other words, the magnates wished to regulate and control

---

109 For the text of the Statute, I have used *Statutes of the Realm*, I, 189—Lapsley also used this text, *E.H.R.*, LVI, 50f. Davies, *Baronial Opposition*, pp. 1-48, offers a good introduction to the Statute, especially to §1, in his discussion of the royal prerogative. Wilkinson, too, presents a good general statement of the problem; *Constitutional History*, II, 113f. Cf. above, n. 2.

lestat del hostel precisely because it was public.[110] The accusations levelled at Piers Gaveston were a criticism of one aspect of
the king's public power, his right to choose his counsellors, who
were members of the household. Essentially, the Ordainers
claimed that the king was getting the wrong advice from his
favorite; he should appoint to his council men who were under
baronial control. Whether they understood the legal theory of
counsel I do not know. But according to the Roman law, and
feudal law too, every prince must consult with counsellors or
experts on important matters of public policy and law and justice. The royal advisers were legally obliged to give good, wise
counsel that was for the public welfare. The problem was, did
subjects have the right to determine whether the counsel given
to the king was good or bad? This cannot be treated here. The
point is that royal counsellors, members of the household, were
members of the government, too.[111] It is likely, then, that the
household was an essential part of the public estate of the king—
so in the intention of the Statute. Hence there was no need of
repeating "lestat del hostel" in the clauses that followed.

§2. *Le poair real* and *lestat de la coronne.* In fact, it is significant that in §2 there is no mention of the estate either of
household or of king in the criticism of the ordinances. It is
stated that examination of the ordinances by king and Parliament showed that they limited the *poair real* and thus blemished
the royal *seigneurie* and the estate of the crown. The weakening of the royal power had in the past resulted in troubles and
wars by which "la terre ad este en peril." Since the king's *potestas* was the *status regis* or its substance in earlier legal thought,
and since its weakness brought on peril to the realm, this language reminds one again that the glossators had said that the
public law, above all in dealing with the magistracy, pertained
to conserving the *status* of the Republic, "ne pereat." An attack
on the *status regis* was a danger to the *status regni*—at least in
the standard theory of monarchy. Hence, again there is a sug-

[110] I assume, of course, that the household of Edward II as an institution was
not very different from that of his father; see Powicke, *Thirteenth Century,* pp.
323f.; and above, to nn. 49-53.

[111] On the king's council as a part of household and government, see Davies,
Baronial Opposition, ch. XI.

gestion that the public *status* or power of the prince is necessary for the *status regni*. And again, the royal power, the royal *seigneurie* (*majestas, dignitas,* or prerogative; not feudal *dominium,* although it too is involved), and the estate of the crown are equivalents of *status regis*.

§3. Here we have the declaration that the king and the whole community of the realm in Parliament have annulled the ordinances, and that the royal statutes made before 1311 shall remain in force. This clause is not important for this study, but its meaning is surely that the old *status regis,* which included the right of the king to make statutes, *ratione utilitatis communis,* with the counsel and consent of his advisers and of the magnates, and, if need be, of all who were touched by a statute, was herewith restored. King and Parliament, not Parliament or any group of subjects without the authority of the king, should legislate.[112]

Now we come to §4. This provision is negative: no subjects of the king or of his heirs shall make any ordinances "on the royal power of our lord the king or of his heirs, or (*ou*) against the estate of our said lord the king or of his heirs, or against the estate of the crown." The fact that *lestat del hostel* is not mentioned is no indication that "lestat nostre dit seignur le roi ou de ses heirs" has taken its place to mean the private aspect of kingship—indeed, the estate of the king is probably the same as, and as public as, the estate of the household. I think the intention of the drafters was to make it clear that unlawful ordinances made by unauthorized persons *on* the *poair real* of king and heirs were also contrary or injurious *to* the royal estate, or to the estate of the crown. *Ou,* "or," does not have to mean that the *poair real* was different from the estate of the king and his heirs; nor that the royal estate was not the same as the estate of the crown. The drafters surely wanted to make it clear to all that the royal power was the essence of the public *status* or office of the king, whether called *status regis* or *status coronae*. If they were guilty of a tautology, which is not strange for men trained in legal thought, it was a useful tautology, reflecting different

---

[112] I have given my views on this in my "Two Laws and the Statute of York," *Speculum,* XXIX, 429-432; see above, ch. VI, nn. 48-58.

ways of looking at the substance of kingship as the highest public office responsible for maintaining the state of the realm. What in fact was an ordinance made by subjects by themselves on the *poair real* was an illegal limitation of and injury to the royal estate and the estate of the crown. Nor does the inclusion of the king's heirs seem to imply a private estate. The heirs were mentioned in order, probably, to stress the continuity of the public power or *status regis* in a monarchy that had become hereditary. We have seen that Edward I, even before coming to the throne, shared in the public estate of Henry III in 1258-1266.

This interpretation is strengthened, in my judgment, by §5, which is affirmative and thereby makes more intelligible the preceding negative provisions. The subjects of the king could not by themselves regulate the power or estate of king and crown; indeed, it was a negation of kingship and the royal prerogative for them to do so. Therefore, in this clause the authors, who of course were champions of the traditional doctrine of kingship, declared that only the king and his subjects in Parliament could provide for the estate of the king and his heirs and for the estate of the realm and the people. Yet there is no mention of the estate of the crown, nor of the *poair real!* A strange omission, on the face of it. But is it strange after all? It is not in the least strange if we assume that the words "pur lestat de nostre seignur le roi et de ses heirs" meant that all provisions for the royal estate included or were those which maintained the royal dignity and power and the rights of the crown. In the following discussion of §5, it will be assumed that the following terms are equivalent to each other: royal estate, estate of the crown, royal dignity, royal power, and prerogative.

Now, no medieval political or legal theory admitted that in a monarchy (or in the Church) subjects by themselves could legislate, "leges novas condere"; they surely could not make and promulgate a law declaring that the king's authority was henceforth subordinate to the great men of the realm. The king was the ultimate authority in making new laws for new situations.[113] He needed counsel and consent; he could not be arbitrary in

---

[113] I am referring to the legists' theory of legislation, which cannot be treated here; but see the *Glos. ord.* to *D.* 1, 4, 2; *C.* 1, 17, 2, 18; and *Auth.* 6, 13 (*Nov.* 84).

making new laws. But he must have the final right to make a statute valid. It would be absurd to think that he could, except momentarily under compulsion, consent to an ordinance initiated by subjects which limited his power or rights of the crown in legislating, judging, and interpreting the law. Therefore, no proposal of a law that restricted or weakened or limited the royal power, the royal *status*, was, shall we say, constitutional (§4). Yet the barons or magnates had tried to set up their own committees to give the "right" advice to the king and had limited the king's right to choose his own counsellors. In a way, they had lawfully appealed from the king poorly informed to the king better informed. But they had gone beyond the public law in forcing the king normally to accept their control of his council, and thus damaging his own powers of magistracy. Apart from having, in the legal thought of the time, the right to be consulted about any business that touched them, they had no right to cripple the right of the king to make the final decision. If the king must consult with them, in great matters touching the realm, they in turn had to consult with the king and obtain his willing or free approval in a business that touched the royal authority. In both cases the *status regis* was superior to their *status*. If the *status* of the king was limited by his duty to maintain the *status regni*, it was enhanced by his right to interpret what was good for the *status* or *commun profit* of realm and people. This right, which was a part of his right and duty to maintain the *status regni*, increased his powers and public *status*. It was the essence of the royal prerogative in the "estate royal." Since his *status* existed for the *status regni*, it was not subject to the power of any group of magnates acting by themselves.[114]

If this is true, it follows that any business that was for, or improved or strengthened, the just powers of the king, was the business of the king as head and of the members of the realm in Parliament. It was a business that profited both the public authority and the welfare of the people, even when it primarily interested the king. And any important act of the king that improved the functioning of the royal jurisdiction and ability to

114 Cf. Davies, *Baronial Opposition*, pp. 1-48, for a like conclusion in different terms and with a great richness of detail.

defend the realm was the business of the *universitas* or *communitas regni*. For in the prevailing ideas of public law, the efficient enforcement of the law in the courts, the maintenance of peace within, and the successful defense of the State were for the *commun profit*, the *utilitas communis et publica*. What therefore profited the public office of the king profited the people and the realm as a whole—so in theory.

Statutes and extraordinary taxes certainly "touched" the *status* of the king with respect to his powers and duties. For example, in the reign of Edward I statutes strengthened his jurisdiction by developing or interpreting the feudal law. A grant of the customs on wool improved the financial basis of the royal government. Extraordinary taxes for the defense of the king and the rights of the crown were equally for the *status regni*. Magnates might object to going on a campaign when the king did not lead in person, or they might argue that a war was unjustified because there was no aggression or emergency. But they did not say that when the king's rights were in actual danger in Gascony that this touched neither their feudal obligations nor the safety of the realm of England. When the king could present a good case of necessity, his plea, based on a long tradition of public law in England as well as on the Continent, that both his dignity and rights of the crown and the *status regni* were concerned met no serious opposition. The king as *caput* and the members of the realm were all in varying degree involved in the common business of facing the threat of an aggressor in order to assure the *status regis et regni*.

What, then, were the matters which the king should establish in Parliament with the assent of the prelates, magnates, and community (*communalte*—which does not mean, but could include, the "commons") of the realm? They were, in the first place, any public business that was "for the Estate of our Lord the King and of his heirs, and for the Estate of the Realm and of the People."[115] To be sure, the business could be the grant of reve-

---

[115] I quote from the translation by G. L. Haskins, *Statute of York*, pp. 95f. As for the community of the realm, I cannot understand why *communalte* is still sometimes translated as the *commons*—as May McKisack interprets the word, *Fourteenth Century*, pp. 71f. The *communalte* is simply, of course, the French

nues for the estate of the king; and in such a case, it has been argued, the royal estate was the material wealth or financial rights of the king—indeed, estate meant property.[116] But again, one must consider the traditional idea that the income of a king was not his estate in the highest, public, sense, but the means of supporting his *dignitas* and *status*, the means of carrying on his public *potestas*. If such revenues were sometimes for the maintenance of *lestat del hostel*, again this estate was either the same as or a part of the public estate of the king's dignity and authority, of the estate of the crown.

In the second place, a business treated and settled by king and Parliament was often that of the royal jurisdiction, of legislation, or of war. Traditionally, I have shown, such a business definitely touched both the public *status* of the king's duties, rights, and powers, or the *status coronae*, and the *status* of people and kingdom. In §5 of the Statute of York, then, establishments for the estate of the king and his heirs were not limited to provisions for the property rights of the household and the royal family. They surely at times were statutes and extraordinary taxes that pertained to and strengthened the public office of the king above all with respect to his right to maintain the *status regni*. If for Henry of Ghent (*ca.* 1280) *ratio status* was the king's use of "right reason" in his power of making statutes for the "evident utility" of the State,[117] how can it be said with

---

for *communitas*, which at times included the *communitates* or *commons*, especially in cases of extraordinary taxation in Parliament and occasionally in legislation. I agree with Professor Strayer, "Statute of York and the Community of the Realm," *A.H.R.*, XLVII, 1-22, that the *universitas regni* or *communitas regni* was chiefly the magnates; but I hold that by the end of the thirteenth century it included the commons in Parliament when a proposed tax or law directly affected their interests—hence the rise of representation of the *communitates*. It will be noted that since 1954 Strayer's argument has in its essence won me over; see *Speculum*, XXIX, 429 n. 45; above, ch. VI, n. 46.

116 Haskins, *Statute of York*, pp. 100-103. His argument is based in part on the belief that the *status Ecclesiae* was the properties of churches and ecclesiastics. But as I am trying to demonstrate in a special study now in preparation, the *status* of the Church was the public welfare and safety of the Church and the faith, but included the instruments necessary for maintaining the faith, namely, the hierarchic *ordo* and government and the property rights and liberties that were deemed necessary for the existence of clergy and Church and its doctrines, all for the salvation of souls.

117 In my "*Ratio publicae utilitatis*," *Welt als Gesch.*, XXI, 88-93; above, ch. V, nn. 124-127.

confidence that the estate of the king in the Statute of York was his *bene essere* only in relation to that part of his administration which looked to his person more than to his crown and was ordinarily carried on through the household organization? How can it be said that the estate of the crown was "the *bene essere* of the king in relation to that part of his administration which looked to his crown and realm rather than his person," as if the estate of the king were different from the estate of the crown?[118]

On the whole, in the light of the prevailing legal theories of public law, kingship, and the State, in the context of coronation oaths and the inalienability of anything necessary for the proper exercise of the royal authority, one must not distinguish sharply, if at all, between *status regis* and *status coronae*. The king, of course, had his private estate in property. But why should it be stressed in Parliament, where normally, as in the time of Edward I, the far more important joint or common businesses of the king's government and the *status regni* had to be treated or debated and settled? The Statute, in §5, dealt positively with public, "national" affairs of king and people, only indirectly with the private aspects of kingship. While it is not literally said, it is implied that the king in Parliament was, as *caput* of the body of the realm, in his highest *status regalis*. The crown was the symbol of those public powers of governing which belonged to the king *ratione status sui* and included rights and revenues necessary to the end. The public estate of the king was the royal dignity and power which were also the estate of the crown. Both belonged to and existed for the estate of the realm, and the care of the estate of the realm belonged to the estate of king and crown.

Lestat du roi, then, in §5 of the Statute of York was surely the traditional public *status* of the king with respect to his supreme authority. Deriving in large part from the Roman law and the glossators, it was that *status magistratus* which was public and existed for the necessity of conserving the *utilitas communis et publica*, the *status Reipublicae*, the *status Regni*. It was that royal estate which Professor George Sayles has said was virtually the same as the prerogative and the crown, which made it law-

[118] *Lapsley, E.H.R.*, LVI, 43.

ful for the king in 1290-1291 to enforce peace on the great lords for the common utility of the realm.[119] What injured the public authority of the king, the royal estate and crown, injured the *status regni*. It was at least similar, this estate of the king, to that *plenitudo imperii* for which, thought Lucas de Penna, the *corona regis* or *diadema* stood as a *signum*: the diadem or crown is the symbol of the king, but does not make the king; the *corona regis* designates the *plenitudo imperii* and is its symbol, but it does not give him the *imperium*.[120] It was that royal estate which Professor S. B. Chrimes, for the fifteenth century, has found in the king's prerogative, power, authority, sovereignty, and duties: "His realm was bound to provide him with the means of maintaining his estate, and hence it was not clear that Parliament had the right to refuse him a grant."[121] In a word, the supreme powers of the king were the highest estate royal.

Finally, these conclusions in part confirm Chrimes's opinion that the "estate of the king meant the mass of rights, duties, and attributes which constituted the kingship." Perhaps the royal estate was the prerogative, although Chrimes may put it better in holding that the prerogative was only one element in the king's estate. But if the *status regis* was above all the *potestas, dignitas, maiestas, corona,* and all the king's public duties and rights in governing in order to maintain and preserve the *status regni,* "lest it perish," it was at times virtually the same as the state of the realm. To repeat the words of Sir Maurice Powicke, Edward I realized "that the state of the king was in the end identical with the well-being of the community of the realm."[122] Edward II probably did not appreciate the true meaning of the "estate royal"; but it can hardly be doubted that his advisers, who were the authors of the Statute of York, fully understood it and deliberately asserted it.

Naturally, in the twelfth, thirteenth, and fourteenth centuries

119 *Select Cases in the Court of King's Bench*, III, xlviii.

120 To *C.* 10, 58, 1 Reos (p. 298, c. 1, no. 5). In another place Lucas emphasizes the *potestas* and *dignitas regis*: it is treason to seize or usurp the "maiorem potestatem et dignitatem regis . . . quia quantum in se est totum reipublicae perturbat ordinem" (to *C.* 11, 53, 1 Si quis; p. 537, no. 39).

121 *English Constitutional Ideas in the Fifteenth Century*, pp. 38-43, 39, 91f.

122 *Thirteenth Century*, p. 37; cf. pp. 6, 67, 514; above to n. 60.

the English monarchy was still in many ways highly feudal and personal, sometimes more a subject of private law than of public. Nonetheless, when Henry II was, with "ira et malevolentia," indulging in personal *vis et voluntas*, he and his counsellors were also aware of the public *iura* that belonged to the *status regis*.[123] And when kings in the thirteenth and early fourteenth century were learning to deal with a business that was common to the *status regis* and the *status regni*, they and their *proceres*, counsellors, and judges in some measure arrived at an appreciation of the public character of the royal majesty, dignity, honor, crown, and estate. Involved in the business of maintaining the state of the realm, the State itself, the "estate royal" was necessarily public, existing *ratione iurisdictionis et gubernationis* and *ratione publicae et communis utilitatis*. The *status regis et regni*, the estates of head and members and of the realm as a whole, belonged to each other and each was indispensable to the other.

John of Salisbury and Richard Fitzneale had long since understood the spirit and even, to some degree, the letter of the revived Roman theory of public law and the State, and had applied it to the kingship of Henry II. If John could not anticipate how Parliament would represent the community or *universitas* of the realm in *ardua negotia* which affected its *status*, he eloquently described the *status regis* as it essentially persisted in the following centuries and was so understood in the royal government in 1322. Let him, therefore, in his Christian-Stoic-Roman way, tell us how the *potestas regis* was public and, sanctioned by God and Nature, was exercised by the king as head for the public and common welfare of people and realm; and how the necessity, health, welfare, and strength of head and members belonged chiefly to the king:

"Unde merito in eum omnium subditorum potestas confertur, ut in utilitate singulorum et omnium exquirenda et facienda sibi ipse sufficiat, et humanae rei publicae status optime disponatur, dum sunt alter alterius membra. In quo quidem

---

[123] See Jolliffe, *Angevin Kingship*, esp. ch. IV. I think that Jolliffe has neglected the understanding of public law in the time of Henry II. Cf. below, ch. IX nn. 36-42.

optimam uiuendi ducem naturam sequimur, quae microcosmi sui, id est, mundi minoris, hominis scilicet, sensus uniuersos in capite collocauit, et ei sic membra subiecit, ut omnia recte moueantur, dum sani capitis sequuntur arbitrium. Tot ergo et tantis priuilegiis apex principalis extollitur et splendescit, quot et quanta sibi ipse necessaria credidit. Recte quidem, quia populo nichil utilius est quam ut principis necessitas expleatur; quippe cum nec uoluntas eius iustitiae inueniatur aduersa. Est ergo, ut eum plerique diffiniunt, princeps potestas publica et in terris quaedam diuinae maiestatis imago. . . .

"Cum enim potestas publica sit . . . omnium uires exhaurit et, ne in se deficiat, incolumitatem omnium debet procurare membrorum. Quot autem in administratione principatus extant officia, tot sunt principalis corporis quasi membra. . . . Nec diu subsistit incolumitas capitis, ubi languor membrorum inualescit."[124]

[124] *Policraticus*, IV, i, xii (ed. Webb, I, 235, 278f.). And on John's appreciation of reason of State see my *"Ratio publicae utilitatis," Welt als Gesch.*, XXI, 20-22; above, ch. V, nn. 32-39.

CHAPTER IX ✦ THE ROMAN LAW AND
THE "INALIENABILITY CLAUSE"
IN THE ENGLISH CORONATION OATH

I N THE preceding chapter we encountered the terminology of the so-called "inalienability" clause of the coronation oath in relation to the *honor, dignitas,* and *status* of king and crown. What was the origin of the principal terms, *iura illibata* and *iura illaesa,* and of the idea of the inalienability of the public rights of the supreme authority in the State? What bearing does the history of the terminology have on dating the first appearance of the clause in the coronation oath?

In recent years a good many historians have been studying that part of the coronation oath in which the king promised or swore to maintain *illibata* or *illaesa* the *iura* of the crown. Mr. H. G. Richardson believes now that an inalienability clause phrased in this or a similar terminology appeared first in the coronation oath of Henry II in 1154, perhaps because of the influence of Nigel, Bishop of Ely; and that the papal chancery, from the time of Pope Alexander III, used the terminology in reference to the fact that kings did add the clause to the traditional promise or oath.[1]

[1] "The Coronation Oath in Medieval England: The Evolution of the Office and the Oath," *Traditio,* XVI (1960), 111-202, esp. 151-169, 174-180. In his earlier study, "The English Coronation Oath," *Speculum,* XXIV (1949), 44-75, he held that the inalienability clause appeared in the time of Henry III. For the background and other views see the following: P. E. Schramm, "Die Ordines der mittelalterlichen Kaiserkrönung," *Archiv für Urkundenforschung,* XI (1930), 285-390; "Die Krönung bei den Westfranken und Angelsachsen von 878 bis um 1000," *Zeitschr. d. Savigny-Stiftung f. Rechtsgeschichte, Kanon. Abt.,* XXIII (1934), 117-242; "Die Krönung in Deutschland bis zum Beginn des Salischen Hauses," *Zeitschr. . . . f. Rechtsgesch., Kanon. Abt.,* XXIV (1935); *A History of the English Coronation; Der König von Frankreich,* 2 vols.; Eduard Eichmann, "Die römischen Eide der deutschen Könige," *Zeitschr. . . . f. Rechtsgesch., Kanon. Abt.,* VI (1916), 140-205; Fritz Hartung, "Die Krone als Symbol der monarchischen

Like other students of the clause, Richardson finds the origin or precedent in the oath of office taken by bishops who were immediately subject to the pope. In fact, by the late eleventh or early twelfth century such bishops swore fealty to the papacy; and bishops in general promised not to alienate the estates of their churches.[2] No doubt, such oaths, along with the whole early tradition of oath-taking, played a role. But a serious difficulty weakens the bishop's oath as a precedent: it was not phrased in such terms as *iura illibata* or *illaesa*.[3]

What, then, is the origin? The logical place to look for the terms is in the *Corpus iuris civilis*, for the laws of late Roman emperors prohibited the alienation of the properties and privileges of churches. And, in fact, it is first in these laws that one finds our terminology on inalienability. Here are the principal texts (the italics are mine):

(*C.* 1, 2, 12; Valentinian and Marcian, *an.* 451) *Privilegia,* quae generalibus constitutionibus universis sacrosanctis ecclesiis . . . retro principes praestiterunt, *firma et illibata in perpetuum decernimus custodiri.*

(*C.* 1, 2, 14, 2; Leo and Anthemius, *an.* 470; after decreeing that the real properties of the Church of Constantinople should not be alienated) *Ea enim quae ad beatissimae ecclesiae iura pertinent* vel posthac forte pervenerint, tamquam ipsam sacrosanctam et religiosam ecclesiam *intacta convenit venerabiliter custodiri, ut,* sicut ipsa religionis et fidei mater perpetua est, *ita eius patrimonium iugiter servetur illaesum.*

Herrschaft im ausgehenden Mittelalter," *Abhandlungen d. Preus. Akad. d. Wissenschaften, Philos.-Histor. Kl.,* no. 13 (1940), 3-46; Ernst Kantorowicz, "Inalienability. A Note on Canonical Practice and the English Coronation Oath in the Thirteenth Century," *Speculum,* xxix (1954), 488-502; Kantorowicz, *King's Two Bodies,* pp. 346-358; Riesenberg, *Inalienability of Sovereignty in Medieval Political Thought,* chs. iv and v; R. S. Hoyt, "The Coronation Oath of 1308," *Traditio,* xi (1955), 235-257; and B. Wilkinson, "The Coronation Oath of Edward II and the Statute of York," *Speculum,* xix (1944), 445-469, and *Constitutional History of England,* iii, pp. 73-83.

[2] Kantorowicz, *King's Two Bodies,* pp. 348-350; Richardson, "Coronation Oath," *Traditio,* xvi, 151-153.

[3] Richardson, *op.cit.,* offers no sources containing the terms. Nor does Kantorowicz, *King's Two Bodies,* pp. 348-350.

Justinian extended this legislation to the Church of Rome (*Nov.* 9; *Auth.*, Coll. 2, t. 4 Ut ecclesia Romana centum annorum gaudeat praescriptione). In this law he referred to the earlier laws without repeating the words quoted above. But he did use other words that are closely related and were to be repeated centuries later: the Roman Church, and churches subject to it, should enjoy the *praescriptio* of a hundred years, "*ut maneant* per totum supradictum tempus [that is, in perpetuity] *integra iura ecclesiastica.*"

The classical jurisconsults had already, with respect to the State, declared that private agreements, *pacta*, were unlawful if they caused public injury, *publica laesio* (*D.* 2, 14, 7, 14). That is, the public welfare, *utilitas publica*, must not be harmed, "publicam non laedi utilitatem" (*D.* 2, 14, 27, 4). (It is interesting to observe here that Azo, with these passages in mind, stated the very principle involved in the inalienability clause: "Si vocas publicum utilitate et auctoritate sine dubio non potest laedi." In other words, what is public from the point of view both of the public utility and of the public authority must suffer no injury. He might well have said that the *auctoritas publica* and the *utilitas publica* should be kept *illaesa*.)[4] Still more important are the laws of Justinian on the duties of imperial judges or magistrates and on their oaths of office. In the famous Praefatio to *Nov.* 8 (*Auth.*, Coll. 2, t. 2), the great emperor spoke of working day and night for the welfare of his subjects in order to relieve them of every burden and "omni damno extrinsecus illato." In §1, Cogitatio, he stated that if his subjects were kept *indempnes* and prosperous by the imperial magistrates, both the *imperium* and the *fiscus* would flourish—the fisc was weakened by the abuses of magistrates. Repeatedly he expressed the pious ideal that all subjects should be kept *illaesi*: "Semper cum dei auxilio omnem facimus providentiam, *ut subiecti* ab eius clementia traditi nobis *illaesi serventur*" (*Nov.* 80, Praef.; *Auth.*, Coll. 6, t. 7 [8]); "Magnum Deum . . . semper invocantes, studemus omnes subiectos nostros . . . illaesos et sine calumnia custo-

---

[4] *Brocardica*, IV De pactis, nos. 11 and 14, at end of vol. containing his *Summa Codicis*, ed. Venice, 1584, cols. 14f.; cf. Irnerius, *Questiones*, ed. Fitting, p. 89.

dire" (*Nov.* 85, 86; Praef. *Auth.*, Coll. 6, t. 13).[5] But if the emperor and his judges should protect subjects from injury, the public rights of the fisc (and of the emperor, of course) must also be kept unharmed. So Justinian declared (*Nov.* 17, c. 1; *Auth.*, Coll. 3, t. 4; c.1 Oportet) that all magistrates should "undique servare ius," keep the *fiscus* unharmed, and vigilantly collect all *fiscalia tributa*, "ne forte fiscus minuatur." For "sicut enim privatos iniustitiam passos adiuvamus, sic et *publicum illaesum* manere volumus."

Possibly *publicum illaesum* is connected with the Roman law on treason. If *majestas laesa*, in the *lex Iulia laesae majestatis* (*D.* 48, 4; *C.* 9, 7), was treason surely the *majestas* of the prince must be kept *illaesa*. In fact, a decretist of the late twelfth or early thirteenth century made the connection when he said that whoever injures magistrates or other public persons injures the *ius publicum*.[6] It is surely significant, moreover, that before 1153 Gilbert Foliot thought of the *majestas illaesa* of Pope Eugenius III, and that Henry II of England was to make use of the idea that princes should "famam suam conservare *illaesam*." Since Henry was accusing Thomas Becket of treason, the implication is that the royal *majestas* must be kept *illaesa*. Indeed, the English chronicler, Ralph de Diceto, associated injury to *fiscalia* (*iura*) with the *laesa majestas principis* (*an.* 1179): "fiscalia supprimentes, et quae principis laederent majestatem, regiam indignationem incurrerent."[7] In other words, if the *fiscus* should remain *illaesus*, all the more should the royal *majestas* and the *iura regis* be kept *illaesa*.

The twofold ideal of maintaining undiminished and unharmed not only the subjects of the emperor but also the rights of the public treasury (prosperous subjects and a prosperous treasury were both necessary for the public and common wel-

---

[5] These passages are quoted by Antonio Rota, "Le fonti del diritto civile e la loro autorità alla metà del XII secolo," in *Studi Sassaresi*, XXIV (1952), 17 n. 5. Rota does not take up the problem of the influence on the coronation oath.

[6] The *ius publicum* looks to the *utilitas publica*, "unde si quod ledat magistratus vel alias publicas personas, dicitur ledere ius puplicum"; *Summa reginensis*, in Vat. MS Reg. 1061, fol. 1f. This is simply another way of speaking of *laesa majestas*. Huguccio also stated this idea, above, ch. VIII, n. 57. Cf. above, to n. 4.

[7] See below, to nn. 31, 32, 39; and *S.C.*, p. 155.

fare of the Empire and of the emperor, the fisc, and the people)[8] was particularly emphasized in the oath which Justinian prescribed for all magistrates. This oath is given in *Nov.* 8, Iusiurandum, "Iuro ego" (*Auth.*, Coll. 2., t. 3 Iuro ego). Every imperial *administrator* must swear by God, etc., that he will serve the Emperor Justinian and the Empress Theodora by doing good work in his office; that he will be zealous and vigilant in looking after all fiscal business; that, insofar as possible, he will everywhere keep subjects unharmed by being *aequus* in all cases, just and fair to both parties; and that he will everywhere preserve the innocent unharmed. These are, for our purpose, the important terms: "Et primum omne habebo studium *ut fiscalia vigilanter inspiciam*, . . . et *subiectos* . . . *illaesos* undique, quantum possibiliter habeo, *custodiabo* . . . *et eos* quidem, qui innoxii sunt, undique *innoxios illaesosque conservabo.*"

In the Roman law, then, and particularly in the legislation of the emperors of the fifth and sixth centuries, the most important terms and the essential principle of the inalienability clause were clearly stated.[9] Do the same terms appear in medieval documents before the twelfth century? So far as I know they do not. Although early synods and popes condemned alienations of ecclesiastical rights and properties, they did not use the words *iura illibata* or *patrimonium illaesum.*[10] Nor were oaths or

---

[8] *C.* 6, 51, 1, 14a, where Justinian states that the welfare (*commodum*) of his subjects belonged to him and was to his profit—and this law is on the rights of the *fiscus* to properties left by men who had no heirs and died intestate.

[9] The terms appear in still other Roman laws, e.g., *C.* 11, 61, 12, Possessores, where Theodosius says that any *ius* granted to a man by the emperor on the emperor's patrimonial property shall "illibatum intemeratumque servari." In *Inst.* 1, 8, 2 ("Expedit enim reipublicae, ne quis sua re male utatur"), it is stated that the *potestas* of owners over their slaves must be *illibata*, but it is to the owners' interest to prevent brutal treatment of slaves. See also *D.* 50, 13, 5, 1.

[10] Richardson, "Coronation Oath," *Traditio*, XVI, 151 n. 3, refers to the early Canon law as given in Ivo of Chartres and in the *Decretum* of Gratian, C. 12, q. 2, esp. cc. 19, 22. Not until the late twelfth and early thirteenth century does any decretist, so far as I have found, use the terms in commenting on the inalienability of the privileges and properties of churches. One decretist connects them not with a king's oath but with the duty of the Church to demand that a king preserve the *iura ecclesiae* unharmed, to C. 12, q. 2, c. 66, ad v. *poposcit*: "Poscere debet ecclesia regem, ut ecclesie iura servet illesa, ut xcvii di. ecclesie"; in the Paris, BN, MS lat. 15393, fol. 145ᵛ. Strangely, the reference is not to the Roman law but to *Decretum*, Dist. 97, c. 1 Ecclesiae, which is a letter of Pope Boniface I asking the Emperor Honorius to protect the Roman Church

promises of bishops and of German kings to the papacy drawn up in these terms.[11] Moreover, while Carolingian kings promised to protect churches and their rights, to do justice to all, and to observe the *leges* and *statuta* for the people, the coronation *ordines* and other kinds of documents do not reflect the literal usage of our terminology.[12] In one instance, however, in 843 a Carolingian king did say that he should be so respected that his

---

and clergy and have care for the *status Ecclesiae*. Apparently the decretist did not think of the Roman laws from which his terms were derived, but the terminology was current and he used it.

Perhaps the author of the gloss just given is Alanus Anglicus—see Kuttner, *Repertorium*, pp. 67-74; and Alfons M. Stickler, "Alanus Anglicus als Verteidiger des monarchischen Papsttums," in *Salesianum*, XXI (1959), 348-350, 371-378. Alanus is certainly the author of another gloss that is interesting in connection with the coronation clause on inalienability. He offers the argument that the pope can depose a secular prince if the situation clearly justifies it and if the "status ecclesie nichilominus illesus permaneret"—to *Decretum*, C. 15, q. 6, c. 3 Alius item, ad v. *deposuit*; quoted by Stickler, *Salesianum*, XXI, 367, col. 2.

Just as in the laws of Justinian the *status* of the fisc (or *iura* of the fisc) and of the emperor and the *status subiectorum* should be kept *illaesus*, so the "state" of the Church must be *illaesus*.

But the fact that Alanus was English is no indication that he had any knowledge of the inalienability of the *iura regni*, etc., in an English coronation oath. As suggested above, he probably got the terms from the currency of them among canonists who studied the Roman law. Of course, other decretists of this period may have used the terms and thus given them to Alanus.

[11] Eichmann, "Römische Eide," *Zeitschr. . . . f. Rechtsgesch., Kanon. Abt.*, VI, 140-205, reveals no such terminology until the late twelfth century. But then the terms appear only in Roger Howden's own words on the oath of fealty of the Emperor Henry VI to the pope, "quod ipse ecclesiam Dei et iura ecclesiastica fideliter servaret illibata, etc." (p. 176). See also Schramm, "Ordines," *Archiv f. Urkundenforschung*, XI, 295 n. 5, for the oath to the Roman people: "se in omnibus leges et dignitates Romanas servaturum illesas"—"illibatas" in another version. The point is that these terms did not remain in the oath, which returned to the traditional form.

On bishops' oaths, also on the oath of the vassal to his lord, see *Decr. Greg.* IX 2, 24, 4 Ego N.; *Decretum*, C. 22, q. 5, c. 18 De forma fidelitatis, and the *Glos. ord.* of Johannes Teutonicus thereto; and the *Libri feudorum*, 2, 5-7.

[12] See, for examples, *M.G.H., Legum S. II, Capitularia*, II, nos. 205, 254, 276, 281, 283, 288, 292; and also Schramm in the studies referred to above, n. 1; Richardson, "Coronation Oath," *Traditio*, XVI, 162f., 174-180; and R. Scheyhing, *Eide Amtsgewalt und Bannleihe*, chs. 1 and 2, and pp. 160-164. Scheyhing does point to the influence, in the twelfth and thirteenth centuries, of a famous law of Justinian, the *Rem non novam* (C. 3, 1, 14), on the tradition of oaths taken by judges. But in this law the judges should swear, on the Gospels, that they will follow the rules of justice in deciding cases; they do not swear to maintain *illaesa* or *illibata* the rights of the fisc and of litigants. On the oath in the early Middle Ages see also M. David, "Le serment du sacre du IXe au XVe siècle," *Revue du moyen âge latin*, VI (1950), 39-180.

honor and *potestas* would remain *inconvulsa*.[13] If this is no indication that he had promised to maintain the royal office and power unharmed, it is a statement of the same principle as that in the later inalienability clause. Perhaps more examples of the kind might be found. Nonetheless, the precise terms seem to be lacking, and it is doubtful in any case that Carolingian sources explain the appearance of the terms in the twelfth century. The terms do not occur in feudal oaths of fealty, nor in any engagement of lords to protect their own rights as well as those of their vassals.

Since, probably, the imperial laws given above largely created the terminology, and Justinian developed a new form of the oaths of magistrates and judges of the Empire, no doubt the main reason for the silence of early medieval sources is the fact that the *Codex* and *Novellae* were not the subject of scientific study before the late eleventh and early twelfth centuries. While it is possible that our terms came into use in the eleventh century, I have not observed them in the polemical literature of the time of Gregory VII, or in the *Anonymous of York*. It was no doubt the teaching of Irnerius and his disciples that caused the Roman terminology to become current as early as the second quarter of the twelfth century. Irnerius and the Four Doctors of Bologna do not stress the terms, but they acquainted their students, some of whom served Frederick Barbarossa and Henry II and other princes (and also the Church and churches), with the twofold concept that the *iura regis et regni* and the *iura ecclesiastica* should be preserved *illibata* and *illaesa*.

The few public documents and letters that I have consulted point to the use of the Roman terminology well before 1154 (the year of the coronation of Henry II) both in Germany and in England. Almost as soon as Frederick Barbarossa was crowned at Aachen in 1152, the royal chancery began to formulate his

---

13 *M.G.H., Legum S. II, Cap.*, II, no. 254: "ut noster honor et potestas regia inconvulsa permaneat." Of course, *honor*, used frequently in the Carolingian age, still often meant the public office of the king. In a sense, therefore, the king held that the *iura regis*, his *potestas*, should be kept *illaesa*.

letters in more terms from the Roman law than had appeared in the reigns of preceding kings and emperors. But did Frederick at his coronation promise or swear to maintain *illibata* or *illaesa* the rights and privileges of churches and of his realm and subjects? I find no evidence that he did so. His *professio* was made apparently in the traditional terms—as the exchange of letters with Pope Eugenius III indicates. He promised to honor the pope and to defend and do justice to the Roman Church and all ecclesiastical persons; and "viduis ac pupillis et universo populo nobis commisso legem et pacem faciamus et conservemus." Not yet, therefore, was the King of the Romans promising to keep the *iura ecclesiastica illibata* and the *iura regis et regni illibata* or *illaesa*, and his subjects *illaesos*, although the substance of the *professio* bears essentially the same meaning. (As emperor, he haughtily told Arnold of Brescia and the Roman citizens that he was not obligated to take oaths to confirm old laws and customs or to defend the *patria*. Perhaps this reflects the idea of the "imperialists" that the emperor was above oath-taking—that kings, however, were lesser magistrates of "provinces" in the Empire and therefore should take an oath of office.)[14]

But in 1153 Frederick condemned the alienation of the properties of the archbishop and church of Cologne, declaring that the emperor should "inviolabiliter conservare" the *iura* of the clergy and churches, and that the *iura* of the church of Cologne should remain "perpetuo robore illibata et inconvulsa"—cf. *C.* 1, 2, 12. The ecclesiastical *iura* so protected, however, were those which were recognized in the imperial courts![15] More significant is the famous *constitutio* of 1154 against the alienation of fiefs. Already in 1136 the Emperor Lothair III had prohibited any future alienations of fiefs, and he had said that it was the duty of the emperor "commoda subiectorum investigare, et eo-

---

[14] A detailed account, with an abundant reference to sources, in H. Simonsfeld, *Jahrbücher des deutschen Reiches unter Friedrich I*, I, 39-43, 122 n. 395. See also *M.G.H., Legum S. IV, Const.*, I, 193f., nos. 137 and 139. On the statement made to Arnold of Brescia, see above, ch. VII, n. 75.

[15] *M.G.H., Legum S. IV, Const.*, I, 204f., no. 146. Note that the king emphasizes the superiority of his *iura* in his courts—implying the principle that the *iura regis et regni* are superior in public law to the *iura ecclesiastica* within the kingdom. See also below, to n. 23.

rum calamitatibus diligenti cura mederi: similiter reipublicae bonum statum ac dignitatem imperii omnibus privatis commodis praeponere."[16] The influence of Justinian in *C.* 6, 51, 1, 14a is evident. But Frederick Barbarossa's law reflects also the legislation of Justinian on the duties and oaths of magistrates. Like Justinian, he balanced the public utility (*regni utilitas*) and the common welfare (*status singulorum*) of his subjects: "Imperialem decet sollertiam ita reipublicae curam gerere, et subiectorum commoda investigare, ut regni utilitas incorrupta persistat, et singulorum status iugiter servetur illaesus."[17]

Let us note also that the words "singulorum status iugiter servetur illaesus" represent the transfer of the Roman law on the inalienability of ecclesiastical property (*C.* 1, 2, 12, 2: "ita eius ecclesiae patrimonium iugiter servetur illaesum") to the inalienability of the welfare and rights of people and realm. According to Rahewin the pope himself promised, through legates, "in nullo regiae dignitati derogare, sed honorem ac iustitiam imperii semper illibatam conservare." In the context this was a statement of the idea that the public powers and laws of the emperor and Empire should not be injured. Moreover, in 1167 Frederick declared that the *status Romani Imperii* and the *status* of the illustrious princes who maintained the glory of the Empire should be "preserved unharmed."[18] And in 1162 he said that he was the *defensor ecclesiarum Dei*, "ut eas et earum iura integra et illesa sub nostro imperiali protectione defendamus."[19]

On the basis of these documents one might well argue that in 1152 Frederick at his coronation had added the new inalienability clause to the traditional *professio*. As remarked above, however, there is no direct evidence that he did so; and no evidence, therefore that he furnished a precedent for Henry II's adding an inalienability clause in 1154. Nonetheless, it is interesting that the Roman terminology of the inalienability clause was appearing by 1153 in Germany. It is still more interesting

---

[16] *Libri feudorum*, 2, 52; *M.G.H., Legum S. IV, Const.,* I, no. 120.

[17] *Libri feudorum*, 2, 55; *M.G.H., Legum S. IV, Const.,* I, no. 148.

[18] Rassow, *Honor imperii*, p. 107 n. 176, Rahewin, to p. 79; also *M.G.H., Legum S. IV, Const.,* I, no. 231: "utriusque status servatur incolumis."

[19] *M.G.H., Legum S. IV, Const.,* I, no. 217.

that Frederick and his advisers were putting to use these Roman concepts of public law: it was not only the duty but the public right of the emperor of the Holy Roman Empire to preserve *illaesa* and *illibata* the public welfare, *status*, of the Empire itself along with the rights and welfare, *status* again, of all subjects, including the clergy and the churches. His *iura* as king and emperor existed chiefly for the defense and maintenance of the public and common welfare—therefore also for the defense of the Church within the State, since the public law was concerned with the magistracy, *sacra*, and priests (cf. *D.* 1, 1, 1, 2 and the *Glos. ord.* thereto). If the supreme authority of the prince included these duties and rights, it included also the right to preserve and strengthen the *status principis*, else he could not keep unharmed the rights of subjects and of the State. Implied, accordingly, if not stated in an inalienability clause, was the principle that the emperor could not alienate what belonged to his necessary authority. *Ratione gubernationis et protectionis, ratione status imperii,*[20] it was the public right of the prince to keep *illibata* and *illaesa* the *iura regni, regis, et coronae.* In a word, the laws of Frederick Barbarossa show that there was already the assumption that if it was the duty and right of the king and emperor to keep unharmed the empire and its subjects, he could not alienate any of that sovereignty which was necessary to the end of maintaining the *status Imperii*, which included the *status ecclesiarum.*[21] His *majestas* must remain *illaesa*—so I venture to put it.

Naturally, the papacy could hardly interpret the German king's rights in this fashion. As Pope Eugenius III said in a letter of 1152, the German bishops should resist any attacks on the Church, "ut . . . et aecclesiae Dei ac regni status in suo decore incolumnis conservetur."[22] The power of the prince was lim-

---

[20] See my *"Ratio publicae utilitatis," Welt als Gesch.,* XXI, 8-28, 71-99; above, ch. v, in general; also ch. VIII.

In 1231 Frederick II reflected the laws of Justinian on magistrates' oaths and on the inalienability of fiscal *iura*—"curie nostre demania et jura quelibet illesa servabunt"; Huillard-Bréholles, *Hist. Dipl. Frid. II,* IV, i (Tit. LXII), pp. 41f.; cf. below, n. 48.

[21] A separate study of *status ecclesiarum* and *Status Ecclesiae* is in preparation. On *laesa* and *illaesa majestas*, see above, to n. 7; also ch. VII, n. 75.

[22] Simonsfeld, *Jahrbücher,* I, 122.

ited by his duty to preserve the *status Ecclesiae*, which in the Pope's mind, as in the Canon law, was superior to the *status regni*. Frederick, however, was expressing the late Roman imperialist doctrine, that it was the emperor's *right* to defend and preserve the *iura* of State and Church, and that the secular prince was the supreme judge with respect to the rights in property of clergy and churches. He intended to enhance the public *iura* or powers of the imperial government, and in some matters, chiefly on the side of property rights, to subject the German churches and clergy to his authority. This intention was expressed in the decision of 1153 concerning the *iura* recognized by the royal court as lawfully belonging to the church of Cologne—only these *iura* were to be kept *illibata* and *inconvulsa*.[23] Above the *iura* of churches were the *iura* of the authority of the prince. Thus again Frederick was in reality, if not always in these words, asserting his right to maintain *illaesa* and *illibata* the *iura regis et regni*.

In England the idea that the *dignitates* and *usus* of king and kingdom should be maintained whole and undiminished had been asserted by Henry I.[24] Did the gradual change to the Roman terminology, *iura illibata-illaesa*, in the time of Henry II and later come from the Holy Roman Empire? Probably the example set by Frederick and the Roman concept of the authority of the prince offered some encouragement to Henry and his counsellors to assert his rights of justice at the expense of ecclesiastical courts. But the principle that a king and others should keep the properties and *iura* of churches *illibata* had long since been stated firmly and explicitly by Popes Innocent II and Eugenius III. Perhaps popes still earlier had used the standard formulas, that the *possessiones* and *bona* of churches and monasteries "firma . . . in perpetuum et illibata permaneant," and "omnia integra conserventur." But from 1137 to 1153 Innocent II and Eugenius III repeatedly stated them in confirming the rights of churches in England and elsewhere—

---

[23] *Ibid.*, 188, no. 138, quoting *M.G.H., Legum S. IV, Const.*, I, 205 no. 146: "ea, que ad nostram cognicionem . . . illibata et inconvulsa permaneant." Cf. above, n. 15.

[24] Hoyt, "Coronation Oath of 1308," *Traditio*, XI, 253.

illibata, therefore, did not originate in the chancery of Frederick Barbarossa.[25] It is interesting (but of no importance for arguing that at his coronation Henry added an inalienability clause for the sake of English churches) that the famous bull of Hadrian IV, 1155-1156, the *Laudabiliter,* which approved Henry's plan for the invasion of Ireland, states that Henry should "jura Ecclesiarum illius terrae illibata et integra conservare."[26] Nor does a decretal of Innocent III, 1202, have any bearing on a coronation oath, although the pope does say that a monastic *ordo* should be kept *illaesus.* (A contemporary decretist says that the *status Ecclesiae* must remain *illaesus.*)[27]

The style used in the papal chancery, then, was one source of the revived Roman terminology. Another source, the letters of Anglo-Norman prelates, resulted from the study of Roman as well as Canon law in Italy, in the court of Archbishop Theobald of Canterbury, and perhaps in the school of Vacarius at Oxford. (But the teaching of Vacarius may not have included an emphasis on the Roman law on the inalienability of church properties; at least I have not found that he used our terms in his *Liber pauperum,* either to *C.* 1, 2, 12 and 14, or elsewhere.) Mr. Richardson, assuming that the inalienability clause was added to the coronation oath in 1154, offers the conjecture that Nigel, Bishop of Ely, was the author.[28] I have not examined the cor-

---

25 There are many examples of the usage. See for a few from the letters of Innocent II, Jaffe-Löwenfeld, nos. 7868, 7877, 7945, and 8005 (in MPL 179, cols. 343, 349, 401, and 449f.); also Rymer, *Foedera,* I, i, 3. For Eugenius III see M.P.L. 180, cols. 1017, 1037, and 1513, nos. 4, 23, and 496; and Rymer, *Foedera,* I, i, 4.

26 Rymer, *Foedera,* I, i, 5f. On the authenticity of the bull see Raymonde Foreville, *L'Eglise et la royauté en Angleterre sous Henri II Plantagenet,* pp. 83-85, 494-499. For another example in a letter of Hadrian IV see Friedberg, *Quinque Compilationes Antiquae, Comp. I,* 3, 26, 15: (*an.* 1154-59) the pope betrayed his succession to St. Peter "si cunctarum iura ecclesiarum integra non debeant illibata servari." This decretal was not included in *Decr. Greg. IX.*

27 Friedberg, *Quinque Comp. Ant., Comp. III,* 3, 24, 5—again this decretal was not included in the *Decr. Greg. IX;* above, n. 10.

28 "Coronation Oath," *Traditio,* XVI, 151-169. I am not sure, as I will indicate more fully below, to nn. 32-37, that Henry took an oath instead of the traditional *professio* or promise. Nor is it certain, I think, that Professor M. David is right about the change from *professio* to *iuramentum* at this time; although he does hold that Henry II made the traditional *professio; La souveraineté et les limites juridiques du pouvoir monarchique du IXe au XVe siècles,* p. 168 nn. 9f. Mr. Richardson argues that Henry II took an oath to which the inalienability clause was added in terms of *iura* or *consuetudines illibatae* or *illaesae.* My argument is that whether there was a traditional *professio* or an oath, it is doubtful

respondence of Nigel and cannot say whether he was familiar with the terms. No doubt he did know them, if only from letters of Archbishop Theobald, Gilbert Foliot of Hereford, and other bishops.

Long before 1154, indeed, Theobald's chancery used *illibata*: the *bona* and *iura* of churches, and gifts to them, should remain *illibata* (several examples 1139-1151).[29] *Illaesa* seems to have been preferred perhaps before 1154, but at any rate, between 1150 and 1161: bad *consuetudines* must be rooted out "et utiles et antiquitus habitas libertates illesas perpetuo conservare"; the *patrimonium* of the Church "illesum debet perpetuo conservari"; and the archbishop should keep the *libertates* and *dignitates* of the church of Canterbury "integras at illesas."[30] Since Theobald participated in the coronation of Henry II, he could have been the author of the inalienability clause—if it was actually added.

Gilbert Foliot, Bishop of Hereford, 1148-1163 (of London after 1163), in a letter to Pope Eugenius III, therefore not later than 1153, hints at the influence of the *lex laesae majestatis* in expressing the wish that the papal *majestas* be preserved *illaesa* and *inoffensa*.[31] In a letter addressed to Bishop Nigel and dated 1148-1160 (hence not necessarily before 1154), he asked for the protection of the rights of Robert de Clare in a church, "ut ecclesiam, quam sibi tuitione vestra possidet, sibi illaesam impurtabatamque patrocinio conservetis."[32] In still another letter he rejoiced that God had kept Joannes de Dinan *illaesum* and that Joannes had maintained God "illaesum in membris suis"

---

that the inalienability clause was used at the coronation. See below, to nn. 36, 45, 48, 49.

We have seen that Bishop Nigel's son, Richard, in the *Dialogue of the Exchequer*, had some acquaintance with terms and concepts from the Roman public law, such as *status regis* and *ratio publicae utilitatis*; above, ch. VIII, nn. 9 and 10, and my "*Ratio publicae utilitatis*," *Welt als Gesch.*, XXI, 71f.

[29] In charters published by Avrom Saltman, *Theobald Archbishop of Canterbury*, pp. 280f., 284, 298, 350, 366 (nos. 54, 55, 58, 73, 128, 144).

[30] Saltman, *Theobald*, pp. 250f., 297, 277 (nos. 23, 72, 50).

[31] Giles, ed., *Gilberti Foliot Ep.*, I, 114, no. 87. Gilbert probably had studied the *Digest* and some early glosses—there was a copy at Hereford about 1160 (Saltman, *Theobald*, p. 175 n. 6). No doubt his copy had been obtained in Italy, or sent to him from there.

[32] Giles, *Gilberti Foliot Ep.*, I, 103, no. 80.

by defending the rights of the clergy of a church.[33] One notes that Gilbert liked *illaesus* better than *illibatus*.

Important, too, is a letter to Pope Alexander III, written, of course, some ten years after the coronation of Henry II, since it relates to the affair of Thomas Becket. Gilbert says that Henry had declared that Thomas could return to England and receive satisfaction from the king "dum tamen in satisfaciendo sibi super his, unde conqueritur, regias sibi, et in quas ipse juratus est, velit dignitates integre conservari."[34] In another letter connected with the controversy Gilbert explains that the royal authority had asserted that it belonged "ad summam regni sui dignitatem" that no prelate should use the weapon of excommunication against any baron engaged in a suit in a royal court, and that the king held that all the bishops of the realm had sworn not to diminish or injure the *privilegia* of the realm.[35] These letters, of course, refer to the famous "promise" of the prelates of the realm in connection with the Constitutions of Clarendon, the "promise" or oath (which Thomas Becket retracted when the Constitutions were promulgated) to respect the *consuetudines, libertates,* and *dignitates* of king and realm.[36] It is thus possible that not only the traditional feudal oath of

33 *Ibid.,* 111, no. 85.
34 *Ibid.,* 240, no. 174; Hoyt, "Coronation Oath of 1308," *Traditio,* XI, 254.
35 Giles, *Gilberti Foliot Ep.,* I, 244f., no. 176.
36 *S.C.,* pp. 163f., and caps. 1 and 7, pp. 164f. On the events of 1163-64 and Henry's obtaining a promise from the prelates, see also Barlow, *Feudal Kingdom of England 1042-1216,* pp. 292-294; Foreville, *L'Eglise et la royauté en Angleterre,* pp. 107-130, 145-153, 249; and Foreville and J. Rousset de Pina, *Du premier Concile du Latran à l'avènement d'Innocent III,* Part 2, pp. 99f. Mlle. Foreville pays insufficient attention to elements of Roman public law that influenced the policy of Henry II: Henry is always *arbitraire,* while Becket simply and rightly represents the Canon law. But it is doubtful that a king, inspired by principles of public law, and claiming the right to exercise his authority both for the *status regis* and for the *status regni,* was any more *arbitraire* than the pope, who could use his power of dispensation in order to maintain the *status Ecclesiae.* Of course, the danger of absolutism was present in State and Church alike. However, in both cases the theory was that the supreme authority should rule in accordance with the law, but was above the positive law in cases of emergency or necessity.
One can consult also, on what happened at Clarendon, David Knowles, *The Episcopal Colleagues of Archbishop Thomas Becket,* pp. 60-66; ch. v on the political problems—there is no reference to the coronation oath of Henry II, nor to the Roman law.

fealty but the Roman magistrate's oath ordered by Justinian is in the background of Henry's policy in 1263-1264.

Whether Henry II's counsellors and his chancery got the Roman terms from the letters of popes and prelates or from a more direct contact with the Roman law I cannot say. But his letters do contain the terms. Indeed, in 1151 at Rouen, as Duke of Normandy, he ordered that those things which the pope had confirmed to the monks of Mortemer should be conserved "integra et illibata."[37] How soon after his coronation the royal chancery employed the terms can be decided only after a study of all his documents. But the quarrel with Thomas Becket probably caused an increasing use of them. For, against the argument of Thomas that the king was not keeping the *iura ecclesiastica illibata*, Henry replied that the pope and the Roman Court in supporting Thomas, who he said was a *proditor* and *infamis*, were injuring the royal *honor* and *dignitas*, as they were injuring the realm and its *iura* and *consuetudines*.[38] He accused the pope of violating his own teaching, that it should be the care of princes "famam suam conservare illesam." He said that he would gladly persevere in his regard for the pope "si nobis et regno nostro eundem honorem et honoris et dignitatis conservationem observaverit." But if anyone attempted to violate the *iura* and *consuetudines* of the realm, the king would reckon him a "publicum hostem et manifestum nominis nostri et honoris et regni . . . inimicum."[39] Henry even spoke of demanding that the pope take public oath that he and his successors would preserve *inconcussae* and *inviolatae* the *regiae consuetudines* of Henry I![40]

Clearly, the king and his advisers were virtually saying that

[37] Delisle and Berger, *Recueil des actes de Henri II*, I, 43f., no. 37.

[38] *Ibid.*, 385, 392, 407 (nos. 237, 246, and 261); cf. the promise made by the pope to Frederick in 1158, above, n. 18.

[39] *Recueil*, I, 392f., no. 246, *an.* 1165. See above, to n. 7, for *laesa* and *illaesa majestas*.

[40] *Recueil*, I, 407f., *an.* 1166. The idea of this perhaps came from the promise made by cardinal-legates to Frederick I, 1158, that the pope would "in nullo regiae dignitati derogare, sed honorem ac iusticiam imperii illibatam conservare"; Rahewin, *Gesta*, III, 24, quoted by Rassow, *Honor Imperii*, p. 107, n. 176, to p. 79; also Simonsfeld, *Jahrbücher*, I, 644 n. 173; cf. above, to n. 18.

the prince in keeping his *fama illaesa* must also preserve *illibata*, *illaesa, inconvulsa,* or *inconcussa* those *iura* of the royal honor and dignity, and of the realm, which were sanctioned by the *consuetudines* of the realm in the time of Henry I. There is a suggestion, moreover, of the concept that the *majestas regis* should be *illaesa,* since a traitor and those who protected him, even if it was the pope himself who abetted the *proditor,* were guilty of *laesa fama regis* if not precisely of *laesa majestas.*

The sources, therefore, show that the Roman terms in the inalienability clause were in circulation and were used in the proper contexts well before 1154 as well as thereafter. But a serious problem remains: was an inalienability clause added to the coronation *professio* (or oath, if it was such) of Henry II? Did the new king swear to maintain *illibata* or *illaesa* the *iura* (or *libertates, consuetudines,* etc.) of king and realm and also the *iura* and *privilegia* of churches? Mr. H. G. Richardson, as we remarked at the outset, thinks that he did, that the inalienability clause first appeared in 1154. As evidence, Richardson offers the Third Recension of the *Leges Edwardi Confessoris* (and dates it 1154-1161),[41] and a letter of Alexander III, 1170.[42] Roger of Howden's statement, that in 1199 John swore to preserve "sanctam ecclesiam et dignitates illius . . . illaesas," could be added.[43] And the sources I have given both for the period before 1154 and for the following years seem to support Mr. Richardson's contention.[44] Certainly, the revival of the Roman law had reinforced the doctrine of inalienability and had fur-

[41] Richardson, "Coronation Oath," *Traditio,* xvi, 167f.: "Debet rex omnes terras et honores, omnes dignitates et iura et libertates corone regni huius in integrum . . . obseruare et defendere. . . ."

[42] *Traditio,* xvi, 163; the argument, probably of Thomas Becket himself, that the king at his coronation promised "ut consuetudines quas auitas dicunt . . . illibatas omni tempore conseruare."

[43] Quoted by Hoyt, "Coronation Oath," *Traditio,* xi, 249 n. 53. For another indication that King John thought in terms of keeping the *libertas* and *dignitas* of the crown *illesa,* see Richardson, *Speculum,* xxiv, 53 n. 54.

[44] Two more sources can now be added: a letter of Alexander III to his legates, that they should effect a reconciliation of Becket and the king, "ita quod sibi et ecclesiae suae antiqua jura et libertates integra et illibata servetis" (in Giles, *Gilberti Foliot Ep.,* ii, 53, no. 331); in 1160 Archbishop Theobald urged the king to preserve *indempnis* the church of Canterbury, for it was the *caput regni* and its *honor* was the *honor regis* (in *Letters of John of Salisbury,* eds. W. J. Millor and H. E. Butler, i, 190f., no. 116).

nished the terminology well before the coronation of Henry II.

Yet, I am not convinced that the new inalienability clause was actually added to the coronation *professio* or oath as early as 1154.[45] Despite the fact that Henry II and Nigel of Ely actively reclaimed the *iura fiscalia* which Stephen had alienated, and that prelates and others had long since been talking about *iura illibata* and the like, no specific statement has come to my attention that Henry and his counsellors and judges were putting into effect what had been sworn to as a principle. The coronation charter itself indicates a traditional promise, not one in the new terminology.[46] Nor does the increasing use of the Roman terms in 1163-1170 prove more than the fact that partisans of the king and of Becket found them useful in arguing about the rights of the king and realm and the rights of the Church. Similarly, there is no certainty that John swore to keep the *libertas* and *dignitas coronae illaesa* even though one source attributes the words to him.[47] And Pope Honorius III's decretal, *Intellecto* (*Decr. Greg. IX* 2, 24, 33), containing the statement that the King of Hungary took a coronation oath that he would maintain unharmed the rights of the crown, is again no positive evidence that the oath was taken in the same terms.[48]

Neither do I fully agree with Professors Wilkinson and Hoyt, who have taken the position that there is no evidence of an inalienability clause added to the English coronation oath before the late thirteenth or early fourteenth century.[49] It is possible that Mr. Richardson is right. It is possible, given the currency of the Roman terminology in the mid-twelfth century, that Henry II—or John or Henry III—added the clause to the oath. But it

45 See above, n. 28.

46 Barlow, *Feudal Kingdom of England*, p. 284.

47 See above, n. 43.

48 As early as 1205 Innocent III ordered that the *jura regni* (of Hungary) "integro conserventur," referring to the *regalia*; Carlyle, *Med. Political Theory*, v, 164 n. 3.

49 Wilkinson, "The Coronation Oath of Edward II and the Statute of York," *Speculum*, XIX, 445-469, and *Constitutional History*, III, 73-83; and Hoyt, "Coronation Oath of 1308," *Traditio*, XI, 235-257. But I agree with them to this extent, that one must treat with caution any use of the terms, outside the coronation oath itself, as evidence of an added inalienability clause. Yet, because of references to an oath couched in the Roman terminology, it is possible that the clause was added to the oath in the thirteenth century—even as early as 1154.

is not certain nor even likely. I therefore leave the problem to be settled by others.

In one sense it is not important to settle the date of the first use of the inalienability clause. It is important, however, to note that the idea of the inalienability of the *iura regis et regni* was asserted by Henry II and his counsellors and supporters. Whether stated in the older terms of defending the *dignitates* and *consuetudines* and *iura* and *libertates* of the crown or of king and realm, or in the newer Roman terms of keeping these *iura illibata* or *illaesa*, the idea was that of a constitutional principle. The public rights of kingship, that *status regis* which was necessary for the *status regni*, must be maintained unharmed, just as the *status regni*, like the *status rei Romanae*, must be preserved, "ne pereat." But Henry II went too fast, and without tact, in trying to reestablish the old superiority that William the Conqueror and Henry I enjoyed over the English church and clergy, and to strengthen it in accordance with the concepts of the *status regis et regni*. The Church at the moment was still too strong for a king to succeed in "nationalizing" the clergy and their churches.

Frederick Barbarossa's policy no doubt encouraged Henry II. But the revival of the Roman law was of great importance to both. In the legislation of late Roman emperors the great secular princes of the twelfth century and their learned advisers began to find new support in striving to consolidate their States. Even more than lesser magistrates or judges, kings should maintain *illaesa* and *illibata* the *iura* of their public authority in order to keep their subjects *illaesos*. Since the public *iura* of the king included his *iura fiscalia*, Richard Fitzneale could say that by the work of the Exchequer "totius regni status indemnis servatur."[50] But the maintenance of the "state of the realm" gave to the king the right (as well as duty) to defend and keep unharmed the *iura* and *privilegia* of ecclesiastical as well as lay subjects; for all, clergy and laity alike, were members of the body of the realm of which the king was the head. The difficulty

---

[50] *S.C.*, p. 205 (I, iv). There is here a similarity to a law of Frederick II, *an.* 1231, that the "curie nostre demania et jura quelibet illesa servabunt"; Huillard-Bréholles, IV, i, *Constitutiones*, 42.

was that if ecclesiastics were subjects of the king they were also members of the Church and subjects of the pope. Naturally, the pope as head of the Church held that his clergy, in matters that pertained to the faith and the *status Ecclesiae*, were not members of the secular State and were not subjects of the king. The pope, not the king, should be the final interpreter of the public law in all matters that touched the Church and its *libertates* and *privilegia*. According to the Canon law, therefore, the king must submit to the pope's interpretation of that public law which dealt with *sacra* and *sacerdotes*: the *iura ecclesiastica* first, thereafter the *iura regis et regni*, must be kept *illibata*. For if the Church was impeded in its work of saving souls, the "state" of king and realm had no value.

This chapter is not intended as a contribution to the history of the relations of Church and State. I have simply wanted to emphasize the origins in the Roman law of the terminology, and of the concepts, in the "inalienability" clause. If Justinian ordered magistrates of the Empire to keep the public *iura* of the emperor *illaesa*, and *subiectos illaesos*, kings and their advisers, from the later twelfth century on, understood very well that it was the right of the prince to keep *illibata* and *illaesa* the *iura* of his public authority, and thereby to keep *illaesos* his subjects and the *status regni*. In other words, the rights and powers belonging to the public *status regis* must not be alienated lest the *status regni* suffer injury. This principle found expression, probably, long before it literally appeared (whenever it did appear) in a coronation oath.

CHAPTER X ✧ PUBLIC LAW, THE
STATE, AND NATIONALISM*

I
N THE twelfth and thirteenth centuries, we have now learned, Roman ideas of public law had been transferred from the universal Empire to the rising feudal monarchies. Kings and their governments, aided by a general awareness of membership in the *universitas* or *communitas regni*, were creating independent States. How these States were at the same time becoming nations and bearers of the ideal of nationalism is now our general subject.

To speak of medieval nationalism, however, violates the accepted historical tradition. Professor Hans Kohn, a distinguished authority on the history of nationalism, has asserted that "nationalism is unthinkable before the emergence of the modern state in the period from the sixteenth to the eighteenth century." Only in the modern age, and above all after the French Revolution, did the prerequisites of nationalism develop—*inter alia*, the territorial and sovereign State, popular sovereignty, "a living and active corporate will," group-consciousness and a mass-psychological state of mind, a supreme loyalty to the nation ("only a few centuries ago man's loyalty was due to his church or religion"), patriotism, and a secularized society.[1]

---

* Published with the title, "Two Notes on Nationalism in the Middle Ages," in *Traditio*, IX (1953), 281-320; now revised. I have revised and added, as the third part of this study, the article entitled " 'Blessed Lady Spain'—Vincentius Hispanus and Spanish National Imperialism in the Thirteenth Century," *Speculum*, XXIX (1954), 198-209. I wish to thank Prof. Brian Tierney for calling attention to errors; I hope that I have corrected them here (see *Traditio*, X, 619 n. 63; cf. below, nn. 182-190).

[1] *The Idea of Nationalism*, pp. 3-19. Other modern historians generally agree with Kohn, e.g., Carlton J. H. Hayes, *The Historical Evolution of Nationalism*; Louis L. Snyder, *The Meaning of Nationalism*; and Boyd S. Shafer, *Nationalism: Myth and Reality*. All, including Kohn, do acknowledge that a few elements of nationalism were manifested sporadically in the Middle Ages—Shafer in par-

[434]

In this chapter nothing will be said about the psychology of the masses. The medievalist, of course, is handicapped by the fact that the sources for the study of the phenomenon are wanting. But in any case it is easy to exaggerate the spontaneity and persistence of patriotism among the masses or "common people." Normally, modern governments have initiated and maintained, by controlling publicity in mass communications, the proper psychological atmosphere of patriotic devotion. From Napoleon to the present, whether the State be monarchic or democratic, governments have had to compel most men to be patriotic enough to pay extraordinary taxes, or to make the supreme sacrifice of fighting and dying for the common fatherland. Conscription is necessary. Patriotism is a product of leadership as well as education.

The assumption in this chapter, therefore, is that patriotism began in the leadership of kings in the new States. Like representation in assemblies, early modern nationalism arose, in the twelfth and thirteenth centuries, at the king's command; and the king and his advisers found inspiration in the law of Rome. Ideas of the public law and the State supported the rise of the national State, and early nationalism at the same time strengthened the public authority of the king exercised as the *status regis* for the *status regni*.

1. *PUGNA PRO PATRIA*

In an excellent article, "*Pro patria mori* in Medieval Political Thought," Ernst H. Kantorowicz has recently called attention to the importance of the concept of *patria* in the rise of the national monarchy and State in the later Middle Ages. No correction is needed, nor, perhaps, any addition. But since he modestly admits that he did not mean to exhaust the subject and does not examine the two laws, and since I had begun to note occasional remarks in the canonists and legists about the *patria* in association with theories of public law and the State, I wish to add some illustrations of the legal thought on the

---

ticular, pp. 5-8, 69ff. But they have not observed the rise of important theories and practices of public law and the State in the twelfth and thirteenth centuries.

subject in the twelfth to fourteenth centuries. These illustrations will supplement, moreover, the essay by Halvdan Koht on nationalism in the Middle Ages.[2]

If the classical *belles lettres* are an important source, as Kantorowicz amply shows, the classical Roman law is another. I shall indicate the appropriate passages in the *Corpus iuris civilis* as they appear in the glosses of the lawyers of the medieval classical period. But the legists and canonists frequently say, to give emphasis to their comments, "Pugna pro patria." For these words their source is not the Roman law, but the moral *Distichs* attributed to Cato and read by school boys throughout the Middle Ages.[3] *Pro patria mori*, of course, presupposes *Pugna pro patria*.

In the early Middle Ages some influence of the Roman law is evident in the barbarian codes, for example, in the Visigothic Code, on the crime of treason "against king, land, or folk—*adversus regem, gentem vel patriam*."[4] The Carolingians repeatedly prescribed punishment for failure to respond to the summons to the army for the *defensio patriae*.[5] The papacy itself admitted that war in defense of the *patria* was lawful even

[2] Kantorowicz's article, in *A.H.R.*, LVI (1951), 472-492; and now his *King's Two Bodies*, pp. 232-272; Koht, "The Dawn of Nationalism in Europe," *A.H.R.*, LII (1947), 265-280. Koht gives as examples for the twelfth and thirteenth centuries Suger's love of France (Suger was himself called *pater patriae*), the *Chanson de Roland* (French valor and *dulce France*), Peter of Blois, Geoffrey of Monmouth (for Britain), Vincent of Cracow for Poland (defense of the common *patria*), Saxo Grammaticus for Denmark, Snorri Sturluson for Norway, and Walther von der Vogelweide for Germany. But one cannot call this feeling nationalism until one learns whether there was at the same time some legal definition of it in association with the idea of kingdoms within Christendom but outside and independent of the universalism attributed to the Holy Roman Empire.

On the subject of medieval origins of independent states there is much of value in von der Heydte, *Geburtsstünde des souveränen Staates*; but the emphasis is on political theories from the late thirteenth century on.

[3] W. J. Chase, *The Distichs of Cato*, p. 12. I find no other source for the exact words *pugna pro patria*, although they are implied by passages in the Roman law.

[4] Floyd Seyward Lear, "The Public Law of the Visigothic Code," *Speculum*, XXVI (1951), 9; other examples in this Code, *ibid.*, 5, 7, 11. See also Kantorowicz, *A.H.R.*, LVI, 476, n. 14.

[5] *Leges Langobardorum* 3, 13 *de his qui ad patriam defendendam ire neglexerint* (etc.) cc. 1 and 3; also, 1, 37, 2—Charlemagne, "de armis intra patriam non portandis."

during Lent—a case of urgent necessity (Nicholas I, 866);[6] and a few years earlier Pope Leo IV assured the Franks that paradise was the reward of those who died "pro veritate fidei, et salvatione patriae, ac defensione Christianorum."[7] Thus the defense of the fatherland justified war, the just war of defense; and these and other papal letters, as well as passages from St. Augustine and St. Ambrose on the subject, were quoted by Gratian: C.23, q.1, c.3; q.2; q.3, c.5, and q.8, cc. 9 and 15.[8]

On these and other passages in the *Decretum* the decretists of the second half of the twelfth and the first quarter of the thirteenth century offer comments that are the more interesting because they refer at times to the Roman law on the defense of the *patria*. Naturally a war is just if it is declared and waged by the prince, in case of inevitable and urgent necessity, either for the *defensio patriae* or for the defense of the faith and the Church—"as when our *orientales*," says a decretist, "are bearing arms against the Saracens."[9] If the cause is just, says Huguccio, famous as a teacher of Innocent III, laymen may engage in war at any time; and, defining the just cause as *necessitas*, he adds that defense of the *patria* ("pro patria tuenda") and winning and preserving the peace are among the necessities or just causes.[10] This supreme necessity of defending the fatherland, it follows, makes lawful many things that are otherwise unlawful; if a man kills his father to defend the *patria* he is to be

---

[6] *Decretum*, C. 23, q. 8, c. 15 Si nulla urget; JE 2812.

[7] C. 23, q. 8, c. 9 Omni timore; JE 2642. Kantorowicz refers to this from the *Decretum* of Ivo of Chartres, but attributes it to Nicholas I; *A.H.R.*, LVI, 481.

[8] On the general theory of the just war, see Robert Regout, *La doctrine de la guerre juste de saint Augustin à nos jours d'après les théologiens et les canonistes catholiques*; and Stephan Kuttner, *Kanonistische Schuldlehre von Gratian bis auf die Dekretalen Gregors IX*, pp. 251ff.

[9] *Summa Coloniensis* (ca. 1169), in Paris, BN, MS lat. 14997, fol. 141–to C. 23, q. 8, c. 9: only public authorities can wage war; "inevitable and urgent necessity" makes a war just "pro defensione tam sua quam patrie"; it is just to fight for the faith and defend the Church, "ut cum orientales nostri contra sarracenas arma ferunt." On this *Summa* see Kuttner, *Repertorium*, pp. 170f.

[10] *Summa*, in Paris, BN, MS lat. 3892, fol. 265, to C. 23, q. 1, c. 1; on the *Summa*, Kuttner, *Repertorium*, pp. 155-160. Also the *Summa Parisiensis* (ca. 1260-70), to C. 23, q. 1: "Sed aliud est ob tuitionem patriae et ob necessitatem hostesque repellendos; aliud propter praedam militare"; ed. Terence P. McLaughlin, p. 210; and Joh. Faventinus, to C. 23, q. 2, c. Quod autem: *ratione rei*, a war is unjust "si non est de repetendis rebus, vel pro defensione patriae . . ."; quoted in the *Glos. ord.* of Joh. Teutonicus.

rewarded rather than punished—so Laurentius Hispanus.[11] Christian soldiers, indeed, says another, should obey the commands even of a Julian the Apostate when he is fighting *pro re publica* against the enemy.[12] Conversely, whoever incites the enemy against the *Respublica* is guilty of treason (*laesa majestas*), and subject to capital punishment (as in Roman law); and whoever flees from the field in a "public war" (i.e., just war) is punishable in the same way—and according to the Canon law is *infamis*.[13] About 1245 Johannes de Deo, in his *Liber poenitentiarius*, says that knights who fight against their own *patria* or are faithless to their lord are guilty of sin.[14]

Furthermore, a king must be ready and able to defend the *patria* or *regnum*. Failure to do so, the decretists explain, was the cause of Pope Zachariah's action in deposing the last of the

11 Paris, BN, MS lat. 15393, fol. 195ᵛ (on Laurentius's *Apparatus*, see Kuttner, *Repertorium*, pp. 76-80), to C. 23, q. 1, c. 3, ad v. *patriae*: "Multa enim licent pro defensione patrie que alias non licent, quia ille qui pro patria defendenda patrem interficit non punitur, immo etiam remuneratur, ff. de religio. minime [*D*. 11, 7, 35]. *la*." Laurentius adds, to c. 15 Si nulla (Nicholas I), ad v. *patriae*: "Magnus est favor patrie defendende, C. de infamibus [=ex quibus causis infamia irrogatur], neminem [*C*. 2, 12, 9], C. libro X, de latoribus, ex varia [*C*. 10, 11, 4], *lau*." On the words of St. Ambrose, "Fortitude is full of justice when in war it defends the *patria* from the barbarians" (23, q. 3, c. 5), the *Glos. ord.* of Joh. Teutonicus has this: "Hoc casu non tenetur, qui patrem proprium interficit, ut ff. de reli. l. minime." Note again the appeal to Roman law.

12 The *Apparatus* "Ius naturale," to C. 11, q. 3, c. 94 Iulianus (in Paris, BN, MS lat. 15393, fol. 138ʳ): "Iulianus imperator et apostata milites habebat sub se Christianos; et si precipiebat eis, ut idola colerent, vel alia mala facerent, non obediebant ei. Si vero precipiebat, ut contra hostes pro re publica dimicarent, obediebant."

13 *Glos. ord.* to C. 6, q. 1, c. 17 Infames: "Tales fugientes sunt rei laesae maiestatis, ut ff. ad le. iul. ma. lege tertia [*D*. 48, 4, 3], et capite puniuntur, nisi quando dominum defendere non potuerunt. . . ." (To *D*. 48, 4, 3, Accursius has this: whoever incites the enemy against the *Respublica* is guilty of *laesa majestas*.) Again, to Dist. 1, c. 10 Ius militare, ad v. *deseratur*: "Secundum canones, qui fugit in bello publico infamis est, ut vi.q.i. Infames. Secundum leges capite punitur, ut ff. de re militari, omne § qui in acie. Joan. Teutonicus."

14 Joh. de Deo (Brit. Mus., MS Royal 11 B v, fol. 139ʳ) Bk. vi, c. *De penitentia simplicium militum et cui debeant confiteri*: ". . . Peccant etiam quia quandoque impungnant propriam patriam, et non servant fidem proprio domino, contra sacros canones, ut probatur xxiii. q. i. c. qui(d) culpatur [c.4], et c. summa milicis (militiae) laus est [c. 7], et xxii. q. v. de forma [c. 18]." To C. 22, q. 5, c. 18 De forma fidelitatis, Joh. Teutonicus says that a vassal cannot aid his lord against his *patria propria* even if he has taken oath to aid him in all suits and against all enemies: "et licet generaliter iuret vasallus domino, scilicet quod in omnibus causis iuvabit ipsum, et contra quemlibet, tamen contra propriam patriam non iuvabit ipsum, ut ff. de rel. l. minime; nec contra papam. . . ."

Merovingians and absolving the Franks from their oaths of fealty to this *roi fainéant*. Gregory VII's letter containing the story (*Decretum* C. 15, q. 7, c. 3 Alius item) was frequently cited by canonists to prove that in special circumstances the pope could intervene in secular affairs, depose kings and emperors, and release subjects and vassals from oaths of homage and fealty. Here we are not interested in the distinction drawn between absolution from oaths to a king when he loses his *dignitas* (public power) and absolution when he is excommunicated. But it is important to note that a prince could be deposed not only *ratione peccati privati*, but also *ratione peccati publici*, for the sin of refusing to defend his realm. Thus Stephen of Tournai, *ca.* 1160-1170, tells how Charles Martel earned his nickname by striking and overcoming enemies, and how he successfully waged war on the enemies of the realm while the king of the Franks was leading a soft and effeminate life. Hence, Charles wrote to the pope, asking for an answer to this question: Who was the more worthy of the royal crown ("corona regni"), he who lived in pleasure and idleness, chambering dissolutely with women, or he who sweated in battle and in camp, constantly fighting "pro regno"? When the pope replied, "he who fought for the kingdom and repelled the enemy," Charles refused the crown for himself, but made his son, Pepin, king, and expelled him who was useless to the kingdom.[15] (We must not worry about the historical accuracy of this version of the story.) Stephen speaks of fighting for the *regnum*; but the author of a different version of the story says, "qui acie pro quiete patrie laboraret," and "qui pro communi salute bella gereret."[16]

---

[15] *Summa*, in Paris, BN, MS lat. 3913, fol. 77ᵛ-78ʳ; I have not consulted the partial edition by J. F. von Schulte; see Kuttner, *Repertorium*, pp. 133-136. Johannes Faventinus copies Stephen in relating the story, Paris, BN, MS lat. 14606, fol. 97ᵛ; Kuttner, p. 145.

[16] In the *Summa* "Elegantius in iure divino," Paris, BN, MS lat. 14997, fol. 109 (cf. Kuttner, pp. 170f.), to C. 15, q.6, c. Alius; I am not sure of the authorship, for the comment is in the form of a gloss to words used by the author of the *Summa*, ad v. *Zacharias*: "Legitur in historia francorum, quod karolus tudes, cum esset princeps militie cuiusdam regis francorum, qui molles et effeminatus otio torpebat, hostes fortiter debellabat. Unde a tundendo hostes sic dictus est, quem ob eandem causam usque hodie francigene martelum vulgariter appellant. Iste remissam regis ignaviam attendens, domino apostolico scripsit, ut responsis

Defense of *patria* or realm was of course a supreme necessity; it was for the common safety and welfare; and it made lawful the ruler's demand for extraordinary taxes to enable him to wage a just war against the aggressor.[17] Usually in their discussion of necessity and lay taxation of the clergy, the canonists speak of *civitas, Respublica,* and *regnum* (*regnum* in a gloss of the late twelfth or early thirteenth century).[18] But Vincentius Hispanus in a gloss (1210-1215) to a decretal of Innocent III associated extraordinary taxation with the poverty or necessity of the *patria,* and he was followed by Johannes Teutonicus.[19]

Turning to the legists—the glossators from Irnerius to Odofredo, and the commentators from Odofredo to Bartolus—we find the love of *patria* stated more often than in the canonists. (It is remarkable, given the frequency of the word in the *Corpus iuris civilis,* that the legists did not discuss it more than they

---

suis docere vellet, quis regno dignior haberetur, qui deliciis luxurie vacaret *an qui acie pro quiete patrie laboraret.* Cumque rescriptum esset eum corona regni digniorem esse, *qui pro communi salute bella gereret,* ignavum illum de regno expulit, et pro eo filium proprium pipinum, postea caroli magni patrem, coronavit." Italics are mine, as in the following quotations.

17 See above, Introduction, and ch. III § 4; v §§ 2, 3; and Le Bras, *L'immunité réelle,* pp. 21-30, 49-148.

18 Le Bras, *op.cit.,* pp. 21-30, observing that the papal legislation on the subject (1179 and 1215) envisaged the Italian commune, finds no extension to kingdoms until the mid-thirteenth century. But the gloss I found is in an early *Apparatus* to *Comp. I* (see Kuttner, *Repertorium,* pp. 323, 338), tit. *De iure patron.,* c. Preterea (3, 34, 29) and specifically mentions the *regnum*: ". . . Tamen in necessitate, puta pro tuitione regni, potest rex a suis hominibus auxilium postulare; moderate tamen . . . infra, de immunitate, non minus" (Paris, BN, MS lat. 15398, fol. 253ᵛ). This gloss was written before 1215, since the *Non minus* of 1179, but not its extension in the *Adversus* of 1215, is mentioned; and after 1188-92, the date of *Comp. I.* See *Decr. Greg. IX* 3, 49, 4 and 7. In 1226 Honorius III permitted Henry III to tax the English clergy for the necessity of war, and thereafter it was assumed that kingdoms as well as *civitates* were covered by the Canon law on taxation and necessity.

19 Vinc. (Bamberg, MS Can. 20, fol. 160ᵛ), *Apparatus* to *Comp. III* (cf. Kuttner, pp. 356, 360), tit. *De censibus et exactionibus,* c. Cum instantia (3, 37, 2; *Decr. Greg. IX* 3, 39, 17): "Ultra facultates enim ecclesie ab aliquo procuratio exigenda non est, x. q. iii. illud [c. 4] *Si enim tenuis est patria tua, extraordinario iuditio est iuvanda,* C. ne nova vec. l. i. [*C.* 4, 42, 1]. Immo a paupere non debent eam exigere . . . nec tenuis vite homines sub pretextu adventus officialium vel militum brevi suppellectili ad eorum usus translata iniuriis vexentur." Note the word *iuditio* (for *iudicio*); it is probably the copier's error and should be *auxilio.* Joh. Teut., *Apparatus* to *Comp. III* (cf. Kuttner, p. 357) in Paris, BN, MS lat. 3930, fol. 183ᵛ, c. cit., ad v. *pregravari*: "Ultra facultatem enim ecclesie ab aliquo procuracio non est exigenda. . . . *Si enim tenuis est patria tua, extraordinario auxilio iure iuvanda est,* C. ne nova vectigalia, l. i. . . ."

did; but they preferred *Respublica*.) Placentinus, in the introduction to his *Summa* on the *Tres Libri* (Books 10-12 of the *Code*), tells how he returned from Montpellier to his *patria*, Mantua; and on the sale or alienation of property belonging to a *civitas* (*C.* 11, 31, 3), his continuator and pupil Pillius says that the *curiales*, or their *maior pars*, must take oath that the sale was for the utility of the *patria*.[20] Like Vincentius Hispanus and Johannes Teutonicus, the great Azo, on *C.* 4, 62, 1, says that for the common utility the emperor can consent to the levy of a new tax "ratione tenuitatis et paupertatis patrie."[21]

In the *Glossa ordinaria* of Accursius (*ca.* 1228), obedience to *patria* and parents, like reverence for God and the right of resisting hostile force, is made a principle of the *ius gentium*. Therefore, "Pugna pro patria!"[22] To every one, says Accursius, his own *patria* is *dulcissima*, and a sentence of exile is naturally a heavy penalty.[23] If the fatherland is sweet and one should fight for it, it is high treason to fight against it or betray it—again

---

[20] Paris, BN, MS lat. 4543, fol. 218.

[21] *Summa Codicis*, fol. 122ᵛ; also in ed. Venice, 1584, col. 449.

[22] To *Inst.* 1, 2, 1 ad v. *omnes gentes utuntur*: "Ut est religio erga deum, ut parentibus et patriae pareamus, ut contra violentiam resistamus. . . ." In *D.* 1, 1, 2, Pomponius says: "Veluti erga Deum religio, ut parentibus et patriae pareamus." To this the *Glos. ord.* ad v. *parentibus*: "Nota, filium debere patri obedire . . ."; ad v. *patriae*: "Pugna pro patria, ut hic, et C. de aboli. l. fallaciter [*C.* 9, 42, 3], et infra, ad leg. Iul. maie. l. pen. [*D.* 48, 4, 10]." The right of self-defense is sometimes made a principle of natural law as well as of *jus gentium* by the canonists; below, n. 62.

[23] To *D.* 32, 1, 99 ad v. *scripsit*: "Hic sequitur Graecum [the Greek words quoted by Scaevola], cuius interpretatio incipit, *patriae meae dulcissimae*. . . . Et nota, cuilibet suam patriam dulcissimam, sic supra, de of. prefec. urb. l. 1. § pen. *Accurs.*" The reference is to *D.* 1, 12, 1, 13 Et Urbe, where it is said that the prefect of Rome can forbid to anyone the city of Rome or Italy or his own province; on which a gloss, ad v. *provincia*: "Si hoc expresse dicat . . . patria sua ei interdici videtur, ut inf. de interd. et rele. l. relegatorum § Constitutum est, que est contra." Here the reference is to *D.* 48, 22, 7, 15, where it is said that if anyone is forbidden his own *patria*, he is forbidden Rome, too; but if forbidden Rome, "patria sua interdictum non videtur"; on this, the glosses ad v. *patria*: "scilicet sua propria"; ad v. *patria sua*: "Ut pote minori" (that is, one's own *patria* or *civitas* other than Rome is inferior to Rome, which, as appears in other glosses, is the *communis patria*; see the following gloss and below where I discuss the scope of *patria*); and ad v. *etiam ab urbe*: "Roma, per excellentiam . . . quae et sua patria est, et quidem maior. . . ." The point is that if a man is exiled from Rome, he is not also exiled from his local *patria* unless it is specifically named by the *praetor*; if exiled from his own *patria*, he is, however, forbidden Rome.

Cato, "Pugna pro patria."[24] *Pro patria mori*, though stated in different words, is glorious. Indeed, those who fall in battle for the *Respublica* live forever in fame and glory, but those who live in exile and shame are dead already. Eternal glory, moreover, is theirs who are killed in tournaments for the entertainment of the public.[25] Thus, in part through the revival of the Roman law, worldly glory appears as an ideal in the thirteenth century along with the equally worldly love of fatherland.

Again, it is no crime if a son kills his father, or the father his son, in defense of the *patria*, as Marcellus says, *D.* 11, 7, 35. But Accursius adds that the son is guilty of parricide unless he kills his father in self-defense.[26] The implication seems to be that the son can lawfully kill his father only if the father directly attacks him, not simply because the father is participating in an attack on the *patria*. Anyone, of course, who attacks or betrays the *patria* is guilty of the *crimen laesae majestatis*, for Cato says, "Pugna pro patria."[27] And anyone who deserts his *patria* is impious.[28]

24 To *D.* 1, 1, 2 (on obedience to parents and *patria*), ad v. *patriae*: "Pugna pro patria ut dixit Cato . . ."; to *C.* 9, 43 (42), 3, 4 Sin autem, on torture in cases of "violata maiestate aut *patria oppugnata, vel prodita*," ad v. *prodita*: "Et iste incidit in crimen laesae maiestatis . . . et Cato, Pugna pro patria"; to *C.* 2, 12, 9 (dishonor, *infamia*, shall attend no one who defends the public business of his *patria*), ad v. *ob defensa*: "In libro Martini est *ob non defensa*; et est plana. Videbatur enim quedam infamia, cum Cato dicat, pugna pro patria. . . . Sed alii habent *ob defensa*. . . ."

25 *Glos. ord.* to *Inst.* 1, 25, § Et constat, ad v. *per gloriam vivere*: "Nota, mortuum vivere per gloriam, ut ff. ad leg. aqui. l. qua actione § si quis in colluctatione [*D.* 9, 2, 7, 4]. Et econtra quis fingitur mortuus, qui vivit per vituperium, ut deportati. . . ." The same thought is expressed in the gloss ad v. *gloriae causa*, *D.* 9, 2, 7, 4: "Per gloriam occiditur, ut hic [that is, killed *in publico certamine*—in this case, tournaments or other combats for public entertainment, as the gloss interprets these words]: et ideo per gloriam vivere potest: licet sic mortuus dicatur, ut Inst. de excu. tut. § j. . . ." Finally, to *D.* 3, 2, 25 (Papinian: ". . . Si quis in bello ceciderit, etsi corpus eius non compareat, lugebitur"), Accursius says, ad v. *ceciderit*: "Qui per gloriam vivere intelligitur, ut Inst. de accusation. tut. in prin." (On tournaments, of course, since they were prohibited by the Church, the canonists taught otherwise.)

26 To *D.* 11, 7, 35 ad v. *occidisset*: "Scilicet, se defendendo: alias tenetur lege Pompeia de parricidiis [*D.* 48, 9, 1] . . . Accursius."

27 *Glos. ord.* to *C.* 9, 43 (42), 3, 4, ad vv. *violatae maiestatis, aut patria oppugnata, vel prodita*: "Et iste incidit in crimen laesae maiestatis . . .; et Cato, Pugna pro patria." Cf. *D.* 48, 4, 10, on the *crimen maiestatis* for betrayal of the city.

28 To *C.* 10, 37, 1 (*curiales* shall not desert their *civitates*; in escaping from their *patria* they are *impii*) ad v. *demonstraverint*: "Et ita notari posset hic,

A famous maxim of Roman law (often repeated by canonists and legists) was that the public welfare must always be preferred to the private—except, normally, the Canon law stated, when the public interest may endanger one's private salvation for the life eternal. No one, therefore, who serves the public utility can at the same time serve private interests. A soldier, for example, because he exists for the *utilitas publica,* cannot act as the agent of his father or mother (*C.* 2, 13, 7). "Everyone," says the author of a summary of this law, "is more closely bound to his *patria* than to his parents, for when it is a question of an act that concerns the *status publicus,* the *patria* is preferred to the parents."[29] Finally, when there are too few *honesti viri,* the necessity of the *patria* may justify the elevation of unworthy men to the municipal decurionate,[30] or even the creation of a minor as decurion.[31] Some men, however, are excused from certain public burdens imposed on others for the common utility of the *patria.* Teachers of the trivium and of medicine do not have to serve as guardians in their own *patria,* and they enjoy the like privilege in the *communis patria,* which is Rome. But doctors of the laws enjoy immunity only in Rome. To these passages (*D.* 27, 1, 7 and 50, 6, 9; *Inst.* 1, 25, 15 Item Romae) the glosses, in which the same use of the word *patria* occurs, add that doctors of the laws are exempt not only in Rome but in Beirut and, of course, Bologna; and that worthy teachers, but not exceeding the number that the *patria* can support, are excused from all public *munera.*[32]

---

quod impium est, relinquere propriam patriam." Cf. *D.* 49, 15, 19, 4: "Nam qui malo consilio, et proditoris animo patria relinquit, hostium numero habendus est."

[29] "Casus . . . Et sic habes, quod quis magis astringitur patriae quam parenti. . . . Nam ubi agitur de statu publico, bene praefertur patria parenti, ut hic. . . ." The *casus* belongs to the late thirteenth or the fourteenth century. The "public state" probably means "public order" or "welfare," not the State.

[30] *D.* 50, 2, 12, and *Glos. ord.* ad v. *petere:* "id est habere. Nec enim honores peti debent, sed offeri . . . ; vel forte in casu loquitur ut *patriae necessitas* hoc exigeret. . . ."

[31] *C.* 2, 42, 1: "scilicet quod *urgentibus patriae necessitatibus* decurio minor annis creatus sit"; gloss ad v. *urgentibus:* "Quia deficiebant idonei: alias minores non admittuntur"—again *patria* is not used by the glossator, but obviously he has it in mind.

[32] See these passages and the glosses, especially to *Inst.* 1, 25, 15, ad v. *grammatici;* and to *D.* 27, 1, 7; cf. *C.* 10, 52, 11.

Odofredo, the first of the great commentators, about the middle of the thirteenth century, adds the specific ideal of the good citizen to the concept of *patria*. "The *bonus civis*," he says, "is he who defends the rights (*iura*) of his *patria*: and it is he, not one hostile to the fatherland, who should be chosen to govern (*ad regimen*)."[33] The Church (that is, local churches and ecclesiastics) is included in the *patria*, and must assume its share of its burdens. In Odofredo, moreover, we find a fuller statement of the theory of Johannes Teutonicus that the duty to defend the *patria* is higher than the feudal obligation of vassal to lord. Is a vassal, he asks, obliged to aid his lord against his own father?[34] No, he answers, for then a father might lawfully kill his son, or a son his father. But if *pro patria* a son can be against his father (*D.* 11, 7, 35),[35] so much the more can a vassal be against his lord in times of just wars, for these wars are waged to defend the *patria* and are always licit (*Decretum*, C. 23, q. 8, c. 15 Si nulla). No one, he continues, may be accused of *infamia* while defending the *iura* of the fatherland, as in *C.* 2, 12, 9.[36] For the *Respublica*, a thing is lawful that otherwise is unlawful, as in *D.* 49, 14, 2;[37] and as Cato says, "Pugna pro patria." A son, finally, must put the *salus Reipublicae* before his filial obligations.[38]

---

[33] *Glossa super pace Constantie*, ad vv. "qui nec contra civitatem, nec nostram maiestatem": "Nota ar. quod ille est bonus civis qui patrie iura tueatur, ut ff. de abol. l. fallaciter [*C.* (not *D.*) 9, 42, 3], de relig. minime [*D.* 11, 7, 35]." I consulted Odofredo's glosses to the Peace of Constance in the Paris, BN, MS lat. 5414A, fol. 14ʳ. In his gloss, as quoted in the commentary of Baldus to the same, there is the addition of the idea of the *bonus civis* in government: "No. arg. quod bonus civis est, qui patriae iura tueatur, et ille ad regimen eligendus, non autem qui est contra patriam. Odof." (Venice edition, 1592, of the *Corpus juris civilis*, v, 505). To *D.* 1, 1, 2-4 Odofredo says: ". . . prius debes obedire patrie quam patri."

[34] To *C.* 10, 48, 3 (on the duty of all, in time of need, to help in building walls and furnishing grain): Odofredo, on the *Tres Libri Codicis*, Lyons, 1550, fol. 46ᵛ; cf. 10, 48, 2; Joh. Teutonicus, to C. 22, q. 5, c. 18; also Joh. de Deo, *Liber poenitentiarius*, vi, c. *De penitentia simplicium militum*; both texts quoted above, n. 14.

[35] This is the passage, referred to above, n. 26 (and repeatedly by canonists and legists), on the right of a son to kill his father in defense of the *patria*.

[36] The law in the *Code* reads: "Neminem sequitur infamia ob defensa publica negotia patriae suae."

[37] One who is a *delator* to the *fiscus* in the name of the *Respublica* is not guilty of *infamia*.

[38] Odofredo, *Summa in usus feudorum*, Compluti (Alcalà de Henarez), 1584, fol. 76ᵛ; I consulted the same treatise under the title *Rationes usus feodorum*, in

The ideal of the *patria* expressed by the legists was being transferred by the middle of the century from Rome and any *civitas* (more on this distinction later) to the kingdoms outside the Holy Roman Empire. In his discussion of the royal authority, legislation, and public law, Bracton associates the *tuitio* or *defensio patriae* with the superior right and power of the king to defend the kingdom of England.[39] Jean de Blanot, *ca.* 1250, claiming for the king of France the same supreme powers of jurisdiction that the emperor has in the Empire, declares that the vassals of the king's vassals are directly subject to the king not by reason of homage, but by reason of this jurisdiction. Hence if a baron should rise against the king and is thus guilty of treason, his vassals shall not aid him. And if the duke of Burgundy is waging war against the duke of Lorraine, while the king of France is fighting the king of Germany (*Alamania*), "who wishes to conquer the crown of France," the vassals of the duke of Burgundy must obey the summons, not of the duke, but of the king, to whom they are subject by reason of his general jurisdiction and his superior tribunal. But they must obey the king's summons to the army above all because it is for the de-

---

the Paris, BN, MS lat. 16008, fol. 86ʳ-86ᵛ; I offer here the text of this title, "Contra quos tenetur vassalus iuvare dominum, et contra quos non," chiefly from the MS, with corrections from the edition of 1584: ". . . Sed quero nunquid contra patrem tenetur vassallus adiuvare dominum? Et videtur quod non, quia tunc pater filium, et filius patrem potest interficere, ff. de relig. et sumpt. fun. l. minime [*D.* 11, 7, 35]. Si ergo contra patrem potest esse filius pro patria, multo plus vassallus potest ["est" in ed.; om. in MS] contra dominum; et enim ["et cum" in ed.] iusta bella, que fiunt pro patria defendenda, unde omni tempore possunt fieri, ut in Decretis xxiij. q. 8, cap. si nulla [c. 15—Pope Nicholas I; cf. n. 6 above]. Nec enim infamatur qui iura patrie defendit, C. de infam. l. nemine [*C.* 10, 57; but the correct reference is in the edition, "C. ex quib. cau. infa. irrog. l. neminem"=*C.* 2, 12, 9]. Sed et pro re publica licet quod alias non liceret, ff. de iure fisci. l. ii. in prin. [*D.* 49, 14, 2], et Cato, 'Pugna pro patria.' Nec distinguo contra quem; et alias filius debet preponere salutem Rei publicae ["Rei publicae" omitted in MS] contra patrem, ut ar. in Auth. ut cum de app. cognosce. § causas vero. vers. si eas pro et contra [Auth. 8.12 § Causas autem, ver. "si eos in criminalibus"=Nov. 115]; sed ar. ff. de fam. l. fi. in prin. et § 1 [*D.* 10, 2, 1, 1—this ref. not in the ed.]; arg. ff. de his qui notant. infa. l. fin. § 1 [*D.*3, 2, 25, 1—this ref. not in MS]. Odofre."

[39] (Ed. Woodbine), II, 19-59, especially p. 28: the waging of war *ad tuitionem patriae* belongs to the prince; and p. 32: the king associates with himself magnates and knights, and girds them with swords, "ut cum rege . . . militent, et defendant patriam et populum dei"; for the sword "significat defensionem regni et patriae."

fense of the crown and for the *bona tocius patrie* or "bonum publicum regni gallie cuius administrationem gerit." They are bound to obey these commands "pugnando pro patria," according to the *ius gentium* (*D.* 1, 1, 2). Again, if it is lawful to fight *pro patria* against one's father, it is the more lawful for the duke's vassals to obey the king. Besides, the duke's summons is only for his own private utility, but the king's is for the public utility, which must be placed above the private (*D.* 17, 2, 65, 5). Only if the king summons them for anything that does not touch the public utility should the vassals obey their overlord, the duke.[40]

This theory is repeated by the French legist of Orléans and Toulouse, Jacques de Révigny, *ca.* 1280, who says that the king of France has no superior, that he is the supreme judge in the realm, and that the vassals of the duke of Burgundy must heed the royal summons, because the *utilitas publica* is preferred to the particular when it is a case of the *tuitio reipublicae*, i.e., of France and the crown.[41] He adds that among the Romans the defense of castles (*castra*) came before the love of children.[42] Then he raises the question of the relative importance of the local *patria*, or native land, and the *patria communis*, Rome. Suppose, he says, that the *Carses*[43] are invading Burgundy and a vassal of the duke is summoned by the duke and the king at the same time. Which call should he heed? In both cases the public utility is concerned. "You may say," Jacques continues, "that if he goes to the king and thus permits the destruction of his sons, land, and property, it will be hard indeed. Now I say that he should not go to the king: he should fight for his own

[40] The text of Jean de Blanot's *Tractatus super feudis et homagiis* is published by J. Acher, "Notes sur le droit savant au moyen âge," *Nouvelle revue historique de droit français et étranger*, xxx (1906), 125-178, especially pp. 160ff.; see also Calasso, *I glossatori e la teoria della sovranità*, 2nd ed., 112-121. The treatise actually is a chapter from Jean's *De actionibus*; see E. M. Meijers, *Responsa doctorum Tholosanorum*, p. vi n. 4.

[41] Pierre de Tourtoulon, *Les oeuvres de Jacques de Révigny* (*Jacobus de Ravanis*) *d'après deux manuscrits de la Bibliothèque Nationale*, pp. 48-50. Tourtoulon edits a part of the text from MS lat. 14350.

[42] He refers here to *D.* 49, 15, 19, 7, "quia disciplina castrorum antiquior fuit parentibus Romanis quam charitas liberorum." The *Glos. ord.* interprets *charitas* as *patria potestas*, introduced into the civil law because of the love of children.

[43] I am unable to identify the *Carses*.

fatherland (*et pugna pro patria*). But they (some *doctores legum*) say that just as Rome is the *communis patria*, so the "corona regni est communis patria," because it is the head (of the kingdom). But if Rome and your own *patria* both summon you, to which will you respond? Rome is the *caput mundi*. "Yet I say that you will remain in your own *patria*. You say that Rome is the common *patria*, and your *patria* is your own. Now you ought to prefer your own to the common *patria*." If the written law (*lex*) is lacking, local custom may be followed. "Therefore one's own *patria* (rather than the *patria communis*) should be preferred. He (the vassal) will therefore first defend his own land." But some hold that "it is worse for the *caput orbis* to be conquered than for a part: consequently you are bound to defend the common rather than your local *patria*." Nonetheless, Jacques concludes, "I say the contrary, as I have said."[44]

Thus Jacques de Révigny raises the question: in case of two necessities or just wars that concern the local and the common *patriae* at the same time, which *patria* has the prior claim on one's loyalty? The local *patria*, he answers. Otherwise, however, in case of a just war for the defense of crown, kingdom, and the common welfare, the kingdom of France is the supreme *patria*. In fact, the French legists held that the common or public utility of the realm was a higher end than that of any part thereof, and the common *patria* of the kingdom therefore superior to any local *patria* of city or province. Such also is the

[44] For most of this theory I have consulted the Paris, BN, MS lat. 14350, fol. 185ʳ–185ᵛ; here Jacques de Révigny is commenting on *Inst.* 4, 6, 13: "Sed pone Carses ingrediuntur Burgundiam, et ego sum homo ducis. Dux . . . scribit pro me, et rex pro me. Quid erit in hoc casu, ad quem vadam ego? Utrinque versatur utilitas publica. Si dicas, tenetur ire ad regem, et permittet destruere filios suos et terram suam et bona sua perire, hoc esset durissimum; hec esset separatio durissima, que vitanda est. Nunc dicerem non ire ad regem . . . ; et pugna pro patria. Ipsi dicunt contrarium . . . quia Roma est communis patria, sic corona regni est communis patria, quia caput. Ego quesivi. Alias Roma vocat te. Ad quem ibis? Patria vocat te. Ad quem ibis? Roma caput est mundi. . . . Dico quod stabis in patria tua. Dices quod Roma est communis patria, et patria tua est propria. Nunc debes preferre patriam propriam patrie communi. . . . Item lex dicit, si lex scripta deficit, inspicienda est consuetudo loci propria; ergo et patria propria preferenda est, ar. l. ff. de leg. et sen. con. l. de quibus, circa prin. [*D.* 1, 3, 32]. Et ideo hic primo defendet terram propriam." Some hold that "deterius quod caput orbis subiugeretur hostibus imperii quam pars; ideo teneris defendere patriam communem, scilicet Romam, quam patriam propriam. Dico tamen contrarium, ut dixi."

implication of Pierre de Belleperche's argument, that Paris is the *communior et excellentior civitas in regno francie*, like Rome in the Empire—he refers to *D.* 50, 1, 33; "Roma communis nostra patria est."[45] "They made Paris their Rome," says Geoffroi de Nés (de Paris) of the men who conducted Philip IV's quarrel with Boniface VIII.[46] The king's jurisdiction, Pierre implies, exercised for the common welfare and defense of the common fatherland of the realm, of which Paris is the center, is supreme, and the more so because he recognizes no superior and is emperor in his own realm. Only the king, therefore, says Jean Faure (Johannes Faber) in the fourteenth century, can levy taxes *ob necessitatem patriae* or *ob utilitatem publicam;* neither *barones* nor towns can do so, although towns and other corporations can levy taxes for local needs from their own members.[47]

If the feudal kingdom is now treated as a *patria communis*, can a Frenchman be loyal to the older, more universal common fatherland, Rome and the Empire? In case of conflict between the two, to which does he owe his loyalty? The lawyers do not, to my knowledge, directly tackle this question, but I think they answer it indirectly. Of course, Pierre Dubois would solve the problem by substituting French for German control of the traditional Empire, by making Philip IV the emperor even outside his own realm.[48] But the French legists, like those supporting other national monarchies, base their answer on the theory that each kingdom is independent of the Empire, for the king has no superior and is emperor in his own realm. Consequently, in the event of a war between such a kingdom and the Empire, or

45 See below, n. 54.

46 Quoted by H. Kämpf, *Pierre Dubois und die geistigen Grundlagen des französischen Nationalbewusstseins*, p. 91:

"Si firent de Paris leur Rome
Ou Saint Pierre oncques ne sist."

47 *Summa Codicis*, Lyons, 1594, to *C.* 4, 62, 1: "Argumentum, quod villa vel collegium non possit indicere collectas, nec barones ob necessitatem patriae. . . . Quod verum est de collegio et universitate super extraneis, sed super illis de sua universitate sic. . . . Sed de barone non credo. . . . Et hoc tenet Hostiensis, videlicet, quod nullus possit indicere, nisi princeps. . . . Item dic, quod nec princeps potest indicere, nisi ob necessitatem vel utilitatem publicam, quin peccet. . . ." He refers, of course, to the great canonist, Henry of Susa. The opinion was common among the legists of the thirteenth century and earlier.

48 See below, n. 158.

between the kingdoms themselves, the subjects of each king must fight for their own common *patria* against the other—each king, of course, will proclaim that he is waging a just war of defense. Thus, each kingdom is a fully independent sovereign nation, and nationalism in the modern sense of the word is almost fully at hand even in legal theory, as it is in fact. Appeals to the pope as the spiritual head of Christendom and as the ultimate arbitrator of national quarrels were futile and could not stop the development.[49]

But let us see how this legal theory of national sovereignty developed—obviously there is no need of explaining how the fact preceded the theory. Of course, the theory of the unity of Christendom in Holy Roman Empire and Church still flourished, and the legists generally held that Rome was the true *Respublica* and *patria communis*, while each *civitas* and kingdom within the Empire was a lesser *Respublica* and a *patria propria*.[50] As Professor Kantorowicz remarks, in Italy *patria* usually meant the city-state, but by the time of Dante and Petrarch it also meant Italy as a whole.[51] Perhaps the idea of Rome as the common fatherland, coupled with the tradition of Rome as the capital of Italy, had some influence on their thought. Anyhow, the distinction between the common and local *patriae* appeared by the early thirteenth century among the decretists.[52] By this time, too, certain canonists were stating another theory that led to the idea that the local *patria* was *communis* for all within it and independent of Rome and the Empire. This was the theory, alluded to already, that the kings of England, France, and Spain recognized no superior on earth, and were emperors in their own realms. It will be treated separately in Part 2 of this chapter—only this much need be said in the present context: in this theory, by implication and by

[49] See below, nn. 101, 107, 155; Jacques de Révigny hesitates to make France independent.

[50] See *D.* 27, 1, 7 and 49, 1, 33 ("Roma communis patria nostra est"), and *Inst.* 1, 25, 15 Item Romae, and the *Glossa ordinaria* thereto; I have referred to some of the glosses above in another connection. As for *Respublica* used for kingdoms and cities, the evidence is too abundant and well known to be discussed here.

[51] *A.H.R.*, LVI, 477 n. 18.

[52] See below, n. 85.

direct statement, the kingdom is not a part of the Roman Empire. Consequently, the public law transferred to the king and kingdom is no longer limited, and the realm becomes an independent state. Finally, when the kingdom is called the *communis patria*, or simply *patria*, the word *patria* loses its connotation of mere *civitas* as it loses that of loyalty to Rome and the Empire of the whole Christian world. It acquires the sense of national localism, of national patriotism indeed, at the very time that the national monarchic State is being constituted. The king becomes the "pater patriae, caput rei publicae."[53] To be sure, the French legists like Jacques de Révigny, Pierre de Belleperche, and Jean Faure can still hesitate to talk of actual conflict between the kingdom and the Empire, but at least they do not envisage the king's obeying the emperor.

In the early fourteenth century and later the idea of *patria* as kingdom found continued expression. Of the numerous sources that might reveal it, I have consulted only a few. For example, Pierre de Belleperche, adviser to Philip IV, drawing the analogy with Rome asserts that Paris is the *communior et excellentior civitas in regno francie*, and refers to *D.* 50, 1, 33 "Roma communis nostra patria est."[54] Publicists and canonists, too, continued to recognize the king's right to extraordinary taxes, even from the clergy, in times of necessity or just wars for the defense

[53] So in a letter of Guillaume de Maire, bishop of Angers, to Philip IV in 1299; Célestin Port, ed., *Le Livre de Guillaume le Maire*, p. 179. The bishop, sending the grievances of his clergy, naturally holds that the prince is subject to divine and human law; otherwise he is a tyrant; and he refers to John of Salisbury, *Policraticus*, IV, 1. *Pater patriae* had been expressed earlier; see Koht, in *A.H.R.*, LII, p. 266; Kantorowicz, *A.H.R.*, LVI, pp. 474, 476.

[54] In Paris, BN, MS lat. 4488, fol. 192ᵛ: ". . . nam quemadmodum in imperio excellentior et communior est civitas romana, ita in regno francie communior et excellentior civitas est parisius." Cf. Joh. de Deo, below, nn. 110f.: "nisi esset in regno aliqua principalis civitas, que esset caput regni, in qua rex iste habuisset domicilium principale." Hence, just as in the empire, a case involving parties in any *civitas*, say Chartres, may be brought to Paris, because it is the common city and there the king's superior jurisdiction is exercised; but the local customs of Chartres should be respected. Pierre concludes, however, that the judge in Paris has the right to decide whether the customs of Chartres should carry weight. Respect for the customs of the local *patria* or *civitas* was a principle of Roman law, and it was repeated in the *Decretum* of Gratian, Dist. 4 c. 2 (Isidore of Seville): "Erit autem lex . . . et secundum consuetudinem patriae loco temporique conveniens . . ."; on which a gloss, *ca.* 1200: "Ut scilicet concordet bonis moribus patrie in qua statuitur . . ." (Paris, BN, MS nouv. acq. lat. 1576, fol. 21ᵛ).

of the *patria* (of course, as I remarked above, nearly all legists, canonists, and publicists discuss this in terms of the *regnum* or *Respublica*). Aegidius Romanus states that the king must serve his subjects by defending the *patria*, and only for this purpose does he dispose of their property; he rules for the common good.[55] Pierre Jame (Petrus Jacobi), in his *Aurea practica libellorum* (1311-1329), offers a lengthy discussion of the independence of the king of France and his powers of taxation for the necessities of war. As Cato says, *Pugna pro patria!*—and it is impious to desert one's own *patria*.[56] In the second half of the fourteenth century the great Neapolitan jurist, Lucas de Penna, calls the defense of the *patria* a *lex virtutis*, and says that nothing is sweeter (*nil dulcius*) than the *patria*, and that everyone is obligated to provide for the *patriae utilitatibus* and work for the *Respublica*.[57] Philip of Leyden wrote a treatise of great importance for the historian of public law, *De cura rei publicae et sorte principis*, and dedicated it to the Count of Holland. He develops fully the theory of the State or of the common welfare and necessity as something above all private interests; and of course, the *defensio patriae* and *salus publica* are the supreme necessity or reason of State.[58] About 1338, in order to help forestall, probably, papal measures against the war plans of Edward III, William of Ockham declared that the pope's *plenitudo potestatis* could not legally prevent the king of England from taxing the clergy for the defense of the *patria*. For the *defensio patriae et iurium regiorum* is a *causa pia*: in such a case of necessity, no special privilege can exempt ecclesiastical property. He appeals to *quod omnes tangit*: since what touches all must be approved of all, and all must take care of what touches all, and since an attack on the kingdom and the rights of the

---

[55] In a treatise attributed to Aegidius, *An et quomodo possint reges bona regni ecclesiis elargiri*, Paris, BN, MS lat. 6786, fol. 22-41ᵛ, especially 24ᵛ–25ᵛ: ". . . Potestates enim terrene sunt ministri dei et serviunt hiis quibus prefiunt, in hoc ipsum videlicet patriam deffendendo. . . . Oportet quod in necessitate habeat omnia illa [property] ad subventionem. . . ." On the authenticity of this treatise see C. Bruni, *Le opere di Egidio Romano*, p. 136, no. 57.

[56] Ed. Cologne, 1575, fol. 277-279, 278ʳ. See below, to n. 152.

[57] *Com. in Tres Posteriores Libros Codicis*, Lyons, 1597, to C. 10, 31, 52; 10, 37, 1; 10, 43, 2.

[58] Eds. R. Fruin and P. C. Molhuysen, pp. 36-41, esp. 38 (casus VI).

king touches all, both clergy and laity, therefore all must offer aid for the defense. Besides, if property is given to churches for pious causes, it is more pious to defend the *patria* than to feed the poor, for the common good is higher than the good of one, and the *bonum totius patriae* is better and more divine than the *bonum pauperum illius patriae*. It is better, then, for the clergy to give money to help the king for the *defensio patriae* than to help the poor, when the laity is not wealthy enough to do so alone.[59]

Not always, however, does the love of *patria* receive praise. In the early thirteenth century Johannes Teutonicus had maintained that all kings were subject to the emperor.[60] More than a century later, Guillaume de Montlauzun († 1343), a French canonist, scornfully said "perchance *favor patrie*, which takes the place of flesh and blood, revealed this to him." But Guillaume himself asserted that *de iure* the king of France and certain other kings did not recognize the emperor as their superior.[61] One detects a bit of French patriotism in this criticism of the Teutonic.

To sum up, the legal sources, like the classics and political treatises, show that the love of *patria* clearly meant fighting for the *patria*—*Pugna pro patria*, as the canonists and legists frequently said, quoting the distich attributed in late antiquity to Cato. And fighting often meant *pro patria mori*. In the thought of some of the lawyers, moreover, by 1300, *de jure* as well as *de facto* the *patria* of the kingdom became the common one for all the people of the kingdom, thus replacing the old universal Rome as the *patria communis*. In the canonists and

[59] *An princeps pro suo succursu, scilicet guerrae, possit recipere bona ecclesiarum, etiam invito papa*, eds. H. S. Offler and R. H. Snape, in *Guillelmi de Ockham Opera Politica*, ed. J. G. Sikes, I, 258-260, 269. Ockham, of course, simply presents what had been the law of the Church itself since 1215, that in cases of necessity the Church should aid the State with a subsidy, but only after the pope consented; Ockham, like some of the polemics who supported Philip IV against Boniface VIII, would make the consent of the pope unnecessary—as it already was in practice. It is interesting that Ockham refers to Cicero and Aristotle, as well as the two laws, in the discussion. His statement of the maxim, *quod omnes tangit*, needs no comment.

[60] See below, nn. 72-81.

[61] To *Clem.* tit. *de iureiur.* c. Romani (2, 9, 1) ad v. *apicem*: ". . . Sed forsan favor patrie, que loco carnis et sanguinis est, hoc sibi revelavit . . ."; Paris, BN, MS lat. 16902, fol. 183; see Schulte, *Quellen*, II, 197. For the context, below, n. 118.

legists, then, we find further evidence of the rise in thought as well as in fact, of the national States in Europe, and this much earlier than once supposed.

The public utility or welfare of all in the community is that *status regni* which has a public right that is superior to and embraces all private rights of king and subjects. The *raison d'être* of the State, it is the principal subject of the public law. It is therefore the duty of the king as chief magistrate, emperor in his realm, to assure this *status* by maintaining law and order within the realm and by defending the realm against aggressors, all to secure peace—the ultimate common welfare on earth. But the royal defense of the *status regni* is at the same time the defense of the *patria*—not only against enemies without, but against enemies within: "It is lawful," says the poet, Geoffroi de Nés (de Paris), urging Philip V of France to crush the provincial leagues, "to repel force with force: fight, therefore, King, for the fatherland"—

> Licitum est vi vim repellere;
> Igitur, rex, pugna pro patria.[62]

Philip IV had already subordinated the love of children (as in the Roman law) to the care and fighting in defense of the *natalis patria*—which thus had become not merely the local but the common fatherland of the kingdom.[63]

2. REX IMPERATOR

In studying the ideal of fighting for the *patria* we noted the problem of the relations of the concept of *patria* with the rise of

[62] Quoted in *Histoire littéraire de la France*, xxxv (1921), 329. He is repeating a principle of natural and civil law as well as the distich of Cato. *Licitum est vim vi repellere* and similar formulas go back to D. 43, 16, 1, 27 ("Vim vi repellere licere Cassius scribit . . .") and D. 9, 2, 45, 4 (Paulus: "Vim enim vi defendere, omnes leges, omniaque iura permittunt"); see Kuttner, *Kanonistische Schuldlehre*, p. 336. To D. 1, 1, 2, ad v. *tripertitum* (threefold origin of private law), the *Glos. ord.* of Accursius: ". . . idem tamen dico de publico, quod est tripertite collectum, secundum Io. et sunt eadem exempla: ut liceat reipublicae vim vi propulsare." See also *Decretum*, Dist. 1, c. 7 Ius naturale, and C. 23, q. 1.

[63] Quoted by Kantorowicz, *A.H.R.*, LVI, p. 479 n. 26, from G. de Lagarde, "La philosophie sociale d'Henri de Gand et Godefroid de Fontaines," *Archives d'histoire doctrinale et littéraire du moyen âge*, XIV (1943-45), 101 n. 1. See also above, to n. 42. Odofredo had said, to D. 1, 1, 1. *Ius gentium*: "et ideo dicit lex prior fuit custodia castrorum quam caritas liberorum."

kingdoms independent of the traditional Roman Empire and with the recognition of this fact in legal opinion. More needs to be said, by way of supplement, about the formulas *rex superiorem non recognoscens* and *rex imperator in regno suo*, because of the strong disagreement still apparent among scholars in their interpretations of the significance of these terms. It needs to be said also because the theory of independent monarchies is vital in the application in turn of the theory of the just war: can kings, as well as the emperor, declare war when it is just, and, if so, can the emperor still arbitrate disputes between them in the hope of preventing war, or must it be the pope who becomes the arbitrator? The connection with the rise of international public law, as opposed to a public law within a universal Empire is obvious. Wars within the Empire, between cities, provinces, or kingdoms, even if sanctioned by the emperor, remain private wars on the level of feuds, for each of these communities is a (fictive) private corporate person, and a subject of private law. But wars between independent States, each of which under its king-emperor possesses a real public law and in its terms has the right to declare a just war of defense without consulting any superior power, become public, international wars: they create the problem, well known today, of a means to limit them as the worst aspect of nationalism. And the idea of the right of an independent king to fight a just war is related to the theory of his public right to levy extraordinary taxes for the defense of the realm.

Of course, the Holy Roman Empire was in fact powerless and could not prevent private wars within, and the theory of universalism in the Middle Ages, in the ideal of one Empire and an emperor superior to all kings, was a failure. The newer theory, that without the emperor the pope was the true superior, was likewise a failure—as Boniface VIII's impotence in stopping the war between Philip IV and Edward I, and the *Unam sanctam*, which denied that the king of France was emperor in his own realm, show quite clearly. It is interesting, therefore, that some thinkers, theologians and lawyers—and at least one pope, who was both theologian and lawyer—observing the facts, began in the twelfth century to adjust the legal theory to them, saying that certain kings recognize no superior, and either said or implied that they are emperors in their realms.

Yet controversy on the meaning of these expressions has long existed. One school—Otto Gierke, Francesco Calasso, and C. N. S. Woolf—holds that *rex imperator* meant in general, at least to the late thirteenth century, that the king within his realm was superior to all others, ruled according to an imitative, limited public law, and was, nonetheless, subject to the emperor; and the kingdom within the Empire was an allodial holding, rather than fief, or was merely a corporate community, a fictive person affected by private law and subject to private law, yet at the same time enjoying some delegated public rights and law.[64] On the other hand some scholars, e.g., Francesco Ercole and Sergio Mochi Onory, go to the other extreme and feel that statements of the kind imply complete independence of the empire.[65] Mochi Onory, indeed, as Meijers and Kuttner point out, stretches too far the opinions of Huguccio, the great canonist of the late twelfth century (and teacher of Innocent III), in order to stress this view.[66] I shall present here, therefore, a brief review of a few of the well-known sources and give some others not so well known, along with my own interpretation. I do not pretend to do more—a new book, based on an examination of all the legal sources, is needed.

In the first place, obviously, the legists of Bologna, e.g., those represented in Accursius's *Glossa ordinaria*, are interested in championing the universal authority of the emperor.[67] Yet on

[64] Gierke, III, 198-210, 267, 350-360, 381-390; Calasso, *Glossatori*, 2nd and 3rd ed., in general, also for bibliography; Woolf, *Bartolus of Sassoferrato*, ch. III and pp. 369-383.

[65] Francesco Ercole, *Da Bartolo all'Althusio*, pp. 70-104, 157-217; Sergio Mochi Onory, *Fonti canonistiche dell'idea moderna dello stato*.

[66] Mochi Onory, *Fonti*, pp. 174-177; E. M. Meijers, book review, in *Tijdschrift voor Rechtsgeschidenis*, XX (1952), 123; Kuttner, "Papst Honorius III. und das Studium des Zivilrechts," in *Festschrift für Martin Wolff*, p. 97, n. 80. Walter Ullmann, "The Development of the Medieval Idea of Sovereignty," *E.H.R.*, LXIV (1949), 1-33, has made a useful contribution but does not treat the early development of the idea.

[67] For example, to the *Libri Feudorum* 2, 53, 1, ad v. *imperio*: "Et ita videtur quod lex ista non habet locum nisi inter illos qui ei subditi sunt. Sed nunquid tenet Francigenas, et alios ultramontanos, qui ei non sunt subditi? Videtur quod non, ex eo quod hic subiicit, 'nostro subiecti imperio, etc.' Sed dicas, quod eos similiter tenet; quoniam licet ei non sint sacramento subditi, sunt tamen

occasion they indicate the realization that the Empire has in fact been divided and some peoples do not use the Roman law.[68] Cino da Pistoia, although generally in favor of the Empire, in the early fourteenth century argues that the Authentic *Habita* does not apply to students at Paris, because the king of France "observat pro libito, cum de facto non recognoscat superiorem in terra."[69] Azo himself reveals that some lawyers of the early thirteenth century were arguing that each king had the same power in his kingdom as the emperor, and therefore could do as he pleased, or at least could act *ratione publice utilitatis*; but he rejects the argument, used for claims of the king of France, and favors the use of a feudal law of Frederick I.[70] Further, the legists at Bologna generally claim for Rome a true public law and a true *Respublica*, but they do concede, with few exceptions, that every *civitas* or kingdom has in a limited sense its public law and can be called a Republic, with its own *fiscus*.[71]

Certain canon lawyers, too, either supported wholeheartedly the universalism of the Empire, or acknowledged a *de facto* independence of kingdoms. Johannes Teutonicus, in the early thirteenth century, was the extreme exponent of the ideal of the Empire as a unity embracing all provinces and kingdoms subject to the emperor as the *dominus mundi*. As a German he liked the

---

ratione imperii Romani, sub quo esse debent, cum ipsi fuerint de imperio Iustiniani. . . ." That is, the French are not vassals of the Emperor Frederick Barbarossa, but they are his subjects because they were in the Roman Empire of Justinian!

68 To *C.* 11, 19 (18), 1: "Hodie imperium est scissum, et studium multis locis fit, maxime Bononiae, quae legalis studii obtinet monarchiam." This is from Pillius's continuation of the unfinished *Summa* of Placentinus on the *Tres Libri*, published as Azo's, Venice, 1584, col. 982: "Verum, cum imperium modernis temporibus scissuram senserit, iste quoque civitates duae [i.e., Beirut and Constantinople] dominationem perdiderint, coeperunt quoque iura quovis loco tradi, et Bononiae maxime, quae legalium studiorum monarchiam tenuit, nec non Mutinae. . . ." But Pillius no doubt has in mind the division of the Empire into the Greek and Western, and would hold that the Roman Empire in the West was a unity, embracing the western kingdoms. Consider also the gloss to *Inst.* 1, 9, 2, ad v. *Romanorum*: "Id est, omnium qui sunt de Rom. imp. Aliae vero gentes quaedam ut servos tenent filios, ut Sclavi; aliae ut prorsus absolutos, ut Francigenae. . . ."

69 Quoted by Savigny, *Geschichte des römischen Rechts im Mittelalter*, VI, 76n.

70 See the discussion by Calasso, *Glossatori*[2], pp. 36-39; full text ed. Landsberg, *Die Quaestiones des Azo*, p. 86; and above, ch. v, nn. 72-75.

71 Gierke, III, 199, 201, 210, 356-360.

idea that the papacy had rightly transferred the Empire from the Greeks to the Germans, who, like the ancient Romans, won the Empire by their superior virtues. His principal thought was expressed about 1215-1220 in glosses to a decretal of Innocent III and to the *Decretum*.[72] Since only the first part of the principal gloss to Innocent III's *Venerabilem*, 1202, is well known,[73] I now give the whole comment: "Sic ergo regimen mundi est translatum ad teuthonicos, nam habent regimen romane ecclesie, ut de con. d. v. in die [*Decretum*, De consecratione, Dist. 5, c. 14]. Et sic patet, quod imperium non est apud grecos, licet largo nomine appelleretur imperator, ut de maio. solite [*Comp. III*, 1, 21, 2; *Decr. Greg. IX* 1, 33, 6], sicut rex scaccorum dicitur rex. Extra ecclesiam autem non est imperium, ut xxiii. q.i. sed illud [24, q. 1, c. 39 Sed illud Augustini]. Est autem imperator super omnes reges, ut vii. q.i. in apibus [c. 41], et omnes naciones sunt sub eo, ut xi. Q. i. hec si quis, ver. volumus [c. 34]; et dicit lex ipse enim est princeps mundi et dominus,[74] ut ff. ad l. ro. deprecatio domine [*D*. 2, 14, 9]. Etiam iudei sub eo sunt, C. de iudeis, iudei [1, 9, 8]; et omnes provincie sunt sub eo, ut lxiii. di. adri. [c. 22], nisi aliquis se doceat exemptum, ut xxiii. Q. viii, c. si in mortem § ecce [p.c. 20]. Nec aliquid regnum potuit prescribere exempcionem, cum non habeat locum in hoc prescrip-

[72] On Joh. Teutonicus see Kuttner, *Repertorium*, pp. 93-99, 357, 370-371, 374-375, and in *Miscellanea Giovanni Mercati*, v, 608-634.

[73] *Appar. to Comp. III*, tit, *de elect.*, c. Venerabilem (1, 6, 19; *Decr. Greg. IX* 1, 6, 34): Schulte, "Literaturgeschichte der Compilationes Antiquae," in *Sitzungsber. d. kais. Akad. d. Wissenschaften zu Wien, Philos.-histor. Kl.*, LXVI (1870), 130-131; G. Post, in *Archiv f. kathol. KR.*, CXVII (1937), 407-408—here I gave a version from a MS in which the words *excepto regimine hyspanie* were interpolated: "Sic enim regimen mundi, excepto regimine hyspanie, translatum est ad teuthonicos." This is in a copy of the *Appar.* of Tancred to *Comp. III*. But other MSS of the *Appar.* that I have seen do not have the words; more important, the *Appar.* of Joh. himself, with the full gloss, in Brit. Mus. MS Royal 11 C. VII, contains no such interpolation. Mochi Onory, *Fonti*, p. 236, is wrong in stressing these words as belonging to Joh. Teut. and indicating that even he weakened the universalism of the empire by making an exception of Spain; he failed to observe that I showed that the words were probably a later insertion, *Arch. f. kathol. KR*, CXVII, 407 n. 3.

[74] The words, "et dicit lex ipse enim est princeps mundi et dominus," are in Bamberg MS Can. 19, fol. 132ᵛ, as given in Tancred's *Appar. to Comp. III*. In the *Appar.* of Joh. himself, in MS Royal 11 C. VII, the words are deep in the margin and do not show clearly in my photograph. Hence I took them from the Bamberg MS.

tio, infra, de prescri. cum ex officii [*Comp. III*, 2, 17, 6; *Decr. Greg. IX* 2, 26, 16]. Nec aliquid regnum[75] potuit eximi ab imperio, quia illud esset acefalum[76] . . . et esset monstrum sine capite. Immo omnes de capite suo imperatori dabunt tributum, nisi in hoc sunt exempti, ff. de censibus, l. ult. [*D.* 50, 15, 8]. Omnia enim sunt in potestate imperatoris, ut viii. di. quo iur. [c. 2]. Fateamur ergo quod teutonici virtutibus promeruerunt imperium, xxviii. Q. ix. ex hiis [c. 14]."[77]

Here, then, is the strongest possible emphasis on the universalism of the Roman Empire. Johannes repeats it in most of his glosses elsewhere. For example, to the decretal, *Per venerabilem* (1202), of Innocent III, on the pope's statement that the King of France recognizes no superior in temporal affairs, he says that nevertheless the king *de jure* is subject to the Roman emperor;[78] and to the *Decretum*, Dist. 1, c. 12 Ius Quiritum, where he says that the emperor is the prince of the world, all kings are under him, and that outside the Roman Empire there can be no legal inheritance, nor any other thing that is sanctioned by the law of the Romans.[79] But in another place Johannes seems to waver and to admit that possibly the kings of Spain are independent, for they "snatched the kingdom from the jaws of the enemy when they were not subject to the Empire."[80] Yet it is possible that this objection was added later by someone else—I have not

[75] *Aliquis regum* in Paris, BN, MS lat. 3930, fol. 107. In MS Royal 11 C. VII the words are hidden in the margin, but one can make out *regnum*. Perhaps *aliquid regnum* is the better reading.

[76] *Falsum* in MS Royal 11 C. VII; *acefalum* in MS lat. 3930.

[77] As indicated in the preceding notes, I have taken the text chiefly from two MSS, Paris, BN, MS lat. 3930, and Brit. Mus., Royal 11 C. VII, in both of which one finds the *Appar.* of Joh. Teut. to *Comp. III*, the decretals of Innocent III; partly also from the *Appar.* of Tancred to the same in Bamberg MS Can. 19.

[78] *Appar.* to *Comp. III*, tit. *Qui filii sint legit.* c. Per venerabilem (4, 12, 2; *Decr. Greg. IX* 4, 17, 13), ad v. *recognoscat*: "De iure tamen subest romano imperatori, ut vii. q. i. in apibus [c. 41], ut dixi supra, de elec. venerabilem."

[79] *Glos. ord.* to Dist. 1, c. 12. This passage is on the idea that the Roman law, *ius Quiritum*, deals with legacies, wardships, contracts, etc.; Joh. ad v. *quod nulli*: ". . . Nam imperator est princeps totius mundi. . . . Sed in diversis provinciis diversi reges sub eo constituti sunt. . . . Qui ergo non vult esse sub Romano Imperio, nec haereditatem habere potest, nec alia quae hic de iure romano enumerantur. . . ."

[80] To Dist. 63, c. 22 Adrianus ad v. *per singulas provincias*: ". . . Fateamur ergo Imperatorem esse dominum mundi. . . . Obstat quod reges Hispaniae, cum non subessent Imperio, regnum ab hostium faucibus eruerunt." See above, n. 73.

examined the manuscripts—for in the main body of the gloss Johannes states that the emperor rules over the provinces of France and Spain, unless they can prove their exemption: for as Gratian said, all men, unless given immunity, owe him tribute (so also in *D.* 50, 15, 8) and have no property rights unless they submit to the Roman Empire.[81] On the whole, therefore, Johannes is unwilling to grant independence even to Spain—one reason, no doubt, for Vincentius Hispanus' violent reaction, as we shall soon see.

More moderate than Johannes Teutonicus, some canonists of the late twelfth and early thirteenth century nonetheless maintained that the French, English, and other "ultramontanes" were subject to the Roman Empire and, at least indirectly, through the Church, to Roman law. Huguccio was the leader of this school. Yet in one place in his *Summa* (1188-1192) to the *Decretum*[82] he says that the pope can depose an emperor, or a king who is not under the emperor (to 15, q. 6, c. 3 Alius item).[83] Nevertheless, in general Huguccio believes that by right all kings and kingdoms are or ought to be under the emperor. His pupil, Innocent III, did not follow the teacher on this point, since he declared in the *Per venerabilem* (1202) that the king of France in temporal affairs recognized no superior (*Decr. Greg. IX* 4, 17, 13).

[81] *Loc. cit.*: "Ergo in Francia et in Hispania. Unus enim imperator . . . ; quod concedo nisi probent se exemptos ab imperatore, ut xxiii. q. viii. c. si in morte § ecce. Unde adhuc de capite suo dabunt tributum imperatori omnes, cum non probent se exemptos ab imperatore, ut ff. de censi. l. ult. Si enim dicunt se non subesse Romano imperio, per consequens dicunt se non habere aliquid proprii, ut infra [for *supra*], dist. j. ius quiritum [see above, n. 79]. Fateamur, etc."

[82] *Summa* to *Decretum*, Dist. 1, c. 12 Ius Quiritum; Causa 6, q. 3, c. 2 Scitote; 7, q. 1, c. 41 In apibus, and 16, q. 6, c. 3 Alius. I have consulted the work in the Paris, BN, MS lat. 3892, but do not need to repeat the passages, for they are in large part quoted by Paul Koschaker, *Europa und das römische Recht*, p. 75; Mochi Onory, *Fonti*, pp. 155, 174-176; Kuttner, in *Festschrift Wolff*, pp. 93, 96 n. 74; and W. Ullmann, "The Medieval Interpretation of Frederick I's Authentic 'Habita,'" *Studi in Memoria di Paolo Koschaker*, p. 102 n. 5. Ullmann exaggerates in saying that late twelfth-century doctrine maintained the unity of the Empire. We shall soon see how Peter the Chanter, and Richard de Mores (Anglicus) held the opposite; and the fact that Alanus in the early years of the thirteenth century believed in the independence of certain kings indicates a background in the twelfth century. On Huguccio see now G. Catalano, "Impero," *Riv. storia dir. ital.* xxx, 3-49.

[83] Mochi Onory, *Fonti*, p. 155.

The author of the *Apparatus* "Ecce vicit leo" (1202-1210) to the *Decretum*[84] goes along with Huguccio in saying that all should be subject to the emperor and Roman law; and he adds that Rome is the *communis patria* of all subjects, since they should use the same law. But, he continues, "today this is not so, for not all are under the emperor, but under the Church."[85] Elsewhere the author says that a *constitutio* or *edictum* can be the legislation of a king in his kingdom as well as of the emperor. However, the emperor alone can make general laws.[86]

One can see that the hesitation of these canonists was in part the result of the fact that the Roman law was not used in certain countries. Hence, Huguccio turns to the idea that the French, English and other "ultramontanes" are nonetheless in the Empire either because they ought to be, or because they use the Latin language, or because of their obedience to the pope and their obligation to live according to those Roman laws that are approved by the Church.[87] But on the other hand, the author of the *Ecce vicit leo* is nearer the theory of independence from the Empire, in spite of believing that all should use the same law. All Christians, however, are subject to the Roman law insofar as it is accepted by the universal Church, and this may account for the small use made of different bodies of customary law by those canonists who argue for the independence of France, Spain, and England, though Vincentius Hispanus declares that Spain has its own legal science, which is one of the

---

84 See Kuttner, *Repertorium*, pp. 59-66.

85 Paris, BN, MS nouv. acq. lat. 1576, fol. 21, to Dist. 1, c. 12 Ius Quiritum, ad v. *proprie sunt romanorum*: ". . . Roma communis omnium subiectorum patria, quia eodem iure debent uti, ut Insti. prologo, in principio. Unde iudei qui sunt subiecti romanis vivunt more romano, ut C. de iudeis, iudei [*C*. 1, 12, 2—but more likely 1, 12, 4 Iussio]. Immo omnes latini debent istis legibus uti, quia unus tantum debet esse imperator, ut vii. q. i. in apibus [c. 41]. Omnes subesse debent illi imperatori. . . . Odie tamen non fit, quia non sunt omnes sub imperatore, sed ecclesia. . . ." Also in Kuttner, in *Festschrift Wolff*, p. 96 n. 76.

86 MS nouv. acq. lat. 1576, to Dist. 2, c. 5: "Quod tamen rex in regno suo, quia quilibet rex in regno suo potest aliquid statuere. . . . Leges autem generales solo imperatori licet condere. . . ." And to Dist. 4, c. 3 In istis temporalibus: "Loquitur secundum antiqua tempora, quando plebs poterat legem condere. Odie solus imperatur. . . ."

87 Kuttner, in *Festschrift Wolff*, p. 96 n. 74; Mochi Onory, *Fonti*, pp. 174-176; A. M. Stickler, "Sacerdotium et regnum, etc.," in *Biblioteca del "Salesianum,"* XXVII (1953), 19, for more evidence.

reasons he advances for the claim of the Spanish to an Empire of their own.[88] Others use the *Super speculam* of Honorius III, 1219 (it forbade the teaching and study of Roman law at Paris and in neighboring cities, because in the Ile-de-France, *Francia*, a region of customary law, it was not needed anyhow, and emphasis should be placed on theology in this university)[89] as additional authority for the fact that many regions do not observe the Roman law, and are therefore outside the Empire. Hostiensis, on the *Super speculam*, lists *Hispania tota*, England, Scotland, Ireland, Germany (*Alamannia*), Denmark (*Dacia*), Sweden, Norway, Hungary, Bohemia, Poland and Bulgaria, as well as France, as provinces that are not subject to Roman law, leaving only Italy and Provençe for the civil law. But he adds that such provinces may use the arguments from the Roman law when their own customs and statutes are wanting[90]—which the kings of England did. Bernard of Parma says that while this is *de facto* true, since some peoples are not under the emperor, they ought *de jure* to be subject to him.[91] Jacobus de Albenga, in his *Apparatus* to *Compilatio V* (decretals of Honorius III) had already said the same: tit. *De privilegiis*, c. *Super speculam* (5, 12, 3; *Decr. Greg. IX* 5, 33, 28), ad v. *imitantur*: "Cum tamen ab omnibus debeant observari, ut C. de legibus et constit. leges sacratissime [*C.* 1, 14, 9]. Hoc verum est de hiis qui sunt ab [= sub]imperio. Franci tamen et yspani et quedam alie provincie, licet de iure debent subesse imperio, ut xi.q.i. volumus [c. 34], et vii. q.i. in apibus, de facto tamen non subsunt."[92]

In general, these canonists acknowledge the *de facto* but not the *de jure* independence of certain kingdoms or provinces— their very use of the word *provincia* indicates their feeling that every kingdom is a part of the Empire. Jacobus de Albenga

[88] Below, n. 190.

[89] I am following here the convincing interpretation of the *Super speculam* by Kuttner in *Festschrift Wolff*, pp. 79-101.

[90] Kuttner, *op.cit.*, p. 98 n. 82.

[91] *Ibid.*, p. 98 n. 81; Bernard adds that the emperor "dominus mundi est," in gloss to *Decr. Greg. IX* 5, 33, 28.

[92] Brit. Mus., MS Royal 11 C. vii, fol. 269ᵛ. On this *Appar.* see Kuttner, *Repertorium*, p. 383. I have not been able to consult the glosses of others to *Comp. V.* Stickler, "Sacerdotium et regnum," *Bibl. "Salesianum,"* xxvii, p. 24, also quotes Jac. de Albenga.

supports this opinion in at least one other gloss to *Comp. V.*[93] While admitting that a king can legislate in his kingdom, like the emperor in the Empire, he implies that his law should not be contrary to imperial law, and that his legislation is on the level of that of the praetorian prefect.[94] Johannes Galensis is of the same opinion.[95]

On the other side, that of the real independence of certain kings and kingdoms, the opinions expressed are not perhaps more abundant, but are significant in relation to the history of the feudal monarchies of England, France, and Spain. That such opinions arose may be related not only to the fact of independence but also to the claims made by some of the kings. As a result of the Reconquest, Alfonso VI styled himself King of Kings and even Emperor, and reflected a fairly old tradition of a Spanish Empire. The pope recognized his title.[96] Even Louis VI of France was called *imperator Franciae* by Galbert of Bruges.[97] Henry II of England, says John of Salisbury, gloried publicly in succeeding to Henry I, his grandfather, "who in his land was king, apostolic legate, patriarch, emperor";[98] and in fact, the *Leges Henrici Primi* had spoken of the "tremendum

[93] To tit. *De censibus* (al. *de immunitate ecclesiarum*) c. *Gravi nobis* (3, 26, 5; not in *Decr. Greg. IX*): "Sed quare papa allegat legem imperatoris ipsi regi [of Portugal], cum ei non subsit? Respondeo, licet ei non subsit, subesse debet tamen. . . . Item lex ista intelligitur esse postquam est per ecclesiam approbata. . . . Et est ar. in decretali ista, quod omnes reges debent subesse imperatori"; in Brit. Mus., MS Royal 11 C. VII, fol. 266ᵛ. Note that Jacobus uses an argument of Huguccio, that at least by reason of approval by the Church, the Roman law may be valid in regions of customary law; above, n. 87.

[94] MS Royal 11 C. VII, fol. 257ᵛ, to *Comp. V* tit. *De iudeis et saracenis*, c. *Intellecto* (5, 3, 1) ad v. *lege perpetua*: "Ita habes quod rex potest facere in terra sua similiter. Prefectus pretorio potest facere legem quam omnes servare tenentur, dummodo non sit legi et constitutioni contraria. . . ."

[95] Kuttner, in *Festschrift Wolff*, p. 98 n. 81; Mochi Onory, *Fonti*, pp. 277-278.

[96] See Merriman, *Rise of the Spanish Empire*, I, pp. 90-91; R. Menendez Pidal, *El imperio hispanico y los cincos reinos*, chs. I-V, VII.

[97] F. L. Ganshof, "Le roi de France en Flandre en 1127 et 1128," *Rev. hist. dr. fr. étr.*, XXVII (1949), 7 n. 2; but on Flanders and its nationalism, *idem* in *Tijdschr. v. Rechtsgeschiedinis*, XVIII (1950), 135-158.

[98] John of Salisbury, *Ep.* 239 (M.P.L., 199.271): Henry II "adeoque gloriatur ut palam dicat se nunc demum avi sui consecutum privilegium, qui in terra sua erat rex, legatus apostolicus, patriarcha, imperator, et omnia quae volebat"; W. Holtzmann, "Das mittelalterliche Imperium und die werdenden Nationen," *Arbeitsgemeinschaft für Forschung des Landes Westfalen*, VII (1953), 19, points this out. But did Henry refer to the Emperor Henry V as his *avus*, even though the German emperor was not his real grandfather?

regie majestatis . . . imperium" as above English customary law.[99] In 1202 King John declared that the "regnum Anglicanum quasi imperio adaequatur," and before 1236 Roger of Wendover in his *Flores Historiarum* attributed to William Rufus the claim that "ipse omnes libertates haberet in regno suo, quas imperator vindicabat in imperio."[100] (But these last two examples may echo the new theory of the canonists rather than the older tradition.) Moreover, the apparent boastfulness of the German canonist Johannes Teutonicus about the superiority of the Teutons and the merits that earned them the Empire, in addition to French bragging in feudal epic and other sources, and to Norman-French crusading imperialism in Spain, Italy, and the Holy Land, no doubt challenged such a response as we shall observe in Vincentius Hispanus. Finally, Mochi Onory may be partly right in his emphasis upon the desire of some canonists and popes to belittle the Roman Empire in order to build up the universal supremacy of papacy and Church. Perhaps the feeling that fact should be justified by theory was as important as anything else.

Now let us review the statements of the opinion that kingdoms were in fact and theory alike independent—that the king recognized no secular superior either in his own realm or outside, in the Roman Empire, and was emperor in his realm.

The French theologian, Peter the Chanter († 1197), discussing the problem of the just war which could be declared, he says, only by the *iudex*, understands the difficulty of the declaration when two equal suzerains, each having no superior, were at war, e.g., the king of the French and the emperor. In such a case only the pope could be the authority for deciding whether the war was just.[101] The pope has the highest authority, but the king is certainly equal to and independent of the emperor.

[99] G. Barraclough, "Law and Legislation in Medieval England," *L.Q.R.*, LVI (1940), 88.

[100] Fritz Schulz, "Bracton on Kingship," *E.H.R.*, LX (1945), 150-151.

[101] Beryl Smalley, *The Study of the Bible in the Middle Ages*, p. 172 n. 1: "Sed si pares non habentes superiores, ut rex Francorum et imperator bellent, periculum est. Ad papam enim recurrendum esset, ut ad maiorem." Was Innocent III, in the *Per venerabilem*, acquainted with Peter the Chanter's words?

The most famous early statement is the well-known one of Alanus, the English canonist of the late twelfth and early thirteenth century.[102] It is in his gloss *(ca.* 1207-1210) to a decretal of Alexander III; it was first published by J. F. von Schulte, and does not need repetition here.[103] But Alanus also wrote an *Apparatus (ca.* 1202) of glosses to the *Decretum*, and to Dist. 96, c. Denique, ad v. *iudicare*; he speaks in words similar to those used on the decretal of Alexander III: "Regulare est, quod laicus clericum non iudicet, ut hic dicitur. Excipitur si laico clerici causa delegetur. . . . Sed nunquid papa posset materialem gladium sibi retinere si vellet? R[espondeo] non, quia dominus gladios divisit, ut hic, et ecclesia ex hoc plurimum turbaretur. Et quod dictum est de imperatore [above, ad v. *Denique*: 'Imperatores rebus humanis tantum president. Ideoque de clericis iudicare non possunt.'], habeatur repetitum de quolibet principe, qui supra se dominum non habet. Unusquisque tantam habet iurisdictionem in regno suo, quantam habet imperator in imperio. Divisio enim regnorum iam iure gentium introducta ['introductum' in the manuscript] a papa approbatur, licet antiquo iure gentium unus imperator in orbe esse debet."[104]

The same opinion is stated in other glosses in Alanus' *Apparatus.* Just as the emperor can legislate, because by the *lex*

102 On his career and works, see Kuttner, *Repertorium*, pp. 67-75, 325; supplementary notes in *Traditio*, I (1943), 289, and VII (1949-51), 339. See also Alfons Stickler, "Alanus Anglicus," *Salesianum*, XXI (1959), 346-406, for a fine critical study; p. 373 for the date of the *Appar.* in the second and better redaction.

103 Schulte, "Literaturgesch. d. Comp. Ant.," *Sitzungsber. d. kais. Akad. d. Wissenschaften zu Wien, Philos.-histor. Kl.*, 66 (1871), 89-90; Mochi Onory, *Fonti*, 191 n. 2.

104 *Apparatus* "Ius naturale" (see Kuttner, *Repertorium*, 67-75; *Trad.* I, 289, n. 52; VII, 339) in Paris, BN, MS lat. 15393, fol. 70. Compare with the last portion of the gloss published by Schulte and Mochi Onory (see preceding note): ". . . Sed numquid papa materialem gladium sibi posset retinere? Resp. non, dominus enim gladios diusit, ut XCVI di. cum ad verum. et praeterea ecclesia ex hoc plurimum turbaretur. Et quod dictum est de imperatore, dictum habeatur de quolibet rege vel principe, qui nulli subest. Unusquisque enim tantum juris habet in regno suo, quantum imperator in imperio. Divisio enim regnorum de jure gentium introductum (a) a papa approbatur, licet antiquo jure gentium imperator unus in orbe esse deberet. A." This gloss belongs to the years 1207-10 (Kuttner, *Traditio*, I, 289 n. 52). Both glosses, therefore, may be influenced by Innocent III's *Per venerabilem*, although Alanus does not cite the decretal. See now Stickler, *op.cit.*, 363, for still another reading of the gloss to Dist. 96, c. Denique—Stickler finds it to c. Cum ad verum.

regia the people conferred the *imperium* upon him, so the king in his kingdom.[105] Again, just as a just war can be declared by the emperor, so it can be declared with full legality (*de iure mero*) only by those princes who have no secular authority above them, although custom permits other, subordinate, princes and cities (Italian) to declare war by their own authority.[106] By implication, in case of a quarrel between two equals, there is no recourse to the supreme arbitration of the emperor to give justice or permission to wage war. Who, then, shall decide which of the two sovereigns has the right to claim that his war is just? The pope, says Alanus, for the pope is the judge ordinary of princes both in spiritual and in temporal matters, and to the pope the prince must go to get justice if possible, or, failing that, to obtain the pope's consent to declare war. But others say, continues Alanus, that the prince does not need to go to the pope for justice before waging war.[107]

Alanus, then, definitely believes that certain kings recognize no secular superior and are emperors in their own kingdoms. In spiritual affairs, of course, and even in temporal, by reason of sin (it is sinful to wage war unjustly), they are subject to the pope. And he states that the pope himself approved their lawful

[105] To Dist. 2, c. 5 Constitutio: "Cum lege regia . . . imperio lata est, populus ei et in eum omne suum imperium et potestatem concessit. . . . Idem et de rege et regno suo." There is here no sense of the emperor's delegating the power of legislation to the king as head of a province. Also to Dist. 8, c. Quo iure ad v. *regum iura*: "Ar. quod reges habeant potestatem condendi leges, sicut et imperatores . . . ," on the words of St. Augustine, who speaks of *imperatores et reges* as equals. See Stickler, *op.cit.*, p. 351.

[106] To C. 23, q. 1, c. 4 Quid culpatur, ad vv. *penes principes sit*: "De iure mero ille habet potestatem indicendi bellum, qui supra se non habet secularem potestatem. Alii autem, quantumcumque magni fuerint, sine superioris auctoritate non possunt, ut infra, q. prox. [23, q. 2, c. 1], et q. v. miles [c. 12]. Consuetudo quorumdam locorum etiam aliis principibus, qui supra se habent dominos, concedit ius indicendi bellum sua auctoritate, et in civitatibus ytalie, et pro eis facit c. infra, e.q.ii. dominus [c. 2];" MS lat. 15393, fol. 181.

[107] To C. 23, q. 1, c. 1 Iustum, ad v. *ex edicto*: the *princeps* "habet ius indicendi bellum . . . ; sine edicto licite gerit bellum, in quo est specialissimum, quod potest iniuriam suam vindicare . . . si aliter iustitia consequi non possit. . . . Et secundum opinionem nostram, quod dominus papa est iudex ordinarius ['dominum papam esse iudicem ordinarium' MS] principum, quo ad spiritualia et quo ad temporalia, ad eum antequam indicat bellum tenetur recurrere, ut per eum iustitiam consequatur si potest, vel eo auctoritatem prestante bellum indicat."

independence of the Empire. (Perhaps he has in mind Pope Innocent III, the *Per venerabilem* of 1202.)

In different words Richard de Mores (Richardus Anglicus) stated essentially the same theory and fact of the independence of certain kings. Writing in the late twelfth century, he says that many kings are not subject to the emperor, for just as some had been subjected to him by force of conquest, they can by the same force or violence regain their freedom. The king is a-nointed, crowned, and given authority in the same way as the emperor; and the king has the power of punishing.[108] A little later, Laurentius, a Spanish canonist, held that the French and Spanish were not bound by the Roman law.[109]

Spanish canonists, indeed, were perhaps more zealous than the English for national pride and independence. Vincentius Hispanus, in ideas expressed between 1215 and 1250, scorned the French and declared that the Germans had lost any claim to the traditional, universal Roman Empire. The Spanish, superior in valor and deeds to French and Germans, were building a separate empire of their own. But Vincentius' thought is so interesting that it will be examined below, in Part 3 of this chapter.

Another important Spanish canonist and theologian, Johannes de Deo, though not so vehement as Vincentius, supports the idea that a king who has no superior is the head of an independent realm and is the equal of the emperor. In his *Liber poenitentiarius*, written in 1245 or 1246, he says that the emperor should confess either to the pope or to someone chosen with the pope's consent. But others say that he should confess to the bishop where he was crowned as king (before the pope crowns him as emperor). Still others, however, say that he can confess to whomever he pleases, so long as he is *sanus*, since the

---

108 See the full text in Mochi Onory, *Fonti*, p. 253, from Gillmann, in *Archiv f. kathol. KR*, CVII, 672 n. 1. On Richard see Kuttner, *Repertorium*, pp. 223-225, 324; and Kuttner and Eleanor Rathbone, "Anglo-Norman Canonists of the Twelfth Century," *Traditio*, VII (1949-51), 329-333, where the earlier identification with Richard de Lacy (*Repertorium*, p. 223) is withdrawn; cf. E. M. Meijers in *Tijdschrift voor Rechtsgeschiedenis*, XX (1952), 89f.

109 Quoted by Kuttner in *Festschrift Wolff*, p. 96 n. 73.

prince is above the law and is the *lex animata* on earth. But Johannes concludes that he should get the pope's special indulgence for his choice of confessor.[110] Practically the same rules apply to the king "qui non habet alium super se." Thus, the statement that some believe that the emperor can confess to whomever he pleases because he is above the law, is fully applied to the king—with one limitation, namely, that if there is a capital city of the kingdom in which the king has his principal *domicilium*, he should get the consent of the bishop of this city to his choice of confessor (just as the emperor should ask the pope's indulgence for his choice).[111]

The eminent secular theologian at Paris, Gérard d'Abbeville, is likewise interesting on the subject of the king of France.[112] In a *Quodlibet* of about 1260, on the duty of a subject to correct, in secret, an erring superior prelate, he refers to St. Bernard's admonishing of Pope Eugenius III, just as Nathan scolded David himself, "qui rex erat et superiorem non habebat, ii° Regum, xii."[113] Obviously, David was never subject to the Roman Empire! In 1265 in a *Quodlibet* on the royal coinage and the public welfare, he refers to Matthew 22.21, "Render therefore unto Caesar, etc.," and Paul, Rom. 13.1-7, to show that the coinage of money belongs to the royal power. Then he says, "Potestas autem regia est potestas sublimior, et maxime regni

[110] Brit. Mus., MS Royal 11 B. v, fol. 138, cap. vi, *De penitentia imperatoris et cui debeat confiteri*. On Joh. de Deo, besides Schulte, *Quellen*, ii, see A. D. de Sousa Costa, *Um mestre portugues em Bolonna no seculo XIII, Joao de Deus: Vida e obras*.

[111] Fol. 138ᵛ, c. *De penitentia regum et cui debent confiteri*: "Dicunt quidam quod rex, qui non habet alium super ["sub" MS] se debet confiteri domino pape, vel de eius licentia sibi eligere providum confessorem, sicut imperator; et habere volunt per decretalem, extra, qui filii sint legitimi, per venerabilem abbatem [*Decr. Greg. IX* 4, 17, 13]. Alii dicunt quod debet confiteri metropolitano per illud capitulum vi. q. iij scitote [c. 2], ubi dicitur, 'Scitote quod certa est provincia que habet decem episcopos et unum regem et unum metropolitanum, etc.' [The passage actually reads, "Scitote certam esse provinciam, quae habet decem aut undecim civitates, et unum regem . . . et unum metropolitanum. . . ."] Tercii dicunt quod debet confiteri cuicumque voluerit, dum est sanus, sicut dictum est de imperatore, nisi esset in regno aliqua principalis civitas, que esset caput regni, in qua rex iste habuisset domicilium principale. Tunc enim ab episcopo illius civitatis debuisset petere licentiam; quod satis poterit sustineri."

[112] See P. Glorieux, *La littérature quodlibétique de 1260 à 1320*, pp. 111-127.

[113] Paris, BN, MS lat. 16405, fol. 119 (the reference is 2 King's [Sam.] 12).

francie, quia sicut dicit capitulum, 'Rex francie superiorem non cognoscit,' " and paraphrases Peter, 1 Epist. 2.13.[114]

I have made no consistent study of the literature of the middle and late thirteenth and the fourteenth centuries. But an illustration or two will suffice to show the continuity of this theory of independence among the canonists. Innocent IV (Italian) and Guillaume Durantis (French) believe in the legal independence of kings who have no superior, and Guillaume also says that, just as no appeal is allowed from the pope or the emperor, so there can be no appeal from a sentence of the French *curia*, since "the king recognizes no superior in temporals."[115] Johannes Andreae says that *propter delictum* a king may be deprived of his kingdom only by the Church when he has no superior—otherwise by his secular superior.[116] Others, e.g., Étienne Troche, Pierre d'Estaing, and Jesselin de Cassagnes, to *Clem.* tit. *De iureiur. c. Romani principes* (2, 9, 1), say that there are many kings, "qui imperatorem in superiorem minime recognoscunt."[117]

To the same decretal Guillaume de Montlauzun observes that "imo de iure Rex francie et quidam alii imperatorem in suum superiorem minime recognoscunt," this being true because Charlemagne, in whose person the Empire was transferred to the Germans, apparently did not intend that his own special patrimony, namely, the Kingdom of France, should be subjected to anyone (i.e., to himself or any other as emperor). If perchance at times the kingdom was the possession (of the emperor), nevertheless in the course of time this situation changed, as the *Per venerabilem* says (and the king of France thus recognizes no superior). (There follows the biting remark already quoted

115 See Ercole, *Da Bartolo*, pp. 174 n. 1, 86 n. 3, 181 n. 4; Calasso, *Glossatori*², pp. 115 n. 92, 116; Ullmann, *E.H.R.*, LXIV, 9f.
116 To *Liber VI* 1, 8, 2 Grandi, ad v. *regis*.
117 Paris, BN, MS lat. 9634, fol. 23; Jesselin, in MS lat. 16902, to the same decretal. On these canonists see Schulte, *Quellen*, II, 199-201, and, for corrections on Etienne Troche and Pierre d'Estaing, P. Fournier, "Notes complémentaires pour l'histoire des canonistes du XIVᵉ siècle," *Nouvelle revue historique de droit français et étranger*, XLIII (1919), 536-44.

about the patriotic fervor of Johannes Teutonicus, who opposed this.)[118]

Certain canonists, then, from the late twelfth century on, laid the foundations of the formulas *rex imperator in regno suo* and *rex superiorem non recognoscens*; and they implied no subordination of kings to the emperor, no inclusion of kingdoms in the Empire. Their theory, along with the transfer of principles of Roman law to the kingdoms, was taken up by the mid-thirteenth century by a few English, French, and Italian jurists who were trained in both laws (Bracton also, of course, and foremost, in the English customary law), and at times were in the service of their kings.

Of all the experts in the law who represented "nationalism" as opposed to universalism, Bracton is of particular interest, for he clearly applied Roman principles of public law to the king and kingdom of England at almost the same time as Jean de Blanot was doing so for France. The king, Bracton says, has no equal in his realm, much less a superior. He should not be under man but under God and the law, for the law makes the king. Since he is the supreme judge, no one shall presume to question his acts —"Nemo quidem de factis suis praesumat disputare."[119] Nor shall any justices or private persons question his charters, for to the king belongs the interpretation, "cum eius sit interpretari cuius est condere."[120] (The statement that only if the king refuses to be under the law does he have a superior on earth, that is, his *curia* of magnates, is probably not by Bracton.)[121] Again, against

---

[118] Paris, BN, MS lat. 16902, fol. 183ʳ, to *Clem.* 2, 9, 1 ad v. *apicem:* "Excedit autem [princeps or emperor] in temporalibus de iure omnes alios. . . . Quod est verum de illis qui sunt de imperio, quia secus de aliis. . . . Et sic nedum de facto, ut . . . per venerabilem; imo de iure rex francie et quidam alii imperatorem in suum superiorem minime recognoscunt, maxime cum karolus magnus, in cuius personam fuit translatum in germanos imperium, non videtur verisimiliter suum speciale patrimonium, quod erat regnum francie, velle alicui subiecisse; quod si forsan aliquibus temporibus fuerit possessio, tamen est per diuturnitatem temporis interversa, ut dicit c. per venerabilem." For the remark about Joh. Teut., see above n. 61.

[119] *De legibus Angliae*, ed. Woodbine, II, 3. For Bracton on kingship see in detail F. Schulz, in *E.H.R.*, LX (1945), 136-176, on *rex imperator* esp. pp. 150f. This statement of Bracton's transfers to the king what the Roman law and the legists said about the emperor, and the canonists about the pope.

[120] *De leg.*, II, 109.   [121] *Ibid.*, 110.

the prince or king, or any other who has no superior except God, the remedy is by petition, not by judicial procedure in court.[122] His power comes from God; but his jurisdiction is limited by the law, despite the saying that "quod principi placet, legis habet vigorem"; and, like the emperor, he judges and legislates with the counsel of his magnates or *proceres*.[123] Undoubtedly, then, Bracton accepts as lawful, even according to the Roman law, the true independence of the king and his realm. He does not call the king emperor in his own realm, but he gives him the attributes of the Roman emperor—perhaps going so far as to paraphrase or vaguely recall the maxim, the prince has *omnia iura in scrinio pectoris sui*, by saying that the king has *omnia iura in manu sua* which belong to his crown and prerogative.[124] The canonists were already saying, it is interesting to note, that the pope, like the emperor, had *omnia iura in scrinio pectoris sui*, that is, such full knowledge of the (common) law when he legislated or gave privileges, that no one could take exception that the pope had overlooked something in the existing laws.[125] Bracton's *iura omnia* surely included the right of the king to interpret the law on the basis of his powers of legislating and judging.

It was very much in line with Bracton's theory that in 1291-1292, in the Great Cause or disputed succession to the throne of Scotland, the court of Edward I decided that, failing clear laws as a basis for a decision, the king could (like the Roman

122 *Ibid.*, III, 43.

123 *Ibid.*, II, 172-174.

124 *Ibid.*, 160: the king has ordinary jurisdiction and *dignitas* and *potestas* over all in the kingdom, "habet enim omnia iura in manu sua, quae ad coronam et laicalem pertinent potestatem et materialem gladium qui pertinet ad regni gubernaculum." I cannot enter into the problem here, except to say that the *iura* may mean laws as well as rights; and this means in general that the king like the emperor, having all laws and rights in his possession that pertain to the crown and the secular or material sword, is absolute in the public sphere of interpreting the law and enforcing it. Cf. McIlwain, *Constitutionalism and the Changing World*, pp. 73-94, 79, 83. Schulz does not discuss this point. On the direct, liturgical origin of *iura in manu sua*, see Kantorowicz, *King's Two Bodies*, p. 153 n. 192.

125 Fr. Gillmann, "Romanus pontifex iura omnia in scrinio pectoris sui censetur habere," *Arch. f. kathol. KR*, XCII (1912), 3-17, and CVI (1926), 156-174. The source is in *C*. 6, 23, 19. The legists were well aware of the principle, e.g., Odofredo, *Com.* on the *Tres Libri*, Lyons, 1550, fol. 9ᵛ, to *C*. 10, 1, 9.

emperor) establish a new law ("condere novam legem") with the counsel of his prelates, *proceres*, and magnates. In this case, according to one source, the king was acting as emperor ("quia hic censetur imperator").[126]

In general, the position held by French legists and political writers is well known.[127] But while Ercole thinks Jean de Blanosco or Blanot stands for the real and legal independence of the French realm, Calasso argues that for this writer the king is emperor within his kingdom while subject to the Roman emperor, who is the lord of the world.[128] Calasso and Woolf believe the same of Jacques de Révigny and Pierre de Belleperche.[129]

Jean de Blanot, writing in 1255 and 1256, says that the king of France has jurisdiction over, though not the right of obtaining homage from, all the vassals in the kingdom, because he has *imperium* over all men in the realm, and the same jurisdiction that the emperor has in the Empire. Moreover, a rebel baron is guilty of treason, just as anyone is who plots the death of a magistrate of the Roman people; and the more so because he acts against the prince, "for *in temporalibus* the prince recognizes no superior." Therefore, because of this supreme jurisdiction, and for the public good of the kingdom or the good of the whole *patria*, the king has the right to demand obedience from all vassals as subjects.[130]

Calasso says that Jean de Blanot thus "merely presents an assimilation of the king of France to the Emperor," but does not give to the king the *plenitudo potestatis imperialis*. This interpretation misses the main point: the king's jurisdiction, accord-

[126] Barnaby C. Keeney, "The Medieval Idea of the State: the Great Cause, 1291-2," *Univ. Toronto Law Journal*, VII (1949), 48-71, 60-61.

[127] See J. Declareuil, *Hist. générale du droit français*, pp. 427-435; Koschaker, *Europa und das römische Recht*, pp. 75-78; Ercole, *Da Bartolo*, pp. 157-217; Calasso, *Glossatori*[2], pp. 31-32, 45-46, 112-125, 152. For early "imperial" claims of French kings see Fawtier, *Capetian Kings*, pp. 79-83.

[128] Ercole, *Da Bartolo*, pp. 157, 184-185; Calasso, *Glossatori*[2], pp. 113-114, 118ff.

[129] *Ibid.*, pp. 31-33, 45-47, 152; Woolf, *Bartolus*, pp. 373-375; but Ullmann, *E.H.R.*, LXIV, 8, says that the majority of the French jurists argued for the *de jure* as well as *de facto* independence of France.

[130] *Tractatus super feudis et homagiis*, ed. Acher, *loc. cit.* (n. 40 above), 159-162; discussed by Calasso, *Glossatori*[2], pp. 112-115, Ercole, *Da Bartolo*, p. 184, and Ullmann, *E.H.R.*, LXIV, 7, 11.

ing to Jean, is supreme in his realm; and the same passages in the
Roman law are cited to show this as those which support the
power, as *dominus mundi*, of the emperor.[131] Even though the
emperor is called *dominus mundi*, his jurisdiction does not
extend to the kingdom of France, as it would if France were
only an allodial holding of the king. The king, then, in effect is
emperor in his own realm (although Jean does not use the
precise words) and he has no superior in temporal affairs.

As for Jacques de Révigny, *ca.* 1270-1280, I am convinced
that on the whole he expresses the theory of independence. To
C. 1, 14, 8 Humanum (Theodosius II and Valentinian, description of the procedure of imperial legislation) he notes that the
emperor cannot legislate without his *proceres*, and adds; "I say
the same for those who do not recognize *de facto* that they have
superiors."[132] *De facto*, not *de jure*, he says, thus failing to assert
that independence from the Empire was sanctioned by law. In
another place, on the question whether any city other than
Rome is a true subject of public law and can recover damages
(restitution), he argues, against Accursius, in the affirmative.
That is to say, other cities than Rome have their own public
law, are public themselves, and can seek restitution—and likewise the Church, for divine and public law walk together ("nam
ius divinum et publicum ambulant pari passu"—a common saying of the lawyers).[133] This does not necessarily indicate independence of the Empire, for many legists admitted the same of
cities within the Empire.

His position is made still more doubtful in his discussion of
imperial privileges granted to provinces. Suppose the pope gives
the king of France the right to collect the tenth of their revenues
from the clergy of the kingdom "pro subsidio terre sancte."

---

131 "Nam sicut omnia sunt imperatoris quantum ad iurisdictionem, cum sit
mundi dominus, sic omnia, que sunt in regno, sunt regis quantum ad iurisdictionem, ut C. de qua. pres. 1. bene a Zenone [*C.* 7, 37, 3], ff. ad 1. ro. de iactu 1.
deprecatio [*D.* 14, 2, 9]." See the famous gloss of Accursius to *C.* 7, 37, 3 ad v.
omnia principis: "Etiam quo ad proprietatem, ut dicit M[artinus] principi apud
Roncaliam, timore vel amore. . . . Sed Bulga[rus] contra etiam ibidem, et hic
expone, ad protectionem vel jurisdictionem . . . Accur."

132 *Commentary* on the *Code*, in Paris, BN, MS lat. 14350, fol. 221ᵛ; Maffei, "I
giuristi francesi," *Annali d. Università di Macerata*, XXIII, 212, 218.

133 *Ibid.*, fol. 206ᵛ-207ʳ.

Now, if a church has a part of its rents in the Empire, and a part in the kingdom, must it pay a tenth of those in the Empire, that is, from property outside the kingdom, as well as a tenth of the rents in the kingdom? Some say yes. Jacques de Révigny holds that to grant a privilege to a province is to grant it to the provincials and the whole territory of the province. Thus, if the emperor grants the *Aurelianenses* immunity from the tribute, he grants it to the territory of Orléans. Therefore, their possessions held outside the province are not immune.[134] It seems, then, that he argues that the clergy of France need not pay a tenth of rents from property held in the Empire, that is, outside the kingdom. Does this mean that the kingdom is outside the Empire? In one sense, it does; but on the other hand, how can he imagine a case in which the emperor gives a privilege to the province of Orléans? It is probable that he does not, in fact, suppose that the emperor can grant a privilege to a French province but is merely engaging in a play of ideas from the Roman law. For he states that certain princes recognize no superior and can legislate just as the emperor does. Further, he considers the crown and king in relation to the public welfare of France, as if the kingdom were independent and outside the Empire, with the full right to wage war with the emperor—or at least with "Germany."[135]

But Calasso and Ercole have stated that for Jacques de Révigny the king is a magistrate of the prince or emperor, and is thus protected by the *Lex Iulia majestatis* against treason, not because he recognizes no superior, for France and Spain were not only at one time (*semel*) but often under the Empire.[136] We must review the whole opinion to place these remarks in context. Jacques begins by saying that all men in the realm are the king's subjects by reason of his ordinary jurisdiction, not by reason of homage. Hence, if vassals obey a rebellious count and attack the king, they are guilty of treason, according to the *Lex Iulia majestatis*, and by this it is proved that the king is *princeps* "quia non cognoscit superiorem." But Jacques goes on to say

---

[134] *Ibid.*, fol. 219ᵛ.
[135] See above, to nn. 41-44.
[136] Calasso, *Glossatori²*, pp. 31 n. 35, 46; Ercole, *Da Bartolo*, p. 167.

that this is treason not because the king is prince, but because he is a magistrate of the prince, for France and Spain were *semel* and *saepe* under the Empire. Then he discusses the problem of loyalty to the king and *patria* in case of war with *Alhimania*.[137]

To me it seems that a different interpretation is possible, that Jacques is simply justifying the application of a principle of Roman public law to the king of France by recalling that France had been under the Empire, and the king can therefore be considered *in this respect* as a magistrate of the emperor, for at one time the delegated authority of the emperor had been exercised in France. But he does not intimate that France and Spain are still within the Empire, and it is doubtful that he felt that the king was in his time simply a *praeses* of an imperial province. If he is a magistrate of the emperor, how can he wage war against *Alhimania*, which is also a part of the Empire? On the whole, then, Jacques de Révigny could hardly be called a champion of the world empire of the Roman emperor.

Pierre de Belleperche (*ca.* 1250-1308), although he served in the government of Philip the Fair, reveals in his works disappointingly little about the French monarchy and its relations with Empire and Church. Ercole and Calasso are in concord in observing that while he admits that *de facto* many peoples recognize no superior, *de jure* the emperor is the *dominus cunctorum*. Ercole quotes a passage, moreover, showing that Pierre believed that no *Respublica* or kingdom but Rome had the full right of restitution.[138] But more needs to be said, for these scholars have overlooked other interesting passages from Pierre's works. For example, on the subject of the just war, at first glance he seems to stand on the side of independence, and in terms recalling Peter the Chanter and some of the canonists. In case of a quarrel, he says, between those who have no superior, when there is no higher judge, they can wage war against each other. Yet he adds that the canonists say that the pope has the supreme jurisdiction when the Empire is without an emperor.[139] No doubt, he thus

137 Pierre de Tourtoulon, *Oeuvres de Jacques de Révigny*, pp. 48-50.
138 Ercole, *Da Bartolo*, pp. 164, 165 n. 2, 166 n. 2, 189-190 n. 3; Calasso, *Glossatori*², p. 32.
139 *Lectura* on the *Inst.*, Paris, 1513, 30ᵛ-31: "Illi qui non habent superiorem:

holds that it is only when there is no emperor that other rulers have no superior.

Again, in another place he says that, for the sake of maintaining a public law, by which, e.g., a road is for public use, it is for the public utility to have one ruler whom the *universus orbis* obeys; and therefore it was necessary to entrust the *regimen* of the world to one man whom all must obey, for otherwise the law (*iura*) could not be enforced. Nor can the subjection of this *terra*, nor the *signum* of its subjection to the prince, be an object of *prescriptio*.[140] But on the other hand, he implies the same principles for the kingdom of France, saying, immediately after his remarks about the Empire and emperor, that in the kingdom of France no one can prescribe his exemption from being subject to the king.[141] Moreover, in another passage, in context with remarks again about the Roman emperor, Pierre states: "And therefore those Lombard cities act badly by not recognizing our king, because they are subject to our king."[142] This is astounding, for his words seem to indicate that the king of France was, as it were, emperor both in his own realm and in Italy ("Lombard" means Tuscany as well as Lombardy proper), during the time when there was no emperor, officially crowned as such by the pope. Is Pierre recalling the situation in the early years of the fourteenth century, when Charles of Valois, with the consent of Philip IV, was acting as Peacemaker for Boniface VIII in Florence (1300-1302)? One can only conjecture. Perhaps a careful study of the French legists in relation to the events of 1296-1303 may bring an answer. At any rate, it is possible that Pierre de Belleperche influenced Pierre Dubois; and like the latter and like Jean de Jandun, he may after all have been im-

---

tales de imperio licite adinvicem possunt debellare: ubi debitor meus vult fugere cum non habeo copiam iudicis, possum ipsum auctoritate propria capere. Ergo cum unus de imperio alii velit rem aufferre cum non habent iudicem adinvicem possunt debellare. . . . Istud posset concedi, si diceremus quod non habent superiorem. Canoniste dicunt quod interim vacante imperio papa habet iurisdictionem. . . ."

[140] *Lectura Inst.*, 4ᵛ-5ᵛ.

[141] *Ibid.*, 6: "Et ideo in regno francie nullus prescribit quin sit subiectus regi"; see Maffei, "I giuristi francesi," *Annali d. Università di Macerata*, XXXIII, 225 f.

[142] *Ibid.*: "Et ideo ille civitates in lombardia male faciunt quod non recognoscunt regem nostrum: quia nostro regi subiecte sunt. . . ."

bued with some ideal of French imperialism as a substitute for the German.[143] (As early as the twelfth century a French canonist had believed that the pope had transferred the Empire to the Franks in the person of Charlemagne, and only after the Carolingian period did the Germans have the Empire, which however did not include France—and this kind of theory may have influenced Guillaume de Montlauzun and the French legists.[144] If so, despite his remarks about the emperor as the ruler of the world, Pierre really holds that the king of France is independent of the Empire. It is possible that the repetition of old theories about the Roman Empire is merely an academic habit, without real reference to France and other countries that had not been within the Holy Roman Empire. Otherwise, it is hard to explain apparent contradictions, or the idea of the kingdom as the *patria communis* with its capital, Paris, the *communior et excellentior* city exactly as Rome was in the Empire.[145]

Of other French legists I have noted only what Jean Faure says († *ca.* 1340). Like the French polemics of the time of Philip the Fair, e.g., the author of the *Questio de potestate Papae*,[146] he stands for national independence: "Today the empire, by God's permission, is divided, and other kings and princes (as well as the emperor) are set up by the people, to whom their election and deposition belongs."[147] Against Hostiensis he asserts that the emperor was not empowered by common right or law (*de iure communi*) to rule outside his territory.[148] Moreover, the pope cannot create doctors of law (Roman law) in the kingdom of France, first, because such a creation does not belong to the spiritual arm, since this science is temporal and imperial, and second, because the pope has no secular power to do so, since the French realm in temporal affairs has no superior, as in the *Per venerabilem*. Who, then, can authorize the doctorate? The

---

143 Below, to n. 158.
144 McLaughlin, ed. *Summa Parisiensis*, pp. 10, 56, 155; Dist. 10, c. 9 De capitulis; Dist. 63, c. 23 In Synodo, c. 30 Ego Ludovicus; C. 11, q. 3, c. 104 Antecessor. See n. 118 above.
145 Above, to nn. 44f., 54.
146 See Calasso, *Glossatori*², p. 62.
147 *Com. in Cod.*, Lyons, 1594, p. 3 no. 8 to *C.* 1, 1 Cunctos populos.
148 *Loc.cit.*

king, for every science is of God, and the *dispensatio* of such a science therefore belongs to that vicar of God who is "maior in terra." Thus the king, as the fact of the discussion to *C.* 1, 17, 2 shows, is made the equal of the emperor.[149]

A contemporary of Jean Faure, Petrus Jacobi (Pierre Jame), French legist and canonist famous for a monumental treatise on drawing up writs (*libelli*) in the early fourteenth century, like-wise says a good deal on the subject that has apparently escaped much attention. On the whole, he believes that France and certain other kingdoms were never subject to the emperor. The *Liber feudorum*, he says, has no validity in France, for the Emperors Lothair and Frederick did not rule over the French kingdom. Yet insofar as these feudal laws are included in the *Authenticae* that are inserted in the *Code*, they are taught in the schools (of France), and they can be used in cases on which the civil and Canon law have nothing to say. The Roman people can no longer make laws, and the French are subject neither to the Roman people nor to the emperor.[150]

More interesting is his discussion of the right of the king of France to tax his subjects, including the clergy, for a just war. Since the king recognizes no superior "de facto, nec de iure," in relation to the Empire, he is, like the king of Aragon and other kings, a *foederatus* or *quasi-foederatus* of the emperor: these kings likewise recognize no superior. (The idea that an independent king is a federate ally or *socius* of Rome comes, of course, from Roman sources, and was stated in the thirteenth century.) Like the emperor, therefore, such kings in case of the just war of defense can summon vassals and subjects to fight, but should pay them in provisions or victuals. They can in addition demand extraordinary subsidies from the inhabitants of the provinces and from all the people of the realm, in cases of dearth

---

[149] *Ibid.*, to *C.* 1, 17, 2 Legislatores: ". . . quo iure creantur doct. legum in regno Franciae, cum nec ad Papam pertineat ex brachio suo spirituali, cum sit scientia temporalis et imperialis. . . . Item nec ex seculari, cum regnum Franciae quo ad temporalitatem non habeat superiorem, ut c. per venerabilem. . . . Sed potest dici, quod cum omnis scientia sit a Deo . . . quod ad eius vicarium qui maior est in terra pertineat dispensatio scientiae etiam huiusmodi. . . ."

[150] *Aurea practica libellorum*, Cologne, 1575, pp. 272-273, nos. 15-18; and 274 no. 21.

or public necessity of war, for the purpose of paying the *milites* for the defense of the *Respublica*. In one way, however, such a king cannot do what the emperor can, namely, exact the ordinary burden of grain, wine, etc., or take silver and gold, from his subjects. (In my opinion this is no indication of the inferiority of the king, but simply a statement of how the power of the emperor in his Empire differs from that of a king who is outside the Empire.) Nonetheless, the king who recognizes no superior can impose extraordinary taxes on his subjects "pro defensione regni," even if they refuse their consent ("etiam ipsis invitis"). His subjects are obliged by the *ius gentium* to pay extraordinary taxes for the defense of the kingdom, for as Cato said, "Pugna pro patria"; and the public law belongs in this respect to the *ius gentium*.[151] Further, it is impious to desert the *patria*. Such taxes, however, should be proportionate to the wealth of each individual.

Kings who have no superior can therefore act in general like the emperor, and have the same powers in their realms as the emperor has in his Empire in cases of necessity. But there are other kings who have neither the *ius* nor the *nomen* of emperor (hence the king of France, who is superior to these kings, is assumed to be an emperor in his own realm), and they succeed to their kingdoms as if to their own patrimony, and have ample personal revenues and income separate (from the public *fiscus*). They cannot institute any *vectigal* or levy taxes for their own profit, for a daughter's dowry, or for any other purpose except the defense of the kingdom or the evident utility of the republic. But a king in this category can obtain any of these extraordinary taxes if the people consent, or if it has been a long-standing custom.[152] Thus, according to Petrus Jacobi there seems to be a hierarchy of kings: some, like the kings of France and Aragon, on the level of the emperor, others of a subordinate kind with ill-defined powers. The basis of this distinction is not clear and needs further study.

It is clear, however, that Petrus Jacobi places the French king

[151] *Ibid.*, pp. 274-278, nos. 21, 38, 39, 40, 42; cap. XII; also see above, to n. 56.
[152] *Ibid.*, pp. 287-289, nos. 43, 44.

at the top. An equal of the emperor and independent of him, the king of France is also superior to other kings in at least one respect. Petrus, referring to the constant wars, exactions, and debasement of the coinage of Philip the Fair, warns the king of France to stop such abuses as unjust subsidies that deprive the churches and ecclesiastics of their liberties—all contrary to the civil and Canon law, for his wars are unjust. When the king does these things he acts not as "rex Franciae, sed ut rex laicus, simpliciter loquendo." It is therefore possible that the king of France is superior to others in part because he has a sacred quality (healing powers?) and is not simply a king who possesses his kingdom as private property.[153] Let the king of France set a high example! For other kings believe that he acts as king of France and they follow his bad example. The pope is to blame for this, because he granted to the French king special exemption from excommunication. The pope and the clergy are above kings, and yet kings inflict unjust *tallia, collectae, mala tolta* and confiscations on the people; and their abuses of the seal and coinage are extortions.[154] It is at least tolerable that kings do not obey the emperor, although they would do well to reflect that, if they were subject to him, he would at least settle their quarrels before they resorted to violence, and he would render justice. But they do not even fear the pope, the judge of all Christian kings! The pope, holding the place of Jesus Christ, would settle their discords, if they would obey him, by means of judgments in the papal court, or by way of transaction, peace and concord. If they obeyed him, the pope could excommunicate the recalcitrant and authorize war against them. But kings do not fear the pope, and (without papal consent to declarations of just wars) they fraudulently demand money that belongs to God and the clergy, and burden the clergy and churches. God will judge them for their inobedience to the pope and for waging unjust wars. They should at least fear God! Alas! they know not the *via pacis*.[155]

[153] See Kämpf, *Pierre Dubois*, pp. 33-53, on the healing powers of the king and his sacred character.

[154] *Aurea practica*, pp. 280-281, 286, nos. 99-100. For the term *malatolta* see Ducange.

[155] *Ibid.*, pp. 278f., nos. 46f.

In sum, Petrus Jacobi, though deploring the results, recognizes the legal and factual independence of a great king like the king of France, who, when he obeys God and the law, is truly an emperor in his own realm. But he also recognizes, with bitterness, the results of this with respect to the Church; in fact, but not of course *de jure*, the king has become independent of the spiritual authority of the pope. More than a century earlier Alanus had been able to state the theory and the fact of *rex imperator in regno suo* without foreseeing such consequences for the universalism of the Church.

For my purpose, chiefly the reexamination of the theory in the earlier period, *ca.* 1150-1275, I have gone too far into the fourteenth century. I must leave the survey of the thought of Marino da Caramanico, Andrew of Isernia, Pierre Dubois, Bartolus, Lucas de Penna, and others, to what has been done by Woolf, Ercole, Calasso, and Ullmann.[156] A new, thorough study of them, however, would be desirable, for Lucas de Penna's inconsistency needs explanation,[157] and it is difficult to decide whether Pierre Dubois believes in the independence of France or, like Jean de Jandun and possibly Pierre de Belleperche, wants to transfer the Empire from the Germans to the French.[158]

But for the twelfth and most of the thirteenth century my conclusion is that Mochi Onory goes too far, Calasso not far enough,[159] in finding expressions of independence of the greater kingdoms from the Empire. Some legists and canonists, of German and Italian origin except for Johannes Galensis, maintained the ideal of the universal authority of the emperor, con-

---

[156] Ercole, *Da Bartolo*, pp. 193-217; Calasso, *Glossatori*², pp. 127-164; Woolf, *Bartolus*, pp. 208-383; Ullmann, *E.H.R.*, LXIV, 18-33.

[157] Ercole, *Da Bartolo*, pp. 214-215. W. Ullmann, *The Medieval Idea of Law as Represented by Lucas de Penna*, does not treat this subject.

[158] See the summary of his thought by C. V. Langlois, in Lavisse, *Histoire de France . . . jusqu'à la Révolution*, III², 284-290; Langlois observes also how Jean de Jandun said that the monarchy of the world belongs to the kings of France (290); also Kämpf, *Pierre Dubois*, pp. 23-26, 45-53, 99. Fritz Kern, *Die Anfänge der französischen Ausdehnungspolitik bis zum Jahr 1308*, refers here and there to the importance of Pierre de Belleperche in helping shape or carry on the foreign policy of Philip IV, but says nothing of Pierre's legal thought and statement about the disobedient Lombards (above to n. 142); on Pierre Dubois, pp. 31-34.

[159] Calasso, in the third ed. of *I glossatori e la teoria della sovranità*, does not change the interpretation we have encountered in the second ed.

ceding only that in fact some kings had no temporal superior (Huguccio, Joh. Galensis, Johannes Teutonicus, Jacobus de Albenga, and Bernard of Parma). Other writers, particularly in the field of polemical treatises around 1300, continued to believe in the ideal of universal Empire, but were prompted by a nationalistic spirit to advocate the transfer of the Empire from the Germans to the French. But a few legists of France, from the mid-thirteenth century on, though falling into some inconsistency because of their training in the Roman law, generally asserted that the king of France was not subject to the emperor and was emperor in his own realm (Jean de Blanot, Jacques de Révigny, Petrus Jacobi, and Jean Faure). Pierre de Belleperche probably favored French domination of Italy and the Empire, hence the substitution of the French for the Germans in control; and yet there are traces of a narrower nationalism in his thought, and certainly he supported French aggression. Bracton, with his grounding in Canon, civil, and customary law, clearly believed that England and the king were in no wise subject to any outside secular prince—as clearly, indeed, as Henry VIII stated absolute independence two and a half centuries later.[160]

The earliest and most ardent statements of the theory of *de jure* as well as *de facto* independence of kingdoms came from canonists and theologians largely of England, Spain and France, from the late twelfth to the mid-thirteenth century and later. Richard de Mores, Alanus Anglicus, Laurentius Hispanus, Vincentius Hispanus, Johannes de Deo, Innocent IV (Italian), Guillaume Durant, and Guillaume de Montlauzun, all in one way or another anticipated or followed Innocent III's statement that the king of France knew no superior *in temporalibus*, and held that the king of France or Spain or England was emperor in his own realm. Not all used the words, *rex imperator in regno suo*, but they implied the equivalent of the formula when they did not state it. The same is true of Peter the Chanter and Gérard d'Abbeville, French theologians.

But if they meant that the king was emperor in his own realm,

[160] McIlwain, *Growth of Political Thought*, p. 268.

did they mean that it was so only in the limited sense, that he was nonetheless subject to the Empire, just as the *pater familias* can be called *rex* in his household but is under higher authorities? Not at all, for such a king ruled according to the independent public law of the realm, even if some of the principles of it were taken from Rome; he had the full right to declare a just war, subject only in theory to papal approval; under no man in temporal matters, he was the equal of the emperor. No one could appeal from him to the emperor, and the emperor's rights of jurisdiction did not extend to the kingdom. The kingdom, moreover, was becoming a *patria communis*: it was no longer a local *patria* within the *patria communis* of Rome.

The canonists who started formulating the theory of the king as an emperor who had no superior were merely reflecting a long tradition. Early medieval kings imitated the late Roman imperial institutions, and legislated like the emperor in their sacred palaces with the counsel of their *proceres*. Spanish kings arrogated to themselves the proud title of *imperator*. By the twelfth century an awareness of independence from the Empire of Charlemagne and his successors had arisen. The universalism of the Church remained, but that of the Roman Empire was weakened and even broken by an important current of thought, as well as by fact, by the middle of the thirteenth century. The kingdom, independent of the Empire, and thus the new common fatherland and common birthplace of all subjects of the king, was now a nation in fact if not yet in name.

3. VINCENTIUS HISPANUS AND SPANISH NATIONALISM

Vincentius Hispanus was mentioned above as important for his love of Spain. His ideas are of particular interest in connection with the history of Spain in his time and with the rise of nationalism in Spain.

It was not uncommon for early medieval kings, for example, in Anglo-Saxon England, to be called emperor, however little the assumption of the title signified. Perhaps in Spain, however, when the kings of Leon and Castile called themselves emperors as early as the tenth century, some concept of separation from the Roman Empire of Charlemagne and Otto the Great may have been involved.[161] It had grown up partly in memory of Visigothic unity, partly (perhaps) in reaction against the claims of the successors of Charlemagne, and partly in the glory derived from the Reconquest. The culmination came in 1135, when Alfonso VII of Leon and Castile assumed the imperial title, and Pope Innocent II, perhaps intentionally, as a blow at the prestige of the Holy Roman Empire, allowed him to call himself King of Kings.[162] St. Ferdinand (1217-1252; 1230-1252 in Leon), fully worthy of the title, aspired to it, but apparently did not actually claim it.[163] His son, Alfonso the Learned, was a candidate for the imperial title, not of Spain but of the Holy Roman Empire. But his efforts ended in fiasco,[164] and during his reign he foolishly alienated those very attributes of the crown that pertained to the strength of the Castilian monarchy in Spain. "He aspired to be emperor, though he was not even able to play the king."[165]

But if Alfonso X failed in this direction, in the *Especulo* and the *Siete Partidas*, a great monument to his scholarly interests, he stated that the king recognizes no superior in temporal matters, and that kings have the same powers in their kingdoms as emperors have in the Empire—[166] a clear reflection of the theory already current, as we have seen, among the canonists and legists. Thus, the old ideal of an Empire of Spain surrendered to the newer theory of the national independence at least of Leon and Castile. Yet the older tradition of empire was na-

---

[161] See Ramon Menendez Pidal, *El imperio hispanico y los cinco reinos*, chs. i-v; also Gifford Davis, "The Incipient Sentiment of Nationality in Mediaeval Castile: The *Patrimonio Real*," *Speculum*, XII (1937), 351-358, esp. p. 352.

[162] Merriman, *Rise of the Spanish Empire*, I, 90; above all, Menendez Pidal, *El imperio hispanico*, ch. vii, esp. pp. 155ff.

[163] Merriman, I, 91.

[164] *Ibid.* and 110ff.; for details, see Charles C. Bayley, *The Formation of the German College of Electors in the Mid-Thirteenth Century*, pp. 69-77, 159-167, 175-181, 193-201.

[165] Merriman, *op.cit.*, 112.

[166] *Siete Partidas*, II, i, 8: ". . . todos aquellos poderes que de suso diximos, que los Emperadores han, e deuen auer en las gentes de su Imperio, que essos mismos han los Reyes en la de sus Reynos, e mayores"; also II, i, 5: "Vicarios de Dios son los Reyes, cada uno in su reyno, puestos sobre las gentes para mantenerlas en justicia, e en verdad quanto en lo temporal, bien assi como el Emperador en su Imperio"; and *Especulo*, I, 13: the king can make laws because "por la merced de Dios non habemos mayor sobre nos en el temporal"; texts also in Carlyle, *Medieval Political Theory*, v, 148; cf. Calasso, *Glossatori*², p. 39 n. 52.

tionalistic too. Indeed, Alfonso X departed from it in trying to win the crown of the Holy Roman Empire, and in a sense was ready to abandon the separate Empire of Spain for the medieval ideal of unity in the Roman Empire. The statement in the *Siete Partidas*, therefore, may be considered as a return, expressed in the formula *rex est imperator in regno suo*, to the tradition of Spanish imperialism.

Paradoxically, the ideal of the Spanish Empire was nationalistic. Yet there was no united kingdom of Spain, and no king after the Visigothic period ruled over the whole Iberian Peninsula until the time of Philip II. If there was an ideal unity in memory of Visigothic Spain and in the goal of Christian reconquest, it never existed in fact in the Middle Ages. For despite the titles of emperor and king of kings, not even the ambitious Alfonso VII could rule over all the kingdoms that arose during the Reconquest. As a result, as the thirteenth century opened there were several kingdoms, of which the most important were Portugal, Leon and Castile, and Aragon. Nevertheless, the sentiment of unity connected with the idea of the Empire as a whole certainly persisted and therefore we may speak of a Spanish nationalism in the twelfth and thirteenth centuries.

If some of this nationalism is to be found in the Spanish chronicles,[167] better evidence of it is furnished by a famous canon lawyer, Vincentius Hispanus.[168] Where he was born is unknown, but it was probably somewhere in Spain. He studied and taught Canon and Roman law at Bologna in the late twelfth and early thirteenth century. He wrote glosses on the *Decretum* (1210-1212), a full *Apparatus* of glosses (1210-1215) to *Compilatio I* and also to *Compilatio III* (1210-1215); moreover, he glossed the Decrees of the Fourth Lateran Council of 1215

---

[167] Davis, "The Incipient Sentiment of Nationality in Mediaeval Castile," *Speculum*, XII, 351-358; the author simply shows how there was some criticism of kings who alienated any territory; there is no study of the problem of alienation in Spanish law. See also by Davis, "The Development of a National Theme in Medieval Castilian Literature," *Hispanic Review*, III (1935), 149ff. Some nationalism may be implied in the chronicles which repeated the legend of Bernardo del Carpio; see below, n. 193.

[168] See Schulte, *Quellen*, I, 191f.; Fr. Gillmann, "Wo war Vincentius Hispanus Bischof?" *Arch. f. kathol. KR.*, CXIII (1933), 99-107; Kuttner, *Repertorium*, I, 374 n. 2.

(1215-1216), and remained active as a scholar long enough to write an *Apparatus* on the *Decretals* of Gregory IX (hence Vincentius was active as a decretalist after 1234).[169] His work shows special knowledge of places in Portugal (Braga, Coimbra, and Lisbon), where he held ecclesiastical provisions. In 1226 he was chancellor to King Sancho II and was elected bishop of Idanha-Guarda in 1229. He died in 1248.[170]

Despite his career in Portugal, there is no doubt that he looked upon himself as a Spaniard and was loyal to the idea of the whole Iberian Peninsula as Spain, of which Portugal was merely a part. He calls himself, in proper humility, "episcoporum Hispanie minimus"—in the introduction to his *Apparatus* to the *Decretals* of Gregory IX.[171] His glorification of Spanish virtues appears as early as 1210-1215: "With deeds, like a Spaniard," he says, "not with words, like a Frenchman."[172] His praise of Spain begins at the same time, for he speaks of "noble Spain."[173] He cannot accept Pope Innocent III's praise of the kingdom of the French. He declares that Spain, not France (the French Church), is greater than other ecclesiastical provinces, for "when Charles with all the northerners (*Francigenae*) wished to invade Spain, the Spanish blocked their passage, overcame them in battle, and killed twelve peers!"[174] (Yet he admitted

[169] Kuttner, I, 54, 326, 356, 370, and 374 n. 2; Gillmann, in *Arch. f. kathol. KR.*, CV (1925), 490, CVI (1926), 161ff., CVIII (1928), 603, CIX (1929), 263, 266.

[170] These details are given by Gillmann, *op.cit.*, CXIII, 99-107; also Pressuti, *Regesta Honorii Papae III*, nos. 1652, 5134, 5136. Javier Ochoa, however, holds that Vincentius was bishop of Saragossa after leaving Bologna; *Vincentius Hispanus*, in general.

[171] Schulte, *Quellen*, I, 191, n. 13; cf. n. 170.

[172] Gillmann, *op.cit.*, CXIII, 100: "Facto, ut ispanus, non autem verbis, ut francigena . . ." (to *Compilatio I*, 2, 20, 29; *Decretals of Gregory IX* 2, 28, 19).

[173] *Ibid.*, p. 101: "Similiter dicitur in nobili yspania: Capre comedunt vineas et asinis amputantur auricule . . ." (to *Compilatio III*, 1, 6, 5; *Decr. Greg. IX* 1, 6, 20).

[174] Innocent III's words, "cum hoc regnum (francorum) benedictum a deo," are in his famous decretal *Novit*, in which he intervened, *ratione peccati*, in the quarrel of Philip II of France and John of England, *Compilatio III*, 2, 1, 3 (*Decr. Greg. IX* 2, 1, 13—here the introductory words are not included). Vincentius's gloss is in his *Apparatus* to *Compilatio III*, and I quote it from the Bamberg MS Can. 20 (P. II. 7) fol. 127 c. 1, ad v. *cum hoc regnum*: "Sic et gallicana ecclesia maior aliis, supra, de magistris, quanto, l. 1 [*Compilatio I*, 3, tit. *De mag.*, c. *Quanto*; *Decr. Greg. IX* 5, 5, 3—where Alexander III praised the Gallican Church as greater than others and forbade payment for the license

that *de jure* the king of France recognized no superior in temporal affairs.)[175]

These remarks were made, we have noted, about 1210-1215. But in this same period of activity as a decretalist Vincentius has nothing of significance to say on Innocent III's famous decretal of 1202, the *Venerabilem*, in which the pope stated his version of the *translatio imperii* from the Greeks to the Germans. As we have seen, it was on the *Venerabilem* that Johannes Teutonicus, after 1217,[176] offered his comment, that all kings and kingdoms are subject to the German, Holy Roman Empire. Why did Vincentius say nothing about Spain in reaction to a decretal that glorified the Germans, when he was writing his *Apparatus* to the *Decretals* of Innocent III and was sharply challenging the idea of the greatness of France? One cannot be sure, but the answer probably lies in Vincentius' resentment towards Johannes Teutonicus as a German patriot. Now, Johannes compiled the *Glossa ordinaria* to the *Decretum* shortly after 1215, and his *Apparatus* to *Compilatio III* (*Decretals* of Innocent III) after 1217,[177] and in these works the German canonist made his sweeping arguments for the supremacy of the German Roman Empire. But Vincentius wrote the glosses in his *Apparatus* to *Compilatio III* before 1215. It seems likely, then, that his failure to react at this time against the right of the Germans to possess the Empire and dominate all kingdoms comes simply from the fact that Innocent III in 1202 acknowledged that certain kings were independent of the emperor (in the decretal, *Per venerabilem*),[178] and in the *Venerabilem* (also 1202) on the *translatio*

---

to teach in cathedral schools]. Immo per hoc colligitur quod hispania est maior aliis provinciis. Cum enim Carolus vellet cum omnibus francigenis intrare hispaniam, ispani ingressu ispanie obviaverunt eis, et superaverunt eos in bello, et occiderunt .xii. paria. Et si vinco vincentem te, vinco te, ff. de diver. et temp. prescrip. de accessionibus [*Dig.* 44, 3]. *Vinc.*"

[175] But this was simply a logical part of Vincentius' belief in the independence of France and Spain alike; independent Spain was superior to independent France—to *Comp. III*, 4, 12, 2 Per venerabilem (*Decr. Greg. IX* 4, 17, 13), ad v. *recognoscat*: "De facto. jo. Immo de iure, supra, de iudic. novit"; Bamberg MS Can. 19, fol. 127. He refers to Johannes Galensis and to the *Novit* of Innocent III (*Decr. Greg. IX* 2, 1, 13).

[176] See Kuttner, *Repertorium*, 357.   [177] *Ibid.*, pp. 93f., 357.

[178] *Decr. Greg. IX* 4, 17, 13: the king of France, he says, recognizes no superior in temporal affairs.

imperii said nothing about kingdoms other than the German, while Johannes Teutonicus' opinions, moreover, were not written until after Vincentius commented on these decretals. Not even Laurentius Hispanus' work on the *Decretum* of Gratian and the *Decretals* of Innocent III (both before 1215), and his acceptance of the *translatio imperii* theory, aroused Vincentius —perhaps, again, because Laurentius did not specifically say, in his theory of the *translatio imperii* to the Germans, that all kingdoms are in the Empire.[179]

But about 1217 Johannes Teutonicus commented on the *Venerabilem* in such a way as to call forth Vincentius' Spanish loyalty. Let us first recall the words of the German canonist. He declared that the government of the world was transferred to the Germans, although the Greek ruler could, *largo nomine*, be called emperor, just as the king of chessmen can be called king, and that the true, German emperor is above all kings and nations; he is the lord of the world, all provinces are under him and all things are in his power. Nor can any kingdom be exempt from the Empire, because it would then be headless and, without a head, a monster. All things are in the power of the emperor. "Let us acknowledge, therefore, that the Teutons by

---

[179] See the gloss, attributed to Laurentius by Gillmann (but I am not certain that it is by Laurentius), to the *Venerabilem*, in Gillmann, *Des Laurentius Hispanus Apparat zur Compilatio III*, pp. 128f.; also in my article, "Some Unpublished Glosses, etc., *Arch. f. kathol. KR.*, CXVII, 407f; cf. my article "The So-called Laurentius-*Apparatus* to the Decretals of Innocent III in *Compilatio III*," *The Jurist*, II (1942), 3-29. Certainly by Laurentius is this, to the *Decretum*, C. 7, 1, 41, ad v. *imperator unus*: "Fuerunt tamen quandoque duo [imperatores] de facto. . . . Quid diceres tu de greculo imperatore? Videtur quod sit imperator, quia constantinus illo transtulit imperium. . . . Et preterea papa ei scribit tanquam imperatori, extra. iii. de maio. et obe. solite [*Decr. Greg. IX* 1, 33, 6]. Videtur contra, quod romanus tantum sit imperator, quia ecclesia romana imperium a grecis transtulit in germanos, extra. iii. de electione, venerabilem, quia greci rebelles et inobedientes erant. Et quod potuit patet, quia ubi secularis est negligens, devolvitur iurisdictio ad ecclesiasticum. . . . Colligitur tamen ex quodam canone, quod iste [imperator] non est nisi yconomus ecclesie romane, de cons., dist. V. in die. *Ia.*"; in Paris, BN, MS lat. 15393, fol. 121. Again, to Dist. 96, c. Si imperator, ad v. *divinitus*: ". . . Sed quis est verus imperator? Dicit B. quod constantinopolitanus. . . . Sed contra, extra. iii. de electione, venerabilem; dicit ibi quod romana ecclesia transtulit dominium vel imperium in occidentem a grecis, et ita iste romanus est verus. *Ia.*"; MS lat. 15393, fol. 70.

their virtues have won the empire" ("Fateamur ergo quod Teutonici virtutibus promeruerunt imperium").[180]

Johannes Teutonicus thus glorifies the Germans by attributing to them the same virtues as those by which the Romans had originally built the Empire—so Gratian, C. 28, q. 1, c. 14 Omnes, § Ex his: "iuxta illud Hieronymi, 'Virtutibus Romani promeruerunt imperium.' "

Perhaps an additional challenge was presented by Jacobus de Albenga, who commented on the *Decretals* of Honorius III (1226). Honorius III in the *Gravi nobis* (1220) warned the king of Portugal against imposing exactions on the clergy and referred to the law of the emperor that granted immunity to the Church. To this Jacobus asks why the pope refers to an imperial law when the king of Portugal is not under the emperor; and he replies that although the king is not under him, he ought to be, and indeed "omnes reges debent subesse imperatori."[181]

But the flaunting of German superiority was more than enough to arouse Vincentius—he was easily moved! In fact, it brought forth an interpolation in the gloss of Johannes Teutonicus perhaps before 1234; in one manuscript I have found the words "excepto regimine hyspanie" inserted thus, "Sic enim regimen mundi, excepto regimine hyspanie, translatum est ad teutonicos."[182] If this insertion was not made by Vincentius (and there is no way of proving that it is his), he definitely revealed his indignation after the *Decretals* of Gregory IX were published by Raymond of Peñafort in 1234. His comment is to the *Venerabilem* (*Decretals* of Gregory IX, 1, 6, 34) and it occurs in his *Apparatus* or commentary. So far as I know, his gloss has not been published.

Vincentius begins his remarks on the *Venerabilem* by quoting literally the earlier opinion of Johannes Teutonicus, namely,

---

[180] See above, nn. 73-81.

[181] Brit. Mus., MS Royal 11 C. VII, fol. 226ᵛ, to *Comp. V*, 3, 26, 5 (Pressuti, *Reg. Hon. III*, no. 2921), ad v. *generali lege*: "Sed quare papa allegat legem imperatoris ipsi regi, cum ei non subsit? Respondeo, licet ei non subsit, subesse debet tamen, ut xi. q. i., in apibus. Item lex ista intelligitur esse postquam est per ecclesiam approbatum, ut C. de veteri iure enucle. l. i, § sed hiis [*C*. 1, 17, 1 § Sed et si]. Et est ar. in decr. ista, quod omnes reges debent subesse imperatori."

[182] Paris, BN, MS lat. 12542, fol. 21; see above, n. 73.

that a kingdom would be a headless monster if independent of the Empire, that all men owe tribute to the emperor, that all things are in his power, and that by their superior virtues the Germans earned the Empire.[183] Now he gives his own opinion: "Make exception, Johannes Teutonicus, of the Spanish, who are exempt by the law itself [i.e., *Dig.* 50, 15, 8, on certain provinces and cities of Spain that were granted immunity from tribute to the emperor]! The Spanish, indeed, refused entrance to Charles and his peers. But I, Vincentius, say that the Germans have lost the empire by their own stupidity[184] [does he refer to the excommunication of Frederick II by Gregory IX in 1239, or to his deposition by Innocent IV at the Council of Lyons in 1245?].[185] For every hut[186] usurps lordship (*dominium*) for itself, and every city contends with the Germans for the same. But the Spanish alone have by their valor (*virtute*) obtained the *imperium*, and they too [the Visigothic kings] have chosen bishops.[187] In France, in England, in Germany, and in Constantinople the Spanish (are renowned because they) rule over the Blessed Lady Spain,[188] of which they are acquiring the lordship and which as lords and masters they are expanding by virtue of their valor and probity. The Spanish, therefore, are aided by their merits and worth. Unlike the Germans, they do not lack a body of

---

[183] *Appar.* to *Decr. Greg. IX* 1, 6, 34 (in Paris, BN, MS lat. 3967, fol. 21, c. 2), ad v. *in germanos*: ". . . Nec aliquid regnum potuit eximi ab imperio, quia illud esset acephalum, ut xxi. di. submittitur [*Decretum*, Dist. XXI, c. 8] et esset monstrum sine capite suo. Debent tributum imperatori nisi in hoc sint exempti, ff. de censibus, l. ult. [*D.* 50, 15, 8]. Omnia enim sunt in potestate imperatoris. . . . Fatetur ego quod theotonici virtutibus prom[er]uerunt imperium. . . ." Cf. Joh. Teut., above, n. 73.

[184] The word is *busnardiam*. My colleague, Professor J. H. Herriott, tells me that the O. Fr. and O. Span. *busnard* (Provençal *busnart*) means "dumb, stupid," and he refers to Meyer-Lübke, in *Romanisches etymologisches Wörterbuch* (3rd ed.), s.v. *buteo*. See also Wartburg, *Französisches etymologisches Wörterbuch*, s.v. *buteo*, from which *buisnart*, "imbécile," in O.F.; and DuCange, s.v. *busio*, from which *buisnart* and *buisnardie*, "stupid, dull."

[185] Naturally I do not pretend to argue a positive connection between Vincentius' gloss and any particular event. Certainly it is doubtful that he wrote his *Appar.* as late as 1245.

[186] In the manuscript *thigurium*.

[187] Here Vincentius refers to the *Decretum*, Dist. LXIII, c. 26 *Cum longe*, which is a decree of a Council of Toledo, specifying the consent of the king in episcopal elections.

[188] The text is difficult here and my translation may be free; but the sense is not altered. See below, n. 190.

prescripts and customs.[189] Who indeed, Spain, can reckon thy glories?—Spain, wealthy in horses, celebrated for food, and shining with gold; steadfast and wise, the envy of all; skilled in the laws (*iura sciens*) and standing high on sublime pillars!"[190]

To understand Vincentius' reaction and the context of his gloss, we must recall the Visigothic tradition and Isidore of Seville's encomium of Spain under the Visigoths,[191] but above

[189] What Vincentius means is that the Spanish law was independent of the Roman law, that indeed the *liber iudiciorum* of Leon forbade on the pain of death the reception of the Roman law. Hence, the Spanish had no need of any Roman law, and Spain was all the more independent of the Roman Empire. Spanish law was the equal of the Roman law, just as the Spanish Empire was the equal of Rome. This meaning is confirmed by an opinion of Vincentius which I overlooked when this study was originally published. Professor Stephan Kuttner has recently sent me the text of the opinion in a gloss in Vincentius' *Commentary* to the *Decr. Greg. IX*, and I quote Kuttner's report of the text— to 5, 33, 28 Super speculam, ad v. *non utuntur*: "in Yspania excellentissima provinciarum prima lex in libro iudiciorum Legionum hec est: 'quicumque recepit (leges) romanas capite puniatur,' et ita de pari contendit cum imperio, etiam cum Francia, quia in eo tempore quo (MS, quod) non erant in Yspania nisi gentiles, in ipso introitu Franchi perierunt cum paribus suis et residui cum rege suo retrocentes dimiserunt ioculatores suos in Vasconia, qui nec locuntur gallicum nec yspanum." See Ochoa, *Vincentius Hispanus*, pp. 16f. (I owe this reference to Professor Kuttner.)

This opinion fits in not only with the gloss translated in my text but also with the gloss quoted above, n. 174.

[190] Paris, BN, MS lat. 3967, fol. 21 c. 2: "Io. theutonice, excipe ipso iure exemptos yspanos, qui karolum non admiserunt, nec eius pares. Sed ego Vinc. dico, quod theutonici per busnardiam perdiderunt imperium. Quodlibet enim thigurium sibi usurpat dominium, et quelibet civitas de dominio cum eis contendit. Sed soli Yspani virtute sua obtinuerunt imperium, et episcopos elegerunt. lxiii. d. cum longe [Dist. 63, c. 25]. Nonne in francia et in anglia et in theotonica et in constantinopoli Yspani dominantur beate [*beate* is in the margin with a sign to indicate its insertion here] domine Yspane, que dominium pariunt, et dominantes audacie et probitatis virtutibus expandunt? Iuvantur ergo Yspani meritis et probitate; nec indigent corpore prescriptionum vel consuetudinum sicut theotonici. Quis valeat numerare, Yspania, laudes tuas, dives equis, preclara cibis auroque refulgens; parca fuge, prudens, et cunctis invidiosa; iura sciens, et stans sublimibus alta columpnis, Vinc." Vincentius in the last sentence may be quoting verses.

[191] In his *Historia de regibus gothorum*, Isidore starts out by describing Spain as the most beautiful of all lands as far as India, as the queen of all the provinces (of the Roman Empire), rich in animals, fruits, harvests, oil, fields, mountains, fish, and precious metals; he admires the beautiful situation and temperate climate; and again Spain is rich in horses ("Tibi cedet Alphaeus equis") and gems. Naturally Golden Rome, *caput gentium*, coveted Spain! And Spain is still happy and flourishing under the Goths. (I owe this reference to Prof. R. L. Reynolds.)

The idea of glorifying Spain thus may have occurred to Vincentius as a result of his reading Isidore's *History*. But his language is sufficiently different

all remember that the period of his career as an important canonist, ecclesiastic, chancellor to the king of Portugal (1226ff.), and bishop of Idanha-Guarda (1229-1248), was also that of great Spanish achievement. If the Albigensian Crusade resulted in greater power for the French monarchy and a check for Aragon in southern France, the victory of Pedro of Aragon at Las Navas de Tolosa (1212), and the expansion of Aragon under James the Conqueror into Valencia (1233-1245) and the Balearics (1229-1235) were adequate compensation. The Reconquest, moreover, was continued with brilliant success by King Ferdinand of Leon and Castile, who took Cordova (1236) and Seville (1248), and conquered Andalusia and Murcia, leaving only the small kingdom of Granada to the Moors. Despite the division of Spain into kingdoms, these were essentially Spanish victories and a legitimate source of Spanish pride. Spaniards, indeed, could boast that their participation in the Crusade of Christendom was as effective and glorious as that of the French and other northern nations in the expeditions to the Holy Land and Constantinople. Vincentius, I am sure, expresses the Spanish pride, nay, patriotism, that arose both from these and earlier achievements, and from the old tradition of the unity of Spain in the Spanish Empire. But the Germans of the same period were involved in futile wars in Italy, and Frederick II's Crusade of 1228-1229 could hardly appeal to the Spanish ideal of fighting the infidel. Therefore, the Spanish, not the Germans, possessed, like the Romans, those virtues by which an Empire is won; and it is the Spanish, not the Germans, who had won and were adding to their Empire. Such is the conclusion of Vincentius Hispanus.

But is this Spanish Empire a universal one that should take the place of the Holy Roman Empire and embrace all kingdoms and nations? Does Vincentius advocate imperialism, in the modern sense of the word, for Spain?

Alexander of Roes, in the later thirteenth century, ardently championed the traditional Empire, but always in German

---

from Isidore's to make one doubt that he had read it. Besides, Isidore looks upon Spain as a province of the Roman Empire.

hands: he wants no German nation or state like France; Germany must be above France (and other kingdoms); world imperialism belongs to the Germans.[192] Thus he continued the ideal of Johannes Teutonicus. In France, a little later, Pierre Dubois countered with his famous plan for French domination in Christendom in order to assure the success of a final crusade. In both instances nationalism becomes a new universalism. But Vincentius had not gone so far. He glorifies Spain and the Spanish and believes that the Spanish are superior to the French and the Germans, and by their virtues merit the empire they have won and are expanding. This empire, however, is not the old, theoretically universal, Holy Roman Empire, which he would transfer from the Germans to the Spanish. It is, I feel, the Empire of Spain, of the Iberian Peninsula. His ideal, therefore, seems to be a continuation of the traditional feeling in Spain of the unity of Spanish history and civilization from the Visigothic period to the Reconquest. His ideal is no doubt limited, moreover, by the theory that the kingdom of Spain is independent of the Holy Roman Empire, for the king recognizes no superior and is emperor in his own realm, and by his own belief that Spain was never ruled by Charlemagne. Not long after Vincentius died, Alfonso the Learned was a candidate for the imperial crown, and perhaps he was inspired by some vague feeling that Spain should be the new center and controlling power of the Holy Roman Empire. Ultimately Spain was in fact the real center when in 1519 Charles I was elected emperor and became Charles V. Yet the true greatness of Spain had been and was being realized in the Aragonese empire in the Mediterranean, in the Portuguese expansion in Africa and the Far East, and in the Castilian conquest of much of the new world. The true Spanish Empire was only by accident joined to the Holy Roman Empire in the person of Charles V. It is with this Empire of Spain, not with Alfonso the Learned's abortive aspiration and the Empire of Charles V, that we must connect the fervid nationalism of Vincentius Hispanus. For the expansion of the Empire of Spain, independent of the Roman Empire, was in his

[192] Herman Heimpel, "Alexander von Roes und das deutsche Selbstbewusstsein des 13. Jahrhunderts," *Archiv für Kulturgeschichte,* XXVI (1935), 19-60.

time already nationalistic and Spanish (Aragonese) supremacy in the western Mediterranean was beginning.

Vincentius Hispanus, then, offers one of the most interesting examples of the expression of the new feeling of patriotism and nationalism in the thirteenth century. His thought is the more remarkable because, as a canon lawyer, he should logically have believed in universalism not only in the Church but also in the State. Proud of Spain, however, and of Spanish achievements, he reacted against German boasts of supremacy. He reacted likewise against French pride.[193] To any French claim of empire and domination in Spain, he responded by declaring that the French were full of words, not deeds, and that the Spanish had defeated the great Charles and killed twelve of his peers. Was Vincentius impatient with the *Song of Roland* and the French imperialism of the feudal epic? Was he simply reflecting Spanish dislike of those French knights who had often assisted in the Reconquest and whose conceit and arrogance frequently aroused resentment in the twelfth and thirteenth centuries? Or was he acquainted with the legend of Bernardo del Carpio in the chronicle of Rodrigo of Toledo (1180-1247; Rodrigo studied at Bologna and Paris, and was bishop in 1209) or with an earlier version of the story told in the Poema de Fernan Gonzalez (1250-2171) of how Bernardo defeated Charles and the twelve peers?[194] Whatever the causes of his national pride, Vincentius will have none of France nor of Germany and the Holy Roman Empire. His common fatherland, his independent kingdom and empire, is Spain —Noble Spain, Blessed Lady Spain!

[193] Odofredo also, to *D.* 2, 14, 7, 7: ". . . olim romani nobiles mittebantur . . . per universas partes mundi regiones sicut hodie fit de nobilibus militibus de francia: ut essent proconsules et presides et in suo reditu portabant infinitum de auro et argento."

[194] See, for the legend of Bernardo, which arose about 1160-1236, hence in the lifetime of Vincentius, Th. Heinermann, *Untersuchungen zur Entstehung der Sage von Bernardo del Carpio*, pp. 108, 28f., 35f., 59f., 75. I cannot go into the subject of the growth of the idea, founded on the attack at Roncesvalles, that Spaniards, rather than Saracens, defeated Charlemagne and his peers. But obviously the Spanish literary tradition may be reflected by Vincentius, as I have indirectly shown. (Prof. Mack H. Singleton kindly gave me the reference above.)

CHAPTER XI ✦ THE NATURALNESS OF SOCIETY AND THE STATE

IN THE general modern theory of the State and nationalism, secularism is considered a necessity for their full development.[1] If the sanction of nature and the natural law is mentioned and the national State is considered to be a natural phenomenon of the social nature of man, such naturalism has no connection with a divine author or religion. State and nationalism resulted in part from the rise of a secular, worldly, naturalistic spirit that removed God from any ordering of the world and man. They could make their first tentative appearance, therefore, only in the late thirteenth century, just when *l'esprit laique* was beginning to manifest itself and to shatter the medieval *Ordo*.

In this study, however, the presumption is that the State and the accompanying nationalism can exist in an age of faith, when men believe in God as the source of nature and the natural ordering of mankind in independent States. They can exist equally well when appeals to God are merely politically expedient. Whether sincere or not (and sometimes it is sincere), the belief that God particularly loves the United States of America is as much a manifestation of nationalism as the opposite assumption that the sovereignty of the national State is supreme in itself, the final end of patriotic devotion. Patriotism can, of course, flourish without the support of a religious faith; but it is often intensified by the conviction that God wills it. Fighting and dying for the fatherland result chiefly from the State's willing it, but the belief that God approves just wars of defense has at times been a moral support both of the heads of State who command and of men who risk their lives in military service. So the State may become supreme whether men hold

[1] See the authorities referred to above, ch. x, n. 1.

that it recognizes no religion or believe that it is sanctified by religion. At any rate, its superiority as a corporate, moral entity that subordinates all, even God and Church, to the end of its safety is often the greater because of the belief that God and the nature that is God's instrument inspired those who created the State and continue to inspire those statesmen who, like Justinian, spend sleepless nights in its service.

The historian must be an Ockhamist, keeping separate the realms of reason and revelation. He can neither prove that God and His natural laws have any connection with the State nor that all human developments can be explained solely in terms of secular naturalism. His duty is that of recognizing the fact that men have often believed that God inspires them and uses them as His instruments, and that God and nature are the ultimate sanction of the State and its laws and its *raison d'être*. In studying the history of the rise of the State and nationalism in the thirteenth century, therefore, the historian must simply record the fact that faith in God and His natural laws was creative. This chapter therefore is based on the presumption that Christian, religious naturalism contributed to the development of the national State in the twelfth and thirteenth centuries, when it was associated with the enterprise of kings, the sentiment of the corporate community of the realm, the principles of public law, and secular naturalism.

A few more remarks are necessary. It is of small importance that the term *natio* was not used for the State—it remained local in its implications. It is important that, as we noted above, the independent kingdom ruled by a king who was emperor in his own realm and recognized no superior was the *patria communis*, the common fatherland of the king and his subjects, and that it was a sovereign community that demanded the subordination of all individual and local rights to its safety and wellbeing. It had become, with the approval of God, a moral and juridical entity that was, *casualiter*, superior to private rights and to private morality. The essence, if not the word of nationalism existed. Finally, there will be no attempt to define nature, natural law, and naturalism except in some of the ways expressed by medieval writers. It is fruitless to examine the whole history of theories of natural law. In this chapter the premise is that in the Middle Ages men of learning almost unanimously accepted God as the author of all things in the world, and that by means of nature and the law of nature as God's instruments the order of the world came into being, an order which included human efforts to organize their societies into States. But this did not prevent their appreciating the derivative but lower secular naturalness of the world and man and of man's creative efforts. The question treated, therefore, is not what we think of God and nature, but what men of the twelfth and thirteenth centuries thought of them in relation to society and to the State.

The preceding chapter has shown that independent, sovereign States were coming into being in the twelfth and thirteenth centuries, that nationalism was beginning to appear in ideals of patriotic loyalty to the State, and that patriotism, loyalty to the common fatherland, was becoming a moral value. The kingdoms of England, France, and Spain, in legal thought as well as fact, were no longer a part of the Holy Roman Empire, nor even autonomous provinces within the Empire. By the later thirteenth century each of these kingdoms was another Rome, a common fatherland, verging on common *natio*, of all the people living in its territory.[2]

Does this mean that, in the political and legal ideas of the age, modern scholars have also found the background of modern nationalism in the belief that nature directly approves the State and thus enhances its value as a moral entity? In general they agree that this element of the naturalness of the State does go back to the Middle Ages, but only to the later period following the great influence of Aristotle's *Politics*, after it was translated into Latin by William of Moerbeke about 1260. Up to that time, they hold, the Stoic-Christian-Augustinian doctrine prevailed, that the State was not natural and good in itself, that it was made necessary by the human perversity and wickedness that resulted from the original sin of Adam and Eve. It was a necessary evil and could not be "naturally" good. God permitted it

[2] On the territorial concept see von der Heydte, *Geburtsstunde des souveränen Staates*, pp. 95f., 407-415. But medieval "territoriality" needs further study.

to develop for the sake of human life on earth; and kings received their power from God to the end of maintaining law, justice, and order for the protection of the innocent against the wicked. Nature, however, was not the cause and sanction of the State.

But with the revival of the *Politics* and its emphasis on man's being by nature a social and political animal, a revolution in political theory took place.[3] Led by St. Thomas Aquinas, the moderate, fully Christian Aristotelians no longer accepted the older tradition of the State's existing chiefly *propter peccatum*, as a conventional institution. For them the State was natural, good in itself, necessary for the good life of men while living in society on earth. Indeed, the higher law of nature that approved society and the State was a gift of God to men and inspired them to create the State. John of Paris, while stressing the multiplicity of naturally independent States in a natural world of differing environments, did not forget that the State, if natural, was perfected by grace and was therefore subject to the spiritual authority of the Church.[4]

The new Aristotelianism, however, caused some thinkers to go to the extreme of accepting Aristotle's separation of nature from theological considerations; they freed the State from any

[3] In general, on the "new Aristotelian" political thought, see Martin Grabmann, "Studien über den Einfluss der aristotelischen Philosophie auf die mittelalterlichen Theorien über das Verhältnis von Kirche und Staat," *Sitzungsber. d. Bayer. Akad. d. Wissenschaften, Phil.-Hist. Abt.*, Heft 2 (1934); Lagarde, *Naissance de l'esprit laique au déclin du moyen âge*, II, 2nd ed. 12-21, and ch. v (also I, ch. x); and Gewirth, *Marsilius of Padua, The Defender of the Peace*, I 18f., 54-56, 88-90. See also Gierke, *Political Theories of the Middle Age*, pp 89-92 and nn. 302, 303; J. Rivière, *Le probleme de l'église et l'état au temps de Philippe le Bel*; Carlyle, *Mediaeval Political Theory*, v, ch. III and pp. 422f., 442; Ewart Lewis, *Mediaeval Political Ideas*, I, 149-161; and von der Heydte, *Geburtsstunde*, 164-190.

Helene Wieruszowski has argued that the *Politics* was known at the court of Frederick II, *Von Imperium zum nationalen Königtum*, Beiheft 30, *Histor. Zeitschr.*, pp. 166-173; but her evidence, that *necessitas* was Aristotelian, is not adequate, for "necessity" as a part of "reason of State" was well known in the preceding centuries—see above, ch. v, n. 17, and Introduction.

[4] Grabmann, "Studien," *SBAW, Phil.-Hist. Abt.* (1934), 33f.; Lagarde, *Naissance*, II, 185-187; Walter Ullmann, "The Medieval Idea of Sovereignty," *E.H.R.*, LXIV (1949), 16f. On Thomas Aquinas, Grabmann, pp. 8-18; and Thomas Gilby, *Between Community and Society. A Philosophy and Theology of the State*, pp. 8, 23f., 116f. Cf. Lewis, *Medieval Political Ideas*, I, 149f.

divine limitation of its sovereignty. The State became self-sufficient, a moral end in itself, no longer subject to a fundamental law of nature having its origin in God. The medieval culmination came in the *Defensor pacis* of Marsiglio of Padua, who made each State so naturally sovereign that it controlled the clergy in its territory and recognized no right of the pope to intervene even in purely religious matters. According to the late Martin Grabmann, Marsiglio and other extreme Aristotelians, starting with the premise of a secular naturalism, founded the *rationale* and ideology of modern statism and nationalism.[5]

It is not my purpose in this study to engage in a debate on the interpretation of Aristotelianism and its consequences from the later thirteenth century on. But the general conclusion, that the medieval theory of the naturalness of society and the State started only with the revival of Aristotle's *Politics*, needs investigation. For it stands to reason that if ancient sources other than Aristotle contained elements of it and were read in the twelfth century, possibly the beginning of social and political "naturalism" can be found during the century and more that preceded the Aristotelianism of the later Middle Ages. It is my purpose, therefore, to examine the appearance of theories of nature and the State in the period of the renaissance of the twelfth century. Nature itself, whether deified or considered as an instrument of God's plan of creation, whether a personification of the natural law or a convenient term for expressing what is simply "natural" in the ordinary sense of the word, was becoming an important theme in the literary, intellectual, and artistic world even before the revival of Greek and Islamic philosophy and science.[6]

[5] Grabmann, *op.cit.*, 41f., 45-48, 54-56. But Gewirth (*Marsilius*, I, 54-56, 88-91) and Lagarde (*Naissance*, first ed., I, ch. 10; and II², ch. 11) are more objective, although still attaching the rise of secularism and naturalism in the political and legal realm to the revival of the *Politics*. See also Gerhart B. Ladner, "Aspects of Mediaeval Thought on Church and State," *The Review of Politics*, IX (1947), 403-422, who says (p. 416) that the State defined as a self-sufficient community, "perfect in itself with regard to population and territory, did not re-emerge before the rediscovery of Aristotle's political thought." Von der Heydte also exaggerates the revolutionary change under the influence of Aristotle, especially in the naturalistic relativism in the Averroists or extreme Aristotelians and in John of Paris, pp. 113-117, 144-150, 179-188, 212f.; on John of Paris, pp. 101-106.

[6] G. Paré, however, in his *Roman de la Rose et la scolastique courtoise*, pp.

THE NATURALNESS OF SOCIETY AND THE STATE

1. SOME SOURCES OF SOCIAL AND POLITICAL NATURALISM IN THE TWELFTH CENTURY

It should not be surprising that some appreciation of the naturalness of society and the State appeared in men of learning of the twelfth century. In this great period of intellectual revival, canonists and legists and writers on politics educated in the cathedral schools of France and in the law schools of Italy were reading, or were learning from those who did read, about nature and society in the Latin Fathers, in the Latin classics, and in the *Timaeus*. This does not mean that all these ancient sources were of equal importance nor that the canonists and legists knew them as well as John of Salisbury did, nor that one can always find direct references to them. But it is useful to give some of the ideas and passages in the principal sources, since at times they influenced jurists who were not "humanists." At least it should be remembered that students who went to the law schools such as Bologna had had a general education in grammar and rhetoric and, of course, in a modicum of Latin literature. Perhaps as usual, when anthologies are the means of teaching literature, familiar quotations may be important in the thinking of those who cannot give references.

In general the Fathers held that man is by nature a social animal only in the sense that men naturally lived in a primitive society before sin made organized societies or States necessary. Hence, while human society is natural, the State is not; "the government of man by man is not part of the natural order of the world."[7] At times, however, the State itself seems to be naturally good precisely because it is necessary in order to give men some security in their social relations. St. Ambrose thought of the State as natural, approved by nature in con-

---

7f., says that nature was discovered from 1150 on. But one must not forget that in the preceding hundred years, men educated in the cathedral schools of France were finding nature and naturalism in Ovid and Claudian; and Neo-Platonic nature was popular at Chartres, as we shall see below, well before 1150.

[7] In general, on natural law and society in the Fathers, see Carlyle, *Med. Polit. Theory*, I, ch. XI (p. 126 for the quotation above); Otto Schilling, *Naturrecht und Staat nach der Lehre der alten Kirche*; and Jean Gaudemet, *L'Eglise dans l'empire romain*, vol. III of Gabriel Le Bras, ed., *Histoire du droit et des institutions de l'église en occident*, pp. 468-492.

formity with the divine will. The *raison d'être* of society, *ratio societatis*, is justice and kindness. This suggests, first, an organized State, with its public law and magistracy, for the end of maintaining law and justice; and second, the Stoic and Ciceronian doctrine of a universal reason that prompts men not only to live in society but to establish good government. Moreover, St. Ambrose praised fortitude in a war waged in defense of the *patria*, and derived it from justice, thus reflecting also the Roman legal thought on natural law, justice, and equity, and anticipating the legists and canonists of our period.[8] St. Augustine, too, in his doctrine of the just war implied the natural right of the State, without any violation of the law of God, to defend itself.[9] Lactantius (*an.* 403-411) had already drawn "the duties of the *animal sociale atque commune* from the dignity of the Son of God, not from contract nor from social necessity." By way of Cicero and Seneca he reflected the Aristotelian idea of the social nature of man, and he held that the State is a postulate of human nature.[10]

This naturalness of society was developed by St. Augustine. Created in the image of God, man was given a soul endowed with reason and intelligence, and reason is the participation of the eternal law, through the natural law, in man—or, as some say, the participation of the rational man in the eternal law. Reason in man becomes the social instinct, natural and divinely ordained, that prompts men to live in association in the political community or secular State. Justice in the State derives from the same divine source of natural law and reason. Stoic "cosmic reason" is made theistic, and by God's special creation of each soul, it becomes a part of men and the human "reason" of society.[11] Hence St. Augustine, more specifically, can say that there is nothing more social by nature than the human race,

8 *De officiis*, I, 22-129; 27, 127-129; 28, 24 and 130-132; and III, 28. See, on St. Ambrose, Schilling, *Naturrecht u. Staat*, pp. 139ff.; Gaudemet, *L'Eglise*, pp. 468f., 487f.; and Regout, *La doctrine de la guerre juste de Saint Augustin à nos jours*, p. 40 n. 1, quoting the *De off.*, I, 22, 129.

9 Regout, *op.cit.*, pp. 39-44.

10 Gilby, *Between Community and Society*, p. 215, from the *Divine Inst.*, VI, 10; also Gaudemet, *L'Eglise*, p. 487.

11 Anton H. Chroust, "The Philosophy of Law of St. Augustine," *Philosophical Review*, LIII (1944), 195-202.

for if a man was made one individual he was not left solitary.[12] God's very command to love one's neighbor is the sanction for love of family, of neighbors, and of peace and well-ordered concord in society. A man's own household is his first care, and the law of nature and society enables him, as it were, to practice charity at home, to avoid injuring others, and to love his neighbors.[13] *Ordinata caritas*, individual and social, is a part of God's law of nature participating in human reason. Like the ancient philosophers, St. Augustine approved the idea that the life of the wise man must be social; but as a Christian he felt that the natural law and reason from God commanded both wise men and saints to live in society in preparation for the City of God.[14]

Further, it is the duty of all men to obey the commands of the ruler of the State so long as they are not against the "society of the city." Indeed, disobedience to kings is against society, because the very *pactum* of human society is to obey them.[15] A *pactum*, of course, is not necessary in a primitive society in which men live strictly according to the law of nature; it is a convention of the organized State, resulting from the sinfulness of men. Nonetheless, one senses in St. Augustine's theory some participation of nature and the natural law in the State. As Professor Jean Gaudemet has recently said, St. Augustine not only did not condemn the State in itself, he accepted organized society as a gift of nature.[16] But to St. Augustine the State was of little importance in comparison with the City of God and he was therefore not interested in any particular kind of State such as the Roman Empire. If governments ruled according to law

[12] *De civitate dei*, XII, 27.

[13] *De civ. dei*, XIX, 14 (*M.P.L.*, 41: 642): God's command to love oneself and one's neighbor and peace, "id est ordinata concordia: cujus hic ordo est, primum ut nulli noceat, deinde ut etiam prosit cui potuerit. Primitus ergo inest ei suorum cura: ad eos quippe habet opportuniorem facilioremque aditum consulendi, *vel naturae ordine, vel ipsius societatis humanae*."

[14] *De civ. dei*, XIX, 5 (*M.P.L.*, 41: 631 f.).

[15] I have taken this from the passage (*Confes.* 2) quoted by Gratian in the *Decretum*, Dist. 8, c. 3 Quae contra mores. Obviously this was a source for similar ideas in the canonists of our period. See also c. 2—on how *iura humana* were given by God to mankind by means of emperors and *rectores*.

[16] *L'Eglise dans l'empire romain*, pp. 490-492; von der Heydte, *Geburtsstunde*, pp. 190-196, also holds that St. Augustine believed that the State was natural; nature and grace sanction it.

and justice, States could differ in size and form in relation to differences of environment. The Heavenly City while on earth called citizens from all "nations," and recognized diversities in language, manners, laws, and institutions—so long as they served to preserve peace and did not hinder the worship of God.[17] St. Augustine does not directly say that all kinds of States are natural societies; but given what he had said elsewhere in the *City of God*, from which this passage is taken, he could very well have held that all States, whatever the customs and institutions that are for justice, exist naturally by God's will. At least this is a kind of natural relativism that could ultimately support independent States rather than a universal empire.

Did John of Paris and other theologians of the late thirteenth and the fourteenth century get this idea only from Aristotelian secularism?[18] It is possible that, since John subjected all kinds of States to the spiritual power, he owed something to St. Augustine. Perhaps both he and others of his time owed something also to the *Decretum*, where not only canonists found, but philosophers might find, a famous statement about the relativism of laws and customs. This came from Isidore of Seville: law (*lex*) should be "according to nature and according to custom, and suitable to the place and time of the *patria*, necessary and useful," as well as honest, just, possible, manifest, and for the common utility of the citizens.[19] "Natural reason," said Johannes Teutonicus, however, *ca.* 1215-1220, is the *natura* mentioned by Isidore.[20]

If the patristic appreciation of nature in the theory of society and the State influenced the new development, the influence of the Latin classics was still more important. From Cicero (and the Roman law) came the idea that nature, in natural reason

[17] *De civ. dei*, xix, 18; note that c. 18 is in Bk. xix, from which I have drawn most of St. Augustine's ideas on the naturalness of society. See also von der Heydte, *Geburtsstunde*, p. 192.

[18] Above, n. 5, end; the idea of relativism and the naturalness of different kinds of States is expressed by Durand de Saint-Pourçain, *Tractatus de legibus*, Paris, 1506, fol. 1f; and Guido Terreni of Perpignan, *Com.* on the *Decretum*, in MS Vat. lat. 1453, fol. 2 c. 1. The whole subject needs investigation in the philosophers and theologians of the fourteenth century.

[19] *Decretum*, Dist. 4, c. 2.

[20] *Glos. ord.* to Dist. 4, c. 2, ad v. *secundum naturam*.

and natural law, was the principal sanction of human society in general, and that, in the *ius gentium*, it furnished the basic principles of the relations of men in their separate societies organized as "peoples." But nature also directly approved the State, for the preservation of the common welfare was a principle of natural law.[21] In the *De officiis*, I, vii, 22, he agrees with Plato that we are born for our *patria* as well as for ourselves; and with the Stoics, that men are born for the sake of men in mutual help. Then he states the thought, which John of Salisbury fully accepted, that "in hoc naturam debemus sequi"—that we should imitate nature by using our skills (*artes*), industry, and talents for the purpose of binding human society more closely together. Here is the idea that nature inspires men to use their reason in the art of developing society and the State.[22] Moreover, like Plato in the Latin version of the *Timaeus*, Cicero says that nature has endowed certain men with the capacity of governing the *Respublica*.[23]

Ovid, in the *Metamorphoses*, I, 5, treated nature as a goddess who helped bring order out of the primeval chaos: "Hanc deus et melior litem natura diremit." Four centuries later Claudian treated nature in much the same way—as a cosmic goddess acting as an intermediary between Zeus and man.[24] As we shall see, the canonists and legists rejected any deification of nature; but, influenced in part by Ovid's words, they personified in nature the natural law that originates in God and thus made nature one of God's instruments in the ordering of human society. Both Ovid and Claudian, moreover, contributed to the "naturalism" that flourished in philosophical poets like Bernard

[21] Ernst Levy, "Natural Law in Roman Thought," in *Studia et documenta historiae et iuris*, Rome, Apollinaris, xv (1949), 1-4. Besides the passages from Cicero's *De officiis* referred to by Levy, see also *De off.*, I, xvi: *ratio* and *oratio* are the bond (*vinculum*) of human society. Thus with Cicero nature was a principle of an organized society, the State; cf. *De off.*, I, iv. See also Carlyle, *Med Polit. Theory*, I, 5f.

[22] On John of Salisbury, below, nn. 40-55.

[23] *De off.*, I, xxi, 72; for the *Timaeus* see below, nn. 28-21.

[24] E. R. Curtius, *European Literature and the Latin Middle Ages*, transl. W. R. Trask, p. 106 on Ovid and Claudian, pp. 106-127 on nature as a goddess in antiquity and in the twelfth century.

Silvester of Tours and Alain de Lille, and in thirteenth-century French literature, especially in the *Roman de la Rose*.[25]

Among other Latin classics, Vergil may have inspired John of Salisbury and Alain de Lille, and perhaps others too, to think of human society as being as natural and good as the society of bees—*Georgics*, IV, 183ff., where Vergil praises bees as the only creatures in the lower orders that share a life in common, live in a "city" according to laws, and are loyal to their *patria*. Seneca, too, is an important source. In his *De beneficiis* one finds that *natura* is simply another name for *deus* and *divina ratio* (IV, vi, 7); that all good things in human life are a gift of God or nature, and therefore that all human *artes* are inspired by nature, that is, by God or divine reason (again, as in Cicero, art imitates nature):

"Ille deus est . . . qui non calamo tantum cantare et agreste atque inconditum carmen ad aliquam tamen observationem modulari docuit, sed tot artes. . . ." (IV, vi, 5.)

"Insita sunt nobis omnium aetatum, omnium artium semina, magisterque ex occulto deus producit ingenia." (IV, vi, 6.)

" 'Natura,' inquit, 'haec mihi praestat.' Non intellegis te, cum hoc dicis, mutare nomen deo? Quid enim aliud est natura quam deus et divina ratio, toti mundo partibusque eius inserta?" (IV, vii, 1.)

"Ergo nihil agis . . . qui te negas deo debere, sed naturae, quia nec natura sine deo est nec deus sine natura, sed idem est utrumque, distat officio." (IV, viii, 2.)

Thus Seneca may have been an additional source for the common saying of canonists and legists, "Natura, id est, deus."

Not only does Seneca hold that nature, or divine reason, is the ultimate source of human arts in general, he holds that human *societas*, without which men would be defenseless, is a gift of nature (IV, xviii, 2-4). As a result of God's gift to all mankind, just as the wind blows for the bad as well as the good,

25 For an emphasis on pagan *natura* see Curtius, *European Literature*, pp. 108-127, treating Bernard Silvester and Alain de Lille. The Christian character of *natura* in these writers is defended by E. Gilson, "La cosmogonie de Bernardus Silvestris," *Arch. d'hist. doct. et litt. du moyen âge*, III (1928), 5-24, and by Theodore Silverstein, "The Fabulous Cosmogony of Bernardus Silvestris," *Modern Philology*, XLVI (1948-49), 92-116.

so cities are founded for all, even for assassins, since city walls protect those who ply their swords on the streets from the public enemy (IV, xxviii, 3-5).

No doubt, other Latin sources of the classical period were of influence in the twelfth century—Quintilian in particular. But enough have been cited for our purpose. It is more important now to turn to a Platonic and Neo-Platonic treatment of nature and society. In the fourth century Chalcidius translated a portion of Plato's *Timaeus* into Latin, and wrote a Latin *Commentary* on the dialogue. (I have found no trace of any influence of Platonism by way of the *Republic*, nor of any influence by way of Averroës' *Commentary*.)[26] Especially in Chalcidius' *Commentary*, the philosophers at Chartres, before 1150, found a neo-Platonized concept of nature according to which nature, while not a goddess, acted as a creative agent of God, or of the Nous, and the World Soul, in bringing order out of the chaos of primeval matter. It is possible that the personification of nature by the philosophical poets resulted from Chalcidian Neo-Platonism as much as from Ovid and Claudian, and that from the school of Chartres, it found its way, along with Ovid's and Seneca's *natura*, into the canonists and legists when they said, "Natura, id est, deus."[27] It is certain, at any rate, that the Chalcidian distinction between *iustitia naturalis* and *iustitia positiva* did pass from the works of philosophers at Chartres into the decretists of the late twelfth and early thirteenth centuries.[28]

[26] Apparently no Latin translation of the *Com.* was made in the thirteenth century; see E. I. J. Rosenthal, *Averroës' Commentary on Plato's Republic*, pp. 1-7. Of course, the *Republic* received no Latin translation in late antiquity or in the Middle Ages.

[27] See also, on *natura* as a creative agent according to the school of Chartres, Frederick Copleston, *History of Philosophy*, II, pp. 170f.; Tullio Gregory, *Platonismo medievale*, Instituto storico italiano per il Medio Evo, *Studi storici*, fasc. 26-27; and the source in Chalcidius's *Commentary* on the *Timaeus*, ed. J. Wrobel, *Platonis Timaeus interprete Chalcidio, cum eiusdem Commentario*, pp. 88f., and ch. XXIII. Other references are given below, nn. 49-51.

[28] Stephan Kuttner, "Sur les origines du terme 'droit positif,'" *Rev. hist. droit fr. étr.*, 4e ser., XV (1936), 736-739; Sten Gagnér, *Studien zur Ideengeschichte der Gesetzgebung (Acta Universitatis Upsaliensis. Studia Iuridica Upsaliensia, 1,)* pp. 210-240. Lagarde, *Naissance*, II², 22, refers to the influence of the *Timaeus*, but only with respect to the idea of natural justice and order in the creation of the universe and man (n. 40).

Nature as "natural justice" was of course Christianized. Nature was an instrument of God, and it represented the divine reason in the natural law. In fact, *iustitia naturalis* was soon interpreted as *ius naturale,* which in the highest sense was the moral commands of God participating in the principles of justice and equity. *Iustitia positiva* became the same thing as the *ius positivum,* the law of human society and the State on earth. Therefore, nature or "natural justice" was not a direct sanction of the State and its institutions.

But if the *Commentary* of Chalcidius was not a source of the concept of the naturalness of the State, possibly the *Timaeus* was. I have found in the Roman and Canon lawyers no direct quotation from the introductory dialogue in the *Timaeus,* where Socrates speaks of a preceding dialogue on political problems (perhaps the *Republic*), and then refers to *natura.* Since, however, the *Timaeus* was well known in the twelfth century, the canonists and legists may have received from discussions in the schools some impression of how nature did directly inspire men in the work of creating the State, even though within the State the positive law was not the same as the natural law. We must therefore examine the opening remarks of Socrates as rendered in Latin by Chalcidius.

To every man, Socrates says, is given *a natura* the skill or occupation that suits him. Therefore, *natura* has given to the guardians of the State (*civitas*) what particularly suits them, the duty or function of protecting or defending the State against all enemies, external and internal, of judging obedient subjects with mercy, and of dealing harshly in battle with enemies. These defenders of the State should be fierce in the *tutela patriae ciuiumque,* wise in religion and in the offices of peace, and kind to their own subjects, but *feroces* against hostile foreigners. Furthermore, nature continuously supports the State by making the family and the rearing of children respond to the needs of the fatherland (*usus patriae*).[29]

---

[29] Wrobel, ed., *Platonis Timaeus,* p. 6: "SO. Tributo nempe ceteris quod cuique eximium a natura datum est, solis his qui pro salute omnium bella tractarent unum hoc munus iniunximus protegendae ciuitatis uel aduersum externos uel aduersum intestinos ac domesticos hostes, mitibus quidem iudiciis

One can object that in these passages nature does not directly cause men to be social animals and organize their society as a State. Yet nature does much more than participate in the State as an eternal norm of justice and equity. It directly approves the defense of the State against enemies, and it subordinates family and the procreation of children to the necessary existence of the State. And surely it is significant that the *civitas* is also called the *patria*. In fact, a glossator of the *Timaeus*, who probably belonged to the school of Chartres, stressed the word *patria* in declaring that the guardians or *magisterium* should act speedily against destroyers (*endirutores*) of the *patria*.[30] In this there is a suggestion, at least, that nature and the natural law sanction the safety of the State. But even if the passage in the Latin *Timaeus* means only that certain men are "naturally" endowed with the capacity to rule and defend the *civitas*, and "naturally" they should fight against enemies and administer justice for the protection of loyal subjects, the *civitas* with its government is the "natural" ordering of human society.

In spite of the Chalcidian distinction between *iustitia naturalis* and *iustitia positiva*, therefore, a reader of the Latin text of the introductory remarks of Socrates could possibly think of nature's participating in the State as a principle of its safety for the sake of the welfare of its members. It is possible, of course, that the emphasis on benevolent justice for loyal subjects and on harsh justice for enemies was understood in part in the tradi-

---

erga oboedientes utpote consanguineos naturaque amicos, asperis autem contra armatas acies in congressionibus Martiis. biformi siquidem natura praeditos: in tutela patriae ciuiumque ferociores, porro in pacis officiis religione sapientes proptereaque mites suis, aduersum alienigenas feroces"; p. 7: "SO. Quid? huius ipsius ancipitis naturae magisterium et quasi quandam nutricationem nonne in exercitio corporum gymnasiorumque luctamine, animorum item placiditatem constituebamus in delinimentis et adfabilitate musicae ceterarumque institutionum, quos adolescentes ingenuos scire par est?" and p. 8: "SO. Ceteros ablegandos alió quondam usui patriae futuros. . . ."

Was Chalcidius possibly influenced by Cicero, *De off.*, I, xxi, 73, in emphasizing nature more than Plato did? Cf. above, to nn. 21-23.

30 Brit. Mus., MS Royal 12 B. XXII, fol. 2ᵛ, ad vv. *naturae magisterium*: "Quasi . . . endirutores patrie, ut promti sint ad laborem et affabiles obedientibus." I was unable to read the word or words before *endirutores*; but possibly one word is *adversum* as in the words of Socrates, above, n. 28, "adversum . . . hostes." As for *endirutores*, I do not find the word in any Latin dictionary; but it probably is a coinage from *diruere, dirutum*.

tional Christian sense—that because of sin, not because of the natural law, the discipline of the State through positive law and justice was necessary in order to protect the innocent from the wicked. But it was easy also to understand this in terms of the law of nature as reason from God participating in men, and thus as reason commanding the magistrates to be just. Indeed, the Epistles of James, IV, 6, and of I. Peter, V, 5, taught that God Himself was gracious to the humble while hostile to the proud; and Vergil, *Aeneid*, VI, 854, "parcere subjectis et debellare superbos," showed how Rome practiced the ideal. St. Augustine quoted these passages at the very beginning of the *De civitate dei*. If these authorities indicated that God approved the principle, and the Romans made it their policy, perhaps this meant to some scholars of the twelfth century that according to the will of God, by way of nature, the natural law, and human reason, the organized State was not only necessary after the Fall but in the new circumstances was natural and was sanctioned by nature. We shall find indications of this kind of thinking in the canonists and legists.[31]

Of all the sources available before the revival of Aristotle's *Politics*, perhaps the Roman law in Justinian's codification, the *Corpus iuris civilis*, was the most important. The Roman jurisconsults generally held that nature and the natural law belonged to the physical world without reference to a divine origin. But the Stoic doctrine of the law of nature as a universal natural reason existing in all men resulted in their belief that the *ius naturale* was common to all peoples in all human societies, and as such it was the *ius gentium* (*D.* 1, 1, 3-6). At times, however, it was also the principle of equity that participated in the law of the State (*ius civile*). In the post-classical period, ending in the codification of the sixth century, this *ius naturale*, under the influence of Christianity, became superior to the *ius civile* and *ius gentium*, and was, apart from its continuing to mean animal instinct, an eternal principle of equity and justice, different from but participating in the *ius gentium* and the positive law of the State. The State was thus not directly ap-

31 Below, sections 3 and 4.

proved by the law of nature.[32] Yet in the ordinary sense of the word, in relation to the physical world, man was *naturally* a social and political animal because of his use of reason and communication in speech—as Cicero put it.[33]

There were passages in the *Digest* on physical nature and man which could be subjected to an interpretation that personified nature as an external power acting on men and prompting them to be social and political. Whether such passages were classical, actually from the works of Ulpian, Gaius, Florentinus, and others, or Byzantine interpolations, scarcely matters in this study, for they were all accepted as fully Roman by the canonists and legists. For example, in *D.* 1, 1, 1, 2 the statement is attributed to Ulpian, that the *ius privatum* comes not only from civil law and the *ius gentium*, but also from "natural precepts." Ulpian probably had no higher law of nature in mind as a source of what was positive law for each State. But the glossators read into his words a principle of equity and justice that participated in the private law; and, as will be observed, some held that the public law of the State also came in part from the natural law.

Another example is the passage from Florentinus, *D.* 1, 1, 3, who says that since *natura* established a *cognatio* (kindred or association) among men, it is wrong for one man treacherously to attack another; and, of course, it is therefore lawful to defend oneself. Natural reason, indeed, other jurisconsults say, permits a man to defend himself against any attack that imperils his life (*D.* 9, 2, 4); and all laws (natural and human) sanction the use of force to repel force (*D.* 9, 2, 44, 4, and 43, 16, 1, 27). And in *D.* 1, 3, 2, we find Marcianus quoting Chrysippus on how *lex* (as a higher law than human law) is the *regula* of the just and the unjust and of those animals which by nature are civil. This version is in a manuscript of the late twelfth or early thirteenth

---

[32] Levy, "Natural Law in Roman Thought," *Studia et documenta historiae et iuris,* xv, 7-19 (cf. above, n. 21); Francesco Calasso, *Medio evo del diritto. I: Le fonti,* pp. 331-333; Carlyle, *Med. Polit. Theory,* I, chs. III, VII.

[33] *De off.,* I, xvi: "Sed, quae naturae principia sint communitatis et societatis humanae . . .; est enim primum, quod cernitur in universi generis humani societate. Eius autem vinculum est ratio et oratio, quae . . . conciliat inter se homines coniungitque naturali quadam societate. . . ."

century (Brit. Mus., MS Royal 11 C. iii, fol. 4ᵛ): ". . . lex omnium est rex et divinarum et humanarum rerum . . . et secundum hoc regula est iustorum et iniustorum, et eorum que natura civilia animalia sunt . . ." (in the modern, Mommsen-Krueger, edition one reads: "Lex . . . oportet autem . . . et ducem et magistram esse animalium, quae natura civilia esse voluit . . ."). The glossators failed to understand from this that nature directly caused men to be political animals. Yet it is striking that the idea was fully available in the *Digest,* and it is possible that it contributed to some emphasis on the naturalness of the State and its law in the twelfth century and later.[34]

But the older Roman theory, that the natural law was, in one meaning, a natural instinct common to animals and men, in another, a higher principle of equity participating in human society by way of the gift of natural reason to men, and in a third, what was common to all peoples (*ius gentium*), remained important. Therefore, when we come to the opinions of canonists and legists, particularly with reference to *D.* 1, 1, 1, 2-3, and 1, 1, 2-6, we must avoid finding a fully naturalistic interpretation of society. There remained a serious distinction between the natural law and the positive law of each organized society. Nonetheless, when the "naturalness" of primitive society yielded to the sinfulness of men and the *ius gentium* appeared to take care of the changed nature of man and provide him with rules common to all peoples (regulating and making lawful property rights, slavery, warfare, and "international" relations), and the positive civil law appeared for the needs of each State, nature, as divine reason in the Stoic-Christian doctrine, did take part in the work of men in the creation of the State. If nature and the law of nature originated in God, it was the duty of men, insofar as possible, to obey natural reason and its moral commands, and to try to make society and its laws conform with a higher natural law and thus imitate nature.

Yet the fact that human laws inevitably, because of the

---

[34] In fact, Johannes (Bassianus?), according to Accursius in the *Glos. ord.* to *D.* 1, 3, 2, ad vv. *natura civilia sunt,* defined *natura* as the "naturalis hominis ingenio," and then said that the *ius naturale* and the *ius civile* are two equivalent but separate species of law. Thus the standard gloss holds here that it is human nature, by the use of reason, that makes man a social animal.

necessities of life in the secular environment, departed from the higher law of nature, means in turn that a lower nature, the very nature of sinful man and of the world and its problems, did sanction organized societies, social changes, and special kinds of law and of government. This nature was a principle of change, of meeting varying human needs according to different circumstances, situations, and environments. In a fashion the *ius gentium* itself, since it was a kind of natural law common to all peoples and approved various kinds of human societies, reflected the idea that nature is change as well as something enduring. The idea will arise that, to care for mankind after the original sin caused the disappearance of the natural, primitive society, God and the higher nature and natural law sanctioned the new nature and naturalness of human organizations in States made necessary by man's wickedness. Perhaps this kind of lower nature, according to which men were of necessity social and political animals for the sake of the common welfare on earth, is not very different from Aristotelian nature. But Christianity in particular, if it recognized, as it did, a secular naturalness, had to insist on its subordination to the higher nature and natural law. Nonetheless, the human social organization of the State and its laws became "naturally" good, despite their failure perfectly to imitate or obey the higher law of nature.

This concept of a lower nature, partly expressed in the classical jurists' definition of nature as the natural law that prompts men to procreate, rear their children, and fight in self-defense against aggressive attack, underlies, of course, the theory that man's social needs are naturally cared for by the State and its strength. But the direct expression of the concept occurs in part in the language used by Justinian and the jurists who compiled the *Corpus iuris civilis*. In the *Prooemium* to the *Codex*, "Cordi Nobis," § 4, Justinian says that no imperial law (*constitutio*) not included in the *Code* should be used (in the courts), "nisi postea varia rerum natura aliquid novum creaverit, quod nostra sanctione indigeat." In *C.* 1, 17, 2, 18, the assertion

is made that "multas etenim formas edere natura novas deproperat," and that new imperial laws can be made for new *negotia*.
And Justinian thus explained his own new legislation (*Nov.*
84): "Multis undique natura novitatibus utens . . . ad opus
multarum nos pertrahit legum." The nature of men and society
therefore demands and makes valid new legislation, for ordinary
nature on earth is constantly changing.

Some of this concept of a lower nature, indeed, may perhaps
underlie Isidore of Seville's theory of law and legislation which
I mentioned above—a theory which certainly was well known
to canonists, legists, and theologians. After explaining (*Etymol.*,
V; *Decretum*, Dist. 4, c. 1) that *leges* are made in order to curb
human wickedness and protect innocence, he said (Dist. 4, c.
2) that a *lex* should be not only proper and just, but also "possibilis, secundum naturam, et secundum consuetudinem patriae," suitable to time and place, necessary and useful, and free
of obscurity; and it should be made "pro communi civium
utilitate." Thus human law itself should be in accord with
natura.[35] Probably, however, Isidore had in mind the Christian
belief that human laws should not violate the natural law, or
the concept that natural reason should participate in the law of
the State. Yet there is a suggestion of the idea that a lower
nature participates in legislation because of the "natural" variety in the environment of local customs and of time and place.
Here, to repeat, is a suggestion, too, that States themselves can
be different in kind, in institutions, and in laws in relation to
differences in the environment. This may very well be one
source of the development of the theory that all kinds of independent, sovereign States can be natural and sanctioned by
nature—by the higher nature through natural reason in men,
and by the lower nature that causes changes and differences in
circumstances and situations and justifies the use of natural
reason to adjust States and their laws to the changing world.

So much for a few of the sources that were known and used
in varying degree in the century preceding the revival of the
Politics. We must now turn to the ways in which they were used.

[35] *Glos. ord.*, to Dist. 4, c. 2; cf. above, to nn. 19, 20.

2. The Twelfth Century: the Anonymous of York, John of Salisbury, and Alain de Lille

A complete history of the rise of "naturalism" in the twelfth century should include the study of the theme of nature in the Latin and vernacular literatures, and in philosophy, science, and art, as well as in legal and political thought. But I must limit myself to a brief consideration of the *Anonymous (Tractates) of York* and of the philosophy of the School of Chartres, before analyzing the ideas of John of Salisbury and Alain de Lille. Thereafter the emphasis will be on the canonists and legists.

The author, or authors, of the *Tractates* of York[36] at the very beginning of the century stressed the *summa lex naturae* as the *divina ratio*. Quoting *Gen.* 1, 26 ("Crescite et multiplicamini et replete terram"), the author of one of the *Tractates*, in order to justify the marriage of the clergy and the right of priests to have children by their concubines, says that this divine command or *benedictio* is the *summa lex naturae*. Thus, every legitimate procreation of offspring is approved by nature and blessed by God. It is good because it results from the "seminal good" of nature; and the "seminal good" is truly lawful since the divine reason, the *summa lex*, and the generative virtue (*vis*) dwell inseparably in it. God, therefore, not the parents, creates; the parents are not the authors but the ministers of God in procreating sons.[37]

If God and nature are the real creators of human life, do they directly participate in and approve, by way of the gift of reason to man, human society and the State? Does the law of nature prompt men to be social and political animals? I find no discussion of the question in the *Tractates*, nor any statement

[36] See G. H. Williams, *The Norman Anonymous of 1100 A.D.*, pp. 88-127; and Norman F. Cantor, *Church, Kingship and Lay Investiture in England 1089-1135*, pp. 174-196. For my purpose, the question of authorship, whether of Gerard of York or William Bona Anima of Rouen, is not important.

[37] M.G.H., *Libelli de lite*, III, 645-650, esp. 650, in Tract. 2: "sine hac igitur benedictione [Gen. 1, 26], que est summa lex nature, nulla hominum generatio sive multiplicatio legitima est per naturam et benedicta a Domino." Procreation is not a vice, "sed de fecunditate seminum . . . de seminali bono nature, quod vere legitimum est, quia divina ratio, que est summa lex, et vis generativa in eo manet inseparabiliter . . . Deus, inquam, creat, non parentes," who are but the *ministri*.

that indicates that society is natural to men. The most one can say is that kingship is sacred in character, and the king, whose power is from God, has the right to control the church and the clergy in his realm.[38] Perhaps the author implies the naturalness of the royal authority, hence in part of the State, in saying that "the power of the king is the power of God. This power, namely, is God's by nature, and the king's by grace."[39] Since the Latin text reads *per naturam,* the meaning seems to be that the power of the king is derived first from the natural law of God, that is, so to speak, the higher reason participating in man, and second, from the grace of God in the particular rulers. The royal power in general is of God through nature and is of grace in the king. Indirectly, it seems, nature participates in the social life of men, for it sanctions the royal authority in the organized society.

Whatever the meaning of nature in relation to the State according to the *Tractates,* it had no apparent influence on later developments. But John of Salisbury is important both for his own theories and for his influence. Educated in part in the school of Chartres and learned in the Latin classics, in his great work on kingship and the State, the *Policraticus,* and in his treatise on education, the *Metalogicon,* he amply reflected the ideas about nature that he found in Cicero, Vergil, and Seneca, in the *Timaeus* and the *Commentary* of Chalcidius, and in the Roman law.[40] The result is that he reveals, in the mid-twelfth

---

38 Besides Williams, *Norman Anonymous,* pp. 148f., and Cantor, *Church, Kingship,* pp. 174-196, on the theory of kingship and independence in the *Tractates,* see the excellent treatment by Kantorowicz, *King's Two Bodies,* pp. 42-61 and p. 51 on the independence of the king and kingdom of England. See also the good discussion by McIlwain, *Growth of Political Thought,* pp. 211-216.

39 Kantorowicz's translation, *King's Two Bodies,* p. 48; n. 11 for the Latin text (*M.G.H., Libelli de lite,* III, 667): "Potestas enim regis potestas Dei est; Dei quidem est per naturam, regis per gratiam. . . ."

40 See, on John as a classical scholar and humanist, Liebeschütz, *Mediaeval Humanism in the Life and Writings of John of Salisbury;* on his political ideas, McIlwain, *Growth of Political Thought,* pp. 319-323; John Dickinson, "The Mediaeval Conception of Kingship as Developed in the Policraticus of John of Salisbury," *Speculum,* I (1926), 307-337; Kantorowicz, *King's Two Bodies,* pp. 94-97. I have depended chiefly on Berges, *Die Fürstenspiegel des hohen und späten Mittelalters,* pp. 40-52, because he stresses nature and the State in John. As for his influence, see W. Ullmann, "The Influence of John of Salisbury on Medieval Italian Jurists," *E.H.R.,* LIX (1944), 384-392. But this deals with the fourteenth century only. John's influence in the thirteenth century needs investigation.

century or shortly after, an early maturity of the theory that man is by nature a social and political animal.

Wilhelm Berges has already remarked on John's appreciation of the naturalness of the State, and on how he foreshadowed the Aristotelian-Christian naturalism of the later thirteenth century. John thought of the State as a natural organism subject to the law of nature, but remaining subordinate to the supernatural end of salvation and to the Church. Nature itself was the ordering of all things in the mind of God, and it was natural reason in man. This reason in human society is the natural law that makes the *Respublica* a kind of body of which the king is the head; and in turn the king must rule according to the higher reason which participates in justice and equity.[41] Indeed, natural reason is in a sense that "reason of State" for which the king is given his public power to govern for the public welfare of the community as a whole and for the common welfare of all its members. The "state of the human republic" is achieved when nature is obeyed by the ruler as the leader, for nature has placed in the head the universal sense (political intelligence, we may say) of all the members, who must be subject to the head in order that all things proceed rightly. The prince himself, in his public authority, is, as it were, the image of the divine majesty. And the Republic, the Kingdom, or the State, is animated by the *beneficium* of the divine gift of natural reason, should be ruled by the *moderamen rationis*, and is the subject of God and nature.[42]

So far I have for the most part followed Berges's interpreta-

---

[41] Berges, *Fürstenspiegel*, pp. 43-46.

[42] *Ibid.*, pp. 46-49. But this association of nature, natural reason, and "reason of State" is partly my own interpretation, inspired by these passages: "Est ergo ... princeps potestas publica et in terris quaedam maiestatis imago"; the prince should obey the law in accepting the burdens of office; "unde merito in eum omnium subditorum potestas confertur, ut in utilitate singulorum et omnium exquirenda et facienda sibi ipse sufficiat, et humanae rei publicae status optime disponatur, dum sunt alter alterius membra. In quo quidem optimam uiuendi ducem naturam sequimur, quae microcosmi sui, id est, mundi minoris, hominis scilicet, sensus uniuersos in capite collocauit, et ei sic uniuersa membra subiecit, ut omnia recte moueantur"; "est respublica corpus quoddam quod diuini muneris beneficio animatur"; and it is ruled by "quodam moderamine rationis"; *Policraticus*, ed. Webb, v, c. 1 and c. 2. See also my "*Ratio publicae utilitatis*, etc.," *Welt als Gesch.*, XXI, 19-22; above, ch. v, nn. 32-38.

tion, but much more needs to be said about John's State both as a direct subject of nature and as a work of art that imitates nature. John holds that if justice and equity come from God by way of natural reason in men, human law, *lex*, is a product of reason, and it should be in conformity with or contain equity and justice (*Policraticus*, IV, 2). Indeed, at this point John reflects *D.* 1, 3, 2, part 2, saying first that *lex* (eternal, universal law), according to Chrysippus, is the control (*compos*) of all things human and divine, that it is responsible for the good and the bad alike, and that it is the *princeps* and *dux* both of things and of men. According to John, Chrysippus' *lex* is really the natural law and natural reason by which God regulates the universe. It is personified by nature. Therefore, the natural reason that descends into man is the command of nature. Nature is the leader (*dux*), the guide; and nature by way of natural reason should be the *moderamen* of government and of society and the State. Moreover, *lex*, that is, natural law and reason, is "the gift of God," "the form of equity, the norm of justice, the image of the divine will, the guardian of safety (*salutis custodia*), the binding, confirming unity (*unio et consolidatio*) of peoples." This *lex* is the *ciuitatis compositio*; and all who engage "in politicae rei universitate" should obey it. So runs, in part, John's reading of *D.* 1, 3, 2, part 1, Nam et Demosthenes.[43] Thus, John goes so far as to attribute to nature, by way of the natural law and reason in men, a direct responsibility for organized human society and its government.

Accordingly, the prince who governs the State as its head and representative should, in terms of *caritas ordinata*, devote himself first of all to God, then, in descending order, to his *patria*, to his parents and relatives, and to foreigners (but very little of himself to these!). And the *ordo caritatis* demands that in cultivating justice the prince should do so for the love of *patria* as well as for the love of his sons. In short, natural reason demands that the prince love and work for the *patria* and do what is

---

[43] *Policraticus*, IV, 2; V, 2; and VII, 17. For the law as a gift of God see also my study, "The Medieval Heritage of a Humanistic Ideal," *Traditio*, XI (1955), 205f. There I failed to observe how *D.* 1, 3, 2 influenced John of Salisbury.

necessary for the *salus subiectorum*.[44] Since this reflection of St. Augustine's doctrine of *caritas ordinata* is combined with the love of fatherland, John again seems to emphasize the direct sanction of the State by God and nature.

In many passages of the *Policraticus* and the *Metalogicon*, however, John of Salisbury stresses a different idea, the idea that the State and the work of the prince in ruling it imitate but are not directly approved by nature. "Art imitates nature"— the theme goes back to Aristotle; but John learned it in Latin sources. For example, Seneca thought of nature as God and as divine reason. But it is as divine reason that nature participates in men, prompting them to the exercise and improvement of their skills (arts). Every human art, therefore, being the result of the combination of human reason and work, imitates nature.[45] Cicero stated the idea in different words and then related it to the State. For, he says, we should "sequi naturam, optimam bene vivendi ducem" (*Lael.* v, 19); and it is by employing our *artes* for the construction of human society that we follow nature. Indeed, it is our duty to follow nature in developing the art of the State (*De off.*, I, vii, 22).[46]

Chalcidius, in his *Commentary* on the *Timaeus*, is another source of this idea. All things, he says, are the work of God, of nature, or of man the *artifex* imitating nature.[47] This statement was repeated by those who studied and taught at Chartres in the early twelfth century.[48] William of Conches declared that every *opus* is the work of God, of nature, or of the "artifex imitans naturam"; using nature as his agent, God made all things in the world. And the work of the *artifex* results in pictures (*imagines*), clothes, and the like, in which man imitates nature.[49] Furthermore, man, in his creation of "positive justice" (or positive law) for the sake of law and order and of the insti-

---

[44] *Policraticus*, IV, 3; IV, 11; and VIII, 5. Possibly John also reflects *D.* 1, 1, 2; cf. below, n. 75.

[45] Above, § 1.

[46] Above, to n. 22.

[47] Quoted by Tullio Gregory, *Platonismo medievale*, p. 89: "Omnia enim quae sunt, vel Dei opera sunt, vel naturae, vel naturam imitantis hominis artificis."

[48] Gregory, *op.cit.*, p. 89; cf. above, nn. 25-30.

[49] J. M. Parent, *La doctrine de la création dans l'école de Chartres*, pp. 127f.

tutions of the State (*instituta reipublicae*), imitates "natural justice" (the law of nature), which is the divine ordering of the world (*conservatio mundi*). His assertion that "natural justice" includes the principle of the "love of parents and the like" suggests also, in the context of the introductory dialogue in the *Timaeus*, that it sanctions the love of the *patria*.[50]

Returning now to John of Salisbury, we find in him a full development of the theme that man is the *opifex* or *artifex* who imitates nature, not only in the liberal arts but in the art of statesmanship. In the *Policraticus* John observes that nature, *diligissima parens*, has arranged certain parts of the human body for the protection of the intestines. Therefore, he adds, it is necessary that "in republica hanc naturae opificis seruari imaginem," that the prince and his counsellors likewise protect and defend all members of the State, and thus, in effect, imitate nature. Indeed, John says, both Cicero and Plato, although differing in their treatment of the Republic, agree that the "*vita civilis* imitates nature"—that nature "which we have repeatedly called the *optima uiuendi dux*." For otherwise, John continues, there can be no civil life. Of all creatures other than man, only the bees imitate nature in their social life and in their loyalty to their *patria*—and, of course, John quotes Vergil, *Georg. IV*, 11. 153-218, on the bees. Men, to be sure, so John implies, are superior to the bees in organizing society and in loving the fatherland. But they, like the bees, imitate nature.[51]

It is in the *Metalogicon* that John of Salisbury fully develops the theme of *ars naturam imitans*. Nature, the "clementissima parens omnium," by giving man the prerogative of reason, elevated him above all other animals. While grace makes nature fruitful, human reason is intent on observing and examining the things created by nature (I, i, 53). The office of nature is strengthened by the exercise of human reason and art (I, i), above all by the art of eloquence (I, vii). Again, nature is aided by *usus, exercitium* and *studium*, for without human effort nature offers little help: "Prodest utique natura, sed eatenus aut

---

[50] Philippe Delhaye, "L'enseignement de la philosophie morale au XII⁰ siècle," *Medieval Studies*, XI (1949), 95f.; see above, nn. 28f.

[51] *Policraticus*, v, 9; VI, 21.

nunquam aut raro, ut sine studio culmen obtineat" (I, viii). This means that art is the proper use of reason, which is a gift of nature, and that nature is therefore, with the aid of reason, the *parens omnium artium* (I, xi). The use of reason in study and exercise aids nature, and this is the origin of all *artes* "Artium natura mater est" (I, xi). But if nature is the mother of the arts, art is not a perfect copy of nature. For art results chiefly from human education (*institutio*), and therefore it only imitates nature. Insofar as art has its origin in nature, however, it desires to conform with nature as much as possible (I, xiv).[52]

Is the State a work of art that imitates nature? Is statesmanship an art? According to John, both in the *Metalogicon* and in the *Policraticus*, the answer is affirmative; and thus the State by imitating nature has its origin in nature. Human society, he says, is in a way the "unica et singularis fraternitas" of the sons of nature (*filiorum nature*). This is because the association of reason and language (*ratio et verbum*) "tot egregias genuit urbes, tot conciliavit et foederavit regna, tot uniuit populos et caritate deuinxit." Anyone who tries to separate what God has joined together for the utility of all, is the public enemy of all. For such a public enemy destroys all liberal studies, attacks philosophy, and tears to pieces the covenant (*foedus*) of human society. Such an enemy is "our Cornificius," who, unskilled in the study of eloquence and the unworthy assailant of it, is attacking all cities and all political life (I, i). But eloquence is one of the greatest gifts of nature (I, vii). As with Cicero, then, *ratio* and *oratio*, gifts of nature, are the cement of human society and the State.[53]

Nature, therefore, through reason and the arts, especially the art of eloquence developed by human exercise, almost directly inspires the making of the State; and again the State is a work of art and reason, and it imitates nature. In fact, in the *Prooemium* to Bk. II of the *Metalogicon*, John states the idea of imitating nature in a startling way: the *leges ciuium* (civil law) commonly receive their force from human *constitutio*, and what is believed to be profitable to the public utility is equivalent to or

[52] The references are to C. C. J. Webb, ed., *Metalogicon*.
[53] See above, n. 21, for Cicero on this.

comparable with natural justice![54] Thus more strongly than William of Conches does John intimate that the *iustitia positiva* in the State, when it is created by men for the public welfare, imitates *iustitia naturalis*, that is, the law of nature. One may venture to conclude, indeed, that John is saying in effect that nature sanctions both the safety and welfare of the State and those human laws that are useful for the maintenance of the State.

If John of Salisbury nonetheless emphasizes in the *Metalogicon* that nature only indirectly sanctions the State by way of the gift of reason to men, and by way of men's using reason to create the art of statecraft, in the *Policraticus* he believes in the naturalness of human society and its organization in the Republic (State). To be sure, he suggests no modern, secular, naturalism. Since nature and natural reason have their origin in God, the human art that imitates nature must be obedient to the divine plan. Society and the State cannot be self-sufficient, unlimited by the law of God and nature. Princes, in their use of reason for the public welfare and safety of the State, must remember that the divine gift of reason to men means that they should obey God's moral commands and practice equity and justice. Nevertheless, God and nature approve that good kind of Republic in which reason participates in the art of governing.[55]

Not nearly so important for his political thought as John of Salisbury, Alain de Lille in the later twelfth century is another example of the classical and Christian tradition of his age and merits notice. Like John he viewed nature as an instrument of God and as the personification of natural reason and natural justice. The human *Respublica*, when it is ruled by reason, is an image (*simulacrum*) of the divine order of the City of God.[56] If in this Alain does not directly associate nature with the State, he makes the association in saying that *natura* proves that there

---

[54] Ed. Webb, p. 60; *M.P.L.*, 199:857: "Nam et leges ciuium ab humana constitutione plerumque uigorem sumunt; et quod publice utilitati creditur expedire, naturali justitie coequatur."

[55] Again see my "*Ratio publicae utilitatis*, etc.," *Welt als Gesch.*, XXI, 19-22; above, ch. v, nn. 32-38.

[56] See the passages from the *De planctu naturae* (*M.P.L.* 210:444f., 453-454); they are quoted by Gregory, *Platonismo medievale*, pp. 145-148.

should be a king, for nature has placed a king over the bees.[57] We can smile because Alain was a poor naturalist, but at least he suggests by his analogy a kind of naturalism of the State.

3. THE DECRETISTS AND DECRETALISTS

John of Salisbury was a classical scholar, and this no doubt explains why we find in him a remarkable theory of the naturalness of society and the State. But in the two laws also, in the Canon law and the Roman law, canonists and legists from about 1150 to 1250 found a relationship between nature and society and developed it so as to contribute a great deal to the appreciation of nature in the political realm. Although chiefly interested in law, they, too, were at least indirectly influenced by the *Timaeus* and the Neo-Platonic doctrines of Chartres; and some of them were acquainted with Ovid on nature if not, except casually, with Cicero and Seneca.[58] Therefore we turn now to the founders of early modern legal science, who, after all, were more directly and practically concerned with Church and State and their problems than any other men of learning.

The decretists, that is, the specialists in the field of the Canon law which Gratian compiled in what we commonly call the *Decretum* (*ca.* 1140), abundantly discussed the meaning of *ius naturale* and *natura* in the passages that Gratian took from Isidore of Seville, Dist. 1, cc. 1 and 7, and in the Words of Gratian, "Humanum genus, etc.," introducing Dist. 1. Isidore (c.7) had defined the natural law as that instinct of nature which is common to all peoples. As such it is expressed, for example, in the union of man and wife, in the procreation and rearing of children, and in the possession of all property in common; and it justifies the repulsion of force with force as natural and right (*aequum*). Gratian himself, departing from the Roman tradition in Isidore, declared that the natural law is what is contained in the *lex* (i.e., the Mosaic law, chiefly the Ten Commandments) and in the Evangels. This law is the moral law of

---

[57] *Summa de arte praedicatoria*, c. xix (*M.P.L.*, 210:150): "Natura convincat esse regem, quod ex aliis animalibus licet cognoscere quibus natura praeficit regem, ut apibus. . . ."

[58] See above, nn. 24-27.

God and is divine. But Isidore, too, Dist. 1, c. 1, said that in the highest sense the natural law is the *lex divina*.

The decretists went further. They held that the *summa lex* or *ius naturae* is the divine reason. The highest nature itself, *summa natura*, is the source of the natural law, and therefore, in a manner of speaking, *summa natura* is God. This, essentially, is what the decretists meant when they occasionally said "Natura, id est, deus."[59] There is nothing pantheistic in their thought.[60] Nature is an agent of God, personifying the divine reason participating in the natural law, and signifying, on the highest level, the moral commands of God. If God can be called *natura*, it is only a way of saying that God is the ultimate source of the laws of nature. Through the gift of reason to the human soul, and through the *lex mosayca* and the Evangels, the law of nature, as God's supreme moral law, is known to men, who should obey it and act as far as possible in accordance with it. In other words, nature and the natural law are instruments of God's reason, by which God orders the world and man; and they are that enduring, unchanging, fundamental law which tells men to use the gift of reason for the achievement of the good, of law and justice, on earth.

Of the decretists of the latter half of the twelfth century, Johannes Faventinus comes nearest to associating *summa natura* and the law of nature with human society. His predecessors,

59 In general on the decretists and the concept, "Natura, id est, deus," see O. Lottin, *Le droit naturel chez Saint Thomas d'Aquin et ses prédécesseurs*, 2nd ed., pp. 11-23, 106-108. For other examples see n. 60 below; also Kuttner, *Repertorium*, p. 202: *ius naturale* "a summa natura proditum est, i.e. a Deo," and "quia a summa natura, que Deus est, proditum est."

60 Several years ago, observing that "Natura, id est, deus" appears in Accursius' *Glossa ordinaria* on the *Corpus iuris civilis*, U. Gualazzini concluded that the concept was so pantheistic that it must have been a later interpolation, probably resulting from pantheistic thought in the sixteenth century—"'Natura, id est Deus,'" in *Studia Gratiana*, III (1955), 412-424. Since then (Professor Stephan Kuttner called this to my attention), Guido Fassio has corrected Gualazzini, showing how the expression was used by the decretists of the twelfth century and later—"Dio e la natura presso i decretisti e decretalisti," in *Il diritto ecclesiastico*, LXVII (1956), 3-10. As will be noted below, I have found an abundant use of "Natura, id est, deus" in the legists or civilians of the late twelfth and early thirteenth century. Accursius himself used it, as the MSS show; see below, nn. 104-110. See now Brian Tierney, "*Natura Id Est Deus*," *Jour. Hist. Ideas*, XXIV (1963), 307-322.

particularly Rufinus and Stephen of Tournai, are important, but their general theory of natural law is well known.[61] Consequently, Johannes Faventinus is the main object of my attention.[62] In his *Summa* (*ca.* 1171) on the *Decretum*, he declares that while the legistic tradition defines the natural law as "what nature has taught all animals" (*D.* 1, 1, 1, 3; *Inst.* 1, 2), he will treat the natural law only as it pertains to men. So the *ius naturale* is a certain *ius* implanted by nature in the human creature. Innate in man, it prompts him to do good and avoid evil. It is a certain part of the divine law, and as such it is that natural law which *summa natura*, "scilicet, deus," has handed down to us and has taught in the *lex mosayca*, the Prophets, and the Evangels.[63] Further, this natural law commands men to love the Lord God, prohibits killing, and so on, as in the Ten Commandments. It sanctions the possession of all things in common, as it does the natural liberty of all. But since the *lex naturalis* does not go beyond the simple nature of things, the existence of iniquity resulted in the necessary modification of natural law by good customs—hence the *coniunctio* of man and woman, permitted by nature, demanded marriage; hence the modification in the civil law on property, such as the private ownership of slaves and fields.

All these things, however, which seem to be contrary to the natural law, Johannes continues, are finally related to it. For,

61 See Lottin, *Le droit naturel*, pp. 11-23, 106-108.

62 On the *Summa* of Johannes and the MSS and editions, see Kuttner, *Repertorium*, pp. 143-146.

63 I have followed the text of the *Summa* in the Brit. Mus., MS Royal 9 E. VII, fol. 2: "Hoc autem ius legistica traditio generalissime diffinit dicens, Ius naturale est, quod natura omnia animalia docuit." But confining his own discussion to mankind, Johannes says: *ius naturale* is a "lex quedam humane creature a natura insita ad faciendum bonum, cavendum contrarium; et est quasi quedam pars divini iuris, vel ei coherens; quod etiam dicitur ius naturale, quod summa natura [*natura* rep. in the MS], scilicet deus, nobis tradidit et per legem et prophetas et per evangelium suum nos docuit." (There is no need of quoting the text further on the standard theory of natural law.) In another place he says (to Dist. 1, c. 1, ad v. *natura*): "Id est, a deo, qui summa natura est, initium habent, vel a naturale equitate non discrepant"; MS Royal 9 E. VII, fol. 2ᵛ e. 1.

It is clear, I think, that Joh. Fav. wanted to correct Ulpian. Where Ulpian had said that the natural law is what nature taught all animals, Joh. says that the higher natural law in men is what God has taught them in the Old and New Testaments. His emphasis is thus altogether Christian, and so is his *summa natura-Deus*.

he says, by way of example, when some men began to throw off all restraint, were living without heads or a *rector*, and were unpunished while doing every conceivable wickedness, it became the custom to war on those who stubbornly rebelled against the authorities (*potestates*) and to enslave them. The discipline of slavery was necessary to make men "abhor *superbia* and *malignitas* and choose innocence and humility." All this derives from the natural law. "The rivers of *honestas* return to the sea of natural law" in such a way that what was totally lost in the first man was regained in the *lex mosayca*, perfected in the Evangels, and decorated *in moribus*.[64]

To be sure, Johannes Faventinus, like Gratian and the glossators, does offer a distinction between the natural law and human *mores* in the *ius gentium* and the *ius civile*. Moreover, his tracing of contraries such as the private ownership of property and slavery ultimately to the natural law itself, another way of explaining them as necessary because of the sins of mankind, reflects traditional Stoic and Christian thought. And his suggestion that the necessity of human life after the Fall caused rulers (*potestates*) to crush the wicked has some reference to the words of Gratian and Isidore of Seville (Dist. 4, c. 1 Factae), that *leges* are made to curb human *audacitas* and to make innocence safe among the wicked. Possibly, however, Johannes also had in mind St. Augustine's quotation of I Peter v. 5 and James IV. 6, and the *Aeneid*, VI. 854, when saying that slavery was necessary to make men abhor pride and wickedness and choose innocence and humility, after remarking on the acephalous condition of society when men were unrestrained in evil, without a *rector*, and implying that rulers must war on rebels and make them slaves.

---

[64] "Omnia tamen hec que iuri naturali videntur adversa, ad ipsum finaliter referuntur, exempli gratia, quia effrenes quidam esse ceperant, et tanquam acephali sine rectore vivebant impune omnia concepta scelera committentes, moribus receptum est, ut qui pertinaciter suis potestatibus rebelles existerent, pulsati bello et capti perpetuo servi essent." The discipline of slavery is necessary to make men "horrere superbiam et malignitatem et eligere innocentiam atque humilitatem." Even this derives from the natural law: "Flumina honestatis redeunt ad mare iuris naturalis, quod ita processit, ut quod in primo homine pene perditum est, in lege mosayca relevaretur, in evangelio perficeretur, in moribus decoraretur"; MS Royal 9 E. VII, fol. 2, c. 2.

Is there not a suggestion, too, of the introductory words of Socrates in the *Timaeus*? To repeat, the guardians of the State should be friendly and kind to obedient subjects, but savage against foreigners in defense of the *patria*.[65] Here also, if indirectly, nature provides for government for the safety of the community and the welfare of obedient subjects; and thus society and its defense against enemies are "natural." Similarly, Johannes Faventinus speaks of government, the safety of society, and war on the wicked, as principles that are derived from the natural law. Indirectly, therefore, even in apparent contradiction, the State, the magistracy, coercive justice, and the just war of defense for the safety of good, obedient subjects and of society, exist by the divine reason that participates through nature in man. But it is surely of some importance that in this kind of thinking there is at the same time a kind of direct sanction of organized society. It is at least unnatural for men to live in an anarchic state. Thus in one sense, an orderly society, the State, is natural.

On the whole, however, we must not go too far in claiming that Johannes' thought directly associates the *summa natura, id est, deus,* with the sanction of the State. Where John of Salisbury developed a Christian naturalism of the State, Johannes Faventinus and other decretists in general accepted Stoic-Christian conventionalism and the Roman-legal idea of the participation of the natural law in the *ius gentium* and the *ius civile*. The *Glossa ordinaria* of Johannes Teutonicus (*ca.* 1215-1220) by and large represents their attitude.[66] Yet the constant

[65] See above, nn. 29f.

[66] Again see Lottin, *Le droit naturel*, pp. 7-23, 106-108; on Huguccio, 110 (*ius naturale* as the *ius divinum* comes from *summa natura, id est, deus*). For other examples see Kuttner, *Repertorium*, p. 202, and W. Ullmann, *Medieval Papalism*, pp. 40f.; Father Alphons Stickler rightly scolds Ullmann for saying (p. 46) that *summa natura-deus* "was a species of Christian pantheism which permeated the canonistic conception of the divine (natural) law." God does not participate in men, but rather the divine reason does so through the natural law. God is *summa natura* only in the sense of being the source of the natural law. For the theory of natural law in the *Lucubratiunculae* of Master Egidius, a canonist of the late twelfth and early thirteenth century, see A. Rota, "Il decretista Egidius e la sua concezione del diritto naturale," *Studia Gratiana*, II, 213-249. In general also, see Kuttner, *Kanonistische Schuldlehre*, pp. 336-338.

emphasis on the participation of natural law or "natural reason"[67] in the *ius gentium* weakened the doctrine of the necessity of society because of sin, and prepared the way for Thomas Aquinas' combination of canonical and Aristotelian theories.

Like the legists then, the decretists occasionally defined the *ius gentium* as a kind of natural law; for in the *Inst.* 2, 1, 11, they observed a passage that attributed the origin of property rights to the *ius naturale*, "quod, sicut diximus, appellatur ius gentium," and thereafter to civil law.[68] One decretist held that the same law can be called natural with respect to its origin, civil with respect to its form (particular application, he perhaps means), and *ius gentium* with respect to its common observance among peoples.[69] In any case, the canonists agreed that the reason from God in the natural law exists in men, and men should use or recall it as the principle of justice and equity in governing the State and in making laws.

More directly, however, a few canonists of the late twelfth century saw in nature and the natural law the vital "reason of society" and its survival. Like most of the Canon lawyers they started with Isidore of Seville's opinion that the natural law permits animals and men to defend themselves against violent attack, and with the similar idea of classical jurisconsults, that every kind of law (the law of nature, the law of peoples, and the civil law of every State), justifies the repulsion of force with force.[70] "For natural reason," a decretalist said, quoting *D.* 9, 2,

[67] Kuttner, *Kanon. Schuldlehre*, p. 339; also "ius naturale pro ratione," and "ius naturale dicitur ratio hominis," in the author of the *Appar.* "Ecce vincit leo," Introduction and to Dist. 1, c. Ius naturale (Paris, BN, MS nouv. acq. lat. 1576, fols. 19ᵛ c. 1 and 20ᵛ c. 1); and the decretalist, Petrus Hispanus: "Nam 'naturalis ratio adversus periculum (permittit se defendere: *Dig.* 9, 2, 4, pr.) . . .'"; Kuttner, p. 347 n. 1. But the equation of the natural law in the highest sense with reason from God imparted to man was common.

[68] *Appar.* "Est ius naturale" to *Decretum*, in Paris, BN, MS lat. 15393, fol. 2ᵛ c. 1; the author refers to *Inst.* 2, 1, 11.

[69] *Summa Monacensis*, quoted by Kuttner, *Kanon. Schuldlehre*, p. 339 n. 1: ". . . nota quod idem ius dicitur tum naturale, tum civile, tum gentium; sc. per diversas causas: naturale origine, civile forma, gentium communi observatione."

[70] Kuttner, *Kanon. Schuldlehre*, pp. 334-339, 337 on the sources in Roman law, *D.* 9, 2, 45, 4 and 43, 16, 1, 27—add *D.* 1, 1, 3.

4 (Gaius), "permits defending oneself against danger."[71] The necessity of self-defense, while approved by all laws, the natural law most fundamentally, in a sense knows no normal application of the positive law; for in such a case of necessity as that of unavoidably killing a thief in the night the human law imposes no penalty.

The canonists sometimes referred to the doctrine of the Roman law and the legists, that in human beings the right of defense against an unjust wrong (*injuria*) comes from the *ius gentium*, and that the right of a society or State to fight a just war of defense, like the origin of States and peoples, also belongs to the *ius gentium*, as Hermogenianus said, *D.* 1, 1, 5.[72] But in general they held that the necessity of defense against *injuria* and violent force was a principle of natural law as reason in man. Human defense against unjust attack is *de iure naturale*.

This theory essentially pertained to private law, in which the natural law participated. Did the canonists apply it in addition to the public law of the State, with respect to its natural right to exist and defend itself? Surely, if every individual man can by natural reason defend himself, the State should also, as a community of men, receive from nature the same right. Yet some attached the right of fighting in a just war of defense to the *ius gentium*, just as the legists did, deriving it only indirectly from the natural law. A few, however, as remarked above, approached or actually stated the idea that nature and the natural law approve the necessity of defending a society of men in war and thereby sanction organized human society itself. To some degree, like Johannes Faventinus, these few were perhaps influenced in this by the *Timaeus* (the guardians are endowed by nature to defend the *patria* or *civitas*). Or they may have remembered something from St. Ambrose and St. Augustine; at least they read their statements about fighting for the *patria* or the State in the *Decretum*.[73] Something, too, came from the classical Roman jurists.

[71] Petrus Hispanus, to *Comp. I,* 2, tit. De appell., c. 35: "Nam naturalis ratio adversus periculum (permittit se defendere . . .)"; quoted by Kuttner, *Kanon. Schuldlehre,* p. 347 n. 1.

[72] Kuttner, *Kanon. Schuldlehre,* pp. 337-343, 338 n. 2.

[73] Above, nn. 8, 13, 28-30; *Decretum,* C. 23, q. 3, c. 5 Fortitudo, and c. 7 Non inferenda. St. Augustine emphasized how God and Christ understood the neces-

We have already taken notice of the influence of the *Timaeus* and the Latin Fathers. How did the Roman law influence the canonists at this point? We must recall that Ulpian and others, while distinguishing between the *ius naturale* and the *ius gentium*, deduced the latter in part from the former, or rather assumed that the natural law was one of the sources of private law and hence participated, as reason in men, in the human law common to all peoples. The legists, we shall see, agreed; and at the same time, some of them argued that the public law of each State contained natural reason, or an element of the natural law.[74] If he did not relate obedience to parents and the *patria* to the law of nature, Pomponius compared it with reverence for the deity.[75] Florentinus (*D.* 1, 1, 3), after saying that we can repulse violent force and injury, declared that it is lawful to protect oneself because *natura* has established such a *cognatio* (kindred, association, natural connection, and the like) between us that it is *nefas*, contrary to the divine law, for man to attack man (literally, for a man to lie in wait for or ambush a man).

A distinguished decretist and decretalist, Damasus (early thirteenth century), quoted Florentinus (*D.* 1, 1, 3), that nature established a *cognatio* among men, and added that it is a holy right (*fas*) to repel violence.[76] In both the classical jurists and in Damasus this natural right thus pertained not only to individuals as such but to individuals because of their association with each other. Although *cognatio* meant sometimes a blood relationship or kindred, in Damasus at least it surely indicates the natural association of men in society. A full generation

---

sity of fighting just wars to preserve peace, of paying tribute to Caesar for the cost of war; further, the *ordo naturalis mortalium*, which exists for peace, demands that princes have the final authority in deciding on war and waging it, and this power comes from God. Men can lawfully fight for peace, if commanded to do so by the ruler; this is not contrary to the will of God—see *Decretum*, C. 23, q. 1, cc. 3-5. Gratian himself, after observing how the Evangels teach that men should not fight (turn the other cheek, etc.), concludes at the end of this *Causa* that *militare*, waging war (if just), is not a sin.

On the general doctrine of the just war and its development see Regout, *Doctrine de la guerre juste*; and Kuttner, *Kanon. Schuldlehre*, pp. 334-379.

[74] Below, § 4. See *D.* 1, 1, ll. 3, 6, 9, 11.

[75] *D.* 1, 1, 2: "Veluti erga deum religio: ut parentibus et patriae pareamus."

[76] Kuttner, *Kanon. Schuldlehre*, p. 337 n. 3; on Damasus see Kuttner, *Repertorium*, pp. 393-396, 428 n. 2.

earlier, however, a decretist paraphrased Florentinus and concluded that nature does establish *societas*, that in a manner the
"social contract" derives from the natural law in the right of
men to defend themselves. In fact, the ideas of the author of
the *Summa Coloniensis*, "Elegantius in iure divino," *ca.* 1169,
are so striking that we must examine them carefully.[77]

Some of his theory of law is familiar enough. There are two
principal kinds of *ius*, the *divinum* and the *humanum*. The
divine law is given in the *lex* (here, the Law of Moses) and in
the Gospels. The human law is made by men and by it equity is
preserved, injury is guarded against, innocence is protected,
violence is curbed, and discord is banished. Human law, in turn,
consists of two kinds of law, the natural and the positive. The
natural law is that which is observed among all men by the
instinct of nature. From this instinct come the union of male
and female, the issue of children, the free acquisition of those
things which are no one's property, the continued and moderate
repulsion of violence with force, and the restitution of what is
held in trust or of a loan.[78] One can readily see that the author
indirectly bases property rights on the law of nature. In fact,
the identification by many canonists of the natural law, as the
moral law of God, with the *lex mosayca* and the Decalogue resulted in the same theory, for if God commands men not to
steal He approves rights in property.[79]

The author's emphasis on the law of nature both in the right
of self-defense and in one aspect of property rights explains,

[77] On the author and the *Summa Colon.* see Kuttner, *Repertorium*, pp. 170-
172. I quote passages from two of the known MSS, the Bamberg MS Can. 39,
fols. 13-144, and the Paris, BN, MS lat. 14997, fols. 1-183.

[78] MS lat. 14997, fol. 1: first the author says that "ius est ars equi et boni"
(cf. Ulpian, *D.* 1, 1, 1), but that *ius* differs from justice in that man is the
author of *ius*, God of justice; *ius* is either *divinum* or *humanum*; "Ius divinum
est quod in lege vel in evangelio; humanum, hominum constitutio, qua equitas
servatur, iniuria propellitur, custoditur innocentia, frenatur violentia, et exulat
discordia"; "Ius humanum aut est naturale, ut quod instinctu nature apud
omnes servatur, puta maris et femine coniunctio, liberorum successio, libera
eorum que in nullius bonis sunt acquisitio, violentia per vim continuata et
moderata repulsio, deposti seu comodati restitutio." The influence of *Inst.* 2, 1
is evident, but this canonist more strongly emphasizes the naturalness of property rights.

[79] Lottin, *Le droit naturel*, pp. 7-40.

perhaps, the way in which he changed the wording of Florentinus's opinion. "All *leges* and *iura*," he continues, "permit repulsing force with force. What anyone has done for the protection of his body, he is said to have done by right." Now, more strongly than Florentinus, our decretist declares that this right comes from nature's "contracting" society among men: "nature has made or contracted so strong an association (*societas*) among men, that it is *nefas* for one to lie in wait for another." But, of course, the right of defending oneself must be free of any spirit of deliberate wrong-doing and love of fighting. Therefore, the vigor of courts and the judgment of public law must not permit anyone who neglects the procedure of lawsuit to seek private revenge for an injury.[80]

Not only does the natural law sanction the private right of defending oneself against bodily harm and injury of one's rights, it sanctions human society itself. Nature, moreover, not only binds men in a kind of social contract, but also stands behind the public law in the form of courts and trials to protect society from the harm that would result from private vengeance, not to mention the harm from giving no man the right, according to the law, to defend himself. If this is said partly in the words of Florentinus, it suggests the principle of natural justice and society in St. Ambrose; and it may be related to the idea in the *Timaeus* and in the Christian tradition that the government by magistrates is natural as a necessity for the defense of the innocent and of society or the *patria* as a whole.

Does the author of the *Summa Coloniensis*, however, weaken his theory of nature and society in his discussion of man-made or positive law? In fact, he adds that the positive law of each city is called civil law, for example, the law that regulates the

---

80 Bamberg, MS Can. 39, fol. 13 (also Paris, BN, MS lat. 14997, fol. 1): "Vim enim vi repellere omnes leges et omnia iura permittunt. Quod quis ob tutelam corporis sui egerit, iure fecisse dicetur. Tantam enim inter homines natura societatem pepigit, ut alterum alteri insidiari nefas sit. Licet ergo vim vi repellere, sed cum moderamine inculpate tutele, et flagrante maleficio, non renovato post rixam bellandi studio. Inde enim iudiciorum vigor, iurisque publici censura in medio est, ne quis post intermissam* litem de illata sibi iniuria permittat ultionem."

* The Paris MS has "post intramissa litem"; the correct reading is in the Bamberg MS.

cult of the gods (*cultus numinum*) and the special form of ceremonies (cf. *D.* 1, 1, 2). But if the positive law deals with different *nationes*, it is called the *ius gentium*. This law of peoples is concerned with the occupation of conquered regions, with the law of war, captivity, slavery, reprisal, redemption of prisoners, and military service; and with the solemnities of waging war and making peace, with military discipline, stipends, rank, honor, division of the spoils, and the portion of the prince.[81] Now, the classical Roman law and the legists tended to assign to the *ius gentium* the actual origin of cities and kingdoms or States.[82] It is therefore noteworthy that our decretist is silent at this point. Since he had just made nature the force that causes men to live in society, it is probable that in his mind society and the State are directly natural. The relations between naturally existing societies, however, are expressed in the *ius gentium*, just as special rules of human conduct within each society are the subject of civil law.

Altogether, then, the author of the *Summa Coloniensis* believed that the association of men in society was inspired by nature. On reflection, we should not be astonished. Of the twelfth century, he belonged to the intellectual atmosphere in which nature and the natural law were descending more often and directly into human affairs. Further, his apparent distinction between the naturalness of States and the human development of the law of relations between States (*ius gentium*) can be observed in other canonists. For example, about 1160 a decretist said that by the *ius gentium* one city, if it has just cause, can attack another, occupy it, and build fortresses in it;[83] and he held that the *ius militare et publicum* derives from the natural

---

[81] In the MSS cit., *loc. cit.*: "Aut est [ius] positivum. Et hoc, si cuius civitatis est proprium, civile dicitur, ut cultus numinum et ceremoniarum ritus specialis. Si enim diversarum sit nationum, ius gentium vocatur, ut sedium devictarum occupatio, belli, captivitatis, servitutis, postliminii, et milicie ius, ut pote belli inferendi sollempnitates, federis facere nexus, signo dato egressio, commissio, receptio, flagitii militaris disciplina, stipendiorum modus, dignitatum gradus, premiorum honor, prede decisio, ac portio principis."

[82] *D.* 1, 1, 5 and 9; and Accursius, *Glos. ord.* to these passages, below, nn. 128-137.

[83] *Summa Parisiensis*, ed. McLaughlin, to Dist. 1, c. 9: "Civitas hoc jure [gentium] si causam habeat civitatem expugnare potest et sedes civitatis occupare ibi suos ponendo et aedificare turres."

law as well as the *ius gentium* and the civil law.[84] Around 1200 another decretist, asserting that a war is just that avenges injuries done to the *Respublica*, intimated that natural justice makes it lawful for the State to defend itself by waging a just war.[85] Johannes Faventinus said that *ratione rei* a war is just *pro defensione patriae*.[86] St. Augustine, indeed, had said that God Himself approved the just war of defense waged by a people or *civitas* (*Decretum*, C. 23, q. 2, c. 2). And even when the canonists attributed the origin of States directly to the *ius gentium* they generally held that after sin came into the world "the natural law now sanctioned, as expedient to sinful men, institutions that it would not have sanctioned had men continued in perfection."[87]

According to the canonists, therefore, the natural law did give men in society the right of organized defense, at the command of the ruler, in a just war. It followed that it was good to fight and die for the *patria*; and killing in its defense, killing one's father if necessary and unavoidable, was not a crime in the thought of the legists or of that of the canonists.[88] The *patria* that men fought for under the authority of the prince, who alone could declare a just war of defense, was, under the influence of the Roman law, becoming the *patria communis*, that is, every independent kingdom ruled by a king who was the prince or emperor in his realm, recognizing no superior outside the realm.[89] Such a common fatherland, the independent State, arising in fact, strongly supported by the legal theory of "nationalistic" canonists, and developed under more effective central governments by kings and their legal advisers, became a

[84] *Ibid.*, p. 3, to Dist. 1, c. 10 Jus militare: "Resp.: Haec duo, jus militare et publicum ex illis tribus speciebus colliguntur"—referring to *ius naturale, ius gentium*, and *ius civile*.

[85] Gloss to *Decretum*, C. 23, q. 2, c. 1: "Iustum esse bellum quod ulciscitur iniurias factas rei publice"; in MS Vat. lat. 2495, fol. 126 c. 2.

[86] In the *Glos. ord.* to Gratian's words, "Quod autem," introducing C. 23, q. 2.

[87] Lewis, *Medieval Political Ideas*, p. 10.

[88] On this, for details, see my study, "Two Notes on Nationalism," *Traditio*, IX, 282-285; above, ch. x, nn. 11, 26; also the excellent treatment by Ernst Kantorowicz of another aspect of the theme, "*Pro patria mori* in Medieval Political Thought," *A.H.R.*, LVI, 472-492, and *King's Two Bodies*, pp. 232-249; and Kuttner, *Kanon. Schuldlehre*, p. 343 n. 2.

[89] "Two Notes on Nationalism," *Traditio*, IX, 296-320; above, ch. x, nn. 44-46, 54.

kind of moral end in itself. This resulted also from the theory that nature and the natural law, originating in God, directly approved it as the chief object of human loyalty on earth and as the means, in its representative (the head, or prince), of defending the safety of its members. Thus, the private natural law of self-defense entered into a kind of public natural law.

One difficulty remains in judging the canonists' doctrine of nature and society. Did the decretist who said, "Tantam enim inter homines natura societatem pepigit, etc.,"[90] have in mind the idea of the primitive society of all men living in common according to the law of nature, before sinfulness resulted in the rise of peoples and States and in a different kind of sanction by the participation of the natural law in the *ius gentium*? It is possible that his theory, like that of the legists, was that of the complete naturalness only of the original *societas*, and the partial naturalness of the human foundation of separate, organized communities or States.[91] Nonetheless, consciously or unconsciously, the decretists transferred much of the naturalness of *societas* in general to the organized, independent *societas*, or *civitas* or *regnum* or *Respublica*, in particular. As we have observed, every kingdom under a king who recognized no superior was a *patria* that had the natural right to fight a just war of defense. The State, then, was already existing as a separate *societas* in accordance with the law of nature. Ptolemy of Lucca, despite the fact that he wrote after Aristotle's *Politics* was well known, reflected the earlier naturalism of canonists and legists when he said that by the law of nature (*de iure naturae*) a king can demand whatever taxes are necessary for the preservation of human society (*ad conservandum societatis humanae*), for it is the duty of the king to care for the common welfare.[92]

To some degree, the canonists, when speaking of nature and society in general, may have had in mind a lower "naturalness" of such human needs as government and the civil law. After all, Isidore of Seville had understood how human laws must be related to the environment (*Decretum*, Dist. 4, c. 2); and per-

90 Above, n. 80.
91 Below, to nn. 107-127.
92 Gierke, *Political Theories*, pp. 190f. n. 323.

haps from this passage (to repeat what was said above), rather than from Aristotle, came the idea that "naturally" various kinds of independent States and polities could lawfully and rightly exist. "Naturally," too, human laws could condone lesser evils forbidden by God and the law of nature lest the greater evil of the destruction of the State result from scandal and anarchy.[93] But were the canonists acquainted with Justinian's doctrine of legislation, that because nature often creates or brings forth new *formae* or situations, the emperor can and should make new laws?[94] No doubt they were: in 1226 Pope Honorius III almost literally quoted the words of Justinian in the bull authorizing the publication of the compilation of his decretals.[95] (At the end of the century Boniface VIII will publish the *Liber Sextus* in similar terms.)[96] Therewith, officially, it was recognized that nature approved papal legislation—but long since the Canon law had stated that councils and popes could "novas canones condere," thus borrowing from the Roman law on the right of emperors "novas leges condere."[97] Shortly after 1226 the decretalist, Jacobus de Albenga, commented on the decretals of Honorius III and referred to Justinian's words in his own theory of the naturalness of new legislation.[98]

93 See above, to nn. 19, 20, and 35; and below, to nn. 146-147, and § 5 in general.

94 See below, nn. 150-165.

95 On this see Kuttner, *Repertorium*, p. 382; E. Friedberg, *Quinque compilationes antiquae*, p. 152. As early as 1163 Pope Alexander III had spoken of how new ills demand the discovery of new medicines, and how new statutes or canons were necessary; *Comp. II*, 3, 27, 1—Friedberg, p. 80. Cf. below, n. 98, on St. Augustine as the source.

96 Gagnér, *Studien zur Ideengeschichte der Gesetzgebung*, pp. 133f.

97 *Decretum*, C. 25, q. 1, c. 6; *D.* 1, 4, 2; *C.* 1, 14, 8.

98 Brit. Mus., MS Royal 11 C. VII, fol. 246; on the *Apparatus* of Jacobus and on the MSS see Kuttner, *Repertorium*, pp. 383f. Jacobus repeats the words of St. Augustine (*Decretum*, Dist. 50, c. 22) on new antidotes and medicines for new ills, and then says that *iura* are needed for *negotia*. Besides, "que de novo emergunt novo consilio indigent . . . Nova res novum consilium desiderat. . . ." No one salve can be used for the eyes of all men (see Dist. 29, c. 3 Necesse). So there must be a variety of punishments according to the variety of delicts and of persons, and "pro varietate culpe debetur ultio. . . ." Logically, then, "leges enim et constitutiones futuris certam est dare formam negotiis" (as in *C.* 1, 14, 7). The very nature of things requires and justifies new remedies and new laws: "Nam cum nichil sit in rerum natura quod stare [this word is illegible in my microfilm of the MS, but it is *stare* in *C.* 1, 17, 2, to which Jacobus refers] possit, natura semper novas [*novat* in the MS] deproperat causas

There is no need of developing this theme now—it will be treated in some detail below when we study the legists. Suffice it to say that the canonists, well before the middle of the thirteenth century, were aware of a lower, secular nature of the State, and held that this nature demands new laws to take care of new kinds of situations. The higher law of nature, of course, is fundamental, unchanging. Yet according to nature in the lower sense, human law can be adapted so as to meet the natural demands of human society and of the State.

One final remark. In general, the canonists of the twelfth and early thirteenth century believed that the social instinct of man was natural, and that nature directly sanctioned the primitive society that was common to all mankind. But they did not attribute the same naturalness to the organized societies or States which developed because of human sinfulness. Nonetheless, they were finding that in some respects, particularly in cases of danger that threatened the common and public safety, the State was a natural good rather than merely a necessary, conventional ordering of society.

4. THE LEGISTS

We have noted that the canonists based their thought in part on the Roman law. How did the legists, especially the glossators from Irnerius to Accursius, treat God and nature in relation to society and the State?

In one sense, of course, they could hardly fail to start with the premise that the Empire (to them often the one true State and bearer and object of the public law) was willed by God and enjoyed always the divine favor. Frederick Barbarossa was probably the first medieval emperor to declare that the *Imperium Romanum* was *sacrum* not only because he and his advisers wished to make it the equal of the Church, but also because in the newly revived Roman law they learned that the law of the State was "sacred"—so Ulpian had said (*D.* 1, 1, 1).

Moreover, Justinian himself had said that he received the

---

edere [*edere* not in MS], ut C. de veteri iure enucl. l. ii. sed quia [*C.* 1, 17, 2]. Et natura introductum est ut plura negocia quam vocabula, ut ff. de prescrip. natura [*D.* 19, 5, 4]. . . ."

government of the Empire from the Celestial Majesty in order to wage war successfully, establish peace, and uphold the *status Reipublicae* (*C.* 1, 17, 1). Among the glossators, by the time of Accursius and the *Glossa ordinaria* (1228), it was a common opinion that the prince was, as it were, "God on earth" and the *lex animata*.[99] As John of Viterbo said, in his *De regimine civitatum* (*ca.* 1228), God on High established the Empire, and the Empire "semper est." But long since, in the *Anonymous of York*, kings had been called the image and vicar of Christ.[100] In effect, the State was something far higher and nobler than a conventional political order made necessary by human sinfulness. It was good in itself.

Logically, then, the legists should have found in nature and the natural law the direct origin of the State. That they did not do so as much as one might have expected can be attributed in part to the influence of the traditional Christian attitude. But the better explanation, no doubt, is that they tried to follow the opinions of the classical jurisconsults in the *Digest*. In general, therefore, they derived separate societies and States directly from the *ius gentium*, indirectly from the *ius naturale*.[101] Since, however, nature and the natural law participated in the "law of peoples," and the *ius gentium* was that natural law which is common to all men but not to all animals, the deduction made was that nature did ultimately sanction the State. For after all, as remarked above, God approved human efforts, and this was true particularly by means of His gift of natural reason in the law and justice which must be practiced by the magistracy. To anticipate, the legists could not but find some sanction of organized societies in accordance with the Christian tradition

99 See Kantorowicz, *King's Two Bodies*, s.v. *lex animata*, for many references. One gloss, to *C.* 1, 2, 10, ad v. *coeleste*, puts it thus: "Id est principis, qui est quasi deus. Coelestis enim Deus in coelis est, ita princeps in terris." For other statements of the same idea see below, nn. 156, 169.

100 John of Viterbo quoted by Berges, *Fürstenspiegel*, p. 30. On the *Anon. of York* see Berges, pp. 28-30; and Kantorowicz, *King's Two Bodies*, pp. 42-61.

101 See the references given above, n. 21, on the Roman theory of natural law. On the theories of the legists see also Calasso, *Medio evo del diritto. I: Le fonti*, pp. 331-333; Carlyle, *Med. Political Theory*, ii, ch. 3; Lewis, *Med. Political Ideas*, i, 7f.; Lottin, *Le droit naturel*, pp. 1-7; and W. Onclin, "Le droit naturel selon les romanistes des XIIe et XIIIe s.," in *Miscellanea moralia . . . Arthur Janssen*, ii, 329-337.

which after all caused them to discover a higher naturalness than the classical jurists could in the *ius gentium* and in the public law of each State. The canonists, of course, were influential.

Like the canonists, in fact, the legists said that in the highest sense nature is, in a manner of speaking, God—again, "natura, id est, deus."[102] The first of the important glossators, Irnerius, held that the *natura* which teaches all animals (Ulpian, in *D.* 1, 1, 1, 3; *Inst.* 1, 2) was divinely promulgated for all, generally and individually; and nature permits the association of man and woman in marriage for the procreation of children.[103] (This idea of the society of man and wife according to natural law may be, in Irnerius as in St. Augustine, the starting point of the argument for the natural law as the sanction likewise for any *societas*, hence for the State.)[104] Placentinus goes a step further in his *Summa* on the *Institutes*. The natural law, he says, is what nature (*natura* in the nominative case) has taught all animals; or it is what has taught all animals by means of nature (if *natura* is read *ablative*; and this statement of the possibility of putting *natura* in the ablative became a commonplace among the legists). Then he adds, "natura, id est, deus, quia facit omnia nasci," and quotes the first words of the familiar passage from Ovid: "Unde Oui. (dius) 'hanc deus et

[102] See above, to nn. 59f.; also Tierney, "*Natura Id Est Deus*," *Jour. Hist. Ideas*, XXIV, 307-322.

[103] To *D.* 1, 1, 1, 3 ad v. *natura*: "Y. divinitus prodita generaliter et singulatim"; in MS Vat. lat. 2705, fol. 5 (but in MS Vat. lat 1406, fol. 2: "Y Scilicet, divinitus prodita generaliter."); ad v. *hinc descendit*: "Y. a natura enim permittitur, ut iungantur et consentientur secundum in permissione est" (MS Vat. lat. 2705, fol. 5; but in E. Besta, *Opera d'Irnerio*, II, 2: ". . . ut iungantur et socientur"—no doubt the better reading; in MS Vat. lat. 1406 the gloss reads: ". . . ut agreguntur et socientur." The words "secundum in permissione est" in MS Vat. lat. 2705 are probably not by Irnerius.

[104] *D.* 1, 1, 10 Iustitia, ad v. *Iustitia*: "Y. (G.) Scilicet, figurate, quia secundum hanc 'constans' quis dicitur, quod enim natura est in eo (naturale est in eo) permanens, quis constare sibi dicitur. . . . Hoc ergo nature (naturale) bonum partim in eo vertitur, ut (uti) pro tuenda hominum societate . . ."; MS Vat. lat. 1408, fol. 3ᵛ (the variants in parentheses are from MS Vat. lat. 1405, fol. 1). Of course, justice, which is a natural good and by nature constant, is only indirectly an indication that the natural law sanctions society. But St. Augustine more directly associated God and the natural law with the State; see the *De civ. dei*, XII, 27; XIX, 14; and on this, Anton Chroust, "The Philosophy of Law of St. Augustine," *Philosophical Review*, LIII, 195-202. Cf. above, nn. 9-17.

melior.'" Nature, he concludes, causes the procreation and rearing (*educatio*) of children.[105] Hugolinus[106] and Azo[107] followed Placentinus in treating the passage in the *Digest* and in the *Inst.*, and also said, in various ways, "Natura, id est, deus." Azo explains that nature is *deus* only in the sense that God taught all animals by means of nature, "per naturam";[108] he thus emphasizes that nature is not the same as God, but is God's instrument. In a discussion of nature and the natural law to be examined below, Azo states the thought in a slightly different manner: "unde dicitur ius naturale quod natura, id est, ipse deus, docuit omnia animalia."[109] In the *Glossa ordinaria*, compiled in the third decade of the thirteenth century and revised in the later years of his life, Accursius included many of the glosses of his predecessors and frequently added his own. One finds, both in manuscripts of the thirteenth century and in editions of the sixteenth, that he, too, said, "natura, id est, deus."[110]

105 *Summa Inst.*, 1, 2 De iure naturali: "Ius naturale est 'quod' nominative, 'natura' ablative, vel 'quod' accusative, 'natura' nominative, docuit cuncta animalia. 'Natura,' id est, deus, quia facit omnia nasci; unde oui. (dius), 'hanc deus et melior. . . .'" I have followed the reading in a thirteenth century MS, Paris, BN, MS lat. 4441, fol. 1ᵛ. The quotation marks, which I have inserted, make clear how Placentinus was aware of the possibility of reading *natura* either in the nominative or in the ablative (Ulpian, *D.* 1, 1, 1, 3: "Ius naturale est quod natura omnia animalia docuit"). The passage is also quoted, from an edition of the sixteenth century, by Carlyle, *Mediaeval Political Theory*, 11, 29. To show that no interpolation was made in modern times, I have preferred to quote from the MS; but see also Fitting, *Juristische Schriften des früheren Mittelalters*, on the *Summa* of Placentinus. For Ovid, see above, n. 24.

106 Gloss to *D.* 1, 1, 1, 3, ad v. *natura*: "Id est, deus natura; 'quod' erit accusativus casus. Vel dic ['quod'] nominativi casus, ['natura'] ablative"; in Paris, BN, MS lat. 4461, fol. 1.

107 MS lat. 4459, fol. 1, to *D.* 1, 1, 1, 3, ad v. *natura*: "Id est, deus, et ita 'quod' erit accusativi casus; vel dic nominativi, et 'natura' sit ablative. *Az.*" The same gloss with the *sigla* of Azo stands also in MS lat. 4451, fol. 9.

108 In Paris, BN, MS lat. 4451, fol. 9—the gloss is interlinear, ad v. *natura*: "Id est deus, vel natura, id est per naturam." I am not certain that this is Azo's gloss, but it is in a MS containing many of his glosses.

109 In his *Summa* on the *Inst.*, ed Venice, 1584, p. 1050. Azo continues with a discussion of *quod* and *natura* in the different cases noted above.

110 I have consulted these MSS: Brit. Mus., MS Royal 11 D. III, fol. 5ᵛ (to *D.* 1, 1, 1, 3); Paris, BN, MS lat. 4426, fol. 1ᵛ (to *Inst.* 1, 2, ad vv. *Hinc descendit, matrimonium appellamus*, and *hinc liberorum procreatio*). I have used also the ed. of Godefroy, Lyons, 1604—the *Corpus iuris civilis*, with the *Glos. ord.*

Professor Stephan Kuttner has kindly given me the following information from a work that was inaccessible to me, Petrus Torelli, *Corpus iuris civilis*

No more than the canonists did the glossators accept any pantheistic doctrine of nature. Their *natura, id est, deus*, simply meant that the highest nature, personifying the *summa lex naturae* and the divine reason, was the instrument by means of which the commands of God participated in the world and in men and their society. Above all, that natural law, *ius naturale*, which was nature's relationship with man, was in a fashion the *ius gentium*, the law of peoples; and while its moral commands entered into the laws (civil or positive law) of each State, it was a fundamental law superior to and outside the civil law. Yet the partial deification of nature meant that the glossators strongly emphasized the connection between God's will and reason, expressed in the natural law, and human reason used in creating the State and its laws. The *ius gentium* was the more natural, responding to the natural need of men to live in societies or States. The result is that nature, more directly than in the classical law, inspired and sanctioned the State.

In developing this theory the glossators may have been influenced by the classics, the *Timaeus*, and the Latin Fathers. But I have found no direct references to these in their comments on nature and society; nor have I found any direct reference to John of Salisbury. One can only say, therefore, that given their education in grammar and rhetoric, they may have learned something of the kind from ideas that were current in their time. But we must let the glossators give their ideas.

Irnerius led the way—and he and his disciples at Bologna may have influenced the decretists. Commenting on Ulpian's famous definition of justice (*D.* 1, 1, 10: "Iustitia est constans et perpetua voluntas ius suum cuique tribuendi"), Irnerius says

---

cum glossa magna Accursii Florentini, fasc. 1: *Institutionum Iustiniani Augusti libri IV* (Bologna, n.d., but perhaps 1940), pp. 18f. Torelli shows that, to *Inst.* 1, 2 ad v. *natura* Accursius said "idest deus" only in the second recension; but ad vv. *Hinc descendit* and *hinc liberorum* he had said in the earlier recension "Idest ab hoc iure naturali, idest Deo, qui . . ." and "Nam deus. . . ." Thus Accursius used the words as early as about 1230—which is not surprising, since his predecessors had long since been doing so. See above, nn. 59, 60. It would be interesting also to study the MSS of the *Glos. ord.* to *D.* 1, 1, 3 in order to learn whether Accursius said "natura, idest deus" in the early recension as well as the later. But it is already evident that he was well acquainted with the words and the idea.

that Justice is *constans* because *natura,* or what is *naturale,* is *permanens* in it, and this "in perpetuum." Nature is also the *naturale bonum* or *bonum naturae,* which is not only in justice but by way of justice is chiefly engaged in the preservation or protection of human society. For, participating in justice and society, it assigns to each one the business that touches or belongs to him.[111] He means, I think, that the natural law that participates in justice protects society by showing men what rightly belongs to them, according to law and justice, and prevents the destructive anarchy that would result from no one's knowing what is rightly his own. Human society, considered generally apart from the Empire or any State, is based on justice and therefore on a principle of natural law. In fact, as Irnerius says, the *ius gentium* contains certain things that are natural.[112]

But if *natura* is the fundamental principle of society in general, it is also the sanction of the "society" of man and woman in marriage. Further, it makes lawful the right of defending oneself either against violent attack or against an unjust wrong (*injuria*).[113] When, however, the natural right of human as-

111 The whole gloss is important, and so far as I know has not been published. Therefore I give it here, using the version in MS Vat. lat. 1408, fol. 3ᵛ, for it seems to offer the best text. In parentheses I indicate important variants in the text found in MS Vat. lat. 1405, fol. 1 (=A), and one or two small variants in Brit. Mus. MS 11 C. III, fol. 1ᵛ (=B), which otherwise gives the same text as in MS Vat. lat. 1408:

Y. Scilicet (not in A and B) figurate, quia secundum hanc 'constans' quis dicitur, quod enim natura (A, *naturale*; B, *nature*) est in eo permanens, quis constare sibi dicitur. Idem (B, *Quod*) et perpetuum est. De hoc in legibus dici solet non est ab re; quod autem vitii est ex nobis incipit et nobiscum desinet. Hoc ergo nature (A, *naturale*) bonum partim in eo vertitur, ut (A, *uti*) pro tuenda hominum societate cuique (B, *suum cuique*; A, *incipiat* follows) quem negotium contingit suum (A, *eas* added; B, *suum* omitted) assignet (A, *signet*), ut de iustitia quidem suum cuiusque (B, *suum cuique*) incipiat esse; de iure vero manifestetur suum esse.

De singulis que iustitie sunt, non est predicabilis [this not in A].

112 To *D.* 1, 1, 1, 4, ad vv. *hoc solis hominibus inter se cummune sit:* "Y. Si videlicet originaliter sit ius gentium, quedam enim in eo sunt naturalia"; in MS Vat. lat. 2705, fol. 5; also in MSS Vat. lat. 1406 and 1408. Besta, *L'Opera di Irnerio,* II, 2, gives this version: "Secundo loco. originaliter fit ius gencium. quedam enim sunt in eo . . . naturalia." See also the glosses quoted by Carlyle, *Mediaeval Political Theory,* II, 43.

113 To *D.* 1, 1, 1, 3, ad v. *natura:* "Y. § divinitus prodita generaliter"; ad vv. *hinc descendit maris atque feminae coniunctio, quam nos matrimonium appellamus:* "Y. § A natura hoc permittitur ut iungentur [*iungantur,* in one or two MSS, and in Besta, *Opera,* II, 2] etiam socientur. § Y. Nam et coitus solo . . .

sociation in society and the natural right of a man to defend himself pass into societies or States, the natural law becomes an essential part of the *ius gentium*. In fact, Irnerius, discussing the opinion of Frontinus (*D.* 1, 1, 3—we have already observed how this passage influenced the decretists),[114] says that the *cognatio* established by nature among men, and the consequent wrongfulness of a man's attacking another, are principles "common to every people (*natio*)." And on the words of Hermogenianus (*D.* 1, 1, 5), he says that the *ius gentium* made lawful the right of waging war to repel an *injuria*, and that it sanctioned men's departing from the *societas* common to all and uniting themselves in particular societies, one society for each people.[115]

For Irnerius, then, there is a distinction between the natural law and the *ius gentium*, and between the formless, but completely natural, primitive society of all men and the "nations" or peoples living in separate, organized, less natural, societies or States. Yet since nature and the natural law are the essence of justice, make self-defense lawful, and prompt men to associate with each other (in the common primitive society), they are the source of another kind of naturalness, that of men's facing the necessity (brought on by their sinfulness and violence) of creating new societies and their laws and governments. If, as he said, what is common to all men is the *ius gentium* in origin (*origi-*

---

causa permittitur." To *D.* 1, 1, 3 (Florentinus), ad v. *propulsemus*: "Y. § Bruta animalia propulsant quidem, sed iniuriam neque pati neque facere intelligentur"; ad v. *ob tutelam*: "Y. § quedam enim licet per se inspecta equa non sunt, ad aliud tamen relata equa sunt, ut aliquem percutere per se inspectum iniquum est, sed ob tutelam sui permissum, ideoque congruum vel equum"; ad v. *nefas*: "§ Y. Igitur depellere insidias fas est, et ideo iure fit." These glosses I have taken from MS Royal 11. C. III, fol. 1; in general this MS offers the best texts, but the same glosses with minor variants are in the MSS Vat. lat. 1406, fol. 2, and 2705, fol. 5.

114 See above, to nn. 76-80.

115 To *D.* 1, 1, 3, ad vv. *cognationem, quandam natura constituit, consequens est*, etc.: "§ Y. Commune omni nationi"; to *D.* 1, 1, 5 ad vv. *Ex hoc iure gentium introducta bella*: "Y. § Ad iniuriam propulsandam, quia tunc permittitur enim bellare"; ad vv. *discretae gentes*: "Y. § Ab illa scilicet soci[e]tate, que omnibus communis erat hominibus, discedere, et specialem unius gentis societatem cohire et utile visum est et iure gentium receptum"; MS Royal 11 C. III, fol. 1.

naliter), certain things in it are *naturalia*.[116] Thus the new, separate *nationes* or peoples in their particular societies, are natural, if in a derived "naturalism."

Some of the glossators who followed distinguished more sharply than Irnerius between the *ius naturale* and the *ius gentium*. Rogerius emphasized the human and secular "naturalness" of the *ius gentium*. He identified the *ius naturale* in part with the law of peoples, in part with equity. For that *ius naturale* which is common to all men and comes from human nature may be called the *ius gentium*. It commands us to revere parents, worship God, and preserve the faith. It is also called the *ius aequissimum*, and in that meaning even civil law can be called *ius naturale*. In fact, the civil law, in its broadest meaning is everything that the *civitas* uses, and as such it can be called both *ius naturale* and *ius gentium*.[117] On the whole, Rogerius seems to combine Roman and Christian and worldly elements: what is natural comes from God but in the State it is in part the worldly needs of men for an orderly society. The State is natural simply because human nature on earth demands its existence.

Hugolinus and Azo clung in part to the classical jurists' tendency to identify, in men, the *ius naturale* and the *ius gentium*; and they further held that the natural law participates not only in the private law but also in the public law of each State.[118] But Azo's theory of natural law merits special attention. In the most general sense, he holds, like the decretists, that the natural

---

[116] See the preceding n.; also *D.* 1, 1, 4, and Irn. ad vv. *quod a naturali recedere*: "Id est, gentium constitutione capiens originem"; and ad vv. *hoc solis hominibus inter se commune sit*: "Y. Si videlicet originaliter sit ius gentium, quedam enim et in eo naturalia sunt"; MS Royal 11 C. III, fol. 1.

[117] *Quaestiones super Institutis*, quoted by H. Kantorowicz, *Studies in the Glossators of the Roman Law*, p. 275.

[118] Hugolinus, in Paris, BN, MS lat. 4461, to *D.* 1, 1, 1, 2, ad vv. *privatum ius tripertitum est* (i.e., derived from the precepts of natural law, the *ius gentium*, and civil law): "Sic et tripertitum credo publicum ius, et negari non potest. Sed immo et de eo non dicit, quia plura traditur de privato quam de publico. *h.*" That is, he means that the jurisconsults were chiefly concerned with private law and discussed its derivation in part from the natural law, and did not discuss the public law in this respect. So also Azo on the same passage: "Idem in publico. *Az.*"; MS Vat. lat. 1408, fol. 3; cf. the *Glos. ord.* On the *ius nat.* as *ius gentium*, Hugolinus to *D.* 1, 1, 1, 3, ad v. *Ius naturale*: ". . . Alias ius naturale ius gentium, ut infra, Inst. de rerum di. (2, 1, 11). *h.*" For Azo see the following nn.

law is what God, by means of nature, has taught all animals.[119]
As the moral law of God, it is contained in the *lex mosayca* and
the Evangels. Apart from natural instinct in animals and men,
it is reason, and it is the highest equity or principle of justice.[120]
But in another sense the natural law, as a result of the natural
reason in men, is the *ius commune*; for reason prompts men to
create law for their own utility in society. Perhaps Azo at this
point is vaguely expressing the idea that legislation is an art that
imitates nature. In the context the *ius commune* is the *ius gentium*, which is also, however, the creation of men.[121] The civil
law of each State is all the laws used by the *civitas*, whether the
natural, the *ius gentium*, and the civil. Insofar as the *ius civile*
includes these kinds of law, one can say that the "civil wisdom"
in law is "a most holy thing."[122] It is the participation of natural
reason and equity in positive law that makes the civil law holy.

As for the *ius gentium*, it differs from that natural law which
is common to all animals in being common to men only, used
by all peoples. It includes religion, or reverence for God, the
duty of obeying parents and fatherland, and the right of repulsing violence and injury. Here Azo is referring both to *D.*
1, 1, 2 (Pomponius, who also associated religion and obedience
to parents and *patria* with the *ius gentium*) and to *D.* 1, 1, 3
(Florentinus); and he now repeats what we have encountered
in the decretists and Irnerius, that the right of self-defense
derives both from the *ius gentium* and from the relationship
which nature established among men.[123] Finally, wars waged by
a prince or by a *populus*, the separate existence of *gentes*, the
foundation of kingdoms, and the division of property, along

---

119 Above, nn. 109-110.

120 *Summa Inst.*, Venice, 1584, p. 1050—to *Inst.* 1, 2; on Azo's theory of the law
of nature see Carlyle, *Med. Polit. Theory*, II, 30-33, 45-49.

121 *Summa*, p. 1050, no. 2.

122 *Ibid.*, p. 1050, no. 3: the *ius civile* in one sense is "omne ius quo utitur
civitas, sive sit naturale, sive civile, sive gentium, et sic accipitur cum dicit lex,
est res sanctissima civilis sapientia, ut ff. de var. et extraord. cog. l. i. §. proinde
[*D.* 50, 13, 1, 5]." Azo, of course, refers in part to the idea that the science of
law in general is *sacratissima*, and its professors are *sacerdotes* who are devoted
to true philosophy (*D.* 1, 1). On this see my "*Philosophantes* and *philosophi* in
Roman and Canon Law," *Archives d'histoire doctrinale et littéraire du moyen
âge* (1954), pp. 135-138.

123 *Summa*, p. 1050, no. 4. Cf. Odofredo, to *D.* 1, 1, 2.

with commerce, contracts, and the like, are all subjects of the *ius gentium*.[124]

Obviously, Azo has drawn on the canonists and early legists. As in them, States or separate societies and the right to wage just wars of defense are directly lawful according to the *ius gentium*. Only the old primitive society and the private right of self-defense within it are directly sanctioned by the natural law. According to Azo, then, are the State and the necessary conventions within it simply expedient, resulting from sin? They are partly natural, too, penetrated by the higher natural law or natural reason participating both in the *ius gentium* and in the *ius civile*. In fact, Azo carefully states that the *ius gentium* did not invent or create property rights, for the Old Testament (he means chiefly the *lex mosayca*) approved property rights and prohibited theft—this idea occurs also in the canonists. Moreover, *pacta* and *obligationes* are subjects both of the natural law and of the law of peoples.[125]

Finally, in a gloss to *D*. 1, 1, 11 (Paulus, on natural law as what is always *aequum* and *bonum*), Azo, like his predecessor, Johannes Bassianus, asks how, if what is always good is from the natural law, it can be said that slavery and usucapion (acquisition of ownership by long use or possession) came from or were introduced for the public good ("de bono publico"). For slavery and *usucapio* are contrary to the natural law, and one may say that they are not good. He replies that it is good that by the natural law all men are free, and that property should not be taken from the owner without just cause ("nulla causa extrinsecus inspecta"). But what is good must be considered also in relation to additional circumstances or causes. Therefore it is better for the *Respublica* that slavery exist than that it should not exist. Without slavery all men captured by the enemy would die; it is better for the Republic that they live as slaves than that they die free men. And if one considers the emergencies (*necessitates*) that would arise without *usucapiones*, it is better to tolerate them, for otherwise *dominium* could not be proved and lawsuits would be endless. "It is good that

124 *Ibid.*, p. 1051, no. 7.
125 *Loc. cit.*

you do not lose your cloak, and good that you lose it before you are killed by a thief."[126]

There are apparent contradictions in Azo. Perhaps they cannot be resolved. But in general it seems that on the one side he believes that the higher nature in the *ius naturale* is the direct source only of that primitive society of all men which knew no need of laws on war, property rights, and the like. But thereafter men quarreled over property rights, claimed ownership by *usucapio*, gathered into separate peoples, developed the laws and institutions of organized societies or States, waged war, and created slavery. If some of these things apparently contradicted the commands of God and nature, nature by way of the natural reason in men caused mankind to formulate the *ius gentium* for the relations between peoples and to adopt laws (civil law) for each people in the State. Although such laws often contradicted the letter of the natural law, they were not a complete violation of the spirit. For these institutions and laws were *relatively* natural and good in relation to the necessity of adapting the law of nature to the lower nature of man and his environment. In any case, the State and its law received the sanction of God and nature insofar as natural reason and justice and equity participated in the civil law and the State.[127]

[126] In MS Vat. lat. 1408, fol. 3ᵛ: "Si semper bonum est, quod est de iure naturali, quomodo ergo dici potest vel servitutem vel usucapionem de bono publico introductam, cum hec iuri naturali sint contraria, et dicantur [MS, *dicat*] non esse bona? Si enim bonum est aliquid esse, ergo malum est ipsum non esse. Respondeo bonum est [MS *hominem*] de iure naturali omnes esse liberos. Item domino suam rem non auferri nulla causa extrinsecus inspecta—sic dicimus bonum est te non amittere cappam. Si autem intellectum referas ad causas supervenientes, melius est rei publice servitutem esse quam non esse. Sic enim omnes capti ab hostibus perirent, et melius esse rei publice eos vivere servos quam mori ingenuos. Item si inspicias necessitates quas quis incurreret nisi usucapiones essent melius est eas tollerari; aliter enim nec probari posset dominium fore, et lites essent infinite. Et bonum est quidem te non perdere cappam, et bonum est te perdere antequam occidaris a latrone. Az."
The same gloss, with a few slight changes, was included by Accursius in the *Glos. ord.*, but without attribution to Azo. The same thought had been expressed by Joh. Bassianus, but without the mention of the good of the *Respublica*; in Paris, BN, MS lat. 4461, fol. 1ᵛ, to *D.* 1, 1, 11.
[127] See n. 122. Azo's thought is thus given in the *Glos. ord.* of Accursius, to *D.* 2, 14, 1 (Ulpian: "Huius edicti aequitas naturalis est . . ."), ad v. *edicti*: "Et quod dicit naturalis, dic, id est, a naturali ingenio vel industria hominum introducta: quod est ius gentium; et sic ponitur ius naturale, inst. de re div. §.

Azo, therefore, like Irnerius and some decretists, made a distinction between the old, higher naturalness of primitive society and the new, lower naturalness of societies made into States. The State is partly natural, not completely conventional. With respect to human nature, the State and its laws and institutions are relatively good; and God and nature inspired men to create them. Human laws and institutions, though still subject to God and nature, were becoming natural in response to the necessities of human life on earth.

In the *Glossa ordinaria* Accursius largely repeated, and made the common property of the legists, the doctrines of the glossators.[128] Indeed, in some respects he emphasized, perhaps more strongly than his predecessors, the naturalness of the State. For, holding that the "law of peoples" is the product of "natural reason," and that individual property rights derive from this, he speaks of the simultaneity of the creation of peoples (*gentes*) by God and nature and of the appearance of the *ius gentium*.[129] Here the old distinction between the *ius naturale* and the *ius gentium* is seriously weakened. Furthermore, Accursius, in order to derive the private ownership of property from the law of nature, identifies the natural law, the *ius gentium*, and the divine precepts given by God to Moses; and in this connection he repeats the idea that the society of peoples (*gentes*) coincided with, and hence was not produced by, the *ius gentium*.[130] But if

---

singulorum (2, 1, 11). Proprie autem non significatur nisi ea aequitas, que communis est omnium animantium . . . Azo. Et quia est hic naturalis aequitas, inducitur naturalis obligatio per pactum. . . ."

128 See the *Glos. ord.* to the passages in *D.* and *Inst.* referred to above.

129 To *Inst.* 2, 1, 1, ad v. *naturali iure*: "id est, iure gentium, quod est naturali ratione inductum [he refers to *D.* 1, 1, 9, Gaius on how *ratio naturalis* caused men to create the *ius gentium*; and to *Inst.* 2, 1, 11]; nam iure naturali primaevo etiam alia essent communia. Accursius." But to *Inst.* 2, 1, 11 Singulorum, ad vv. *rerum natura prodidit*, after saying "natura id est, Deus": "Statim cum procreavit Deus gentes, statim fuit ius gentium. Accur."

As to the gloss to *Inst.* 2, 1, 1, another edition gives this version: "Id est, iure gentium, quod est instinctu naturae inductum. . . ." I have not examined MSS of the thirteenth century, and therefore have no way of knowing which is the original version.

130 *D.* 1, 1, 5 Ex hoc iure gentium, *Glos. ord.* ad vv. *dominia distincta*: "Imo et secundum ius naturale sunt distincta: quia secundum ius diuinum aliquid erat proprium. dicitur enim, Furtum non facies. Item non concupisces rem proximi tui. . . . Et si dicatur, omnia sunt communia iu. natur. expone. id est,

property rights are natural, it is also a command of the law of nature that no one enrich himself to the detriment of another. (A *regula iuris, D.* 50, 17, 106, had stated that the principle was naturally equitable.)[131]

In still another and perhaps more important way Accursius forgot the usual separation of the natural law from the *ius gentium* and the *ius civile*. The Roman jurisconsults, we have often noted, had said that *ratio naturalis* and nature made lawful the right of defending oneself against aggressive attack (*D.* 1, 1, 3 and *D.* 9, 2, 4). Irnerius, like the decretists, even derived from nature the sanction of war in defense of society.[132] Accursius made this principle of natural law a principle also of the public law of the State. Commenting on Ulpian's statement about the threefold origin of private law in the *ius naturale*, the *ius gentium*, and the *ius civile*, Accursius attributes the right of the *Respublica* to defend itself to the natural law: the public law, like the private law, is derived from the *ius naturale, ius gentium*, and *ius civile*; therefore "it is lawful for the Republic to repel force with force." And he gives as his authority a glossator of the late twelfth century, Johannes Bassianus.[133] In effect, the right of the State to wage a just war of defense is sanctioned by nature.

In fact, God and nature give the State, whether the Empire or any kingdom or *civitas*, the lawful right to defend itself.[134] So Accursius, on *D.* 1, 1, 5 (that by the *ius gentium* peoples and *regna* arose), says that *regna* were founded by peoples who

---

communicanda. sed respon. etiam tunc quando haec praecepta diuina dabantur Moysi a Deo, erat ius gentium: et secundum illud dicebatur aliquid meum. nam cum essent gentes iam coniunctae, erat ius gentium. . . ."

131 To *D.* 1, 1, 2, ad vv. *ex naturalibus praeceptis*: from the law of nature, "ut nemo fiat locupletior cum aliena iactura"; also ad v. *tripertitum*: ". . . et ut cum iniuria eius alter non lucupletetur: item et circa usucapiones."

132 See above, nn. 58-86, on the decretists, and n. 115 for Irnerius.

133 To *D.* 9, 2, 4, ad v. *naturalis ratio*: "id est, ius gentium . . . ut supra, de iustitia et iure, l. iii [*D.* 1, 1, 3 Florentinus] . . ."; to *D.* 1, 1, 2, ad v. *tripertitum*: just as the private law is derived from the natural, *ius gentium*, and civil law, "idem tamen dico de publico, quod est tripertite collectum, secundum Io. [hannem Bas.], et sunt eadem exempla: ut liceat reipublicae vim vi propulsare. . . ."

134 The canonists were more ready to recognize States other than the Empire as independent; but there are traces of this in the legists—see my "Two Notes on Nationalism," *Traditio*, IX, 297-309; above, ch. x, nn. 67-71; also *D.* 1, 1, 5.

elected kings for themselves. After all (perhaps he had this partly in mind), the Hebrews chose Saul as their king, and King David, as Gérard d'Abbeville said, had no superior.[135] If, as Ulpian said (quoting Cassius, *D.* 43, 16, 1, 27), *natura* approves repelling force with force, it makes lawful the repulsion of armed force with armed force (*arma armis*). On this Accursius says that *natura* means the natural law.[136] But *arma* suggests the military power of the State. Again, therefore, the natural law as the *ius gentium* sanctions the right of each State to defend itself: it is lawful for the Republic to repel force with force.[137]

To sum up the theories of the glossators, the very belief that God directly founded princely and royal authority, that the prince is as it were "God on earth," is an indication that the State was positively good and natural with respect to the environment of man on earth. The emphasis, moreover, on the participation of God's will and reason in nature and the natural law, on the participation of natural reason in men, and therefore on the participation of nature, natural law, and natural reason in the *ius gentium*, "international" law, resulted in bringing closer together, not in separating, the natural law and the *ius gentium*.[138] The participation of nature and natural reason in the State and its law, both by way of the gift of reason to every man and by way of the moral commands of God, re-

---

[135] To *D.* 1, 1, 5, ad v. *regna condita*: "a singulis gentibus, quae sibi reges elegerunt." On Gérard d'Abbeville see my "Two Notes on Nationalism," *Traditio*, IX, 309; above, ch. X, n. 113.

[136] *Glos. ord.*, to *D.* 43, 16, 1, 27.

[137] To *D.* 1, 1, 2, ad v. *tripertitum*: public law is derived from the natural law, *ius gentium*, and civil law; e.g., "ut liceat reipublicae vim vi propulsare"; and to *Inst.* 1, 1, 3, ad v. *tripertite*: the right of the State to defend itself belongs both to natural law and the *ius gentium*, "ut ecce a iure naturali, ut non locupletetur cum iactura alterius respublica; a iure gentium, ut liceat reipublicae propulsare iniuriam."

[138] Von der Heydte, it seems to me, goes too far in holding that before the revival of Aristotle's *Politics* the *ius gentium* was so much between the *ius naturale* and the human law in each State that it was separate from the natural law, that the influence of Aristotle brought the *ius gentium* into the realm of natural law—*Geburtsstunde d. souveränen Staates*, pp. 144-148. Of course, the *ius gentium* was not the same as the natural law. But usually, the glossators viewed it as being that part of the natural law which pertained to all men, and which in part pertained to their separate societies and States and controlled their relations. The usual interpretation is the same as that of von der Heydte, e.g., Carlyle, *Med. Political Theory*, II, chs. III-V and VII.

sulted in some emphasis on the natural lawfulness of property rights, on the ideal of fair trial in accordance with equity and justice and with the right of every one to defend himself, and on the duty and right of the government to legislate, judge, and administer for the public and common welfare of all subjects, and to defend the State. In the realm of the public law of the State, the concept of "natural" reason resulted in strengthening the right of the ruler to use "reason of State," especially in cases of necessity or dire emergency, or "reason" of the public and common welfare, for the maintenance of the *status Reipublicae* —"lest it perish—*ne pereat*," said the glossators to D. 1, 1, 1, 2.[139]

The State was already becoming a supreme moral entity on earth, and it could demand the sacrifice of human lives for its safety. Like the canonists, the glossators had developed the concept of the glory of fighting and dying for the common fatherland (*patria communis*) of the independent State.[140] If there was no sin in killing the enemy while defending the State, nor even in a son's unavoidably killing his father fighting against the *patria*, surely the State was already natural, recognized by God and nature as a good end in itself.

It was the glossators, as well as the canonists, of the twelfth and early thirteenth century who gave this concept of nature's approving war in defense of the fatherland, the State, to the ensuing age. Ptolemy of Lucca (*ca.* 1300), for example, derived from the law of nature a king's right to tax his subjects for the sake of preserving *societas humana* (he means the State).[141] In 1316 Bartholomew of Capua, logothete in the kingdom of Naples, in a speech in favor of the king's request for money from the cities for the arming of ships, directly drew from the Roman

---

[139] See my "Ratio publicae utilitatis," *Welt als Gesch.*, XXI, 97; above, ch. v, n. 131; also the *Glos. ord.* of Accursius to D. 1, 1, 1, 2, ad v. *status Rei romanae.* I have found the statement made also by Hugolinus and Azo, to the same passage. See above, ch. VII, n. 7.

[140] Details in my "Two Notes on Nationalism," *Traditio*, IX, 281-296; above, ch. x, nn. 11, 22, 26. To the glossators, the State was the Empire.

[141] Quoted by Gierke, *Political Theories of the Middle Age*, n. 323, p. 191: the king "de iure naturae" can demand "omnia necessaria ad conservationem societatis humanae"; and this also because of the king's duty to care for the common welfare—a constant theme in the Roman law and glossators on the right and duty of the prince.

law his appeal to the *ius naturale*, which he equated with the *ius gentium*. The king, he said, was waging a just war of defense. But such a war is in defense of the *patria*. It is right to fight for the *patria*, because by the *ius naturale*, which is called the *ius gentium*, everyone is enjoined to defend the fatherland. For, as one reads at the beginning of the *Digest*, the natural law, or the *ius gentium*, commands us piously to obey our parents and the fatherland. As Cato says, "Fight for the fatherland!" And as the law says (that is, the Roman law), the art of defending fortresses is more ancient than the love of children.[142]

Bartholomew was inspired not by Aristotelian naturalism, but by the very passages from the *Digest* (1, 1, 2; 1, 1, 1, 4; 1, 1, 3) which canonists and legists frequently referred to before 1230 when they were closely associating, and even identifying, the *ius naturale* and the *ius gentium* in their theory of the State. It is interesting, too, that Bartholomew, like the legists, recalled the old maxim attributed to Cato, "Pugna pro patria!"[143]

But the same legal tradition, in the theory of the naturalness of the State with respect to its being approved by that nature which participated in the *ius gentium* and in the public law of each State, had been understood by the government of Frederick II. Petrus de Vinea, who drafted the Constitutions of Melfi (*Liber Augustalis*, 1231), reflecting the ideas of earlier legal thought,[144] appealed to natural reason and to necessity and utility as sanctions of the imperial authority and of the City (Rome)—hence, of the Empire.[145] So Frederick declared, in the words of Petrus de Vinea, "both all-powerful Reason, who commands kings, and Nature impose upon us the obligation to

---

[142] See the whole speech in August Nitschke, "Die Reden des Logotheten Bartholomäus von Capua," *Quellen u. Forschungen aus Ital. Arch. u. Bibl.*, XXXV (1955), 266-273. Cf. Odofredo, to *D.* 1, 1, 1-4.

[143] "Two Notes on Nationalism," *Traditio*, IX, 281-296; above, ch. X, § 1.

[144] See Kantorowicz, *King's Two Bodies*, pp. 97-107.

[145] Helene Wieruszowski, *Vom Imperium zum nationalen Königtum*, pp. 167, 169 n. 88, and 170ff., thought that appeals to nature resulted from the knowledge of the *Politics* in the court of Frederick II. The earlier tradition in legal thought more easily accounts for it.

On reason and nature in the documents and laws of Frederick see also E. Kantorowicz, *Kaiser Friedrich der Zweite*, p. 232, and the *Ergänzungsband*, p. 106; and now Kantorowicz, *King's Two Bodies*, p. 106 n. 55.

enhance in the time of our *imperium* the glory of the City."[146]
Furthermore, recalling the *natura* of Ovid and of the school of
Chartres, Petrus made nature a creative power.[147] Two genera-
tions later Bartholomew of Capua, commenting on the words
of Petrus in the *Liber Augustalis*, quoted Ovid just as Placentinus had done and saw in creative nature, "id est, deus," and
the divine providence the principle of law and order in the
world and in human reason.[148]

It is too strong to say that Petrus de Vinea and Bartholomew
of Capua deified nature. Petrus, at any rate, subordinated nature
to God, holding that nature was an agent of Providence in
creating man in Its image and in making man the *dignissima
creatura*, only a little lower than the angels.[149] But nature and
natural reason, through the agency of men, were the direct
author of order in the State. If the State was a work of art that
imitated nature, it was also directly approved by nature.

[146] Quoted and translated by Kantorowicz, *King's Two Bodies*, pp. 105f.—from
Huillard-Bréholles, *Historia diplomatica Friderici Secundi*, v, 162.

[147] Huillard-Bréholles, *Historia diplom.*, IV, i, 3, Const. Fred. II, 1, 1, 1: "Post
mundi machinam Providentia divina formatam, et primordialem materiam
nature melioris conditionis officio in rerum effigies distributam, qui facienda
previderat facta considerans et considerata commendans, a globo circuli lunaris
inferius hominem creaturarum dignissimam creaturam, ad imaginem propriam
effigiemque formatam, quem paulo minus minuerat ab Angelis, consilio propenso
disposuit preponere ceteris creaturis . . . et homo quem Deus rectum et simplicem
procreavit. . . ." Of course, there is also the Biblical influence in this.

[148] *Commentaria* and glosses to the *Constitutiones regni utriusque Siciliae*,
Venice, 1580, p. 1, to 1, 1, 1 Post mundi, ad vv. *materiam naturae melioris*:
"Potest intellegi active de natura naturante, id est, Deo, in quo omnia certa
sunt, scilicet tam praeterita quam praesentia et futura. . . . Quem intellectum
videtur habuisse Ovidius, unde ista verba sumpta fuerunt, ait enim. Hanc Deus,
et melior litem natura diremit. A divina namque providentia mundi totius
elementa processerunt. . . ." In the Ant. Cervone ed. of the *Constitutiones*,
Naples, 1773, the gloss seems to be attributed to Marinus de Caramanico (pp.
1f.). From this ed. I refer to other interesting statements—ad vv. *primordialem
materiam*: this is *chaos*, the formless and "confusa congeries omnium rerum"
which the philosophers call *hyle*, "quam dicunt esse inter aliquid et nihil"; and,
ad vv. *naturae melioris*, after the passage from Ovid and the words *a divina . . .
processerunt*, the author adds: "et eorum dispositio in orbem terrarum producta
est. . . . Posset etiam legi passive de natura naturata, scilicet rerum. . . ." Clearly
these words reflect both the Neo-Platonists of Chartres and the ideas about
nature and God in the glossators of the twelfth and early thirteenth century.
But the words, "A divina namque providentia mundi totius elementa processerunt," come from Justinian, *C.* 1, 17, 1, where, however, it is the *providentia
summae trinitatis*.

[149] Above, n. 147.

5. The Secular Naturalness of the State and New Laws

Gradually the canonists and legists felt their way toward the doctrine that God, by means of nature and the natural law, gave His approval to men's use of the divine gift of natural reason in creating States. Another kind of nature, however, a more secular one, began to play an important role. This in part was because of the very theory that the State, although sanctioned by the higher nature, was inevitably in the world and therefore could not be a perfect image of the natural order of the universe, nor could it perfectly copy and enforce the moral, natural law of God. Consequently, separate societies and States were natural in a lower meaning, that in this world of things and men nature is a principle of change. Sometimes, so we have seen in the decretists, this resulted in a distinction between the higher naturalness of the primitive society common to all men and the lower naturalness of separate societies of peoples living in a state of sinfulness. These societies, organized into States, enjoyed some sanction of the higher nature in the *ius gentium*, but they were also merely natural in relation to the weakness of human nature. That is to say, they naturally developed in response to the natural needs of men living in a sinful world. In other words, *summa natura* directly approved and prompted the social instinct of men living in primitive society, but the ordinary nature of sinful men thereafter caused them to become separate peoples or organized societies or States.

If *summa natura* and the natural law and natural reason continued in some respects to command men to obey God and the moral law of nature, and to practice justice in the relations of their States and in each State itself, lower human nature justified compromises. In each State new situations, new kinds of cases, represented a nature that was frequently changing; and therefore, new laws made by the supreme legislative authority in the State were naturally necessary. The positive law of the State was itself natural, even though it must not directly run contrary to the higher natural law. In other words, new human laws should not violate the moral commands of God embodied in the higher natural law. But the canonists recognized that some human weaknesses or sins were so natural in a lower sense that the State could not exist without tolerating them.[150] Lesser evils sometimes had to be condoned lest the greater evil of the destruction of Church or State result. This really meant that, again, the State was a higher moral value. Thomas Aquinas understood this, and not exclusively in Aristotelian terms. In the early fourteenth century Nicholas de Lyra, the great commentator on the Bible, understood the principle very well indeed. Prostitution, he said, referring to St. Augustine, is contrary to the law of nature; but it is lawful in the State lest the natural *libido* of men cause anarchy and destroy the public welfare and the State itself. Such a *malum*, and other *minora mala*, are permitted lest greater evils arise; and the greatest evil, with respect to human welfare on earth, would be the destruction of the State.[151] Obviously, in this kind of thinking no human law can declare that immoral acts are good. But some human sinfulness is so "natural" that it must be tolerated and even regulated for the sake of the State, which also is natural, but natural in a higher and better sense.

[150] Guido de Baysio, *ca.* 1300, commenting on the *Decretum*, Dist. 4, c. Causa vero, summed up this view—in his *Rosarium*, Venice, 1577, fol. 6, nos. 3, 4, and 6: measure should be observed in human *lex* (as in Aristotle, Bk. x of the *Metaphysics*); "diversae leges imponuntur hominibus secundum rerum conditionem"; as Isidore of Seville says: "lex debet esse possibilis secundum naturam et secundum consuetudinem, etc."; "lex autem humana imponitur multitudini, in qua maior pars hominum imperfecta: et ideo lege humana non prohibentur omnia vitia, a quibus virtuosi abstinent: sed solum graviora, a quibus impossibile est maiorem partem multitudinis abstinere, et precipue que sunt in nocumentum aliorum, sine quorum prohibitione conservari non potest societas"—e.g., homicide, theft, and the like.

[151] For Thomas Aquinas see Lottin, *Le droit naturel*; and Gagnér, *Studien*, pp. 193-207, 270-283. Nicholas de Lyra, *Postilla super Evangelia* (edition printed by Johannes de Puzpach at Mantua, 1477—there are many editions, but this one was available to me), in his introduction to the *Postilla* on Matthew: ". . . Ita in legibus que communitati seruande imponuntur aliqua mala minora permittuntur ut maiora euitentur. Sicut lex ciuilis meretrices in ciuitatibus permittit, ne respublica propter imperfectionem multitudinis que castitatem conseruare non potest, dissensionibus que propter libidinem insurgerent conturbetur. Unde dicit Aug. in libro de ordine: 'Aufer meretrices a ciuitatibus et omnia conturbabis libidinibus.' Verum ista mala que bono modo auferre non potest, relinquit diuino iudicio punienda. Unde dicit Aug. primo de libero arbitrio: 'Lex ista que regendis ciuitatibus fertur, multa concedit atque impunita relinquit, que per diuinam prouidentiam uindicantur.'"

If this tradition goes back to St. Augustine, it goes back also to Justinian's theory of legislation. (We have already observed that Honorius III and Jacobus de Albenga, *ca.* 1226, understood and repeated the words of Justinian.)[152] No doubt, Ulpian and other ancient jurisconsults furnished the essential idea, for Ulpian asserted that by the very nature of things there are more *negotia* than *vocabula* (*D.* 19, 5, 4)—on the word *vocabula* Accursius offers *actiones*, or kinds of suits, as the definition. Justinian developed the concept. He declared that if *varia natura* should create a new situation, the emperor could make a new law.[153] Nature is continually bringing forth new "forms." Hence, although divine things are perfect, the condition of human law is always indefinite and impermanent. New kinds of business or difficulties emerge, therefore, which old laws do not regulate. Wherefore God Himself put the imperial "state" in charge of human affairs, in order that the emperor take care of all new contingencies by means of suitable rules.[154] Further, since *natura* everywhere causes many novelties, it forces upon the emperor the necessity of making many laws (*leges*). In fact, Justinian said this by way of explaining a new law on heirs and inheritance. Finally, our whole *status* (human estate) is in perpetual motion, and nothing is so stable and immobile among men that no change can be suffered. Therefore, the *varietas* of human nature often makes it necessary to moderate law (*lex*) by means of exceptions in order that *lex* itself may remain unmoved.[155] Apparently the meaning is that the changing nature

---

[152] Above, to nn. 95-98. Gagnér, *Studien*, pp. 128-135, 195-210, fails to observe that the theory was stated in terms from Justinian long before the publication of the *Liber Sextus* of Boniface VIII.

[153] *Prooem.* to the *Codex* (ed. Mommsen-Krueger, p. 4), "Cordi nobis," § 4: no *constitutio* outside the *C.* is to be used (or added to the official body of imperial laws), "nisi postea varia rerum natura aliquid novum creaverit, quod nostra sanctione indigeat. . . ."

[154] *C.* 1, 17, 2, 18: ". . . multas etenim formas edere natura novas deproperat, etc."

[155] *Auth.*, Coll. 6, t. 12 (*Nov.* 84): "Multis undique natura novitatibus utens . . . ad opus multarum nos pertrahit legum"; and *Auth.*, Coll. 2, t. 1, c. 2 (*Nov.* 7): "Ut autem lex ad humanae naturae varietatem, et quod semper venit, moderata, per omnia immota permaneat (quid enim erit stabile inter homines et ita immobile ut nullam patiatur mutationem: cum omnis noster status sub perpetuo motu consistat?), necessarium existimavimus quasdam exceptiones dari legi cum

of human conditions requires new laws lest the very principle of law become a fleeting thing.

The early glossators did not overlook these passages. Johannes Bassianus repeated the thought of Justinian, saying that nature is always hastening to bring forth new "forms," that is, new situations. God on High established the emperor on earth in order to adapt *leges* to the *varietas naturae*. Accordingly, Justinian promulgated the new laws incorporated in the *Novellae*, and medieval emperors made new laws on fiefs.[156] Azo in his *Commentary* on the *Code*, held that the *Novellae* were useful because they dealt with new *negotia* and were approved both by custom and by the interpretation of jurisprudents, and because "natura enim tota die novas edit formas."[157] Before the middle of the thirteenth century Roffredo of Benevento, referring to *Auth.* Coll. 6, t. 12 (*Nov.* 84), declared that because nature does approve *novitates*, new things are daily and *de novo* brought forth.[158] In a gloss written after the time of the *Glos. ord.* of Accursius, perhaps after the Latin translation of the *Politics* appeared (yet containing no Aristotelian naturalism), a legist repeated the words of Roffredo and added that new solicitude is necessary for new things. He said further that the care for new things adds to art, for every *artificium*, every art, grows with its frequent exercise; and, as in D. 32, t. De leg. et fideicom., 65, 3, this agrees with human nature.[159] Therefore, nature has caused

---

multis vigiliis et subtilitate adinventas: ut eas habens in auxilio lex nequaquam moveatur."

[156] *Summa Auth.*, with additions of Accursius, ed. in the Venice, 1584, ed. of Azo's *Summa Codicis*, cols. 1219-1287, col. 1221, to Coll. 1: "Quia natura deproperat semper novas edere formas, ut C. de vet. iu. enucl. 1. 2. §. sed quia [1, 17, 2, 18]. propterea Deus de coelis Imperatorem constituit in terris, ut leges adaptet secundum naturae varietatem . . .'"; and (col. 1219, in the Prooem.) the *Nov.* of Justinian comprise "omne id novum, quod varia rerum natura creavit, et nova negotia" which had not been "laqueis iuris innodata" before the compilation of the book of the *Nov.* was made. Johannes also speaks of the *leges novae* of the emperors Frederick and Henry on fiefs. (This *Summa* may belong to another glossator.)

[157] *Com.* on the *Code*, Paris, 1577, p. 4, to Prooem.; also *Summa Codicis*, p. 7: ". . . Sed quia multas formas edere natura deproperat. . . ."

[158] *Tractatatus libellorum*, Lyons, 1561, p. 3, *Prooem.*: ". . . Verum quia natura quotidie multis novitatibus utitur: et de novo nova quotidie procreantur, ut in Auth. de consangui. et uter. fra. in princ. col. vj. . . ."

[159] Vat., MS Ross. 582, fol. 4, to *C.*, *Prooem.*, "Cordi nobis," § 4, ad vv. *nisi*

the creation of the whole book of the *Authenticae*.[160] Thus, here is the concept we have in part met with in John of Salisbury. The art of legislation in the State, like the art of creating and maintaining the State, imitates nature.

But Accursius had seen how this kind of nature might come into conflict with unchanging, eternal, *summa natura*. Constantly changing nature, he said, while it causes *facta* to change, does not mean any change in the *ius naturae*.[161] What he means can be gathered from the fact that on the unchanging character of the law of nature he refers to a famous passage in the *Inst.*, 1, 2, 11, which states that those *naturalia* which are equally obeyed among all peoples (i.e., the *ius gentium*)[162] and were established by divine providence are forever constant and immutable; but those *iura* which each *civitas* makes for itself are often changed either by the tacit consent of the people or by later legislation. It is interesting that a decretist of the late twelfth century had stated the same principle, but allowed for exceptions, e.g., when the law on slavery is *scienter* contrary to the law of nature.[163]

The legists, then, like the canonists, were acquainted with two kinds of nature, the higher, eternal, unchanging, nature in the fundamental, natural law, and the lower nature of the world and man in the naturalness of changing conditions and facts,

postea varia rerum natura aliquid novum creaverit: "Nota, quod natura, etc. [referring to the words of Rof. Benev., above, n. 154]. Nam pro novis nova sollicitudo exigitur, pro qua ad exercitium provehimur [MS, provetamur]; quod quidem arti tribuit incrementum, quia omne artificium propter nimium exercitium suscipit incrementum, ff. de le. iij. l. servis legatis. §. ornatricibus." The reference is to *D*. 32, 65, 3: ". . . et omne artificium incrementum recipit: quod magis optinere debet, quia humanae naturae congruum est." Azo, *Summa Codicis*, Venice, 1584, col. 1, had already developed this theory.

160 MS Ross. 582, fol. 4: "sicut est hodie de libro autenticorum."

161 *Glos. ord.* to *Auth.*, Coll. 6, t. 12 (*Nov.* 84) ad vv. *Multis undique natura novitatibus utens*: "Quia facta mutantur secundum cursum naturae. . . . Non autem ius naturae mutatur: ut Inst. de iu. natu. §. pen. [1, 2, 11]. Accursius"; also to *Auth.*, Coll. 2, 1, 2 (*Nov.* 7), ad v. *inter homines*: ". . . aliud est in divina natura. . . ."

162 Here is a strong emphasis on the idea that the *ius gentium* is essentially the natural law that participates in and sanctions all human societies and States.

163 *Summa Parisiensis*, ed. McLaughlin, p. 4, to Dist. 4, c. 2 (Isidore on how a *lex* should be *secundum naturam*): "ut non contradicat juri naturali nisi scienter et praedicantur contra jus naturale fiat ut est de servitutibus."

in the naturalness of men's industry and art in imitating nature, and in the naturalness of the human legislation needed to take care of this changing nature. A kind of secular naturalism therefore played an important role in the new theory and practice of legislation in Church and in State.[164] This theory, in addition to the well-known Roman theory of the right of the ruler to make laws for the necessity and utility of people and State, and to make new laws when new kinds of cases emerged,[165] resulted in the development of a moderate, or Christian-secular, positivism during the century that preceded the revival of the *Politics*.

One question remains. Did the new, secular, *varia natura* take the place of *summa natura* in sanctioning the State and its laws? I have found no statement that could be so interpreted. Not even Marsiglio of Padua was so secular in his thought that he could deny the importance of the eternal and natural laws— he simply intended, as he says, to discuss those laws that men made for the State; and he did not argue that human laws could openly violate the law of nature. In brief, God and the higher nature remained superior to and a limitation of the State and the *ius civile*. But at the same time, by the participation of the natural law of God in human reason used in governing the State, God and nature directly approved the public law that was administered by princes for the preservation of the *status Reipublicae*, "lest it perish—*ne pereat*."[166] Henry II of England may at one moment have reached the logical conclusion: what nature permitted him to do was not unlawful.[167]

[164] For the actual practice of legislation see Plucknett, *Legislation of Edward I*, pp. 2-5, 158-160; Powicke, "Reflections on the Medieval State," *Trans. Royal Hist. Society*, XIX, 12-14; Gagnér, *Studien*, sections II and III; and Barnaby C. Keeney, "The Medieval Idea of the State: the Great Cause," *Univ. Toronto Law Journal*, VIII (1949), 48-71, esp. 60f. n. 35.

[165] On legislation in relation to customary law, to necessity and utility, and to new, emerging situations not covered by older laws, see *D.* 1, 1 ll. 6, 9, 11; 1, 2 ll. 1, 14, 15, 25, 32, 35-40; 1, 3, 2; 2, 1; 2, 14 and 15; 2, 25; 2, 32, 1; 2, 35; 2, 40; and *C.* 1, 14, 8. Of course, the right of the prince to be the ultimate interpreter of the law, with the advice of his counsellors and legal experts, was a kind of legislation; and judges, too, in the courts, legislated by way of interpreting law and custom.

[166] See above, n. 139.

[167] "Non videtur illicitum, quod mihi est a natura permissum"; quoted by Berges, *Fürstenspiegel*, pp. 127f., from Peter of Blois, *Dialogus cum rege Henrico*, in *Opera omnia*, ed. J. A. Giles.

6. Conclusions

In one sense there has been no need of studying how the naturalness of society and the State was appearing in the legal thought of the century and more before 1260. The fact is that practical statesmen as well as theorists assumed that communities from guilds and cathedral chapters to cities and kingdoms were, by the nature of things on earth, good for human society. And since God approved kings and their sacrosanct office, it followed that the rising monarchic States were more of a positive good than a necessary evil. Above all, in the twelfth century the developing appreciation of the world, the expression of secular values in the political, economic, and social revival, and the confident application of creative activities to political as well as intellectual, artistic, and architectural ends, both resulted from and intensified a relatively new kind of secularism and naturalism. If all these activities remained subordinate, generally speaking, to God and the ultimate spiritual goal, they nonetheless flourished and were receiving some intellectual and rational appreciation and justification. It has therefore been interesting to trace a small part of the history of the ideas, even though in fact men were displaying some confidence in themselves and their world by starting the creation of the State.

As if summing up the contributions of the philosophers and lawyers of the preceding century, in 1231 Frederick II solemnly declared that all-powerful reason and nature obliged him to enhance the glory of the City; and reason and nature prompted him to promulgate new laws both for the City and for the kingdom. Petrus de Vinea, who composed Frederick's statement, reflected a tradition that had been developing in the twelfth and early thirteenth centuries. This tradition, arising from the earlier tradition in the Latin Fathers, the classics, Plato's *Timaeus*, and the Roman law, was created by John of Salisbury and by the canonists and legists.

John of Salisbury is truly remarkable, as it were symbolizing the "modernness" of the twelfth century. On the one side he stressed the theory that God and nature and the natural law directly sanctioned the State as a natural body and natural organization of human society. Men, like bees, but superior to bees, are by nature social creatures. But on the other side he also held that nature and reason inspire men to develop the art of the State, and that the State, therefore, imitates nature but is not the work of nature itself. Despite this inconsistency, John on the whole thought that society and the State were natural. But if the State was natural, it was subordinate to God's will that men obey His commands and strive for justice.

The canonists and legists, perhaps because they were not classical humanists like John of Salisbury, were not so "modern." In fact, at first glance they seem to adhere to the traditional conventionalism of society and the State, holding that the higher nature of the natural law was only an indirect sanction. Yet, by way of their Christian treatment of nature and its close connection, and even confusion with, the *ius gentium*, they tended to think that if nature provided the rules of "international" relations, and at the same time participated in the public law of each State on the right to preserve itself against an enemy, nature itself, like God, did sanction the State. The natural law was in fact the source of that positive, public law which gave to the government both the right and the duty to maintain the State and the public and common welfare. As a result, in times of great danger or dire emergencies, the safety of the State was a necessity that knew no law (*Necessitas legem non habet* had literally become a principle of public law), and the prince and State were above ordinary laws in such cases precisely because they were obeying the higher law of nature.

God, men thought, viewed the State as naturally good for the common welfare on earth and therefore it was right for men to fight and die for the fatherland. It was right also, because God commanded it, that the prince should have the supreme authority in the State. As a glossator of the twelfth century said, God established the emperor on earth so that laws could be made for men because of the *varietas naturae*.[168] John of Viterbo (about 1228) went further: God founded the *Imperium* (Empire), which exists forever; emperors received from God the permis-

[168] Above, n. 156.

sion to make laws; and God placed the emperor above the law (human law, no doubt), sending him to men as the *lex animata*. His contemporary, Boncompagno, intimated that the emperor was the interpreter of the natural as well as positive law, thus suggesting that in a sense he was above the law of nature itself.[169] Kings who were emperors in their own realms, ruling over their own sovereign States, enjoyed the same direct approval of God; and their kingdoms were, if not founded by God, a natural consequence of the divine favor.

There remained, to be sure, some of the Stoic-Christian tradition of the conventional character of the State. Nonetheless, man was by nature a social animal. It is not important that the canonists and legists did not say this literally. It is important, however, that some of them, from Irnerius on, spoke of the naturalness of that peculiar primitive society that had been common to all men until sinfulness broke it up into separate societies or peoples and States. But since the "law of peoples" (*ius gentium*) was that natural law which is common to men as men rather than as animals, the new societies, organized as States, were likewise natural as subjects of one aspect of the natural law.

At the same time, a lower, more secular, nature and naturalism appeared in the legal thought. For, in the first place, States were a natural result of weak human nature. In the second place, the lower nature of man in a naturally changing environment justified necessary compromises with the higher, moral law of nature for the sake of the common welfare of men on earth and for the sake of the safety of the State. *Varia natura* made it "natural" for a royal government to legislate by making new laws. *Summa natura* furnished that natural reason according to which kings should devote themselves to the art of statecraft and legislation. If art imitated nature, nature in the highest sense inspired the creative art itself and therewith approved the State,

---

169 F. Hertter, *Die Podestàliteratur Italiens im 12. und 13. Jahrhundert (Beiträge zur Kulturgeschichte des Mittelalters und der Renaissance*, 7), p. 70: "Imperium enim deus de celo constituit; imperium autem semper est, Imperatores vero proferendi leges a deo licentiam acceperunt; deus subiecit leges Imperatori et legem animatam eum misit hominibus." Cf. Kantorowicz, *King's Two Bodies*, pp. 122, 130; p. 131 for Boncompagno.

even though the State was not the direct work of nature. Nature helped those who helped themselves by using natural reason in the art of imitating nature. Thus, the State as a work of art appeared in medieval thought long before the time of the Italian Renaissance. Finally, Aristotle's *Politics*, no doubt, was welcomed partly because the canonists and legists had prepared the minds of scholastic philosophers for its emphasis on the naturalness of human society and the State.

REFLECTIONS

T IS perhaps one of the ironies of history that the law of the Roman Empire gave to feudal monarchs and Italian communes the *rationale* of sovereign, independent States and thus contributed to the dissolution of the noble ideal of Christendom in Holy Roman Empire and Holy Roman Church. To be sure, the ideal persisted—and not only in Dante. Henri Daniel-Rops has eloquently described how the Florentine painter, Andrea, in the middle of the fourteenth century, "gave expression to the whole ideal of medieval society," a hierarchy of order under God. "A noble image indeed," he continues, "on which humanity may gaze with yearning; for we have lost the idea of end and means. We struggle vainly to re-establish order; but it is precisely our rejection of the hierarchic system which has landed us in tragedy and ruin. . . . Such, for about three hundred years [1050-1350], was mankind's vision of the world. . . . For three long centuries its law held sway; nor can we assign to chance the fact that, between those years, society enjoyed what may be considered the richest, most fruitful, most harmonious epoch in all the history of Europe."[1]

One cannot help sympathizing with the famous Academician's vision of the twelfth and thirteenth centuries. Both in fact and in the novel disseizin by each independent *Respublica* of Roman principles and ideals of the public law—a disseizin in effect declared lawful by kings in their High Courts and Councils and by Italian communal governments—the secular hierarchy of order, such as it was, already in large measure belonged not to one universal State but to the rising national and city-states. If the spiritual hierarchy of order briefly seemed to give Christendom a higher unity than had been possible in the Holy Roman Empire, the *ratio status regis et regni*, "reason of State" in the hands of every king who was emperor in his own realm,

[1] *Cathedral and Crusade. Studies of the Medieval Church 1050-1350* (transl. by John Warrington of *L'Eglise de la Cathédrale et de la Croisade*), pp. 1f.

was actively threatening the universal *status Ecclesiae.* The localism of the early Middle Ages found legal confirmation in the creation of independent States, and a new ordering of Europe was appearing. If the lower nature of the world and man, aided by natural and legal reason and by the art of statesmanship, was the immediate cause, *summa natura,* "id est, deus," approved.

The revival of the Roman law, however, was only a part of the environment that favored the development of sovereign States. Combined with traditional theories of kingship (which should not be called theocratic) and with the survival in the early Middle Ages of the Roman idea of the public welfare, which it was the king's duty to maintain, elements of feudalism were at hand for the use of such able monarchs as Henry II of England and Philip Augustus of France and their successors in the effort to assert the public rights of king and realm. At the same time, a more prosperous economic life provided royal governments with those revenues which were a necessary foundation of the "estate royal" and the rights of the crown, of those public rights without which the "state of the realm" might suffer harm and perish. Important, too, was the personal ambition, if it accompanied skill in law and politics, of men who wanted to convert theoretical into actual powers of office. Sir Maurice Powicke, in his great chronicle of England in the thirteenth century, has, with the learning of a distinguished historian of the twentieth century and with the spirit of Matthew Paris, shown in remarkable detail how the making of the English State was the work of men who in the midst of political strife were conscious of their responsible membership in the *universitas regni.* He has shown, moreover, how vital to the development of the English State was Edward I's appreciation of the common interests of the "estate royal" and the "state of the realm." In sum, the historical background, the general environment, and the personal qualities of great men, along perhaps with chance, go far toward explaining the evolution of the State and its public law.

Nonetheless, it is impossible to imagine how one can fully treat the history of the early modern State without considering the Roman law and its influence on those who participated in creating its institutions. If some kind of State was bound to develop in response to the challenge of disorder, how can the historian describe it and its legal functions except in such Roman terms as *utilitas publica, status civitatis* or *regni, status regis,* and *ratio status?* How can he speak of corporate communities, representation, and consent except in such Roman terms as *universitates, communitates, plena potestas,* and *quod omnes tangit?* It is easy to say that, because Latin was the official language, and vernacular equivalents would have served as well (as they sometimes did—e.g., *commun profit, pleniere pooste,* and *lestat du roialme),* the terminology is of no fundamental significance. But the fact is that the Latin of the Roman law furnished a set of concepts and principles as well as words, and that the Roman law acquainted men of legal learning in royal and city governments with a context of ideas about problems of public law and the State—a context that was vague or poorly understood or practiced in the age of feudalism.

Legal history, in particular the history of the ideas which medieval jurists and kings found in the Roman law, explains in part how representation and consent arose and changed the feudal into a national assembly, and how the consent both of the greater men of the realm and of representatives of lesser men in their communities was ultimately subordinate to the public rights of the royal government exercised in the public interest of the State, *ratione status regis et regni.* The Roman law, and also the Canon law of the Church, furnished the legal theory and practice of corporations and corporate agency. In the feudal system individualism and individual rights precluded a formal representation of communities, except insofar as the nobility pretended to represent them. When, therefore, the members of guilds, corporations, towns, and shires felt the need of defending their interests in courts and councils, it was the two laws which instructed them, as it instructed the authorities who decided that they should be summoned. First the Roman and then the Canon law offered the precedent of corporate representation by agents who were given full powers of attorney.

In cases involving the rights of corporate communities, full powers of attorney, *plena potestas*, meant that the constituents, through their representatives, consented to the court's interpretation of their rights according to the law. Their consent was procedural in nature, including the right to defend rights before the court and the necessity of accepting the jurisdiction of the judge and his decision—appeal, however, being possible from a lower to the highest court of the prince. Voluntary consent, too, although implicit in feudal contractual relations between lords and vassals, found additional support in the Roman law. The Roman maxim, *quod omnes tangit*, could express either procedural or voluntary consent. But because the prince, whether king or pope, was the supreme judge in all cases touching the rights of magnates, prelates, and communities of lesser men, the right of voluntary consent was weakened. It was weakened especially when private rights came into conflict with the public "right of State," or the public interest of the community of the realm. If individual and corporate rights and voluntary consent had succeeded in limiting the royal prerogative in cases involving the public and common welfare, the "estate royal" would hardly, according to the prevailing theory of kingship, have been strong enough to maintain the "state of the realm"; and the "state of the realm" would have suffered harm so long as no other *status, id est, magistratus* existed as the supreme authority.

Again it was the Roman law which offered the solution that was adaptable to the feudal monarchy; and as a result, consent either in general or in local assemblies became almost as procedural as in cases belonging to the realm of private law. According to the Roman public law, the ruler had the public right to demand support for all actions that were deemed necessary for the public welfare of the State. It was the right and duty of the magistracy to administer, legislate, and judge so as to maintain the public and common welfare. The *raison d'être* of king and realm demanded the constant use of "right reasoning" in all proper spheres of government. But whenever an important business (*ardua negotia*) was the common concern of the "estate royal" and the "state of the realm," whenever an emergency, just cause, or necessity touched both estates, that is, the public powers of the monarch and the public welfare of the kingdom, "right reasoning" was that "reason of State" which gave to the king the prerogative described in terms of *status regis* or *status coronae*. The public law that pertains to the *Respublica*, said a decretist in the later twelfth century, is concerned "with the prerogative of the emperor and priests and others to whom the defense of the *Respublica* chiefly belongs."[2] In other words, the prerogative was the ensemble of those public powers of the prince by which the public welfare of the State and the common welfare of the people could be preserved unharmed. The prerogative vested in the *status regis* was therefore superior to private rights and the right of consent.

In political fact, of course, powerful subjects often questioned the royal interpretation of the public welfare and the use of "reason of State"; and probably communities such as French towns in Languedoc, failing to appreciate the public welfare of the realm as a whole, understood how to maintain a passive if not active resistance to the king's demands. English magnates, not to mention others, sometimes held that the king was poorly advised and did not truly understand the public interest. In the legal thought of the age, however, the king enjoyed in his public office as head of the realm, and in his prerogative, the final right to interpret, to judge, and to decide what belonged to the public law of the State. For the sake of the safety of the realm, therefore, it was his right and duty to do what was necessary for the public and common welfare; and in public cases of necessity to demand the consent of the community of the realm, that is, of magnates, prelates, and communities, to what should be done. On the basis of rights which were affected by the *negotia regis et regni*, by a great necessity or emergency that touched *status regis* and *status regni* in common, great men and representatives of communities of other men who had rights and privileges should be summoned and given the opportunity to treat (*tractare*), debate, and thus defend their interests by arguing against the king's alleged case of necessity, or by asking for a lesser

2 *Summa*, "Antiquitate et tempore," in the Vat. MS Pal. 678, fol. 37, to Dist. 1, c. 11: *ius publicum* pertains to the *Respublica*—"Hoc autem est, quod est de prerogativa imperatoris et sacerdotum et aliorum, quorum precipue est tueri enim rempublicam et ei providere in sacris . . . et sacerdotibus . . . et magistratibus." See Kuttner, *Repertorium*, p. 178.

burden of taxation than the king proposed, or by presenting petitions for the remedy of grievances—or by a combination of pleas. Nevertheless, presiding in and over his High Court and Council in Parliament or in Estates General (or, in France, presiding by means of baillis and seneschals over local assemblies), the kings of England and France—and also in general the kings of Aragon and Castile—could in spite of grumblings demand and usually receive consent to what was deemed necessary by the royal government for the defense of the State. If in the fourteenth century resistance to the authority of the king became serious, in legal theory the prerogative of the king remained as a nucleus for the continued growth of the idea of the crown and "estate royal" as the supreme public authority in the State.

Consent, then, was not a democratic reflection of the will of the people. It did not so limit the royal authority that the king became a mere symbol or a glorified chairman presiding over an assembly. The prevailing theory of procedural consent did reflect the traditional ideal of law and justice, that it was the duty of the government to give all rightful individuals and communities of individuals a hearing before king and court and council. But when the public welfare or "state" of the State was the issue, the public "right of State," which the king as head represented and must defend, gave to the royal government (or the government of a city-state) the superior right to demand the sacrifice of private rights in times of necessity. Necessity, the public necessity of the State, knew no law that enabled private interests to weaken or injure the public welfare of the corporate body of the State and the common welfare of the collective membership. Higher justice demanded that the royal judge make his decisions in favor of the *status regis* and the *status regni*. If the king could not injure, by alienating, the public rights of his prerogative without injuring the public "right of State," neither could he injure the "estate royal" or rights of the crown by giving up his right to obtain consent to what he decided was necessary for the maintenance both of the "estate royal" and the "state of the realm." *Lestat du roi* in all its integrity was deemed essential to *lestat du roialme. La com-*

munalte should cooperate with the king, as the king should work for it; but the king was the head, and in his "body politic" he possessed the right to interpret the rules of cooperation in the interest of the State. The Roman law, in sum, had provided much of the legal thought which, on the one hand, helped free men to belong to corporate and quasi-corporate communities and obtain the representation of their rights before courts or in councils and assemblies, and, on the other, aided the efforts of kings to subordinate local and individual rights to the public welfare of the community of the realm and thus to create the substance if not all the accidents of the State.

In still another way, by 1300, the State was being created in the image of the Roman Empire. It was acquiring the sovereignty of the Roman *patria communis;* it was itself an Empire and it was becoming a national State. The Roman public law, now becoming the essence of the public law of the national State, gave to the monarchy the legal right to demand patriotic loyalty to king and realm—a loyalty which was quite different from the old personal loyalty of vassal to lord. When at the same time both God and the law of nature were sanctioning the State as the good end of human society on earth, so much the greater was the public right of the ruler to demand patriotic devotion even of the many who did not feel or understand it, and to demand, rather than ask for, consent to whatever was done *ratione status regis et regni.*

Such in general was the theory of public law and the State in the legal thought, and often in the acts of kings and of city-states, of the twelfth and thirteenth centuries. In Germany and Italy the emperors lacked the power and means for enforcing the public law of the Empire, and feudal princes, communes, and the papacy prevented the creation of a great State of the Roman Empire. But neither Germany nor Italy could become a national State. *Ständestaaten* arose in Germany, while in Italy the more powerful communes became city-states, each of which demanded so much patriotic loyalty for itself that little was left for Italy as a whole; in neither region could any ruler furnish the headship and leadership necessary for the maintenance of a national State. It was in England and France, and in Spain, that the feudal monarchy was most successful in applying the principles of public law and in compelling the private rights of feudalism to submit measurably to the practice of the public interest of the State. If one finds it strange that the kingdom of England, the land of the common law, was the most complete State in the thirteenth century, one must recall that Roman principles of public law were likely to be most successful where a strong kingship, in an environment of some awareness of a general membership in a territorial *regnum*, was able to assert its right to govern for the public and common welfare of realm and people.

Nowhere, however, we must repeat, was the practice of the art of the State efficient. Nowhere could royal governments exact that obedience of subjects which is generally obtained by the State in the twentieth century. But if this is true of the medieval State, it is also in small part true of the modern State. The public and private aspects of government can never be so sharply distinguished as theorists dealing with the modern State like to believe. Henry VIII, Louis XIV, and Napoleon, not to mention many another great prince, were not above letting their private, personal pleasures and *ira et voluntas* influence actions alleged to be for the public interest. Indeed, displays of private emotion have often been instruments of public policy. It is not necessary to assume that personal wrath and arbitrariness were a practice only of feudal monarchs. The private "body" of the ruler has been of great public importance whether at Versailles or in the Kremlin. Even in the United States the private estate of the President and household is not always kept separate from the public estate of the presidency. The White House is more than a residence: it is a public, "sacred," palace. But in it presidents and their families have sometimes found it difficult to keep distinct their private and public life. How often, moreover, have presidents, senators and representatives and their wives spent public money, and used transportation paid for by public taxation, in pursuit of private relaxation! Naturally the personal well-being of higher magistrates and their families may be necessary for "right reasoning" in the practice of the art of statesmanship in the public interest.

For better or for worse, the private estate of the head can still affect the exercise of the public powers belonging to his public estate, as it can affect the "state" of the Nation. And privileges, granted *ratione publicae utilitatis*, still serve the State.

In the feudal monarchy of the twelfth and thirteenth centuries there was, of course, far more of the personal and private, far more of the feudal and proprietary, than in governments of States in the twentieth century. In these studies, however, I have assumed that the private elements are so well known that it was permissible to stress the rise of important ideas belonging to the realm of public law. I have therefore tried to present, not a story of the confusion of private and public in a medieval "government at work," but an interpretation of the history of a few of the ideas that played a significant role in the gradual formation of the medieval, early modern State. Long before the Italian Renaissance, the concept, and some practice, of the "State as a work of art" had become manifest during the great medieval renaissance of the twelfth and thirteenth centuries.

BIBLIOGRAPHY

Manuscripts are occasionally listed more than once, partly because a manuscript may contain works of several authors, partly because the classification according to subject matter may be helpful to the student. In the case of printed sources, the title of a collection or the name of the author is usually given rather than the name of the editor. With few exceptions the secondary works listed are those referred to in the *Studies*.

A. Manuscripts

I. Manuscript sources pertaining to medieval Roman Law

Pre-Accursian glosses (before *ca.* 1230) to the *Digest* (chiefly of Irnerius, Bulgarus, Jacobus, Martinus, Placentinus, Pillius, Johannes Bassianus, Hugolinus, and Azo—on these legists and others listed below, see Savigny, *Gesch. d. röm. Rechts im MA*), consulted in the following manuscripts:

Bamberg, Staatsbibl., Jur. 11, 12, 14, 15, 17, 19, 20, 21;
London, Brit. Mus., Royal 11 C. III;
Paris, Bibl. Nat., lat. 4429, 4450, 4451, 4454, 4455, 4458, 4458A, 4461, 4487A, 4536;
Vatican City, Bibl. Vaticana, Vat. lat. 1405, 1406, 1407, 1408, 2313, 2511, 2512, 2705, 9665; Borghes. 225, 373; Pal. lat. 733; Ross. 586.

Post-Accursian glosses (*ca.* 1230-1350) to *D.* (Odofredo, Jacques de Révigny, Jacobus de Arena, Dinus de Mugellano, Martinus Syllimanus, Pierre de Belleperche, Jacobus de Belvisio, Ubertus de Bobbio, and Jacobus Butrigarius), in these manuscripts:

Bibl. Vat., Pal. lat. 733, 753; Urb. lat. 163.

Pre-Accursian glosses to the *Codex*, Bks. 1-9 and the *Tres Libri*, Bks. 10-12 (Irnerius, Martinus, Bulgarus, Jacobus, Pillius, Albertus, Johannes Bassianus, Azo, Hugolinus), in the following:

Paris, BN, lat. 4429, 4517, 4518, 4528, 4536, 4546;
Bibl. Vat., Vat. lat. 1427, 11152; Borghes. 273; Pal. lat. 761, 763.

[571]

Post-Accursian glosses to *C.* (Odofredo, Jacques de Révigny, Guido de Suzaria, Richardus de Isernia, Bartholomew of Capua, and others), in manuscripts:

Bibl. Vat., Vat. lat. 1428; Borghes. 374; Regin. lat. 120; Ross. 582.

Pre- and post-Accursian glosses to the *Inst.*, in manuscripts:

Bibl. Vat., Vat. lat. 4424, 4429, 8782; Borghes. 374, 435.

Glosses to the *Authenticae*, in manuscripts:

Paris, BN, lat. 4429; Bibl. Vat., Borghes. 273.

Glosses to the *Libri Feudorum* and the *Lex lombardorum*, in manuscripts:

Paris, BN, lat. 4616; Bibl. Vat., Vat. lat. 3980.

Placentinus, *Summa Codicis*, and *Summa Inst.*:
Paris, BN, lat. 4441, 4539; Bibl. Vat., Chis. E. VII. 217.

Johannes Bassianus, *Summa Auth.*, Paris, BN, MSS lat. 4542, 4543.

Pillius, *Summa Inst.*, Paris, BN, MS lat. 4429; *Distinctiones*, Paris, MS nouv. acq. lat. 2376, fols. 120^v-126^v; *Quaestiones*, MS Vat. lat. 2661, fols. 39-56.

Hugolinus, *Summa super usibus feudorum*, Rome, Bibl. Casanatense, MS 108 (A. IV. 10), fols. 263^v-269^v; *Distinctiones*, Bibl. Vat., MS Pal. lat., 656, fols. 187-202^v, and Bibl. Casanatense, MS 1910, fols. 91-110^v.

Azo, *Quaestiones*, MS Vat. lat. 2661, fols. 56-59.

Odofredo, glosses to the *Peace of Constance*, Paris, BN, MS lat. 5414A; *Rationes usus feodorum (Summa in usus feudorum)*, MS lat. 16008; *Repetitiones*, MS lat. 4545; *Quaestiones*, MS lat. 4604, fols. 95-101.

Jean de Blanot (Johannes de Blanosco), *Summa de actionibus*, Bibl. Vat., MSS Vat. lat. 2329 and Borghes. 149; *Summa super usibus feudorum*, MS Vat. lat. 2642.

Jacques de Révigny, *Lectura* on Bks. 1-4 of the *Codex*, Paris, BN, MS lat. 14350, fols. 213-415 (ed. in 1519 as the work of Pierre de Belleperche); *Commentaria* or *Lectura* on the *Inst.*, MS lat. 14350, fols. 144-213; on the *Dig. Novum*, MS lat. 14350, fols. 1-143; *Repetitiones*, MS lat. 4488, fols. 257-317.

Pierre de Belleperche, *Repetitiones* on the *Dig. Vetus*, Paris, BN, MS lat. 4888, fols. 139ff.

Guido de Suzaria, *Suppletiones et quaestiones de facto super digesto veteri*, Paris, BN, MS lat. 4489, fols. 3-29; *Lectura in Codicem*, MS lat. 4489, fols. 30-76.

Bertrand de Déaux (Bertrandus de Deocio), Bernardus de Deutio (see Index, *s. n.* Bertrand de Déaux), *Quaestiones disputatae,* Bibl. Vat., MS Vat. lat. 2642, fols. 116ᵛ-124.
Libellus ordinis iudiciarii, Paris, BN, MS lat. 18420.

II. MANUSCRIPT SOURCES PERTAINING TO THE CANON LAW

(on the literature of Canon law see above all Kuttner, *Repertorium,* and Schulte, *Quellen*)

1. Glosses and *Apparatus* of gl. to Gratian's *Decretum,* before 1215

Glosses of Johannes Faventinus, Huguccio, Laurentius, Alanus, and others, consulted in the manuscripts Bamberg Can. 13; Paris, BN, MS lat. 14317; Rome, Bibl. Angelica, 1270; Vat. lat. 1367, 2495; Vat., Ross. 595; Monte Cassino 66.
Appar. "Ecce vicit leo," Paris, BN, MS nouv. acq. lat. 1576.
Appar. of Alanus, "Ius naturale," Paris, MS lat. 15393 (see Kuttner, "Bernardus Compostellanus, etc." *Traditio,* I, 289 and Stickler, "Alanus Anglicus," *Salesianum,* XXI, 346-404).
Appar. of Laurentius Hispanus, Paris, MS lat. 15393.
Glossa Palatina, Bibl. Vat., MSS Pal. lat. 658 and Reg. lat. 977.

2. Summas and other works on the *Decretum* (for any editions see Bibl. B. II)

Paucapalea, *Summa,* Brit. Mus., MS Royal 11 B. II.
Stephen of Tournai, *Summa,* Bibl. Vat., MS Borghes. 287.
Johannes Faventinus, *Summa,* Brit. Mus., MS Royal 9 E. VII, MS Borghes. 71, and MS Casanatense 1105.
Simon of Bisignano, *Summa,* Brit. Mus., MS Royal 10 A. III, and Rome, Bibl. Angelica, MS 1270.
Sicardus of Cremona, *Summa,* Paris, BN, MS lat. 4288, and Bibl. Vat., MS Pal. lat. 653.
Huguccio, *Summa,* Paris, BN, MSS lat. 3892 and 15396-15397; Vat. lat. 2280.
Summa Reginensis, Bibl. Vat., MS Reg. 1061.
Summa Casinensis, Monte Cassino, MS 396.
Summa "Elegantius in iure divino" (*Summa Coloniensis*), Bamberg, MS Can. 39, and Paris, BN, MS lat. 14997.
Summa "Antiquitate et tempore," Bibl. Vat., MS Pal. lat. 678.
Summa "Tractaturus magister," Paris, BN, MS lat. 15994.
Laborans, Cardinal, *Compilatio decretorum,* Bibl. Vat., MS Arch. Basil. S. Petri C. 110.
Guido Terreni of Perpignan, *Commentaria,* MS Vat. lat. 1453.

3. Glosses and *Apparatus* to the *Quinque Compilationes Antiquae* (papal decretal letters compiled *ca.* 1188-1226; see Friedberg, *Quinque Comp. Ant.*, and Kuttner, *Repertorium*, pp. 323-385)

> *Comp. I*, glosses of Petrus Hispanus, Richardus Anglicus (de Mores), Damasus, Alanus, Laurentius, Vincentius, and Tancred, in the following manuscripts: Bamberg, Can. 19, 20; Halle, Universitätsbibl., Ye 52; Leipzig, Universitätsbibl., 968, 983; Monte Cassino, 46; Paris, BN, lat. 3930, 3932, 15398; Bibl. Vat., Pal. lat. 288, 652, 653, 696.
>
> *Comp. II*, glosses of Albertus, Alanus, Vincentius, Laurentius, Johannes Galensis, and Tancred, in MSS Bamberg Can. 19, Paris lat. 3930 and 3932.
>
> *Comp. III*, glosses of Silvester, Johannes Galensis, Laurentius, Vincentius, Johannes Teutonicus, and Tancred, in MSS Bamberg Can. 19, 20; Brit. Mus., Royal 11 C. VII; Paris, lat. 3930, 3932, 15398, 15399; Monte Cassino 46; Vat. lat. 1377, 1378; Vat., Chis. E. VII. 207.
>
> *Comp. IV*, with the *Appar.* of Johannes Teutonicus, in MSS Bamberg Can. 19, 23; Brit. Mus., Royal 11 C. VII; Vat. lat. 1377.
>
> *Comp. V, Appar.* of Jacobus de Albenga, MS Royal 11 C. VII.

4. Other works of decretalists, before 1234

> Ambrosius, *Summa*, MS Casanatense 1910.
> Damasus, *Summa*, MSS Paris, BN, lat. 14320; Casanatense 1910.
> Honorius of England, Paris, BN, MS lat. 14591.
> Raymund of Peñafort, *Summa*, Bibl. Vat., MS Borghes. 261.

5. Decretalists' works relating to the *Decr. Greg. IX* (1234) and to later collections of papal decretals from Innocent IV to John XXII

> Vincentius Hispanus, *Apparatus* to *Decr. Greg. IX*, Paris, BN, MS lat. 3967.
> Abbas Antiquus (Bernard de Montmirat), *Apparatus* or *Lectura* to *Decr. Greg. IX*, MSS Paris, BN, lat. 3992, 4011A; Bibl. Vat., Borghes. 260, Vat. lat. 2542; *Lectura* and *Distinctiones* on the *Constitutiones* of Inn. IV in Borghes. 260 and Vat. lat. 2542.
> Johannes Hispanus de Petesella, *Summa* on *Decr. Greg. IX*, MS Vat. lat. 2343.
> Johannes Garsias Hispanus, *Commentaria* on *Decr. Greg. IX* and on *Decr. Inn. IV*, MSS Paris, BN, lat. 8923; Bibl. Vat., Pal. lat. 629.

Lectura (author not identified) on *Decr. Greg. IX*, Bibl. Vat., MS Pal. lat. 655.

Guido de Baysio, *Apparatus* or *Commentaria* to the *Liber Sextus*, MSS Paris, BN, lat. 8024, 11719; Vat. lat. 1452.

Guillaume de Montlauzun, *Lectura* on the *Clementinae*, Paris, BN, MS lat. 16902.

Pierre Bertrand, *Apparatus* to the *Liber Sextus*, the *Clementinae*, and the *Extravagantes*, Paris, BN, MS lat. 4085.

Etienne Troches and Pierre de l'Estaing, *Lectura*, or *Reportationes*, or *Repetitiones*, on the *Clementinae*, Paris, BN, MS lat. 9634.

Paulus de Liazariis, *Apparatus* to the *Clementinae*, MSS Paris, BN, lat. 4102; Vat. lat. 1437.

III. MISCELLANEOUS

Damasus, *Summa de ordine iudiciario*, Paris, BN, MS lat. 3925A, fols. 81-94; *Quaestiones*, Bamberg MS Can. 42, and Bibl. Vat., MS Borghes. 261; *Brocardica super iure canonico*, MSS Borghes. 261 and Casanatense 108.

Bartholomew of Brescia, *Quaestiones dominicales* and *Quaestiones veneriales*, MSS Paris, BN, lat. 15424 and Casanatense 1094.

Johannes de Deo, *Libellus dispensationum*, MS Casanatense 108; *Liber poenitentiarius*, MS Royal 11 B. v; *Quaestiones de facto*, MS Borghes. 260.

Aegidius Romanus (Giles of Rome), *Tractatus quomodo reges et principes possunt possessiones et bona regni peculiaria ecclesiis elargiri*, Paris, BN, MS lat. 6786, fols. 22-41.

Gérard d'Abbeville, *Quodlibeta*, Paris, BN, MS lat. 16405.

Henry of Ghent, *Quodlibeta*, Paris, BN, MS lat. 15350, fols. 251-290.

Glosses to the *Timaeus*, Brit. Mus., MS Royal 12 B. XXII.

Formulary of Bec, Brit. Mus., MS Cotton Dom. A. XI.

Ludovicus de Corthosiis (de Padua), *De principibus*, Paris, BN, MS lat. 4612.

B. Printed Sources

I. MEDIEVAL ROMAN LAW

Accursius. *Glossa ordinaria* to the *Corpus Iuris Civilis*, D., C. 1-9 and 10-12 (*Tres Libri*), *Auth.* (*Nov.*), and *Inst.*, and to the *Libri*

Feudorum, 5 vols.; Lyons, 1604. (There are many editions of the *C.I.C.* accompanied by the *Glos. ord.*; I have used several in various libraries, but chiefly the one given above.)

Albericus de Rosciate (Rosate). *Super Codice Commentarium.* Lyons, 1545.

———. *Super Digesto Vetere Commentarium.* Lyons, 1541.

———. *Super Digesto Novo Commentarium.* Lyons, 1545.

———. *Commentaria de statutis*, in *Tract. Univ. Juris*, II, 2-85 (see *Tract.*, below).

Azo (Azzo). *Summa Codicis.* Venice 1584 and 1610, and many other editions.

———. *Summa Inst.* Venice, 1584, etc. (after the *Summa C.*).

———. *Lectura ad singulas leges XII librorum Codicis.* Paris, 1577, and Lyons, 1596 (by Hugolinus on Bks. 10-12, *Tres Libri*).

———. *Brocardica.* Venice, 1584 (at end of vol. containing other works of Azo).

———. *Quaestiones*, E. Landsberg (ed.). *Die Quaestionen des Azo*; Freiburg i.-B., 1888.

Baldus Ubaldus (de Ubaldis). *Commentarius in Codicem.* 4 vols.; Venice, 1586.

———. *Commentarius* on *D., Inst.*, and *C.* Venice, 1616.

———. *In feudorum usus commentaria.* Venice, 1580.

———. *Glossa ordinaria* to *De pace Constantiae* in the *Volumen legum* in vol. v of the *Corpus Iuris Civilis.* Lyons, 1604.

Bartolus de Saxoferrato. *Opera omnia.* 11 vols.; Venice, 1602-1603.

———. *Apparatus* of glosses to the *Extravagantes* in the *Volumen legum* in vol. v of the *Corpus Iuris Civilis.* Lyons, 1604.

Bencivenne. *Summa de ordine judiciorum*, ed. Bergmann (*q. v.*) as the work of Pillius.

Bergmann, F. C. (ed.). *Pillii, Tancredi, Gratiae libri de iudiciorum ordine.* Göttingen, 1842.

Bernardus Dorna, *Summa libellorum*, ed. Wahrmund, *Quellen*, I, i (see Wahrmund).

Bibliotheca iuridica (see Gaudenzi).

Brachylogus, ed. E. Böcking. Berlin, 1829.

Bulgarus. *Ad digestorum titulum de diversis regulis juris antiqui Commentarius*, ed. F. G. C. Beckhaus. Bonn, 1865.

Corpus Iuris Civilis (*D., C., Inst., Nov.*), eds. Th. Mommsen, P. Krüger, R. Schoell, and G. Kroll. 3 vols.; new printing, Berlin, 1954, of 12th ed., 1911.

Cynus (Cino da Pistoia). *Super Codice et Digesto Veteri lectura.* Lyons, 1547.

———. *Commentarium.* Frankfurt, 1578.

Dissensiones dominorum (*sive controversiae veterum iuris Romani interpretatum qui glossatores vocantur*), ed. G. Haenel. Leipzig, 1834.

Gaudenzi, A. (ed.). *Bibliotheca iuridica medii aevi*: *Scripta, anecdota glossatorum.* 3 vols.; Bologna, 1888-1901.

Glossa ordinaria (see *Corpus Iuris Civilis, Corpus Juris Canonici,* Accursius, Bernard of Parma, and Johannes Teutonicus).

Gratia. *Ordo iudiciorum* (see Bergmann).

Gross, C. (ed.). *Incerti auctoris Ordo judiciarius.* Innsbruck, 1870.

Haenel, G. (see *Dissensiones*).

Hugolinus. *Summa* of the *Digest*, in the Venice, 1584, and other editions of Azo, *Summa Codicis* (wrongly attributed to Johannes Bassianus).

————. *Lectura* on the *Tres Libri* (see Azo, *Lectura*).

Irnerius. E. Besta, *L'Opera di Irnerio.* 2 vols.; Turin, 1896.

————. G. Pescatore, *Die Glossen des Irnerius.* Greifswald, 1888.

————. *Summa Codicis* (see Rogerius).

————. H. Fitting (ed.). *Quaestiones de iuris subtilitatibus des Irnerius.* Berlin 1894.

Iuris interpretes saeculi XIII (see Meijers, Bibl. C.)

Jacobus de Arena. *Commentarium in universum ius civile.* Lyons, 1541.

Jacobus de Belvisio. *Summa Authenticarum* and *Usus feudorum.* Lyons, 1511.

Jacobus Buttrigarius. *Lectura in Digesto Veteri.* Rome, 1606, 1611.

————. *Lectura in Codicem.* Paris, 1516.

Jacobus Columbi. *Summa super usibus feudorum,* ed. J. B. Palmieri, *Scripta anecdota glossatorum,* II, 183-194 (see Gaudenzi; Palmieri wrongly attributes the work to Hugolinus—see H. Kantorowicz in *Zeitschr. Sav.-Stift., Röm. Abt.,* L [1930], 474).

Jacques de Révigny. *Commentarias* on the *Codex.* Paris, 1519 (wrongly attributed to Pierre de Belleperche).

Jean Faure (Johannes Faber). *Breviarium in Codicem.* Paris, 1545 and Lyons, 1594.

————. *Commentarius in Institutiones.* Lyons, 1593.

Johannes Bassianus. *Summa libri Authenticarum,* ed. Venice, 1584 (in the volume containing the *Summa* of Azo, etc.; see Azo).

————. *Summa* of the *Digest* (see Hugolinus).

Lo codi, eds. H. Fitting and H. Suchier. Halle, 1906.

Lucas de Penna. *Commentaria in tres posteriores libros Codicis Iustiniani* (the *Tres Libri*). Lyons, 1597.

Odofredo. *Lectura*: on the *Digestum Vetus,* Lyons, 1550 and 1552; on the *Dig. Infortiatum,* Lyons, 1550 and 1552; on the *Dig. Novum.*

Lyons, 1552; on the *Codex*, Lyons, 1550 and 1552; on the *Tres Libri*, Lyons, 1517.

――――. *Summa in usus feudorum*. Compluti (Alcalá de Henares), 1584.

Oldradus (Oldrado da Ponte). *Consilia*. Venice, 1571.

Ordo judiciarius Bambergensis (see Bamberg *Ordo*, Bibl. B. ii).

Ordo judiciarius "Scientiam," in Wahrmund, *Quellen*, ii, i (see Wahrmund).

Pierre de Belleperche. *Commentaria* on *D. Vetus* and *D. Novum*, and *Repetitiones* on the *Codex*. Frankfurt, 1571.

――――. *Lectura* or *Com.* on the *Inst.* Lyons, 1536 and Paris, 1513.

Pierre Jame (Petrus Jacobi), *Aurea practica libellorum*; Cologne, 1575.

Pillius, on the *Tres Libri* (see Placentinus).

Placentinus. *Summa Codicis*, ed N. Rhodius. Mainz, 1536.

――――. *Summa Institutionum*, ed. Fitting, *Juristische Schriften* (see Fitting, in Bibl. C); also Mainz, 1535.

――――. *Summa* of the *Tres Libri*. Venice, 1584, in the vol. containing the *Summa Codicis* of Azo, pp. 934-1042; the work was finished by Pillius.

――――. *Summa "Cum essem Mantua,"* ed. G. Pescatore. Greifswald, 1897.

Rainerius of Perugia. *Ars notariae*, ed. Wahrmund, *Quellen,* iii, ii (see Wahrmund).

Rogerius. *Summa Codicis*, ed. H. Fitting as the work of Irnerius. Berlin, 1896.

Rolandinus Passagerii. *Summa totius artis notariae*. Venice, 1574.

Scripta, anecdota glossatorum (see Gaudenzi).

Tractatus ex variis juris interpretibus collecti. 18 vols.; Lyons, 1549.

Tractatus universi juris. 29 vols.; Venice, 1584.

Vacarius. *Liber pauperum*, ed. F. de Zulueta (Selden Society, xliii). London, 1927.

Wahrmund, L. *Quellen zur Geschichte des römisch-kanonischen Processes im Mittelalter*. Innsbruck, 1905ff.

Wunderlich, Agathon. *Anecdota quae ad processum civilem pertinent*. Göttingen, 1841.

II. Medieval Canon Law

Abbas Antiquus (Bernard de Montmirat). *Commentarius* on *Decr. Greg. IX*. Venice, 1588.

Aegidius de Fuscarariis. *Ordo iudiciarius*, ed. Wahrmund, *Quellen,* iii, i (see Wahrmund, Bibl. B. i).

Arnulphus, Magister. *Summa minorum*, ed. Wahrmund, *Quellen,* i, ii.

Augustinus, Antonius (Agustino, Antonio). *Antiquae collectiones decretalium*. Ilerdae, 1576.

Bamberg *Ordo iudiciarius*, ed. J. F. v. Schulte, *Sitzungsber. d. Kais. Akad. Wien, Philos.-Hist. Cl.*, LXX (1872).

Bernard de Montmirat (see Abbas Antiquus).

Bernard of Compostella. *Commentaria* on Bk. 1 of *Decr. Greg. IX*. Venice, 1588 (with *Com.* of Abbas Antiquus, *q.v.*).

Bernard of Parma. *Glossa ordinaria* to *Decr. Greg. IX*. Lyons, 1558 and 1572, and Paris, 1553 (there are many editions—see also *Corpus Juris Canonici*).

Bernard of Pavia. *Summa decretalium*, ed. E. A. T. Laspeyres. Ratisbon, 1860 (includes also Bernard's *Summa de electione*).

Boich (Bohic), Henricus. *In quinque libros decretalium libros Commentaria* (*Distinctiones* on *Decr. Greg. IX*). Venice, 1576.

Corpus Juris Canonici, ed. E. A. Friedberg. 2 vols.; Leipzig, 1879-1881 (vol. I, *Decretum* of Gratian; II, *Decr. Greg. IX, Liber Sextus, Clementinae*, and *Extravagantes communes* of John XXII).

Curialis, ed. Wahrmund, *Quellen*, I, iii (see Wahrmund).

Damasus. *Brocarda sive regulae canonicae*, in *Tractatus universi juris*, XVIII, 506ff. (see *Tract. univ. juris*).

Decretum of Gratian (see *Corpus Juris Canonici* and Johannes Teutonicus, *Glossa ordinaria*).

Dinus Mugellanus (Dino de Mugello). *Commentarius in regulas iuris pontificii*. Lyons, 1545.

Friedberg, E. A. (ed.). *Quinque Compilationes Antiquae*. Leipzig, 1882.

Geoffrey of Trani (Goffredus Tranensis). *Summa Decr. Greg. IX*, ed. J. B. Ziletto. Venice, 1564.

Guido de Baysio (Archidiaconus). *Rosarium* (*Com.* on the *Decretum*). Venice, 1577.

Guillaume Durantis. *Speculum iuris* (*Speculum judiciale*). 4 vols.; Venice, 1602.

———. *In sacrosanctum lugdunense concilium sub Gregorio X . . . Commentarius*. Fano, 1569.

Henricus Boich (see Boich).

Henry of Susa (Hostiensis). *Summa aurea*. Lyons, 1542 and Basel, 1573.

———. *Lectura* or *Commentaria* on *Decr. Greg. IX*. Paris, 1512.

Hostiensis (see Henry of Susa).

Innocent IV. *Apparatus super libros decretalium*. Venice, 1481, 1578, and Frankfurt, 1570.

Jacobus de Ardizone. *Summa feudorum*, in *Tract. univ. juris*, XIV (x, P. 1)

Jean Lemoine (Johannes Monachus). *Glossa aurea* (*Apparatus*), to *Liber Sextus*. Paris, 1535 and Venice, 1585.

———. Glosses to the *Extravagantes communes,* vol. III of *Corpus Juris Canonici,* ed. Lyons, 1559.

Johannes Andreae. *Novella Commentaria* on *Decr. Greg. IX.* 5 vols.; Venice, 1581.

———. *Novella Commentaria* on the *Liber Sextus.* Lyons, 1584.

Johannes Teutonicus. *Glossa ordinaria* to the *Decretum.* Lyons, 1553 (there are many editions).

Lyndwood, William. *Provincialia.* Oxford, 1679.

Panormitanus. *Commentaria in decretalium libros.* 3 vols.; Venice, 1571.

Paucapalea. *Summa,* ed. J. F. v. Schulte. Giessen, 1890.

Quinque Compilationes Antiquae (see Friedberg; and Bibl. A. II).

Raymund of Peñafort. *Summa de casibus.* Rome, 1603.

———. *Summa de iure canonico,* ed. J. Rius Serra, *S. Raymundi Penyafort Opera omnia,* vol. I. Barcelona, 1945.

Rhetorica ecclesiastica, ed. Wahrmund, *Quellen,* I, iv (see Wahrmund).

Richardus Anglicus (de Mores). *Summa de ordine iudiciario,* ed. Wahrmund, *Quellen,* II, iii.

Roffredo of Benevento. *Tractatus aureus ordinis iudiciarii, Opus libellorum super iure pontifico,* and *Quaestiones Sabbatinae.* Lyons, 1561.

Rufinus. *Summa decretorum,* ed. H. Singer. Paderborn, 1902.

Simon of Bisignano. *Summa,* ed. J. Juncker, "Die Summa des Simon von Bisignano und seine Glossen," *Zeitschr. d. Sav.-Stift. f. Rechtsgesch., Kan. Abt.,* XV (1926).

Stephen of Tournai. *Summa,* ed. J. F. v. Schulte. Giessen, 1891.

Summa on *Decretum,* wrongly attributed to Rufinus, by J. F. v. Schulte, ed. Giessen, 1892.

Summa parisiensis, ed. Terence P. McLaughlin, *The Summa Parisiensis on the Decretum of Gratian.* Toronto, 1952.

Summa "Ut nos minores," ed. J. G. C. Joosting, "Die Summa Ut nos minores. Nach der Leidener Handschrift herausgegeben," *Zeitschr. d. Sav.-Stift. f. Rechtsgesch., Kan. Abt.,* XVII (1928).

Tancred. *Ordo iudiciorum* (see Bergmann, Bibl. B. I).

Wahrmund, L. "Der 'Parvus ordinarius,' " *Archiv f. kath. Kirchenrecht,* LXXXI (1901).

William of Drogheda. *Summa aurea,* ed. Wahrmund, *Quellen,* II, ii (see Wahrmund).

Zabarella, Franciscus. *Commentaria super libris decretalium.* Venice, 1602.

Acta capitulorum provencialium Ordinis Fratrum Praedicatorum, ed. C. Douais. Toulouse, 1894.

Actes de la province ecclésiastique de Reims, ed. Th. Gousset, vol. III. Paris, 1843.

Alain de Lille. *De planctu naturae*, M.P.L., 210.

———. *Summa de arte praedicatoria*, M.P.L., 210.

Andrew (Andreas) of Isernia. *Commentaria*, or *Peregrina lectura*, *super constitutionibus et glossis Regni Siciliae*, ed. Cervone (see *Constitutiones Regni Siciliarum*).

———. *In usus feudorum commentaria*. Frankfurt, 1598.

Annales monastici: I. *Annales de Burton*; III. *Annales prioratus de Dunstaplia*, ed. H. R. Luard (Rolls Series). London, 1864, 1868.

Anonymous of York (see *Tractatus Eboracenses*).

Bartholomew of Capua. *Commentaria* on the *Constitutiones Regni Siciliae*. Venice, 1580 (also ed. Cervone; see *Const. Regni Siciliarum*).

Beaumanoir. *Coutumes de Beauvaisis*, ed. A. Salmon. 2 vols.; Paris, 1899-1900.

Bernard of Clairvaux. *De consideratione libri quinque ad Eugenium Tertium*, M.P.L., 182.

Boncompagno. *Rhetorica novissima*, ed. A. Gaudenzi (see Gaudenzi, Bibl. B. 1).

Bracton, Henry of. *De legibus et consuetudinibus Angliae*, ed. G. E. Woodbine. 4 vols.; New Haven and London, 1915-1942; also ed. Sir Travers Twiss (Rolls Series). 6 vols.; London, 1878-1883.

Catálogo. Colección de Cortes de los antiguos reinos de España por la Real Academia de la Historia. Madrid, 1855.

Chartularium Universitatis Parisiensis, eds. H. Denifle and E. Chatelain. 4 vols.; Paris, 1889-1897.

Chase, W. J. *The Distichs of Cato*. Madison, Wis., 1922.

Codigos antiguos de España, ed. M. M. Alcubilla. Madrid, 1885.

Cole, H. *Documents Illustrative of English History in the Thirteenth and Fourteenth Centuries* (Record Commission). London, 1844.

Colección de documentos inéditos del Archivo General de la Corona de Aragón. 41 vols.; Barcelona, 1847-1910 (vols. I-XVII ed. by Prospero de Bofarull y Mascaro).

Colección de fueros municipales, ed. T. Muñoz y Romero. Madrid, 1847.

Coluccio dei Salutati, *De tyranno*, ed. Fr. Ercole. Bologna, 1942.

Constitutiones et acta publica imperatorum et regum, M.G.H., Legum Sectio IV.

Constitutiones Regni Siciliarum Libri III, ed. Antonius Cervonius (Cervone). Naples, 1773 (also ed. Huillard-Bréholles, *Hist. diplom. Frid. Secundi,* IV, i—see Huillard-Bréholles).

Consuetudines Curiae Romanae, ed. L. Wahrmund, *Archiv f. kath. Kirchenrecht,* LXXIX (1899).

Cortes de los antiguos reinos de Aragón y de Valencia y principado de Cataluña. Madrid, 1896ff.

Cortes de los antiguos reinos de León y de Castilla. 5 vols.; Madrid, 1861-1903 (*Introducción* by Colmeiro, *q.v.,* Bibl. C).

Coutumiers de Normandie, ed. E. J. Tardif. 2 vols.; Rouen and Paris, 1881-1903.

Delaborde, H.-F., Petit-Dutaillis, Ch., and Monicat, J. (eds.). *Recueil des actes de Philippe Auguste.* 2 vols.; Paris, 1916-1943.

Delaborde, H.-F. *Oeuvres de Rigord et Guillaume le Breton.* Vol. I, Paris, 1882.

Delisle, L., and Berger, E. *Recueil des actes de Henri II.* Vol. I, Paris, 1916.

Denifle, H. "Die Constitutionen des Predigerordens vom Jahre 1228," *Archiv für Litteratur- und Kirchengeschichte des Mittelalters,* I (1885).

Diplomata regum et imperatorum Germaniae, M.G.H., *Dipl.*

Drogo de Altovillari. *Summa de omni facultate,* ed. Pierre Varin, in *Archives législatives de la ville de Reims* (*Documents Inédits*), 1re partie, *Coutumes.* Paris, 1840.

Etablissements de Saint Louis, ed. P. Viollet. 4 vols.; Paris, 1881-1886.

Fleta, eds. H. G. Richardson and G. O. Sayles (Selden Society). 2 vols.; London, 1955.

Formulae, M.G.H., *Legum Sectio V.*

Gilbert Foliot. *Epistolae,* ed. J. A. Giles (*Patres Eccl. Angl.*). Oxford, 1845.

Giovanni da Botero. *Della ragion di stato* (see *Scrittori politici*).

Giovanni Villani. *Cronica,* ed. Celestino Durando. 8 vols.; Turin, 1880.

Giry, A. (ed.). *Documents sur les relations de la royauté avec les villes en France de 1180 à 1314.* Paris, 1885.

Glanville. *De legibus et consuetudinibus regni Angliae,* ed. G. E. Woodbine. New Haven, 1932.

Guibert de Tournai. A. de Poorter (ed.). *Guibert de Tournai, O. F. M., Le traité Eruditio regum et principum* (*Les philosophes belges,* IX). Louvain, 1914.

Guido Faba. *Summa dictaminis* (see Rockinger, *Briefsteller*).

Guillaume du Breuil. *Stilus Curie Parlamenti,* ed. F. Aubert. Paris, 1909.

Guillaume le Maire. Célestin Port (ed.). *Le Livre de Guillaume le Maire.* Paris, 1874.

Henry of Ghent. *Quodlibeta—Magistri Henrici a Gandavo aurea quodlibeta.* Venice, 1608, 1613.

Huillard-Bréholles, J. L. A. *Historia diplomatica Friderici Secundi.* 7 vols.; Paris, 1852-1861.

Isambert. *Recueil général des anciennes lois françaises.* Vol. I, Paris, 1822.

Jean de Blanot. *Tractatus super feudis et homagiis,* ed. J. Acher, "Notes sur le droit savant au moyen âge," *Nouv. rev. hist. de droit français et étranger,* xxx (1906), 125-178.

John of Paris. *Tractatus de potestate regia et papali.* Paris, 1506; also ed. Jean Leclerq, *Jean de Paris et l'ecclésiologie du XIIIᵉ siècle* (Part 2). Paris, 1942.

John of Salisbury. *Policraticus,* ed. C. C. J. Webb. 2 vols.; Oxford, 1909 (also in *M.P.L.,* 199).

———. *Metalogicon,* ed. C. C. J. Webb. Oxford, 1929.

———. *Letters,* eds. W. J. Millor and H. E. Butler, *The Letters of John of Salisbury* (revised by C. N. L. Brooke). Vol. I, *The Early Letters.* London, 1955.

Jusselin, M. "Lettres de Philippe le Bel relatives à la convocation de l'assemblée de 1302," *Bibliothèque de l'Ecole des Chartes,* LXVII (1906).

Leges Visigothorum antiquiores (Fontes iuris germanici antiqui), ed. K. Zeumer. Hannover and Leipzig, 1894.

Liber Augustalis (see *Const. Regni Sicil.*).

Libri feudorum (see Accursius, *Glossa ordinaria*).

Literae cantuarienses—The Letter Books of the Monastery of Christ Church, Canterbury, ed. J. B. Sheppard (Rolls Series). Vol. III, London, 1889.

Mansi. *Concilia—Sacrorum conciliorum nova et amplissima collectio,* eds. J. D. Mansi and others. Florence and Venice, 1759-1798.

Marinus de Caramanico. *Glossa ordinaria* to the *Constitutiones Regni Siciliae (Liber Augustalis),* ed. Cervone (see *Const. Regni Sicil.*).

Marsiglio of Padua. *Defensor Pacis,* ed. C. W. Previté-Orton. Cambridge, 1928.

Martène, E., and Durand, U. *Thesaurus novus anecdotorum.* 3 vols.; Paris, 1717.

Matthew Paris. *Chronica majora,* ed. H. R. Luard (Rolls Series). 6 vols.; London, 1876-1882.

Memoranda de Parliamento, ed. F. W. Maitland. London, 1893.

Modus tenendi parliamentum, ed. T. D. Hardy. London, 1846.

Nicholas de Lyra. *Postilla super Evangelia.* Mantua, 1477.

Norman Anonymous (see *Tractatus Eboracenses*).

Ockham (see William of Ockham).

Oculus pastoralis, in L. A. Muratori, *Antiquitates italicae medii aevi*, IV, 95-109.

Otto of Freising and Rahewin. *Gesta Friderici I. Imperatoris*, ed. G. Waitz in *M.G.H., SS in Usum Scholarum*. Hannover, 1884.

Otto Morena. *Historia Frederici I.*, ed. F. Güterbock in *M.G.H., SS*, N.S., VII, Berlin, 1930.

Pantin, W. A. (ed.). *Documents Illustrating the Activities of the General and Provincial Chapters of the English Black Monks* (Camden Third Series). London, 1931-1937.

Parliamentary Writs, ed. F. Palgrave. 2 vols. in 4, London, 1827-1834.

Peckham, Johannes. *Registrum epistolarum*, ed. C. T. Martin. 3 vols.; London, 1882-1885.

Philippus de Leyden. *De cura rei publicae et sorte principantis*, ed. R. Fruin and P. C. Molhuijsen. 's-Gravenhage, 1900.

Pierre Bertrand, *De origine iurisdictionum, seu de duabus potestatibus*, in *Tractatus universi juris*, III (see *Tractatus univ. juris*, Bibl. B. I).

Picot, G. *Documents relatifs aux états généraux et assemblées reunis sous Philippe le Bel*. Paris, 1901.

Pierre d'Auvergne (see Thomas Aquinas, *In libros Politicorum expositio*).

Pierre Dubois, *De recuperatione Terrae Sanctae*, ed. Ch.-V. Langlois. Paris, 1891.

Regesta pontificum romanorum: to 1198, eds. Ph. Jaffe and S. Loewenfeld, 2nd ed., Berlin, 1885-1888; 1198-1304, A. Potthast, Berlin, 1874-1875.

Regesta Honorii Papae III, ed. P. Pressutti. Rome, 1888-1895.

Register of S. Osmund, ed. W. H. Rich Jones (Rolls Series). 2 vols.; London, 1883-1884.

Registres of Popes Gregory IX, Innocent IV, Alexander IV, and other popes of the thirteenth and early fourteenth centuries, published in the series *Bibliothèque des Ecoles Françaises d'-Athènes et de Rome*, Paris, 1884ff.—still in progress.

Richard Fitzneale. *De necessariis observantiis scaccarii dialogus* (*Dialogus de scaccario*), eds. A. Hughes, C. G. Crump, and C. Johnson. Oxford, 1902.

――――. *Dialogus de scaccario*, ed. and transl. Charles Johnson (Nelson's Medieval Classics). London, 1950.

Rockinger, L. *Briefsteller und Formelbücher des eilften bis vierzehnten Jahrhunderts* (*Quellen zur bayerischen und deutschen Geschichte*, IX). Munich, 1863.

Rolls of the Justices in Eyre . . . Gloucestershire, etc., ed. Doris May Stenton (Selden Society Publications, LIX). London, 1940.

Rotuli Literarum Clausarum, ed. T. D. Hardy. 2 vols.; London, 1833-1844.

Rotuli Parliamentorium. Vol. I, London, 1767.

Rotuli Parliamentorum Anglie hactenus inediti, eds. H. G. Richardson and G. O. Sayles (Camden Third Series, LI). London, 1935.

Rymer, Thomas. *Foedera, Conventiones, etc.,* Vol. I, London, 1816.

Scrittori politici. Milan, 1839 (includes Giovanni da Botero, *q.v.*).

Select Cases in the Court of King's Bench, ed. G. O. Sayles (Selden Society), LV, LVII-LVIII. London, 1936-1939.

Shirley, W. W. (ed.). *Royal and Other Historical Letters Illustrative of the Reign of Henry III* (Rolls Series). 2 vols.; London, 1862-1866.

Siete partidas, ed. A. de San Martin, in *Los codigos españoles.* 2 vols.; Madrid, 1848ff.; 2nd. ed., 1872.

Statutes of the Realm (Record Commission). Vol. I, London, 1810.

Stubbs, W. *Select Charters,* 9th ed., rev. H. W. C. Davis. Oxford, 1929.

Theiner, A. *Codex diplomaticus dominii temporalis Sanctae Sedis.* Rome, 1861.

Thomas Aquinas. ed. A. P. d'Entrèves. *San Tommaso d'Aquino, Scritti politici.* Bologna, 1946.

———. *In libros Politicorum expositio,* ed. Raymundus M. Spiazzi. Rome, 1951 (with the continuation by Pierre d'Auvergne of Thomas's commentary).

Thomas of Capua. *Ars dictandi,* ed. E. Heller, *Sitzungsber. d. Heidelberger Akad. d. Wissenschaften, Philos.-hist. Kl.* Heidelberg, 1929.

Thomas of Walsingham. *Gesta Abbatum Sancti Albani,* ed. H. T. Riley. Vol. I, London, 1867.

Thorndyke, Lynn. *University Records and Life in the Middle Ages.* New York, 1944.

Tractatus Eboracenses (Tractates of York), M.G.H., Libelli de lite, III (also called the Anonymous of York and the Norman Anonymous).

Varin, Pierre. *Archives législatives de la ville de Reims (Documents inédits).* Paris, 1840.

Villehardouin. *Conquête de Constantinople,* ed. Edmond Faral. Vol. I, Paris, 1938.

Wilkins, D. *Concilia Magnae Britanniae et Hiberniae.* 4 vols.; London, 1737.

William of Ockham. *Opera politica,* ed. J. G. Sykes. Vol. I, Manchester, 1940.

Wrobel, Johann (ed.). *Platonis Timaeus, interprete Chalcidio, cum eiusdem interpretatio.* Leipzig, 1876.

Zurita, Jerónimo. *Anales de la Corona de Aragón.* 2nd ed., Saragossa, 1610.

C. Secondary Works

Acher, Jean. "Notes sur le droit savant au moyen âge," *Nouvelle revue historique de droit français et étranger*, xxx (1906).

Adams, G. B. *Constitutional History of England.* New York, 1921.

Altamira y Crevea, R. *Cuestiones de historia del derecho.* Madrid, 1914.

———. *History of Spanish Civilization.* Transl. by P. Volkov. London, 1930.

Aubert, Jean-Marie. *Le droit romain dans l'oeuvre de Saint Thomas* (Bibliothèque Thomiste, xxx). Paris, 1955.

Baldwin, J. F. *The King's Council in England during the Middle Ages.* Oxford, 1913.

Ballesteros y Beretta, D. Antonio. *Historia de España.* 5 vols.; Barcelona, 1918-1929.

Barker, E. *The Dominican Order and Convocation.* Oxford. 1913.

Barlow, Frank. *The Feudal Kingdom of England, 1042-1216.* London, 1955.

Baron, Hans. *The Crisis of the Italian Renaissance: Civic Humanism and Republican Liberty in an Age of Classicism and Tyranny.* 2 vols.; Princeton, 1955.

Barraclough, Geoffrey. *History in a Changing World.* Oxford, 1955.

———. "Law and Legislation in Medieval England," *Law Quarterly Review*, LVI (1940).

———. "Praxis beneficiorum," *Zeitschrift der Savigny-Stiftung für Rechtsgeschichte, Kan. Abt.*, xxvii (1937).

Bataillard, Charles. *Les origines de l'histoire des procureurs et des avoués.* Paris, 1868.

Bayley, Charles C. *The Formation of the German College of Electors in the Mid-Thirteenth Century.* Toronto, 1949.

———. "Pivotal Concepts in the Political Philosophy of William of Ockham," *Journal of the History of Ideas*, x (1949).

Bémont, Charles. *Chartes des libertés anglaises (1100-1305).* Paris, 1892.

Benedito, C. M. "Nuevas behetrías de León y Galicia y textos para el estudio de la curia regia leonesa," *Anuario de historia del derecho español*, vi (1929).

Berger, E. *Saint Louis et Innocent IV.* Paris, 1893.

Berges, Wilhelm. *Die Fürstenspiegel des hohen und späten Mittelalters.* Stuttgart, 1938 and 1952.

Besta, E. *L'Opera di Irnerio.* 2 vols.; Turin, 1896.

Bethmann-Hollweg, M. A. von. *Der Civilprozess des gemeinen Rechts in geschichtlicher Entwickelung.* 6 vols.; Bonn, 1864-1874.

Birdsall, Paul. " 'Non Obstante'—A Study of the Dispensing Power of English Kings," *Essays in History and Political Theory in Honor of Charles Howard McIlwain,* ed. Carl Wittke. Cambridge, Mass., 1936.

Bisson, Thomas N. "An Early Provincial Assembly," *Speculum,* XXXVI (1961).

Bligny-Bondurand, E. *Les coutumes de Saint-Gilles.* Paris, 1915.

Bluntschli, J. K. *Theory of the State* (transl. of sixth German edition). Oxford, 1885.

Boase, T. S. R. *Boniface VIII.* London, 1933.

Bofarull y Romaña, Manuel de. *Las antiguas cortes.* Madrid, 1912; 2nd ed., Alcalá de Henares, 1945.

Bouix, L'Abbé D. *Du concile provinciale.* Paris, 1850.

Bresslau, H. *Handbuch der Urkundenlehre für Deutschland und Italien.* 2nd ed., 2 vols.; Leipzig, 1912-1931.

Bruni, C. *Le opere di Egidio Romano.* Florence, 1936.

Brunner, H. *Forschungen zur Geschichte des deutschen und französischen Rechtes.* Stuttgart, 1894.

Brunner, Otto. *Land und Herrschaft.* Brunn, München, Wien, 1943.

Brys, J. *De dispensatione in iure canonico.* Bruges, 1925.

Buckland, W. W. *The Main Institutions of Roman Private Law.* Cambridge, 1931.

———. *Textbook of Roman Law from Augustus to Justinian;* 2nd ed., Cambridge, 1932.

———. and A. D. McNair. *Roman Law and Common Law: A Comparison in Outline.* Cambridge, 1936.

Buisson, Ludwig. *Potestas und Caritas. Die päpstliche Gewalt im Spätmittelalter.* Cologne, 1958.

———. *König Ludwig IX. der Heilige und das Recht.* Freiburg, 1954.

Burckhardt, Jacob. *Die Kultur der Renaissance in Italien.* Vol. v of the *Gesamtausgabe,* ed. Werner Kaegi. Stuttgart, Berlin, and Leipzig, 1930; also Vol. III of *Gesammelte Werke.* Basel, 1955.

———. *The Civilization of the Renaissance in Italy.* Transl. S. G. C. Middlemore. 2 vols. New York, 1955.

Caillemer, E. *Le droit civil dans les provinces anglo-normandes au XIIe siècle.* Caen, 1883.

———. *"Jean de Blanot,"* *Mélanges Ch. Appleton.* Lyons and Paris, 1903.

Calasso, Francesco. *I Glossatori e la teoria della sovranità.* 2nd ed., Milan, 1951; 3rd ed., Milan, 1957.

———. *Medio evo del diritto*: I. *Le Fonti.* Milan, 1954.

———. *Gli ordinamenti giuridici del rinascimento medievale*; 2nd ed., Milan, 1949; Reprint, 1953.

———. "Origini italiane della formola 'rex in regno suo est imperator,'" *Riv. di storia del diritto italiano*, III (1930).

Calisse, C. *Storia del parlamento in Sicilia.* Turin, 1887.

Cam, Helen M. "L'assiette et la perception des indemnités des représentants des comtés dans l'Angleterre médiévale," *Rev. hist. de droit français et étranger*, 4e sér., XVIII (1939).

———. "The Community of the Vill," *Medieval Studies Presented to Rose Graham.* Oxford, 1950.

———. "The Evolution of the Medieval English Franchise," *Speculum*, XXXII (1957).

———. "The Relation of English Members of Parliament to their Constituencies in the Fourteenth Century," *L'Organisation corporative du moyen âge* (Etudes présentées à la Commission Internationale pour l'Histoire des Assemblées d'États, III). Louvain, 1939.

Cantini, Joannes A. "De autonomia judicis saecularis et de romani pontificis plenitudine potestatis in temporalibus secundum Innocentium IV," *Salesianum*, XXIII (1961).

Cantor, Norman F. *Church, Kingship, and Lay Investiture in England, 1089-1135.* Princeton, 1958.

Carlyle, A. J. "Some Aspects of the Relation of Roman Law to Political Principles in the Middle Ages," *Studi di storia e diritto in onore di Enrico Besta.* Vol. III, Milan, 1937-1939.

Carlyle, R. W., and A. J. *A History of Mediaeval Political Theory.* 6 vols.; Edinburgh and London, 1903-1936.

Cassirer, Ernst. *The Myth of the State.* New Haven, 1946.

Catalano, Gaetano. "Impero, regni e sacerdozio nel pensiero di Uguccio da Pisa," *Riv. di storia del diritto italiano*, XXX (1957).

Chabod, Federico. *Machiavelli and the Renaissance.* Transl. by David Moore. London, 1958.

Checchini, Aldo. "L'ordinamento processuale romano nell'alto medioevo," *Atti del Congresso Internazionale di Diritto Romano*, I (1934).

Cheney, C. R. *English Synodalia of the Thirteenth Century.* London, 1941.

Chénon, E. "Le droit romain à la *curia regia* de Philippe Auguste à Philippe le Bel," *Mélanges Fitting.* Vol. I, Montpellier, 1907.

———. *Histoire générale du droit français public et privé.* Paris, 1926.

Cheyette, Fredric. "Procurations by Large-Scale Communities in Fourteenth-Century France," *Speculum*, XXXVII (1962).

Chrimes, S. B. *English Constitutional Ideas in the Fifteenth Century*. Cambridge, 1936.

———. *An Introduction to the Administrative History of Mediaeval England*. Oxford, 1959.

Chroust, Anton-Hermann. "The Corporate Idea and the Body Politic in the Middle Ages," *Review of Politics*, IX (1947).

———. "The Philosophy of Law of St. Augustine," *Philosophical Rev.*, LIII (1944).

Clarke, Maude V. *Medieval Representation and Consent*. London, 1936.

Clementi, D. "That the Statute of York is no Longer Ambiguous," in *Album Helen Maud Cam* (Etudes Présentées à la Commission Internationale pour l'Histoire des Assemblées d'Etats, XXIV). Vol. II, Louvain and Paris, 1961.

Cohen, Hermann Joseph. *A History of the English Bar and Attornatus to 1450*. London, 1929.

Collinet, Paul. *La procédure par libelle*. Paris, 1932.

Colmeiro, Don Manuel. *Cortes de los antiguos reinos de Leon y de Castilla, Introducción*. Vol. I, Madrid, 1912 (see *Cortes, etc.*, Bibl. B. III).

Congar, Yves M.-J. "Quod omnes tangit, ab omnibus tractari et approbari debet," *Rev. hist. de droit français et étranger*, 4e sér., XXXVI (1958).

Conrat, M. *Geschichte der Quellen und Literatur des römischen Rechts im früheren Mittelalter*. Leipzig, 1891.

Copleston, Frederick. *History of Philosophy*. Vol. II, Westminster, Md., 1955.

Coville, A. *Les états de Normandie. Leurs origines et leur développement au XIVe siècle*. Paris, 1894.

Crook, John A. *Consilium principis. Imperial Councils and Counsellors from Augustus to Diocletian*. Cambridge, 1955.

Crosara, F. "Respublica e respublicae: cenni terminologici dall' età romana all' XI secolo," *Atti del Congresso Internazionale di Diritto Romano e di Storia del Diritto*. (Verona, 1948), IV (Milan, 1953).

Curtius, Ernst. *European Literature and the Latin Middle Ages*. Transl. W. R. Trask. London, 1953.

Daniel-Rops, Henri. *Cathedral and Crusade. Studies of the Medieval Church, 1050-1350*. Transl. John Warrington. London and New York, 1957.

David, M. *La souveraineté et les limites juridiques du pouvoir monarchique du IXe au XVe siècles*. Paris, 1954.

David, M. "Le serment du sacre du IXe au XVe siècle," *Rev. du moyen âge latin*, VI (1950).

Davies, J. C. *The Baronial Opposition to Edward II. Its Character and Policy.* Cambridge, 1918.

Davis, Gifford. "The Incipient Sentiment of Nationality in Mediaeval Castile: the *Patrimonio Real*," *Speculum*, XII (1937).

———. "The Development of a National Theme in Medieval Castilian Literature," *Hispanic Rev.*, III (1935).

Davy, M. M. "La situation juridique des étudiants de l'Université de Paris au XIIIe siècle," *Rev. d'hist. de l'Eglise en France*, XVII (1931).

Declareuil, J. *Histoire générale du droit français.* Paris, 1925.

Delhaye, Philippe. "L'Enseignement de la philosophie morale au XIIe siècle," *Medieval Studies*, XI (1949).

Dempf, Alois. *Sacrum Imperium.* Munich, Berlin, 1929; 2nd ed., 1954.

Denifle, H. *Die Entstehung der Universitäten des Mittelalters bis 1400.* Berlin, 1885.

Dickinson, John. "The Mediaeval Conception of Kingship and Some of Its Limitations, as Developed in the *Policraticus* of John of Salisbury." *Speculum*, I (1926).

Digby, K. E. *An Introduction to the History of the Law of Real Property.* 3rd ed., Oxford, 1884.

Dowdall, H. C. "The Word 'State,' " *Law Quarterly Rev.*, XXXIX (1923).

Duff, P. W. *Personality in Roman Private Law.* Cambridge, 1938.

Dupré-Theseider, Eugenio. *L'Idea imperiale di Roma nella tradizione del medioevo.* Milan, 1942.

Dupuy, P. *Histoire du différend d'entre le pape Boniface VIII et Philippe le Bel, roy de France.* Paris, 1655.

Edwards, J. G. "*Confirmatio Cartarum* and Baronial Grievances in 1297," *E.H.R.*, LVIII (1943).

———. "The *Plena Potestas* of English Parliamentary Representatives," *Oxford Essays in Medieval History Presented to H. E. Salter.* Oxford, 1934.

———. "Taxation and Consent in the Court of Common Pleas, 1338," *E.H.R.*, LVII (1942).

Egenter, Richard. "Gemeinnutz vor Eigennutz. Die soziale Leitidee im 'Tractatus de bono communi' des Fr. Remigius von Florenz († 1319)," *Scholastik*, IX (1934).

Ehrlich, Eugen. *Beiträge zur Theorie der Rechtsquellen. I. Das jus civile, jus publicum, jus privatum.* Berlin, 1902.

Ehrlich, L. *Proceedings against the Crown* (Oxford Studies in Legal and Social History, VI, xii). Oxford, 1921.

Eichmann, Eduard. "Die römische Eide der deutschen Könige," *Zeitschr. d. Sav.-Stift. f. Rechtsgesch., Kan.-Abt.*, VI (1916).

Emden, A. B. (see Rashdall, *Universities*).

Engelmann, Woldemar. *Die Wiedergeburt der Rechtskultur in Italien durch die wissenschaftliche Lehre*. Leipzig, 1938.

Ercole, F. *Da Bartolo all'Althusio*. Florence, 1932.

Erdmann, C. "Zur Entstehung der Formelsammlung des Marinus von Eboli," *Quellen u. Forschungen aus Ital. Archiven u. Bibl.*, XXI (1929-1930).

Ermini, G. *I parlamenti dello stato della chiesa dalle origini al periodo Albornoziano*. Rome, 1930.

Eschmann, I. Th. "A Thomistic Glossary on the Principle of the Preëminence of a Common Good," *Mediaeval Studies*, V (1943).

Esmein, A. *Cours élémentaire du droit français*. Paris, 1892.

Ewald, W. *Siegelkunde* (G.v. Below and F. Meinecke, *Handbuch der mittelalterlichen und neueren Geschichte*). Berlin, 1914.

Fagnan, Prosper. *Commentaria in Libros Decretalium*. 3 vols.; Venice, 1729.

Fairman, Charles. "The Law of Martial Rule and the National Emergency," *Harvard Law Review*, LV (1942).

Fassio, Guido. "Dio e la natura presso i decretisti e decretalisti," *Il diritto ecclesiastico*, LXVII (1956).

Fawtier, Robert. *The Capetian Kings of France*. Transl. L. Butler and R. Adam. London, 1960.

Fichtenau, Heinrich. "Arenga. Spätantike und Mittelalter im Spiegel von Urkundenformeln," *Mitteilungen des Instituts für österreichische Geschichtsforschung, Ergänzungsband*, XVIII (1957).

———. "Byzanz und die Pfalz zu Aachen," *Mitteil. Inst. f. österr. Geschichtsforsch.*, LIX (1951).

Ficker, J. *Forschungen zur Reichs- und Rechtsgeschichte Italiens*. 4 vols.; Innsbruck, 1868-1874.

Fitting, H. *Juristische Schriften des früheren Mittelalters*. Halle, 1876.

Foreville, Raymonde. *L'Eglise et la royauté en Angleterre sous Henri II Plantagenet (1154-1189)*. Paris, 1943.

———., and Rousset de Pina, F. *Du premier Concile du Latran à l'avènement d'Innocent III*. Paris, 1953.

Fournier, P. *Les officialités au moyen âge*. Paris, 1880.

———. "Notes complémentaires pour l'histoire des canonistes du XIVe siècle," *Nouv. rev. hist. de droit français et étranger*, XLIII (1919).

Fraser, Constance M. "Prerogative and the Bishops of Durham, 1267-1376," *E.H.R.*, LXXIV (1959).

Friedlaender, Ina. *Die päpstlichen Legaten in Deutschland und Italien am Ende des XII Jahrhunderts* (Historische Studien, Heft 177). Berlin, 1928.

Friedrich, C. J. *Constitutional Reason of State.* Providence, 1957.

Fuente, Vicente de la. *Estudios criticos sobre la historia y el derecho de Aragón.* 3 vols.; Madrid, 1884-1886.

Fustel de Coulanges, N. *Histoire des institutions politiques de l'ancienne France.* Vol. III, 3rd ed., Paris, 1905.

Gagnér, Sten. *Studien zur Ideengeschichte der Gesetzgebung (Acta Universitatis Upsaliensis. Studia Iuridica Upsaliensis, 1).* Stockholm, 1960.

Galbraith, G. R. *The Constitution of the Dominican Order, 1216-1360.* Manchester, 1925.

Ganshof, Francois-L. "Les origines du concept de souveraineté nationale en Flandre," *Tijdschr. v. Rechtsgesch.,* XVIII (1950).

———. "Le roi de France en Flandre en 1127 et 1128," *Rev. hist. de droit français et étranger,* XXVII (1949).

Garcia de Diego, E. "Historia judicial de Aragón en los siglos VIII al XII," *Annuario de historia del derecho español,* XI (1937).

Gaudemet, Jean. *L'Eglise dans l'empire romain* (vol. III of G. Le Bras [ed.]. *Histoire du droit et des institutions de l'Eglise en occident*). Paris, 1958.

———. "Utilitas publica," *Rev. hist. de droit français et étranger,* XXIX (1951).

Genuardi, L. "Il Papa Eugenio III e la cultura giuridica in Roma," *Mélanges Fitting.* Vol. II, Montpellier, 1908.

Gewirth, Alan. *Marsilius of Padua, The Defender of the Peace.* Vol. I, New York, 1951.

Gierke, Otto. *Das deutsche Genossenschaftsrecht.* 4 vols.; Berlin, 1868-1914.

———. *Natural Law and the Theory of Society, 1500-1800.* Transl. E. Barker. Cambridge, 1934 and Boston, 1957.

———. *Political Theories of the Middle Age.* Transl. F. W. Maitland. Cambridge, 1900.

———. "Über die Geschichte des Majoritätsprinzips," *Essays in Legal History,* ed. P. Vinogradoff. Oxford, 1913.

Gilbert, A. H. *Machiavelli's Prince and Its Forerunners.* Durham, N.C., 1938.

Gilbert, Felix. "Florentine Political Assumptions in the Period of Savonarola and Soderini," *Jour. Warburg and Courtauld Inst.,* XX (1957).

Gilby, Thomas. *Between Community and Society. A Philosophy and Theology of the State.* London, New York, and Toronto, 1953.

———. *Principality and Polity. Aquinas and the Rise of State Theory in the West.* New York, 1958.

Gillet, P. *La personnalité juridique en droit ecclésiastique.* Malines, 1927.

Gillmann, Franz. *Des Laurentius Hispanus Apparat.* Mainz, 1935.

———. "Johannes Galensis als Glossator, insbesondere der Compilatio III, *Archiv f. kath. Kirchenrecht,* CV (1925).

———. "Romanus pontifex iura omnia in scrinio pectoris sui censetur habere," *Archiv,* XCII (1912), and CVI (1926).

———. "Wo war Vincentius Hispanus Bischof?" *Archiv,* CXIII (1933).

Gilmore, Myron P. *Argument from Roman Law in Political Thought, 1200-1600.* Cambridge, Mass., 1941.

Gilson, E. "La cosmogonie de Bernard Silvestris," *Arch. d'hist. doctrinale et littéraire du m. â.,* III (1928).

Giry, A. *Manuel de diplomatique.* Paris, 1925.

Glorieux, P. *La littérature quodlibétique de 1260 à 1320.* 2 vols.; Le Salchoir-Kain, 1925-1935.

———. *Répertoire des maîtres en théologie de Paris au XIIIe siècle.* 2 vols.; Paris, 1933-1934.

Goebel, Julius, Jr. "The Matrix of Empire," Introductory Essay to Joseph Henry Smith, *Appeals to the Privy Council from the American Plantations.* New York, 1950.

Grabmann, M. "Studien über den Einfluss der aristotelischen Philosophie auf der mittelalterlichen Theorien über das Verhältnis von Kirche und Staat," *Sitzungsber. d. Bayer. Akad. d. Wissenschaften, Phil.-Hist. Abt.,* Heft 2 (1934).

Gregory, Tullio. *Platonismo medievale.* Rome, 1958.

Gualazzini, U. " 'Natura, id est Deus,' " *Studia Gratiana,* III (1955).

Güterbock, C. *Bracton and His Relations to the Roman Law.* Trans. Brinton Coxe. Philadelphia, 1866.

Halphen, Louis. "Les débuts de l'Université de Paris," *Studi medievali,* Nuova ser., II (1929).

———. "L'Idée de l'état sous les Carolingiens," *Revue historique,* CLXXXV (1939).

Hartung, Fritz. "L'Etat c'est moi," *Histor. Zeitschr.,* CLXIX (1949).

———. "Die Krone als Symbol der monarchischen Herrschaft im ausgehenden Mittlelalter," *Abhandlungen d. Preus. Akad. d. Wissenschaften, Philos.-Hist. Kl.,* no. 13 (1940).

Hashagen, J. *Staat und Kirche vor der Reformation.* Essen, 1931.

Haskins, G. L. *Growth of English Representative Government.* Philadelphia, 1948.

———. *The Statute of York and the Interest of the Commons.* Cambridge, Mass., 1935.

Haskins, G. L. "The Petitions of the Representatives in the Parliaments of Edward I," *E.H.R.*, LIII (1938).

———. "Three English Documents Relating to Francis Accursius," *Law Quarterly Rev.*, LIV (1938).

———. "Francis Accursius; a New Document," *Speculum*, XIII (1938).

Hayes, Carlton J. H. *The Historical Evolution of Modern Nationalism.* New York, 1931.

Heckel, R. von. "Das Aufkommen der ständigen Prokuratoren an der päpstlichen Kurie im 13 Jht.," *Miscellanea Francesco Ehrle.* Vol. II, Rome, 1924.

———. "Beiträge zur Kenntnis des Geschäftsgang der päpstlichen Kanzlei im 13. Jht.," *Festschrift Albert Brackmann*, ed. L. Santifaller. Weimar, 1931.

———. "Der Libellus petitionum des Kardinals Guala Bichieri," *Archiv f. Urkundenforschung*, I (1908).

Hefele, C.-J. *Histoire des Conciles.* Transl. H. Leclercq. Vols. V and VI, Paris, 1913-1915.

Heimpel, Herman. "Alexander von Roes und das deutsche Selbstbewusstsein des 13. Jahrhunderts," *Archiv f. Kulturgeschichte*, XXVI (1935).

Heinermann, Th. *Untersuchungen zur Entstehung der Sage von Bernardo del Carpio.* Halle, 1927.

Hertter, F. *Die Podestàliteratur Italiens im 12. und 13. Jahrhundert (Beiträge zur Kulturgeschichte des Mittelalters und der Renaissance, 7).* Leipzig and Berlin, 1910.

Hessel, A. *Geschichte der Stadt Bologna.* Berlin, 1910.

Hexter, J. H. "*Il principe* and *lo stato*," *Studies in the Renaissance*, IV (1957).

Heydte, F. A. Freiherr von. *Die Geburtsstunde des souveränen Staates.* Regensburg, 1952.

Hinschius, P. *Das Kirchenrecht der Katholiken und Protestanten in Deutschland.* Part I. *Das katholische Kirchenrecht.* 6 vols. in 7; Berlin, 1869-1897.

Hof, Alfred. " 'Plenitudo potestatis' und 'Imitatio imperii' zur Zeit Innozenz III," *Zeitschr. f. Kirchengesch.*, LXVI (1954-1955).

Holdsworth, W. S. *History of English Law.* 13 vols., London, 1922-1935.

Holtzmann, W. "Das mittelalterliche Imperium und die werdenden Nationen," *Arbeitsgemeinschaft für Forschung des Landes Westfalen*, VII (1953).

Hourlier, Jacques. *Le chapitre général jusqu'au moment du grand schisme.* Paris, 1936.

Hoyt, R. Stuart. *The Royal Demesne in English Constitutional History, 1066-1272*. Ithaca, N.Y., 1950.

——. "The Coronation Oath of 1308," *Traditio*, XI (1955).

——. "Royal Taxation and the Growth of the Realm in Mediaeval England," *Speculum*, XXV (1950).

Jacob, E. F. *Essays in the Conciliar Epoch*. Manchester, 1943.

——. "Changing Views of the Renaissance," *Trans. Royal Hist. Soc.*, XVI (1931).

——. *Studies in the Period of Baronial Reform and Rebellion, 1258-1267*. Oxford, 1925.

Jenkinson, C. H. "*The First Parliament of Edward I*," *E.H.R.*, XXV (1910).

Jolliffe, J. E. A. *Angevin Kingship*. London, 1955.

——. *The Constitutional History of England*. London, 1937.

Jolowicz, H. F. *Historical Introduction to the Study of Roman Law*. Cambridge, 1932.

Jordan, Karl. "Die Entstehung der römischen Kurie," *Zeitschr. d. Sav.-Stift. f. Rechtsgesch., Kan. Abt.*, XXVIII (1939).

Kämpf, Helmut. *Pierre Dubois und die geistigen Grundlagen des französische Nationalbewusstseins um 1300*. Leipzig and Berlin, 1935.

Kantorowicz, Ernst. *Kaiser Friedrich der Zweite*. 2nd ed., Berlin, 1928; *Ergänzungsband*, Berlin, 1931.

——. *The King's Two Bodies*. Princeton, 1957.

——. "Christus-Fiscus," *Synopsis: Festgabe für Alfred Weber*. Heidelberg, 1948.

——. "Pro patria mori in Medieval Political Thought," *A.H.R.*, LVI (1951).

——. "Inalienability. A Note on Canonical Practice and the English Coronation Oath in the Thirteenth Century," *Speculum*, XXIX (1954).

——. "Mysteries of State: an Absolutist Concept and Its Late Mediaeval Origins," *Harvard Theol. Rev.*, XLVIII (1955).

——. "Invocatio nominis imperatoris," *Bollettino del Centro di Studi Filologici e Linguistici Siciliani*, III (1955).

——. "Zu den Rechtsgrundlagen der Kaisersaga. 1. Ein angebliches Testament Kaiser Friedrichs II," in *Deutsches Archiv f. Erforschung des M.A.*, XIII (1957).

——. "Kingship under the Impact of Scientific Jurisprudence," *Twelfth Century Europe and the Foundations of Modern Society* (eds. M. Clagett, G. Post, R. L. Reynolds). Madison, Wis., 1961.

Kantorowicz, Hermann. *Bractonian Problems*. Glasgow, 1941.

——. *Studies in the Glossators of the Roman Law*. Cambridge, 1938.

Kantorowicz, Hermann. "The Quaestiones disputatae of the Glossators," *Rev. d'hist. du droit (Tijdschr. v. Rechtsgesch.)*, XVI (1939).

———. "Accursio e la sua biblioteca," *Riv. di storia del diritto italiano*, II (1929).

Ke Chin Wang, H. "The Corporate Unity Concept (or Fiction Theory) in the Year Book Period," *Law Quarterly Rev.*, LVIII (1942).

Keeney, Barnaby C. "The Medieval Idea of the State: the Great Cause," *Univ. of Toronto Law Journal*, VIII (1949).

———. "Military Service and the Development of Nationalism in England, 1272-1327," *Speculum*, XXII (1947).

Kelsen, Hans. *General Theory of Law and State*. Trans. Anders Wedberg. Cambridge, Mass., 1945.

Ker, N. R. *Medieval Libraries of Great Britain*. London, 1941.

Kern, Fritz. *Gottesgnadentum und Widerstandsrecht im früheren Mittelalter*. Leipzig, 1914.

———. *Recht und Verfassung im Mittelalter*. New printing, ed. E. Anrich. Tübingen, 1952 (from *Historische Zeitschrift*, CXX [1919]).

———. *Kingship and Law in the Middle Ages*. Transl. S. B. Chrimes (of *Gottesgnadentum* and *Recht und Verfassung*; see above). Oxford, 1939.

Kibre, Pearl. *The Nations in the Mediaeval Universities*. Cambridge, Mass., 1948.

———. *Scholarly Privileges in the Middle Ages*. Cambridge, Mass., 1962.

Kienast, Walter. "Die Anfänge des Europaischen Staatensystems im späteren Mittelalter," *Hist. Zeitschrift*, CLIII (1936).

———. "Untertaneneid und Treuvorbehalt," *Zeitschr. d. Sav.-Stift. f. Rechtsgesch.*, Ger. Abt., LXVI (1948).

Knowles, David. *The Episcopal Colleagues of Archbishop Thomas Becket*. Cambridge, 1951.

Koeppler, H. "Frederick Barbarossa and the Schools of Bologna," *E.H.R.*, LIV (1939).

Köstermann, E. "Status als politischer Terminus in der Antike," *Rheinisches Museum f. Philologie*, N.F., LXXXVI (1937).

Kohn, Hans. *The Idea of Nationalism*. New York, 1946.

Koht, Halvdan. "The Dawn of Nationalism in Europe," *A.H.R.*, LII (1947).

Koschaker, Paul. *Europa und das römische Recht*. Berlin, 1947.

Krey, A. C. "William of Tyre," *Speculum*, XIV (1941).

Kuttner, Stephan. *Kanonistische Schuldlehre von Gratian bis auf die Dekretalen Gregors IX*. Città del Vaticano, 1935.

———. *Repertorium der Kanonistik*. Città del Vaticano, 1937.

Kuttner, Stephan. "Bernardus Compostellanus Antiquus. A Study in the Glossators of the Canon Law," *Traditio*, I (1943).

———. "Sur les origines du terme 'droit positif,'" *Rev. hist. de droit français et étranger*, 4ᵉ sér., xv (1936).

———. "Wer war der Dekretalist 'Abbas Antiquus'?" *Zeitschr. d. Sav.-Stift. f. Rechtsgesch.*, *Kan. Abt.*, xxvi (1937).

———. "Les débuts de l'école canoniste française," *Studia et documenta historiae et juris* (1938).

———. "Johannes Teutonicus, das vierte Laterankonzil und die Compilatio Quarta," *Miscellanea Giovanni Mercati*, v, Città del Vaticano, 1946.

———. "Papst Honorius III und das Studium das Zivilrechts," *Festschrift für Martin Wolff*. Tübingen, 1952.

———. "Pope Lucius III and the Bigamous Archbishop of Palermo," *Studies Presented to Aubrey Gwynn, S.J.* Dublin, 1961.

———., and Rathbone, E. "Anglo-Norman Canonists of the Twelfth Century," *Traditio*, vi (1949-1951).

———., and Smalley, Beryl. "The 'Glossa ordinaria' to the Gregorian Decretals," *E.H.R.*, lx (1945).

Lacger, L. de. "Statuts inédits d'un concile de la province de Bourges au XIII siècle," *Rev. histor. de droit français et étranger*, 4ᵉ sér., v (1926).

———. "La primatie et le pouvoir métropolitain de l'archevêque de Bourges au XIIIᵉ siècle," *Rev. d'hist. ecclés.*, xxvi (1930).

Ladner, Gerhart B. "Aspects of Mediaeval Thought on Church and State," *Rev. of Politics*, ix (1947).

Lagarde, G. de. *La naissance de l'esprit laïque au déclin du moyen âge*. 6 vols.; vol. i, 3rd ed., Louvain and Paris, 1956; vol. ii, 2nd ed., 1958; vol. iv, *Guillaume d'Ockham*, 1962.

———. "Individualisme et corporatisme au moyen âge," *L'Organisation corporative du moyen âge à la fin de l'ancien régime (Etudes présentées à la Commission Internationale pour l'Histoire des Assemblées d'Etats*, ii). Louvain, 1937.

———. "L'Idée de représentation dans les oeuvres de Guillaume d'Ockham," *Histoire des assemblées d'états (Bull. Intern. Committee of Historical Sciences*, ix). Paris, 1937.

———. "La philosophie sociale d'Henri de Gand et de Godefroid de Fontaines," *Arch. d'hist. doctrinale et littéraire du moyen âge*, xiv (1943-1945); also in *L'Organisation corporative du moyen âge à la fin de l'ancien régime; Etudes . . . Com. Int. . . . Assemblées d'Etats*, vii); Louvain, 1943.

Langlois, Ch.-V. *Saint Louis—Philippe le Bel—Les derniers Capétiens directs* (see Lavisse).

Langlois, Ch.-V. "Formulaires de lettres du XIIe, du XIIIe et du XIVe siècle," *Notices et extraits des manuscrits de la Bibliothèque Nationale*, XXXIV (1891).

Lapsley, G. T. "Knights of the Shire in the Parliaments of Edward II," *E.H.R.*, XXXIV (1919).

——. "The Interpretation of the Statute of York," *E.H.R.*, LVI (1941).

——. *Crown, Community, and Parliament in the Later Middle Ages*, eds. Helen M. Cam and G. Barraclough. Oxford, 1951.

Lavisse, E. (ed.). *Histoire de France . . . jusqu'à la révolution.* 9 vols. in 18; Paris, 1900-1911. Vol. III, ii, by Ch.-V. Langlois, *Saint Louis—Philippe le Bel—Les derniers Capétiens directs*.

Lear, F. S. "The Public Law of the Ripuarian, Alemannic, and Bavarian Codes," *Medievalia et Humanistica*, II (1944).

——. "Contractual Allegiance vs. Deferential Allegiance in Visigothic Law," *Illinois Law Rev.*, XXXIV (1940).

——. "The Idea of Majesty in Roman Political Thought," *Essays in History and Political Theory in Honor of Charles Howard McIlwain*. Cambridge, 1936.

——. "The Public Law of the Visigothic Code," *Speculum*, XXVI (1951).

Le Bras, Gabriel. *L'Immunité réelle*. Paris, 1920.

Leclerq, Jean. *Jean de Paris et l'écclésiologie du XIIIe siècle*. Paris, 1942.

Lefebvre, Ch. "Hostiensis," *Dictionnaire de droit canonique*, V (1953).

Lefebvre, G. (see Petit-Dutaillis).

Le Foyer, Jean. "Deux problèmes de la formation de la théorie de l'apanage royal en France," *Tijdschr. v. Rechtsgesch.*, XIII (1934).

Lehmann, Karl. *Las langobardische Lehnrecht*. Göttingen, 1896.

Leicht, P.-S. "Introduction des villes dans les assemblées d'états en Italie," *Histoire des assemblées d'états (Bull. International Com. Historical Sciences*, IX). Paris, 1937.

——. "Un principio politico medievale," in *Rendiconti d. R. Accademia Nazionale dei Lincei, Classe di Scienze Morali, Storiche*, ser. 5, XXIX; Rome, 1920.

——. "La posizione giuridica dei parlamenti medievali Italiani," *L'Organisation corporative du moyen âge (Etudes . . . Commission Intern. pour l'Hist. des Assemblées d'Etats*, II). Louvain, 1937).

Levy, Ernst. "Natural Law in Roman Thought," *Studia et documenta historiae et iuris*, XV (1949).

Lévy-Ullmann, H. *The English Legal Tradition*. London, 1935.

BIBLIOGRAPHY

Lewis, Ewart. "Organic Tendencies in Medieval Political Thought," *Amer. Political Science Rev.*, XXXII (1938).

Liebeschutz, Hans. *Mediaeval Humanism in the Life and Writings of John of Salisbury* (Studies of the Warburg Institute, 17). London, 1950.

Lehmann, K. *Die Entstehung der Libri Feudorum.* Rostock, 1891.

Lodge, Eleanor C., and Thornton, Gladys A. *English Constitutional Documents.* Cambridge, 1935.

Lottin, O. *Le droit naturel chez Saint Thomas d'Aquin et ses prédécesseurs.* 2nd ed., Bruges, 1931.

Lousse, E. "Parlementairisme ou corporatisme? Les origines des assemblées d'états," *Rev. hist. de droit français et étranger*, XIV (1935).

———. "Les caractères essentiels de l'état corporatif médiéval," *Les études classiques*, VI (1937).

———. *La société d'ancien régime.* Louvain and Bruges, 1943.

Lowery, Edith Clark. "Clerical Proctors in Parliament and Knights of the Shire, 1280-1374," *E.H.R.*, XLVIII (1933).

Lucas, H. S. "The Machinery of Diplomatic Intercourse," in Morris, *English Government*, I (see Morris).

Luchaire, A. *Innocent III.* Vol. VI. *Le Concile de Latran et la réforme de l'Eglise.* Paris, 1908.

———. *Les communes françaises à l'époque des capétiens directs.* Paris, 1890.

Lunt, W. E. *Financial Relations of the Papacy with England to 1327* (Studies in Anglo-Papal Relations during the Middle Ages, I). Cambridge, 1939.

———. "Consent of the Lower Clergy to Taxation during the Reign of Henry III," *Essays in Honor of George Lincoln Burr.* New York, 1931.

McIlwain, C. H. *The High Court of Parliament and Its Supremacy.* New Haven, 1910.

———. *Growth of Political Thought in the West.* New York, 1932.

———. *Constitutionalism and the Changing World.* New York, 1939.

———. *Constitutionalism Ancient and Modern.* New York, 1940.

———. "Medieval Estates," in *C.M.H.*, VII.

———. "Medieval Institutions in the Modern World," *Speculum*, XVI (1941).

———. "The Present Status of the Problem of the Bracton Text," *Harvard Law Review*, LVII (1943).

MacIver, R. M. *The Modern State.* London, 1926.

McKechnie, W. S. *Magna Carta. A Commentary on the Great Charter of King John.* Glasgow, 1914.

McKisack, May. *The Parliamentary Representation of the English Boroughs during the Middle Ages.* London, 1932.

———. *The Fourteenth Century.* Oxford, 1961.

Maffei, Domenico. "I giuristi francesi e il 'Constitutum Constantini' al tempo di Filippo il Bello," *Annali della Università di Macerata,* XXIII (1957).

Maitland, F. W. *History of English Law* (see Pollock).

———. *Selected Passages from the Works of Bracton and Azo* (Selden Soc., VII). London, 1895.

Mann, H. K. *Lives of the Popes.* Vol. XV, London, 1929.

Marcuse, A. *Die Repräsentativverfassung in Europa bis zum Durchbruck des Absolutismus* (Histor. Studien, Fasc. 277). Berlin, 1935.

Marichalar, A., and Manrique, C. *Historia de la legislation y recitaciones del derecho civil de España.* Vol. IV, Madrid, 1862.

Marongiu, Antonio. *L'Istituto parlamentare in Italia dalle origini al 1500.* Milan, 1949.

———. *Storia del diritto pubblico.* Milan, 1956.

———. "Note Federiciane. Manifestazioni ed aspetti poco noti della politica di Federico II," *Studi Medievali,* XVIII (1952).

Meijers, E. M. *Etudes d'histoire de droit,* eds. R. Feenstra and H. F. W. D. Fischer. 3 vols.; Leiden, 1959.

———. *Responsa doctorum Tholosonarum.* Leiden, 1938 (now also in *Etudes d'hist. de droit,* III; see above).

———. "De Universiteit van Orléans in de XIIIᵉ eeuw," *Tijdschr. v. Rechtsgesch.,* I (1918-1919), II (1920-1921).

———. "Sommes, lectures et commentaires (1100-1250)," *Atti del Congresso internaz. di diritto romano, Bologna-Roma, 1933.* Vol. I, Pavia, 1934.

———. *Iuris Interpretes saeculi XIII.* Naples, 1925.

———. "Les glossateurs et le droit féodal," *Tijdschr. v. Rechtsgesch.,* XIII (1934).

Meinecke, Friedrich. *Die Idee der Staatsräson in der neueren Geschichte.* Munich and Berlin, 1924; 3rd ed., 1929; 4th ed., ed. W. Hofer, 1957 (Friedrich Meinecke, *Werke,* Vol. I).

———. *Machiavellism. The Doctrine of Raison d'Etat and Its Place in Modern History.* Transl. Douglas Scott. London, 1957.

Menéndez Pidal, R. *El imperio hispanico y los cinco reinas.* Madrid, 1950.

Mercati, Angelo. "La prima relazione del Cardinale Nicolò de Romanis sulla sua legazione in Inghilterra," *Essays in History presented to Reginald Lane Poole,* ed. H. W. C. Davis. Oxford, 1927.

Merriman, R. B. *The Rise of the Spanish Empire in the Old World and the New.* Vol. I, New York, 1918.

Meyer, A. O. "Zur Geschichte des Wortes Staat," *Die Welt als Geschichte*, x (1950).

Meyer, Ernst. *Römischer Staat und Staatsgedanke*. Zurich, 1948.

Meyer, Georg. *Das Recht der Expropriation*. Leipzig, 1868.

Mitteis, Heinrich. *Der Staat des hohen Mittelalters*. 3rd ed., Weimar, 1948.

Mochi Onory, Sergio. *Fonti canonistische dell'idea moderna dello stato*. Milan, 1951.

Morrall, John B. *Political Thought in Medieval Times*. 2nd ed., London, 1960.

Morris, W. A. (ed.). *The English Government at Work, 1327-1336.* Vol. I, Cambridge, Mass., 1940.

————. "Magnates and Community of the Realm in Parliament, 1264-1327," *Medievalia et Humanistica*, I (1943).

Mosse, George L. *The Holy Pretence*. Oxford, 1957.

Müllejans, Hans. *Publicus und Privatus im römischen Recht und im älteren kanonischen Recht unter besonderer Berücksichtigung der Unterscheidung Ius publicum und Ius privatum*, in *Münchener Theologische Studien*, III. Kanon. Abt., XIV, Munich, 1961.

Muñoz y Romero, T. *Colección de Fueros Municipales*. Madrid, 1847.

Neilson, Nellie. "The Early Pattern of the Common Law," *A.H.R.*, XLIX (1944).

Nitschke, August. "Die Reden des Logotheten Bartholomäus von Capua," *Quellen u. Forschungen aus Ital. Arch. u. Bibl.*, XXXV (1955).

Ochoa, J. "Problemas biograficos de Vincentius Hispanus," *Congrès de droit canonique médiéval, Louvain et Bruxelles, 1958*. Louvain, 1959.

————. *Vincentius Hispanus. Canonista boloñes del siglo XIII.* Rome-Madrid, 1960.

Onclin, W. "Le droit naturel selon les romanistes des XIIe et XIIIe s.," *Miscellanea moralia . . . Arthur Janssen*. Vol. II, Louvain, 1948.

Otway-Ruthwen, J. "The Constitutional Position of the Great Lordships of South Wales," *Trans. Royal Hist. Soc.*, Ser. 5, VIII (1958).

Pacaut, Marcel. *La théocratie. L'Eglise et le pouvoir au moyen âge.* Paris, 1957.

Palmer, R. R. *The Age of the Democratic Revolution*. Princeton, 1959.

Paré, G. *Les idées et les lettres au XIIIe siècle: Le Roman de la Rose* (University of Montreal, Bibliothèque de Philosophie). Montreal, 1947.

Paré, G. *Le Roman de la Rose et la scolastique courtoise* (Publ. Inst. d'Etudes Médiévales d'Ottawa). Paris and Ottawa, 1941.

Parent, J.-M. *La doctrine de la création dans l'Ecole de Chartres* (Publ. Inst. d'Etudes Médiévales d'Ottawa, VIII). Paris and Ottawa, 1941.

Parkinson, G. H. R. "Ethics and Politics in Machiavelli," *Philosophical Quarterly*, V (1955).

Pasquet, D. *An Essay on the Origins of the House of Commons.* Transl. R. G. D. Laffan. Cambridge, 1925.

Patetta, F. "Contributi alla storia del diritto romano nel medio evo," *Bull. dell' Istituto di Diritto Romano*, IV (1891).

Pertile, A. *Storia del diritto italiano.* 2nd ed., 6 vols.; Turin, 1891-1903.

Petit-Dutaillis, Ch. *Etude sur la vie et le règne de Louis VIII (1187-1226).* Paris, 1896.

————., and Lefebvre, G. *Studies and Notes Supplementary to Stubbs' Constitutional History.* Manchester, 1930.

Plucknett, T. F. T. *Statutes and Their Interpretation in the First Half of the Fourteenth Century.* Cambridge, 1922.

————. *Concise History of the Common Law*; 2nd ed. Rochester, N.Y., 1936; 5th ed., London, 1956.

————. *Legislation of Edward I.* Oxford, 1949.

————. "The Lancastrian Constitution," *Tudor Studies Presented to . . . Albert Frederick Pollard.* London, 1924.

————. "Words," *Cornell Law Quarterly*, XIV (1928-1929).

————. "Parliament," in Morris, *English Government* (*q.v.*).

————. "The Relations between Roman Law and English Common Law down to the Sixteenth Century," *Univ. of Toronto Law Journal*, III (1939).

Pollard, A. F. *The Evolution of Parliament.* 2nd ed., London, 1926.

Pollock, F., and Maitland, F. W. *The History of English Law.* 2nd ed., 2 vols.; Cambridge, 1898.

Poole, R. L. *The Exchequer in the Twelfth Century.* Oxford, 1922.

Post, G. "Alexander III, the *licentia docendi*, and the Rise of the Universities," *Haskins Anniversary Essays in Mediaeval History.* Boston and New York, 1929.

————. "Some Unpublished Glosses (*ca.* 1210-1214) on the *Translatio Imperii* and the Two Swords," *Archiv f. kath. Kirchenrecht*, CXVII (1937).

————. "Additional Glosses of Johannis Galensis and Silvester," *Archiv f. kath. Kirchenrecht*, CXIX (1939).

————. "The So-Called Laurentius Apparatus to the Decretals of Innocent III in *Compilatio III*," *The Jurist*, II (1942).

Post, G. *"Philosophantes* and *Philosophi* in Roman and Canon Law," in *Archives d'histoire doctrinale et littéraire du moyen âge* (1954).

———., with Kimon Giocarinis and Richard Kay. "The Medieval Heritage of a Humanistic Ideal," *Traditio*, XI (1955).

Power, Eileen. *The Wool Trade in English Medieval History.* London, 1941.

Powicke, F. M. *The Loss of Normandy (1189-1204).* Manchester, 1913; rev. ed., 1960.

———. *Stephen Langton.* Oxford, 1928.

———. *King Henry III and the Lord Edward. The Community of the Realm in the Thirteenth Century.* Oxford, 1947.

———. *The Thirteenth Century,* 1216-1307. Oxford, 1953.

———. "Reflections on the Medieval State," *Trans. Royal Hist. Soc.* XIX (1936).

———. and Rashdall (see Rashdall, *Universities*).

Prentout, Henri. *Les états provinciaux de Normandie.* 2 vols.; Caen, 1925-1926.

Queller, Donald E. "L'Evolution du rôle de l'ambassadeur: les pleins pouvoirs et le traité de 1201 entre les croisés et les Vénétiens," *Le moyen âge,* no. 4 (1961).

———. "Thirteenth Century Envoys: *Nuncii* and *Procuratores,"* *Speculum,* XXXV (1960).

Radin, Max. *Handbook of Anglo-American Legal History.* St. Paul, Minn., 1936.

Ramos, Demetrio. *Historia de las cortes tradicionales de España.* Burgos, 1944.

Rashdall, Hastings. *The Universities of Europe in the Middle Ages;* 3 vols.; Oxford, 1895; new ed. by F. M. Powicke and A. B. Emden, Oxford, 1936.

Rassow, Peter. *Honor Imperii. Die neue Politik Friedrich Barbarossas 1152-1159.* Munich and Berlin, 1940.

Rathbone, Eleanor. "Anglo-Norman Canonists" (see Kuttner).

Regout, R. *La doctrine de la guerre juste, de S. Augustin à nos jours d'àpres les théologiens et les canonistes catholiques.* Paris, 1935.

Richardson, H. G. "An Oxford Teacher of the Fifteenth Century," *Bull. John Rylands Library,* XXIII (1939).

———. "The Oxford Law School under John," *Law Quarterly Rev.,* LVII (1941).

———. "Azo, Drogheda, and Bracton," *E.H.R.,* LIX (1944).

———. "Tancred, Raymond, and Bracton," *E.H.R.,* LIX (1944).

———. "The English Coronation Oath," *Speculum,* XXIV (1949).

———. "The Coronation Oath in Medieval England: The Evolution of the Office and the Oath," *Traditio,* XVI (1960).

BIBLIOGRAPHY

Richardson, H. G., and Sayles, G. O. "The Origins of Parliament," *Trans. Royal Hist. Soc.*, XI (1929).

———., and Sayles. "Parliamentary Documents from Formularies," *Bull. Inst. Historical Research*, XI (1934).

———., and Sayles. "Parliaments and Great Councils in Medieval England," *Law Quarterly Rev.* (1961); reprinted, London, 1961.

———., and Sayles. "The Early Statutes," *Law Quarterly Rev.*, L (1934).

———., and Sayles. "The King's Ministers in Parliament," *E.H.R.*, XLVI (1931).

Riesenberg, Peter. *Inalienability of Sovereignty in Medieval Political Thought.* New York, 1956.

Riess, Ludwig. *History of the English Electoral Law in the Middle Ages.* Transl. K. L. Wood-Legh. Cambridge, 1940.

Rivière, J. *Le problème de l'église et l'état au temps de Philippe le Bel.* Louvain and Paris, 1926.

Roberts, M. "The Political Objectives of Gustavus Adolphus in Germany, 1630-1632," *Trans. Royal Hist. Soc.*, 5th ser., VII (1957).

Roby, J. J. *Roman Private Law in the Times of Cicero and the Antonines.* 2 vols.; Cambridge, 1902.

Roman, J. *Manuel de sigillographie française.* Paris, 1913.

Rosenthal, E. I. J. (ed. and transl.). *Averroes' Commentary on Plato's Republic.* Cambridge, 1956.

Rota, Antonio. "Le fonti del diritto civile e la loro autorità alla metà del XII secolo," *Studi Sassaresi*, XXIV (1952).

———. "L'Influsso civilistico nella concezione dello stato di Giovanni Salisberiense," *Riv. di storia del diritto italiano*, XXVI-XXVII (1953-1954).

———. "Il decretista Egidius e la sua concezione del diritto naturale," *Studia Gratiana*, II (1954).

Ruess, Karl. *Die Rechtliche Stellung der päpstlichen Legaten bis Bonifaz VIII.* Paderborn, 1912.

Saltman, Avrom. *Theobald Archbishop of Canterbury.* London, 1956.

Sarti, M., and Fattorini, M. *De claris Archigymnasii Bononiensis professoribus.* New ed. by C. Albicini and C. Malagola, 3 vols.; Bologna, 1888-1896.

Savigny, F. C. v. *Geschichte des römischen Rechts im Mittelalter.* 2nd ed., 7 vols.; Heidelberg, 1834-1851.

Sayles, G. O. "Representation of Cities and Boroughs in 1268," *E.H.R.*, XL (1925).

———., and Richardson (see Richardson, H. G., for joint works of R. and Sayles).

Scheyhing, R. *Eide Amtsgewalt und Bannleihe.* Cologne, 1960.

Schilling, Otto. *Naturrecht und Staat nach der Lehre der alten Kirche*. Berlin, 1914.

Scholz, R. *Die Publizistik zur Zeit Philippe des Schönen und Bonifaz VIII* (Kirchenrecht.-Abh., II, 6-8). Stuttgart, 1903.

Schramm, Percy E. *Kaiser, Rom und Renovatio*. 2 vols.; Leipzig, 1929.

——. *A History of the English Coronation*. Transl. E. G. Legg. Oxford, 1937.

——. *Der König von Frankreich*. 2 vols.; Weimar, 1939.

——. *Herrschaftszeichen und Staatssymbolik* (*Schriften der M.G.H.*, XIII, 1-3). 3 vols.; Stuttgart, 1956.

——. "Die Ordines der mittelalterlichen Kaiserkrönung," *Archiv f. Urkunderforschung*, XI (1930).

——. "Die Krönung bei den Westfranken und Angelsachsen von 878 bis um 1000," *Zeitschr. d. Sav.-Stift. f. Rechtsgesch., Kan. Abt.*, XXIII (1934).

——. "Die Krönung in Deutschland bis zum Beginn des Salischen Hauses," *Zeitschr. d. Sav.-Stift. f. Rechtsgesch., Kan. Abt.*, XXIV (1935).

Schulte, J. F. v. *Die Geschichte der Quellen und Literatur des canonischen Rechts von Gratian bis auf die Gegenwart*. 3 vols.; Stuttgart, 1875-1877.

——. "Zur Geschichte der Literatur über das Dekret Gratians," *Sitzungsber. d. Kais. Akad. d. Wissenschaften zu Wien, Philos.-Hist. Cl.*, LXIII (1869), LXIV (1870).

——. "Johannes Teutonicus," *Zeitschr. f. Kirchenrecht*, XVI (1881).

——. "Literaturgeschichte der *Compilationes Antiquae*," *Sitzungsber. . . . zu Wien, Philos.-Hist. Cl.*, LXIV (1870).

——. "Die Glosse zum Dekret Gratians von ihren Anfängen bis auf die jüngsten Ausgaben," *Denkschriften d. kais. Akad. der Wissenschaften zu Wien, Philos.-Hist. Cl.*, XXI, ii (1872).

Schulz, Fritz. *Principles of Roman Law*. Oxford, 1936.

——. "Critical Studies on Bracton's Treatise," *Law Quarterly Rev.*, LIX (1943).

——. "A New Approach to Bracton," *Seminar* (Annual Extraordinary Number of *The Jurist*), II (1944).

——. "Bracton on Kingship," *E.H.R.*, LX (1945).

——. "Bracton and Raymond de Peñafort," *Law Quarterly Rev.*, LXI (1945).

——. "Bracton as a Computist," *Traditio*, III (1945).

Scrutton, T. E. *The Influence of the Roman Law on the Law of England*. Cambridge, 1885.

Seeger, J. *Die Reorganisation des Kirchenstaates unter Innocenz III.*
Kiel, 1937.

Senior, W. "Roman Law in England before Vacarius," *Law Quarterly Rev.*, XLVI (1930).

————. "Roman Law MSS. in England," *Law Quarterly Rev.*, XLVII (1931).

————. "Roffredo da Benevento," *Law Quarterly Rev.*, L (1934).

Shafer, Boyd S. *Nationalism: Myth and Reality.* New York, 1946.

Sherman, C. P. *Roman Law in the Modern World.* 2 vols.; Boston, 1917, New Haven, 1922.

Silverstein, Theodore. "The Fabulous Cosmogony of Bernardus Silvestris," *Modern Philology*, XLVI (1948-1949).

Simonsfeld, H. *Jahrbücher des deutschen Reiches unter Friedrich I.* Vol. 1, Leipzig, 1908.

Smalley, Beryl. *Study of the Bible in the Middle Ages.* Oxford, 1941.

————. "Glossa ordinaria" (see Kuttner).

Smith, A. L. *Church and State in the Middle Ages.* Oxford, 1913.

Snyder, Louis L. *The Meaning of Nationalism.* New Brunswick, N.J., 1954.

Solmi, A. *Storia del diritto italiano.* 3rd ed., Milan, 1930.

Sousa Costa, A. D. de. *Um mestre portugues em Bolonha no seculo XIII, Joao de Deus: Vida e obras.* Braga, 1957.

Sproemberg, Heinrich. "Das Erwachen des Staatsgefühls in den Niederlanden. Galbert von Brügge," *L'Organisation corporative du moyen âge à la fin de l'ancien régime* (Etudes . . . Commission Internationale pour l'Histoire des Assemblées, III). Louvain, 1939.

Stephenson, Carl. "Les 'aides' des villes françaises," *Le moyen âge*, XXIV (1922).

Stickler, Alfons M. "Concerning the Political Theories of the Medieval Canonists," *Traditio*, VII (1949-1951).

————. "Sacerdotium et regnum nei decretisti e primi decretalisti," *Salesianum*, XV (1953).

————. "Sacerdozio e Regno nelle nuove ricerche attorno ai secoli XII e XIII nei decretisti e decretalisti fino alle decretali di Gregorio IX," *Miscellanea Historiae Pontificiae*, XVIII (1954).

————. "Alanus Anglicus als Verteidiger des monarchischen Papsttums," *Salesianum*, XXI (1959).

Stölzel, A. "Glosenapparat des Vacarius Pragensis zu den Digestentiteln 43, 24, 25 und 39, 1," *Festschrift f. Heinrich Brunner.* Munich and Leipzig, 1914.

Strayer, Joseph R. *The Administration of Normandy under Saint Louis.* Cambridge, Mass., 1932.

————., and Taylor, C. H., *Studies in Early French Taxation.* Cambridge, Mass., 1939.

Strayer, Joseph R., and Taylor, C. H. "Laicization of French and English Society in the Thirteenth Century," *Speculum*, xv (1940).

———. "The Statute of York and the Community of the Realm," *A.H.R.*, xlvii (1941).

———. "Defense of the Realm and the Royal Power in France," *Studi in onore di Gino Luzzato*. Milan, 1949.

———. "Philip the Fair—A 'Constitutional' King." *A.H.R.*, lxii (1956).

———., and Rudisill, George, Jr. "Taxation and Community in Wales and Ireland, 1272–1327," *Speculum*, xxix (1954).

Stubbs, William. *Constitutional History of England*. 5th ed., 3 vols.; Oxford, 1891-1903.

Stutz, U. "The Proprietary Church as an Element of Mediaeval Germanic Ecclesiastical Law," in *Mediaeval Germany. Essays by German Historians*. Transl. G. Barraclough. 2 vols; Oxford, 1938.

Svennung, Joseph. *Orosiana (Uppsala Universitets Årsskrift, 1922. Filosofi, Språksvetenskap och Historiska Vetenskaper, 5)*. Uppsala, 1922.

Tamassia, N. *Odofredo*. Bologna, 1895.

Tangl, M. *Die päpstlichen Kanzleiordnungen von 1200-1500*. Innsbruck, 1894.

Tardif, Jules. *Etudes sur les institutions politiques et administratives de la France*. Vol. 1, Paris, 1881.

Taylor, C. H. "Some New Texts on the Assembly of 1302," *Speculum*, xi (1936).

———. *Studies in Early French Taxation* (with J. R. Strayer, *q.v.*).

Thorne, S. E. "Statuti in the Post-Glossators," *Speculum*, xi (1936).

———. "Gilbert de Thornton's Summa de legibus," *Univ. of Toronto Law Journal*, vii (1947).

Tierney, Brian. *Foundations of the Conciliar Theory. The Contribution of the Medieval Canonists from Gratian to the Great Schism*. Cambridge, 1955.

———. "Grosseteste and the Theory of Papal Sovereignty," *Journal of Ecclesiastical History*, vi (1955).

———. "*Natura Id Est Deus*: Juristic Pantheism," *Jour. Hist. Ideas*, xxiv (1963).

Torelli, Pietro. "Glosse preaccursiane alle Istitutione. Nota secunda: glosse di Bulgaro," *Riv. di storia del diritto italiano*, xv (1942).

———. "Glosse preaccursiane . . . Nota terza: Iacobo ed Ugo," *Rendiconto delle Sessioni d. R. Accademia d. Scienze dell' Istituto di Bologna. Classi di Scienze morali*, viii (1946).

Tourtoulon, Pierre de. *Etudes sur le droit écrit. Les oeuvres de Jacques de Révigny (Jacobus de Ravanis) d'après deux manuscrits de la Bibliothèque Nationale*. Paris, 1899.

Tout, T. F. *Chapters in the Administrative History of Mediaeval England*. Vols. I and II; Manchester and London, 1920.

Treharne, R. F. "The Significance of the Baronial Reform Movement," *Trans. Royal Hist. Soc.*, XXV (1943).

Trueman, John H. "The Statute of York and the Ordinances of 1311," *Medievalia et Humanistica*, X (1956).

Tunmore, H. P. "The Dominican Order and Parliament," *Catholic Hist. Rev.*, XXVI (1941).

Ullmann, Walter. *The Medieval Idea of Law as Represented by Lucas de Penna*. London, 1946.

———. *Medieval Papalism*. London, 1949.

———. *The Growth of Papal Government in the Middle Ages*. London, 1955.

———. *Principles of Government and Politics in the Middle Ages*. London, 1961.

———. "The Influence of John of Salisbury on Medieval Italian Jurists," *E.H.R.*, LIX (1944).

———. "The Medieval Idea of Sovereignty," *E.H.R.*, LXIV (1949).

———. "The Medieval Interpretation of Frederick I's Authentic 'Habita,'" *Studi in memoria di Paolo Koschaker*: *L'Europa e il diritto romano*. Vol. I, Milan, 1953.

Usón y Sesé, M. "Un formulario latino de la cancillería real aragonesa (siglo XIV)," *Anuario de historia del derecho español*, VI (1929).

Valls-Taberner, F. "Le juriste catalan Pierre de Cardona," *Mélanges Paul Fournier*. Paris, 1929.

Vickers, K. H. *England in the later Middle Ages*. 4th ed., London, 1926.

Vinogradoff, P. *Roman Law in Medieval Europe*. 2nd ed. by F. de Zulueta; Oxford, 1929.

———. "Les maximes dans l'ancien droit commun anglais," *Rev. hist. de droit français et étranger*, 4e sér., II (1923).

———. "The Roman Element in Bracton's Treatise," *Collected Papers*. Vol. I, Oxford, 1928; also in *Yale Law Jour.*, XXXII (1933).

Viollet, Paul. *Histoire des institutions politiques et administratives de la France*. 3 vols.; Paris, 1890-1903.

Waley, Daniel. *The Papal State in the Thirteenth Century*. New York, 1961.

Walker, L. J. *The Discourses of Niccolò Machiavelli*. 2 vols.; London, 1950.

Wenger, L. *Institutes of the Roman Law of Civil Procedure*. Transl. O. H. Fisk. New York, 1940.

Weske, Dorothy. *Convocation of the Clergy*. New York, 1937.

White, A. B. *The Making of the English Constitution*. 2nd ed., New York and London, 1925.

———. *Self-Government at the King's Command*. Minneapolis, 1933.

———. "Some Early Instances of Concentration of Representatives in England," *A.H.R.*, XIX (1913).

———., and Notestein, W. *Source Problems in English History*. New York and London, 1915.

Wieruszowski, Helene. *Vom Imperium zum nationalen Königtum* (*Histor. Zeitschr.*, Beiheft 30). Munich and Berlin, 1933.

———. "Roger II of Sicily, *Rex-Tyrannus*, in Twelfth Century Political Thought," Speculum, XXXVIII (1963).

Wilkinson, B. *Studies in the Constitutional History of the Thirteenth and Fourteenth Centuries*. Manchester, 1937.

———. *Constitutional History of England, 1216-1399*. 3 vols.; New York and London, 1948-1958.

———. "The Coronation Oath of Edward II and the Statute of York," *Speculum*, XIX (1944).

———. "The 'Political Revolution' of the Thirteenth and Fourteenth Centuries in England," *Speculum*, XXIV (1949).

Wilks, Michael J. *The Problem of Sovereignty in the Later Middle Ages*. Cambridge, 1963.

———. "The Idea of the Church as 'Unus homo perfectus' and its Bearing on the Medieval Theory of Sovereignty," *Miscellanea Historiae Ecclesiasticae*. Stockholm, 1960.

Williams, G. H. *The Norman Anonymous of 1100 A.D.* (*Harvard Theological Studies*, 18). Cambridge, Mass., 1951.

Williams, James. "Latin Maxims in English Law." *Law Magazine and Rev.*, XX (1895).

Woodbine, G. E. "The Roman Element in Bracton's *De adquirendo rerum domino*," *Yale Law Jour.*, XXXI (1921-1922).

Woolf, C. N. S. *Bartolus of Sassoferrato*. Cambridge, 1913.

INDEX

The innumerable references to glosses and to specific passages in the Roman and Canon law, have been omitted in this index, for I thought it best to let the subject matter guide the reader to them. In fact, the emphasis is on the subject matter; but because of its complicated nature it is not completely presented in all the variety of concepts and themes. Where the subject is repeated in text and footnotes on the same page, references to the footnotes are usually omitted. The listing of the names of persons and places is as complete as is necessary for their connection with the subject matter. The abbreviations are standard: abp., archbishop; bp., bishop; emp., emperor; k., king—except that *q.o.t.* is used for *quod omnes tangit*.

—G. P.